READINGS IN
ORGANIZATIONAL DECLINE

**BALLINGER SERIES
ON
INNOVATION AND ORGANIZATIONAL CHANGE**

Series Editors:

Michael Tushman and Andrew Van de Ven

Readings in Organizational Decline

Frameworks, Research, and Prescriptions

Edited by

Kim S. Cameron
Robert I. Sutton
David A. Whetten

BALLINGER PUBLISHING COMPANY
Cambridge, Massachusetts
A Subsidiary of Harper & Row, Publishers, Inc.

International Standard Book Number: 0–88730–223–8 (CL)
0–88730–270–X (PB)

Library of Congress Catalog Card Number: 87–27136

Printed in the United States of America

Library of Congress Cataloging-in-Publication Data

Readings in organizational decline : Frameworks, research, and
    prescriptions / edited by Kim S. Cameron, Robert I. Sutton,
    David A. Whetten.
              p.   cm. — (Ballinger series on innovation and
    organizational change)
        1. Organizational change.   I. Cameron, Kim S.   II. Sutton,
    Robert I.   III. Whetten, David A. (David Allred), 1946–
    IV. Organizational decline.   V. Series.
    HD58.8.R37   1988   87–27136
    658.4′06 — dc 19

    ISBN 0–88730–223–8
    ISBN 0–88730–270–X (pbk.)

Contents

Acknowledgments

The idea for this book arose out of frustration with trying to find the key articles on organizational decline for our individual research projects. We each had invested several years in conducting research on organizational decline and death, yet in our conversations together, we were continually being surprised by work that one of us knew about that another did not. That frustration, along with our collective conviction that the topic of organizational decline needed additional research attention, motivated us to compile this book. (It should be noted that the listing of editors' names is alphabetical and does not reflect magnitude of contribution to this project.)

We owe an intellectual debt to a great many individuals for their ideas, critiques, and stimulating conversations on the topics of organizational decline and death. In particular, the contributions of Dan Alpert, Leonard Greenhalgh, Robert Kahn, Anne Lawrence, Louis Pondy, and Mayer Zald have been influential in developing our ideas. The study group on creative responses to retrenchment at the University of Illinois and the organizational studies division at the National Center for Higher Education Management Systems have also influenced our work. In addition, we acknowledge our dependence on the ideas of the authors whose work is represented in this book. Their collective contributions have formed important bases for our own thinking. Finally, we gratefully acknowledge the encouragement and support of Marjorie Richman, our editor at Ballinger Publishing Company. Despite the fact that edited books are often risky undertakings for publishers, Marjorie became convinced along with us that such a book was needed in the organizational sciences.

This project was prepared while Robert I. Sutton was a fellow at the Center for Advanced Study in the Behavioral Sciences. He wishes to acknowledge financial support provided by the Carnegie Corporation of New York and the William and Flora Hewett Foundation. Kim S. Cameron received financial support from the U.S. Army Research Institute and from the National Center for the Improvement of Teaching and Learning at the University of Michigan. He gratefully acknowledges the assistance of Sarah Freemen in proofreading and bibliographic assistance.

PART I

Introduction

Issues in Organizational Decline

Kim S. Cameron
Robert I. Sutton
David A. Whetten

Organizational decline is emerging as one of the most important topics addressed by organizational research. Consider, for example, that the number of business failures more than quadrupled from 1979 to 1985, while the number of new businesses incorporated increased only 25 percent in the same period. As a result, the index of net business formation declined 14 percent from 1979 to 1985.[1]

American manufacturing has declined rapidly. Over two million manufacturing jobs have been lost since 1980 due to offshore competition. The steel and automobile industries closed so many plants that the industrial Midwest became known as the "rust bowl." And in 1983 Brock Yates was able to write seriously about *The Decline and Fall of the American Automobile Industry,* a book that would have been pure fiction in the 1950s and 1960s. Indeed, it appears that American managers have been poorly prepared to cope with such widespread financial woes and with the associated human suffering. These hard times may continue because many American managers have not learned how to retain competitive advantage nor how to regain it once it is lost. To illustrate, leaders of once wildly successful high technology companies such as Advanced Micro Devices, Control Data, Atari, and even Hewlett-Packard believed that their firms would never suffer from organizational decline because they were more skilled than their counterparts in the smokestack industries. Yet almost one million jobs have been lost to overseas competitors in high technology industries since 1980. The decline of silicon-chip manufacturers has been especially dramatic. Whereas eight years ago U.S. chipmakers held almost 80 percent of the world's market, they now rank second to the Japanese in world market share.

A recent opinion poll brings more bad news to American manufacturers. American consumers were asked which product they would buy if they knew only that one brand was made in the United States and the other was made in Japan. A majority of consumers would purchase the

3

Japanese product on the assumption that it was of higher quality.

Unfortunately, the threat of decline is not limited to manufacturing industries. Portions of the service sector are also being buffeted by decline. In the financial-services sector, for example, trends similar to manufacturing are apparent. The 200 bank failures that occurred between 1980 and 1985 exceeded the total for the previous forty years. Moreover, this decline appears to be accelerating; in 1986 alone over 130 banks failed and over 1,000 branches closed. One bank each day is being added to the list of "problem banks," which now totals almost 1,500. Approximately 10 percent of the banks on this list will eventually fail. The Japanese have now captured over 8 percent of the U.S. banking market, or about $170 billion per year in revenues. Seven of the ten largest commercial banks in the world are now Japanese and only one is American, a dramatic reversal from a decade ago.

The total number of jobs is increasing in America's service sector. But this is a mixed blessing. Wages in the service sector average less than 80 percent of the goods-producing sector wages. Thus, future buying power and economic expansion are also threatened as this country becomes increasingly dependent on a service economy. These trends have led some commentators to predict that American organizations are following a path to second-rate status. Lester Thurow (1984: 9) captures the essence of this point of view:

> America faces a problem that is simply put. The huge technological edge enjoyed by Americans in the 1950s and 1960s has disappeared. Whereas America once had effortless economic superiority, we are now faced with competitors who have matched our achievements and may be in the process of moving ahead of us. If present trends continue, America's standard of living will fall relative to those of the world's new industrial leaders and we shall become simply another country like Egypt, Greece, Italy, Portugal, Spain, and England—all of which once led the world but do no longer.

Avoiding organizational decline, and managing it once it occurs, have also emerged as challenges for leaders in industries not faced with overall decline. Deregulation has increased competition in the airline industry so much that former success stories such as Braniff (Nance 1984) and Eastern have come close to organizational death. The shakeout in this industry is so severe that People Express, which was born and initially flourished because of the opportunities created by deregulation, eventually went into a sharp decline and disappeared as a corporate entity since being acquired by Texas Air. The health-care industry is under severe pressure to cut costs, which is leading to widespread layoffs and other efficiency measures (White 1985). The shift in college-student preferences toward professional programs and away from liberal arts programs, along with the decreasing number of traditional college-aged 18–26-year-olds, threatens the survival of up to 700 small colleges in the next decade (Cameron & Ulrich 1986). And the current wave of "merger mania" has led successful firms such as CBS, Goodyear, and Atlantic Richfield to experience at least short-term decline (Hirsch in press). Such firms have responded to hostile-takeover bids with defensive maneuvers to raise cash, including the sale of profitable units, layoffs, and paycuts. In short, there is hardly a sector of the U.S. economy that has avoided the challenges of retrenchment and decline, regardless of past and current patterns of growth.

U.S. culture is one that has traditionally emphasized growth and progress (Whetten 1980; see also Chapter 8). Despite arguments that "small is beautiful" (Schumacher 1973), U.S. managers and management theorists still appear to believe that bigger is better. This success-through-growth ethic is so deeply ingrained in American culture, in fact, that managers avoid the subject of decline whenever possible. Even terms like decline, retrenchment, and downsizing are replaced in most corporate communications by euphemisms such as resizing, redesign, and reorganization.

Yet the harsh events of the past decade have forced both managers and management scholars to learn about retrenching, closing, and divesting, as well as about turnaround and recovery. These lessons are reflected in the increasing numbers of popular writings on the subject. Publications including the *Wall Street Journal, Business Week, Fortune, Harvard Business Review,* and the *New York Times* often carry reports about turnaround strategies, plant closings, bankruptcies, layoffs, and other issues faced by declining organizations. Lee Iacocca's (1984) turnaround of the Chrysler Corporation is among the most popular books about management ever published. Other popular books have been written about troubled banks (Sprague 1986), the collapse of Braniff Airlines (Nance 1984), the troubles of International Harvester (Marsh 1985), and the bankruptcy of Osborne Computers (Osborne & Dvorak 1984). One book even teaches strategies for detecting, avoiding, and profiting from bankruptcy (Platt 1985).

The Emerging Scholarly Literature on Organizational Decline

Researchers and theorists in a wide range of disciplines have also been responsive to the financial and social problems caused by organizational decline. Indeed, scholarly attention to decline has increased exponentially in the past decade. Approximately 75 percent of the academic literature on organizational decline has appeared since 1978. In preparing this book, we have reviewed hundreds of articles and books on declining organizations in the literatures on organizational behavior, organizational theory, organizational development, management strategy, psychology, sociology, public health, education, and public administration. Typical of most new research areas, this literature is uneven in quality, rarely cumulative, and widely dispersed.

Our aim is to present the best writing and research in this emerging area, to provide guidance for organizing this diverse literature, and to sug-

gest pathways for enhancing future work. It is intended to be a source book that can both stimulate and guide scholarly thinking and research on this critical topic. Further, our hope is that it will help to facilitate the emergence of a cumulative literature. To accomplish these ends, the following chapters present twenty-two of the best and most representative articles on organizational decline and commentaries by three well-known scholars about these writings. We have included previously published articles to help readers identify a representative core of past writing on organizational decline. We also help interpret and summarize that literature in this introduction and critique it in the three commentaries at the end of the book.

Our review of the decline literature led us to conclude that three key issues both inhibit a cumulative literature on organizational decline from developing and impede theory building and research. First, confusion exists about the definition of organizational decline. The conceptual boundaries of decline, as well as its operationalization in research, have been neither consensual nor clear. Second, numerous approaches have been taken in the decline literature and no common organizing framework exists to codify them. This leads to further noncumulation and diversity among contributions. Third, several impediments exist that may deter investigators from studying and writing about declining organizations. Even though this topic is of considerable importance from both applied and theoretical perspectives, several practical and psychological roadblocks may mean that decline will continue to be underinvestigated.

The remainder of this introduction addresses these three crucial issues, and provides an overview of the remaining parts of the book.

Defining Organizational Decline

Our literature review suggested a wide variety of possible definitions of organizational decline, although the articles that we reviewed rarely offered

Figure 1. The Decline Process

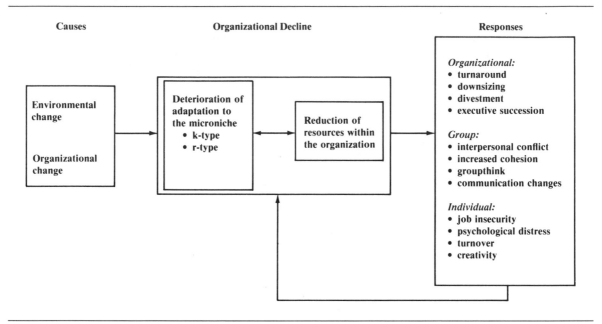

formal definitions. Nonetheless, depending on the type of organization and the preferred language, decline has been characterized as shrinking markets and increased competition (Porter 1980; Harrigan 1982); as budget cuts (Chapter 18; Behn 1983); and as workforce reduction—especially layoffs (Chapter 13; Cornfield 1983). In schools, decline has been defined as shrinking student enrollment (Freeman & Hannan 1975), and shrinking revenues (Cameron 1983). Other descriptions include loss of legitimacy (Benson 1975), maladaptation to a shrinking environmental niche (Greenhalgh 1983), stagnation (see Chapter 8), and deteriorating and unsatisfactory organizational performance that causes members and clients to become disgruntled (Hirschman 1970; Kolarska & Aldrich 1980).

As this list indicates, there are many possible definitions and no consensus about the best way to define decline. In contrast to other concepts that have also been ambiguously defined in the organizational literature, such as organizational effectiveness (see Cameron & Whetten 1983; Good-

man, Pennings & Associates 1977), we believe that it is possible to offer a working definition of organizational decline that integrates prior efforts to study and define decline and that will help guide future empirical research.

Figure 1 diagrams this definition of organizational decline. Decline is defined as a two-stage phenomenon in which, first, an organization's adaptation to its domain, or microniche, deteriorates (Greenhalgh 1983; Zammuto & Cameron 1985), and second, resources are reduced within the organization. Following Wilson's (1980) writings in sociobiology, such deterioration may be "k-type" or "r-type." Deterioration of the "k-type" occurs because an organization is part of a macroniche inhabited by a population of organizations (McKelvey 1982), or is part of an industry (Harrigan 1982), that is shrinking or shifting. The U.S. cigarette industry is an example of a macroniche that has been experiencing k-type decline (Miles & Cameron 1982), and the decline of American Brands cigarette business from 1950 to 1970 is an example of a firm in this industry that has experienced k-type decline—that is, shifting market demand away from nonfilter cigarettes. In contrast, deterioration of the "r-type" occurs when an organization is in a stable or growing population or macroniche but has taken actions, such as introducing poor-quality products or engaging in criminal acts, that have led to a deterioration in adaptation. As of this writing, a failing biotechnology firm would be an example of "r-type" deterioration. Biotechnology is a growing industry, but some individual companies are experiencing financial difficulties.

Both k-type and r-type deterioration mean that the organization has become less well adapted to its microniche and is less successful at exchanging its outputs for new inputs. As a result, there is a reduction of available resources within the organization (see Chapter 10). As Figure 1 indicates, organizations, groups, and individuals affected by decline respond in a number of ways, some functional, others dysfunctional.

The perspective portrayed in Figure 1 helps clarify two potential sources of confusion about what organizational decline is and what it is not. First, this definition applies to the organizational level analysis. It focuses specifically on organizational adaptation to a microniche, not on the level of adaptation of a population to the macroniche. As Cameron and his colleagues observe in Chapter 10, environmental decline—that is, k-type deterioration of a macroniche—may or may not affect resources in a given organization. If an organization is part of an industry characterized by shrinking consumer demand, it cannot be described as "declining" if it is maintaining sales by increasing its market share.

Second, this definition helps researchers distinguish responses to decline from decline itself. This definition spotlights exchanges between the organization and environment as well as the flow of resources into the organization that results from such exchanges. Decline is indicated when there is an objective decrease in the flow of resources. Perhaps the most direct measures of decline are financial data such as changes in sales figures or yearly budgets. But indirect measures may also prove revealing, such as decreases in student enrollment in schools (e.g. Freeman & Hannan 1975) or decreases in customers of service organizations.

Figure 1 also indicates that organizational, group, and individual responses to a given episode of decline may influence subsequent levels of decline. To illustrate, top management may try to engineer a turnaround by introducing new products or services that enhance the fit between the organization and its niche, and thus increase the level of resources within the organization. The Apple Computer Corporation, for example, was experiencing decline in 1985 because sales of its Macintosh personal computer had slowed in the education market and attempts to break into the corporate market had met with little success. But the introduction of the Mac Plus in 1986 (a new and more powerful member of the Macintosh product family) led to a substantial increase in sales in the educational market and enabled Apple to break into corporate markets. In terms of Figure 1, this attempt at turnaround enhanced the organization's adaptation to its microniche and increased resources within the organization.

We do not wish to imply, however, that only the responses of top management can affect subsequent levels of decline. The responses of other organizational participants can accelerate, slow, halt, or even reverse a given episode of decline. For example, local governments can affect the course of decline by lowering or raising taxes. Unions may further deplete resources within the organization by demanding pay raises and going on strike. Or unions may slow the decline by accepting paycuts, reductions in benefits, or layoffs.

Moreover, the actions listed in Figure 1 may influence subsequent levels of decline regardless of whether such responses are intentional or unintentional. The implementation of strategic decisions such as changes in domain (Zammuto & Cameron 1985) and work-force reduction (Greenhalgh, Lawrence & Sutton in press) are examples of intentional responses that can influence subsequent levels of decline. In contrast, groupthink (Janis 1982) and the resistance to change that results from job insecurity (see Chapter 15) are examples of responses that are usually unintentional, but may nevertheless affect subsequent levels of decline.

Many of the responses presented in Figure 1 — executive succession or psychological distress, for example — are clearly distinct from decline. But other responses to decline are often confused with decline itself. Therefore, to help clarify what organizational decline is not, we differentiate decline from four other concepts that are commonly confused with it in the literature.

First, decline can be distinguished from downsizing or retrenchment. These two terms generally pertain to some type of reduction in work force or reduction in services provided by an organization. Downsizing and retrenchment are the terms most frequently confused with decline. As Greenhalgh and his colleagues make clear (Greenhalgh 1983; Greenhalgh, Lawrence & Sutton in press), work-force reduction is a strategic response to the work-force oversupply often caused by decline, but it should not be conceptualized as decline itself. Similarly, retrenching the services provided by an organization (e.g., trimming travel budgets, reducing executive perquisites) may be motivated by decline, but it need not be, and retrenchment is clearly not a synonym for decline.

As with other responses listed in Figure 1, downsizing or retrenchment can be functional or dysfunctional. Choosing the wrong strategy, or implementing the correct strategy poorly, can decrease organizational adaptation and further hamper the flow of resources. Waves of layoffs, for example, may create a job-insecurity crisis that increases psychological strain and decreases productivity. This crisis also encourages the employees with the most marketable skills to "jump ship" and obtain employment elsewhere (Greenhalgh & Rosenblatt in Chapter 15; Sutton, Eisenhardt & Jucker 1986).

In contrast, downsizing or retrenchment can enhance adaptation in other settings. Layoffs and attrition programs can cut costs and act as symbolic signals to key participants such as customers and stockholders that the organization is responding correctly to decline. For example, the Chrysler Corporation helped reverse its steep decline by cutting its work force in half (Iacocca 1984), and a majority of the Fortune 500 firms have engaged in some kind of downsizing or retrenchment activity in the last five years, irrespective of their objective growth or decline pattern.

Second, decline can be distinguished from turbulence. Conceptually, these two concepts are distinctive, but the literature has often confused them operationally. The most common measurement pattern for decline, for example, is to subtract levels of resources at one point in time (T_1) from levels at a later point in time (T_2) without considering the patterns of fluctuations in between. When T_2 is less than T_1, decline is said to have occurred. Cameron and his colleagues (see Chapter 10), for example, found important differences between the effects of decline and turbulence on organizational functioning; yet much of the literature has failed to account for different patterns of resource fluctuation over time.

Third, decline can be distinguished from scarcity. Scarcity involves a lack of available resources in the microniche and is, therefore, a property of the external environment, not the organization. Zammuto and Cameron (1985), for example, identified four types of environmental decline: erosion, dissolution, contraction, and collapse. Each of these four conditions is a characteristic of the environment; thus each is more accurately characterized as a form of scarcity than a form of organizational decline.

Fourth and finally, organizational decline can be distinguished from organizational ineffectiveness, which is broader than our concept of decline. The extent to which an organization is perceived as effective or ineffective at a given moment varies widely, depending on which effectiveness criteria are being applied, which constituencies are consulted, and the preferences of those constituencies (Cameron & Whetten 1983; Goodman, Pennings & Associates 1977). Indeed, Goodman, Atkin, and Schoorman (1983) have proposed that the concept of effectiveness is so complex and there is so little consensus about what it comprises that studies of effectiveness per se are not likely to be fruitful in the future. Our hope is that the relatively narrow view of decline as reduction of internal resources will mean that future research on decline will be characterized by greater consensus and less confusion than past work on organizational effectiveness.

Approaches to the Study of Decline

We have defined organizational decline as deterioration in an organization's adaptation to its microniche and the associated reduction of resources within the organization. Given this definition of decline, we can turn now to approaches for the study of decline.

As mentioned earlier, the noncumulative nature of the decline literature is, in part, a product of the absence of an overall organizing framework. Typical of many emerging research areas, most studies are conducted with little regard for their cumulative contribution. The result is a literature that is fragmented, confusing, and frequently contradictory. For example, one study finds that decline leads to rigidity, conflict, and turnover (Chapter 10); another finds that it produces innovation and stimulus for expansion (MacMillan 1985). One field study finds that layoffs reduce productivity among remaining employees (Greenhalgh 1982), while a series of laboratory studies suggests that layoffs lead to increased productivity among "survivors" (Brockner, Davy & Carter in Chapter 14; Brockner in press). One perspective argues that decline in some populations is inevitable (Hannan & Freeman 1977; Chapter 4), while another author recounts effective turnaround strategies in declining populations (Whetten 1984). Of more concern than the contradictions is the fact that many of these studies do not try to explain, or even acknowledge, the differences in their findings relative to others. For this reason, we feel it is important to propose an organizing framework for the decline literature at the outset of this book.

In the following three parts of this book, chapters are divided into three categories: conceptual, empirical, and normative. These categories do not, however, represent an organizing framework. Instead, they identify the orientation taken by the authors. The objective of an organizing framework is to help guide research and theory and to stimulate cumulation. Therefore, instead of merely categorizing work by type, a more substantive framework must be devised.

Our review of the organizational decline literature suggests that it can be usefully classified along two dimensions: (1) the *phenomena* being considered and (2) the *form of the theory* used to describe the phenomena. Regarding phenomena, there are studies that focus on the *causes* of decline versus studies that concentrate on the *consequences* of decline. Regarding the form of the theory, there are studies using *variance* approaches versus studies using *process* approaches. These two dimensions, we believe, provide guidance for classifying existing theory, research, and practice, and for identifying topics for future scholarly work on decline.

The Phenomena: Causes versus Consequences of Decline

The distinction between the causes of decline and the consequences of decline follows from the definition of decline presented above and portrayed in Figure 1. Because decline is deterioration in adaptation and the associated reduction of internal resources, this phenomenon has been examined as both a cause and an effect. Some researchers who study the causes of decline (e.g., population ecologists, life-cycle theorists) have been interested in the environmental inertial forces that predict which organizations will live and which will die. For example, Carroll and Delacroix (see Chapter 9) studied the economic and political conditions preceding the formation of newspapers. They found that those formed under tumultuous political conditions and periods of noneconomic expansion had higher mortality rates than those formed under political stability and economic expansion. Zammuto (1984) examined changes in the population of U.S. colleges and universities that occurred between the early 1970s and the early 1980s. He found that decline and failure rates were strongly associated with the type of institutional environment; for example, private liberal-arts schools declined more than public comprehensive schools.

Other investigators of the causes of decline have addressed the internal forces that may explain the onset of a downturn. Starbuck, Greve and Hedberg (1978), for example, identified a "success-breeds-failure" syndrome among organizations. An uninterrupted pattern of growth, they discovered, led managers to be less successful in adapting to severe decline than a more saw-toothed organizational history. Organizations having previous experience with periods of decline were inoculated against large downturns more often than were continuously successful firms. Masuch (1985) discussed various "vicious circles" in organizations that led to organizational decline and decay. The vicious circle of bureaucracy, for example, is identified as one precursor to decline. Other factors — such as formalization, maturation, growth, boldness of leadership, and so on — also were proposed to lead to decline when caught in a deviation-amplifying cycle.

Investigators of the consequences of decline, on the other hand, have been interested in phenomena that result from decline. Some studies have centered on structural consequences at the organization level. For example, Hambrick and Schecter (see Chapter 16) investigated the management strategies that were most effective in helping declining firms to recover. They discovered that efficiency-oriented moves were associated with successful turnaround from decline, but not with entrepreneurial initiatives. Levine, Rubin and Wolohojian (1981; 1982) studied the political and organizational consequences of decline in several large U.S. cities. In New York City, Oakland, and Cincinnati, for example, they found that decentralization and politicization resulting from decline blocked effective retrenchment strategies. Conflict among special-interest groups also inhibited effective coping.

Other investigators of the aftermath of decline have emphasized psychological and behavioral consequences for groups and individuals. For example, Brockner and his colleagues (see Chapter 14) used a laboratory experiment to study how survivors reacted to the layoff of a coworker. They discovered that "survivor guilt" caused employees who remained after a layoff, particularly those with low self-esteem, to increase their productivity. Cobb and Kasl's (1977) longitudinal study of workers displaced by two plant closings identified a variety of negative effects on well-being, including hypertension, anxiety, and loss of income.

The Form of the Theory: Variance in Decline versus the Process of Decline

The distinction between variance and process descriptions of decline in organizations is based on work by Mohr (1982). A variance theory is composed of variables. It seeks to explain which independent variable, or variables, determines variation in some dependent variable. In a variance theory, each independent variable is necessary and sufficient to affect the dependent variable. In addition, the time ordering among independent variables in a variance theory is usually unimportant.

A study by Altman and his colleagues (1977) illustrates the logic of variance theories. They developed models for predicting which firms would fail and which would survive by explaining variation in the dependent variable of financial failure. Each of their independent variables, such as debt/equity ratio, was necessary and sufficient to bring about failure. Furthermore, the time ordering of the variables was immaterial to the model; Altman and his colleagues simply entered them simultaneously into a multiple-regression equation. This approach is typical of classical variance methodologies.

In contrast, a process theory tells a story about how some outcome occurs. Rather than dealing with variables, process theories are composed of discrete states and events. The precursors in a process theory are each necessary to bring about the outcome of interest, but any given precursor is insufficient alone. In addition, the time ordering among contributing events is generally critical to the outcome.

An example of a process theory is Sutton's (1984; 1987) model of organizational death. He specifies three sequential sets of tasks: the struggle for organizational survival, the disbanding of the organizational arena, and the reconnection of the people and things that composed the organization with other social systems. This is a process theory because it tells a story about how organizational death comes about; it does not seek to explain differences between organizations that live and die. The theory is composed of discrete events (e.g., announcements of organizational death) and states (e.g., disbanding), rather than of variables. Each event or state is necessary but not sufficient to bring about organizational death; for example, it is proposed that all dying organizations first struggle for survival. But it is *not* proposed that struggle alone is sufficient to cause organizational death. Finally, as with most process theories, the time ordering among the stages is essential: reconnection of people and things cannot occur before they are removed from the dying organization.

The Organizing Framework

Figure 2 portrays an integration of these two primary dimensions. The major benefit of such a framework is that it identifies areas in which progress is being made and areas in which more empirical and theoretical work is needed. We have placed a representative reference in each cell. The listed references do not always fit within a single cell since some studies may consider both cause and effect, both process and variance, as well as a variety of levels of analysis. In constructing Figure 2, however, we have sought to place each listed article in a cell that is consistent with its dominant theme.

We also have restricted the references listed in the figure to those articles presented here. Because of the usual space considerations, many high-quality conceptual, empirical, and practical papers could not be included in this book; nevertheless, those chosen represent important streams of thought and research on decline and are among the best available. In addition, because these papers are intended to be representative, only eight of the twenty-two articles included in this book are cited in Figure 2.

Cell A identifies studies that have investigated variables that precede or cause decline in organizations. Nystrom and Starbuck's case studies (see Chapter 17) revealed that past success can set the stage for organizational decline because "as successes accumulate, organizations emphasize efficiency, grow complacent, and learn too little." They propose that top managers' "encased learning" is a malady within organizations that may lead to full-blown crises because such blindness and rigidity may hamper organizations' ability to recognize and adapt to organizational crises. Nystrom and Starbuck suggest that organizations in crisis must often remove top managers so that obsolete dominating ideas and standard operating procedures can be unlearned. These authors contend that organizations can avoid crises —and top managers can thus keep their jobs—if unlearning occurs routinely through listening to dissents, exploiting opportunities, and experimenting.

A study of external causes of decline using a variance approach is illustrated by a study of Irish and Argentine newspaper survival by Carroll and Delacroix (Chapter 9). It focused on industry maturity, political turmoil, and economic expansion as predictors of organizational birth and death and was briefly summarized earlier. Most studies of external causes of decline have adopted a population ecology or macroeconomic perspective and some impressive theoretical progress has been made. However, relatively few studies that investigate the internal and external factors leading to organizational decline have appeared in the literature, and much of the work is still propositional or theoretical.

Cell B contains papers that focus on the processes that lead to decline in organizations. Greenhalgh and Rosenblatt (Chapter 15) propose that layoffs are part of a vicious circle (Masuch 1985)

Figure 2. An Organizing Framework for the Literature on Organizational Decline

PHENOMENA CONSIDERED

		Causes of Decline		Consequences of Decline	
		Internal	External	Organizational/ Structural	Individual/ Behavioral
FORM OF THE THEORY	Variance Approaches	Nystrom and Starbuck 1984	Carroll and Delacroix 1982	Cameron, Kim, and Whetten 1987	Brockner, Davy, and Carter 1985
	Process Approaches	Greenhalgh and Rosenblatt 1984	Sutton and Callahan 1987	Staw, Sandelands, and Dutton 1981	Krantz 1985

of internal events that can cause or accelerate organizational decline. They further propose that layoffs lead to a job-insecurity crisis among organizational members, causing reduced productivity, increased turnover of valuable members, and resistance to change. These internal changes reduce organizational efficiency and adaptability, leading to the need for more layoffs. Thus, Greenhalgh and Rosenblatt propose a model of the causes of decline that focuses on a chain of actions and reactions within organizations.

In contrast, Sutton and Callahan's paper (Chapter 12) on the stigma evoked by Chapter 11 of the Federal Bankruptcy Code emphasizes causes of decline that occur outside of the organization or, more precisely, it considers factors that cause decline to accelerate. But both papers in cell B stress process approaches. Sutton and Callahan's case studies led them to propose a sequence in which: (1) the fact of Chapter 11 is discovered by key members of the organizational audience (e.g., suppliers and customers); (2) the image of

the firm and its top management is spoiled; (3) members of the organizational audience have negative reactions including disengaging from the firm, demanding a more favorable exchange relationship, and denigrating the firm and its leaders; and (4) these negative reactions further increase the probability of organizational death. Sutton and Callahan's study is one of the few empirical investigations that attempts to investigate the causes of decline using a process approach. Indeed, of the four cells represented in Figure 2, the least amount of empirical work has been done on the internal and external processes that cause organizations to decline.

Far more studies have appeared that are representative of cell C. These studies identify the organizational and individual consequences of decline, and they often contain prescriptions about effective adaptive strategies for managing organizational decline. (In fact, the prescriptive literature—much of which is nonempirical or based on consulting experiences—is the single largest category of writing on decline to date. An abundance of writing advising managers on how to turn a business around now exists.) The study of 335 colleges and universities by Cameron, Kim and Whetten (see Chapter 10) is illustrative of the empirical work emphasizing the organizational consequences of decline. They identified twelve organizational attributes that changed as a result of decline. One finding was that conflict, conservatism, scapegoating, turnover, and resistance to change increased in organizations encountering decline, while morale, innovation, and the credibility of leaders decreased compared to growing organizations. The study by Brockner and his colleagues (Chapter 14), summarized earlier, illustrates an emerging literature on the aftermath of restricted resources on the individual level. Their finding that — at least for people with low self-esteem — layoffs may actually increase productivity among "survivors" challenges the assumptions held by many managers. Despite the relatively large number of articles represented by cell B, however, this literature is by no means well developed; on the contrary, it remains fragmented and largely noncumulative.

Cell D depicts studies that have described the processes that can unfold as a result of decline. Staw, Sandelands and Dutton's (1981) paper on the threat-rigidity thesis describes such a sequence of organizational changes. They contend that perceptions of external threat — such as reduction of internal resources — can lead to a sequence of organizational-level changes including greater formalization of communication, greater centralization of decisionmaking, and increased use of efficiency measures. Such changes are proposed to lead, in turn, to restriction of information processing, constriction of control, and conservation of resources.

Krantz's case studies emphasized the consequences of decline for group and individual processes in declining organizations. He identified the psychological fears and anxieties that resulted from severe cutbacks in two organizations. The subsequent group-defense mechanisms used to contain these maladaptive — but perhaps unavoid-

able — responses to decline were described in terms of Bion's theory of effective group functioning. Krantz's work is of unusually high quality because his case studies were used to generate theory. Unfortunately, although our literature search uncovered numerous case studies describing the process of decline in a single school, firm, or institution, the case studies that represent cell D are rarely integrative and typically make little or no theoretical contribution to the study of decline.

In sum, relatively few studies exist using the process approach to decline and relatively few studies covering the causes of decline have been conducted. Ignorance about the causes of decline is particularly disturbing given the frightening statistics cited earlier. And, while we are most knowledgeable about the organizational and structural consequences of decline, much more theory-building and testing is needed before our understanding of the variables associated with cell C is adequate. Nonetheless, organizational scholars know much more than they did a decade ago about the causes and consequences of decline.

Impediments and Inducements for Future Work on Decline

Thus far, we have described the importance and prevalence of organizational decline for American management; we have proposed a working definition of organizational decline; and we have offered a framework for integrating past theory and research on decline and for guiding future work. Throughout this discussion we have implied that researchers *should* put forth greater efforts to study declining organizations. However, we have not yet considered the forces that influence whether or not researchers *will* study decline. Next we cover the set of strong impediments and inducements that organizational scholars who choose to study declining organizations will encounter.

Impediments for Decline Research

Our experiences, and those of our colleagues, over the past eight years suggest that difficult roadblocks impede the development of a coherent body of literature on decline and identification of practical tools for decline managers. We discuss next the stigma of decline and the problem of obtaining sufficient resources to study decline, two of the most formidable impediments.

The stigma of decline. Whetten (1980: 579–80) has observed that the American culture is preoccupied with growth and progress:

> We are told that, through the *Power of Positive Thinking* (Peale, 1952) we can *Think and Grow Rich* (Hill, 1967). It follows that if success can be willed, then failure must reflect a lack of desire. Hence, admitting failure is practically a national taboo.

Indeed, we contend that there is a stigma associated with the topic of organizational decline that causes researchers to avoid studying the topic, management educators to avoid teaching the subject, and managers to resist participating in such research.

While not all researchers shun the topic of decline, there is an overall tendency in the organizational-studies literature to focus on the birth and growth of organizations rather than their decline and death. This tendency is surprising since, in any large population of organizations over a long period of time, there will be a large number of declining and dying organizations. In fact, we noted earlier that recent statistics indicate that the rate of business failure in the United States is at an all-time high.

Organizational-decline research has increased during the last decade in response to foreign competition in the private sector and cutbacks in the public sector. But far more organizational research and theory-building still emphasize organizational birth and growth. As noted earlier, published organizational life-cycle models still focus almost exclusively on organizational birth and growth (Quinn & Cameron 1983; Whetten in Chapter 1).

Furthermore, we continue to be surprised by the discomfort that the topics of organizational decline and death evoke among some of our colleagues. Some colleagues have confided that they could never study such a depressing topic. Other colleagues have suggested that we "work on something optimistic for a change."

This discomfort seems to be most pronounced with respect to organizational death and bankruptcy, topics that especially challenge the "national taboo" of failure. In particular, it seems impossible to discuss these topics comfortably unless audiences are given opportunities to joke and laugh. The presence of such "gallows humor" is consistent with classical psychological (Freud 1960) and anthropological (Radcliffe-Brown 1952) arguments that laughter and joking serve to release tension in distressing situations.

The stigma of decline may also explain why organizational decline is not taught widely in man-management classes (Zammuto 1982). There has been an increase in the teaching of decline in the past five years, stressing in particular Harrigan's work (see Chapter 7; 1982) on declining industries. But we do not know of a single master's-degree course in the United States that thoroughly covers the management of decline, and few introductory organizational behavior classes include even a single session on the subject. This view is consistent with a set of recent *Wall Street Journal* articles (December 15, 1986) that argued that—despite some exceptions—most business schools do not teach the management of decline because of the American taboo against failure.

Finally, the tendency of U.S. managers to avoid talking about organizational decline—particularly their own association with this set of transitions—means that this subject is more difficult to study than organizational growth or effectiveness. Salancik's (1979: 641) simple field-stimulation demonstrates that managers would rather participate in a study of success than failure:

> We asked firms to fill out a short questionnaire, inquiring about nothing more than the name of the organization, its sales, size, and the average return on its common stock. For ten firms the cover letter introduced a study of why firms fail; for another ten it said the study addressed organizational success. Two of the fail questionnaires were returned compared to six of the success questionnaires.

Indeed, Sutton and his colleagues experienced refusals so often in their studies of organizational death (Harris & Sutton 1986; Sutton & Schurman 1985) and of bankruptcy (Chapter 12) that they developed special methods for gathering data produced by informants who refused to participate.

Even when managers and other employees agree to participate in research on decline, data collection can be more difficult because informants who feel the sting of failure may display more red-hot emotion than do members of successful organizations (Sutton & Schurman 1985). For example, Harris and Sutton found that nine out of twenty-three managers who completed a questionnaire about their reactions to organizational death reported that the experience was equivalent to divorce or the death of a spouse. Such intense emotional demands mean that even cooperative informants or respondents will require more time and care to work with. Further, the accuracy of self-reports may be even more suspect than in research on less threatening topics.

Obtaining resources to study decline. We also contend that the study of declining and dying organizations requires more resources and that such resources are more difficult to obtain. The above discussion suggests that response rates are lower in research on organizational decline and death. This increases research costs because—in comparison to studies of growing, successful organizations—more hours of research time must be invested for each completed interview or returned questionnaire.

The fiery emotions expressed by participants in research on organizational decline and death also increase research costs because more skilled —and thus more highly paid—field workers are required. Furthermore, more time must be devoted to developing strategies for working with distraught informants and allowing members of the research team to provide one another with emotional support (Sutton & Schurman 1985).

On the other side of the ledger, financial support for research on organizational decline may be more difficult to obtain. In the private sector,

managers are often willing to support research about their firms. As Whetten (1980) points out, growing companies are far more likely to have the resources to support research than are declining companies. A variety of strong inducements prevent declining organizations from supporting research. Few declining organizations have the discretionary resources to support research about topics such as their structure, strategy, processes, and leadership. In fact, funds for research and development on new products and services are usually among the first to be cut in a declining organization. Research conducted by either internal or external investigators on management issues is typically even more difficult to support since decisionmakers are likely to view it as pure luxury.

Resistance to funding research on decline may also arise because leaders worry that it will be the equivalent of airing dirty laundry. And, despite researchers' assurances of confidentiality, such fears may have a basis in reality. The shortcomings of human information processing (Nisbett & Ross 1980) may cause observers to blame top managers for poor organizational performance, regardless of the extent to which leaders may deserve such blame (Pfeffer 1977; Meindl, Ehrlich & Dukerich 1985). Since most leaders understand that they will be perceived by internal and external organizational actors as responsible for failure as well as success, they may be wise to veto funding for any study that evaluates a declining firm's strategy, structure, or leadership. (Conversely, it is usually in the best interests of leaders of successful organizations to fund such research.)

Inducements to the Study of Decline

The above discussion paints a bleak picture for aspiring decline researchers. We have done so to help researchers anticipate the hazards of studying decline. However, it is also essential to note that investigating declining organizations can be especially rewarding, both to researchers as individuals and to the organizational-studies literature as a whole. We consider three such inducements below: working with knowledgeable and interested informants; the opportunity to make a substantial scholarly contribution; and the opportunity to make a substantial practical contribution.

Working with knowledgeable and interested informants. We discussed above the problems associated with convincing people to participate in such research and the problems of working with distraught research subjects. Nonetheless, our experience, and the experience of other decline researchers, indicates that there are also great advantages to working with such informants.

First, people who are key figures in declining or dying organizations are typically knowledgeable about the phenomenon. The problems and challenges of the management of decline are so visible in an organization that information is readily available. Thus, while we as organizational researchers may sometimes study topics such as leadership style or centralization that informants have never thought of, members of declining organizations typically have a vast store of knowledge about the subject at hand.

Second, we have also discovered that, although the initial refusal rate is high in studies of declining or dying organizations, informants or respondents are usually remarkably helpful once they have chosen to participate in the research. Such cooperation occurs, we believe, because the subject of the research is usually a central issue in the informant's life.

We have often been surprised by the amount of time that overloaded informants have taken to speak with us. One of us recalls a top-level administrator who spent an entire day organizing and explaining thousands of pages of records data. These were records from a defunct organization that the administrator had first tried to save and then had to disband. He put aside a day to help us because "this was an important part of my life. I want you to understand what happened." We doubt that this fellow would have been so cooperative if he had believed that we were studying "leadership style" or "centralization."

The opportunity to make a substantial scholarly contribution. Our discussion of the organizing framework presented in Figure 2 indicates that organizational decline is an area that is, on the whole, badly in need of new theory and research. Quantitative or qualitative research that makes comparisons across organizations, rather than describing a single case, is especially needed.

Perhaps as a result of the stigma of decline and problems with acquiring resources, or perhaps because this is a relatively new area of scholarly research, people who build and test theories about declining organizations have an array of opportunities to make new contributions. In comparison to other areas that primarily offer scholars the chance to make incremental contributions, scholars who focus on organizational decline have greater opportunities for developing new theories, or testing theories for the first time. For example, Whetten's (Chapter 8) review of the literature on organizational life cycles indicated that numerous theories and studies describe how the processes of organizational birth and growth unfold, but that very little work examines the converse processes of organizational death and decline.

Moreover, declining organizations are excellent natural laboratories for studying other organizational phenomena. Albert and Whetten (1985) propose that issues of organizational identity (i.e., the organization's claimed central character, distinctiveness, and continuity over time) usually remain latent during periods of stability and growth. But issues of "who we are," "who we are not," and "who we should be in the future" become of central importance when members are confronted with evidence that their organization's character may be flawed. The debate over such issues becomes especially heated when choices must be made about which parts of the organization should be eliminated and which parts should be retained.

The opportunity to make a substantial practical contribution. Finally, we hope that scholars will be moved to conduct research on declining organizations because both American and foreign managers need such information badly. Most managers are not trained to avoid organizational decline or to manage it once it occurs. Surely this fact of organizational life should be an inducement for researchers. We believe that they would be rewarded both intrinsically and extrinsically if, as they chose topics for the empirical study of declining and dying organizations, they focused on research questions that can ultimately guide managerial practice. We need (1) better evidence and theory to write better popular books and articles for decline managers; (2) better management education for future and current managers; and (3) better consultation, provided by change agents, for declining organizations.

Overview of the Book

The remainder of this book is divided into four main parts. The following three parts contain twenty-two previously published articles on decline. We sought to meet two goals in our efforts to compile these parts: (1) to select the highest quality articles and (2) to best represent the range of literature on declining and dying organizations. The fourth and final part contains three original reviews and commentaries.

Part II, entitled *Conceptual Foundations,* contains two sets of articles. The first set deals with organizational decline as a special case of organizational decline processes, addressing factors such as the organizational life cycle, metamorphic change, and structural inertia. The second set centers on the context of decline; particularly threat-rigidity effects, environmental change, and organizational atrophy and entropy.

Part III presents *Empirical Foundations.* Section A of this part comprises three reports of empirical investigations from the macro perspective, including articles that predict variation in both the occurrence and the effects of decline and death. Section B includes four articles that describe decline from the micro perspective, emphasizing the psychological and behavioral reactions of individuals and groups during decline.

Normative Foundations, Part IV, includes seven articles offering theory-based prescriptions for recovery and turnaround, downsizing and retrenching, and divesting, terminating, and closing organizations. Since no one response is best in all declining organizations, and since decline can require a battery of complex responses, the articles included discuss when and how various alternatives should be selected.

The final part, *Commentaries,* contains articles written by three well-known scholars: Bill McKelvey, Alan Meyer, and L. L. Cummings. These authors each review the decline literature from a different level of analysis, and use their vantage points to identify major contributions, blind spots, weaknesses, and pathways for future theory-building and research. Bill McKelvey reviews the literature from the standpoint of organizational populations, Alan Meyer assesses writings on decline in terms of the organizational level of analysis, and Larry Cummings evaluates this literature from the perspective of small groups and individuals.

Note

1   These and the following statistics in this chapter regarding the decline of American organizations and job loss can be found in Cameron and Ulrich (1986), "The Hollow Corporation" (1986), "The Push for Quality" (1987), and Thurow (1984).

References

Albert, S., and D. Whetten. 1985. "Organizational Identity." In *Research in Organizational Behavior,* Vol. 7, edited by L.L. Cummings and B.M. Staw. Greenwich, CT: JAI Press, pp. 263–96.

Altman, E.I., R.G. Haldeman, and P. Narayanan. 1977. "Zeta Analysis: A New Model to Identify Bankruptcy Risk of Corporations." *Journal of Banking and Finance* 1: 29–54.

Behn, R. 1983. "The Fundamentals of Cutback Management." In *What Role for Government: Lessons from Policy Research,* edited by R. Zeckhauser and D. Leebaert, pp. 310–22. Durham, N.C.: Duke University Press.

Benson, J.K. 1975. "The Interorganizational Network as a Political Economy." *Administrative Science Quarterly* 20: 229–49.

Brockner, J. In press. "The Effects of Work Layoffs on Survivors: Research, Theory, Practice. In *Research in Organizational Behavior,* Vol. 10, edited by B.M. Staw and L.L. Cummings. Greenwich, Conn.: JAI Press.

Cameron, K.S. 1983. "Strategic Responses to Conditions of Decline: Higher Education and the Private Sector." *Journal of Higher Education* 54: 359–80.

Cameron, K.S., and D.O. Ulrich. 1986. "Transformational Leadership in Colleges and Universities. In *Higher Education: Handbook of Theory and Research,* Vol. 2, edited by John R. Smart. New York: Agathon.

Cameron, K.S., and D.A. Whetten. 1983. *Organizational Effectiveness: A Comparison of Multiple Models.* New York: Academic Press.

Cobb, S., and S.V. Kasl. 1977. *Termination: The Consequences of Job Loss.* U.S. Department of Health, Education, and Welfare. HEW Publication no. 77-224.

Cornfield, D.B. 1983. "Chances of Layoff in a Corporation: A Case Study." *Administrative Science Quarterly* 28: 503–20.

Freeman, J., and M.T. Hannan. 1975. "Growth and Decline Processes in Organizations." *American Journal of Sociology* 40: 215–28.

Freud, S. 1960. *Jokes and Their Relation to the Unconscious.* London: Pergamon Press.

Goodman, P.S., R.S. Atkin, and D.F. Schoorman. 1983. "On the Demise of Organizational Effectiveness Studies." In *Organizational Effectiveness: A Comparison of Multiple Models,* edited by K.D. Cameron and D.A. Whetten, pp. 162–83. New York: Academic Press.

Goodman, P.S., J.M. Pennings, and Associates. 1977. *New Perspectives on Organizational Effectiveness.* San Francisco: Jossey-Bass.

Greenhalgh, L. 1982. "Maintaining Organizational Effectiveness During Organizational Retrenchment." *Journal of Applied Behavioral Science* 18: 155–70.

———. 1983. "Organizational Decline." In *Research in the Sociology of Organizations,* Vol. 2, edited by S.B. Bacharach, pp. 231–76. Greenwich, Conn.: JAI Press.

Greenhalgh, L., A.T. Lawrence, and R.I. Sutton. In press. "Determinants of Workforce Reduction Strategies." *Academy of Management Review.*

Hannan, M.T., and J.H. Freeman. 1977. "The Population Ecology of Organizations." *American Journal of Sociology* 82: 929–64.

Harrigan, K.R. 1982. "Exit Decisions in Mature Industries." *Academy of Management Journal* 25: 707–32.

Harris, S.C., and R.I. Sutton. 1986. "Functions of Parting Ceremonies in Dying Organizations." *The Academy of Management Journal* 29, no. 1: 5–30.

Hill, N. 1967. *Think and Grow Rich.* New York: Hawthorn.

Hirsch, P.M. In press. *Pack Your Parachute.* Reading, Mass.: Addison-Wesley.

Hirschman, A.O. 1970. *Exit, Voice, and Loyalty.* Cambridge, Mass.: Harvard University Press.

"The Hollow Corporation." 1986. *Business Week* (March 3) 57–85.

Iacocca, L. 1984. *Iacocca: An Autobiography.* New York: Bantam.

Janis, I.L. 1982. *Groupthink.* Boston: Houghton Mifflin.

Kolarska, L., and H. Aldrich. 1980. "Exit, Voice and Silence: Consumers' and Managers' Responses to Organizational Decline." *Organization Studies* 1, no. 1: 41–58.

Levine, C.H., I.S. Rubin, and G.G. Wolohojian. 1981. "Resource Scarcity and the Reform Model: The Management of Retrenchment in Cincinnati and Oakland." *Public Administration Review* 42: 619–27.

———. 1982. "Managing Organizational Retrenchment: Preconditions, Deficiencies, and Adaptations in the Public Sector." *Administration and Society* 14: 101–36.

MacMillan, I.C. 1985. *Progress in Research on Corporate Venturing.* Research Report Series, Center for Entrepreneurial Studies, New York University.

Marsh, B. 1985. *A Corporate Tragedy: The Agony of International Harvester Company.* Garden City, N.Y.: Doubleday.

Masuch, M. 1985. "Vicious Circles in Organizations." *Administrative Science Quarterly* 30: 14–33.

McKelvey, B. 1982. *Organizational Systematics.* Berkeley: University of California Press.

Meindl, J.R., S.B. Ehrlich, and J.M. Dukerich. 1985. "The Romance of Leadership." *Administrative Science Quarterly* 30: 78–102.

Miles, R.H., and K.S. Cameron. 1982. *Coffin Nails and Corporate Strategy.* Englewood Cliffs, N.J.: Prentice-Hall.

Mohr, L. 1982. *Explaining Organizational Behavior.* San Francisco: Jossey-Bass.

Nance, J.J. 1984. *Splash of Colors: The Self-Destruction of Braniff International.* New York: Morrow.

Nisbett, R., and L. Ross. 1980. *Human Inference: Strategies and Shortcomings of Social Judgment.* Englewood Cliffs, N.J.: Prentice-Hall.

Osborne, A., and J. Dvorak. 1984. *Hypergrowth:*

The Rise and Fall of Osborne Computer Corporation. Berkeley, Calif.: Idthekkethan Publishing Company.

Peale, N.V. 1952. *The Power of Positive Thinking.* Englewood Cliffs, N.J.: Prentice-Hall.

Pfeffer, J. 1977. "The Ambiguity of Leadership." *Academy of Management Review* 2: 104–12.

Platt, H.D. 1985. *Why Companies Fail.* Lexington, Mass.: Lexington Books.

Porter, M.E. 1980. *Competitive Strategy.* New York: Free Press.

"The Push for Quality." 1987. *Business Week* (June 8) 130–44.

Quinn, R.E., and K.S. Cameron. 1983. "Organizational Life Cycles and Shifting Criteria of Effectiveness: Some Preliminary Evidence." *Management Science* 29: 33–51.

Radcliffe-Brown, A.R. 1952. *Structure and Function in Primitive Society.* New York: Free Press.

Salancik, G.R. 1979. "Field Stimulations for Organizational Behavior Research." *Administrative Science Quarterly* 24: 638–49.

Schumacher, E.F. 1973. *Small is Beautiful.* New York: Colophon Books.

Sprague, I.H. 1986. *Bailout: An Insider's Account of Bank Failures and Rescues.* New York: Basic Books.

Starbuck, W.H., A. Greve, and B.L.T. Hedberg. 1978. "Responding to Crisis." *Journal of Business Administration* 9: 111–37.

Sutton, R.I. 1984. "Organizational Death." Ph.D. diss., The University of Michigan, Ann Arbor.

———. 1987. "The Process of Organizational Death: Struggling, Disbanding, and Reconnecting." Typescript.

Sutton, R.I., K.M. Eisenhardt, and J.V. Jucker. 1986. "Managing Organizational Decline: Lessons from Atari." *Organizational Dynamics* 14: 17–29.

Sutton, R.I., and S.J. Schurman. 1985. "On Studying Emotionally Hot Topics: Lessons from an Investigation of Organizational Death." In *Clinical Demands of Research Methods,* edited by D. Berg and K. Smith. Beverly Hills: Sage.

Thurow, L. 1984. "Revitalizing American Industry: Managing in a Competitive World Economy." *California Management Review* 28: 9–41.

Whetten, D.A. 1980. "Organizational Decline: A Neglected Topic in Organizational Science." *Academy of Management Review* 5: 577–88.

———. 1984. "Effective Administrators." *Change* (November–December) 38–43.

White, E.C. 1985. "Administrators Shrink Their Hospitals to Withstand Competitive Pressures." *Modern Healthcare* 15, no. 23: 66–71.

Wilson, E. 1980. *Socio-Biology.* Cambridge, Mass.: Harvard University Press.

Yates, B. 1983. *The Decline and Fall of the American Automobile Industry.* New York: Empire Books.

Zammuto, R.F. 1982. "Organizational Decline and Management Education." *Exchange* 7: 5–12.

———. 1984. "Are Liberal Arts Colleges an Endangered Species?" *Journal of Higher Education* 55: 184–211.

Zammuto, R.F., and K.S. Cameron. 1985. "Environmental Decline and Organizational Response." In *Research in Organizational Behavior,* Vol. 7, edited by L.L. Cummings and B.M. Staw. Greenwich, Conn.: JAI Press.

PART *II*

Conceptual Foundations of Decline: Change Processes and Context of Decline

Until recently, organizational theorists and researchers could largely ignore decline. Most theories about organizational performance, and most criteria for measuring effectiveness, were based implicitly on assumptions of growth and enlargement. That was because most organizations generally grew and expanded. Decline was viewed as objective evidence of ineffectiveness and failure. Successful organizations enlarged operations, elaborated structures, and added boundary-spanning units. Successful managers accounted for more sales, higher profits, and greater numbers of employees year after year.

Decline can no longer be defined as merely a departure from effective performance, however, nor as an unusual phenomenon typical of weak or sick organizations. Not only have more organizations gone out of business in the last five years alone than in the previous 30 years, but a majority of the Fortune 500 corporations have implemented downsizing activities in the 1980s. Never before have so many organizations consciously engaged in decline strategies—for example, reducing employees, consolidating production capacity, cutting administrative overhead—in order to enhance their effectiveness.

This trend, however, has highlighted a fundamental weakness in most current organizational theories: While they do reasonably well in accounting for organizational growth, most do not account for organizational decline. Assumptions that growth and expansion are natural consequences of effective performance have dominated organizational sciences. The prevailing assumption has been that the major issues organizations encounter result from expansion and enlargement, and that environmental challenges (e.g., increasing turbulence and complexity) are best addressed through addition, augmentation, or diversification. Theories of organizational design based on information processing, resource dependency, bureaucracy, or organizational development, for example, all assume that adaptive organizational design changes lead to increasing information-processing capacity, resource acquisition, divisionalization, and so on.

When a decreasing supply of resources is available to organizations over time, when getting smaller may be more effective than getting larger, or when downsizing and cutback may be the preferred design alternatives, little guidance is available from organizational theory for effective organizational performance. For example, do declining organizations follow a reverse pattern of lifecycle stages from that of organizations that are growing? Or do they abandon product-based organizational designs in favor of more rudimentary functionalized designs?

Recently, organizational theorists have begun to address conditions of decline more thoughtfully. Foundations for models of organizational performance accounting for conditions of downsizing, decline, and death are being laid. These theorists have begun to consider how and why decline occurs, what organizational processes accompany decline, and how it can best be managed. This part of the book includes eight chapters that address these conceptual foundations. The selections represent theoretical perspectives upon which much of the decline literature is being built. The chapters are divided into two sections: those in Section A cover decline as a change process, and those in Section B focus on the context of decline.

Section A considers decline as a special case of organizational change, but each chapter takes a different approach to the explanation and dynamics of decline. These approaches include discussion of the stages of organizational development, frame-breaking or metamorphical change, and structural inertia and ecological change. Section B contains chapters on the organizational and environmental context that accompanies decline. The authors consider precursors to as well as antecedents of organizational decline. The discussions include threat-rigidity responses, technological and sociological changes, environmental-niche changes, and organizational processes such as atrophy and entropy.

In Chapter 1, David A. Whetten reviews the decline and growth literature. He begins by pointing out the continuing debate on the applicability of the biological metaphor to organizational growth and decline. Some scholars accept quite literally the idea that organizations follow stages of development similar to living organisms. Others are critical of that perspective. Whetten helps bring these two opposing viewpoints together by discussing stages of development as clusters of problems that organizations face as they grow or decline. These problem clusters are not linear, nor are they hierarchically superior to one another. Thus, stages of development in organizations do not necessarily indicate increased maturity, since stages may also be recursive.

In his chapter, Whetten organizes the growth and decline literatures on the basis of two major themes: (1) causes and consequences of growth and decline, and (2) the effective management of growth and decline. He points out both functions and dysfunctions of growth (e.g., growth creates economies of scale, but it also creates inflexibility), as well as the difficulties in measuring growth (e.g., size is usually used as a measure of growth, but it varies widely in its operationalization). Similarly, he points out functions and dysfunctions of decline (e.g., decline may stimulate organizational renewal, but it also may lead to a threat-rigidity response), and also the differences between environmentally induced decline (e.g., reduced customer demand may cause decline) and internally induced decline (e.g., the "success-breeds-failure" syndrome may cause decline).

The second chapter focuses specifically on decline as part of the organizational life cycle. Kim S. Cameron and David A. Whetten review organizational life-cycle models and examine their application to colleges and universities. These authors suggest that organizational life-cycle stages are predictable patterns of change, especially typical of early development in organizations or that occur after a major discontinuity. Life-cycle changes involve alterations of structures, strategies, leadership patterns, and cultures. They are explained as emerging from the same dynamics that foster group-stage development.

A review of the group-stage development literature produced a model of six consensual stages that are quite consistent with the major models of organizational life cycles. A consensual four-stage model for organizational change was also identified from a review of the organizational life-cycle literature, and the congruence between group and organizational life-cycle models is demonstrated in this chapter.

The third chapter, by Michael L. Tushman, William H. Newman, and Elaine Romanelli, represents a contrary viewpoint to the predictions of the life-cycle models in Chapters 1 and 2. It exemplifies a stream of research by Tushman and his colleagues relating to discontinuous change in organizations. They argue that organizations are more likely to experience revolutionary changes *of* systems (i.e., reformed organizational values and mission, altered power and status relationships, revised interaction patterns, and new management) than to engage in predictable patterns of change through life-cycle stages. This kind of change is called metamorphical change and is necessitated when the organization becomes incongruent with its environment, requiring reestablishment of equilibrium. Metamorphical change is dysfunctional in times of growth and success, but it is necessary under conditions of decline in order to reestablish effectiveness.

The fourth chapter represents a different perspective on change associated with organizational decline. Michael T. Hannan and John Freeman argue that organizations are characterized by structural inertia — that is, pressures toward stability and status quo resulting from both internal and external forces. Inertia is evidenced when organizations change relatively slowly (or not at all) in response to threats and opportunities in their environment. This condition, according to the authors, characterizes all effective organizations.

In brief, Hannan and Freeman argue that effective organizations are reliable (i.e., reproduce collective action with little variance) and accountable (i.e., governed by norms of rationality). These two characteristics create conditions in which routines of behavior (structures) in organizations become ritualized and associated with moral value. Pressure to change organizations creates strong normative and value-laden resistance. Organizational growth and death, therefore, are best explained by ecological selection dynamics. Organizations that grow represent organizational types that are selected by the environment as adaptable because of this inertial quality. Organizations that decline and die do so because they lack structural inertia. They do not have the capacity to reproduce themselves or maintain appropriate levels of accountability for action. Single organizational decline, according to Hannan and Freeman, is not nearly as important an issue for scholars as is decline in organizational populations and organizational forms, since the latter is a product of ecological selection processes.

The second set of chapters begins with a discussion of the threat-rigidity phenomena in Chapter 5 by Barry M. Staw, Lance E. Sandelands, and Jane E. Dutton. These authors propose that in threatening circumstances, individuals, groups, and organizations respond by becoming more rigid: dominant behavioral responses are emitted, flexibility is reduced, information flows are constricted, scapegoating occurs, self-protection predominates, and so on. This response is supported in their reviews of the literature on individual-level behavior dealing with stress, anxiety, and disasters. It also is confirmed at the group level in reviews of the literatures on group cohesiveness, group leadership and control, and pressures toward uniformity in groups. At the organization level, support was found in a survey of the crisis, information-processing, control process, and efficiency literatures.

In brief, the chapter points out that across these multiple levels of analysis, threat-rigidity effects are prevalent. And, to the extent that decline is considered threatening, similar individual, group, and organizational responses are expected to occur when it is encountered. Whereas not all rigidity is dysfunctional, Staw and his coauthors argue that many instances of organizational breakdown and death are directly attributable to this effect.

Chapter 6 expands the idea of threat-rigidity by identifying four different types of decline that occur as a result of changes in the environment. Kim S. Cameron and Raymond F. Zammuto suggest that not all types of decline produce threat and rigidity. Rather, organizational decline results from two main changes in the environment: (1) a reduction in the size of a niche (e.g., fewer resources available) or (2) a change in the shape of the niche (e.g., a shift in preferences or demand). They also suggest that these changes can be distinguished as continuous (i.e., predictable from past trends) or discontinuous (i.e., a deviation from past trends). Combining these two dimensions—type of environmental change and continuity of change—results in a typology in which four patterns of decline occur.

One type of decline is *erosion,* defined as a continuous decline in niche size, in which decline is gradual and predictable. A second is *contraction,* defined as a discontinuous decline in niche size, in which decline occurs suddenly and unpredictably. A third is *dissolution,* defined as a continuous change in niche shape, in which a predictable shift occurs from one niche to another. A fourth is *collapse,* defined as discontinuous change in niche shape, in which a rapid and dramatic alteration of the niche requires the abandonment of that niche. Different reactions are likely to occur within each environmental condition, and different strategies are likely to be effective.

Chapter 7, by Kathryn Rudie Harrigan, is representative of a series of investigations of declining industries she has conducted. Here, Harrigan identifies three main dimensions that serve as the core of her decline model. The first is the *favorability of the environment* as determined by the causes of decline: technological obsolescence, sociological or demographic change, or changing fashion. These conditions create different patterns of decline—for example, quick deterioration of demand for products or services, slowly diminishing demand, plateaued demand, or zero demand—which determine environmental favorability. Industry environments are classified as favorable, intermediate, or unfavorable based on these conditions. The second dimension is the *competitive strength of the industry,* or industry attractiveness. Competitive strength is based on factors such as brand loyalty, strong distribution systems, technological leadership, economies of scale, favorable location of raw materials, and so on. Industries are rated as high, medium, or low in competitive strength and attractiveness. These environmental and industry conditions give rise, according to Harrigan, to the third dimension: five *types of strategies* that must be matched with the environment and industry. The chapter suggests that when an appropriate match between strategy and conditions exist, a 92 percent success rate results. When strategies and conditions are not matched, an 85 percent failure occurs. The strategies are: (1) increase investment and expand the organization, (2) hold firm and defend the business, (3) reposition by selecting new market niches, (4) milk current investments, or (5) exit the industry. A summary matrix matching strategies to conditions is discussed.

The final chapter in this section, Chapter 8, is by David A. Whetten, in which he examines the sources, responses, and effects of decline. After summarizing major themes in the population and organizational literatures, Whetten identifies four main sources of decline that have been examined by organizational scholars: (1) organizational atrophy (as illustrated by the "success-breeds-failure" syndrome), (2) vulnerability (as illustrated by the "liability-of-newness" phenomenon), (3) loss of legitimacy (as illustrated by the power generated by political slack), and (4) environmental entropy (as illustrated by loss of niche capacity). Responses to decline are also categorized into four types depending on the extent to which change is defined positively or negatively and the extent to which action is proactive or reactive: (1) preventing decline (negative proactive), (2) defending against decline (negative reactive), (3) reacting to decline (positive reactive), and (4) generating decline (positive proactive).

These categories of sources and responses are examined in terms of the differences that appear in public-sector organizations versus private-sector organizations. In the private sector, decline and death are defined as suicide, while in the public sector they are viewed as homicide. Private-sector decline is most often attributed to managerial incompetence, while public sector decline is attributed to environmental scarcity. In the private sector, positive proactive responses are more prevalent than in the public sector, where negative reactive responses are most likely.

1

Organizational Growth and Decline Processes

David A. Whetten

Introduction and Historical Context

The increasing emphasis on the temporal aspects of organizations represents a significant trend in the study of organizations. Authors stress the need to examine dynamic, evolutionary processes within single organizations (Cameron & Whetten 1981, Kimberly & Quinn 1984, Miller & Friesen 1980, Kimberly & Miles 1980, Tushman & Romanelli 1985, Singh et al. 1986), as well as in populations of organizations (Freeman & Hannan 1975, Tushman & Anderson 1986). Evidence of this trend is reflected in the extensive use of the organizational life cycles analogy, which focuses on the natural, metamorphic processes associated with birth, maturation, decline, and death in organic systems.

Recent efforts to organize strands of organizational theory taxonomically have made clear that theories can be categorized as either mechanistic or organic. Further, some writers see a general trend in the field from mechanistic to organic views of organizations (Van de Ven & Astley 1981, Perrow 1979, Scott 1981). Although economists have drawn on the biological analogies of natural selection and birth and death processes for decades (Marshall 1920, Boulding 1950) and isolated early organizational theorists urged their adoption (Haire 1959, Katz & Kahn 1966, Lippitt & Schmidt 1967), such analogies did not gain widespread use in organization research until the 1970s.

Clearly the most hotly contested issue in the life cycles literature is how literally the biological analogy should be applied to social systems. In his early work, Kenneth Boulding advocated a fairly extreme position in favor of a strong, literal adoption of the biological model (1950). He argued that economics should move beyond its prevailing paradigm, which he characterized as a static equilibrium theory of maximizing behavior, to adopt an ecological approach to economics. He described society as a large "ecosystem," in which every organism (organization) behaves according to the interplay between an "inner law of growth and survival" and "a complex hostile-friendly external environment of other organisms" (p. 6). He further argued that economics should develop a life cycle theory which was cognizant of disequilibrium and "the irreversible processes of (decline) and entropy" (p. 37). Indeed, Boulding contended that for all organisms ("individuals, families, firms, nations, and civilizations") there is an "inexorable and irreversible movement towards the equilibrium of death" (p. 38).

This position prompted a strong rebuttal from an early organizational theorist, Edith Penrose (1952). She asserted that "the data" simply do not support organizational analogies either to the natural selection process or to biological life cycles. She maintained that there was no evidence to support the claim that all organizations must die or that life cycle stages are a function of age. Penrose argued that the literal adoption of the biological analogies by social scientists "suggest[s] explanations of events that do not depend upon the conscious willed decisions of human beings" (p. 808). Further, she argued that the search for general laws predetermining individuals' choices missed the mark, because it would "rid the social sciences of the uncertainties and complexities that arise from the apparent 'free will' of man and would endow them with that more reliable power of prediction which for some is the essence of 'science'" (p. 818).

Debate over Life Cycle "Stages"

The debate between voluntaristic and deterministic theories of human behavior within organizations is still active today (Van de Ven & Astley 1981), and it is evident in the unresolved question of how literally the life cycles model should be applied to the study of organizations. The central issues in the current writing on this topic are the number of stages in the life cycles model, and the deterministic nature of these stages, including whether movement through the stages is linear or recursive.

One of the major challenges to a serious discussion of these issues is the proliferation of life cycle models. Quinn & Cameron (1983) and Cameron & Whetten (1983) have published reviews of close to 30 life cycle models from the group development and organizational development literatures. The resulting summary model contains four stages: entrepreneurial (early innovation, niche formation, high creativity), collectivity (high cohesion, commitment), formalization and control (emphasis on stability and institutionalization), and elaboration and structure (domain expansion and decentralization).

The most distinctive feature of this summary model is that it covers only the "growth stages," roughly from birth through maturity. This highlights the lack of attention devoted to the stages of decline and death in these literatures, particularly during the growth oriented decades of the 1960s and 1970s (Whetten 1980a). However, it also simplifies the debate over the deterministic nature of OLC stages. Several contemporary authors (e.g. Filley & Aldag 1980, Freeman 1982, Starbuck 1968, Tichy 1980) echo the conviction of Edith Penrose that organizational changes cannot be predicted in advance and that current organizational characteristics do not necessarily foretell future characteristics. Still, a review of this literature by McEvoy (1984) indicates there is considerably more consensus about sequential movement through these early stages of development than through the later stages of decline and death.

Part of the reason for disagreement over this issue is the different interpretations of "stages of development" in the literature. Those who choose a fairly narrow definition, analogous to biological development, are most opposed to its application to social systems. These authors object to the deterministic logic reflected in organizational life cycle models which is based on a dialectical view of problem solving (e.g. Greiner 1972). They also feel that the summary models of stage development, containing three to five stages, are overly simplistic and therefore of little predictive value (beyond denoting gross developmental processes approximating common sense views of youth, adolescence, maturity, and old age).

A less controversial view suggests that these "stages" are simply clusters of issues or problems that social systems must resolve, and that the inherent nature of these problems suggests a roughly sequential ordering (Miller & Friesen 1980, Cameron & Whetten 1983, Tushman & Romanelli 1985). That is, problem B logically follows problem A in the evolution of a typical organization. In addition, it is argued that these problem sets should be specified at the level of organizational subsystems (e.g., management, technology, structure) to avoid the implication that all facets of an organization proceed simultaneously, in lock-step fashion, through a small number of organization-level developmental stages. This is especially true of mature organizations in which the subsystems become increasingly loosely coupled. An example of a subsystem evolutionary sequence is the need to solve the problem of poor coordination between several organizational units, or product lines, which logically follows an earlier period of structural expansion.

If we define stages as clusters of subsystem problems or issues that are linked sequentially and embedded within the natural evolutionary processes of organizations, then there is considerable logical, as well as empirical, support for this view of organizational development (Lyden 1975, Kimberly 1979, Quinn & Cameron 1983) — with three important qualifications.

First, critics of social evolution theories have consistently objected to the normative connotation of "more advanced" associated with terms like progression and development (Timasheff 1967). It is, therefore, important to note in the life cycle literature that movement from one stage to the next need not be viewed as progression to a higher, more effective, or more sophisticated level of development.

Second, it is important to distinguish between sequential and nonrecursive development. Linear movement implies one direction only. In the life cycle literature no compelling reason argues that the problems present at one stage can only be resolved by moving toward the next stage. Research on group stage development has shown that a recycling phenomenon often occurs when groups in their latter stages of development encounter major crises (Cameron & Whetten 1983). A similar phenomenon undoubtedly occurs in organizations. As the result of a merger, a substantial decrease in resources, or the loss of key personnel, a mature institution may appropriately revert to an earlier set of problems.

Third, it is important to differentiate between growth stages, or problems and decline stages. As noted earlier, life cycle stage models to date have emphasized primarily the growth side of the developmental process. There are several possible explanations for this lack of attention to decline processes in the organizational sciences literature (Whetten 1980a). These include: (a) the practical problems of gaining access to collect data in dying organizations; (b) researchers' cultural biases stemming from the association between growth processes and our society's preoccupation with youth, vigor and virility; (c) the fact that social science research on organizations is largely supported by an entrenched establishment in which managers are rewarded primarily for their ability to foster and sustain organizational growth; and (d) the obvious conclusion that not all mature organizations decline and die, which has undoubtedly discouraged some authors from adding additional stages to the standard life cycle model.

This reluctance to concentrate on decline and death stages ignores important findings in the life cycle literature. Research on the effective management of declining organizations has shown that the problems associated with shrinking economic resources and moral support are qualitatively different from problems associated with growth (Cameron, Whetten & Kim 1987, Nystrom & Starbuck 1984). This important observation suggests the need to develop a series of problem sets capturing the essence of organizational decline and recovery, or death, which are not causally linked to the birth and growth stages.

Although a coherent, empirically grounded model of organizational decline and death stages has not been proposed thus far, rudimentary bits and pieces are starting to emerge (Whetten & Cameron 1985, Sutton 1983, DeGreene 1982).

In examining this literature, it is important both to understand the largely unresolved controversy over the empirical support for patterned development and to look beyond the debate to examine the theoretical and practical benefits derived from the life cycle stages analogy. The literature has identified four important applications for the analogy (Cameron & Whetten 1983). First, it serves as a very useful diagnostic tool, in the sense that awareness of an organization's current life cycle stage conveys information about problems and experiences probably encountered previously by organizational members. Second, it sensitizes us to the fact that goals, priorities, and even the appropriate criteria of effectiveness shift over the course of an organization's life span. Third, it is an important source of contextual information that must be factored into the analysis of organizational research results. That is, the structural properties and internal processes observed in rapidly growing organizations are very different from those found in declining organizations. Fourth, at a practical level, an understanding of the clusters of problems one is likely to encounter at different stages of organizational development, as well as insights for effectively managing the transitions between stages, represent important aids for organizational leaders.

In reviewing the life cycles literature, it is apparent that in addition to debating these conceptual issues, the discussion of growth and decline processes has focused on two major themes. A number of authors have examined the *causes and consequences* of organizational growth and decline as one way of assessing the extent to which different life cycles stages are qualitatively different. Others have chosen to focus on the *effective management* of the growth and decline processes —arguing that management initiatives influence the incidence and amplitude of the growth and decline cycles, as well as blunt or exacerbate their

natural consequences. We discuss in turn the literature addressing each of these themes.

Causes and Consequences of Growth and Decline Stages

Causes of Growth

Organizations grow for a variety of reasons. However, as Pfeffer and Salancik (1978) point out, it is often difficult to assess the true motivations for growth after the fact. That is, one must avoid the pitfall of attempting to extrapolate causes from consequences. Gaining consensus on the reasons for the observed growth in a specific organization can, therefore, be a formidable task. However, three general explanations for organizational growth have been highlighted in the literature (Child & Kieser 1981).

The first and most self-evident explanation is that growth can occur as a by-product of other strategies. As organizations successfully satisfy needs for their services, this success fosters growth.

Second, growth is frequently sought directly because it facilitates the internal management of an organization. Increased surplus resources resulting from growth make it easier to obtain commitment to organizational goals and priorities from various factions and to resolve conflicts between those factions (Pfeffer & Salancik 1978). In addition, growth and expansion increase opportunities for promotion (Dent 1959), provide greater challenge for (and utilization of) managers (Starbuck 1965, Penrose 1959), and satisfy needs for higher salaries and prestige (Roberts 1959).

Third, growth enables an organization to attenuate its dependence on the environment by reducing either uncertainty or external control. Research studies have shown that the performance of larger organizations tends to be more consistent and stable (Caves 1970, Ferguson 1960, Marris & Wood 1971). The likelihood of an organization being either taken over or allowed to go out of business also declines with size (Singh 1971, Steindl 1945). The strategic advantage of large size stems from a variety of factors. For example, in cases where economies of scale can be achieved in the production process, growth makes the organization more efficient and therefore more competitive. Growth also provides the resources for the diversification that enables an organization to spread its risk across several product lines or even industries. Further, growth supplies large organizations with the resources necessary to fund the development of new projects or to produce and market more economically designs pioneered by smaller firms. Taking all these factors into consideration, Child and Kieser (1981: 32) have concluded that "Growth is therefore [pursued by organizations as] a basis for security."

Before leaving this topic, it is important to point out two basic problems with the measurement of size and growth. First, studies often do not differentiate between the two (Scott 1981). Size is an absolute measure of the scale of an organization, generally based on number of employees or total revenues (Kimberly 1976). In contrast, growth is a relative measure of size, as observed over time. Consequently, it is important that we treat with caution conclusions about the causes or consequences of growth (like those noted above) based on cross-sectional studies of the correlates of size. Research studies on the correlates of large size represent a fertile ground for extrapolating hypotheses for longitudinal studies of the advantages of growth, but there are a variety of reasons why the two approaches might produce different results.

For example, Filley & Aldag (1978) argue that many of the studies correlating size and various measures of success do not control for type of organization (industry, organizational form, or technology); consequently, the correlation between size and outcomes may be spurious. Penrose (1959) also noted several constraints on growth that must be taken into consideration: (a) some types of business are unsuited to large size, such as service organizations; (b) large firms may protect small operations through protective pricing; (c) situations in which easy entry and exit and high mortality rates preclude the achievement of large size; (d) a large business may ignore certain small businesses who could be driven out of business and thus encourage smallness.

The second problem with the traditional approach to measuring growth is that it typically does not examine what Boulding (1953) calls population growth. Because growth is not randomly distributed across a population of organizations, it is bound to create a differential strategic advantage (or disadvantage), Boulding argues. This line of reasoning anticipated the contemporary population ecology perspective which argues that outcomes or characteristics of population members can be presumed to have strategic value only in reference to others in the population and to the carrying capacity of the ecological niche (Hannan & Freeman 1978, Freeman 1982). This argument demonstrates the need to measure growth of an organization relative to others in its population, if one is interested in assessing the impact of growth on other organizational properties related to survival.

Consequences of Growth

One of the most controversial issues in the literature on the consequences of growth is whether there is an inevitable point of diminishing returns, past which the advantages of growth become less evident until gradually growth becomes disadvantageous. A common and enduring theme in the sociology of organizations literature has been the dysfunctional consequences of large size. Extremely large organizations are perceived by outsiders as too complex, too rigid, too impersonal, too inefficient, and too inaccessible. Consequently, many researchers consider growth beneficial only up to a point (Perrow 1979, Hedberg, Nystrom & Starbuck 1976, Meyer 1977). This view was borne out in Pfeffer & Salancik's (1978) review of this topic in which they found that profitability increased in growing organizations up to a point and then tapered off. Warwick (1975) also observed a steady decline in flexibility and responsiveness due to bureaucratic growth in the U.S. State Department, despite reforms designed to curb it. This is consistent with Aldrich & Auster's (1986) observation that the rate of innovation diminishes with organizational size.

There are basically three prevailing explanations for these apparent dysfunctional outcomes of large size. First, many point to the diminished capacity for changes, and increased bureaucratic ossification, inherent with the aging process. Because organization age and size are positively correlated, consequences of large size are often confused with advanced age. Inkson, Pugh and Hickson (1970) found that fourteen organizations in England increased their level of bureaucratization over a four-to-five year period, independent of changes in their size. Starbuck (1965) has argued that this process reflects organizational learning, in which organizations learn to cope with their growth by routinizing and formalizing critical communication and coordination activities. The resulting increased efficiencies encourage further bureaucratization, which over time rigidifies more and more of the organization's processes.

Second, several authors have argued that the loss of responsiveness associated with increased size is the result of the substitution of the personal, self-centered goals of key leaders for the original organizational goals emphasizing service and quality. This argument is exemplified by Michels' (1962) "iron law of oligarchy," which grew out of his investigation of the shift towards more conservative goals in the German Socialist party, in response to its leaders' desire for greater security. A related leader-driven bureaucratization process was proposed by Weber (1947) in his discussion of the "routinization of charisma" process. He argued that as organizations founded by charismatic leaders grew, the founder would institute a system of hierarchical offices as a means of legitimizing his or her power and in order to increase its efficiency and continuity through routinization.

Third, as young organizations mature, their growth often reflects adaptation to the dominant societal institutions. Several studies of the maturation process in reform government organizations have observed a pattern of liberal goals and flexible, open structures transformed by the give-and-take associations with established opposing groups (Selznick 1949, Lipset 1950, Cahn & Cahn 1964).

Fourth, undermanning theory suggests that mature, large organizations tend to become less motivating environments for employees because jobs become highly specialized and so provide less autonomy, variety, and task identity (Wicker et al. 1976).

Although this "curvilinear benefits of growth" viewpoint pervades the field, others have argued that the relation between growth and effectiveness is moderated by other organizational factors. For example, organizations with routine technologies can capitalize on growth to increase their economies of scale, but rapid growth in nonroutine job shops creates debilitating coordination problems (Filley & Aldag 1980). Zald and Ash (1966) have made a similar argument for the impact of organizational goals, or domain. Contrary to the prevailing view that growth inevitably leads to increased conservatism in organizations, they argued that social-movement organizations with exclusive membership rules and a remote chance of reaching their goals in the near future will likely adopt very radical organizing processes. Others have also argued that growth produces the serious dysfunctional consequences, connoted by "bureaucracy," only in organizations that are poorly managed. In other words, it is not growth per se that causes the problems, but rather poor management (Child & Kieser 1981).

Up to this point, we have examined the consequences of growth primarily in terms of their strategic implications, that is, whether growth increases or decreases an organization's chances of survival. Another segment of this literature focuses on the consequences of growth on internal organizational processes — without reference to their strategic implications. This area has its own controversies, focusing primarily on the causal relationships between size, technology, and structure (Aldrich 1972). However, Child and Kieser identify several commonalities in the literature on the effect of organization growth on structure. These include: "a rising level of internal differentiation into specialized roles, functions, and divisions; a growing complexity in terms of occupations and skills employed; increased delegation and an emphasis on solving problems through direct, lateral communications rather than hierarchical communications; an increasing use of formal systems and procedures; and a rising proportion of employees concerned with administrative and staff functions" (1981: 38). They also observed three general changes in organizational technology associated with organizational growth: a shift to mass production of goods and services, the increased utilization of knowledge technology (e.g. computers), and the application of new specialist techniques (1981: 42).

Consequences of Decline

Several authors writing on the topic of life cycles have argued that more attention needs to be given to the nongrowth periods of organizational development and evolution (Whetten 1980a, Green halgh 1983, Zammuto & Cameron 1985). In response, an extensive literature on the management of decline has emerged within business administration (Starbuck et al. 1978, Taber et al. 1978), as well as in the related fields of public administration (Levine 1978, Biller 1980), hospital administration (Jick & Murray 1982) and educational administration (Petrie & Alpert 1983, Cyert 1978, Berger, 1983).

Unfortunately, there is little agreement in this literature on the definition of organizational decline. Authors typically focus on decreases in the number of employees or financial resources. However, some combinations of organizational size, performance, and resource levels are extremely difficult to categorize. For example, if a professional football team's win-loss record drops, but its revenues increase (possibly due to the employment of a star quarterback with broad fan appeal), is the organization declining? And what about a liberal arts college that reduces its enrollment, culls its course offerings, and fires several of its faculty, all in the process of becoming a more prestigious and higher-priced institution?

Or a drug rehabilitation center whose clientele (and staff) increases while its cure rate drops? The resolution of these issues is beyond the scope of this review. The interested reader is referred to Cameron et al. (1987). For our immediate purposes, we will use the common definition of decrease in profit or budget.

Thus far, little empirical research has investigated the individual and organizational consequences of decline. Writers have limited their discussions largely to case studies, theoretical treatises, model development, or demographic trend analyses (Zammuto & Cameron 1985, Jick & Murray 1982, Whetten 1980b, Hirschhorn 1983). With the exception of the research on the impact of retrenchment on administrative ratios (Freeman & Hannan 1975, Ford 1980) relatively little empirical research has examined the antecedents or consequences of decline in organizations. There is virtual consensus in the literature, however, that decline produces dysfunctional consequences at both individual and organizational levels. It is argued that conflict, secrecy, rigidity, centralization, formalization, scapegoating, and conservatism increase, and that morale, innovativeness, participation, leader influence, and long-term planning decrease (Cameron et al. 1987). The logic of these dysfunctional "outcomes of decline" is explained as follows.

Conditions of decline inherently involve restricted resources and pressures to retrench. Levine (1978, 1979), Whetten (1980b), Hermann (1963), and others have noted the intensification of conflict under these conditions as fights over a smaller resource base and consequent attempts to protect turf predominate. Pluralism, or the development of organized and vocal special interest groups, increases as organizations become politicized (Pfeffer & Salancik 1978, Pfeffer 1981a, Whetten 1981). Morale worsens as a "mean mood" becomes wide-spread (Bozeman & Slusher 1979, Levine et al. 1981, Starbuck et al. 1978). Attempts to ameliorate conflict and increase morale often involve the use of slack resources to meet operational needs, hence slack and redundancy (and, therefore, flexibility) are eliminated. Managers generally prefer across-the-board cutbacks, rather than selective, prioritized cuts, to appease conflicting demands and minimize the political fallout of retrenchment (Whetten 1980b, Cyert 1978, Boulding 1975).

Authors also have suggested that conservatism and short-term orientation result from decline (i.e. the threat-rigidity response), and efficiency takes priority over effectiveness (Staw et al. 1981, Cameron 1983, Whetten 1981, Rubin 1979, Bozeman & Slusher 1979). Innovation is more likely to be blamed for decline than seen as a solution to it. As a result, risk taking and creativity decrease (Boyd 1979, Starbuck & Hedberg 1977). Centralization of decision-making increases because mistakes become more visible and costly when resources are scarce, and decisions are pushed up the hierarchy. Participation consequently decreases. Centralization restricts communication channels and increases the likelihood that leaders will be scapegoated by frustrated organizational members who feel uninformed. Leader credibility suffers, and this often leads to high rates of leader turnover and "leadership anemia" (Whetten 1981, Hermann 1963, Greenhalgh & Rosenblatt 1984, Levine 1979).

In sum, despite the lack of extensive empirical verification, general consensus exists in the literature that declining organizations are characterized by a wide range of dysfunctional organizational processes. These outcomes of decline erode organizational effectiveness and undermine member satisfaction and commitment. The management of decline is characterized, therefore, as both difficult operationally and hazardous politically.

This is not to say that decline cannot stimulate organizational renewal through increased productivity, prioritization of organization commitments, and renewed personal dedication. Indeed, a sizable literature has emerged during the past decade codifying the procedures for turning around declining organizations (Hofer 1980, Schendel et al. 1976, Bibeault 1982), and several authors have argued that the key stimulant for major change and innovation in mature organizations is the shock of failure in the marketplace

(Nystrom & Starbuck 1984). However, it is evident from this literature that, as its name implies, turnaround management involves taking an organization that has been buffeted by the vagaries of diminished resources and setting it upon a new course. With rare exception, organizations are turned around only after the internal organizational and personal consequences of decline are so pervasive and severe that a consensus on the need for drastic action has grudgingly emerged.

Research on the consequences of organizational decline and death suggests an important linkage between the organizational life cycles and population ecology literatures. To date research on micro (organizational) processes has not linked very well with that on macro (population) birth and death rates. Multilevel studies of organizational morbidity would enable us to examine in fine-grained detail the causes of changes in the size and composition of populations of organizations, as well as the aggregate impact of individual organizational processes. They would also allow us to examine important public policy issues, such as: How can the components of defunct organizations be used most efficiently to stimulate the generation of new organizations?

Causes of Decline

In considering the causes of decline, one must keep in mind the distinction between environmental and organizational decline. The model of decline proposed by Zammuto & Cameron (1985) highlights the two major forms of environmental decline: (a) decrease in a niche's carrying capacity for current activities and (b) a qualitative shift within a niche to support new activities. From a population ecology perspective, these environmental decline conditions will precipitate organizational decline among members of a population who are unable to compete successfully for a shrinking resource base in condition (a), or who fail to shift into new activities supported under condition (b) (Hannan & Freeman 1984).

This leaves open the question of why some organizations fail to adapt to these shifting environmental conditions, while others hold their own or even flourish. Obviously, we must look at the management practices within organizations to understand fully the causes of organizational decline. Information about environmental conditions is, therefore, necessary but not sufficient for understanding the causes of organizational decline.

The literature on the internal causes of organizational decline tends to focus on two themes. First, Starbuck and his associates (Starbuck & Hedberg 1977, Nystrom & Starbuck 1984) have examined numerous cases of organizational decline within the American and European business community to try to better understand the organizational decline process. They coined the phrase "success breeds failure" to explain a frequently observed pattern of decline. Their argument is that very successful organizations often become over-confident of their ability to dominate a market. This over-confidence is manifest in a reduction in both product development and emphasis on quality, insensitivity to negative feedback from customers, failure to monitor trends in basic research and product innovation, and discounting of the seriousness of short-term drops in sales. In essence, these organizations do a poor job of anticipating problems, or even of responding to them in their nascent stage. Instead, they wait until erosion of their competitive position has reached a crisis level, and then they tend to over-react with draconian actions to save a product or, in some cases, the entire company.

This argument goes further. The tendency to discount pressing environmental problems is not the result of all forms of growth ("success"). Rather it is the natural outcome of earlier spectacular and continuous growth. That is, this dysfunctional over-confident mind-set is brought on by the absence of any disconfirming evidence. In a sense, it is a form of the Midas Touch problem, in that senior officials become convinced that any task they set their mind to will turn to gold, and this egotistical view is reinforced by their very impressive track record.

The second explanation for organizational decline focuses on organizations with a very different growth pattern. These are mature institutions who have maintained a steady, though generally modest, growth rate. However, in the process they have fallen prey to the liabilities of large size and complexity discussed in an earlier section. They have become so cumbersome and rule-bound that they are unable to respond quickly to changing environmental conditions. Furthermore, a feeling of complacency pervades the organization. This condition has been referred to as decline-as-stagnation (Whetten 1980b). In contrast to the mercurial rise and precipitous fall of the decline-as-crisis organizations described by Starbuck, most members of these latter organizations are unaware of the slight changes in growth or decline. Whereas the bottom seems to fall out of the first organization's growth, the second organization slides almost imperceptibly into trouble. An example of this form of gradual erosion is a large state university whose annual increases in operating expenses from the legislature do not keep pace with inflation. In this situation it generally takes several years to detect a significant impact on organizational performance, and even in those cases where an astute administration points to the problem early on, they have difficulty generating a mandate for change.

Effective Management of Growth and Decline

Organizational Growth

Thus far we have determined that authors in this field generally agree that members of organizations view growth as a desirable objective to pursue; there is considerably less agreement on the merits of growth once it is achieved. This discussion of motives and consequences still leaves open the question of means, that is, "How do organizations grow effectively?" In this section we review the most common growth mechanisms, or means, used by organizations. The larger question of how managers can mitigate the organizational and personal dysfunctional consequences of growth (or large size) is beyond the scope of this review. Access to this extensive literature can be gained through the articles proposing life cycle models summarized in Quinn and Cameron (1983), or through DeGreene (1982), Miller and

Friesen (1983, 1980), Tushman and Romanelli (1985), or Child and Kieser (1981).

There are at least four distinct vehicles for organizational growth—two strategic and two operational (suggested by Child & Kieser 1981).

The first is growth in an organization's existing domain. The trend towards greater concentration in most industries suggests that many organizations strive for monopoly within their field of activity. This can be done either through competitive or noncompetitive strategies (Pennings 1981). The latter include contracting, co-opting, and coalescing (forming joint partnerships) (Thompson 1967).

Second is growth through diversification into new domains. Diversification is a well-known strategy for spreading risk in business organizations, or for increasing legitimacy (political support) among government organizations (Peabody & Rourke 1965). Aggressive diversification has been particularly characteristic of big businesses and appears in a variety of forms, including development of new products and services, vertical integration, concentric diversification, and conglomerate diversification (Ansoff 1965, Rumelt 1974, Wood 1971).

Third is growth through technological development. The history of organizational development since the industrial revolution has to a large extent been one of adaptation to technological progress. This has resulted in a substantial increase in average firm size (Child & Kieser 1981). The trend is evident in both business and nonbusiness organizations (Perrow 1965), although the causal direction between increases in size and changes in technology is sometimes difficult to determine (Mansfield 1968).

Fourth is growth through improved managerial techniques. As we noted earlier, one of the early explanations for organizational growth was that it served as a means for utilizing excess managerial talent (Penrose 1952). It follows that increases in the efficiency of the management process would provide the impetus for further growth. Again, it is often hard to separate cause from effect, but there are strong position statements in the literature arguing that improved management fosters organizational development (Hedberg et al. 1976, Weick 1977, Staw 1977, Porter 1980, Tushman & Romanelli 1985).

Organizational Decline

Because the literature on the effective management of decline is less well formed than the comparable literature for organizational growth, we review it in more detail. In reviewing the material on this subject, the distinction in the biological ecology literature between r-extinction and k-extinction is a useful organizing device (Wilson 1980). A key concept in the ecology literature is that ecological niches have an inherent carrying capacity. The upper limit "K" represents the maximum population size that can be supported by the resource base in that niche. Organizations that decline short of this upper limit are generally victims of poor management (r-extinction). Their failure to remain competitive is self-induced. In contrast, organizations that decline at the zenith of the carrying capacity curve are victims of a depleted resource pool (k-extinction). They are having problems coping, but so are most other members of the population. In today's economy, the death of a software manufacturing firm would generally represent a case of r-extinction, whereas the failure of a coal mine would represent k-extinction.

The literature on the management of decline typically addresses one of these two conditions. The extensive treatment of turnaround management typically focuses on the problems of r-decline (Hofer 1980). A single organization has made a serious strategic miscalculation and needs to remedy the situation. One of the early studies on this topic distinguished operational from strategic responses to decline (Schendel et al. 1976). These authors found that a common mistake made by businesses is that they respond to strategic (effectiveness) problems with operational (efficiency) remedies. Recent research has underscored the importance of this distinction. Hambrick & Schecter (1983) identified three successful turnaround strategies among a sample of approximately 260 businesses experiencing declines: asset/cost surgery, selective product/market pruning, and piecemeal strategy. All three strategies were used widely in this sample, depending primarily on the business' level of production capacity utilization.

Based on his extensive practical experience with turnaround management, Bibeault (1982) identified a four-stage process: management change, evaluation, emergency actions, and stabilization and return-to-normal growth. This model explicitly argues that successful turnaround strategies can only be implemented by new management. This has been a fairly controversial subject in the literature (Whetten 1984, Starbuck & Hedberg 1977), but the general consensus is that when the cause of an organization's problems is widely attributed to current management, both external and internal support for a turnaround strategy is contingent on a change in top personnel. In other words, problem causers have little credibility as problem solvers (Pfeffer & Blake-Davis 1986, Salancik & Meindl 1984).

The symbolic value of a change in management is emphasized in Chaffee's (1984) work on strategic management in universities and colleges. She distinguishes between the traditional view of strategic management (which she refers to as adaptive) and an interpretive approach. The adaptive strategy for turning around an organization focuses on taking substantive action to reconcile inconsistencies and imbalances between organizational components and environmental conditions. The interpretive approach focuses on the management of meaning and underscores the value of symbolism. While the specific actions may be similar under both approaches, the emphasis of the interpretive approach is on anticipating the ways in which planned actions will be interpreted by critical constituencies (see also Pfeffer 1981b).

Zammuto & Cameron (1985) have used a different approach in analyzing turnaround strategies. Building on a typology of business strategies proposed by Miles & Cameron, they clustered successful turnaround efforts into five categories.

Domain defense is oriented towards preserving the legitimacy of the existing domain of activities and buffering the organization from hostile environmental conditions, possibly through the formation of coalitions with similar organizations. Domain offense focuses on expanding those activities that the organization already does well. Domain creation supplements current domain activities with new domains, primarily through diversification. Domain consolidation involves reducing the size of the domain occupied by the organization, by cutting back to the core products or services. Domain substitution involves replacing one set of activities with another; such a substitution occurred when the March of Dimes shifted its orientation from polio to birth defects.

In contrast, the work on managing organizations in declining industries (k-decline) focuses on a different set of issues. The principal theme in this literature is selecting the appropriate response to the dwindling resource base available to the population (Harrigan 1980, Porter 1980). The options typically include: taking a leadership position in terms of gaining a larger share of the dwindling market, creating a specific niche in which the organization can exploit a unique competitive advantage, "harvesting" the organization by managing a controlled divestiture, and exiting quickly through immediate liquidation. In considering these choices, firms must confront several "barriers to exit." There are financial, legal, structural, emotional, and informational obstacles to selling a firm and leaving the industry (Harrigan 1982, Porter 1976).

The literature on managing population decline has stimulated considerable interest in the divestment process in large corporations. Studies have focused on the deterrents to divestiture (Harrigan 1981), factors influencing the divestment decision (Duhaime & Grant 1984), and methods for increasing cooperation between the corporate headquarters and the divesting operation (Nees 1981).

There are two bodies of literature on the management of decline that cross-cut the distinctions between r and k decline. These focus on the effective management of retrenchment (down-sizing), and, when necessary, of organizational death.

Organizational Retrenchment. The retrenchment literature has primarily dealt with the internal management of decline, rather than with strategic responses to it. It is not surprising that this literature is concentrated in the areas of public, health care, and educational administration. In these contexts the recommendations for turning-around an organization or exiting a domain are generally inappropriate. The administration of a school district with shrinking enrollments can do little to turn that situation around, and many underfunded government agencies cannot ignore their legislative mandate and close their doors. Consequently, the only option left in these situations is to manage the downsizing process effectively.

The recommendations in this literature for managing retrenchment effectively can be grouped into roughly three sequential stages (Whetten 1984, Whetten & Cameron 1985). First, it is proposed that management should strive for "early warning and detection" of the impending problem. Effective anticipation of an emerging budget problem can often allow administrators to conserve resources and thereby blunt the impact of the cuts (Levine 1979). Once the problem has been identified, it is important for management to report an accurate and credible account of the causes of the problem and to seek out the experience of others who have encountered similar problems (Behn 1980). It is also critical for the administration to demonstrate their willingness to come to grips with the problems early on, to avoid the appearance of lack of moral conviction or political courage (Warren 1984).

The second stage involves "seizing the initiative." Once the need for change is clear, leaders are urged to convey a clear message that the organization is capable of handling the crisis (Behn 1980). This helps dispel the confidence-shaking attribution, typical of these situations, that the organization is being buffeted by its environment and has no control over its destiny (Salancik &

Meindl 1984, Levine 1978). One way to convey this message is to open up the communication and decision-making processes (Gilmore & Hirschhorn 1983). Crises create uncertainty, and uncertainty is reduced by information. Managers are also encouraged to promote critical thinking within the organization regarding alternative courses of action (Warren 1984, Perry 1986). At a time when the normal reaction is to become very conservative and essentially opt for doing less of the same, opportunities for revitalizing and overhauling old organizations are often overlooked (Biller 1980, Whetten 1981). A key element in this process is encouraging the high-quality members of the organization to remain. The best way to do this seems to be through co-opting them into key leadership positions (formal or informal) and assuring them that quality will not be compromised during the retrenchment process (Behn 1980). Another aspect of seizing the initiative is creating, and then focusing attention on, a clear vision of the future opportunities within the organization (Cyert 1978). Shifting the attention of members from survival to excellence is a key to circumventing the tendency to mourn one's losses (Sutton et al. 1986, Walton 1986).

The final stage in the retrenchment process involves effectively "implementing the downsizing program." It is argued that a key aspect of any retrenchment process is creating incentives for reducing or redirecting organizational activities. The tendency to become defensive and suspicious must be countered by overarching goals, personal incentives to cooperate, and social mechanisms for integrating "winners and losers" (Krantz 1985, Biller 1980). It is also important during this period to establish mechanisms for helping members cope with their insecurity, stress and anxiety (Gilmore & Hirschhorn 1983, Greenhalgh & Rosenblatt 1984, Brockner et al. 1985). A key element in effective retrenchment management appears to be preserving some organizational slack for stimulating ongoing innovation (Behn 1980, Cyert 1978). Innovation is the life blood of most organizations and the source of considerable personal satisfaction and pride. It must, therefore, be sustained during periods of retrenchment (Greenhalgh et al. 1986).

Organizational Death. Probably the most understudied aspect of the growth and decline process in organizations is organizational death. Although the prediction of bankruptcy is a popular topic in the business finance (Altman et al. 1977, Argenti 1976) and business strategy fields (Miller 1977, Sharma & Mahajan 1980), very little research has examined the behavioral aspects of actually managing the close-out process (Slote 1969, Loving 1979, Mick 1975). However, this void is rapidly being filled (Harris & Sutton 1986, Sutton 1983). One of the most important contributions on this topic thus far has come from the research on employee behaviors during the organizational closing process (Sutton 1983). This work has shown that many of the negative expectations and suspicions held by managers during this time are incorrect. For example, managers typically believe that once a plant closing has been announced, productivity and quality will plummet, employee sabotage and stealing will increase, the best employees will leave, rumors will abound, anger toward management will become the dominant emotion, conflict will increase, and employees will have difficulty accepting the fact that the closing is going to occur. Sutton reports evidence that some of these anticipated reactions never occur and that others occur only under special circumstances (see also Nees 1981).

Sutton's (1983) work has also examined the dilemmas and paradoxes encountered by management during the closing process. These include accepting blame versus deflecting it to external causes; disbanding the organization while at the same time needing to sustain high morale and productivity; informing openly and broadly versus shielding interested parties from all but the most essential information; and finally, giving hope versus taking it away. These issues effectively portray the complex challenges facing managers of closing facilities. Fortunately, research

on strategies for effectively managing the disengagement process should provide significant aids for these managers. Promising disengagement mechanisms include shared symbolic events, such as "parting ceremonies" (Harris & Sutton 1986, Albert 1984), and the establishment of interorganizational social support and outplacement programs (Taber et al. 1979).

A slightly different perspective on the task of closing down an organization is provided in the program termination literature in public administration (Behn 1980, Kaufman 1976). It offers several suggestions for accomplishing the seemingly impossible task of terminating a public policy or program. These include the following. Don't float a trial balloon and give your opposition a chance to muster support against your proposal—act quickly and decisively. Enlarge the policy or program's constituency to incorporate interest groups supporting your position. Focus attention on the policy's harm. Inhibit the natural tendency to compromise with opponents. Recruit an outside administrator/terminator. Buy off the beneficiaries of the current program to reduce their opposition. Advocate the adoption of a new (replacement) program, rather than the abolition of the current one.

There is an important distinction between the close-out literature that has emerged in the private and public sectors. The public administration recommendations tend to focus on the termination decision-making process, specifically, how to achieve consensus for your position, or at least how to minimize opposition to your stated objectives. In contrast, research done on the close-out process in the private sector has tended to focus on the effective implementation of the decision. That is, how to minimize the costs, in terms of human capital, of your decision to close a facility.

One of the more promising new topics for study related to organizational death is employee buy-outs (O'Toole 1979, Hochner & Granrose 1985). This research has thus far examined the effects of employee ownership on employee attitudes (Stern & Hammer 1978) and productivity

(Conte & Tannenbaum 1978), and the requirements for effectively initiating employee ownership (Stern & Hammer 1978, Hochner & Granrose 1985, Woodworth 1982), including financial support, adequate leadership and management expertise, favorable responses from the parent organization, and union support. Future work in this area should focus on building bridges to the broader streams of research on management succession, organizational innovation, owner control, and management of change.

Conclusion

The organizational life cycles literature to date has focused primarily on the early development phases of growing organizations. This has spawned considerable controversy over the legitimate use of the life cycle stages concept to characterize evolutionary processes in older, larger organizations. Recent writing on this subject suggests that the concept of stages should be loosely interpreted to mean a set of problems that logically follows an earlier set but is not determined by that set. Furthermore, the application of this problem-tracking approach appears to be most useful at the subsystem level of organizations. It is also evident that more effort needs to be focused on identifying the sets of problems unique to organizational decline and death.

The research on the causes and consequences of growth and decline processes in organizations has focused on the role of environmental, structural, and individual factors. Indeed, the distinction between internal and external causes has been particularly problematic in the decline literature. In general, our knowledge of the antecedents and outcomes of growth far surpasses our understanding of organizational decline. Important breakthroughs in this area await the development of comprehensive models and concrete operationalizations of key terms.

The literature on the management of growth and decline is the least well developed. Here again, our knowledge about the effective management of growth far surpasses what we know about re-trenchment or downsizing. Due to the lack of large-scale research on this subject, prescriptions for managers are largely based on sketchy, anecdotal evidence. This is an especially promising area for future research.

Literature Cited

Albert, S. 1984. A delete-design model for successful transitions. In *Managing Organizational Transitions,* ed. J. Kimberly, R. Quinn, pp. 169–91. Homewood, Ill.: Irwin.

Aldrich, H.E. 1972. Technology and organizational structure: A re-examination of the findings of the Aston group. *Admin. Sci. Q.* 17: 26–43.

Aldrich, H., Auster, E. 1986. Even dwarfs started small: Liabilities of age and size and their strategic implications. In *Research in Organizational Behavior,* ed. L.L. Cummings and B.M. Staw, 8: 165–98. Greenwich, Conn.: JAI.

Altman, E.I., Haldeman, R., Narayanan, P. 1977. Zeta-analysis: A new model to identify bankruptcy risk of corporations. *J. Bank. Finan.* 1: 29–54.

Ansoff, H.I. 1965. *Corporate Strategy.* New York: McGraw Hill.

Argenti, J. 1976. *Corporate Collapse: The Causes and Symptoms.* New York: Wiley.

Behn, R. 1980. How to terminate public policy: A dozen hints for the would be terminator. In *Managing Fiscal Stress,* ed. Charles H. Levine, pp. 313–26. Chatham, N.J.: Chatham House.

Berger, M. 1983. Retrenchment policies: Their organizational consequences. *Peabody J. Educ.* 60(2): 49–63.

Bibeault, D.B. 1982. *Corporate Turnaround.* New York: McGraw Hill.

Biller, R.P. 1980. Leadership tactics for retrenchment. *Public Admin. Rev.* Nov./Dec., pp. 604–9.

Boulding, K.E. 1950. *A Reconstruction of Economics.* New York: Wiley.

Boulding, K.E. 1953. Toward a general theory of growth. *Can. J. Econ. Polit. Sci.* 12(3): 326–40.

Boulding, K. 1975. The management of decline. *Change* 64: 8–9.

Boyd, W.L. 1979. *Retrenchment in American education: The politics of efficiency.* Presented at Am. Educ. Res. Assoc. Meeting, San Francisco.

Bozeman, B., Slusher, E.A. 1979. Scarcity and environmental stress in public organizations: A conjectural essay. *Admin. Soc.* 11: 335–56.

Brockner, J., Davy, J., Carter, C. 1985. Layoffs, self esteem, and survivor guilt: Motivational, attitudinal, and affective consequences. *Organ. Behav. Hum. Decision Processes* 36: 229–44.

Cahn, E.S., Cahn, J.C. 1964. The war on poverty: A civilian perspective. *Yale Law J.* 73: 1317–52.

Cameron, K.S. 1983. Strategic responses to conditions of decline: Higher education and the private sector. *J. Higher Educ.* 54: 359–80.

Cameron, K.S., Sutton, R.I., Whetten, D.A. 1987. Issues in organizational decline. In *Organizational Decline: Frameworks, Research, and Applications,* ed. K.S. Cameron, R.I. Sutton, D.A. Whetten. Cambridge, Mass.: Ballinger. In press.

Cameron, K.S., Whetten, D.A. 1981. Perceptions of organizational effectiveness over organizational lifecycles. *Admin. Sci. Q.* 26(4): 525–44.

Cameron, K.S., Whetten, D.A. 1983. Models of the organizational life cycle: Applications to higher education. *Rev. Higher Educ.* 6(4): 269–99.

Cameron, K.S., Whetten, D.A., Kim, M. 1987. Organizational dysfunctions of decline. *Acad. Manage. J.* 30: 126–38.

Caves, J. 1970. Uncertainty, market structure and performance: Galbraith's conventional wisdom. In *Industrial Organizations and Economic Development,* ed. J.W. Markham, G.F. Paparek, pp. 282–302. Boston: Houghton Mifflin.

Chaffee, E.E. 1984. Successful strategic management in small private colleges. *J. Higher Educ.* 55: 212–41.

Child, J., Kieser, A. 1981. Development of organizations over time. In *Handbook of Organizational Design,* ed. P.C. Nystrom, W.H. Starbuck, pp. 1928–64. New York: Oxford Univ. Press.

Conte, M., Tannenbaum, A.S. 1978. Employee-owned companies: Is the difference measurable? *Monthly Labor Rev.* 101: 23–28.

Cyert, R.M. 1978. The management of universities of constant or decreasing size. *Public Admin. Rev.* 38: 345.

DeGreene, K.B. 1982. *The Adaptive Organization. Anticipation and Management of Crisis.* New York: Wiley.

Dent, J.K. 1959. Organizational correlates of the goals of business management. *Personnel Psychol.* 12: 365–93.

Duhaime, I.M., Grant, J.H. 1984. Factors influencing divestment decision-making: Evidence from a field study. *Strategic Manage. J.* 5: 301–18.

Ferguson, C.E. 1960. The relationship of business size to stability: An empirical approach. *J. Ind. Econ.* 9: 43–62.

Filley, A.C., Aldag, R.J. 1978. Characteristics and measurement of an organizational typology. *Acad. Manage. J.* 21:578–91.

Filley, A.C., Aldag, R.J. 1980. Organizational growth and types: Lessons from small institutions. In *Research in Organizational Behavior,* ed. B.M. Staw, L.L. Cummings, 2: 279–320. Greenwich, Conn.: JAI.

Ford, J.D. 1980. The occurrence of structural hysteresis in declining organizations. *Acad. Mgmt. Rev.* 5(4): 589–98.

Freeman, J. 1982. Organizational lifecycles and natural selection processes. In *Research in Organizational Behavior,* ed. B.M. Staw, L.L. Cummings, 4: 1–33. Greenwich, Conn.: JAI.

Freeman, J.H., Hannan, M.T. 1975. Growth and decline processes in organizations. *Am. Sociol. Rev.* 40: 215–28.

Gilmore, T., Hirschhorn, L. 1983. Management challenges under conditions of retrenchment. *Human Resourc. Manage.* 22(4): 341–57.

Greiner, L.E. 1972. Evolution and revolution as organizations grow. *Harvard Bus. Rev.* 4 (July–August): 37–46.

Greenhalgh, L. 1983. Organizational decline. In *Research in Sociology of Organizations,* ed. S. Bachrach, 2: 231–76. Greenwich, Conn.: JAI.

Greenhalgh, L., McKersie, R.B., Gilkey, R.W. 1986. Rebalancing the workforce at IBM: A case study of redeployment and revitalization. *Organ. Dynam.* (Spring): 30–47.

Greenhalgh, L., Rosenblatt, Z. 1984. Job insecurity: Toward conceptual clarity. *Acad. Mgmt. Rev.* 9: 438–48.

Haire, M. 1959. Biological models and empirical histories of the growth of organizations. In *Modern Organization Theory,* ed. M. Haire, pp. 272–306. New York: Wiley.

Hambrick, D.C., Schechter, S.M. 1983. Turnaround strategies for mature industrial product business units. *Acad. Manage. J.* 26: 231–48.

Hannan, M.T., Freeman, J.H. 1978. The population ecology of organizations. In *Environments and Organizations,* ed. M.W. Meyer and associates, pp. 177–99. San Francisco: Jossey-Bass.

Hannan, M.T., Freeman, J. 1984. Structural inertia and organizational change. *Am. Sociol. Rev.* 29: 149–64.

Harrigan, K.R. 1980. *Strategies for Declining Businesses.* Lexington, Mass.: Heath.

Harrigan, K.R. 1981. Deterrents to divestiture. *Acad. Manage. J.* 24(2): 306–23.

Harrigan, K.R. 1982. Exit decisions in mature industries. *Acad. Manage. J.* 24(4): 707–32.

Harris, S.G., Sutton, R.I. 1986. Functions of parting ceremonies in dying organizations. *Acad. Manage. J.* 29(1): 5–30.

Hedberg, B.L.T., Nystrom, P.C., Starbuck, W.H. 1976. Camping on see-saws: Prescriptions for a self-designing organization. *Admin. Sci. Q.* 21: 41–65.

Hermann, C.F. 1963. Some consequences of crisis which limit the viability of organizations. *Admin Sci. Q.* 16: 533–47.

Hirschhorn, L. 1983. *Cutting Back.* San Francisco: Jossey-Bass.

Hochner, A., Granrose, C.S. 1985. Sources of motivation to choose employee ownership as an alternative to job loss. *Acad. Manage. J.* 28(4): 860–75.

Hofer, C.W. 1980. Turnaround strategies. *J. Bus. Strategy* Summer, pp. 19–31.

Inkson, J.H., Pugh, D.S., Hickson, D.J. 1970. Organizational context and structure: An abbreviated replication. *Admin. Sci. Q.* 15: 318–408.

Jick, T.D., Murray, V.V. 1982. The management of hard times: Budget cutbacks in public sector organizations. *Organ. Stud.* 3: 141–69.

Katz, D., Kahn, R.L. 1966. *The Social Psychology of Organizations.* New York: Wiley.

Kaufman, H. 1976. *Are Government Organizations Immortal?* Washington, D.C.: Brookings Inst.

Kimberly, J.R. 1976. Organizational size and the structuralist perspective: A review, critique and proposal. *Admin. Sci. Q.* 21: 571–97.

Kimberly, J.R. 1979. Issues in the creation of organizations: Initiation, innovation and institutionalization. *Acad. Manage. J.* 22: 437–57.

Kimberly, J.R., Miles, R.H. 1980. *The Organizational Life Cycle.* San Francisco: Jossey-Bass.

Kimberly, J.R., Quinn, R. 1984. *Organizational Transitions.* Homewood, Ill.: Irwin.

Krantz, J. 1985. Group processes under conditions of organizational decline. *J. Appl. Behav. Sci.* 21(1): 1–17.

Levine, C.H. 1978. Organizational decline and cutback management. *Public Admin. Rev.* 38: 316–25.

Levine, C.H. 1979. More on cutback management: Hard questions for hard times. *Public Admin. Rev.* 39: 179–83.

Levine, C.H., Rubin, I.S., Wolohojian, G.G. 1981. *The Politics of Retrenchment.* Beverly Hills, Calif.: Sage.

Lippitt, G.L., Schmidt, W.H. 1967. Crises in a developing organization. *Harvard Bus. Rev.* 45: 417–38.

Lipset, S.M. 1950. *Agrarian Socialism.* Berkeley: Univ. Calif. Press.

Loving, R. 1979. W.T. Grant's last days. In *Life in Organizations,* ed. B.A. Stein, R.M. Kanter, pp. 400–11. New York: Basic Books.

Lyden, F.J. 1975. Using Parsons' functional analysis in the study of public organizations. *Admin. Sci. Q.* 20: 59–70.

Mansfield, E. 1968. *Industrial Research and Technological Innovation.* New York: Norton.

Marris, R.L., Wood, A. 1971. *The Corporate Economy.* London: Macmillan.

Marshall, A. 1920. *Principles of Economics.* London: Macmillan. 8th ed.

McEvoy, G.M. 1984. *The organizational life-cycle concept: Approaching adolescence or drawing near death?* Work. Pap. Dep. Bus. Admin. Utah State Univ.

Meyer, M.W. 1977. *Theory of Organizational Structure.* Indianapolis: Bobbs-Merrill.

Michels, R. 1962. *Political Parties.* New York: Collier.

Mick, S.S. 1975. Social and personal costs of plant shutdowns. *Indust. Relat.* 14: 203–08.

Miles, R.H., Cameron, K.S. 1982. *Coffin Nails and Corporate Strategies.* Englewood Cliffs, N.J.: Prentice Hall.

Miller, D. 1977. Common syndromes of business failure. *Bus. Horizons* 20 (December): 43–53.

Miller, D., Friesen, P. 1980. Archetypes of organizational transition. *Admin. Sci. Q.* 25: 268–99.

Miller, D., Friesen, P. 1983. Sucssful and unsuccessful phases of the corporate life cycle. *Organ. Stud.* 4: 339–56.

Nees, D. 1981. Increase your divestment effectiveness. *Strategic Manage. J.* 2: 119–30.

Nystrom, P.C., Starbuck, W.H. 1984. To avoid organizational crisis, unlearn. *Organ. Dynam.* Spring: 53–65.

O'Toole, J. 1979. The uneven record of employee ownership: Is worker capitalism a fruitful opportunity or an impractical idea? *Harvard Bus. Rev.* 57(9): 185–97.

Peabody, R.L., Rourke, F.E. 1965. Public bureaucracies. In *Handbook of Organizations,* ed. J.G. March, pp. 802–37. Chicago: Rand McNally.

Pennings, J. 1981. Strategically interdependent organizations. In *Handbook of Organizational Design,* ed. P.C. Nystrom, W.H. Starbuck, 1: 433–55. London: Oxford Univ. Press.

Penrose, E.T. 1952. Biological analogies in the theory of the firm. *Am. Econ. Rev.* 4: 804–19.

Penrose, E. 1959. *The Theory of the Growth of the Firm.* Oxford: Blackwell.

Perrow, C. 1965. Hospitals: Technology, structure and goals. In *Handbook of Organizations,* ed. J.G. March, pp. 910–71. Chicago: Rand McNally.

Perrow, C. 1979. *Complex Organizations: A Critical Essay.* Glenview, Ill.: Scott Foresman. 2nd ed.

Perry, L.T. 1986. Least-cost alternatives to layoffs in declining industries. *Organ. Dynam.* (Spring): 48–61.

Petrie, H.G., Alpert, D.A. 1983. What is the problem of retrenchment in higher education? *J. Manage. Stud.* 20: 97–119.

Pfeffer, J. 1981a. *Power in Organizations.* Marshfield, Mass.: Pitman.

Pfeffer, J. 1981b. Management as symbolic action: The creation and maintenance of organizational paradigms. In *Research in Organizational Behavior,* ed. L.L. Cummings and B.W. Staw, 3: 1–52. Greenwich, Conn.: JAI.

Pfeffer, J., Davis-Blake, A. 1986. Administrative succession and organizational performance: How administrator experience mediates the succession effect. *Acad. Mgmt. J.* 29(1): 72–83.

Pfeffer, J., Salancik, G.R. 1978. *The External Control of Organizations: A Resource Dependence Perspective.* New York: Harper & Row.

Porter, M.E. 1976. Exit barriers and strategic organizational planning. *Calif. Manage. Rev.* 19(2): 21–33.

Porter, M. 1980. Competitive strategy in declining industries. In *Competitive Strategy,* ed. M. Porter, pp. 254–74. New York: Free Press.

Quinn, R.E., Cameron, K.S. 1983. Organizational lifecycles and shifting criteria of effectiveness: Some preliminary evidence. *Mgmt. Sci.* 29(1): 33–51.

Roberts, D.R. 1959. *Executive Compensation.* Glencoe, Ill.: Free Press.

Rubin, I.S. 1979. Retrenchment, loose structure, and adaptability in the university. *Sociol. Educ.* 52: 211–22.

Rumelt, R.P. 1974. *Strategy, Structure and Economic Performance in Large American Industrial Corporations.* Boston: Grad. School Bus. Admin. Harvard Univ.

Salancik, G.R., Meindl, J.R. 1984. Corporate attributions as strategic illusions of management control. *Admin. Sci. Q.* 29(2): 238–54.

Schendel, D., Patton, G.R., Riggs, J. 1976. Corporate turnaround strategies: A study of profit decline and recovery. *J. Gen. Manage.* 3: 3–11.

Scott, W.R. 1981. *Organizations: Rational, Natural, and Open Systems.* Englewood Cliffs, N.J.: Prentice Hall.

Selznick, P. 1949. *TVA and the Grass Roots.* Berkeley: Univ. Calif. Press.

Sharma, S., Mahajan, V. 1980. Early warning indicators of business failure. *J. Marketing* 44: 80–89.

Singh, A. 1971. *Take-overs.* Cambridge, Engl.: Cambridge Univ. Press.

Singh, J.V., House, R.J., Tucker, D.J. 1986. Organizational change and organizational mortality. *Admin. Sci. Q.* 31: 171–93.

Slote, A. 1969. *Termination: The Closing at Baker Plant.* Indianapolis: Bobbs-Merrill.

Starbuck, W.H. 1965. Organizational growth and development. In *Handbook of Organizations,* ed. J.G. March, pp. 451–533. Chicago: Rand McNally.

Starbuck, W.H. 1968. Organizational metamorphosis. In *Promising Research Directions,* ed. R.W. Millner, M.P. Hottenstein, pp. 113–32. State Park, Penn.: Acad. Mgmt.

Starbuck, W., Greve, A., Hedberg, B.L.T. 1978. Responding to crisis. *J. Bus. Admin.* 9: 111–37.

Starbuck, W., Hedberg, B.L.T. 1977. Saving an organization from stagnating environments. In *Strategy + Structure = Performance,* ed. H. Thorelli, pp. 249–59. Bloomington: Indiana Univ. Press.

Staw, B.M. 1977. The experimenting organization. *Organ. Dynam.* 6(2): 30–46.

Staw, B.M., Sandelands, L.E., Dutton, J.E. 1981. Threat-rigidity effects in organizational behavior: A multilevel analysis. *Admin. Sci. Q.* 26: 501–24.

Steindl, J. 1945. *Small and Big Business.* Oxford. Blackwell.

Stern, R.N., Hammer, T.H. 1978. Buying your job: Factors affecting the success or failure of employee acquisition attempts. *Human Relat.* 31: 1101–11.

Sutton, R.I. 1983. Managing organizational death. *Human Resource Manage.* 22(4): 377–90.

Sutton, R.I., Eisenhardt, K.M., Jucker, J.V. 1986. Managing organizational decline: Lessons from Atari. *Organ. Dynam.* (Spring): 17–29.

Taber, T.D., Walsh, J.T., Cooke, R.A. 1979. Developing a community-based program for reducing the social impact of a plant closing. *J. Appl. Behav. Sci.* 20: 133–55.

Thompson, J.D. 1967. *Organizations in Action.* New York: McGraw Hill.

Tichy, N. 1980. Problem cycles in organizations and the management of change. In *The Organizational Lifecycle,* ed. J.R. Kimberly, R.H. Miles, pp. 164–83. San Francisco: Jossey-Bass.

Timasheff, N.S. 1967. *Sociological Theory. Its Nature and Growth.* New York: Random House.

Torbert, W.R. 1974. Pre-bureaucratic and post-bureaucratic stages of organizational development. *Interpers. Dev.* 5: 1–25.

Tushman, M.L., Romanelli, E. 1985. Organizational evolution: A metamorphosis model of convergence and reorientation. In *Research in Organi-*

zational Behavior, ed. B.M. Staw, L.L. Cummings, 7: 171–222. Greenwich, Conn.: JAI.

Tushman, M.L., Anderson, P. 1986. Technological discontinuities and organizational environments. *Admin. Sci. Q.* 31: 439–65.

Van de Ven, A.H., Astley, W.G. 1981. Mapping the field to create a dynamic perspective on organizational design and behavior. In *Perspectives on Organizational Design and Behavior,* ed. A.H. Van de Ven, W.F. Joyce, pp. 409–18. New York: Wiley.

Walton, R.E. 1986. A vision-led approach to management restructuring. *Organ. Dynam.* (Spring): 4–16.

Warren, D.A. 1984. Managing in crisis: Nine principles for successful transitions. In *Managing Organizational Transitions,* ed. J. Kimberly, R. Quinn, pp. 85–106. Homewood, Ill.: Irwin.

Warwick, D.P. 1975. *A Theory of Public Bureaucracy.* Cambridge, Mass.: Harvard Univ. Press.

Weber, M. 1947. *The Theory of Social and Economic Organization,* trans. and ed. A.M. Henderson, J. Parsons. London: Oxford Univ. Press.

Weick, K.E. 1977. Organizational design: Organizations as self-designing systems. *Organ. Dynam.* 6(2): 30–46.

Whetten, D.A. 1980a. Organizational decline: A neglected topic in the organizational sciences. *Acad. Manage. Rev.* 4: 577–88.

Whetten, D.A. 1980b. Sources, responses, and the effects of organizational decline. In *The Organizational Lifecycle,* ed. J. Kimberly, R. Miles, pp. 342–74. San Francisco: Jossey-Bass.

Whetten, D.A. 1981. Organizational responses to scarcity: Exploring the obstacles to innovative approaches to retrenchment in education. *Educ. Admin. Q.* 17: 80–97.

Whetten, D.A. 1984. Effective administrators: Good management in the college campus. *Change* Nov./Dec., pp. 38–43.

Whetten, D.A. 1986. *Effective management of retrenchment.* Work. Pap., Coll. Commerce Bus. Admin. Univ. Ill., Champaign.

Whetten, D.A., Cameron, K.S. 1985. Administrative effectiveness in higher education. *Rev. Higher Educ.* 9(1): 35–49.

Wicker, A., Kirmeyer, S.L., Hanson, L., Alexander, D. 1976. Effects of manning levels on subjective experiences, performance, and verbal interaction in groups. *Organ. Behav. Human Perform.* 17: 251–74.

Wilson, E. 1980. *Sociobiology.* Cambridge, Mass.: Harvard Univ. Press.

Wood, A. 1971. Diversifications, mergers and research expenditures: A review of empirical studies. In *The Corporate Economy,* ed. R. Marris, A. Wood, pp. 428–53. Cambridge, Mass.: Harvard Univ. Press.

Woodworth, W. 1982. *Collective power and liberation of work.* Paper presented Tenth World Congress Sociol., Mexico City.

Zald, M.N., Ash, R. 1966. Social movement organizations: Growth, decay and change. *Soc. Forc.* 44: 327–41.

Zammuto, R.F., Cameron, K.S. 1985. Environmental decline and organizational response. In *Research in Organizational Behavior,* ed. B.M. Staw, L.L. Cummings, 7: 223–62. Greenwich, Conn.: JAI.

2

Models of the Organizational Life Cycle: Applications to Higher Education

Kim S. Cameron

David A. Whetten

The Carnegie Council for Policy Studies (1980) has pointed out that if we take the year 1530 as a starting point (the year the Lutheran Church was founded), there are 66 institutions that existed then in the Western World and that still exist today in a recognizable form. They are the Catholic and Lutheran Churches, the Parliaments of Iceland and the Isle of Man, and 62 universities. This remarkable resiliency on the part of at least a few universities helps support the contention of Bennis (1964) that the general structure and design of institutions of higher education is much more adaptive and restorative than are traditional bureaucracies and hierarchical systems. They are

The research reported here was supported by a contract (#400-80-0109) from the National Institute of Education. This is an edited version of a longer published article.

Condensed with permission from *Review of Higher Education,* Vol. 6. © 1983 Association for the Study of Higher Education.

loosely coupled (Weick, 1976), fluid systems (Cohen & March, 1974) that have a great capacity to survive environmental disruptions.

On the other hand, colleges and universities have no immunity to organizational demise. In fact, the annual rate of death for institutions of higher education is actually higher than for business organizations and federal government bureaus. Katz and Kahn (1978), for example, reported that business failures between 1924 and 1973 averaged 57 per 10,000 firms. Kaufman (1976) reported a government bureau death rate of 28 per 10,000. Zammuto (1984), on the other hand, found the mortality rate of colleges and universities in the United States to be 117.6 per 10,000 between 1971 and 1981. Moreover, Zammuto also found that the number of deaths among colleges and universities has increased since the early 1970s. He concluded that some kinds of institutions (e.g., small, private comprehensive institutions) may need to be put on an "endangered species list" because of their unusually high mortality rates.

These statistics point out that even with the capacity to be resilient and adaptive, many institutions operate in ways that do not take advantage of these capacities, and they subsequently find themselves unable to adjust to environmental changes. When unusual circumstances arise in the environment, some institutions find that they have become incapable of maintaining resiliency.

Transitions and the Organizational Life Cycle

One reason for the loss of resiliency and for the emergence of dysfunctional characteristics under conditions of institutional stress is the mismanagement of the transitions that occur throughout the organizational life cycle. The effective management of those transitions is critical to institutional survival.

Transitions in institutions occur when there is a mismatch between environmental demands, institutional attributes, and strategies being pursued. These mismatches usually arise from changes in the external environment (e.g., changes in consumer demand may dictate more need for engineering or high technology training in schools as opposed to liberal arts training), or from self-generated changes in the institution itself (e.g., conflicting coalitions may lead to alterations in structure, such as the formation of a union). Managing these transitions so as to produce rigidity and inflexibility is one of the main reasons for high rates of institutional death among colleges and universities (Whetten, 1981).

Miller and Friesen (1980) studied the types of transitions in which organizations engage, and they described certain "archetypes" that recurred regularly in a wide variety of situations. The conclusion of their investigation was that the kinds of transitions required of organizations are relatively few.

> Perhaps the most arresting finding of this study is that the same types of transitions keep cropping up with impressive frequency in an extremely diverse sample of organizations. Furthermore, there do

not appear to be a very great number of common transition types. Therefore it might eventually be possible to discover the fundamental building blocks or response behaviors constituting the elementary dynamics of organizational change. (p. 288)

Miller and Friesen's results lend support to the claims of a number of writers who have tried to identify these elementary dynamics of organizational change, and to outline models of the major transitions that occur in organizations. These models have been labelled "organizational life cycle models," and they identify the major transitions required of organizations as they develop over time. We review the various models of organizational life cycles that have been proposed and discuss several of the major issues surrounding the presence of predictable transitions over a life cycle. We conclude by pointing out some implications of life cycle models for effective institutional adaptation.

The Concept of Organizational Life Cycle

The term "organizational life cycle" refers to predictable change in organizations from one state or condition to another. It focuses on evolutionary change in the sense that the development of organizations is assumed to follow an *a priori* sequence of transitions rather than to occur randomly or metamorphically.

The concept of the organizational life cycle has achieved popularity only relatively recently (Kimberly & Miles, 1980). This recency reflects an increasing emphasis among organizational theorists and researchers both on process of organizational decline and retrenchment, and on processes involved with organizational birth. In higher education, both these phenomena are prevalent, as evidenced by the fact that during the decade of the 1970s, approximately 20 percent of all institutions experienced a decline in enrollment (the highest in history), as well as the highest mortality rate in history (Zammuto, 1983). At the same time, however, Trow (1979) pointed out that the prevalence of organization births still outstripped organizational deaths.

The extraordinary phenomenon of high fertility and high mortality rates among institutions of higher learning is still with us. Between 1969 and 1975, some 800 new colleges (many of them community colleges) were created, while roughly 300 were closed or consolidated, leaving a net gain of nearly 500 in just six years. (p. 272)

Organizational birth and death are not new phenomena, of course, but past researchers have treated them largely as static occurrences. Tabulated frequencies rather than descriptions of transitions from one organizational state to another are the most prevalent outcomes of research. As Kimberly suggested (1980), the dynamic properties of organizations largely have been ignored in scholarly inquiry in favor of cross-sectional, snap-shot views.

Two different factors have led to a consideration of the dynamic life cycle properties of organizations in recent years. The first is the extension and elaboration of the biological metaphor as it pertains to organizations; the second is the literature on group development.

Whereas biological analogies have a long history in the organizational sciences, and social evolution has been a recurring theme in the social sciences (Spencer, 1897; Parsons, 1964; Miller, 1978; Campbell, 1969, 1975; McKelvey, 1982), recent authors have become both more insistent of the applicability of this theme, and more ardent in arguing that biological analogies can inform the analysis of organizational change processes. Writers such as Aldrich (1979), Hannan and Freeman (1978), and McKelvey (1982) have developed a population ecology perspective of organizations which relies heavily on biological science. These theorists focus on the dynamics of survival and demise of populations of organizations in a similar way to biologists' focus on the survival and extinction of species of living organisms. That is, the characteristics of the species and the extent of its adaptability determines survival or extinction. Katz and Kahn (1978), Miller and Rice (1967), and Weick and Daft (1983), are among the theorists who take the organization level of analysis (as opposed to the population level) and also argue that properties of living (biological) systems

are similar to organizational development. Just as living organisms pass through predictable stages of development and undergo a series of predictable transitions (e.g., stages of child development), so also are organizations claimed to possess similar properties. Though the debate is still lively regarding the appropriateness of biological analogies for organization change and development, these analogies have nevertheless provided impetus for interest in organizational life cycles.

The second stimulus for considering the life cycle properties of organizations has come from research and theory on group development. Beginning with Dewey's (1933) emphasis on five (cognitive) stages of learning and Freud's (1921) analysis of children's (affective) responses to authority figures, theorizing and research have proliferated relative to cognitive and affective changes in groups over time. Writers on group development have observed a variety of different types of groups with varying compositions. For example, problem-solving, therapy, and interpersonal growth groups have been studied ranging from one session lasting several hours to multiple sessions over several years. Group membership has varied widely in the research—with members from 3 to 70 years old, mental patients and normals, managers and subordinates, students and instructors, and volunteers and forced-participants. Analysis has focused on personal role behaviors, on group processes, on unconscious processes among members, on problem solving strategies, on interpersonal needs, and so on (Cameron, 1976). Despite this variety, models of group development proposed by these various writers have been strikingly similar.

For example, widespread agreement has been found in the group development literature that groups progress predictably through a series of six sequential stages. Table 1 summarizes those models and compares their proposed stages. These six summary stages are:

(1) Isolation, orientation, and testing stage—in which group members try to identify acceptable roles for themselves, dependence on a leader is present, individuals feel isolated,

Table 1. A Comparison of Eighteen Models of Group Stage Development

Summary Model	[1]Isolation, Orientation, and Testing Stage	[2]Formation of "Groupness" and Unity Stage	[3]Conflict and Counter-Dependence Stage	[4]Conflict Resolution and Coordination Stage	[5]Separation, Elaboration, and Independence Stage	[6]Effective Group Functioning (or Termination) Stage
Barron and Krulee (1948)			[1]Initial resistance	[2]Understanding and acceptance		[3]Well-organized and productive group
Stock and BenZeev (1948)	[1]Exploration and definition stage	[2]Intense feelings and creativity stage		[3]High task involvement stage		[4]Group and task centered stage
Thelen (1949)	[1]Individual orientation		[2]Frustration and conflict stage	[3]Cohesiveness and sweetness stage		
Bales and Strodtbeck (1951)	[1]Problems of orientation stage		[2]Problems of evaluation stage	[3]Problem of control stage		
Theodorson (1953)	[1]Few norms, friendships, role differentiations stage			[2]Many rules, linkages, interdependencies stage		
Bennis and Shephard (1956)	[1]Dependence and submission stage		[2]Counterdependence stage	[3]Resolution stage	[4]Enactment and [5]Disenchantment stage	[6]Consensual validation stage
Modlin and Faris (1956)		[1]Structuralization stage	[2]Unrest, friction, and disharmony stage		[3]Change stage	[4]Integration stage
Martin and Hill (1957)	[1]Isolation stage	[2]Asyndectic stage	[3]Stereotyping, [4]Reaction, and [5]Conflict stage	[6]Here-&-now and [7]Interpersonal focus stage	[8]Self-analysis stage	[9]Problem solution and [10]Competence stage
Schutz (1958)	[1]Problems of inclusion stage			[2]Problems of control stage		[3]Problems of affection stage
Smith (1960)	[1]Independence and low task orientation stage			[2]Interdependence and task orientation stage	[3]Independence and task resolution stage	

	[1]	[2]	[3]	[4]	[5]	[6]
Kaplan and Roman (1963)	One-to-one relationships stage	Concern for the group stage	Sub-group coalition formation stage	Pairing and intimacy stage	Maturity stage	
Schroeder and Harvey (1963)	Absolutistic dependency stage	Negative independence stage	Conditional dependence stage	Positive independence stage		
Mills (1964)	Personal frustration and hostility stage	Internalization and affection stage	Work orientation stage	Termination stage		
Tuckman (1965)	Dependence, testing, and orientation stage	Conflict and emotional response stage	Cohesion and exchange stage	Role and problem solution stage		
Slater (1966)	Unconscious stage	Bonding with leader stage	Revolt and guilt stage	Common experience and intimacy stage	Consciousness stage	
Mann (1967)	Initial complaining stage	Premature enactment stage	Confrontation stage	Internalization stage	Separation stage	Terminal review stage
Dunphey (1968)	Absolutistic dependency stage	Rivalry and aggression stage	Coordinated structural patterns stage			

information gathering activity is focused on, and members become familiar with rules and expectations.

(2) Formation of "groupness" and unity stage — in which members begin feeling integrated and a part of the group, group issues take precedence over individual issues, and feelings of cohesion and unity develop.

(3) Conflict and counter-dependence stage — in which group members react against the "sweetness" that has developed, the leader of the group is resisted, and rivalry and dissatisfaction increase.

(4) Conflict resolution and coordination stage — in which rivalry and competitiveness is resolved, individual roles are coordinated into a smooth functioning group, and pairing and intimacy occur among group members.

(5) Separation, elaboration, and independence stage — in which group member roles are differentiated, unique identities of individuals are re-established, and entrepreneurial activity increases.

(6) Effective group functioning (or termination) stage — in which problem solving occurs effectively, personal issues among group members and role conflicts are resolved, and efficient task accomplishment occurs.

These group stages follow a sequential pattern except when major disruptions occur such as a change in group leadership, membership, or resources. The group may then re-cycle back to earlier stages and develop through the sequence again.

The importance of these sequential group stages is that similar transitions have been found at more macro (organizational) levels of analysis. Group phenomena often generalize to more aggregated units in organizations. And because there is a great deal of empirical evidence confirming the presence of sequential stages on the group level, interest in organizational life cycle stages has emerged as well.

Models of Organizational Life Cycles

Despite the empirical evidence supporting the sequential development of groups through predict-able transitions, the notion that organizations pass through separate, sequential stages is controversial among organization theorists. Organizations are more complex entities than groups, they are affected more by external environments, and their purposes and tasks are generally more elaborate. Therefore, it is questionable whether the same change processes apply.

One group of writers, for example, suggests that organizational changes cannot be predicted in advance and that present characteristics of organizations cannot foretell future characteristics (Filley & Aldag, 1980; Freeman, 1982; Starbuck, 1968). Tichy (1980) argues, for example, that "the biological analogy of a system going through predictable phases of development does not hold up to empirical scrutiny. Organizations do not follow predictable biosocial stages of development" (p. 164).

The alternative proposed by these writers is that organizations make adjustments to their environments over time, but those adjustments cannot be anticipated. For example, Filley and Aldag (1980) proposed that organizational transitions are not sequential, and that advanced prediction of what form an organization will take is not possible.

> In general it appears that organizations do experience shifts in their basic character, that common patterns of structure and growth are to be found in various forms of human organization, and that unlike the case with organisms, the patterns need not follow each other in a prescribed order. (p. 283)

On the other hand, other writers adopt a position similar to group stage development researchers by arguing that sequential stage development accurately maps organizational transitions over time. Lavoie and Culbert (1978) summarized this view.

1. In most organizations, the changes that characterize development follow more or less the same sequential pattern.
2. Under normal circumstances, changes that are progressive will not easily reverse themselves.

3. Developmental change is a change in the quality of responses (format, pattern, structure, etc.) and not merely in the frequency of correctness according to an external criterion such as profitability.
4. Developmental changes affect a broad range of organizational activities and responses.
5. Development change is hierarchical, that is, latter forms will dominate and integrate earlier ones. (p. 418–19)

At least ten different models of sequential life cycle development have been proposed by writers. None of the models is identical to the others, but like the group stage development models, they all identify a common set of problems and characteristics that are typical of organizational transitions over time.

These ten models have focused on different organizational phenomena (e.g., changes in structure, functional problems, leadership issues, individual "mentalities," control mechanisms), and authors have considered different types of organizations (e.g., federal government bureaus, medical schools, colleges, businesses) in their proposals. But these differences do not discriminate among the various models. All ten models suggest similar life cycle stages. The models contain an *entrepreneurial stage* (early innovation, niche formation, creativity), a *collectivity stage* (high cohesion, commitment), a *formalization and control stage* (stability and institutionalization), and a *structure elaboration and adaptation stage* (domain expansion and decentralization). The summary model in Table 2 enumerates the common organizational characteristics typical of each of these stages.

For an organization to exist in any one of these life cycle stages creates problems that can be solved by moving to the next stage of development. For example, the problem created by the entrepreneurial stage is a lack of coordination and cohesion. Organization members work for their own goals and outcomes. The main problem created by the collectivity stage is a need for efficiency, coordination, and control of the production process. Stage 3, the formalization and

control stage, presents problems of rigidity, lack of participation, and non-adaptability. The final stage, structure elaboration and adaptation, presents problems from all three of the previous stages and, therefore, may perpetuate a recycling or a subdivision of units into different stages. Organizations are able to maintain effectiveness in spite of these problems by progressing to the next stage of the life cycle.

Some of the authors in Table 2 divide these four major stages into multiple sub-stages (e.g., Adizes' adolescent, prime, and mature organizational stages are all in the formalization and control stage); some authors ignore either the first or the last stage (e.g., Katz and Kahn do not include the entrepreneurial stage in their model; and Downs, Lyden, Adizes and Kimberly do not include the fourth stage — elaboration of structure — in their models). But as a group, there seems to be some consensus in the models about the characteristics of certain developmental stages as organizations progress through their life cycles. This consensus is reflected in the Summary Model in Table 2.

With the exception of Adizes' model, none of the life cycle models is concerned with organizational decline. All assume an unending growth curve, or at least stability. In addition, the length of time that organizations remain in particular stages of development is not specified by the authors. However, research by Kimberly (1979), Cameron and Whetten (1981), Miles and Randolph (1980), Neal (1978), and Quinn and Cameron (1983) suggest that the stages can occur in rapid sequence (e.g., maturity can be reached quickly) or they can be very slow in developing (Downs, 1967). Lippitt and Schmidt (1967) even hold that organizational age and stage of development are poorly correlated and all organizations do not progress through all stages of the model.

Unlike many of the group stage development models, organizational development models have not been based on systematic empirical investigation. Instead, they were proposed only on the basis of observations and experiences of the authors themselves. As a result, much more controversy

Table 2. An Integration of Ten Life Cycle Models

Summary Model

1. Entrepreneurial Stage
- Marshalling of resources
- Multiple and diverse ideas
- Entrepreneurial activities
- Little planning and coordination
- Formation of a "niche"
- "Prime mover" has power

2. Collectivity Stage
- Informal communication and structure
- Sense of collectivity
- Long hours spent
- Sense of mission
- Innovation continues
- High commitment

3. Formalization & Control Stage
- Formalization or rules
- Stable structure
- Emphasis on efficiency and maintenance
- Conservatism
- Institutionalized procedures

4. Elaboration of Structure Stage
- Elaboration of structure
- Decentralization
- Domain expansion
- Adaptation
- Renewal

Downs: Motivation for Growth (1967)

Struggle for Autonomy Stage
- Legitimize the function to the external environment
- Obtain autonomy from parent or competing bureaus
- Stabilize resources
- Achieve survival threshold

Rapid Growth Stage
- Innovators and climbers have control
- Emphasis on innovation and expansion
- Occurrence of an "age lump" in membership

Deceleration Stage
- Increased size and complexity causes coordination problems
- Innovation is deemphasized
- Smoothness and predictability are emphasized
- "Conservers" have control
- Formalized and elaborate role systems
- Reduced flexibility

Lippitt & Schmidt: Critical Managerial Concerns (1967)

Birth
- One-man rule
- Short-range perspective
- Concerned with survival
- Confidence in personal abilities
- Personal control

Youth
- Emphasis on stability and service
- Team decision making
- Efficiency emphasized
- Goal setting and planning occur
- Systematic control

Maturity
- Emphasis on adaptability
- Contribution to society is valued
- Growth opportunities are sought

Scott: Strategy and Structure (1971)

Stage 1
- One-man rule
- Paternalistic reward system
- Subjective evaluation criteria
- No formal structure

Stage 2
- Functional specialization
- Institutionalized procedures
- Systematic reward system
- Impersonal evaluation
- Formalized structure

Stage 3
- Diversified product markets
- Search for new products and growth opportunities
- Semi-autonomous divisionalized structure

Greiner: Problems Leading to Evolution and Revolution (1972)

Creativity Stage
- Emphasis on producing a product
- Long hours of work with modest rewards
- Informal communication and structure

Direction Stage
- Functional structure established
- Accounting system set up
- Specialization of tasks
- Formalized rules and policies

Delegation Stage
- Decentralization of structure
- Decision making pushed lower in the hierarchy
- Management by exception

Coordination Stage
- New systems arise
- Product groups form
- Long term planning
- Profit sharing programs

Collaboration Stage
- Team Action
- Spontaneity in management
- Confrontation in interpersonal problems

Adizes: Major Organizational Activities (1979)

Courtship Stage
- Founders are dreaming up "what we might do"
- Entrepreneurial activities

Infant Organization Stage
- Emphasis on production
- Time pressures keenly felt
- No tradition
- Few meetings
- Little planning

Go-Go Organization Stage
- Rapid expansion
- Personalized leadership
- Some planning
- Fast, frequent, intuitive decision making

Adolescent Organization Stage
- Planning and coordination are important
- Administrative activities increase at the expense of entrepreneurial activities and production
- Stability and conservatism
- Formalized rules and policies

Prime Organization Stage
- Emphasis on efficiency
- Increasing loss of touch with the environment
- Thick organization boundaries
- Aspirations remain stable, no desire to grow or change
- Stability and predictability are valued

Maturity Stage
- Paternalistic, comfortable organizational climate
- Low emphasis on production
- Formalized relationships
- Little innovation

Table 2 (Continued)

Kimberly: Internal Social Control, Structure of Work and Environmental Relations (1979)

First Stage
- Marshalling of resources
- Creation of an ideology

Second Stage
- Obtaining support for the external environment
- Choice of a "prime mover"
- Staffing of the organization
- Frequent, discrete decisions are made

Third Stage
- Formation of identity
- Sense of collectivity of family
- High member commitment and involvement in the organization
- Pursuit of organizational mission
- Postponing individual need fulfillment temporarily

Fourth Stage
- Formalized structure
- Policies and rules set up
- Internal organizational competition
- Stabilized external relations
- Conservative trend
- High personal investment questioned

Child and Kieser: Markets, Transactions, and Structure (1981)

First Stage
- No formal structure
- Personal direction
- No differentiation or specialization
- One product

Second Stage
- Integration of transactions
- Functional specialization
- Single product or market

Third Stage
- Multiple products and markets
- Product specialization
- Fragmentation of transactions

Fourth Stage
- Grid or matrix structure
- Fragmented markets

Torbert: Mentality of Members (1974)

Fantasies Stage
- Individual visions and fantasies
- Free-floating conversation
- Diffused perceptions by members

Investment Stage
- High investment by individual
- No clear leadership style
- Validity and depth of commitment examined

Experiments Stage
- Plans, schedules, roles, and governance established
- Rational decision making

Openly Chosen Structure Stage
- Collaboration among levels
- Reflection about deeper issues
- Creativity and innovative methods
- Flexibility in procedures

Determination Stage
- Group goals and structure set up
- Group unity prevalent
- Psychological contracts set up

Predefined Productivity Stage
- Focus on task performance as defined by others
- Fixed rules, structures, and authority system

Foundational Community Stage
- Shared spiritual, behavioral, and theoretical qualities among members
- Organization becomes a spiritual community

Liberating Disciplines Stage
- Individuals and the organization are engaged in self renewal
- Inclusive not exclusive boundaries
- Organization seeks challenges

Lyden: Functional Problems (1975)

First Stage
- Emphasis on adaptation to the external environment

Second Stage
- Emphasis on resources acquisition

Third Stage
- Emphasis on goal attainment

Fourth Stage
- Emphasis on pattern maintenance and institutionalization

Katz and Kahn: Organizational Structure (1978)

Primitive System Stage
- Cooperation endeavors based on common needs and expectations of members

Stable Organization Stage
- Coordination and formalization
- Authority systems arise
- Informal structure arises
- Rule enforcement
- Maintenance systems arise

Elaborative Supportive Structures Stage
- Adaptation systems are formed, i.e., procurement systems, disposal systems, institutional relations system

Table 3. A Comparison of the Group and Organization Life Cycle Stage Models

Group Level	Characteristics	Organization Level
1. Isolation, orientation, and testing stage	• dependence on the leader • a "prime mover" has power • little coordination or planning • abundance of diverse ideas	1. Creation and entrepreneurial stage
2. Formation of "groupness" and unity stage	• sense of collectivity and group identity • high commitment to the group • informal interaction and co-ordination	2. Collectivity stage
3. Negative reactions, counter-dependence, and conflict stage	• counter-dependence toward the leader • subgroups and coalitions form • confrontation, conflict, and tension	
4. Conflict resolution, coordination, and cohesion stage	• coordination of activities • formalization of rules • stability and conservatism • cohesion and exchange	3. Formalization and control stage
5. Separation, elaboration, and independence stage	• decentralization and independence • experimentation and expansion • elaboration of structure • healthy discontent with the status quo	4. Elaboration of structure stage
6. Effective group functioning (or termination) stage	• problem solving competence • high task accomplishment • review of termination issues	

surrounds the validity of life cycle models for describing organizational transitions than is the case for models of group transitions. Whereas a large amount of empirical evidence exists for the presence of group stage development (Slater, 1955; Dunphey, 1968; Tuckman, 1965), similar evidence has not yet been produced for organization stage development.

On the other hand, since these various models were proposed, evidence that supports the existence of sequential stages has been uncovered by several authors. Similarities between group and organization transitions, and case studies of organizational change over time, are illustrations of this evidence.

Evidence for Sequential Life Cycle Stages

Table 3 compares the characteristics of the summary group development model with the summary organization life cycle model. Whereas the organization-level model contains fewer stages, similar characteristics are common to both models. These similarities are important because, as Lyden (1975) suggested, "the same functional requirements or problems must be dealt with at every level of system organization" [p. 59]. Groups or sub-systems face the same problems and transitions as does the broader organization; therefore, it is reasonable to assume that stage development models will be similar.

More compelling support comes, however, from the life cycle research of authors who investigated organizational changes over time. For example, Quinn and Cameron (1983) analyzed the birth and early history (i.e., the first six years) of a state agency in New York. They chronicled the development of the organization from its first stage (the creation and entrepreneurial stage) — when characteristics existed such as fluid and non-bureaucratic methods of task assignment, strong personal power and no formal office for the director, a strong emphasis on creativity, and no formal organization chart — through the second stage of development (the collectivity stage) where work teams were formed, a missionary zeal and dedication to the organization were developed, and high cohesion and interaction occurred both among organization members and between members and outside constituencies. The events leading to the development of the third stage (the formalization and control stage) also were analyzed along with the organizational trauma that resulted from the transition from stage 2 to stage 3. It was concluded that the characteristics prescribed by the life cycle model did occur as predicted.

Kimberly's (1979) analysis of the life cycle development of a medical school provides another example. He analyzed the preconditions leading to the birth of the organization and the subsequent presence of stage 1 characteristics (such as the presence of a powerful leader, riskiness, entrepreneurial activity, and innovation). Stage 2 characteristics were found to develop later (close, informal coordination of various groups of doctors and medical school staff, increasing sense of mission, designs of a unique, innovative curriculum), and stage 3 characteristics began emerging at the close of the investigation (e.g., institutionalization of procedures, conservative trends established, formalized evaluations, differentiation and specialization of tasks). Kimberly suggested that institutional characteristics acquired in one stage of development may actually serve to impede the transitions into later stages.

A third example is Neal's (1978) analysis of an adult education organization. She described the pre-conditions that led to the establishment of the institution, and then traced transitions through each of four sequential stages prescribed in the model. Neal concluded that group development theory was a good predictor of the phenomena that she observed. Stages of development were followed sequentially, and the fact that the organization's death occurred after only three years helped transitions from one stage to another occur more rapidly.

Other examples of sequential life cycle development can be found in Cameron and Whetten (1981), Miles and Randolph (1980), Lyden (1975), and Child and Kieser (1981).

Implications of Life Cycle Models for Higher Education

Having briefly reviewed the major issues surrounding the concept of organizational life cycle and the various models that have been proposed, we can now turn to a discussion of their implications for institutions of higher education during periods of transition. Two major insights can be drawn from the life cycle literature.

First, a greater understanding of the life cycle stages, and the pitfalls and opportunities associated with each, can help institutions make these transitions less traumatic. Transitions in institutions of higher education are motivated by imbalances or crises. Greiner (1972) argued that each life cycle stage is culminated by a major crisis that ushers in the next stage of development. New stages are reached by solving the major problems of the previous stage, but those solutions create new organizational problems. An understanding of this dialectical view of organizational change aids the effective management of transitions by guiding the problem solving process. Specifically, the appropriateness of a response to major crises is often a function of the organization's life cycle stage of development. When the crisis appears to stem from the dysfunctional consequences of the current mode of operation, administrators would do well to consider making changes that are consistent with the next level of development. For example, an institution in the second stage of life cycle development (i.e., cohesion and commitment are high, a sense of family exists, the identity of the institution is a crucial concern) should explore the possibility of increasing formalization and control (i.e., moving towards the formalization stage). Greiner (1972), Lyden (1975), and others suggest that when these conditions exist, institutional responses that don't lead to the next developmental stage are less likely to be effective.

Bourgeois, McAllister, and Mitchell (1978) found evidence for this proposition when they investigated the responses made by newly formed divisions of a large organization to certain environmentally induced crises. Contrary to contingency theory (Lawrence & Lorsch, 1969), but consistent with the life cycle model, successful divisions responded to turbulence and uncertainty by becoming more mechanistic, rather than more organic in structure. The apparent cause for the success of this strategy was that these organizations were at an early stage in their development (stage 2) where they needed increased formalization and control (stage 3) to cope effectively with environmental problems.

This is not to say, of course, that all crises can be resolved only by moving toward the next level of development. Research on group stage development has shown that a recycling phenomenon often occurs when groups in their latter stages of development encounter major crises. A similar phenomenon undoubtedly occurs in organizations. As the result of a merger, a substantial decrease in resources, a major loss of personnel, and so on, a mature institution may appropriately revert to an earlier stage of development. The strategies implemented dictate which previous stage will be returned to. A consolidation and centralization strategy, for example, will lead the institution back to the formalization and control stage (stage 3) where the major institutional problems will then center on how to maintain adaptability, creativity, and participativeness. Strategies oriented toward increasing morale, commitment, and individual initiative may lead back to stage 2 (the collectivity stage) where major institutional problems then center on how to maintain control, efficiency and coordination.

This recycling phenomenon explains why some writers find evidence that sequential transitions are characteristic of organizations whereas others argue that sequential change does not occur. Transition through organizational life cycle stages is observed mainly in the early history of organizations, whereas evidence that life cycle stages do not occur comes totally from older, mature organizations (Filley & Aldag, 1980; Penrose, 1952; Tichy, 1980). Both phenomena probably occur, inasmuch as recycling through life cycle stages after organizations become mature may be interpreted as being an absence of sequential transitions. Moreover, the elaboration of structure stage (stage 4) often leads to decentralization and loose coupling, especially in colleges and universities, so that different subunits may progress at different rates through the recycling process, or they may shift back to different stages. Institutional diversity may make a consistent transition pattern on the organizational level difficult to identify (Freeman, 1982).

A second insight gained from the life cycle literature is that *the criteria of institutional effectiveness applicable in one stage of development are not necessarily appropriate in other stages of development.* Because the major problems and activities of institutions change with each new stage, judgments of institutional success also are based on different criteria. For example, Cameron and Whetten (1981) found that the criteria of effectiveness held by participants in simulated organizations changed as the organizations progressed from birth to maturity. Early on, participants tended to focus on factors important to them as individuals, but gradually their emphasis shifted to the work group and subunit level, and finally to the organization as a whole. Also, their initial ratings of effectiveness were geared to success in procuring resources, while later their concern shifted to the successful disposal of outputs. Cameron and Whetten concluded that "the simulated organizations developed through stages similar to those experienced by real organizations" (p. 537) and that "significant variation existed in the ratings [of effectiveness] of the individual, department, and organization levels, depending on the organization's stage of development" (p. 534).

Another study (Quinn & Cameron, 1983) also found evidence for a shift in the importance of effectiveness criteria depending on the life cycle stage. They investigated the transitions engaged in by a state government agency and tried to determine which criteria of effectiveness were most important in which stage of development. Four different models of effectiveness were used, each of which relies on different indicators to judge effectiveness — the rational goal model, the open systems model, the human relations model, and the internal processes model. They found that in stage 1 (the entrepreneurial stage), the open systems model criteria were most important. In stage 2 (the collectivity stage), human relations and open systems model criteria took precedence. In stage 3 (the formalization stage) rational goal and internal process model criteria were paramount, and in stage 4 (the elaboration of structure stage) open systems and rational goal model criteria were relied on most to judge effectiveness.

One reason for this shift in the importance of effectiveness criteria was that in different stages of development, different constituencies were more or less dominant. In early stages, for example, resource providers were more important than regulators, but in later stages the reverse was true. What this suggests for colleges and universities is that the institution must adopt the primary criteria of effectiveness espoused by the dominant constituency in order to survive. In a study of college and university effectiveness, for example, Cameron (1983) discovered that the most successful institutions were those that satisfied the preferred criteria of effectiveness held by the most powerful constituencies.

This shift in criteria of effectiveness from one stage to another also points out the need to match the characteristics of top institutional administrators with the unique challenges facing a college or university at a particular point in its development history. That is, some administrators may be able to manage effectively in one stage of life cycle development but not in another. In his study of the early history of English private schools founded by entrepreneurs, for example, Pettigrew (1979) found that once the school became well-established, the future well-being of the institution depended on the founder stepping down and installing a "steady state manager" in his place. In those cases where the entrepreneur insisted on retaining operational control of the school once it reached stage 3 or 4, it suffered from a lack of attention to internal management details. In other words, entrepreneurial leaders are most effective when success is defined by innovation and resource acquisition (i.e., stage 1), but less effective when criteria of success focus on stability, control, and efficiency (i.e., stage 3).

A similar result was found by Chaffee (1982) in her study of institutional recovery from revenue decline. In *every case,* successful recovery schools replaced old administrators (who had managed the institution under conditions of growth and expansion) with a new management team. A new stage of organization development made old ways of administering ineffective. Administrative style must change, therefore, or else new administrators who can manage the demands of a new stage of development must be installed, when major institutional transitions occur. Administrators who refuse to acknowledge the need for change, and who tenaciously cling to anachronistic policies and programs applicable to earlier stages of organizational development, will generally be replaced once the organization enters a new life cycle phase. The prospect of being able to avert a necessity of leadership turnover represents one of the strongest motivations for developing a greater understanding of the life cycle model of organizations.

References

Adizes, I. 1979. Organizational passages: Diagnosing and treating life cycle problems in organizations. *Organizational Dynamics* 9: 3–25.

Aldrich, H.E. 1979. *Organizations and environments.* Englewood Cliffs, N.J.: Prentice-Hall.

Bales, R., & Strodtbeck, F.L. 1951. Phases in group problem solving. *Journal of Abnormal and Social Psychology* 46: 485–95.

Barron, M., & Krulee, G. 1948. Case study of a basic skill training camp. *Journal of Social Issues* 4: 10–30.

Bennis, W.G. 1964. *Organizational developments and the fate of bureaucracy.* Invited address at the American Psychological Association.

Bennis, W.G., & Shepard, H.A. 1956. A theory of group development. *Human Relations* 9: 415–37.

Bourgeois, L.J., McAllister, D.W., & Mitchell, T.R. 1978. The effects upon decisions about organizational structure. *Academy of Management Journal* 28: 508–14.

Cameron, K.S. 1976. *Organizational diagnosis and group stage development.* Discussion paper, Yale University, 1976.

Cameron, K.S. 1983. *An empirical investigation of the multiple constituencies model of organizational effectiveness.* Working paper, National Center for Higher Education Management Systems.

Cameron, K.S., & Whetten, D.A. 1981. Perceptions of organizational effectiveness over organizational life cycles. *Administrative Science Quarterly* 26: 525–44.

Campbell, D.T. 1969. Variation and selective retention in sociocultural evolution. *General Systems* 16: 69–85.

Campbell, D.T. 1975. On the conflicts between biological and social evolution and between psychology and moral tradition. *American Psychologist* 30: 1103–26.

Carnegie Council for Policy Studies. 1980. *Three thousand futures.* San Francisco: Jossey-Bass.

Chaffee, E.E. 1982. *Case studies in college strategy.* Boulder, Colo.: National Center for Higher Education Management Systems.

Child, J., & Kieser, A. 1981. Development of organizations over time. In P.C. Nystrom & W.A. Starbuck (Eds.), *Handbook of organizational design,* Vol. 1. New York: Oxford University.

Cohen, M.D., & March, J.G. 1974. *Leadership and ambiguity: The American college president.* New York: McGraw-Hill.

Dewey, J. 1933. *How we think.* Boston: Heath.

Downs, A. 1967. *Inside bureaucracy.* San Francisco: Little, Brown and Company.

Dunphey, D.C.. 1968. Phases, roles, and myths in self-analytic groups. *Journal of Applied Behavioral Sciences* 4: 195–225.

Filley, A.C., & Aldag, R.J. 1980. Organizational growth and types: Lessons from small institutions. In B.M. Staw & L.L. Cummings (Eds.), *Research in organizational behavior,* Vol. 2. Greenwich, Conn.: JAI Press.

Freeman, J. 1982. Organizational life cycles and natural selection processes. In B.M. Staw & L.L. Cummings (Eds.), *Research in organizational behavior,* Vol. 4. Greenwich, Conn.: JAI Press.

Freud, S. 1921. *Group psychology and the analysis of the ego.* Hogarth Press.

Greiner, L. 1972. Evolution and revolution as organizations grow. *Harvard Business Review* 49: 37–46.

Hannan, M.T., & Freeman, J.H. 1978. The population ecology of organizations. In M.W. Meyer & Associates (Eds.), *Environments and organizations: Theoretical and empirical perspectives.* San Francisco: Jossey-Bass.

Hedberg, B.L.T., Nystrom, P., & Starbuck, W. 1976. Camping on seesaws: Prescriptions for a self-designing organization. *Administrative Science Quarterly* 21: 41–65.

Kaplan, S.R., & Roman, M. 1963. Phases of development in an adult therapy group. *International Journal of Group Psychotherapy* 13: 10–26.

Katz, D., & Kahn, R.L. 1978. *The social psychology of organizations.* New York: John Wiley & Sons.

Kauffman, J.F. 1982. *Some perspective on hard times.* Presidential address at the Association for the Study of Higher Education meetings.

Kaufman, H. 1976. *Are government organizations immortal?* Washington, D.C.: Brookings Institute.

Kimberly, J.R. 1979. Issues in the creation of organizations: Initiation, innovation, and institutionalization. *Academy of Management Journal* 22: 437–57.

Kimberly, J.R. 1980. The organizational life cycle: Constructive concept or misguided metaphor? In J.R. Kimberly & R.H. Miles (Eds.), *The organizational life cycle.* San Francisco: Jossey-Bass, Inc.

Kimberly, J.R., & Miles, R.H. 1980. *The organizational life cycle.* San Francisco: Jossey-Bass, Inc.

Lavoie, D., & Culbert, S.A. 1978. Stages in organization and development. *Human Relations* 31: 417–38.

Lawrence, P.R., & Lorsch, J.W. 1969. *Organization and environment.* Homewood, Ill.: Irwin.

Lippitt, G.L., & Schmidt, W.H. 1967. Crises in a developing organization. *Harvard Business Review* 47: 102–12.

Lyden, F.J. 1975. Using Parsons' functional analysis in the study of public organizations. *Administrative Science Quarterly* 20: 59–70.

Mann, R.D. 1967. *Interpersonal styles and group development.* New York: John Wiley & Sons.

Martin, E.A., & Hill, W.F. 1957. Toward a theory of group development: Six phases. *International Journal of Group Psychotherapy* 7: 20–30.

McKelvey, B. 1982. *Organizational systematics: Taxonomy, evolution, classification.* Berkeley, Calif.: University of California Press.

Miles, R.H., & Randolph, W.A. 1980. Influence of organizational learning styles on early development. In J.R. Kimberly & R.H. Miles (Eds.), *The organizational life cycle.* San Francisco: Jossey-Bass, Inc.

Miller, D., & Friesen, P. 1980. Archetypes of organizational transition. *Administrative Science Quarterly* 25: 268–99.

Miller, E.J., & Rice, A.K. 1967. *Systems of organization.* London: Fairstock Institute.

Miller, J.G. 1978. *Living systems.* New York: McGraw-Hill.

Mills, T.M. 1964. *Group transformation.* Englewood Cliffs, N.J.: Prentice-Hall.

Modlin, H.C., & Faris, M. 1956. Group adaptation and integration in psychiatric team practice. *Psychiatry* 19: 97–103.

Neal, J.A. 1978. *The life cycles of an alternative organization.* Boston: Intercollegiate Case Clearinghouse.

Parsons, T. 1964. Evolutionary universals in society. *American Sociological Review* 29: 339–57.

Penrose, E.T. 1952. Biological analogies in the theory of the firm. *American Economic Review* 42: 804–19.

Pettigrew, A.M. 1979. On studying organizational cultures. *Administrative Science Quarterly* 24: 570–81.

Quinn, R.E., & Cameron, K.S. 1983. Organizational life cycles and shifting criteria of effectiveness: Some preliminary evidence. *Management Science* 29: 33–51.

Schroeder, H.M., & Harvey, O.J. 1963. Conceptual organization and group structure. In O.J. Harvey (Ed.), *Motivation and social interaction.* New York: Ronald Press.

Schutz, W.C. 1958. *FIRO.* New York: Rhinehart & Co.

Scott, B.R. 1971. *Stages of corporate development, Part 1.* Case No. 9-371-294. Boston: Intercollegiate Case Clearinghouse, Harvard Business School.

Slater, P.E. 1966. *Microcosm.* New York: John Wiley & Sons, Inc.

Slater, P.E. 1955. Role differentiation in small groups. *American Sociological Review* 20: 300–10.

Smith, A. 1960. Development study of group processes. *Journal of Genetic Psychology* 97: 29–39.

Spencer, H. 1897. *The principles of sociology,* Vol. 1.

New York: Appleton, Century, Crofts.

Starbuck, W. 1968. Organizational metamorphosis. In R.W. Milman & M.P. Hottenstein (Eds.), *Promising research directions.* State College, PA: Academy of Management.

Starbuck, W.H., Greve, A., & Hedberg, B.L.T. 1978. Responding to crisis. *Journal of Business Administration* 9: 111–37.

Stock, D., & BenZeev, S. 1958. Changes in work and emotionality during group growth. In D. Stock & H.A. Thelan (Eds.), *Emotional dynamics and group culture.* New York: New York University Press.

Thelen, H.A. 1949. Stereotypes and the growth of groups. *Educational Leadership* 6: 309–16.

Theodorson, G.A. 1953. Elements in the progressive development of small groups. *Social Forces*: 311–20.

Tichy, N. 1980. Problem cycles in organizations and the management of change. In J.R. Kimberly & R.H. Miles (Eds.), *The organizational life cycle,* pp. 164–83. San Francisco: Jossey-Bass, Inc.

Torbert, W.R. 1974. Pre-bureaucratic and post-bureaucratic stages of organization development. *Interpersonal Development* 5: 1–25.

Trow, M. 1979. Aspects of diversity in American higher education. In H.J. Gans, N. Glazer, J.R. Gusfield, & C. Gencks (Eds.), *On the making of Americans: Essays in honor of David Reisman.* Philadelphia: University of Pennsylvania Press.

Tuckman, B.W. 1965. Developmental sequences in small groups. *Psychological Bulletin* 63: 384–99.

Weick, K.E. 1976. Education organizations as loosely coupled systems. *Administrative Science Quarterly* 21: 1–19.

Weick, K.E. 1982. Administering education in loosely coupled schools. *Phi Delta Kappan* 64: 673–76.

Weick, K.E., & Daft, R. 1983. The effectiveness of interpretation systems. In K.S. Cameron & D.A. Whetten (Eds.), *Organizational effectiveness: A comparison of multiple models,* pp. 71–94. New York: Academic Press.

Whetten, D.A. 1980. Organizational decline: A neglected topic in the organizational sciences. *Academy of Management Review* 4: 577–88.

Whetten, D.A. 1981. Organizational responses to scarcity: Exploring the obstacles to innovative approaches to retrenchment in education. *Educational Administration Quarterly* 17: 80–97.

Zammuto, R.F. 1983. Growth, stability, and decline in American college and university enrollments. *Education Administration Quarterly* 19: 83–99.

Zammuto, R.F. 1984. Are liberal arts colleges an endangered species? *Journal of Higher Education* 55: 184–211.

3

Convergence and Upheaval: Managing the Unsteady Pace of Organizational Evolution

Michael L. Tushman

William H. Newman

Elaine Romanclli

A snug fit of external opportunity, company strategy, and internal structure is a hallmark of successful companies. The real test of executive leadership, however, is in maintaining this alignment in the face of changing competitive conditions.

Consider the Polaroid or Caterpillar corporations. Both firms virtually dominated their respective industries for decades, only to be caught off guard by major environmental changes. The same strategic and organizational factors which were so effective for decades became the seeds of complacency and organization decline.

The authors thank Donald Hambrick and Kathy Harrigan for insightful comments and the Center for Strategy Research and the Center for Research on Innovation and Entrepreneurship at the Graduate School of Business, Columbia University, for financial support.

Recent studies of companies over long periods show that the most successful firms maintain a workable equilibrium for several years (or decades), but are also able to initiate and carry out sharp, widespread changes (referred to here as reorientations) when their environments shift. Such upheaval may bring renewed vigor to the enterprise. Less successful firms, on the other hand, get stuck in a particular pattern. The leaders of these firms either do not see the need for reorientation or they are unable to carry through the necessary frame-breaking changes. While not all reorientations succeed, those organizations which do not initiate reorientations as environments shift underperform.

This article focuses on reasons why for long periods most companies make only incremental changes, and why they then need to make painful, discontinuous, system-wide shifts. We are particularly concerned with the role of executive leadership in managing this pattern of convergence punctuated by upheaval.

Here are four examples of the convergence/upheaval pattern:

- Founded in 1915 by a set of engineers from MIT, the General Radio Company was established to produce highly innovative and high-quality (but expensive) electronic test equipment. Over the years, General Radio developed a consistent organization to accomplish its mission. It hired only the brightest young engineers, built a loose functional organization dominated by the engineering department, and developed a "General Radio culture" (for example, no conflict, management by consensus, slow growth). General Radio's strategy and associated structures, systems, and people were very successful. By World War II, General Radio was the largest test-equipment firm in the United States.

  After World War II, however, increasing technology and cost-based competition began to erode General Radio's market share. While management made numerous incremental changes, General Radio remained fundamentally the same organization. In the late 1960s, when CEO Don Sinclair initiated strategic changes, he left the firm's structure and systems intact. This effort at doing new things with established systems and procedures was less than successful. By 1972, the firm incurred its first loss.

  In the face of this sustained performance decline, Bill Thurston (a long-time General Radio executive) was made President. Thurston initiated system-wide changes. General Radio adopted a more marketing-oriented strategy. Its product line was cut from 20 different lines to 3; much more emphasis was given to product-line management, sales, and marketing. Resources were diverted from engineering to revitalize sales, marketing, and production. During 1973, the firm moved to a matrix structure, increased its emphasis on controls and systems, and went outside for a set of executives to help Thurston run this revised General Radio. To perhaps more formally symbolize these changes and the sharp move away from the "old" General Radio, the firm's name was changed to GenRad. By 1984, GenRad's sales exploded to over $200 million (vs. $44 million in 1972).

After 60 years of convergent change around a constant strategy, Thurston and his colleagues (many new to the firm) made discontinuous system-wide changes in strategy, structure, people, and processes. While traumatic, these changes were implemented over a two-year period and led to a dramatic turnaround in GenRad's performance.

- Prime Computer was founded in 1971 by a group of individuals who left Honeywell. Prime's initial strategy was to produce a high-quality/high-price minicomputer based on semiconductor memory. These founders built an engineering-dominated, loosely structured firm which sold to OEMs and through distributors. This configuration of strategy, structure, people, and processes was very successful. By 1974, Prime turned its first profit; by 1975, its sales were more than $11 million.

  In the midst of this success, Prime's board of directors brought in Ken Fisher to reorient the organization. Fisher and a whole new group of executives hired from Honeywell initiated a set of discontinuous changes throughout Prime during 1975–1976. Prime now sold a full range of minicomputers and computer systems to OEMs and end-users. To accomplish this shift in strategy, Prime adopted a more complex functional structure, with a marked increase in resources to sales and marketing. The shift in resources away from engineering was so great that Bill Poduska, Prime's head of engineering, left to form Apollo Computer. Between 1975–1981, Fisher and his colleagues consolidated and incrementally adapted structure, systems, and processes to better accomplish the new strategy. During this convergent period, Prime grew dramatically to over $260 million by 1981.

  In 1981, again in the midst of this continuing sequence of increased volume and profits, Prime's board again initiated an upheaval. Fisher and his direct reports left Prime (some of whom founded Encore Computer), while Joe Henson and a set of executives from IBM initiated wholesale changes throughout the organization. The firm diversified into robotics, CAD/CAM, and office systems; adopted a divisional structure; developed a more market-driven orientation; and increased controls and systems. It remains to be seen how this "new" Prime will fare. Prime must be seen, then, not as a 14-year-old firm, but as three very different organizations, each of which was managed by a different set of executives. Unlike General Radio, Prime initiated these discontinuities during periods of great success.

- The Operating Group at Citibank prior to 1970 had been a service-oriented function for the end-user areas of the bank. The Operating Group hired high school graduates who remained in the "back-office" for their entire careers. Structure, controls, and systems were loose, while the informal organization valued service, responsiveness to client needs, and slow, steady work habits. While these patterns were successful enough, increased demand and heightened customer expectations led to ever decreasing performance during the late 1960s.

  In the face of severe performance decline, John Reed was promoted to head the Operating Group. Reed recruited several executives with production backgrounds, and with this new top team he initiated system-wide changes. Reed's vision was to transform the Operating Group from a *service*-oriented back office to a *factory* producing high-quality products. Consistent with this new mission, Reed and his colleagues initiated sweeping changes in strategy, structure, work flows, and culture. These changes were initiated concurrently throughout the back office, with very little participation, over the course of a few months. While all the empirical performance measures improved substantially, these changes also generated substantial stress and anxiety within Reed's group.

- For 20 years, Alpha Corporation was among the leaders in the industrial fastener industry. Its reliability, low cost, and good technical service were important strengths. However, as Alpha's segment of the industry matured, its profits declined. Belt-tightening helped but was not enough. Finally, a new CEO presided over a sweeping restructuring: cutting the product line, closing a plant, trimming overhead; then focusing on computer parts which call for very close tolerances, CAD/CAM tooling, and cooperation with customers on design efforts. After four rough years, Alpha appears to have found a new niche where convergence will again be warranted.

These four short examples illustrate periods of incremental change, or convergence, punctuated by discontinuous changes throughout the organization. Discontinuous or "frame-breaking"

change involves simultaneous and sharp shifts in strategy, power, structure, and controls. Each example illustrates the role of executive leadership in initiating and implementing discontinuous change. Where General Radio, Citibank's Operating Group, and Alpha initiated system-wide changes only after sustained performance decline, Prime proactively initiated system-wide changes to take advantage of competitive/technological conditions. These patterns in organization evolution are not unique. Upheaval, sooner or later, follows convergence if a company is to survive; only a farsighted minority of firms initiate upheaval prior to incurring performance declines.

The task of managing incremental change, or convergence, differs sharply from managing frame-breaking change. Incremental change is compatible with the existing structure of a company and is reinforced over a period of years. In contrast, frame-breaking change is abrupt, painful to participants, and often resisted by the old guard. Forging these new strategy-structure-people-process consistencies and laying the basis for the next period of incremental change calls for distinctive skills.

Because the future health, and even survival, of a company or business unit is at stake, we need to take a closer look at the nature and consequences of convergent change and of differences imposed by frame-breaking change. We need to explore when and why these painful and risky revolutions interrupt previously successful patterns, and whether these discontinuities can be avoided and/or initiated prior to crisis. Finally, we need to examine what managers can and should do to guide their organizations through periods of convergence and upheaval over time.

The Research Base

The research which sparks this article is based on the abundant company histories and case studies. The more complete case studies have tracked individual firms' evolution and various crises in great detail (e.g., Chandler's seminal study of strategy and structure at Du Pont, General Motors, Standard Oil, and Sears[1]). More recent studies have dealt systematically with whole sets of companies and trace their experience over long periods of time.

A series of studies by researchers at McGill University covered over 40 well-known firms in diverse industries for at least 20 years per firm (e.g., Miller and Friesen[2]). Another research program conducted by researchers at Columbia, Duke, and Cornell Universities is tracking the history of large samples of companies in the minicomputer, cement, airlines, and glass industries. This research program builds on earlier work (e.g., Greiner[3]) and finds that most successful firms evolve through long periods of convergence punctuated by frame-breaking change.

The following discussion is based on the history of companies in many different industries, different countries, both large and small organizations, and organizations in various stages of their product class's life-cycle. We are dealing with a widespread phenomenon — not just a few dramatic sequences. Our research strongly suggests that the convergence/upheaval pattern occurs within departments (e.g., Citibank's Operating Group), at the business-unit level (e.g., Prime or General Radio), and at the corporate level of analysis (e.g., the Singer, Chrysler, or Harris Corporations). The problem of managing both convergent periods and upheaval is not just for the CEO, but necessarily involves general managers as well as functional managers.

Patterns in Organizational Evolution: Convergence and Upheaval

Building on Strength: Periods of Convergence

Successful companies wisely stick to what works well. At General Radio between 1915 and 1950, the loose functional structure, committee management system, internal promotion practices, control with engineering, and the high-quality, premium-price, engineering mentality all worked together to provide a highly congruent system. These internally consistent patterns in strategy, structure, people, and processes served General Radio for over 35 years.

Similarly, the Alpha Corporation's customer driven, low-cost strategy was accomplished by strength in engineering and production and ever more detailed structures and systems which evaluated cost, quality, and new product development. These strengths were epitomized in Alpha's chief engineer and president. The chief engineer had a remarkable talent for helping customers find new uses for industrial fasteners. He relished solving such problems, while at the same time designing fasteners that could be easily manufactured. The president excelled at production — producing dependable, low-cost fasteners. The pair were role models which set a pattern which served Alpha well for 15 years.

As the company grew, the chief engineer hired kindred customer-oriented application engineers. With the help of innovative users, they developed new products, leaving more routine problem-solving and incremental change to the sales and production departments. The president relied on a hands-on manufacturing manager and delegated financial matters to a competent treasurer-controller. Note how well the organization reinforced Alpha's strategy and how the key people fit the organization. There was an excellent fit between strategy and structure. The informal structure also fit well — communications were open, the simple mission of the company was widely endorsed, and routines were well understood.

As the General Radio and Alpha examples suggest, convergence starts out with an effective dovetailing of strategy, structure, people, and processes. For other strategies or in other industries, the particular formal and informal systems might be very different, but still a winning combination. The formal system includes decisions about grouping and linking resources as well as planning and control systems, rewards and evaluation procedures, and human resource management systems. The informal system includes core values, beliefs, norms, communication patterns, and actual decision-making and conflict resolution patterns. It is the whole fabric of structure, systems, people, and processes which must be suited for company strategy.[4]

As the fit between strategy, structure, people, and processes is never perfect, convergence is an ongoing process characterized by incremental change. Over time, in all companies studied, two types of converging changes were common: fine-tuning and incremental adaptations.

Converging Change: Fine-Tuning. Even with good strategy-structure-process fits, well-run companies seek even better ways of exploiting (and defending) their missions. Such effort typically deals with one or more of the following:

- *Refining* policies, methods, and procedures.
- Creating *specialized units and linking mechanisms* to permit increased volume and increased attention to unit quality and cost.
- *Developing personnel* especially suited to the present strategy—through improved selection and training, and tailoring reward systems to match strategic thrusts.
- Fostering individual and group *commitments* to the company mission and to the excellence of one's own department.
- Promoting *confidence* in the accepted norms, beliefs, and myths.
- *Clarifying* established roles, power, status, dependencies, and allocation mechanisms.

The fine-tuning fills out and elaborates the consistencies between strategy, structure, people, and processes. These incremental changes lead to an ever more interconnected (and therefore more stable) social system. Convergent periods fit the happy, stick-with-a-winner situations romanticized by Peters and Waterman.[5]

Converging Change: Incremental Adjustments to Environmental Shifts. In addition to fine-tuning changes, minor shifts in the environment will call for some organizational response. Even the most conservative of organizations expect, even welcome, small changes which do not make too many waves.

A popular expression is that almost any organization can tolerate a "ten-percent change." At any one time, only a few changes are being made; but these changes are still compatible with the prevailing structures, systems, and processes. Examples of such adjustments are an expansion in sales territory, a shift in emphasis among products in the product line, or improved processing technology in production.

The usual process of making changes of this sort is well known: wide acceptance of the need for change, openness to possible alternatives, objective examination of the pros and cons of each plausible alternative, participation of those directly affected in the preceding analysis, a market test or pilot operation where feasible, time to learn the new activities, established role models, known rewards for positive success, evaluation, and refinement.

The role of executive leadership during convergent periods is to reemphasize mission and core values and to delegate incremental decisions to middle-level managers. Note that the uncertainty created for people affected by such changes is well within tolerable limits. Opportunity is provided to anticipate and learn what is new, while most features of the structure remain unchanged.

The overall system adapts, but it is not transformed.

Converging Change: Some Consequences. For those companies whose strategies fit environmental conditions, convergence brings about better and better effectiveness. Incremental change is relatively easy to implement and ever more optimizes the consistencies between strategy, structure, people, and processes. At AT&T, for example, the period between 1913 and 1980 was one of ever more incremental change to further bolster the "Ma Bell" culture, systems, and structure all in service of developing the telephone network.

Convergent periods are, however, a double-edged sword. As organizations grow and become more successful, they develop internal forces for stability. Organization structures and systems become so interlinked that they only allow compatible changes. Further, over time, employees develop habits, patterned behaviors begin to take on values (e.g., "service is good"), and employees develop a sense of competence in knowing how to get work done within the system. These self-reinforcing patterns of behavior, norms, and values contribute to increased organizational momentum and complacency and, over time, to a sense of organizational history. This organizational history — epitomized by common stories, heroes, and standards — specifies "how we work here" and "what we hold important here."

This organizational momentum is profoundly functional as long as the organization's strategy is appropriate. The Ma Bell and General Radio culture, structure, and systems — and associated internal momentum — were critical to each organization's success. However, if (and when) strategy must change, this momentum cuts the other way. Organizational history is a source of tradition, precedent, and pride which are, in turn, anchors to the past. A proud history often restricts vigilant problem solving and may be a source of resistance to change.

When faced with environmental threat, organizations with strong momentum

- may not register the threat due to organization complacency and/or stunted external vigilance (e.g., the automobile or steel industries), or
- if the threat is recognized, the response is frequently heightened conformity to the status quo and/or increased commitment to "what we do best."

For example, the response of dominant firms to technological threat is frequently increased commitment to the obsolete technology (e.g., telegraph/telephone; vacuum tube/transistor; core/semiconductor memory). A paradoxical result of long periods of success may be heightened organizational complacency, decreased organizational flexibility, and a stunted ability to learn.

Converging change is a double-edged sword. Those very social and technical consistencies that are key sources of success may also be the seeds of failure if environments change. The longer the convergent period, the greater these internal forces for stability. This momentum seems to be particularly accentuated in those most successful firms

in a product class (e.g., Polaroid, Caterpillar, or U.S. Steel), in historically regulated organizations (e.g., AT&T, GTE, or financial service firms), or in organizations that have been traditionally shielded from competition (e.g., universities, not-for-profit organizations, government agencies and/or services).

On Frame-Breaking Change

Forces Leading to Frame-Breaking Change.
What, then, leads to frame-breaking change? Why defy tradition? Simply stated, frame-breaking change occurs in response to or, better yet, in anticipation of major environmental changes — changes which require more than incremental adjustments. The need for discontinuous change springs from one or a combination of the following:

- *Industry Discontinuities* — Sharp changes in legal, political, or technological conditions shift the basis of competition within industries. *Deregulation* has dramatically transformed the financial services and airlines industries. *Substitute product technologies* (such as jet engines, electronic typing, microprocessors) or *substitute process technologies* (such as the planar process in semiconductors or float-glass in glass manufacture) may transform the bases of competition within industries. Similarly, the emergence of industry standards, or *dominant designs* (such as the DC-3, IBM 360, or PDP-8) signal a shift in competition away from product innovation and towards increased process innovation. Finally, *major economic changes* (e.g., oil crises) and *legal shifts* (e.g., patent protection in biotechnology or trade/regulator barriers in pharmaceuticals or cigarettes) also directly affect bases of competition.
- *Product-Life-Cycle Shifts* — Over the course of a product class life-cycle, different strategies are appropriate. In the emergence phase of a product class, competition is based on product innovation and performance, where in the maturity stage, competition centers on cost, volume,

and efficiency. Shifts in patterns of demand alter key factors for success. For example, the demand and nature of competition for minicomputers, cellular telephones, wide-body aircraft, and bowling alley equipment was transformed as these products gained acceptance and their product classes evolved. Powerful international competition may compound these forces.

- *Internal Company Dynamics*—Entwined with these external forces are breaking points within the firm. Sheer size may require a basically new management design. For example, few inventor-entrepreneurs can tolerate the formality that is linked with large volume; even Digital Equipment Company apparently has outgrown the informality so cherished by Kenneth Olsen. Key people die. Family investors may become more concerned with their inheritance taxes than with company development. Revised corporate portfolio strategy may sharply alter the role and resources assigned to business units or functional areas. Such pressures, especially when coupled with external changes, may trigger frame-breaking change.

Scope of Frame-Breaking Change. Frame-breaking change is driven by shifts in business strategy. As strategy shifts so too must structure, people, and organizational processes. Quite unlike convergent change, frame-breaking reforms involve discontinuous changes throughout the organization. These bursts of change do not reinforce the existing system and are implemented rapidly. For example, the system-wide changes at Prime and General Radio were implemented over 18–24-month periods, whereas changes in Citibank's Operating Group were implemented in less than five months. Frame-breaking changes are revolutionary changes *of* the system as opposed to incremental changes *in* the system.

The following features are usually involved in frame-breaking change:

- *Reformed Mission and Core Values*—A strategy shift involves a new definition of company mission. Entering or withdrawing from an industry may be involved; at least the way the company expects to be outstanding is altered. The revamped AT&T is a conspicuous example. Success on its new course calls for a strategy based on competition, aggressiveness, and responsiveness, as well as a revised set of core values about how the firm competes and what it holds as important. Similarly, the initial shift at Prime reflected a strategic shift away from technology and towards sales and marketing. Core values also were aggressively reshaped by Ken Fisher to complement Prime's new strategy.

- *Altered Power and Status*—Frame-breaking change always alters the distribution of power. Some groups lose in the shift while others gain. For example, at Prime and General Radio, the engineering functions lost power, resources, and prestige as the marketing and sales functions gained. These dramatically altered power distributions reflect shifts in bases of competition and resource allocation. A new strategy must be backed up with a shift in the balance of power and status.

- *Reorganization*—A new strategy requires a modification in structure, systems, and procedures. As strategic requirements shift, so too must the choice of organization form. A new direction calls for added activity in some areas and less in others. Changes in structure and systems are means to ensure that this reallocation of effort takes place. New structures and revised roles deliberately break business-as-usual behavior.

- *Revised Interaction Patterns*—The way people in the organization work together has to adapt during frame-breaking change. As strategy is different, new procedures, work flows, communication networks, and decision-making patterns must be established. With these changes in work flows and procedures must also come revised norms, informal decision-making/conflict-resolution procedures, and informal roles.

- *New Executives*—Frame-breaking change also involves new executives, usually brought in from outside the organization (or business unit) and placed in key managerial positions. Commitment to the new mission, energy to overcome prevailing inertia, and freedom from prior obligations are all needed to refocus the organization. A few exceptional members of the old guard may attempt to make this shift, but habits and expectations of their associations are difficult to break. New executives are most likely to provide both the necessary drive and an enhanced set of skills more appropriate for the new strategy. While the overall number of executive changes is usually relatively small, these new executives have substantial symbolic and substantive effects on the organization. For example, frame-breaking changes at Prime, General Radio, Citibank, and Alpha Corporation were all spearheaded by a relatively small set of new executives from outside the company or group.

Why All at Once? Frame-breaking change is revolutionary in that the shifts reshape the entire nature of the organization. Those more effective examples of frame-breaking change were implemented rapidly (e.g., Citibank, Prime, Alpha). It appears that a piecemeal approach to frame-breaking changes gets bogged down in politics, individual resistance to change, and organizational inertia (e.g., Sinclair's attempts to reshape General Radio). Frame-breaking change requires discontinuous shifts in strategy, structure, people, and processes concurrently—or at least in a short period of time. Reasons for rapid, simultaneous implementation include:

- *Synergy* within the new structure can be a powerful aid. New executives with a fresh mission, working in a redesigned organization with revised norms and values, backed up with power and status, provide strong reinforcement. The pieces of the revitalized organization pull together, as opposed to piecemeal change where one part of the new organization is out of synch with the old organization.
- *Pockets of resistance* have a chance to grow and develop when frame-breaking change is implemented slowly. The new mission, shifts in organization, and other frame-breaking changes upset the comfortable routines and precedent. Resistance to such fundamental change is natural. If frame-breaking change is implemented slowly, then individuals have a greater opportunity to undermine the changes and organizational inertia works to further stifle fundamental change.
- Typically, there is a *pent-up need for change*. During convergent periods, basic adjustments are postponed. Boat-rocking is discouraged. Once constraints are relaxed, a variety of desirable improvements press for attention. The exhilaration and momentum of a fresh effort (and new team) make difficult moves more acceptable. Change is in fashion.
- Frame-breaking change is an inherently *risky and uncertain venture*. The longer the implementation period, the greater the period of uncertainty and instability. The most effective frame-breaking changes initiate the new strategy, structure, processes, and systems rapidly and begin the next period of stability and convergent change. The sooner fundamental uncertainty is removed, the better the chances of organizational survival and growth. While the pacing of change is important, the overall time to implement frame-breaking change will be contingent on the size and age of the organization.

Patterns in Organizational Evolution. This historical approach to organization evolution focuses on convergent periods punctuated by reorientation—discontinuous, organization-wide upheavals. The most effective firms take advantage of relatively long convergent periods. These periods of incremental change build on and take advantage of organization inertia. Frame-breaking change is quite dysfunctional if the organization is successful and the environment is stable. If, however, the organization is performing poorly and/or if the environment changes substantially, frame-breaking change is the only way to realign the organization with its competitive environment. Not all reorientations will be successful (e.g., People Express' expansion and up-scale moves in 1985–86). However, inaction in the face of performance crisis and/or environmental shifts is a certain recipe for failure.

Because reorientations are so disruptive and fraught with uncertainty, the more rapidly they are implemented, the more quickly the organization can reap the benefits of the following convergent period. High-performing firms initiate reorientations when environmental conditions shift and implement these reorientations rapidly (e.g., Prime and Citibank). Low-performing organizations either do not reorient or reorient all the time as they root around to find an effective alignment with environmental conditions.

This metamorphic approach to organization evolution underscores the role of history and precedent as future convergent periods are all constrained and shaped by prior convergent periods. Further, this approach to organization evolution highlights the role of executive leadership in managing convergent periods *and* in initiating and implementing frame-breaking change.

Executive Leadership and Organization Evolution

Executive leadership plays a key role in reinforcing system-wide momentum during convergent periods and in initiating and implementing bursts of change that characterize strategic reorientations. The nature of the leadership task differs sharply during these contrasting periods of organization evolution.

During convergent periods, the executive team focuses on *maintaining* congruence and fit within the organization. Because strategy, structure, processes, and systems are fundamentally sound, the myriad of incremental substantive decisions can be delegated to middle-level management, where direct expertise and information resides. The key role for executive leadership during convergent periods is to reemphasize strategy, mission, and core values and to keep a vigilant eye on external opportunities and/or threats.

Frame-breaking change, however, requires direct executive involvement in all aspects of the change. Given the enormity of the change and inherent internal forces for stability, executive leadership must be involved in the specification of strategy, structure, people, and organizational processes *and* in the development of implementation plans. During frame-breaking change, executive leadership is directly involved in *reorienting* their organizations. Direct personal involvement of senior management seems to be critical to implement these system-wide changes (e.g., Reed at Citibank or Iacocca at Chrysler). Tentative change does not seem to be effective (e.g., Don Sinclair at General Radio).

Frame-breaking change triggers resistance to change from multiple sources. Change must overcome several generic hurdles, including:

- Individual opposition, rooted in either anxiety or personal commitment to the status quo, is likely to generate substantial individual resistance to change.
- Political coalitions opposing the upheaval may be quickly formed within the organization. During converging periods a political equilibrium is reached. Frame-breaking upsets this equilibrium; powerful individuals and/or groups who see their status threatened will join in resistance.
- Control is difficult during the transition. The systems, roles, and responsibilities of the former organization are in suspension; the new rules of the game—and the rewards—have not yet been clarified.
- External constituents—suppliers, customers, regulatory agencies, local communities, and the like—often prefer continuation of existing relationships rather than uncertain moves in the future.

Whereas convergent change can be delegated, frame-breaking change requires strong, direct leadership from the top as to where the organization is going and how it is to get there. Executive leadership must be directly involved in: motivating constructive behavior, shaping political dynamics, managing control during the transition period, and managing external constituencies. The executive team must direct the content of frame-breaking change *and* provide the energy, vision, and resources to support, and be role models for, the new order. Brilliant ideas for new strategies, structures, and processes will not be effective unless they are coupled with thorough implementation plans actively managed by the executive team.[6]

When to Launch an Upheaval

The most effective executives in our studies foresaw the need for major change. They recognized the external threats and opportunities, and took bold steps to deal with them. For example, a set of minicomputer companies (Prime, Rolm, Datapoint, Data General, among others) risked short-run success to take advantage of new opportunities created by technological and market changes. Indeed, by acting before being forced to do so, they had more time to plan their transitions.[7]

Such visionary executive teams are the exceptions. Most frame-breaking change is postponed until a financial crisis forces drastic action. The momentum, and frequently the success, of convergent periods breeds reluctance to change. This commitment to the status quo, and insensitivity to environmental shocks, is evident in both the Columbia and the McGill studies. It is not until financial crisis shouts its warning that most companies begin their transformation.

The difference in timing between pioneers and reluctant reactors is largely determined by executive leadership. The pioneering moves, in advance of crisis, are usually initiated by executives within the company. They are the exceptional persons who combine the vision, courage, and power to transform an organization. In contrast, the impetus for a tardy break usually comes from outside stakeholders; they eventually put strong pressure on existing executives—or bring in new executives—to make fundamental shifts.

Who Manages the Transformation

Directing a frame-breaking upheaval successfully calls for unusual talent and energy. The new mission must be defined, technology selected, resources acquired, policies revised, values changed, organization restructured, people reassured, inspiration provided, and an array of informal relationships shaped. Executives already on the spot will probably know most about the specific situation, but they may lack the talent, energy, and commitment to carry through an internal revolution.

As seen in the Citibank, Prime, and Alpha examples, most frame-breaking upheavals are managed by executives brought in from outside the company. The Columbia research program finds that externally recruited executives are more than three times more likely to initiate frame-breaking change than existing executive teams. Frame-breaking change was coupled with CEO succession in more than 80 percent of the cases. Further, when frame-breaking change was combined with executive succession, company performance was significantly higher than when former executives stayed in place. In only 6 of 40 cases we studied did a current CEO initiate and implement multiple frame-breaking changes. In each of these six cases, the existing CEO made major changes in his/her direct reports, and this revitalized top team initiated and implemented frame-breaking changes (e.g., Thurston's actions at General Radio).[8]

Executive succession seems to be a powerful tool in managing frame-breaking change. There are several reasons why a fresh set of executives are typically used in company transformations. The new executive team brings different skills and a fresh perspective. Often they arrive with a strong belief in the new mission. Moreover, they are unfettered by prior commitments linked to the status quo; instead, this new top team symbolizes the need for change. Excitement of a new challenge adds to the energy devoted to it.

We should note that many of the executives who could not, or would not, implement frame-breaking change went on to be quite successful in other organizations — for example, Ken Fisher at Encore Computer and Bill Podusk at Apollo Computer. The stimulation of a fresh start and of jobs matched to personal competence applies to individuals as well as to organizations.

Although typical patterns for the when and who of frame-breaking change are clear — wait for a financial crisis and then bring in an outsider, along with a revised executive team, to revamp the company — this is clearly less satisfactory for a particular organization. Clearly, some companies benefit from transforming themselves before a crisis forces them to do so, and a few exceptional executives have the vision and drive to reorient a business which they nurtured during its preceding period of convergence. The vital tasks are to manage incremental change during convergent periods; to have the vision to initiate and implement frame-breaking change prior to the competition; and to mobilize an executive who can initiate and implement both kinds of change.

Conclusion

Our analysis of the way companies evolve over long periods of time indicates that the most effective firms have relatively long periods of convergence giving support to a basic strategy, but such periods are punctuated by upheavals — concurrent and discontinuous changes which reshape the entire organization.

Managers should anticipate that when environments change sharply:

- Frame-breaking change cannot be avoided. These discontinuous organizational changes will either be made proactively or initiated under crisis/turnaround conditions.
- Discontinuous changes need to be made in strategy, structure, people, and processes concurrently. Tentative change runs the risk of being smothered by individual, group, and organizational inertia.
- Frame-breaking change requires direct executive involvement in all aspects of the change,

usually bolstered with new executives from outside the organization.
- There are no patterns in the sequence of frame-breaking changes, and not all strategies will be effective. Strategy and, in turn, structure, systems, and processes must meet industry-specific competitive issues.

Finally, our historical analysis of organizations highlights the following issues for executive leadership:

- Need to manage for balance, consistency, or fit during convergent period.
- Need to be vigilant for environmental shifts in order to anticipate the need for frame-breaking change.
- Need to effectively manage incremental as well as frame-breaking change.
- Need to build (or rebuild) a top team to help initiate and implement frame-breaking change.
- Need to develop core values which can be used as an anchor as organizations evolve through frame-breaking changes (e.g., IBM, Hewlett-Packard).
- Need to develop and use organizational history as a way to infuse pride in an organization's past and for its future.
- Need to bolster technical, social, and conceptual skills with visionary skills. Visionary skills add energy, direction, and excitement so critical during frame-breaking change.

Effectiveness over changing competitive conditions requires that executives manage fundamentally different kinds of organizations and different kinds of change. The data are consistent across diverse industries and countries; an executive team's ability to proactively initiate and implement frame-breaking change *and* to manage convergent change are important factors that discriminate between organizational renewal and greatness versus complacency and eventual decline.

Notes

1   A. Chandler, *Strategy and Structure* (Cambridge, MA: MIT Press, 1962).

2   D. Miller and P. Friesen, *Organizations: A Quantum View* (Englewood Cliffs, NJ: Prentice-Hall, 1984).

3   L. Greiner, "Evolution and Revolution as Organizations Grow," *Harvard Business Review* (July/August 1972), pp. 37–46.

4   D. Nadler and M. Tushman, *Strategic Organization Design* (Homewood, IL: Scott Foresman, 1986).

5   T. Peters and R. Waterman, *In Search of Excellence* (New York: Harper and Row, 1982).

6   Nadler and Tushman, op, cit.

7   For a discussion of preemptive strategies, see I. MacMillan, "Delays in Competitors' Responses to New Banking Products," *Journal of Business Strategy,* 4 (1984): 58–65.

8   M. Tushman and B. Virany, "Changing Characteristics of Executive Teams in an Emerging Industry," *Journal of Business Venturing* (1986).

4

Structural Inertia and Organizational Change

Michael T. Hannan

John Freeman

Most prominent organization theories explain variability in organizational characteristics, that is, diversity, through reference to the history of adaptations by individual organizations. Earlier (Hannan and Freeman, 1977), we challenged this view and argued that adaptation of organizational structures to environments occurs principally at the *population* level, with forms of organization replacing each other as conditions change. This initial statement of population ecology theory rested on a number of simplifying assumptions. A major one was the premise that individual organizations are subject to strong inertial forces, that is, that they seldom succeeded in making rad-

ical changes in strategy and structure in the face of environmental threats.

How strong are inertial forces on organizational structure? This question is substantively interesting in its own right. It is also strategically important, because the claim that adaptation theories of organizational change should be supplemented by population ecology theories depends partly on these inertial forces being strong.

Many popularized discussions of evolution suggest that selection processes invariably favor adaptable forms of life. In fact the theory of evolution makes no such claim, as we made clear earlier (Hannan and Freeman, 1977; Freeman and Hannan, 1983). This paper goes beyond our earlier theory in acknowledging that organizational changes of some kinds occur frequently and that organizations sometimes even manage to make radical changes in strategies and structures. Nevertheless, we argue that selection processes tend to favor organizations whose structures are difficult to change. That is, we claim that high levels

The work reported here was supported by National Science Foundation grants SES-8109382 and ISI-8218013. We would like to acknowledge the helpful comments of Terry Amburgey, Gary Becker, Jack Brittain, Glenn Carroll, James Coleman, Susan Olzak, Jeffrey Pfeffer, Arthur Stinchcombe, and three referees on earlier drafts.

Reprinted with permission from *American Sociological Review,* Vol. 49, April 1984. © American Sociological Association.

of structural inertia in organizational populations can be explained as an outcome of an ecological-evolutionary process.

In addition to deriving structural inertia as a consequence of a selection process, this paper explores some of the details of inertial forces on organizational structure. It considers how inertial forces vary over the life cycle, with organizational size, and with complexity, and suggests some specific models for these dependencies.

Background

Our earlier formulation of an ecological theory of organizational change pointed to a variety of constraints on structural change in organizations:

> ... for wide classes of organizations there are very strong inertial pressures on structure arising from both internal arrangements (for example, internal politics) and from the environment (for example, public legitimation of organizational activity). To claim otherwise is to ignore the most obvious feature of organizational life. (Hannan and Freeman, 1977: 957).

Some of the factors that generate structural inertia are internal to organizations: these include sunk costs in plant, equipment, and personnel, the dynamics of political coalitions, and the tendency for precedents to become normative standards. Others are external. There are legal and other barriers to entry and exit from realms of activity. Exchange relations with other organizations constitute an investment that is not written off lightly. Finally, attempting radical structural change often threatens legitimacy; the loss of institutional support may be devastating.

We continue to believe that inertial pressures on most features of organizational structure are quite strong—much stronger than most theorists acknowledge. Moreover, the assumption that organizations rarely make fundamental changes successfully has proven to be a useful strategic simplification. It has allowed a rich and evocative set of ecological theories and models to be applied to the problem of changes in organizational form

over time (see, e.g., Brittain and Freeman, 1980; Carroll, 1983; Carroll and Delacroix, 1982; Freeman, 1982; Freeman and Hannan, 1983; Freeman et al., 1983).

However, the claim that organizational structures rarely change is the subject of dispute. March (1981: 563) summarizes his review of research on organizational change by asserting:

> Organizations are continually changing, routinely, easily, and responsively, but change within organizations cannot be arbitrarily controlled.... What most reports on implementation indicate ...is not that organizations are rigid and inflexible, but that they are impressively imaginative.

The contemporary literature contains at least three broad points of view on organizational change. Population ecology theory holds that most of the variability in organizational structures comes about through the creation of new organizations and organizational forms and the replacement of old ones (Hannan and Freeman, 1977; Freeman and Hannan, 1983; McKelvey, 1982). A second view, which might be called rational adaptation theory, proposes that organizational variability reflects designed changes in strategy and structure of individual organizations in response to environmental changes, threats, and opportunities. There are numerous variants of this perspective which differ widely on other dimensions. Contingency theories emphasize structural changes that match organizational structures to technology-environment pairs (Thompson, 1967; Lawrence and Lorsch, 1967). Resource-dependence theories emphasize structural changes that neutralize sources of environmental uncertainty (Pfeffer and Salancik, 1978). An institutionally oriented version of this perspective holds that organizational structures are rationally adapted to prevailing, normatively endorsed modes of organizing (Meyer and Rowan, 1977; DiMaggio and Powell, 1983). Marxist theories of organization typically assert that organizational structures are rational solutions for capitalist owners to the problem of maintaining control over labor (Edwards, 1979; Burawoy, 1979). The third broad perspective, which might be called random transformation theory, claims that organizations change their structures mainly in response to endogenous processes, but that such changes are only loosely coupled with the desires of organizational leaders and with the demands and threats of environments (March and Olsen, 1976; March, 1981; Weick, 1976).

Progress in explaining organizational diversity and change requires understanding both the nature of organizational change and the degree to which it can be planned and controlled. Here we concentrate mainly on the first issue: does most of the observed variability in organizational features reflect changes in existing organizations, whether planned or not, or does it reflect changes in populations with relatively inert organizations replacing each other? In other words, does change in major features of organizations over time reflect mainly adaptation or selection and replacement?

The selection and adaptation perspectives are so different that it is hard to believe that they are talking about the same things. Scott (1981: 204) claims that they are not:

> . . . the natural selection perspective seems to us to be particularly useful in focusing attention on the core features of organizations, explaining the life chances of smaller and more numerous organizations, and accounting for changes in organizational forms over the long run. By contrast the rational selection or resource dependency approach emphasizes the more peripheral features of organizations, is better applied to larger and more powerful organizations, and stresses changes occurring over shorter periods of time.

This contrast provides a useful point of departure for an attempt to clarify the conditions under which the two perspectives apply.

Transformation and Replacement

All accepted theories of biotic evolution share the assumption that innovation, the creation of new strategies and structures, is random with respect to adaptive value. Innovations are not produced because they are useful; they are just produced. If an innovation turns out to enhance life chances, it will be retained and spread through the population with high probability. In this sense, evolution is blind. How can this view be reconciled with the fact that human actors devote so much attention to predicting the future and to developing strategies for coping with expected events? Can social change, like biotic evolution, be blind?

Almost all evolutionary theories in social science claim that social evolution has foresight, that it is Lamarckian rather than Darwinian in the sense that human actors learn by experience and incorporate learning into their behavioral repertoires (see, e.g., Nelson and Winter, 1982). To the extent that learning about the past helps future adaptation, social change is indeed Lamarckian—it transforms rather than selects. In other words, major change processes occur *within* behavioral units.

Even when actors strive to cope with their environments, action may be random with respect to adaptation as long as the environments are highly uncertain or the connections between means and ends are not well understood. It is the *match* between action and environmental outcomes that must be random on the average for selection models to apply. In a world of high uncertainty, adaptive efforts by individuals may turn out to be essentially random with respect to future value.

The realism of Darwinian mechanisms in organizational populations also turns on the degree to which change in organizational structures can be controlled by those ostensibly in command. Suppose that individuals learn to anticipate the future and adapt strategies accordingly and that organizations simply mirror the intentions of rational leaders. Then organizational adaptations would be largely nonrandom with respect to future states of the environment. On the other hand, if March and others are right, organizational change is largely uncontrolled. Then organizations staffed by highly rational planners may behave essentially randomly with respect to adaptation. In other words, organizational outcomes may be decoupled from individual intentions; organizations may have lives of their own. In this case it is not enough to ask whether individual humans learn and plan rationally for an uncertain future. One must ask whether organizations as collective actors display the same capacities.

The applicability of Darwinian arguments to changes in organizational populations thus depends partly on the tightness of coupling between individual intentions and organizational outcomes. At least two well-known situations generate loose coupling: diversity of interest among members and uncertainty about means-ends connections. When members of an organization have diverse interests, organizational outcomes depend heavily on internal politics, on the balance of power among the constituencies. In such situations outcomes cannot easily be matched rationally to changing environments.

When the connections between means and ends are obscure or uncertain, carefully designed adaptations may have completely unexpected consequences. Moreover, short-run consequences may often differ greatly from long-run consequences. In such cases, it does not seem realistic to assume a high degree of congruence between designs and outcomes.

Structural Inertia

To this point we have adopted the frame of reference of the existing literature, which asks whether organizations learn and adapt to uncertain, changing environments; but we think this emphasis is misplaced. The most important issues about the applicability of evolutionary-ecological theories to organizations concern the *timing* of changes.

Learning and adjusting structure enhances the chance of survival only if the speed of response is commensurate with the temporal patterns of relevant environments. Indeed, the worst of all possible worlds is to change structure continually only to find each time upon reorganization that the environment has already shifted to some new configuration that demands yet a different structure. Learning and structural inertia

must be considered in a dynamic context. Can organizations learn about their environments and change strategies and structures as quickly as their environments change? If the answer is negative, replacement or selection arguments are potentially applicable.

Three things must be known in order to answer questions about the applicability of selection theories to populations of organizations. The first issue is the *temporal pattern of changes in key environments*. Are typical changes small or large, regular or irregular, rapid or slow? The second issue is the *speed of learning mechanisms*. How long does it take to obtain, process, and evaluate information on key environments? The third issue is the *responsiveness of the structure to designed changes*. How quickly can an organization be reorganized?

To claim that organizational structures are subject to strong inertial forces is not the same as claiming that organizations never change. Rather, it means that organizations respond relatively slowly to the occurrence of threats and opportunities in their environments. Therefore, structural inertia must be defined in relative and dynamic terms. It refers to comparisons of the typical rates of change of the processes identified above. In particular, structures of organizations have high inertia when the speed of reorganization is much lower than the rate at which environmental conditions change. Thus the concept of inertia, like fitness, refers to a correspondence between the behavioral capabilities of a class of organizations and their environments.

Our definition of structural inertia implies that a particular class of organizations might have high inertia in the context of one environment but not in another. For example, the speed of technical change in the semiconductor industry has been very high over the past twenty years. Firms that would be considered remarkably flexible in other industries have not been able to reorganize quickly enough to keep up with changing technologies.

One of the most important kinds of threats to the success of extant organizations is the creation of new organizations designed specifically to take advantage of some new set of opportunities. When the costs of building a new organization are low and the expected time from initiation to full production is short, this kind of threat is intense (unless there are legal barriers to the entry of new organizations). If the existing organizations cannot change their strategies and structures more quickly than entrepreneurs can begin new organizations, new competitors will have a chance to establish footholds. Other things being equal, the faster the speed with which new organizations can be built, the greater is the (relative) inertia of a set of existing structures.

Even such a successful and well-managed firm as IBM moves ponderously to take advantage of new opportunities. Granted, IBM eventually moved into the market for minicomputers and microcomputers and appears poised to dominate them. Still, the protracted period of assessing these markets, waiting for technologies to stabilize, and reorganizing production and marketing operations created the opportunity for new firms to become established. As a consequence, the structure of the computer industry is almost certainly different than it would have been had IBM been willing and able to move quickly. The point is that IBM did change its strategy somewhat, but this change took long enough that new firms using different strategies and structures were able to flourish.

Reproducibility, Inertia, and Selection

As we have emphasized elsewhere, organizations are special corporate actors. Like other corporate actors, they are structures for accomplishing collective action as well as repositories of corporate resources. Unlike other collective actors, organizations receive public legitimation and social support as agents for accomplishing specific and limited goals. Although individual members often manipulate organizations to serve private goals and organizations pursue other goals in addition to their public goals, the basis on which organizations mobilize resources initially and gain support from society is their *claim* to accomplish some

specific set of ends (e.g., making a profit, treating the sick, producing basic scientific research).

Creating an organization means mobilizing several kinds of scarce resources. Organization builders must accumulate capital, commitment of potential members, entrepreneurial skills, and legitimacy (see Stinchcombe, 1965). Once such resources have been invested in building an organizational structure, they are difficult to recover. Although one can sell the physical assets of a disbanded organization and sometimes its name, most resources used to build it are lost when it is dissolved. Not only are the costs of starting an organization nontrivial, but organizations continually use substantial portions of their resources in maintaining and reproducing their structures rather than in performing collective action. Just as in the case of biotic creatures, there is a substantial metabolic overhead relative to the amount of work performed. Thus the creation of a permanent organization as a solution to a problem of collective action is costly compared to other alternatives.

Why do individuals and other social actors agree to commit scarce resources to such expensive solutions to problems of collective action? A number of answers to this question have been put forth (see Scott, 1981: 135–63, for an insightful review). The new institutional economics argues that organizations arise to fill the gaps created by market failure (Arrow, 1974). Williamson's (1975) influential analysis proposes that organizations are more efficient than markets in situations in which economic transactions must be completed in the face of opportunism, uncertainty, and small-numbers bargaining. Although sociologists tend to deny that organizations arise mainly in response to market failures, they tend to agree that organizations have special efficiency properties, but emphasize their efficiency and effectiveness for coordinating complex tasks (Blau and Scott, 1962; Thompson, 1967).

Although these efficiency arguments are plausible, it is not obvious that they are correct. Many detailed accounts of organizational processes raise serious doubts that organizations minimize the costs of completing many kinds of transactions. Indeed, there appears to be a strong tendency for organizations to become ends in themselves and to accumulate personnel and an elaborate structure far beyond the technical demands of work. Moreover, many organizations perform very simple tasks that involve low levels of coordination. In contrast, collections of skilled workers collaborating in ad hoc groups can often complete quite complex tasks. From the perspective of the performance of a *single,* complex collective action, it is not obvious that a permanent organization has any technical advantage.

We emphasize different kinds of competencies. The first of these is *reliability.* Organizations have unusual capacities to produce collective products of a given quality repeatedly. In a world of uncertainty, potential members, investors, and clients may value reliability of performance more than efficiency. That is, rational actors may be willing to pay a high price for the certainty that a given product or service of a certain minimum quality will be available when it is needed. Reliability depends on the *variance* of performance (including its timeliness) rather than its average level.

Organizations have higher levels of reliability than ad hoc collectives in two senses: one cross-sectional and the other temporal. Cross-sectional reliability means that an outcome chosen at random from a population of organizations will have lower variance than one chosen at random from a population of other kinds of producers. Temporal reliability means the variability over time in the quality (including timing of delivery) of an outcome is lower for those produced by organizations than for those produced by ad hoc groups. Overall, we argue that the distinctive competence of organizations is the capacity to generate collective actions with relatively small variance in quality.

Organizations have a second property that gives them an advantage in the modern world: *accountability.* The spread of general norms of rationality in the modern world (Weber, 1968) and a variety of internal and external contingencies demand that organizations be able to account rationally for their actions. This means both that they must be able to document how resources have been used and to reconstruct the sequences of organizational decisions, rules, and actions that produced particular outcomes. It does not necessarily mean that organizations must tell the truth to their members and to the public about how resources were used or how some debacle came about. What matters is that organizations can make internally consistent arguments that appropriate rules and procedures existed to reproduce rational allocations of resources and appropriate organizational actions.

Norms of procedural rationality are pervasive in the modern world. Organizational legitimacy, in the sense of high probability that powerful collective actors will endorse an organization's actions (Stinchcombe, 1968), depends on ostensible conformity to these norms. Coleman (1974) has argued that corporate actors favor other corporate actors over individuals. We add that corporate actors especially favor other corporate actors that give signals of procedural rationality and accountability.

Testing for accountability is especially intense during organization building, the process of initial resource mobilization. Potential members want assurance that their investments of time and commitment will not be wasted. When membership involves an employment relation, potential members often want guarantees that careers within the organization are managed in some rational way. Potential investors (or supporters) also assess accountability. In fact, the profession of public accountancy arose in the United States in response to the desires of British investors in American railroads for assurances that their investments were being managed in appropriate ways (Chandler, 1977). Demands for accounting rationality in this narrow sense are both widespread and intense in modern societies. For example, the federal government will not allocate research grants and contracts to organizations that have not passed a federal audit, meaning that they have given evidence of possessing the appropriate rules and procedures for accounting for the use of federal funds.

Accountability testing is also severe when resources contract. Members and clients who would otherwise be willing to overlook waste typically change their views when budgets and services are being cut.

In our judgment, pressures for accountability are especially intense when (1) organizations produce symbolic or information-loaded products (e.g., education, branded products versus bulk goods)—see DiMaggio and Powell (1983); (2) when substantial risk exists (e.g., medical care); (3) when long-term relations between the organization and its employees or clients are typical; and (4) when the organization's purposes are highly political (Weber, 1968). Our arguments presumably apply with special force to organizations in these categories. Still, we think that pressures towards accountability are generally strong and getting stronger. The trend toward litigating disputes and pressures for formal equality in modern polities intensifies demands for accountability. All organizations seem to be subject to at least moderate levels of accountability testing.

We argue that the modern world favors collective actors that can demonstrate or at least reasonably claim a capacity for reliable performance and can account rationally for their actions. These forces favor organizations over other kinds of collectives and they favor certain kinds of organizations over others, since not all organizations have these properties in equal measure. Selection within organizational populations tends to eliminate organizations with low reliability and accountability. The selection processes work in several ways. Partly they reflect testing by key actors and environments in the organization-building stage. Potential members, investors, and other interested parties apply tests of reliability and accountability to proposed new ventures. Such testing continues after founding. Unreliability and failures of accountability at any stage in a subsequent lifetime threatens an organization's ability to maintain commitment of members and clients and its ability to acquire additional resources.

Assumption 1. *Selection in populations of organizations in modern societies favors forms with high reliability of performance and high levels of accountability.*

When does an organization have the capacity to produce collective outcomes of a certain minimum quality repeatedly? The most important prerequisite is so commonplace that we take it for granted. Reliable performance requires that an organization continually reproduce its structure—it must have very nearly the same structure today that it had yesterday. Among other things, this means that structures of roles, authority and communication must be reproducible from day to day.

Assumption 2. *Reliability and accountability require that organizational structures be highly reproducible.*

A structure can conceivably be reproduced repeatedly by negotiation and conscious decision making. The members of an organization with such practices might happen to decide each day to re-create the structure that existed the previous day. But this seems unlikely. Reproducibility is far more likely under different conditions. In general, organizations attain reproducibility of structure through processes of institutionalization and by creating highly standardized routines.

The first solution, institutionalization, is a two-edged sword. It greatly lowers the cost of collective action by giving an organization a taken-for-granted character such that members do not continually question organizational purposes, authority relations, etc. Reproduction of structure occurs without apparent effort in highly institutionalized structures. The other edge of the sword is inertia. The very factors that make a system reproducible make it resistant to change. In particular, to the extent that an organization comes to be valued for itself, changes in structural arrangements become moral and political rather than technical issues. Attempts at redesigning structures in organizations built on moral commitment are likely to spark bursts of collective opposition premised on moral claims in favor of the status quo. Even if such opposition does not prevail, it delays change considerably.

As a brake on structural change, institutionalization applies both to the organization as a whole and to its subunits. But what about the diversity among sets of differentiated activities within the organization? Some kinds of organizations perform diverse sets of activities, sometimes in parallel and sometimes sequentially. Military organizations provide a striking example; they maintain "peacetime" and "wartime" structures.[1] Similarly, labor unions gear up for organizing drives or for waves of strikes and then return to more placid bread-and-butter collective bargaining. Manufacturing firms sometimes concentrate on redesigning products and at other times concentrate on marketing an extant set of products. Each phase of organizational activity involves mobilizing different kinds of structures of communication and coordination. In a real sense these kinds of organizations can be said to use different structures in different phases.

Does this mean that these organizations have somehow escaped inertial tendencies? We think not, at least from the perspective of attempts at building theories of organizational change. These organizations have multiple *routines;* they shift from one routine (or set of routines) to another in a fairly mechanical fashion. We think that organizations have high inertia both in the sets of routines employed and in the set of rules used to switch between routines.

According to Nelson and Winter (1982: 96) routines are the "source of continuity in the behavioral patterns of organizations." They are patterns of activity that can be invoked repeatedly by members and subunits. One way of conceiving of routines is as organizational memory—an organization's repertoire of routines is the set of collective actions that it can do from memory. Nelson and Winter emphasize that organizations *remem-*

ber by doing. Like knowledge of elementary algebra or high school Latin, collective knowledge is the basis of organizational routines and decays rapidly with disuse. Even occasional use reveals some decay in recall and demonstrates the need to reinvest in learning to keep skills at their former levels. Organizations that have the capacity to use a broad repertoire of routines do so by virtue of large investments in keeping their routines sharp. For example, peacetime armies devote a great deal of their resources to simulating wartime situations and training. Armies that fail to make such an investment experience great difficulty in making the transition to battle readiness.

The fact that organizational routines decay with disuse implies that organizations face the classic specialism–generalism dilemma in deciding how many routines to maintain at any fixed level of resources. Generalists (those with many routines) are no less inert than specialists in the manner in which they adapt to environmental change in the sense that they still use a limited number of routines. As Nelson and Winter (1982: 134) put it:

> . . . it is quite inappropriate to conceive of firm behavior in terms of deliberate choice from a broad menu of alternatives that some outside observer considers to be "available" to the organization. The menu is not broad, it is narrow and idiosyncratic. . . . Efforts to understand the functioning of industries and larger systems should come to grips with the fact that highly flexible adaptation to change is not likely to characterize the behavior of individual firms.

We think that it is a reasonable first approximation to think of organizations as possessing relatively fixed repertoires of highly reproducible routines. Then the present argument can be applied either to the organization as a whole, where the issue is the diversity of the repertoire, or to the individual routine.

Thus we argue that the properties that give some organizations reproducibility also make them highly resistant to structural change, whether designed or not. As we noted above, this means that some aspects of structure can be changed only slowly and at considerable cost (many resources must be applied to produce structural change). Such structures have a dead-weight quality; there are large lags in response to environmental changes and to attempts by decision makers to implement change. Since lags in response can be longer than typical environmental fluctuations and longer than the attention spans of decision makers and outside authorities, inertia often blocks structural change completely.

The inertia of reproducible organizations is usually viewed as a pathology. A classic statement of this position is Merton's (1957) essay on the "dysfunctions of bureaucracy." High levels of inertia may produce serious mismatches between organizational outcomes and the intentions of members and clients in situations in changing environments. But, as we argued earlier (Freeman and Hannan, 1983), organizations that frequently try to reorganize may produce very little and have slight chances of survival. Here the issue is the cause of structural inertia rather than its consequences. Our argument is that resistance to structural change is a likely by-product of the ability to reproduce a structure with high fidelity:

Assumption 3. *High levels of reproducibility of structure generate strong inertial pressures.*

The three assumptions form the core of our first argument. Taken together they imply:

Theorem 1. *Selection within populations of organizations in modern societies favors organizations whose structures have high inertia.*

This theorem states that structural inertia can be a *consequence* of selection rather than a precondition. All that is required is that some organizations in an initial population have high levels of reproducibility (hence high levels of inertia) and that selection pressures be reasonably strong. Under such conditions, selection pressures in modern societies favor organizations whose structures are resistant to change, which makes selection arguments all the more applicable.

A Hierarchy of Inertial Forces

So far we have considered organizations as unitary actors, either adapting to their environments or remaining inert. This is simplistic in that it ignores the obvious fact that some parts of organizations change more quickly than others and that adaptive changes are sometimes not difficult to discern or implement. Universities, for example, are constantly changing the textbooks used for instruction. They do so in an adaptive way, keeping up with the constantly evolving knowledge bases of their various fields. Persuading a university faculty to abandon liberal arts for the sake of vocational training is something else again.

Why would the university's curriculum be so difficult to change? A number of answers come quickly to mind. The curriculum embodies the university's identity with reference both to the broader society and to its participants (i.e., faculty, students, staff, administration, alumni). The kinds of courses offered and the frequency with which they are offered serve as a statement of purpose which is articulated with society's value system. The curriculum also represents one of the bases on which resources are distributed. A change toward a more vocationally oriented set of courses threatens entrenched interests. Professors of classics and other humanistic fields that would have a lesser role in such an institution can be expected to resist such a change. The curriculum is difficult to change, then, because it represents the core of the university's organizational identity and underlies the distribution of resources across the organization. In these ways, it can be said to lie at the university's "core."

This view of organizations as having a core which is more difficult to modify than more peripheral parts of its structure is not new. As Parsons (1960: 59–69) pointed out, organizational authority hierarchies are not continuous: qualitative breaks occur between the technical, managerial, and institutional levels. The technical system is that part of the organization that directly processes the "materials" used by the organization.

The resources used by the technical system to do the organization's basic work are allocated by a broader organizational apparatus, the managerial or administrative system, which also relates those technical activities to the public served. While each depends on the other, the managerial level stands in a superordinate position. It both controls and services the technical level's operations, while the reverse is less often the case.

The third part, the institutional system, articulates the whole organization with the broader society. Parsons emphasized its role in legitimating the organization. Boards of trustees and directors are responsible for long-run policy and for the conduct of the organization with regard to its reputed goals. Because the institutional and managerial levels of the organization stand prior to the technical level in controlling the flow of resources, any important change in their operations leads to changes in the details of the operations of the technical system, while the reverse is less often true.

Thompson (1967) adopted these distinctions in arguing that organizations are built in such a way as to protect structural units carrying out the primary technology from uncertainties emanating from the environment. Thompson, however, drew core-periphery distinctions with reference to the organization's operating technology. Since we think that the importance of technology in determining structure varies greatly across kinds of organizations, we emphasize institutional characteristics more than technical ones. In this way our approach is closer to Parsons than to Thompson.

An argument similar to ours has been advanced by Downs (1967: 167–68) in his use of the metaphor of organizational depth:

> . . . organizations have different structural depths. Our analysis recognizes four "organizational layers." The shallowest consists of the specific actions taken by the bureau, the second of the decision-making rules it uses, the third of the institutional structure it uses to make those rules, and the deepest of its general purposes.

The layers supposedly differ in characteristic speeds of response.

We conceptualize organizational structure as composed of hierarchical layers of structural and strategic features that vary systematically in flexibility and responsiveness. Our theory emphasizes the claims used to mobilize resources for beginning an organization and the strategies and structures used to maintain flows of scarce resources. Thus we classify items of structure according to their bearing on resource mobilization. From the perspective of resource mobilization, the core aspects of organization are (1) its stated *goals*—the bases on which legitimacy and other resources are mobilized; (2) *forms of authority* within the organization and the basis of exchange between members and the organization; (3) *core technology,* especially as encoded in capital investment, infrastructure, and the skills of members; and (4) *marketing strategy* in a broad sense—the kinds of clients (or customers) to which the organization orients its production and the ways in which it attracts resources from the environment. The four characteristics stand in a rough hierarchy, with publicly stated goals subject to the strongest constraints and marketing strategy the weakest. Thus we expect the likelihood of change by transformation to decline as one proceeds up the hierarchy.

These four properties provide a possible basis on which to classify organizations into forms for ecological analysis. An organization's initial configuration on these four dimensions commits it to a certain form of environmental dependence and to a long-term strategy. Once an organization has made a public claim to mobilize resources, has induced individuals to cede some control in return for specific inducements, has invested in physical and human capital of specific types, and has designed a product or service to appeal to a certain audience, it has greatly limited its range of feasible transformations.

Although organizations sometimes manage to change positions on these dimensions, such changes are both rare and costly and seem to subject an organization to greatly increased risks of death. Thus these characteristics serve as a possible basis for selection and replacement within populations of organizations.

Although the four properties listed above encompass much of organizational strategy and structure, they do not come close to exhausting the dimensions of structure that interest social scientists. In particular, the list does not include structure in the narrow sense of numbers and sizes of subunits, number of levels in authority structures, span of control, patterns of communication, and so forth. Nor does it contain what Scott (1981) calls peripheral structures, the detailed arrangements by which an organization makes links with its environment and tries to buffer its technical core (for example, interlocking directorates and joint ventures).

We think that properties of organization charts and patterns of specific exchanges with actors in the environment are more plastic than the core set. They tend to change as organizations grow and decline in size, as technologies change, and as competitive and institutional environments change. They can be transformed because attempts at changing them involve relatively little moral and political opposition within the organization and in the environment and do not raise fundamental questions about the nature of the organization. In short, inertial forces on these aspects of structure and on peripheral or buffering activities tend to be weaker than those on core features.

Most organization theories assume that peripheral structures are premised on and adapted to a core structure. Changes in core structures usually require adjustment in the peripheral structures. However, the reverse is not true.[2] If a core structure is subject to strong selection pressure, peripheral structures will also be subject to at least weak (indirect) selection. In such cases, ecological theory applies at least indirectly to changes in peripheral structures. The tighter the coupling between the core and peripheral structures, the more direct is the applicability of our theory.

Overall we are inclined to agree with Scott that evolutionary-ecological theories apply more appropriately to core properties than to others. But we think that is because the strength of inertial pressures differ rather than because selection pressures on core and peripheral structures differ.

In addition to varying by aspects of structure, the strength of inertial forces may also vary with life-cycle phase, size, and complexity. The remainder of the discussion considers these issues.

Life-Cycle Variations in Inertia

Newly created organizations apparently have lower levels of reproducibility than older ones. As Stinchcombe (1965) pointed out, new organizations typically have to rely on the cooperation of strangers. Development of trust and smoothly working relationships take time. It also takes time to work out routines. Initially there is much learning by doing and comparing alternatives. Existing organizations have an advantage over new ones in that it is easier to continue existing routines than to create new ones or borrow old ones (see the discussion in Nelson and Winter, 1982: 99–107). Such arguments underlie the commonly observed monotonically declining cost curve at the firm level—the so-called learning curve.

In addition, the reliability and accountability of organizational action depend on members having acquired a range of organization-specific skills (such as knowledge of specialized rules and tacit understandings). Because such skills have no value outside the organization, members may be reluctant to invest heavily in acquiring them until an organization has proven itself (see Becker, 1975). Once an organization survives the initial period of testing by the environment, it becomes less costly for members to make investments in organization-specific learning—early success breeds the conditions for later success. Thus collective action may become more reliable and accountable with age simply because of a temporal pattern of investments by members. Moreover, the collective returns to investments in organization-specific learning may take time to be realized, just like the case for other forms of human capital. For both of these reasons, the levels of reliability and accountability of organizational action should increase with age, at least initially.

Once members have made extensive investments in acquiring organization-specific skills, the costs of switching to other organizations rise. Consequently the stake of members in keeping the organization going tends to rise as it ages.

Finally, processes of institutionalization also take time. In particular, it takes time for an organization to acquire institutional reality to its members and to become valued in its own right.

Assumption 4. *Reproducibility of structure increases monotonically with age.*

Theorem 2. *Structural inertia increases monotonically with age.* (From Assumptions 2 and 4)

Theorem 3. *Organizational death rates decrease with age.* (From Assumption 4 and Theorem 1)

Theorem 3, often called the "liability of newness" hypothesis (Stinchcombe, 1965), has been well documented empirically (see Freeman et al., 1983). Death rates appear to decline approximately exponentially as organizations age. One explanation for this finding is that reproducibility rises roughly exponentially with age over the early years in an organization's life.

Processes of external legitimation also take time. Although an organization must have some minimal level of public legitimacy in order to mobilize sufficient resources to begin operations, new organizations (and especially new organizational forms) have rather weak claims on public and official support. Nothing legitimates both individual organizations and forms more than longevity. Old organizations tend to develop dense webs of exchange, to affiliate with centers of power, and to acquire an aura of inevitability. External actors may also wait for an initial period of testing to be passed before making investments in exchange relations with new organizations. Thus processes of institutionalization in the environment and exchange relationships with relevant sectors of the environment may account for the relationships stated in Theorems 2 and 3. The argument to this point cannot distinguish between the internal and external sources of the relationships.

Size and Inertia

We argued above that dampened response to environmental threats and opportunities is the price paid for reliable and accountable collective action. If this argument is correct, organizations respond more slowly than individuals on average to environmental changes. However, some organizations are little more than extensions of the wills of dominant coalitions or individuals; they have no lives of their own. Such organizations may change strategy and structure in response to environmental changes almost as quickly as the individuals who control them. Change in populations of such organizations may operate as much by transformation as selection.

Except in exceptional cases, only relatively small organizations fit this description. An organization can be a simple tool of a dominant leader only when the leader does not delegate authority and power down long chains of command. Failure to delegate usually causes problems in large organizations. Indeed, the failure of moderate-sized organizations is often explained as resulting from the unwillingness of a founder-leader to delegate responsibility as the organization grew.

One way to conceptualize the issues involved is to assume that there is a critical size, which may vary by form of organization (and also, perhaps, by age), at which failure to delegate sharply limits its viability. In such a threshold model, organizations may be quite responsive below the threshold level of size. Above the threshold, organizations tend to have higher inertia. Or the relationship between size and inertia may be roughly continuous. Downs (1967: 60) argues that for the case of public bureaus: "...the increasing size of the bureau leads to a gradual ossification of its action ...the spread and flexibility of its operation steadily diminish." Whether there is a threshold as we have suggested or a continuous relationship as Downs suggested, it seems clear to us that size does affect inertia.

Assumption 5. *The level of structural inertia increases with size for each class of organization.*

Assumption 5 seems to suggest that selection arguments are more appropriate for large organizations than for small ones, contrary to widespread opinion (Aldrich, 1979; Perrow, 1979; Scott, 1981; Astley and Van de Ven, 1983). However, the situation is more complex than this. The likelihood that an organization adjusts structure to changing environmental circumstances depends on two factors: the rate of undertaking structural change and the probability of succeeding in implementing change, given an attempt. Assumption 5 suggests that the first quantity, the rate of attempting change, is higher for smaller organizations. But what about the second quantity?

It is helpful in answering this question to complicate the model slightly. Fundamental change—change in core aspects of structure—rarely occurs overnight. More commonly, an organization spends some period of time reorganizing, either by design or happenstance. Usually there is a period of time during which existing rules and structures are being dismantled (or successfully challenged) and new ones are being created to replace them. Similarly, existing links with the environment are cut and new links forged. During such periods, organizations have elements of both old and new structures. The presence of multiple rules and structures greatly complicates organizational action; so too does a shifting set of environmental relations. Such changes increase the likelihood of conflict within an organization as contending parties seek to shape rules to benefit their self-interests.

Fundamental reorganization may sometimes occur gradually and imperceptibly, but sometimes sharp breaks with the past can be discerned, and one can identify the approximate time of onset of the reorganization. One clear example is a declaration of bankruptcy in order to obtain relief from creditors during a period of attempted reorganization. In many other circumstances, organiza-

Figure 1. State Space for the Process of Fundamental Change in Organizational Structure

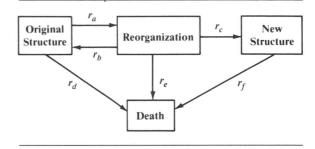

Note: The r_j's are instantaneous transmission rates.

tional leaders announce planned shifts in strategy and structure such as entries into new markets and internal restructuring. In such cases it may be helpful to introduce a new state into the model: the state of attempting fundamental reorganization. Figure 1 depicts the possible transitions in this expanded state space. The parameters associated with each transition, the r's, are instantaneous transition rates. In terms of this representation, Assumption 5 states that the rate of moving to the state of reorganization decreases with size. But it says nothings about the other rates.

The processes of dismantling one structure and building another make organizational action unstable. Consequently, the variance of quality and timeliness of collective action decline during reorganization.

Assumption 6. *The process of attempting reorganization lowers reliability of performance.*

Assumptions 1 and 6 together imply:

Theorem 4. *Attempts at reorganization increase death rates.*

Organizations undergoing structural transformation are highly vulnerable to environmental shocks. Large size presumably enhances the capacity to withstand such shocks. Small organizations have small margins for error because they cannot easily reduce the scope of their operations much in response to temporary setbacks. Indeed, the claim that death rates decrease with size is nothing more than a restatement of the idea advanced earlier (Hannan and Freeman, 1977) that longer time spans must be used to study replacement in populations of large organizations.

Assumption 7. *Organizational death rates decrease with size.*

We assume that size has qualitatively similar effects on all three death rates in Figure 1: r_d, r_e, and r_f. Thus small organizations are assumed to be more likely than large ones to enter the state of reorganization, but are also more likely to exit this state by death.

Finally, there is the issue of success at implementing change (the rate of moving from "reorganization" to "new structure"). An organization undertaking reorganization can successfully make the transition to the new state or it can drift back to its original structure, assuming that it does not die. The model in Figure 1 contains two rates that pertain to these processes: r_c, the rate of moving to the new structure, and r_b, the rate of returning to the old one. The effect of size on these rates is unclear. On the one hand, the greater inertia of large organizations might lower the rate of successes at reorganization. On the other hand, successes at reorganization might depend on the magnitude of resources applied to the task. Since large organizations typically have more resources than small ones, this line of reasoning suggests that the rate of achieving structural change increases with size.

The relationship between size and the rate of structural change is indeterminate in our theory for two reasons. The first is ignorance about the effects of size on rates of completing structural reorganization, conditional on having attempted it. The second source of indeterminacy is the implication that small organizations are more likely to attempt structural change but are also more likely to die in the attempt. Although our analysis does not offer an answer to the main question about size and inertia, it does not support the widespread

view that ecological arguments are particularly appropriate for the study of change in populations of *small* organizations.

The model in Figure 1 may be substantively interesting in its own right, assuming that approximate information on dates of leaving states of reorganization can be obtained. It provides a framework for addressing a variety of questions about inertia and change. It has the advantage of transforming what have been mainly rhetorical questions about the applicability of the ecological perspective into specific research questions.

Consider again the question of life-cycle variations discussed in the previous section. Recall that we assume that reproducibility increases with age (Assumption 4) because routines become worked out, role relations stabilize, and so forth. What effect, if any, does structural reorganization have on these processes? We think that reorganization is sometimes tantamount to creating a new organization (with a given level of resources). When reorganization is that fundamental, work groups are reshuffled, bringing strangers into contact, routines are revised, and lines of communication are reshaped. In this situation reorganization robs an organization's history of survival value. That is, reorganization reduces the reliability of performance to that of a new organization. The stability of the previous structure does not contribute to reducing variability with new sets of procedures, role relations, etc.

If internal processes are solely responsible for the tendency of organizational death rates to decline with age (Theorem 3), the death rate for an organization that has just entered the state "new structure" should be no lower than the death rate of a completely new organization with that structure (and levels of resources). In this sense, reorganization sets the "liability of newness" clock back towards zero.

Assumption 8. *Structural reorganization produces a liability of newness.*

In order to make this argument concrete, we consider its implications for one kind of parametric model for liability of newness. A variation of the

Markham model fits data on age-variations in organizational death rates well (Freeman et al., 1983; Carroll and Delacroix, 1982). This model has the form

$$r_d(t \mid t_0) = \alpha + \beta e^{-\gamma(t - t_0)},$$

where t_0 is the time of founding and γ is positive. The liability of newness in this model is expressed by β, because the initial death rate is $\alpha + \beta$ and the asymptotic death rate is α. Imagine an organization created at time t_0 that successfully changes its structure at t_n, that is, it enters the state "new organization" at that time. The argument that the liability-of-newness clock is set back towards zero implies that its death rate at time t approximates that of a new organization with the same structure. In particular, suppose that the death rate of a new organization with structure like this one has the following age-dependence in death rates

$$r_d(t \mid t_0) = \alpha' + \beta' e^{-\gamma'(t - t_0)},$$

where $\gamma' \geq 0$. Then for the case of an organization born at t_0 that switches to this structure at $t_n > t_0$, the death rate is given by

$$r_d(t \mid t_n) = \alpha' + \beta' e^{-\gamma'(t - t_0)}.$$

That is, development over the period (t_0, t_n) has no impact on its death rate, other things being equal.

The argument in the preceding paragraphs can be viewed as one way to formalize some long-standing notions about organizational crises. Child and Kieser (1981: 48) put the issue as follows: "To some extent, a crisis successfully overcome may represent a new birth, in the sense that changes initiated are sufficiently radical for a new identity to emerge." We suggest that such questions be viewed in terms of shifts in age-dependencies in organizational death rates.

External processes may also account for the tendency of death rates to decline with age. For example, we mentioned the tendency for organizations to acquire legitimacy simply by virtue of longevity as well as the fact that it takes time for organizations to develop enduring exchange relations with key actors in the environment. Some sorts of changes in strategy and structure strain external relations, especially when the changes imply a shift is ostensible goals. But, simple structural reorganization, without any apparent change of goals, does not rob an organization's history of its value for public legitimacy and does not necessarily upset exchange relations with the environment. Old organizations can presumably count on their existing exchange partners for support during and following such structural change.

If the liability of newness reflects internal processes, the death rate will jump with structural changes. In contrast, if the decline in the death rate with age reflects mainly the operation of external processes of legitimacy and exchange, the death rate will not jump when structural changes do not imply a change in basic goals. That is, arguments about internal and external processes lead to different predictions about the effect of structural reorganization on the death rate. Therefore the study of such effects may shed light on the relative importance of internal and external processes in accounting for age variation in the death rate in selected organizational populations.

Finally, there is no reason to suspect that the death rate declines with duration in the state "reorganization." Quite the contrary—as the length of time over which reorganization is attempted increases, the costs (especially the opportunity costs) of reorganization increase. As the fraction of organizational resources devoted to reorganization increases, the capacity of the organization to produce collective products declines along with its capacity to defend itself from internal and external challenges. Hence protracted periods of reorganization disrupt organizational continuity and increase the risk of death.

Assumption 9. *The death rate of organizations attempting structural change rises with the duration of the reorganization.*

A model consistent with this assumption is the classic Gompertz model:

$$r_e(t \mid t_r) = \theta e^{k(t - t_r)},$$

where t_r is the time of entering the state of reorganization and $k > 0$. This sort of model can perhaps elucidate another claim in the organizations literature. March (1981: 567), referring to the work of Hermann (1963) and Mayhew (1979), states that

> ...organizations facing bad times will follow riskier and riskier strategies, thus simultaneously increasing their chances of survival and reducing their life expectancy. Choices that seek to reverse a decline, for example, may not maximize expected value. As a consequence, for those that do not survive, efforts to survive will have speeded up the process of failure.

It is hard to imagine how an action can both increase a survival probability and increase the death rate in conventional models for the death rate (since life expectancy is a monotonically decreasing function of the death rate). However, the framework introduced above is consistent with this sort of pattern.

Consider the case in which the death rate of organizations in some environment rises precipitously at a certain moment t_1 (due perhaps to some discontinuous change in the environment). The death rate of organizations that retain their structures, r_d, will gradually decline to an asymptote that is considerably higher than the asymptotic rate in the old environment.

Suppose that some organizations in the population attempt structural change at t_1. Consider two kinds of trajectories of death rates by age. The dashed trajectory in Figure 2 depicts the death rate of an organization that successfully implements the new structure at t_3. The dotted trajectory pertains to an organization that reverts to the old structure at t_4. In a collection of histories like those in Figure 2, one would see that strategic action to promote survival exposes an organization to great risks (thereby "reducing its life expectancy"). But, because the death rate declines rapidly with duration in the new structure, a successful transformation eventually leads to a lower death rate (seeming to "increase chances of survival")— even lower than the death rates of organizations that retain the original structure. However, it is not clear that structural change necessarily increases unconditional life expectancy. This depends on the various rates. Still, introducing the

Figure 2. Hypothetical Death-Rate Functions for a Population of Organizations Exposed to a Shift in Selection Pressures at t_1

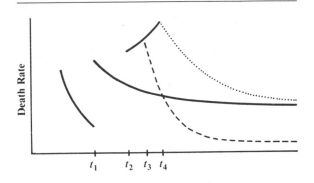

Notes: The solid decreasing curves represent the death rates of organizations that retain their strategies and structures. The rising solid curve represents the death-rate function of organizations that undergo attempts at reorganization at t_2. The dashed curve represents the new (better adapted) strategy and structure at t_3. The dotted curve represents the death-rate function of organizations that revert to their old strategies at t_4.

competing risks of death and reorganization allows one to deal systematically with this complicated problem.

Environmental Change, Size, and Inertia

Assumption 5 states that large organizations are less likely than small ones to initiate radical structural change. Does this mean that larger organizations have greater inertia, as Downs (1967) and others have claimed? If inertia is equated with low absolute rates of initiating structural change, it does. When inertia is viewed in comparative terms, as we argue it should be, the relationship of size to inertia is more complicated than the literature has indicated.

According to Assumption 7, the death rate declines with size. This statement is equivalent to the proposition that time-scales of selection processes stretch with size, as we noted earlier. One way to visualize such a relationship is to consider environmental variations as composed of a spectrum of frequencies of varying lengths—hourly, daily, weekly, annually, etc. Small organizations are more sensitive to high-frequency variations than large organizations. For example, short-term variations in the availability of credit may be catastrophic to small businesses but only a minor nuisance to giant firms. To the extent that large organizations can buffer themselves against the effects of high-frequency variations, their viability depends mainly on lower-frequency variations. The latter become the crucial adaptive problem for large organizations. In other words, the temporal dimensions of selection environments vary by size.

We proposed above that inertia be defined in terms of speed of adjustment relative to the temporal pattern of key environmental changes. Although small organizations are less ponderous than large ones (and can therefore adjust structures more rapidly), the environmental variations to which they are sensitive tend to change with much higher frequency. Therefore, whether the adjustment speeds of small organizations exceed those of large ones compared to the volatility of relevant environments is an open question. One can easily imagine cases in which the reverse is true, in which elephantine organizations face environments that change so slowly that they have relatively less inertia than the smallest organizations.

Complexity and Inertia

The complexity of organizational arrangements may also affect the strength of inertial forces. Although the term complexity is used frequently in the literature to refer to the numbers of subunits or to the relative sizes of subunits, we use the term to refer to patterns of links among subunits. Following Simon (1962), we identify a simple structure with a *hierarchical* set of links, which means that subunits can be clustered within units in the fashion of Chinese boxes (what mathematicians call a lattice).

Hierarchical systems have the property that flows (of information, commands, resources) are localized: an adjustment within one unit affects only units within the same branch of the hierarchy. Simon (1962) argued that hierarchical patterns appear frequently in nature ("nature loves hierarchy") because the probability that a complex assembly is completed in an environment subject to periodic random shocks is higher when stable subassemblies exist, as in a hierarchy. More complex structures do not have many subassemblies and thus are vulnerable to shocks during the whole developmental sequence.

Recent work on population ecology supports Simon's argument. For example, May (1974), Šiljak (1975), and Ladde and Šiljak (1976) show analytically and with simulation experiments that ecological networks are destabilized when links (of predation, competition, or symbiosis) are introduced. Both the number of links and the complexity of the pattern affect stability.

We think that similar arguments apply to structural change within organizations. When links among subunits of an organization are hierarchical, one unit can change its structure without requiring any adjustment by other units outside its branch. However, when the pattern of links is nonhierarchical, change in one subunit requires adjustment by many more subunits. Such adjustment processes can have cycles; change in one unit can set off reactions in other units, which in turn require adjustment by the unit that initiated the change. Long chains of adjustments may reduce the speed with which organizations can reorganize in response to environmental threats and opportunities.

Although slow response does not necessarily imply a lower rate of attempting structural change, it seems likely that this is the tendency. As we noted above, a slow speed of response increases the likelihood that the environment will have changed before an organization can complete a process of reorganization. Knowledge of this fact may dissuade organizational leaders from initiating change and may serve as a powerful objection to proposed change by parties who benefit from the status quo.

Complex systems have slow response times not because they are any slower than simpler systems in detecting environmental threats and opportunities but because the process of adjustment takes longer. In terms of the framework developed in earlier sections, this argument implies:

Assumption 10. *Complexity increases the expected duration of reorganization.*

That is, once a complex organization has begun structural change, it will tend to be exposed to a longer period of reorganization than a simpler organization attempting similar changes. Assumptions 9 and 10 imply:

Theorem 5. *Complexity increases the risk of death due to reorganization.*

A complete analysis requires consideration of the effects of complexity on rates of initiating change and of its effects on success in implementing change (as we discussed above in the analysis of the effects of size). We are not yet ready to make any claims about effects of complexity on these rates. Still, the result in Theorem 5 suggests that population-ecological analysis might be more appropriate for explaining change in populations of complex organizations than in populations of simple ones because complexity increases inertia by at least one mechanism. This result, like that on size, disagrees with the conventional wisdom.

Conclusions

We have attempted to clarify when it is reasonable to assume that organizational structures have inertia in the face of environmental turbulence. We have argued that selection pressures in modern societies favor organizations that can reliably produce collective action and can account rationally for their activities. A prerequisite for reliable and accountable performance is the capacity to reproduce a structure with high fidelity. The price paid for high-fidelity reproduction is structural inertia. Thus if selection favors reliable, accountable organizations, it also favors organizations with high levels of inertia. In this sense, inertia can be considered to be a by-product of selection. Our argument on this point may be considered an instance of the more general evolutionary argument that selection tends to favor *stable* systems (see Simon, 1962).

Of course, the claim that selection favors organizations with high inertia is not a warrant for assuming that most organizations have high inertia. Selection pressures often may not be strong enough to screen exhaustively for the "most fit" organizations. Moreover, most organizational populations are replenished more or less continuously by an inflow of new members. Younger organizations tend to have less inertia than older ones, and new organizations are more likely to adopt structures that differ greatly from those that would dominate any steady-state of the process subject to selection and closed to new entries.

Organizational selection operates on many dimensions besides reproducibility of structure. If selection pressures on specific features of structure are sufficiently strong, organizations with the characteristics appropriate to the environment are favored even if they have relatively low levels of reproducibility.

By the same token, environments in which change is turbulent and uncertain may not constitute a systematic regime of selection. The traits that are favored may shift frequently enough that no clear trend emerges. Such settings may favor organizational forms that can take quick advantage of new habitats. The capacity to respond quickly to new opportunities presumably competes with the capacity to perform reliably and accountably (Brittain and Freeman, 1980; Freeman, 1982). Such dynamics may dilute the importance of reliability and accountability in organizational selection. We will address these issues in subsequent papers.

For all these reasons, it is not sufficient to assume that selection processes favor organizations with high inertia and to proceed as though observed populations contain only such organizations. These considerations lead naturally to consideration of systematic variation within populations in the strength of inertial pressures. Existing theory provides some insights into these matters. One line of reasoning, which we pursued, suggests that inertial pressures increase with age—that organizations tend to ossify as they grow older. We suggest that the more fundamental process is that reproducibility increases with age. It follows from our general perspective that the death rate declines with age.

The effects of size on inertia are problematic in our revised theory. It is widely agreed that larger organizations are more ponderous than small ones. We think that analysis of the effects of size on inertia must consider several kinds of transition rates. One is simply the rate (in an absolute time scale) of attempting fundamental structural change. Another transition concerns success in implementing change. There is also the effect of attempting change on the death rate. We argue that small organizations are not only more likely than large ones to attempt change, but are also more likely to die in the process. Without further information on the magnitudes of the rates, it is not clear whether small or large organizations have higher overall rates of successfully implementing change. Our analysis suggests that it is premature to conclude that ecological theory may be applied more readily to small than large organizations. Clearly this matter deserves more theoretical and empirical attention.

Notes

1 Janowitz (1960) discusses various conflicting demands of organizing military activities in peacetime and war. Etzioni (1975) discusses the shifts in control problems that arise in armies and labor unions as a result of such changes.

2 Hawley's (1968) principle of isomorphism makes a similar argument concerning the relationship between "key functions" and other organizational structures.

References

Aldrich, Howard E. 1979. Organizations and Environments. Englewood Cliffs, NJ: Prentice-Hall.

Arrow, Kenneth J. 1974. The Limits of Organization. New York: Norton.

Astley, W. Graham and Andrew Van de Ven. 1983. "Central perspectives and debates in organization theory." Administrative Science Quarterly 28: 245–73.

Becker, Gary S. 1975. Human Capital. Second edition. New York: Columbia University Press.

Blau, Peter M. and W. Richard Scott. 1962. Formal Organizations. San Francisco: Chandler.

Brittain, Jack and John Freeman. 1980. "Organizational proliferation and density-dependent selection." Pp. 291–338 in John Kimberly and Robert Miles (eds.), Organizational Life Cycles. San Francisco: Jossey-Bass.

Burawoy, Michael. 1979. Manufacturing Consent Changes in the Labor Process Under Monopoly Capitalism. Chicago: University of Chicago Press.

Carroll, Glenn R. 1983. "Concentration and specialization: dynamics of niche width in populations of organization." Unpublished manuscript.

Carroll, Glenn R. and Jacques Delacroix. 1982. "Organizational mortality in the newspaper industries of Argentina and Ireland: an ecological approach." Administrative Science Quarterly 27: 169–98.

Chandler, Alfred D. 1977. The Visible Hand: The Managerial Revolution in American Business. Cambridge: Belknap.

Child, John and Alfred Kieser. 1981. "Development of organizations over time." Pp. 28–64 in William H. Starbuck and Paul C. Nystrom (eds.), Handbook of Organizational Design, Volume 1. Oxford: Oxford University Press.

Coleman, James S. 1974. Power and the Structure of Society. New York: Norton.

DiMaggio, Paul J. and Walter W. Powell. 1983. "The iron cage revisited: institutional isomorphism and collective rationality in organizational fields." American Sociological Review 48: 147–60.

Downs, Anthony. 1967. Inside Bureaucracy. Boston: Little, Brown.

Edwards, Richard. 1979. Contested Terrain: The Transformation of the Work Place in the Twentieth Century. New York: Basic Books.

Etzioni, Amitai. 1975. The Comparative Analysis of Complex Organizations. Second edition. New York: Free Press.

Freeman, John. 1982. "Organizational life cycles and natural selection processes." Pp. 1–32 in Barry M. Staw and Lawrence L. Cummings (eds.), Research in Organizational Behavior, Volume 4. Greenwich, CT: JAI Press.

Freeman, John, Glenn R. Carroll and Michael T. Hannan. 1983. "The liability of newness: age-dependence in organizational death rates." American Sociological Review 48: 692–710.

Freeman, John and Michael T. Hannan. 1983. "Niche width and the dynamics of organizational populations." American Journal of Sociology 88: 1116–45.

Hannan, Michael T. and John Freeman. 1977. "The population ecology of organizations." American Journal of Sociology 82: 929–64.

Hawley, Amos H. 1968. "Human ecology." Pp. 328–37 in David L. Sills (ed.), International Encyclopedia of the Social Sciences. New York: Macmillan.

Hermann, C.F. 1963. "Some consequences of crisis which limit the viability of organizations." Administrative Science Quarterly 8: 61–82.

Janowitz, Morris. 1960. The Professional Soldier. Glencoe, IL: Free Press.

Ladde, G.S. and D.D. Šiljak. 1976. "Stability of multispecies communities in randomly varying environments." Journal of Mathematical Biology 2: 165–78.

Lawrence, Paul and Jay Lorsch. 1967. Organization and Environment. Cambridge: Harvard University Press.

March, James G. 1981. "Footnotes on organizational change." Administrative Science Quarterly 26: 563–97.

March, James G. and Johan P. Olsen. 1976. Ambiguity and Choice in Organizations. Bergen, Norway: Universitetsforlaget.

May, Robert M. 1974. Stability and Complexity in Model Ecosystems. Second edition. Princeton: Princeton University Press.

Mayhew, L.B. 1979. Surviving the Eighties. San Francisco: Jossey-Bass.

McKelvey, Bill. 1982. Organizational Systematics. Berkeley: University of California Press.

Merton, Robert K. 1957. Social Theory and Social Structure. Second edition. Glencoe, IL: Free Press.

Meyer, John W. and Brian Rowan. 1977. "Institutionalized organizations: formal structure as myth and ceremony." American Journal of Sociology 83: 340–63.

Nelson, Richard R. and Sidney G. Winter. 1982. An Evolutionary Theory of Economic Change. Cambridge: Belknap.

Parsons, Talcott. 1960. Structure and Process in Modern Society. Glencoe, IL: Free Press.

Perrow, Charles. 1979. Complex Organizations: A Critical Essay. Second edition. Glencoe, IL: Scott Foresman.

Pfeffer, Jeffrey and Gerald Salancik. 1978. The External Control of Organizations: A Resource Dependence Perspective. New York: Harper & Row.

Scott, W. Richard. 1981. Organizations: Rational, Natural, and Open Systems. Englewood Cliffs, NJ: Prentice-Hall.

Šiljak, D.D. 1975. "When is a complex ecosystem stable?" Mathematical Bioscience 25: 25–50.

Simon, Herbert A. 1962. "The architecture of complexity." Proceedings of the American Philosophical Society 106: 67–82.

Stinchcombe, Arthur S. 1965. "Social structure and organizations." Pp. 153–93 in James G. March (ed.), Handbook of Organizations. Chicago: Rand McNally.

———. 1968. Constructing Social Theories. New York: Harcourt, Brace & World.

Thompson, James D. 1967. Organizations in Action. New York: McGraw-Hill.

Weber, Max. 1968. Economy and Society: An Outline of Interpretive Sociology. Three volumes. New York: Bedmeister.

Weick, Karl. 1976. "Educational organizations as loosely coupled systems." Administrative Science Quarterly 21: 1–19.

Williamson, Oliver E. 1975. Markets and Hierarchies: Analysis and Antitrust Implications. New York: Free Press.

5

Threat-Rigidity Effects in Organizational Behavior: A Multilevel Analysis

Barry M. Staw

Lance E. Sandelands

Jane E. Dutton

Recent economic trends have engendered interest in how organizations cope with adversity. Some researchers have taken an evolutionary perspective on the issue, examining the life span of a large number of organizations under varying environmental conditions (e.g., Hannan and Freeman, 1977; Aldrich, 1979). Others have taken a more policy-oriented perspective, examining how specific organizations have successfully or unsuccessfully adapted to threatening environments (Argenti, 1976; Rubin, 1977; Starbuck and Hedberg, 1977). This paper will also address the question of organizational adaptation in the face of adver-

sity. However, rather than simply concentrating upon organizational actions in a social or market context, we will focus upon how adversity affects the adaptability of multiple layers of an organizational system.

At present, sociological theory notes that organizations attempt to cope with potential sources of adversity (Thompson, 1967; Pfeffer and Salancik, 1978) by adjusting their internal structure or by taking actions to enhance their position in the environment. Many of these market strategies and buffering techniques (e.g., Thompson, 1967) have a rather anthropomorphic quality to them and could be construed as the product of a policy-making group or even a single decision maker. While it can be argued that sociological rather than psychological theories are best equipped to explain macro-level phenomena, there are, as Miller (1978) has noted, many effects that appear

The authors wish to thank Jeanne Brett, Larry Cummings, Joanne Martin, J.P. Miller, and the anonymous *Administrative Science Quarterly* reviewers for their insightful comments on an earlier version of this paper.

to generalize across levels of analysis. The reaction of entities to threat or adversity may be just such a phenomenon. The anthropomorphic quality of macro-level propositions may be the product of parallels in the effect of threat upon individual, group, and organizational behavior. Anthropomorphism may also result from the fact that organizational actions are often initiated by individual and group forces, such that social and psychological effects indirectly influence organization-level phenomena.

Not only do current models emphasize organizational and not individual or group responses to adversity, but they also take a functional stance. It is commonly assumed that methods of coping with adversity are appropriate and increase the survival prospects of the organization (Thompson, 1967; Pfeffer and Salancik, 1978) or protect local interests (Cyert and March, 1963). What is missing is the identification of maladaptive or pathological cycles of behavior (Merton, 1967; Hall, 1976). This article will therefore examine evidence for a maladaptive tendency in reacting to adversity and will examine the case for this pathology from multiple levels of analysis.

The Threat-Rigidity Thesis

Many well-publicized corporate collapses can be viewed as failures to alter response in the face of environmental change. The Penn Central Railroad, for example, continued paying dividends until cash flow dried up completely (Altman, 1971); Chrysler Corporation, when faced with the oil crisis and rising gasoline prices, continued large (but efficient) production runs on its largest and most fuel-inefficient cars until inventories overflowed (*Business Week,* 1979; *Fortune,* 1979); the *Saturday Evening Post* continued to raise its prices as circulation dropped (Hall, 1976). At the individual level of analysis, some of these same pathologies may also exist. When placed in a threat situation, an individual's most well-learned or dominant response may be emitted (Zajonc, 1966), but this response may be grossly inappropriate if the

task or learning environment has changed. Similarly, decision-making groups may reduce their flexibility under a stress situation, sealing off new information and controlling deviant responses (Janis, 1972).

As illustrated in these several examples, there may be a general tendency for individuals, groups, and organizations to behave rigidly in threatening situations. As we will explore in the review of several disparate literatures, there may be two types of effects. First, a threat may result in restriction of information processing, such as a narrowing in the field of attention, a simplification in information codes, or a reduction in the number of channels used. Second, when a threat occurs, there may be a constriction in control, such that power and influence can become more concentrated or placed in higher levels of a hierarchy. Thus, it is hypothesized that a threat results in changes in both the information and control processes of a system, and, because of these changes, a system's behavior is predicted to become less varied or flexible.

Data bearing on the threat-rigidity thesis will be presented from studies conducted at the individual, group, and organizational levels of analysis. Throughout the discussion, we will treat threat as an environmental event that has impending negative or harmful consequences for the entity (cf. Lazarus, 1966). However, in order to bring together sufficient literature to assess the threat-rigidity effect across multiple levels of analysis, it will be necessary to consider streams of research that overlap but do not match perfectly this definition of threat. Also, although we will consider information processing and control as determinants of rigidity, operationalizations of these variables will not be isomorphic across all levels of analysis. Such slippage in definitional precision will make our review conclusions more speculative than we would like, but this ambiguity is inevitable in searching for parallel and molar effects that span levels of analysis.

As outlined in Figure 1, the general thesis we will explore in this article is that a threat to the

Figure 1. Threat-Rigidity Cycles

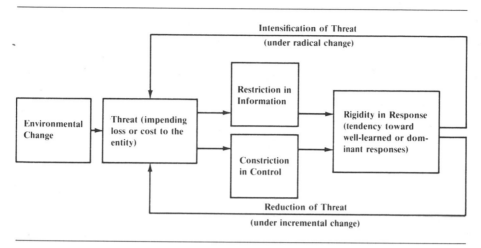

vital interests of an entity, be it an individual, group, or organization, will lead to forms of rigidity. It is further proposed that threat-rigidity effects can be maladaptive. When the environment has changed radically, flexibility and diversity in response have survival value (Campbell, 1965; Weick, 1979). Thus, maladaptive cycles are predicted to follow from threats which encompass major environmental changes since prior, well-learned responses are inappropriate under new conditions. In contrast, when a threat does not involve major environmental change (e.g., when no basic causal relationships have been altered), rigidity in response may not be dysfunctional. A rigid yet previously successful response may in fact be appropriate to a threatening situation that does not involve major changes. After reviewing the evidence bearing on the threat-rigidity thesis, we will return to this issue of the functional versus the dysfunctional nature of threat-rigidity effects.

Individual-Level Effects

The individual literature most relevant to threat deals with the effects of stress, anxiety, and arousal. Because threat is so frequently associated with these individual reactions, it has been used as the means to manipulate these variables. Studies frequently employ a threatening experience to alter states of stress, anxiety, and arousal, and then the effects of these manipulations are assessed upon individual cognition and behavior. Although stress, anxiety, and arousal are no doubt the immediate consequences of threat, we will consider them as virtual manipulation checks of whether a threatening stimulus has been presented.

Psychological Stress

The effects of psychological stress on individual behavior have received much attention (for reviews, see Janis, 1958; Lazarus, 1966; Appley and Trumbell, 1967; Sarason and Spielberger, 1975; McGrath, 1976; Beer and Newman, 1978). While the construct of stress has been interpreted in many divergent ways (e.g., stressful behaviors, adverse stimuli, and aspects of the social or physical environment), the research that is most relevant to threat involves the manipulation of an experimental context. Psychological stress has been manipulated by administering performance-failure feedback on preceding experimental tasks (Postman and Bruner, 1948; Cowen, 1952a, 1952b; Osler, 1954; Smock, 1955), by excess pacing of experimental tasks and time pressure (Lazarus and Eriksen, 1952; Castaneda and Palermo, 1955; Palermo, 1957), by threats of electrical shock (Pronko and Leith, 1956), and by varying the formality, warmth, and friendliness of experimental settings (Cowen, 1952a, 1952b).

Effects of stress relevant to the threat-rigidity hypothesis can be found in three streams of research. In the area of perception, research indicates that psychological stress interferes with the ability of subjects to identify and discriminate among visual stimuli (e.g., Postman and Bruner, 1948; Postman and Brown, 1952; Smock, 1955). Under stress, individuals perceive unfamiliar stimuli in terms of previously held "internal hypotheses" about the identity of stimulus objects, whereas persons not subjected to stress conditions are better able to identify and discriminate unfamiliar stimuli.

In the area of problem solving and learning, studies have used Luchins' (1942) water jar test to examine whether stress induces problem-solving rigidity. This test requires subjects to develop strategies for solving an arithmetic problem, and rigidity is measured by adherence to a previously learned solution, even when that solution is no longer appropriate for the problem at hand. Subjects in stress conditions have been found to be less flexible in their choice of solution methods than nonstress subjects (Cowen, 1952a, 1952b).

Finally, in the area of motor performance, research has shown an interaction between stress and training. Trained subjects in a stress condition perform better than subjects in nonstress conditions, but untrained subjects in a stress condition perform less well than nonstress subjects (e.g., Castaneda and Palermo, 1955; Pronko and Leith, 1956; Palermo, 1957). Some authors (e.g., Pronko and Leith, 1956) have concluded that psychological stress leads to behavioral-response rigidities, but, in the case of the trained subjects, the rigidified response is appropriate for task performance. These findings also support the Hull–Spence theory of motivation in which psychological stress may act to increase drive level and stimulate dom-

inant habituated responses (cf. Taylor and Spence, 1952; Farber and Spence, 1953; Spence and Farber, 1953). Task performance is enhanced in cases in which dominant responses are performance-relevant but hindered in the cases in which dominant responses are irrelevant or detrimental.

Anxiety

The relationship between anxiety and behavior can be categorized into two substreams of research. On the one hand are correlational studies relating measured states of anxiety (e.g., Taylor's Manifest Anxiety Scale) to various performance indicators. For example, studies of visual discrimination and learning have found that highly anxious subjects are less sensitive to visual stimulation (Goldstone, 1955) and are less discriminating of visual detail (Korchin, Singer, and Ballard, 1951; Korchin and Basowitz, 1954). On the other hand, many studies of anxiety have used experimental manipulations similar to studies of stress (e.g., electric shock and performance-failure feedback). This body of research indicates that anxiety, like psychological stress, interferes with visual discrimination (Eriksen and Wechsler, 1955), motor performance involving vigilance (Wachtel, 1968), and intellectual test performance (Mandler and Sarason, 1952; Sarason, Mandler, and Craighill, 1952; Wine, 1971).[1]

Physiological Arousal

Although arousal is a physical rather than psychological state of the organism, the concepts of stress, anxiety, and arousal are complementary aspects of human functioning (Schlosberg, 1954; Duffy, 1962). During periods of threat, individuals become physiologically activated in addition to experiencing psychic stress and anxiety. In fact, it is likely that arousal is ultimately responsible for the behavioral effects observed under conditions of stress and anxiety, although there is still considerable debate about whether arousal precedes or follows from more cognitively based emotional reactions (Schachter and Singer, 1962; Zajonc, 1980).

Arousal researchers have investigated many of the same aspects of human functioning as those working in the areas of stress and anxiety. Frequently studied are the effects of arousal upon perception (Duffy, 1932, 1962; Bacon, 1974; Pallak et al., 1975), learning (Yerkes and Dodson, 1980; Berry, 1962; Obrist, 1962; Kleinsmith and Kaplan, 1963; Eysenck, 1975), and motor performance (Thorner, Gibbs, and Gibbs, 1942; Huxtable, White, and McCartor, 1946; Stennett, 1957). As summarized by Easterbrook (1959), the effect of arousal upon perception is to narrow the range of cues processed by decreasing sensitivity to peripheral cues. In terms of learning and performance, arousal may also reduce flexibility and induce responses that are well-learned or habituated (for reviews see Duffy, 1962; Broadbent, 1971; Eysenck, 1976).

Disaster Research

While research on stress, anxiety, and arousal has been primarily laboratory-based, the largest source of field data related to threat comes from disaster-research studies. In the early 1950s, the U.S. government sponsored studies of communities that experienced tornadoes (Wallace, 1956), floods (Danzig, Thayer, and Galanter, 1958), major coal mining accidents (Beach and Lucas, 1963), and other disasters. While this literature provides some insight into the reactions of individuals in threat situations, the evidence is often anecdotal and speculative. Nonetheless, from the available case studies and clinical analyses of behavior in disaster situations, two themes are prevalent. First, most authors agree that the primary psychological effects of crisis are to create feelings of stress and anxiety in affected individuals (Bettelheim, 1943; Boder, 1954; Janis, 1954, 1962; Menninger, 1954; Glass, 1955; Wallace, 1956; Wolfenstein, 1957; Withey, 1962; Beach and Lucas, 1963). Second, the anxiety and stress brought on by a crisis elicits behavioral responses of withdrawal (Menninger, 1954; Glass, 1955), reductions in critical information processing (Menninger, 1952; Danzig et al., 1958), and constriction in behavioral responses

(Menninger, 1952; Glass, 1955). In a review of disaster studies, Withey (1962: 118), for example, concluded that the anxiety individuals experience in crisis situations leads to "a narrowing of the perceptual field and a limitation of the information that can or will be received" and that a more persistent threat may lead to even "greater constriction of cognition, rigidity of response, and primitive forms of reaction."

Summary of Individual Effects

We have only briefly reviewed the extensive body of research that relates to individual responses in threat situations. However, because the convergence of data across the research areas is so strong, it is possible to construct a summary model. Figure 2 depicts relationships between the theoretical constructs of stress, anxiety, physiological arousal, and cognitive and behavioral effects. Three aspects of this model are central: (1) the link between threat situations and psychological stress and anxiety; (2) the nature of cognitive manifestations of stress/anxiety/arousal; and (3) the link between cognitive manifestations of stress/anxiety/arousal and properties of individual behavior.

As shown in Figure 2, it is posited that threat leads to psychological stress and anxiety. This linkage is explicit in the disaster literature since symptoms of psychological stress and anxiety are found to be widespread in communities afflicted by disaster. This linkage is also implicit in the experimental literature, because manipulations such as electric shock, failure feedback, excessive time pressure, and threatening ambience are unpleasant, personally aversive events.

A second important feature of the model depicted in Figure 2 concerns the cognitive and motivational manifestations of psychological stress, anxiety, and arousal. The effects of these factors can be delineated between information and control processes. In threat situations, restrictions in information have been shown to result from tendencies on the part of individuals to emphasize prior expectations or internal hypotheses about

Figure 2. A Model of Individual Response to Threat

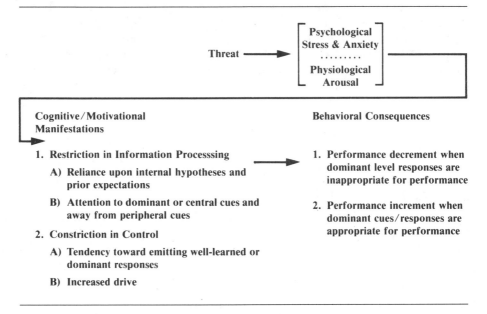

their environment (Postman and Bruner, 1948; Postman and Brown, 1952; Smock, 1955), and from tendencies to narrow attention to include dominant cues and exclude peripheral cues (Easterbrook, 1959; Wachtel, 1968; Wine, 1971; Eysenck, 1976). Likewise, constrictions in control correspond to the tendency of individuals to emit dominant, well-learned or habituated responses in threat situations (Beier, 1951; Cowen, 1952a, 1952b; Farber and Spence, 1953; Schaffer, 1954; Castaneda and Palermo, 1955; Eriksen and Wechsler, 1955; Pronko and Leith, 1956; Palermo, 1957; Zajonc, 1965; Pallak et al., 1975).

A final aspect of the model that bears discussion is the link between the cognitive and behavioral consequences of threat situations. In the disaster literature, anecdotal evidence has suggested that threatened individuals may fail to heed warnings or follow directions (Wolfenstein, 1957) and may even "freeze up" or fixate in their behaviors (Glass, 1955). These observations are consistent with findings from experimental psychology that suggest that psychological stress, anxiety, and arousal often result in poor task performance and

a tendency to persevere in well-learned courses of action. Significantly, however, the psychological literature cautions that the performance effects of stress, anxiety, and arousal are not general. Whether an individual performs a task well in a threat situation depends on performance relevant cues being central in the environment (as opposed to peripheral) and on performance relevant responses being dominant for the individual. This of course means that threats resulting from common or familiar problems may induce effective coping responses from individuals, while threats arising from radical environmental change may bring on a maladaptive reaction. This also means that practice or drill may not lead to effective coping mechanisms, except when the parameters of threat situations are well known or when the drills can, in fact, train individuals for cognitive flexibility under adverse circumstances.

Group-Level Effects

Threats to the interest and purposes of groups often occur, some so severe as to cause the breakup of a collectivity or loss to each of its members. For this reason, there may be parallels between the individual-level effects of threat and effects on the group level of analysis. However, because group research has not directly investigated this issue, it is necessary to examine several seemingly divergent subareas in order to explore such parallels.

The Effects of Threat upon Group Cohesiveness

One of the long accepted hypotheses of group behavior is that an external threat draws group members together and increases group cohesiveness. Much of the research supporting this contention comes from studies of intergroup conflict. The best known and one of the earliest illustrations of this effect was Sherif's boys' camp studies (Sherif and Sherif, 1953; Sherif et al., 1961). When two groups were placed in a competitive situation, the sociometric choices of group members shifted to an intragroup basis, with very few affective or social linkages persisting across the competitive groups. The rivalry between groups appeared to increase the liking and social bonds within each group and such positive intragroup affect was directly associated with intergroup hostility. Although some researchers (e.g., Rabbie and Wilkins, 1971; Rabbie and Huggen, 1974) have contested these findings on the grounds that they result from a relatively uncontrolled field experiment, laboratory experiments in which intergroup rivalry is manipulated also support Sherif's early conclusions (for a review see Dion, 1979).

Although competition between groups has been found to increase intragroup cohesiveness, this does not mean that adversity always draws group members together. When two groups compete for resources, the losing group may suffer a decrease in intragroup cohesiveness, while the winners may increase their cohesion further (Wilson and Miller, 1961; Ryen and Kahn, 1975; Worchel, Lind, and Kaufman, 1975). Thus, competition that threatens the loss of resources can lead to increased cohesiveness while the *actuality* of such a loss may lead to dissension. It would seem, therefore, that intergroup rivalry may focus attention

on intragroup relationships and make group membership more salient, but it can only assure a relatively short-term increase in cohesiveness. More sustained cohesiveness may result from *successful* competition.

The literature on group problem solving also addresses the intragroup consequences of group success or failure, although these data are derived from task performance rather than competition with a rival group. A large number of studies have found success on a group task to lead to positive affect toward other members of the group while task failure reduces intragroup cohesiveness (for reviews see Shaw, 1976; Zander, 1979). There are some exceptions to this general finding, but few studies have demonstrated that group failure leads to increased cohesion, and such increases could be viewed as a short-term reaction rather than a long-run consequence of failure.

In summary, an outside threat is posited to lead to an increase in the salience of intragroup relationships and a decrease in intergroup ties. This increased focus upon intragroup membership and processes will generally also lead to an increase in cohesiveness and liking for other group members. However, we would hypothesize that increases in cohesiveness may be short-lived if a group fails to meet outside challenges, either in terms of an intergroup rivalry or a problem facing the group. In the case of sustained and clearcut failure, the increased focusing upon in-group process may only serve to exacerbate a loss in cohesiveness. On the other hand, a group which is successful, or at least not failing to meet an outside challenge, may sustain cohesiveness at a high level.

The Effect of Threat upon Group Leadership and Control

Although group membership by itself can be stress reducing (Schachter, 1959), an external threat facing a group would be expected to raise anxiety about the attainment of group goals and individual interests as they relate to collective achievements. One way to meet such an outside challenge or reduce the threat might be increased reliance upon a group leader.

The effect of external threat upon leadership is not straightforward. Worchel, Andreoli, and Folger (1977) found that members of competing groups identified fewer members as leaders than did members of cooperating groups, implying a centralization of authority under threat. However, in Hamblin's (1958) research, groups were exposed to an outside threat or crisis, and he observed the replacement rather than a strengthening of existing group leadership. The threat in Hamblin's study consisted of radical changes in the rules of an experimental game, making it impossible for a group to succeed on the task or even to predict what behaviors were necessary for group success. In this experiment, there was a tendency for those who were initially most influential to lose some of their power and for those who were initially second in group influence to attain the leadership role. Other research by Hollander and his associates showed that a failure experience increased the influence of an elected leader but not that of an appointed leader (Hollander, Fallon, and Edwards, 1974). However, even for elected leaders, continued failure caused a significant erosion in their influence over time.

From existing data, it can be hypothesized that external threat focuses the attention of group members upon the actions of a leader and others high in influence. If external threat is translated into a clear-cut failure experience, the leader may be blamed and his or her influence reduced. However, replacement of the group leader does not necessarily mean a decentralization of power within the group. If anything, an external threat probably increases reliance upon those high in influence, and, as Hamblin (1958) has shown, failure may cause those who already possess substantial influence (e.g., second in power) to gain in power, while those with the least initial influence continue to rely on others.

Research on leadership and group threat appears to contradict observations that support for leaders increases under threatening situations. For example, it has been hypothesized that support for a national leader increases during times of war (Hertzler, 1940; Korten, 1962) and that the influence of labor leaders increases during a strike against management (Walton and McKersie, 1965). How are these observations reconciled with the available literature on group behavior?

Some of the confusion on this topic results from the lack of distinction between external threat and failure. In real-world settings, threat may persist for a long period of time before failure information is received, allowing a leader to take action or mobilize efforts before any negative consequences have materialized. In contrast, most laboratory experiments have manipulated failure information so that the erosion of collective goals or interests has already occurred. A second difference between laboratory studies and real-world observations has to do with the external nature of a threat. In experimental studies using failure experience, it is not often clear whether a threat to collective welfare is due to an external force or internal incompetence. The leader may therefore be justifiably blamed when a group fails or cannot solve a problem. In contrast, many of the most salient examples of threat in the real world (e.g., warfare) are clearly introduced by an external agent. Leaders are rarely blamed for provoking a war or precipitating a strike, although they are sometimes accused of not taking strong enough action to alleviate the outside threat. Thus, support for group leaders in real-world settings may stem from the external attribution of a setback as well as the anticipation of eventual goal achievement. In contrast, laboratory evidence of derogation of the leader may stem from the internal attribution of threat and the anticipation of failure.

The Effect of Threat upon Pressures toward Uniformity

Early theoretical work by Festinger (1950) posited that pressures toward uniformity arise because group members perceive uniformity as necessary to move toward a collective goal. Festinger hypothesized that groups will exert pressure upon deviants in order to reach consensus on opinions and beliefs and that pressures for uniformity will increase as a collective goal increases in importance or as group members become increasingly dependent upon the group. Thus, as a logical extension, it would seem that a threat to group interests would also heighten pressures toward uniformity.

Festinger posited that when individuals deviate on important issues the group will increase communication with and exert pressure upon the deviant to change. However, if the deviant fails to come into line with the rest of the group, communication may become sharply reduced and he or she may become excluded from important group tasks. In an elegant empirical study, Schachter (1951) validated Festinger's predicted changes in communication with deviants and showed how pressures for uniformity can lead to exclusion of deviants from vital group functions. In a cross-cultural study, Schachter et al. (1954) also showed that pressures for uniformity increase as a group goal is threatened and that such pressures increase as the magnitude of threat or value of the goal increases.

Janis' (1972) historical analysis of top-level decision-making groups can also be interpreted in terms of the effect of threat upon pressures for uniformity. Janis posited that many of the worst decisions by the U.S. government (e.g., the Bay of Pigs invasion, the decision to cross the 38th Parallel during the Korean War, and the escalation of the Vietnam War) were a product of "groupthink." As defined, groupthink is a syndrome of process characteristics present in highly cohesive policy groups. But at the heart of the groupthink syndrome are the outcroppings of pressures toward uniformity, such as direct influence upon group members whose opinions deviate from consensus beliefs, self-censorship of deviant beliefs by group members, exclusion of divergent information or possible critical input to the group, and a shared illusion of unanimity concerning central beliefs or collective judgments. While Janis (1972) portrays these processes as a product of group cohesiveness, they can be viewed simply as indications of pressures for uniformity. Moreover, in each of the cases used by Janis to illustrate groupthink, an external threat was present. Thus, it may be prudent to consider threat as the variable that initiates pressures for uniformity rather than group cohesiveness, as originally formulated by Janis. Adding some support to this position is an experiment by Flowers (1977) in which increased group cohesiveness did not adversely affect decision processes as predicted by Janis' model.

Summary of Group Effects

Figure 3 outlines some of the principal effects of an external threat upon group processes. When a threat has been attributed to an external source and it is thought likely for a group to successfully meet the threat, then increased cohesiveness, leadership support, and pressure for uniformity is predicted. The group will seek consensus and in so doing will generally support the policies or position of the existing group leadership. Reaching consensus, however, will often entail the restriction of information, ignoring divergent solutions and downplaying the role of deviant positions. Consensus seeking also involves a constriction of control, such that the opinions of the dominant members may prevail and their influence may become more centralized. Such changes in information and control processes may, of course, lead to faulty group decision making.

If a threat is attributed to internal deficiencies or the group is perceived as unlikely to succeed, then neither cohesiveness nor consensus are likely to follow. Failure experiences breed dissensus and leadership instability, both of which can be viewed as providing new information or a loosening of control. What frequently follows from such instability is the appearance of new leaders or group consensus, which promises a turnaround of group fortunes and/or success against the external threat.

Figure 3. A Model of Group Response to Threat

Organization-Level Effects

The study of threat to organizational systems can draw upon several research literatures. Research on natural disasters has been extended to the analysis of organizational responses to crisis (e.g., Brouillette and Quarantelli, 1971; Turner, 1976). Likewise, political scientists have been concerned with how governmental bodies react to national threats and how crisis decision making may deviate from a rational-choice model (Snyder and Paige, 1958; Hermann, 1963; Holsti, 1971; Paige, 1972). Finally, of late there has been increasing attention devoted to decline processes in public organizations, brought on by budgetary cutbacks in universities (Rubin, 1977; Manns and March, 1978) and governmental agencies (Mitnick, 1978; Bozeman and Slusher, 1979). In the private sector, there has been a similar concern with industrial decline or retrenchment (Khandwalla, 1972; Schendel, Patton, and Riggs, 1976; Starbuck and Hedberg, 1977; Starbuck, Greve, and Hedberg, 1978; Whetten, 1980). In many cases, severe resource constraints have created a situation in which the welfare or viability of an organization is threatened.

Crisis or Threat?

Much of the organization-level work on threat has made use of the theoretical construct of crisis. The most prevalent definition is Hermann's (1963) classification in which a crisis is said to occur when three conditions are present: (1) there is a major threat to system survival; (2) there is little time to react; and (3) the threat is unanticipated. This three-part scheme has endured within this literature, even though empirical support for the scheme has been limited. For example, perceptions by U.S. State Department officials of the characteristics of a crisis did not reveal such a tripartite classification (Lentner, 1972). Notably missing from the Foreign Service officers' perceptions of crisis were opinions that a threat must be unanticipated to constitute a crisis. Even Hermann's (1965) own research did not confirm the anticipation dimension of the definition of crisis. As a result, some researchers have substituted the idea that a crisis must be ill-structured rather than unanticipated (e.g., Turner, 1976), or that a crisis is perceived when there is a disruption for which no specific plans have been made (Billings, Milburn, and Schaalman, 1980). Meanwhile, other researchers have attached the crisis label to a range of phenomena such as information overload (Meier, 1962) and financial adversity (Rubin, 1977; Starbuck and Hedberg, 1977). For simplicity, we will avoid any syndrome-like definition of crisis and will instead deal with the effects of threat. In our view, threat is probably the driving force behind most of the events that the term *crisis* attempts to explain. Although time pressure or anticipation may interact with threat in affecting actions, most research has shown a simple, direct effect of the extent of potential loss upon the perception of a crisis (e.g., Lentner, 1972; Billings, Milburn, and Schaalman, 1980).

The Effect of Threat upon Informational Processes

In research on decision making during international conflicts it has been posited that a threat to security results in a restriction of the number of alternatives considered by policy makers (Snyder and Paige, 1958; North et al., 1963; Holsti, 1964). The reason for a restriction in alternatives is not yet clear. Smart and Vertinsky (1977) suggested that fewer sources of information are consulted in a crisis, which explains why there are fewer alternatives available. In contrast, Williams (1957) proposed that new information that cannot be easily assimilated to information already possessed is assigned a low value. The net effect of this tendency is to restrict alternatives to those that are similar to information that the organization already possesses and, as Paige (1972) observed, for decision makers to rely heavily on past experience or prior knowledge.

As we noted in our discussion of individual-level effects, there is a tendency for individuals to identify a dominant and familiar precept in a threat situation and then to assimilate new information into it. This tendency has also been observed by researchers who have sought to understand governmental decision making under threat. Holsti (1971), for example, noted that policy makers tend to adopt a single approach to problem solving and then supplement this mode of problem solving by collecting objective information supporting it. He further noted the tendency for policy makers, confronted by threat, to simplify and stereotype assessments of the situation. In a similar vein, Lasswell et al. (1949) found an effect of external threat upon the simplification of language. By content analyzing editorials in prominent newspapers from various countries, he found that when these countries were confronted with serious international threats, the editorial content of newspapers tended to become simplified and repetitive. Suedfeld and Tetlock (1977), in a content analysis of public speeches and diplomatic communications, also found a reduction in cognitive complexity in conflict situations leading to the outbreak of war.

Although an external threat appears to produce simplification and a reduction in alternatives considered by policy makers, it does not appear to reduce search behavior. The available data on search activity indicate that search for information follows a wave pattern over time. Initially, at the detection of a threat, more information is sought to confirm the presence of the threat. This tendency was vividly illustrated by officials at Pearl Harbor prior to the Japanese attack. When these officials first learned of the possibility of an attack, they searched intensively for information to confirm the existence of the threat (Wohlstetter, 1962; Paige, 1972). However, as the threat became a reality, the search for information appeared to decrease. This reduction in search could have been due to the overloading of communication channels that often occurs at the onset of threat. Holsti (1964), for example, found evidence of information overload in the crisis preceding World War I. The central decision units were physically overloaded, and, hence, information search attempts were blocked. North et al. (1963) found a similar occurrence in their study of the crisis preceding World War I, as did Williams (1957) in his study of communication patterns in a natural disaster.

Search for information may reintensify as soon as a decision has been made on how to cope with a threat. However, the type of information sought is not information on alternatives nor information about the threat, but instead is support information confirming policy choices that have already been made. For example, Paige (1972), in his study of Korean and Cuban decisions, found that when confronted with crisis decisions, decision makers solicited advice from subordinates, presumably only to confirm their decision outcomes or preferences. Similarly, Rubin (1977) found an increased search for information by members of university departments who were faced with severe financial-cutback decisions. She attributed the increase in information search to both the decreased tolerance for error in cutback decisions and the need to justify decisions, once they are made. One might interpret the behavior of the secretary of state during the Cuban missile crisis in a similar way. Larson (1963), for example, noted that the U.S. secretary of state communicated with over 75 governments during the Cuban missile crisis, and these communication efforts may have been intended to collect information supporting the U.S. position.

The preceding discussion suggests that an external threat can have a somewhat paradoxical impact on information processes within an organization. As we have noted, search for information may change as a threat develops, from an initial flurry when a threat is recognized, to a low point as channels become overloaded, and on to a second peak as decisions are confirmed or implemented. However, throughout these changes in information search, the number of genuinely new or novel alternatives considered by the organization may still be relatively low. Even when search is increased, information received is likely to be similar to that of the past, due to heavy reliance on standard operating procedures, previous ways of understanding, or communication that is low in complexity (Starbuck, Greve, and Hedberg, 1978).

Control Processes

A second major effect of threat appears to be a mechanistic shift (Burns and Stalker, 1961) in which there is increased centralization of authority, more extensive formalization, and standardization of procedures. Although many researchers have noted these organizational reactions to threat (Hermann, 1965; Smart and Vertinsky, 1977; Bozeman and Slusher, 1979), very limited attention has been paid to why the effects have been observed. It seems logical that when threat confronts an organization, a major concern would be the enhancement of control and coordination of organizational action. In general, as the importance of decisions increases, they are made at progressively

higher levels within an organizational hierarchy, presumably because top-level decision making is less likely to differ from the core values or goals of the organization (Kanter, 1977). Similarly, increased formalization and standardization of procedures can insure coordination of organizational action when lower-level participants must carry out the decisions of others (Katz and Kahn, 1978). Thus, because threat makes salient the possibility of substantial error or loss, we should expect increases in both organizational coordination and control.

The centralization of authority in response to crisis is the most widely acknowledged aspect of the mechanistic shift. Hermann (1963) argued that increased centralization is manifested by contraction in authority, reduction in the number of decision participants, and decision making at higher levels of the organization. In his simulation studies, he found no actual reduction in the number of decision makers during a crisis decision (although contraction possibilities were limited in his experimental groups of five persons), but he did find a perceived reduction in the number of participants. In case studies of international crises, Paige (1972) and Holsti (1971) did find a reduction in the size of decision bodies during times of threat. Likewise, the data of Starbuck, Greve, and Hedberg (1978) in a case study of a declining firm, Rubin's (1977) research on responses to budget cutbacks in universities, and Khandwalla's (1972) research on organizational response to malevolent environments all show increasing centralization in times of threat. Pfeffer and Leblebici (1973) found that a stressful environment with a high degree of market competition, coupled with a rapid degree of environmental change, was associated with taller organizational structures and increased review and control of decision making.

An interesting exception to the centralization effect was found by Brouillette and Quarantelli (1971) in their investigation of how organizations deal with natural disasters. They found that divisions or units of public-work organizations became more autonomous during a threat period, decisions being made without consultation with higher officials. However, within each of these autonomous units an informal administrative core emerged to make decisions, suggesting that debureaucratization may be accompanied by increased centralization *within* each of the units. The key point may be that the centralization may vary according to whether the threat affects a subunit or an entire organization.

As an extension of the Brouillette and Quarantelli findings, one might hypothesize that a threat may force a control response that results in the strengthening of tightly coupled links within organizations and the dissolution of weak links. Therefore, in a diversified or decentralized organization, a threat may induce a control response that dissolves weak links to the top while strengthening intraunit links, giving the appearance of a debureaucratization process. In contrast, within a functional or traditionally structured organization, threat may stimulate a control response that strengthens links to the top while dissolving weak links between departments or units, producing a more obviously centralized structure. This hypothesized strengthening of strong links and weakening of loose links between departments and levels of an organization would be analogous to the observed dominant-response effect (Zajonc, 1965) at the individual level of analysis.

Other indications of a mechanistic shift in response to threat include an increased use of formalized procedures and greater standardization of activities. In Rubin's (1977) study of responses of a university to budget cutbacks, departments tended to use more explicit decision-making criteria and systemized their allocation criteria. Similarly, in a study of corporate turnaround strategies (Schendel, Patton, and Riggs, 1976), firms made profit responsibilities more explicit in response to profit decline. Also, Khandwalla (1972) found that organizations, when faced with adverse environmental conditions, increased the use of standardized and routinized practices. Finally, a laboratory simulation by Bourgeois, McAllister, and Mitchell (1978) showed that business students

actually preferred mechanistic over organic structures when acting as a manager facing turbulent environments.

Thus, threat appears to be accompanied by a change in organizational structure that resembles a mechanistic shift. This change is evident in increased centralization, formalization, standardization and routinization. From available evidence at the organizational level, the shift to a more rigid structure seems to be due to decision makers' attempts to enhance control so as to insure that organizational members act in a concerted way in meeting a threat situation.

Dominance of Efficiency Concerns

There is some support for the predominance of efficiency concerns in organizations during times of threat. Efficiency concerns are manifested in the tightening of available budgets, increased emphasis on cost cutting, and intensification of efforts to insure accountability. These effects are often brought about by a severe decline in performance and a reduction in slack resources within the organization. For example, Starbuck and Hedberg's (1977) case study data indicate that decline is accompanied by a high premium placed upon efficiency measures. The two companies in their sample used temporary expedients such as cost cutting, budget tightening and the restriction of marginal activities to deal with severe financial adversity. Similarly, Schendel, Patton, and Riggs (1976) documented the increased use of firings and greater budget and cost control as measures employed by companies faced by persistent decline in market performance. Rubin's (1977) study of universities plagued by budget cutbacks indicates a similar tendency with respect to the dominance of efficiency concerns. In universities faced with financial constraints, allocation criteria for resource distribution become highly salient. Finally, Bozeman and Slusher (1979) noted that in times of sustained resource scarcity in the public sector there is increased technological efficiency and increased pressures for accountability which

Figure 4. A Model of Organizational Response to Threat

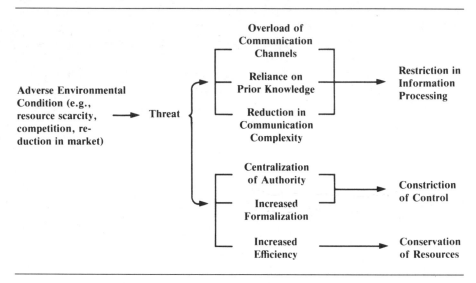

Summary of Organized Effects

Figure 4 summarizes the predicted effects of threat on organization-level phenomena. As shown in the figure, threat has generally been conceived as a result of an adverse condition in the environment, such as resource scarcity, competition, or reduction in the size of the market. The consequences of threat on the organization can be placed in three groups. First, due to an overload of communication channels, reliance on prior knowledge, and a reduction in communication complexity, there may be a restriction in the information-processing capacity of the organization. Second, due to a centralization of authority and increased formalization of procedures, there may be a constriction in control. Finally, there may be increased efforts to conserve resources within the system through cost-cutting and efforts for greater efficiency.

Toward a Multilevel Theory

In a review of the evidence, the threat-rigidity thesis finds support at multiple levels of analysis. At

may, in turn, eliminate the use of creative or novel strategies in decision making.

the individual level, there are strong indications of constrictions in information processing and behavioral response in the face of threat. At the group level, there is evidence of similar effects when a threat is perceived as external to the group and when there is some expectation of successfully resisting the threat. Finally, at the organization level, there is evidence of a mechanistic shift, restricting information and moving control to higher levels in the system. Although the concepts and operationalization of effects vary both within and especially between levels of analysis, it does appear possible to draw some generalizations from the data.

At present, most of the evidence underlying the threat-rigidity thesis is interpreted in psychological or sociological theories at either micro- or macro-levels of analysis. For example, there are delimited or "middle-range" theories (Merton, 1967) about how individuals react to stress, how groups deal with failure experiences, and how organizations cope with adversity. The advantage of these delimited models is that they allow a rather fine-grained analysis of a particular subject group and capitalize on preexisting disciplinary boundaries. The primary disadvantage of these delimited models is that they are level-specific and tend to restrict our ability to see general patterns across social entities.

A Systems Approach

Given the generality of threat-rigidity effects, a systems-theory explanation would seem appealing. One could treat each entity, be it an individual, group, or organization, as a relatively autonomous system attempting to cope with its own idiosyncratic environment. The relatively consistent findings at the three levels of analysis would thus support a general explanation of reactions to threat, in language that is devoid of psychological or sociological terms but is instead translated into the description of general social systems (e.g., Miller, 1978).

As an example of a systems explanation, one could utilize a fundamental principle of cybernetics to show how rigidity can result from threat. First, as outlined by Weiner (1948) and Ashby (1956), the number of output discriminations of a system (i.e., its behavioral repertoire) is limited by the variety of information inherent in its input. Second, as is well known (e.g., Arrow, 1974), there are costs associated with the gathering, use, and maintenance of information by a system. Thus, under a threat situation, a system is likely to economize in information processing by decreasing the use of nonessential peripheral channels and by reducing the number and complexity of information codes employed. Such a reduction in complexity and variety of input may, therefore, lead to a concomitant reduction in system response capability or a narrowing in the behavioral repertoire.

Using the systems metaphor, it can also be seen how the effect of threat upon internal control mechanisms may induce system rigidity. Under threat, the necessity of system response is great, and input processes may be subordinated to output and control processes. Information channels and codes that are normally used for inputting information from the environment may become oc-cupied by signals aimed at controlling and coordinating the behavior of system subunits. Again, the effect of increased control may be to decrease discriminability and thereby narrow the behavioral repertoire.

By mixing the systems approach with a social-evolutionary perspective (e.g., Campbell, 1965; Weick, 1979), it is easy to see how pathological responses can develop in the face of environmental change. When a threat occurs, the entity focuses attention on the source of danger, economizing on nonrelevant input and processing functions and responding with well-learned or salient behavioral responses. While such a response pattern works well for threats of a known or repeated nature (for which a well-learned response is likely to be correct), it is less appropriate for threats of unknown dimensions. A change in the basic patterning or cause-effect relations in an environment requires diversity in input mechanisms and variety in response. For example, when market parameters change or task and learning environments are radically different, the entity cannot adapt by narrowing its input and response repertoire. As noted by advocates of social-evolutionary models (e.g., Campbell, 1965; Weick, 1979; Aldrich, 1979), only variety in input and diversity in response insures survival under conditions of radical change.

Cross-Level Effects

As we have noted, disciplinary theories (e.g., psychological or sociological models of stress and coping) can provide an in-depth analysis of single-level phenomena, while a systems approach can address generalities that appear across levels of analysis. What is missing in both these perspectives, however, is an understanding of effects that cross levels of analysis. Are there, for example, individual effects that affect group processes under threat or group processes that affect organizational responses to threat? Such questions are difficult to answer but may in fact explain much of the consistency of threat-rigidity effects that appear to cross levels of analysis.

Individual-Level Effects in Group Settings

When individuals are brought together to reach a decision about an issue (e.g., in a policy-making group), the inputs or knowledge brought to the decision are, in large part, the cognitions and information of individuals. Although group interaction may become a new input of its own, the abilities and skills of group members are crucial to group performance (Shaw, 1976). Even some of the group processes themselves may depend on the array of individual characteristics brought into the group setting. Polarization effects, for example, depend upon the diversity and extremity of opinion before a group is convened, rather than upon a processing feature such as strength of argumentation or diffusion of responsibility (Lamm and Myers, 1978). Therefore, if individuals restrict their cognitions and narrow their response repertoire in threat situations, we should expect similar group-level effects. Rather than treating group rigidities as created only by social process, at least some of this apparent group-level effect may thus be explained by cognitive changes in the individuals composing the group.

Group Effects in Organizational Settings

Janis (1972), in his work on "groupthink," has characterized many decisions and actions in organizations as the product of policy-making groups. For top governmental decision making, there are formal groups (e.g., The National Security Council) ready for use in threat situations, and there are many similar counterparts in industry (e.g., weekly meetings of the president and executive vice presidents). Given the increase in affiliative tendencies in threat situations (Schachter, 1959) and the objective need to coordinate policy, it is likely that groups will be convened to deal with a threat situation. Thus, any rigidities generated by group process under threat may also be manifested in organizational actions.

Individual Effects in Organizational Settings

Although groups are often convened to deal with crisis situations, many major decisions still originate with administrators acting alone or in consultation with very few others. For example, when organizations seek control in threat situations, individual actors are the ones who clamor for influence, and they are the ones who refer crucial decisions up the hierarchy. A serious threat to an entire organization also challenges the interests of individual actors and may exacerbate the power differential between subunits and the administrators who head them. Such a threat may result in more centralized control, not because of an organizational process or formation of a particular coalition, but because top level administrators demand more control in coping with the situation.

Organizational members can be viewed as having central or peripheral interests in the welfare of an organization and the subunit in which they are employed. Members who tie their own personal welfare to that of the organization can therefore be expected to act for the organization in relatively the same way as they would for their own idiosyncratic interests. Immersed in their roles as agents of the organization, some top administrators may even act to defend the interests of the collectivity when their own personal welfare is not immediately obvious. In contrast, middle-level administrators frequently express more loyalty to the organizational subunit or work group, while the interests of the lowest-level members of the organization are often peripheral to the organization. Thus, by viewing organizational action as a function of the welfare of individual actors (cf. Olson, 1968), it is easy to see why macro-organizational behavior often so closely resembles individual coping responses. Organizational actions in the environment (e.g., reduction of uncertainty and threat) are predicated upon the interests of top-level administrators, which are, in turn, nearly isomorphic with the welfare of the organization as a collectivity. Because lower-level personnel have more heterogeneous interests, it is also easy to see why a threat situation instills greater coordination and control. Unreliable or divergent behavior is viewed as something to be avoided by top-level administrators whose interests are more directly threatened.

The Dual Nature of Threat-Rigidity Effects

Throughout our discussion of the effects of threat, we have focused on possible maladaptive reactions by individuals, groups, and organizations. We have emphasized that restrictions in information and control may hinder adaptation to new environmental conditions, thereby bringing more substantial losses to the entity. However, it can be argued that the maladaptive nature of threat-rigidity effects are limited. For example, dysfunctions may be most graphically demonstrated in laboratory settings since, in those situations, experimenters can abruptly change causal rules so that prior behavior is no longer appropriate. In other environments, because causal relationships are more stable, it may be functional to rely on well-learned theories and action sequences that have been reinforced in the past.

The key to whether a threat-rigidity effect is functional or not may rest on the nature of the threat itself. In order to accumulate evidence, we necessarily treated threat as a broad construct that included any impending negative consequences for an entity. However, it may be important to distinguish between cases in which the level of known variables has changed and those in which basic causal relationships have been altered. As shown in Figure 1, either incremental or radical environmental change can cause a threat to an entity. But, depending on the source of threat, response rigidities can serve to either reduce or intensify the threat. The net results, of course, can be either a functional adaptation to the environment or a maladaptive cycle of threat-rigidity effects.

As an example of the dual nature of threat-rigidity effects, it is interesting to reconsider what happens to organizations in times of resource scarcity (Staw and Szwajkowski, 1975). The general reaction of organizations to increase efficiency and control (Whetten, 1980) would certainly be functional when the parameters of the environment are well known and coping mechanisms clear. However, when adversity results from a radical change in the environment, it may be dysfunctional for an organization to tighten controls and press efficiency. In their discussion of the reaction of public agencies to budget restraints, Bozeman and Slusher (1979: 346) well summarized the problem:

> Scarcity-induced stress causes organizations to behave as if complex, dynamic and interrelated environments are in fact simple, static and unrelated. These behaviors include narrower domain definitions, reductions in labor intensive technology, increasing specializations of technologies and more mechanistic structures with tighter administrative control. The public organization's turbulent environment is essentially demanding an increased domain. However, the organization's response is to constrict its domain.

Therefore, although an organization's reaction to scarcity can insulate it against immediate failure, increased efficiency and control can prove maladaptive when scarcity is symptomatic of more fundamental change. In essence, doing better at what one already knows is at best a mixed blessing.

Conclusion

We have attempted in this article to bring some widely varied literature to bear on a rather simple but important problem. Although threat-rigidity effects are not always dysfunctional, many systematic breakdowns (Hall, 1976) do appear to fit a threat-rigidity cycle. In a sense, threat-rigidity effects may be a two-edged mechanism in which both the survival and extinction potentials of organizations are amplified. Thus, there is a clear need for research that can specify conditions under which restrictions in information and constriction of control will prove functional or dysfunctional.

There is also room for much more research on the specification of individual, group, and organizational effects of threat, as well as on effects that may cross levels of analysis. Our integration of prior findings and theoretical speculations, therefore, should be viewed as simply a starting point rather than a summary of work on this topic.

Note

1 The fact that psychological stress and anxiety have been identified with a common set of experimental operations suggests a problem of discriminant validity (Campbell and Fiske, 1959). However, we cite the stress and anxiety literatures separately because they are treated separately within psychology, and because we are concerned primarily with the general effects of threat rather than the distinctions between these two constructs.

References

Aldrich, Howard E. 1979. Organizations and Environments. Englewood Cliffs, NJ: Prentice-Hall.

Altman, Edward I. 1971. Corporate Bankruptcy in America. Lexington, MA: Heath Lexington Books.

Appley, Mortimer, and I. Trumbell. 1967. Psychological Stress: Issues in Research. New York: Appleton-Century Crofts.

Argenti, John. 1976. Corporate Collapse. New York: Halstead.

Arrow, Kenneth J. 1974. The Limits of Organization. New York: Norton.

Ashby, William Ross. 1956. An Introduction to Cybernetics. New York: Wiley.

Bacon, Stephen J. 1974. "Arousal and the range of cue utilization." Journal of Experimental Psychology, 102: 81–87.

Beach, H.D., and R.A. Lucas, eds. 1963. Individual and Group Behavior in a Coal Mine Disaster. Disaster Study #13. Washington, DC: National Academy of Sciences, National Research Council.

Beer, Terry A., and John E. Newman. 1978. "Job stress, employee health, and organizational effectiveness: A facet analysis, model, and literature review." Personnel Psychology, 31: 665–99.

Beier, Ernest G. 1951. "The effect of induced anxiety on flexibility of intellectual functioning." Psychological Monographs, 65(9), Whole No. 326: 1–26.

Berry, R.N. 1962. "Skin conductance levels and verbal recall." Journal of Experimental Psychology, 63: 275–77.

Bettelheim, Bruno. 1943. "Individual and mass behavior in extreme situations." Journal of Abnormal and Social Psychology, 38: 417–52.

Billings, Robert S., Thomas W. Milburn, and Mary Lou Schaalman. 1980. "A model of crisis perception: A theoretical and empirical analysis." Administrative Science Quarterly, 25: 300–16.

Boder, David P. 1954. "The impact of catastrophe." Journal of Psychology, 38: 3–50.

Bourgeois, L.J., III, Daniel W. McAllister, and Terence R. Mitchell. 1978. "The effects of different organizational environments upon decisions about organizational structure." Academy of Management Journal, 21: 508–14.

Bozeman, Barry, and E. Allen Slusher. 1979. "Scarcity and environmental stress in public organizations: A conjectural essay." Administration and Society, 2: 335–55.

Broadbent, Donald E. 1971. Decision and Stress. London: Academic Press.

Brouillette, John R., and E.L. Quarantelli. 1971. "Types of patterned variation in bureaucratic adaptations to organizational stress." Sociological Inquiry, 41: 39–45.

Burns, Thomas, and G.M. Stalker. 1961. The Management of Innovation. London: Tavistock.

Business Week. 1979. "Is Chrysler the Prototype?" August 20: 102–10.

Campbell, Donald T. 1965. "Variation and selective retention in socio-cultural evolution." In H.R. Barringer, G.I. Blanksten, and R. Mack (eds.), Social Change in Developing Areas: 19–49. Cambridge, MA: Schenkman.

Campbell, Donald T., and Donald W. Fiske. 1959. "Convergent and discriminant validation by the multi-trait–multi-method matrix." Psychological Bulletin, 56: 81–105.

Castaneda, Alfred, and David S. Palermo. 1955. "Psychomotor performance as a function of amount of training and stress." Journal of Experimental Psychology, 50: 175–79.

Cowen, Emery L. 1952a. "The influence of varying degrees of psychological stress on problem solving rigidity." Journal of Abnormal and Social Psychology, 47: 512–19.

———. 1952b. "Stress reduction and problem solving rigidity." Journal of Consulting Psychology, 16: 425–28.

Cyert, Richard M., and James G. March. 1963. A Behavioral Theory of the Firm. Englewood Cliffs, NJ: Prentice-Hall.

Danzig, E.R., P.W. Thayer, and Lila P. Galanter.

1958. The Effects of a Threatening Rumor on a Disaster Stricken Community. Disaster Study #10. Washington, DC: National Academy of Sciences, National Research Council.

Dion, Kenneth. 1979. "Intergroup conflict and intragroup cohesiveness." In William G. Austin and Stephen Worchel (eds.), The Social Psychology of Intergroup Relations: 211–24. Monterey, CA: Brooks/Cole.

Duffy, Elizabeth. 1932. "The relationship between muscular tension and quality of performance." American Journal of Psychology, 44: 535–46.

———. 1962. Activation and Behavior. New York: Wiley.

Easterbrook, James A. 1959. "The effect of emotion on cue utilization and the organization of behavior." Psychological Review, 66: 183–201.

Eriksen, Charles W., and Henry Wechsler. 1955. "Some effects of experimentally induced anxiety upon discrimination behavior." Journal of Abnormal Social Psychology, 51: 458–63.

Eysenck, Michael W. 1975. "Arousal and speed of recall." British Journal of Social and Clinical Psychology, 14: 269–77.

———. 1976. "Arousal, learning, and memory." Psychological Bulletin, 83(3): 389–404.

Farber, I.E., and Kenneth W. Spence. 1953. "Complex learning and conditioning as a function of anxiety." Journal of Experimental Psychology, 45: 120–25.

Festinger, Leon. 1950. "Informal social communication." Psychological Review, 57: 271–82.

Flowers, Matie L. 1977. "A laboratory test of some implications of Janis' groupthink hypotheses." Journal of Personality and Social Psychology, 35: 888–96.

Fortune. 1979. "Chrysler's pie-in-the-sky plan format for survival." October 22: 46–52.

Glass, A.J. 1955. Psychological Considerations in Atomic Warfare. No. 560. Washington, DC: Walter Reed Army Medical Center.

Goldstone, Sanford. 1955. "Flicker fusion measurements and anxiety level." Journal of Experimental Psychology, 49: 200–2.

Hall, Richard I. 1976. "A system pathology of an organization: The rise and fall of the old *Saturday Evening Post*." Administrative Science Quarterly, 21: 185–211.

Hamblin, Robert L. 1958. "Leadership and crises." Sociometry, 21: 322–35.

Hannan, Michael T., and John H. Freeman. 1977. "The population ecology of organizations." American Journal of Sociology, 82: 929–64.

Hermann, Charles F. 1963. "Some consequences of crisis which limit the viability of organizations."

Administrative Science Quarterly, 8: 343–58.

———. 1965. "Crisis in foreign policy making: A simulation of international politics." Unpublished Ph.D. dissertation, Northwestern University.

Hertzler, J.D. 1940. "Crises and dictatorship." American Sociological Review, 5: 157–69.

Hollander, Edwin P., B.J. Fallon, and M.T. Edwards. 1974. "The influence and acceptability of appointed and elected leaders under conditions of group success or failure." Paper presented at the Annual Eastern Psychological Association Meeting.

Holsti, Ole R. 1964. "An adaptation of the 'general inquirer' for the systematic analysis of political documents." Behavioral Science, 9: 382–88.

———. 1971. "Crisis, stress, and decision making." International Social Science, 23: 53–67.

Huxtable, Zelma L., Miriam H. White, and Marjorie A. McCartor. 1946. "A reperformance and reinterpretation of the Arai experiment in mental fatigue with three subjects." Psychological Monographs, 59(5), Whole No. 275: 1–52.

Janis, Irving L. 1954. "Problems of theory in the analysis of stress behavior." Journal of Social Issues, 10: 12–125.

———. 1958. Psychological Stress. New York: Wiley.

———. 1962. "Psychological effects of warnings." In G.W. Baker and D.W. Baker (eds.), Man and Society in Disaster: 55–92. New York: Basic Books.

———. 1972. Victims of Groupthink. Boston: Houghton-Mifflin.

Kanter, Rosabeth. 1977. Men and Women of the Corporation. New York: Basic Books.

Katz, Daniel, and Robert L. Kahn. 1978. The Social Psychology of Organizations, 2d ed. New York: Wiley.

Khandwalla, Pradip. 1972. "Environment and its impact on the organization." International Studies of Management and Organizations, 2: 297–313.

Kleinsmith, Louis J., and Stephen Kaplan. 1963. "Paired associate learnings as a function of arousal and interpolated interval." Journal of Experimental Psychology, 65: 190–93.

Korchin, Sheldon J., and Harold Basowitz. 1954. "Perceptual adequacy in a life stress." Journal of Psychology, 38: 495–502.

Korchin, Sheldon J., Jerome L. Singer, and Robert G. Ballard. 1951. "The influence of frustration on the reproduction of perceived forms." Personality, 1: 54–66.

Korten, David C. 1962. "Situational determinants of leadership structure." Journal of Conflict Resolution, 6: 222–235.

Lamm, Helmut, and David G. Myers. 1978. "Group induced polarization of attitudes and behavior." In Leonard Berkowitz (ed.), Advances in Experimental Social Psychology, 2: 145–95. New York: Academic Press.

Larson, David L. 1963. The Cuban Crisis in 1962. Boston: Houghton Mifflin.

Lasswell, Harold D., N. Leites and Associates. 1949. Language of Politics. New York: George Stewart.

Lazarus, Richard S. 1966. Psychological Stress and the Coping Process. New York: McGraw-Hill.

Lazarus, Richard S., and Charles W. Eriksen. 1952. "Effects of failure stress upon skilled performance." Journal of Experimental Psychology, 43: 100–5.

Lentner, Howard H. 1972. "The concept of crisis as viewed by the United States Department of State." In C. Hermann (ed.), International Crises: Insights from Behavioral Research: 112–13. New York: Free Press.

Luchins, Abraham S. 1942. "Mechanization in problem solving." Psychological Monographs, 54(6): 1–95.

Mandler, George, and Seymour B. Sarason. 1952. "A study of anxiety and learning." Journal of Abnormal and Social Psychology, 47: 166–73.

Manns, Curtis, and James G. March. 1978. "Financial adversity, internal competition, and curriculum change in a university." Administrative Science Quarterly, 23: 541–52.

McGrath, Joseph E. 1976. "Stress and behavior in organizations." In M. Dunnette (ed.), Handbook of Industrial and Organizational Psychology: 1351–96. Chicago: Rand-McNally.

Meier, Richard L. 1962. "Overload at the stock exchange." In Richard L. Meier (ed.), A Communications Theory of Urban Growth: 72–83. Cambridge, MA: MIT Press.

Menninger, Karl A. 1954. "Regulatory devices of the ego under major stress." International Journal of Psycho-Analysis, 35: 412–20.

Menninger, William C. 1952. "Psychological reactions in an emergency (flood)." American Journal of Psychiatry, 109: 128–30.

Merton, Robert K. 1967. On Theoretical Sociology. New York: Free Press.

Miller, James G. 1978. Living Systems, New York: McGraw-Hill.

Mitnick, Barry M. 1978. "Deregulation as a process of organizational reduction." Public Administration Review, 38: 350–57.

North, Robert C., Ole R. Holsti, M. George Zaninovich, and Dina A. Zinnes. 1963. Content Analysis. Evanston, IL: Northwestern University Press.

Obrist, Paul A. 1962. "Some autonomic correlates of serial learning." Journal of Verbal Learning and Verbal Behavior, 1: 100–4.

Olson, Mancur. 1968. The Logic of Collective Action. New York: Schocken Books.

Osler, S.F. 1954. "Intellectual performance as a function of two types of psychological stress." Journal of Experimental Psychology, 47: 115–21.

Paige, Glenn D. 1972. "Comparative case analysis of crisis decisions in Korea and Cuba." In Charles Hermann (ed.), International Crises: Insights from Behavioral Research: 39–55. New York: Free Press.

Palermo, David S. 1957. "Proactive interference and facilitation as a function of amount of training and stress." Journal of Experimental Psychology, 53: 293–96.

Pallak, Michael S., Thane S. Pittman, Jack F. Heller, and Paul Munson. 1975. "The effects of practice and irrelevant stress on Stroop Color-Noun Task Performance." Bulletin of the Psychonomic Society, 6: 248–50.

Pfeffer, Jeffrey, and Huseyin Leblebici. 1973. "Executive recruitment and the development of interfirm organizations." Administrative Science Quarterly, 18: 449–61.

Pfeffer, Jeffrey, and Gerald R. Salancik. 1978. The External Control of Organizations: A Resource Dependence Perspective. New York: Harper & Row.

Postman, Leo, and Donald R. Brown. 1952. "The perceptual consequences of success and failure." Journal of Abnormal and Social Psychology, 47: 213–21.

Postman, Leo, and Jerome S. Bruner. 1948. "Perception under stress." Psychological Review, 55: 314–23.

Pronko, W.H., and W.R. Leith. 1956. "Behavior under stress: A study of its disintegration." Psychological Reports Monograph Supplement, 5.

Rabbie, Jacob M., and Karel Huggen. 1974. "Internal disagreements and their effects on attitudes toward in- and outgroups." International Journal of Group Tensions, 4: 222–46.

Rabbie, Jacob M., and Gerard Wilkins. 1971. "Intergroup competition and its effect on intra- and intergroup relations." European Journal of Social Psychology, 1: 215–34.

Rubin, Irene. 1977. "Universities in stress: Decision making under conditions of reduced resources." Social Science Quarterly, 58: 242–54.

Ryen, Allen H., and Arnold Kahn. 1975. "The effects of intergroup orientation on group attitudes and proxemic behavior: A test of two models." Journal of Personality and Social Psychology, 31: 302–10.

Sarason, Irwin G., and Charles D. Spielberger, eds. 1975. Stress and Anxiety II. New York: Wiley.

Sarason, Seymour B., George Mandler, and Peyton G. Craighill. 1952. "The effect of differential instructions on anxiety and learning." Journal of Abnormal and Social Psychology, 47: 561–65.

Schachter, Stanley. 1951. "Deviation, rejection, and communication." Journal of Abnormal and Social Psychology, 46: 190–207.

———. 1959. The Psychology of Affiliation. Stanford, CA: Stanford University Press.

Schachter, Stanley, J. Nuttin, C. Monchaux, P. Maucorps, D. Osmen, H. Duijker, R. Rommetveit, and J. Israel. 1954. "Cross-cultural experiments on threat and rejection." Human Relations, 7: 403–39.

Schachter, Stanley, and Jerome E. Singer. 1962. "Cognitive, social and physiological determinants of emotional state." Psychological Review, 69: 379–99.

Schaffer, H. Rudolph. 1954. "Behavior under stress: A neurophysiological hypothesis." Psychological Review, 61: 323–33.

Schendel, Dan, G.R. Patton, and James Riggs. 1976. "Corporate turnaround strategies: A study of profit decline and recovery." Journal of General Management, 3: 3–11.

Scholsberg, Harold. 1954. "Three dimensions of emotion." Psychological Review, 61: 81–88.

Shaw, Marvin E. 1976. Group Dynamics: The Psychology of Small Group Behavior, 2d ed. New York: McGraw-Hill.

Sherif, Musafer, O.J. Harvey, B. Jack White, William R. Hood, and Carolyn W. Sherif. 1961. Intergroup Cooperation and Competition: The Robbers Cave Experiment. Norman, OK: University Book Exchange.

Sherif, Musafer, and Carolyn W. Sherif. 1953. Groups in Harmony and Tension: An Introduction to Studies in Intergroup Relations. New York: Harper & Row.

Smart, Carolyne, and Ian Vertinsky. 1977. "Designs for crisis decision units." Administrative Science Quarterly, 22: 640–57.

Smock, Charles D. 1955. "The influence of stress on the perception of incongruity." Journal of Abnormal and Social Psychology, 50: 354–56.

Snyder, Richard C., and Glenn D. Paige. 1958. "The United States decision to resist aggression in Korea: The application of an analytical scheme." Administrative Science Quarterly, 3: 341–78.

Spence, Kenneth W., and I.E. Farber. 1953. "Conditioning and extinction as a function of anxiety." Journal of Experimental Psychology, 45: 116–19.

Starbuck, William H., Arent Greve, and Bo L.T. Hedberg. 1978. "Responding to crises." Journal of Business Administration, 9: 111–37.

Starbuck, William H., and Bo L.T. Hedberg. 1977. "Saving an organization from a stagnating environment." In H. Thorelli (ed.), Strategy + Structure = Performance: 249–58. Bloomington, IN: Indiana University Press.

Staw, Barry M., and Eugene Szwajkowski. 1975. "The scarcity-munificence component of organizational environments and the commission of illegal acts." Administrative Science Quarterly, 20: 345–59.

Stennett, Richard G. 1957. "The relationship of performance level to level of arousal." Journal of Experimental Psychology, 54: 54–61.

Suedfeld, Paul, and Philip E. Tetlock. 1977. "Integrative complexity of communications in international crises." Journal of Conflict Resolution, 21: 427–41.

Taylor, Janet A., and Kenneth W. Spence. 1952. "The relationship of anxiety level to performance in serial learnings." Journal of Experimental Psychology, 44: 61–64.

Thompson, James. 1967. Organizations in Action. New York: McGraw-Hill.

Thorner, M., F.A. Gibbs, and E.L. Gibbs. 1942. "Relation between the EEG and flying ability." War Medicine, 2: 255–62.

Turner, Barry A. 1976. "The organizational and interorganizational development of disasters." Administrative Science Quarterly, 21: 378–97.

Wachtel, Paul L. 1968. "Anxiety, attention and coping with threat." Journal of Abnormal and Social Psychology, 73: 137–43.

Wallace, A.F.C. 1956. Tornado in Worcester: An Exploratory Study of Individual and Community Behavior in an Extreme Situation. Disaster Study, #3. Washington, DC: National Academy of Sciences, National Research Council.

Walton, Richard E., and Robert B. McKersie. 1965. A Behavioral Theory of Labor Negotiation. New York: McGraw-Hill.

Weick, Karl E. 1979. The Social Psychology of Organizing, 2d ed. Reading, MA: Addison-Wesley.

Weiner, Norbert. 1948. Cybernetics. Cambridge, MA: MIT Press.

Whetten, David A. 1980. "Organizational decline: Antecedents and consequences." In J. Kimberly and R.H. Miles (eds.), Organizational Life Cycles: 342–74. San Francisco: Jossey Bass.

Williams, Harry B. 1957. "Some functions of communication in crisis behavior." Human Organization, 16: 15–19.

Wilson, Warner, and Norman Miller. 1961. "Shifts in evaluations of participants following intergroup competition." Journal of Abnormal and Social Psychology, 63: 428–31.

Wine, Jeri. 1971. "Test anxiety and direction of attention." Psychological Bulletin, 76: 92–104.

Withey, Stephen B. 1962. "Reaction in uncertain threat." In George W. Baker and Dwight W. Chapman (eds.), Man and Society in Disaster: 93–123. New York: Basic Books.

Wohlsetter, Roberta. 1962. Pearl Harbor: Warning and Disaster. Stanford, CA: Stanford University Press.

Wolfenstein, Martha. 1957. Disaster: A Psychological Essay. Glencoe, IL: Free Press.

Worchel, Stephen, Virginia A. Andreoli, and Robert Folger. 1977. "Intergroup cooperation and intergroup attraction: The effect of previous interaction and outcome of combined effort." Journal of Experimental Social Psychology, 13: 131–40.

Worchel, Stephen, E. Lind, and K. Kaufman. 1975. "Evaluations of group products as a function of expectations of group longevity, outcome of competition, and publicity of evaluations." Journal of Personality and Social Psychology, 31: 1089–97.

Yerkes, Robert M., and J.D. Dodson. 1980. "The relation of strength of stimulus to rapidity of habit formation." Journal of Comparative and Neurological Psychology, 18: 459–82.

Zajonc, Robert B. 1965. "Social facilitation." Science, 149: 269–74.

———. 1966. Social Psychology: An Experimental Approach. Belmont, CA: Wadsworth.

———. 1980. "Feeling and thinking." American Psychologist, 35: 151–75.

Zander, Alvin. 1979. "The psychology of group process." Annual Review of Psychology: 417–52. Palo Alto, CA: Annual Reviews.

6

Matching Managerial Strategies to Conditions of Decline

Kim S. Cameron

Raymond F. Zammuto

Interest in organizational decline has grown in recent years as taxpayer revolts, a stagnating worldwide economy, federal cutbacks, and problems of an aging population have become common fare in the mass media. Not only are bankruptcies at an all-time high for private sector organizations, but organizations in the public sector also are being buffeted by increasing demands for services while receiving proportionally fewer resources (Levine, Rubin, and Wolohojian, 1981; Starbuck and Nystrom, 1981). Frequently, however, those who write about decline treat it as an aberration from expected organizational growth patterns, or as a temporary inconvenience to be endured until things get better (Taylor, 1982). Much of the literature in the organizational sciences continues to assume growth as the dominant, and desirable, mode for organizations.

Whetten (1980a) pointed out, for example, that two of the most popular organization design models, produced by Galbraith (1977) and by Lawrence and Lorsch (1969), contain implicit biases toward growth. Both models are based on the assumption that organizations are successful to the extent to which they match environmental conditions. As turbulence, uncertainty, and increasing amounts of information are encountered by organizations, the prescriptions of these models are to differentiate and add boundary spanning or information processing units — that is, to expand or grow. Under conditions of decline, with diminishing resources and organizational slack, such strategies often are both impossible and unlikely to improve organizational adaptability.

Other examples are models of organizational change as organizations progress through their life cycles. Of the ten models of life cycle development reviewed by Quinn and Cameron (1983), only one paid any attention to organizational decline (Adizes, 1979). The other nine either ignored the

From *Human Resource Management,* Vol. 22. © 1983 John Wiley & Sons, Inc. Reprinted with permission.

phenomenon or assumed an unending pattern of growth for organizations. The bias toward growth as a natural and desirable state of organizations permeates these models.

This implicit emphasis on growth among organizational scholars has inhibited the development of theories of adaptation to decline, and much of the literature on the subject still lacks integration. A recent bibliography by Zammuto (1982a) shows, for example, that most of the literature on decline has appeared since 1979, and no unified or consensual perspective has been produced. Little integration or model-building has occurred, and much of the writing is still armchair theorizing, personal recollections of managers, or descriptions of isolated case studies.

A survey of this literature makes it clear that these case study descriptions and accounts of personal experiences in declining organizations are not always describing the same types of phenomena. Decline in the oil refinery industry, for example, is not at all the same as decline in public school systems. Causal factors as well as managerial responses differ dramatically. We concluded that if decline were to be taken seriously as a continuing fact of organizational life, a framework or typology of different decline phenomena would be needed as a first step in identifying the most successful ways to manage it. The intent of this article is to examine such a typology, and to show how different managerial strategies can be matched with different types of decline. Our intent is to suggest guidelines for managers that can be used as they diagnose and help their organizations adapt to conditions of decline.

Developing a Typology of Decline

We first began to notice that organizations experience different types of decline in our investigations of the U.S. automobile industry (Zammuto, 1982b), the U.S. tobacco industry (Miles and Cameron, 1982), and American colleges and universities (e.g., Cameron, 1983; Zammuto, 1983). Moreover, we noted a wide variety of strategic and tactical responses that were associated with those various decline conditions, some of which

were successful and some of which were not. Some of the successes could be accounted for by particular organizational strengths, outstanding managerial competencies, or just plain luck. But it also became evident that characteristics of the external environment played a dominant role in determining successes and failures of managerial responses during periods of decline. As conditions in the environment changed, different kinds of constraints were imposed on organizations and different organizations experienced qualitatively different conditions of decline.

It seemed appropriate, therefore, to identify characteristics of the environment that produced different types of decline and then to identify managerial responses that appeared to be most appropriate in each of those conditions. Our typology of decline, therefore, is based on changes in the external environment. We ignore the kinds of decline that result from mismanagement or mistakes in organizations, and instead consider only the kinds of decline that are induced environmentally. This emphasis on changes in the external environment as the precursor to decline points out that nearly all organizations may face these conditions at some time, and they are not just aberrations from an expectation of continued growth.

Decline as a Product of the Environment

To understand our typology of decline, it is first necessary to discuss the nature of the environment of organizations and to explain the types of changes that occur in that environment. The environment can be thought of as being composed of an assemblage of *niches*. A niche is a segment of the larger environment (Hutchinson, 1957) that is bounded by such factors as the availability of resources to support an organization's activities, constraints such as technology and culture, and the presence of consumer demand for organizations' outputs (see Zammuto and Cameron, 1983, for a more extensive discussion).

The level and types of organizational performance that a niche will support is continually being altered as resource availability, constraints, and output demand change over time. These changes create the conditions of both growth and decline for organizations. We are particularly interested in the situation where these changes reduce the size of a niche or modify its configuration, creating conditions of decline. These changes may take many forms, including decreased demand for products or services, increased government regulation, technological development rendering current products or services obsolete, or a decrease in the general level of resources in the environment. While many types of changes can create conditions of decline, we focus primarily on resource scarcity and the changing acceptance of organizational outputs as its major causes.

Two types of changes can occur in niches that cause decline: decreased resource availability that reduces the size of a niche, or changes in preferences for the outcomes of organizational performance that result in decreasing demand. This latter condition constrains the types of performance in which an organization can engage. In the first condition, a smaller niche requires a lower level of organizational activities because of a declining resource base. In the second condition, the niche is changing so that it no longer supports the types of activities in which organizations have engaged. The original niche may evolve into a different niche which supports a different set of organizational activities or it may cease to exist entirely.

Figure 1 depicts a niche shrinking from A to B because of a declining resource base. Niche B cannot support the same level of organizational activity as could niche A, because of either reduced availability of raw materials (input shrinkage) or a reduction in the demand for the organization's outputs (output shrinkage).

An example of a reduction in niche size is provided by the case of the city of Oakland, California, in the late 1970s. The reduction of resources available to the city reduced the size of the niche supporting municipal services. The resource base eroded because of a precipitous decline in population during the 1970s, a higher than average rate of unemployment in the city, a doubling of the proportion of minorities—many of whom were marginally employed—a slowing of growth in sales tax revenues, and the passage of Proposition

Figure 1. Change in the Size of an Environmental Niche

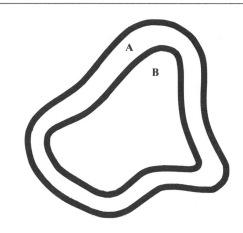

13 which limited the property tax base of the city (Levine, Rubin, and Wolohojian, 1981). These conditions all combined to create a niche much smaller than before, so that lower levels of organizational activity were required in order to survive in the smaller niche.

Figure 2 represents a niche undergoing a qualitative change in configuration. This figure reflects the evolution of niche A into niche B; niche A is abolished or is subsumed by niche B. Only the area of intersection between A and B is left of the

Figure 2. Change in the Shape of an Environmental Niche

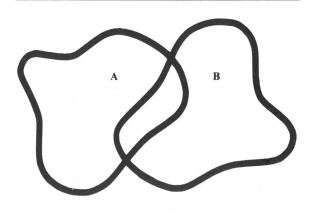

original niche. The implication is that new forms of performance are required of an organization in niche A if it is to survive the transition to niche B.

The experience of the American automotive companies during the 1970s provides a good example of one niche evolving into another, or of shrinkage in one niche resulting in the expansion of another. Historically, the U.S. automotive manufacturers produced large, relatively fuel-inefficient vehicles for the U.S. market. Through the late 1960s and early 1970s, changes in several conditions occurred that led to decline: the growing internationalization of the global automotive industry, increased government regulation, increased gasoline prices in the U.S., and increased import competition in the U.S. market (Zammuto, 1982b; Doz, 1981). By the late 1970s, the niche had evolved so that while the American manufacturers could still sell some large automobiles (the previous niche), the bulk of the market had shifted to smaller, more fuel-efficient vehicles by the end of the decade (the new niche).

In addition to changes in the size and configuration of a niche, another factor closely related to decline is the continuity with which decline occurs. That is, a decline in the availability of resources can occur suddenly, or there can be a sustained, continuous decline in resource availability. Schendel and his associates (Schendel and Patton, 1976; Schendel, Patton, and Riggs, 1976) suggested that the pattern of change in the external environment is an important factor in determining managerial responses to decline. Two patterns of change can be discerned in their findings: continuous change and discontinuous change. Continuous change represents relatively smooth change; change is largely uninterrupted, and past trends are good predictors of the future. Discontinuous change represents sudden change where the past is not a good predictor of the future. A major shift occurs in the trends experienced in the past. When a continuous decline occurs, organizations have more opportunity to plan for adaptation than when discontinuous decline occurs. Hence, organizations often are affected differently by conditions of decline depending on whether it is continuous or discontinuous. These two conditions are really opposite ends of a continuum. But for purposes of simplicity, we treat them as discrete in discussing their effects on organizations.

A Typology of Decline and Managerial Responses

In Figure 3, we present our typology of decline based on the two factors discussed above—the continuous or discontinuous nature of decline, and the type of change occurring in a niche. In each condition of decline, human resource issues arise within the organization that require unique managerial strategies to resolve them. For example, it is generally acknowledged that conflict increases within organizations that face decline (Whetten, 1980a), but our model suggests that the underlying sources of that conflict may vary depending on the types of decline being faced. Similarly, working relationships between managers and subordinates are almost always changed by decline (Levine, 1978, 1979), but different types of relationships may emerge under different conditions of decline.

For example, organizations that encounter continuous decline in their niche's size experience *erosion*. Frequently, decline is gradual and predictable. In this situation, stagnation and a progressive reduction in resources serve to heighten conflict over who will get less. While pressured to become more centralized, managers can remain consultative with subordinates since organizational survival is not immediately threatened. There is time to consider multiple alternatives and upward information flow is not entirely constricted.

Organizations that encounter discontinuous decline in their niche's size experience *contraction*. Because a sudden reduction in resource availability occurs, the organization's survival is in jeopardy. Conflict within the organization is a product of the experienced threat to existence, and autocratic management results. That is, there is little time for participative decision-making or information search, so management becomes highly centralized.

Figure 3. A Typology of Decline and Some Human Resource Issues

CONTINUITY OF ENVIRONMENTAL CHANGE

	Continuous Change	Discontinuous Change
TYPE OF CHANGE IN NICHE CONFIGURATION	*EROSION*	*CONTRACTION*
	SOURCE OF CONFLICT	**SOURCE OF CONFLICT**
	Stagnation	Threat
Change in Niche Size	**MANAGER-SUBORDINATE RELATIONS**	**MANAGER-SUBORDINATE RELATIONS**
	Consultative	Autocratic
	DISSOLUTION	*COLLAPSE*
	SOURCE OF CONFLICT	**SOURCE OF CONFLICT**
	Contention	Confusion
Change in Niche Shape	**MANAGER-SUBORDINATE RELATIONS**	**MANAGER-SUBORDINATE RELATIONS**
	Coalitional	Chaotic

Dissolution is the type of decline experienced when change results in a gradual shift from one niche to another. Organizations' outputs progressively become less acceptable within the environment. Conflict arises over what new directions the organization will take to survive. As in a political process, coalitions form around various alternatives for changing the products or services of the enterprise. Upward information flow can continue inasmuch as the dissolution occurs slowly, but manager-subordinate relationships become more coalitional in nature.

Collapse refers to a rapid and dramatic condition of decline. Niche shape is altered suddenly and extensively, and the original niche often dissipates in a very short time. Confusion over what is the best path toward organizational survival contributes to increased levels of conflict. Managerial relationships with subordinates are generally chaotic and disorderly. It is difficult to determine what information is valid and reliable

because of the constricted time frame in which the organizations must operate. Therefore, decisive leadership tends to be replaced by turmoil.

Usefulness of the Typology of Decline

The usefulness of identifying a typology of decline is that it can help managers select appropriate responses when their organizations face reductions in resource availability or output acceptance. No single strategy is appropriate for each of the four conditions. Rather, the four types of decline require different managerial approaches if successful outcomes are to be achieved.

The literature on decline provides a wide variety of prescriptions for managing cutback conditions, yet many of these prescriptions are contradictory to one another. Some authors advise that managers take one stance toward decline, while others advise the polar opposite stance. For example, managers are told to be entrepreneurial and innovative on the one hand (e.g., Galbraith, 1982; Tyler, 1982), and cautious on the other (e.g., Campbell, 1982). Some authors prescribe managerial action that is rational and systematic (e.g., Levine, Rubin, and Wolohojian, 1981), while others advocate questioning, randomness, and playfulness under the threat of decline (e.g., Hedberg, Nystrom, and Starbuck, 1976; Weick, 1977). Some authors have reported evidence for successful adaptation as a result of implementing certain prescribed strategies (e.g., Cameron, 1983; Chaffee, 1983; Harrigan and Porter, 1983), yet other authors have indicated that none of the strategies are very effective. Thurow (1981) indicated, for example,

> Nothing has worked very well when it comes to coping with economic decline. . . . My suspicion would be that no institutions manage decline very well. A look at private companies in areas where markets are contracting will show that they are almost always badly managed. . . . The standard business advice is to move out of the sunset areas of the economy and into the sunrise areas. But this advice obviously is of no value to an enterprise such as government that is locked into a particular geographic region or a particular service line. . . . Thus there may be no solution to the problem of how to manage decline well. It may simply be impossible.

One advantage of our typology of decline is that the divergent prescriptions for responding to decline are shown to be complementary, not contradictory. Each set of prescriptions is found to be appropriate in certain conditions of decline, but not others. The typology, therefore, serves a useful integrating function for adaptive decline strategies.

Under conditions of decline, managers are not only faced with varying prescriptions for how to respond, but they also are faced with personal and organizational pressures that make *any* intentional management response difficult to implement. The credibility and competence of the managers themselves are often called into question when decline occurs, and political forces become more organized, vocal, and pervasive. Resistance to change is an initial reaction in threatened firms

as past successes are relied on to justify current positions. Innovativeness is usually dampened, and an aversion to risk takes over. The well-known threat-rigidity response is typical of managerial action (i.e., managers become more closed and rigid when threatened), and "turf" consciousness leads to persistent self-protective behaviors. In turn, this leads to an increase in discord within the organization and to sagging morale. Information flow is almost always constricted, especially information from lower levels in the organization upward (see Staw, Sandelands, and Dutton, 1981; Whetten, 1980a, 1980b, 1981; Hermann, 1963; Billings, Milburn, and Schaalman, 1980, for elaborations of these points).

Under these conditions, guidelines that help managers both diagnose and respond appropriately to different types of decline are especially useful. Without some kind of framework or legend to help identify appropriate strategies, managers are pressured to engage in behaviors that frequently are productive neither for the organization nor for its individual members. Our model of decline is proposed so that both diagnostic and prescriptive guidelines can be provided for managers faced with these conditions of decline.

Managerial Responses to Decline

Successful managerial responses to decline can be organized along two main dimensions—behavioral tactics and domain selection strategies. Behavioral tactics are the immediate, short-term actions taken by managers when they become aware of the condition of decline. These tactics involve relatively minor adjustments and changes compared with domain selection strategies, which involve major adjustments in the organization and its activities and are usually long term in scope. Tactics are specific managerial actions that may lead to a strategic change (Thompson and Strickland, 1980).

Managers' tactics vary according to the condition of decline being faced. For example, managers generally are more inclined toward reactivity and defensiveness when the decline is discontinu

Figure 4. Managerial Responses to Conditions of Decline

CONTINUITY OF ENVIRONMENTAL CHANGE

	Continuous Change	Discontinuous Change
TYPE OF CHANGE IN NICHE CONFIGURATION		
	EROSION	*CONTRACTION*
	TACTICS	**TACTICS**
	Proactive	Reactive
Change in Niche Size		
	STRATEGIES	**STRATEGIES**
	Domain Offense	Domain Defense or Consolidation
	DISSOLUTION	*COLLAPSE*
	TACTICS	**TACTICS**
	Enactive	Experimental
Change in Niche Shape		
	STRATEGIES	**STRATEGIES**
	Domain Creation	Domain Substitution

ous than when it is continuous. That is, when decline occurs suddenly, protective reactions are a likely first response. When the decline threatens the very existence of the niche (changes in configuration) as opposed to simply reducing the resource base (changes in size), managers are usually inclined toward proactivity rather than reactivity. This is because the manager must lead the organization into a new domain if it is to survive, and finding a new supportive niche requires initiatory rather than responsive behavior.

Tactics can be organized into four categories, as shown in Figure 4—enactive, reactive, proactive, and experimental. Each is associated with a different type of decline. Enactive tactics refer to instrumental activities that implement new kinds of managerial behaviors. Not only are new activities proposed, they are enacted or implemented. Reactive tactics are those implemented in direct response to a decline event, and not until it occurs. Proactive tactics attempt to anticipate environmental events and are implemented aggressively. Proactivity connotes taking the offensive.

Experimental tactics are similar to trial-and-error actions taken when no clear alternative or model is present. Tentative actions are taken without much validating information.

The strategies employed in response to decline also vary under different conditions. In this discussion, we refer to *domain selection strategies* as being the particular kind of strategy that is most relevant.

Managers select specific domains that are supported by the resources present in the niche in which their organizations exist. Organizational domains refer to the population served, the technology employed, and the service rendered by the organization (Meyer, 1975). They are identified by examining the major activities pursued by the organization (Cameron, 1981). Most organizations have a core domain or a "primary task" (Rice, 1965) that defines the character of the organization. In conditions of decline, this core domain may be threatened by a reduction in the resources available in the niche (changes in niche size) and by the evolution of the niche itself (changes in niche configuration). Different types of decline require different types of domain strategies ranging from defending a current domain to creating a new domain or substituting a new domain for an old one.

The four types of domain selection strategies associated with the four types of decline are domain offense, domain defense or consolidation, domain creation, and domain substitution (see Figure 4). Domain offense strategies expand the current domain of the organization and are designed to create organizational slack. Domain defense or consolidation strategies are designed to reduce the size of the domain occupied by the organization and to protect the core domain from being abolished. Domain creation involves diversifying and supplementing the current domain with other more protected domains. Domain substitution strategies completely replace the current domain with another existing domain.

Managing Conditions of Decline

In a condition of *erosion,* organizations are faced with a continuous shrinkage in the size of their niche which is not likely to present an immediate threat to organizational survival. A climate of stagnation exists. Wildavsky (1972) suggests that such conditions provide managers with the opportunity to establish new priorities, to alter resource or product mix, or to pursue new activities aggressively. Under normal conditions, organizational inertia inhibits many new activities to be pursued, but a condition of gradual resource cutback provides the impetus for proactive managerial action. In a condition of erosion, therefore, successful managerial action tends to be *proactive,* leading toward *domain offense* strategies, or the expansion of the organization's domain.

An example of the management of erosion is provided by Miles and Cameron's (1982) and Hopkins' (1984) studies of the U.S. tobacco industry. Over the 30-year period studied by Miles and Cameron, the six U.S. tobacco firms displayed several different kinds of tactics and strategies as

their environmental conditions changed, and several types of decline were encountered. Hopkins, however, identified a particular time period when erosion was the dominant condition of decline faced by these firms (1965–1970). That is, per capita consumption of cigarettes was gradually declining in each of these years, and average tobacco acreage harvested gradually shrunk as well. Continuous shrinkage of niche size differentiated this period from others faced by the tobacco industry previously or afterward.

During this period of erosion, tobacco firms were characterized by proactive management and domain offense strategies. For example, Ansoff (1965) suggested three types of domain offense strategies that can be implemented by product-oriented firms: product development strategies (i.e., new, improved, or differentiated products for present customers), market penetration strategies (i.e., present products for present customers), and market development strategies (i.e., present products for new customers). Tobacco firms engaged in each of these three strategies under conditions of erosion significantly more than at any other time. That is, new cigarette brands were introduced at an accelerated rate (product development), advertising expenditures increased markedly (market penetration), and exports of cigarettes overseas grew substantially (market development) (see Miles and Cameron, 1982, and Hopkins, 1984, for supporting empirical data).

In a condition of *contraction,* organizations face a discontinuous, often unexpected, decline in resource availability. The niche is suddenly smaller, which leads to a threat-rigidity response on the part of managers. Staw, Sandelands, and Dutton (1981) documented a *reactive* response on the part of individuals faced with discontinuous decline in a variety of settings. Reactive behaviors dominate among managers as conservatism, across-the-board cuts, and other protective measures are used in an attempt to preserve organizational position within the niche. The manager is expected to buckle down and weather out what is often perceived to be a temporary inconvenience. The major concern is to conserve current resource levels until better times arrive. These reactive tactics employed by managers tend to lead to *consolidation* and *defense* of the traditional domain of the organization. Strategies are oriented toward the preservation of the organization's core until either conditions change or until strategic planning can occur.

An example of a condition of contraction is provided by the oil refinery industry in the United States. Clark (1976) identified four distinct time periods that this industry has encountered since 1950, based on an analysis of productive refinery capacity, expandable oil resources, petroleum costs, production levels, and other factors. These periods range from surplus and rapid buildup (1950–1957) to contraction (1973–1974) as a result of the Arab oil embargo.

The reaction of the 149 firms in this industry to the period of contraction was analyzed by Hopkins (1984). He used three different kinds of criteria to indicate domain defense or consolidation — cost reduction strategies, discontinued operations, and the narrowing of the range of investments. The purpose was to determine the extent to which firms trimmed "organizational fat," consolidated around their core domains, and became protective when facing a sudden reduction in the size of the environmental niche. His analyses confirmed that the most successful (profitable) firms did, in fact, engage in the predicted tactics and strategies as they encountered this period of contraction. Significant differences were found between the behaviors of these oil firms during this contraction period compared with periods before or after. Operations were discontinued, high cost and marginal activities were curtailed, and investments were withdrawn from unrelated (unconsolidated) subsidiaries. Less successful firms did not follow these tactics and strategies to the same extent.

The condition of *dissolution* is qualitatively different from erosion and contraction in that the environmental niche does not just get smaller, it threatens to evolve into a completely different niche. The acceptability of the outputs of the organization is in question. Managers find that they must enact or implement new alternatives in order for the organization to move into a new, supported niche. New resources are pursued, and new domains of activity are sought that may find legitimacy and acceptability. Because the decline is continuous, it usually can be predicted in advance and adjustments can be planned for. *Enactive* tactics are required of managers, then, which lead to *domain creation* strategies, or the diversifying of the organization's risk.

A recent example of dissolution involves small, private liberal arts colleges in the United States. Facing a changing economy and job market, liberal arts colleges in the 1970s began experiencing a gradual shift in student demand away from liberal arts courses and toward professional programs and the applied sciences. The liberal arts were criticized as lacking in relevance, and unemployed Ph.D.s in classics or philosophy became almost a cliche.

Chaffee (1983) studied the responses of 14 small, private liberal arts institutions to conditions of decline and found that successful institutions facing conditions of dissolution responded as suggested by the model. Rally College, for example, created management-oriented business and economics departments as well as programs in criminal justice and hotel/food service management when student enrollments began to decline (only 20% of Rally's students are now liberal arts majors). (Names of institutions in Chaffee's report are fictitious to preserve confidentiality for the institutions. All other data are accurate, however.) Prairie College maintained its liberal arts emphasis but implemented computer literacy requirements, a pre-med curriculum, and a career counseling service for all students at the school. Heartland College established joint programs with nearby universities and medical centers for purposes of career development. Crossroads College changed its name, dropped several liberal arts majors, and gave increased emphasis to technical and vocational programs. In fact, seven of the fourteen institutions studied by Chaffee successfully recovered from decline, and in every case, new domains were created and administrators enacted new internal changes as a response to their potentially dissolving niche.

The final condition of decline, *collapse,* refers to an immediate threat to the survival of the organization. Discontinuous change occurs in the shape of the environmental niche producing such catastrophic conditions that managers within the organizations are likely to have no previous experience to call upon for guidance. Past assumptions about cause-and-effect relationships are shaken. Managerial behaviors (tactics) are expected to be oriented toward *experimentation,* since the adaptations that will work under conditions of collapse are unknown. The lack of predictability and the suddenness with which the decline occurs, coupled with a desire to have the organization survive the collapse of the niche, result in random trial-and-error responses by managers. New domains are tried on an *ad hoc* basis in hopes of finding a domain to *substitute* for the one that has collapsed. There is no time to plan for domain creation, so existing domains which have the needed environmental support are sought as substitutes for the nonsupported domain. Managers must be concerned primarily with finding resources and with identifying a domain that will be supported by a new niche. The first satisfactory alternative encountered is likely to be accepted (Simon, 1976; Hall and Mansfield, 1971; Hermann, 1963; Whetten, 1981).

An example of a collapse in an environmental niche can be found in the U.S. wristwatch industry, particularly as it affected U.S. Time Corporation. U.S. Time, the maker of Timex watches, had captured almost 50% of the domestic watch market by 1960 (Barney, 1978). Timex watches had become highly standardized with interchangeable parts, and they were manufactured and assembled only with U.S. Time's uniquely designed tools. Therefore, they were produced more rapidly and less expensively than any other watches on the market at the time.

The introduction of the first quartz digital watch in 1968 marked a radically different approach to watch-making, however. Whereas Timex watches had 98 movable parts (compared with about 120 for most other watches), the simplest electronic watch had 5 parts, none of which moved. Prices for electronic watches, however, were running from about $800 to $2000, far beyond the $7.95 Timex watches ("Why watch makers...," 1970). In 1971, Timex even introduced its own quartz digital watch that sold for less than $200, far below the price of its competitors ("The mainspring in Timex," 1971).

In 1975, however, an unpredicted niche collapse occurred for both expensive quartz watches and for inexpensive mechanical watches ("Digital watches...," 1975). Semiconductor companies (e.g., Texas Instruments, Hughes Aircraft, National Semiconductor) introduced digital watches for under $30. A year later in 1977, Texas Instruments introduced a digital watch for under $10. *Business Week* reported that "Timex...does not have a choice. It has to find a way to compete. The speed at which digital watch prices are falling forces Timex to buy a semiconductor company now" ("The $20 digital...," 1976). This is exactly what Timex did. Consistent with the predictions of the decline model, it substituted a new domain for its old domain by purchasing an already established semiconductor technology from RCA ("Buy of RCA's...," 1976).

Conclusion

This discussion of conditions of decline explains why there is such diversity in the literature regarding prescriptions for adaptation. As we have illustrated, some conditions suggest that proactive responses are most effective, whereas other conditions suggest that the opposite kinds of responses (i.e., reactive) are more appropriate for organizational success. This model leads to the conclusion that the prescriptions of various authors for coping with decline, which previously have seemed contradictory, are in reality complementary. Incompatibilities in the literature can be explained by the fact that they address the phenomenon of decline from different perspectives. No one prescription for managerial behavior is applicable or appropriate in every condition since they focus on different aspects of decline.

We do not claim, of course, that the strategies and tactics suggested by our typology of decline are the *only* ones that are effective, nor that all successful managers and organizations implement them in adapting to decline. The tactics and strategies are presented, rather, as dominant responses that frequently appear in successful organizations that are faced with different environmental conditions. Their implementation has been found to be associated with successful performance, but they are by no means sufficient conditions for effectiveness in decline. Our purpose in pointing out these tactics and strategies is simply to help managers resist the pressures that arise from conditions of decline to become rigid, conservative, and self-protective. They may do so by having other alternatives in mind that have been found to be successful elsewhere.

Our discussion of the four conditions of decline also provides a model for diagnosing organizational environments. Whereas decline has generally been thought of as an aberration from the normal conditions of growth, we have pointed out that conditions of decline are a common environmental occurrence, and that different forms of decline present interesting new possibilities for organizations which may not be available during conditions of stability or growth. Given recent economic and government trends, it is less productive to think of decline as an exception to the desirable condition of growth, and more productive to consider ways to understand and manage its various forms well. Moreover, because decline is a multidimensional phenomenon, considering only one set of factors in diagnosing and responding to it may prove detrimental to long-term organizational survival. Managers should find this model useful, therefore, in identifying the nature of the decline that exists in their environment, and

in selecting types of tactics and strategies for coping with that decline.

References

Adizes, I. 1979. Organizational passages: Diagnosing and treating life cycle problems in organizations. *Organizational Dynamics* 86: 3–25.

Ansoff, H.I. 1965. *Corporate strategy.* New York: McGraw-Hill.

Barney, J. 1978. The electronic revolution in the watch industry: A decade of environmental changes and corporate strategies. Working Paper Series C, Yale University School of Organization and Management.

Billings, R.S., Milburn, T.W., and Schaalman, M.L. 1980. A model of crisis perception: A theoretical and empirical analysis. *Administrative Science Quarterly* 25: 300–16.

Buy of RCA's LCD line by Timex expected today. *Electronic News,* April 12, 1976, p. 53.

Cameron, K.S. 1981. Domains of organizational effectiveness in colleges and universities. *Academy of Management Journal* 24: 25–47.

Cameron, K.S. 1983. Strategic responses to conditions of decline: Higher education and the private sector. *Journal of Higher Education* 54: 359–80.

Campbell, S.D. 1982. Responses to financial stress. In C. Frances (Ed.), *Successful responses to financial difficulty.* San Francisco: Jossey-Bass.

Chaffee, E.E. 1983. *Case studies in college strategy.* Boulder, CO: National Center for Higher Education Management Systems.

Clark, S. 1976. *Oil industry earnings, 1950–1975.* Claremont, CA: Claremont College Press.

Digital watches: Bringing watchmaking back to the U.S. *Business Week,* October 27, 1975, pp. 79–92.

Doz, Y.L. 1981. The internationalization of manufacturing in the automobile industry. *Social Science Information* 20: 857–81.

Galbraith, J.R. 1977. *Organizational design.* Reading, MA: Addison-Wesley.

Galbraith, J.R. 1982. Designing the innovating organization. *Organizational Dynamics* 11: 5–25.

Hall, D.T., and Mansfield, R. 1971. Organizational and individual responses to external stress. *Administrative Science Quarterly* 16: 533–46.

Harrigan, K.R., and Porter, M.E. 1983. End-game strategies for declining industries. *Harvard Business Review* 61: 111–20.

Hedberg, B.L.T., Nystrom, P.C., and Starbuck, W.H. 1976. Camping on seesaws: Prescriptions for self-designing organizations. *Administrative Science Quarterly* 21: 41–65.

Hermann, C.F. 1963. Some consequences of crisis which limit the viability of organizations. *Administrative Science Quarterly* 8: 61–82.

Hopkins, W. 1984. Strategic adaptation to decline in two U.S. industries. Unpublished doctoral dissertation, University of Colorado.

Hutchinson, G.E. 1957. Concluding remarks. *Cold Spring Harbor Symposium on Quantitative Biology* 22: 415–27.

Lawrence, P.R., and Lorsch, J.W. 1969. *Organization and environment.* Homewood, IL: Irwin.

Levine, C.H. 1978. Organizational decline and cutback management. *Public Administration Review* 38: 316–25.

Levine, C.H. 1979. More on cutback management: Hard questions for hard times. *Public Administration Review* 39: 179–83.

Levine, C.H., Rubin, I.S., and Wolohojian, G.G. 1981. *The politics of retrenchment: How local governments manage fiscal stress.* Beverly Hills, CA: Sage.

The mainspring in Timex. *New York Times,* December 5, 1971, p. F7.

Meyer, M.W. 1975. Organizational domains. *American Sociological Review* 40: 599–615.

Miles, R.H., and Cameron, K.S. 1982. *Coffin nails and corporate strategies.* Englewood Cliffs, NJ: Prentice-Hall.

Quinn, R.E., and Cameron, K.S. 1983. Organizational life cycles and shifting criteria of effectiveness: Some preliminary evidence. *Management Science* 29: 33–51.

Rice, A.K. 1965. *Learning for leadership.* London: Tavistock.

Schendel, D.E., and Patton, G.R. 1976. Corporate stagnation and turnaround. *Journal of Economics and Business* 28: 236–41.

Schendel, D.E., Patton, G.R., and Riggs, J. 1976. Corporate turnaround strategies: A study of profit decline and recovery. *Journal of General Management* 3: 3–11.

Simon, H.A. 1976. *Administrative behavior,* 3rd ed. New York: Free Press.

Starbuck, W.H., and Nystrom, P.C. 1981. Designing and understanding organizations. In P.C. Nystrom and W.H. Starbuck (Eds.), *Handbook of organizational design.* New York: Oxford University Press.

Staw, B.M., Sandelands, L.E., and Dutton, J.E. 1981. Threat-rigidity effects in organizational behavior: A multilevel analysis. *Administrative Science Quarterly* 26: 501–24.

Taylor, B. 1982. Turnaround, recovery, and growth: The way through the crisis. *Journal of General Management* 8: 5–13.

The $20 digital watch arrives a year early. *Business Week,* January 26, 1976. pp. 27–28.

Thompson, A.A., and Strickland, A.M. 1980. *Strategy formulation and implementation.* Dallas: Business Publications, Inc.

Thurow, L. 1981. Review of Charles H. Levine (Ed.), *Managing fiscal stress,* in *Journal of Economic Literature:* 1105–6.

Tyler, R.W. 1982. Dynamic response in a time of decline. *Phi Delta Kappan:* 655–58.

Weick, K.E. 1977. Organization design: Organizations as self-designing systems. *Organizational Dynamics* (Autumn): 31–46.

Whetten, D.A. 1980a. Organization decline: Neglected topic in organizational science. *Academy of Management Review* 4: 577–88.

Whetten, D.A. 1980b. Sources, responses, and effects of organizational decline. In J.R. Kimberly and R.H. Miles (Eds.), *The organizational life cycle.* San Francisco: Jossey-Bass.

Whetten, D.A. 1981. Organizational responses to scarcity: Exploring the obstacles to innovative approaches to retrenchment in education. *Educational Administration Quarterly* 17: 80–97.

"Why watch makers are all wound up," *Business Week,* October 3, 1970, pp. 86–87.

Wildavsky, A. 1972. The self-evaluating organization. *Public Administration Review* 32: 509–20.

Zammuto, R.F. 1982a. *Bibliography on decline and retrenchment.* Boulder, CO: National Center for Higher Education Management Systems.

Zammuto, R.F. 1982b. *Assessing organizational effectiveness: Systems change, adaptation, and strategy.* Albany, NY: SUNY Press.

Zammuto, R.F. 1983. Growth, stability, and decline in American college and university enrollments. *Educational Administration Quarterly* 19: 83–99.

Zammuto, R.F., and Cameron, K.S. 1983. A typology of environmental decline and organizational response. In B.M. Staw and L.L. Cummings (Eds.), *Research in Organizational Behavior,* Vol. 7. Greenwich, CT: JAI Press.

7

Strategies for Declining Industries

Kathryn Rudie Harrigan

About fifteen years ago, eight large U.S. firms committed an average of $10 million each to the construction of new plants that used an experimental technology to manufacture products for several customers who held long-term contracts. However, "bugs" in this technology cut these plants' maximum output to levels below their engineered capacity. Two years later, a rival technology relying upon different raw materials was commercialized, and the firms' own raw materials prices quadrupled. As a result, industrywide consumption of the product dwindled.

Seeing this change, one firm wrote off its plant immediately and contracted for supplies consumed internally from a competitor. It broke even. Another firm was locked into production with customers who would not renegotiate their contracts. It suffered losses. A third firm managed to satisfy its contractual customers by retiring its own plant and leasing a competitor's plant that was of a smaller, more appropriate capacity for its customers' needs. It prospered.

About the same time, several even larger U.S. companies were heavily invested in a basic technology when a major technological breakthrough that could spawn several subsequent generations of product improvements was announced. The firms had been planning to erect highly automated plants for these basic products to lower the cost of their domestic labor forces. The newer technology had not yet been commercialized and was quite expensive. But it would definitely make their basic product obsolete in the future.

One firm sold its patents and ideas to foreign producers who could import the product less expensively than it could be produced in the United States. It prospered. A second firm used the product internally. It made the investment in automated plants and helped its competitors to exit. It prospered too.

Less than ten years ago, over thirty U.S. firms were caught completely off guard when a new version of a consumer product was merchandised with great fanfare. Although the new version was quite expensive, it made their version obsolete overnight.

The author would like to acknowledge the assistance of Dr. Michael E. Porter and The Division of Research, Harvard Business School, in completing this study, and the editorial assistance of Dr. Charles Hofer, New York University, for his contributions to the completion of this article.

From the *Journal of Business Strategy,* Vol. 1. © 1980 Warren, Gorham & Lamont, Inc. Reprinted with permission.

One firm which produced inexpensive models of the older consumer product increased its output and prospered. Another firm which produced very high quality models of the consumer product slowly reduced its output as the newer product caught on, but continued to market the "obsolete" model. It prospered, too. A third firm's models looked very similar to those of the newer version. Unfortunately, retailers would not carry them because they seemed redundant. That firm lost money despite its low operating costs.

Each of these situations involved a declining industry and the types of competitive strategies used to respond to that situation. Some firms prospered, some did not. A key question, then, is: What types of strategies are most appropriate for businesses that face environments of declining demand? The study reported in this article investigated this question in some detail. In particular, it examined the various characteristics of declining industry environments and the types of strategies which firms used for responding to industry decline. Also, given the various characteristics of a particular declining industry, the study identified the types of strategy alternatives most appropriate for different firms within that environment, and it explored how firms actually selected the strategy alternatives they used. It found that appropriateness of particular strategies for dealing with decline depended upon the characteristics of the industry in question, the firm's competitive posture within that industry, and the timing of competitors' decisions;[1] and it developed a model for prescribing the types of strategies that a firm should use for the circumstances it faced. Overall, the model was supported quite strongly as more than 92 percent of the firms that followed its directions were successful, while over 85 percent of those who violated its precepts failed.[2]

Types of decline

Observation suggests that product or industry demand may decline in many ways. It may deteriorate quickly, as was the case with rubber baby panties when disposable diapers were commercialized; or it may diminish slowly, like cigar consumption, which has been "declining" intermittently for half a century. Similarly, demand may plummet to a lower level and plateau, as has occurred with baby food consumption which has fallen with the declining U.S. birthrate, and with various other products that are sustained by a core of replacement demand; or demand may decline to zero without pausing. Also, there may be substantial uncertainty regarding a product's revitalization, as in the case of millinery equipment for ladies' hats; or there may be relative certainty that the product is indeed obsolete, as in the case of electronic receiving tubes (vacuum tubes).

Observation also suggests that there are different ways to respond to declining demand. Some firms, such as E.I. duPont de Nemours in rayon, exited quickly after recognizing demand for the product was deteriorating. Other firms "milked" their end-game businesses, like PPG Industries in synthetic soda ash, and exited later when they were better prepared to do so. Still other firms, such as Regal Ware, Inc. in percolator coffee-makers, stuck it out to the end, when most competitors had discontinued their products, and reaped the benefits of doing so. Since these firms had clearly devised more than one way of responding to declining demand, it seemed that additional research concerning strategies for declining demand was needed to improve understanding of this phenomenon.

Surveying Sixty Firms in Eight Industries

The purpose of the research was to study patterns of declining demand for products which were made obsolete by technological, cultural, or demographic change, and to study firms' responses to these patterns to see whether there were some responses to decline that were more (or less) successful than other responses. Several declining industries were studied to see whether certain strategies were always successful, or successful in only some situations.

The study tried to probe beyond the existing writings on decline by developing hypotheses, gathering data concerning firms' behaviors, and comparing the successes and failures of these firms with the outcomes the hypotheses would have predicted.[3]

The sample included sixty firms in eight industries. The industries were chosen to cover the broadest range of situations and to contrast three key structural traits: the degree of product differentiation in the industry, the relative height of the industry's exit barriers, and the degree of concentration of the industry. These industries (and the firms within them) also differed in a number of secondary factors as is indicated in Exhibit 1.

In gathering data for this study, the strategic actions and plans of these firms were traced back to a common base year selected to contrast periods of relatively stable demand with the period(s) of decline. Thus, the base year in the study of cigars was 1964, a near-historic peak in U.S. cigar consumption and the year in which the Surgeon General announced that cigarette smoking was carcinogenic. The responses of seven of the major competitors in this industry to the subsequent decline in demand were compared in the years following that base year through 1978. Public source data concerning exit from the industry, plant closings (or expansions), product line deletions, mergers, and other similar activities by major industry competitors were supplemented by analyses of annual reports (and other financial data), studies by investment analysts, and interviews with some of the industry executives, their suppliers, and their customers, in order to ascertain how the different competitors responded to declining demand. These data were then used to develop descriptions of the declining industries and strategy/response profiles for each of the major firms in these industries.

The strategies identified through these field studies were then matched against each firm's relative success at the horizon year, 1978. The final results were profiles of responses similar to those shown in Exhibit 2, which were compared with the predictions in order to test the effectiveness of the model.

What the Study Found

Overall, there were six broad findings that emerged from the research, as well as a number of particular findings. The broad findings were as follows:

- There were a number of different types of decline. Some types were better than others because they represented superior opportunities to prosper during the decline or to exit successfully from the decline.
- A number of different strategies were used during decline. There was no single road to success. Also, many innovative ways of retrieving the value of a firm's assets were found, and a variety of tactics for executing these different strategies proved effective.
- A firm's relative success during decline was affected by its relative competitive strengths as well as by the structure of the industry it was in.
- The appropriate strategies for coping with decline varied according to the firm's strengths and whether its industry environment was favorable for prolonged participation and relatively easy exit.
- There were a few exceptions to the general patterns observed. Some firms discovered unique ways to beat the laws of the marketplace.
- Firms did not always adopt the most economically appropriate strategies because competitors' actions sometimes shifted the balance in an industry seeming to be favorable or unfavorable, because they sometimes misread the signals which would have suggested an alternative action plan, and because they were sometimes willing to live with lower levels of performance as a result of the central importance of the business involved to their corporate portfolios.

Causes of Decline

Overall, there were three major reasons for the declines that occurred. These were (1) technological obsolescence, (2) sociological or demographic changes, and (3) changing fashion. In general, de-

Exhibit 1. Sample Design for the Study of Declining Industries

Degree of Product Differentiation	Height of Exit Barriers	Degree of Concentration	Industries Studied	Firms Studied	Demand Uncertainty	Rapidity of Demand Decline	Pockets of Demand
Differentiated	High	Concentrated	Rayon and acetate	American Enka	Great	Fluctuating	Apparel
				Avtex Fibers	Great	Fluctuating	Apparel
				Beaunit	Great	Fluctuating	Velvets
				Celanese	Great	Fluctuating	Apparel
				Courtaulds	Great	Fluctuating	Apparel
				DuPont	Great	Rapid	Few
				Industrial Rayon	Great	Rapid	Few
				Tennessee Eastman	Little	Slow	Filters
		Fragmented	Cigars	American Cigar	Little	Slow	Premium
				Bayuk Cigar	Little	Slow	None
				Consolidated Cigar	Little	Slow	Premium
				Culbro Co.	Little	Slow	Premium
				Havatampa Cigar	Little	Slow	None
				Jno. H. Swisher & Son	Little	Slow	Low priced
				Tampa Cigarmakers	Some	Slow	Premium
Differentiated	Low	Concentrated	Baby foods	Abbott Laboratories	Great	Slow	Formula
				Beech-Nut Foods	Great	Moderate	None
				Gerber Products	Great	Moderate	Formula
				Mead-Johnson	Great	Slow	Formula
				H.J. Heinz	Great	Moderate	None
				Swift & Co.	Great	Moderate	None
		Fragmented	Electric percolator coffee-makers	Corning Glass Works	Little	Rapid	Premium
				S.W. Farber	Little	Rapid	Premium
				General Electric	Little	Rapid	Discounters
				Mirro Aluminum	Some	Moderate	Low priced
				Proctor-Silex	Little	Very fast	None
				Regal Ware	Some	Moderate	Low priced
				Sunbeam Appliance	Little	Rapid	Discounters
				West Bend	Little	Rapid	None
Commodity	High	Concentrated	Electronic receiving tubes	General Electric	Little	Moderate	Replacement
				GTE Sylvania	Little	Moderate	Replacement
				RCA Corporation	Little	Moderate	Replacement
				Raytheon	Little	Moderate	Distributors
				Westinghouse Electric	Little	Moderate	Few
		Fragmented	Acetylene	Air Products & Chemicals	Some	Moderate	Welders
				Air Reduction (AIRCO)	Great	Rapid	Contract
				American Cyanamid	Great	Slow	Internal
				Chemetron	Some	Moderate	Welders
				Diamond Shamrock	Little	Rapid	Internal
				Dow Chemical	Some	Slow	Internal
				DuPont	Great	Rapid	Internal
				Monochem	Little	Slow	Internal
				Monsanto	Great	Slow	Internal
				Rohm & Haas	Little	Moderate	Internal
				Tenneco Chemical	Little	Rapid	Few

Import Competition	Number of Segments Served	Relative Competitive Strengths	Price Levels	Strength of Rivalry	Reinvestment Requirements	Government Regulations	Markets for Sale of Assets
Severe	Several	Moderate	Volatile	Strong	Pollution Control	Environmental	Few
Severe	Many	Weak, but big	Volatile	Strong	Pollution Control	Environmental	Few
Severe	Few	Weak	Volatile	Strong	Pollution Control	Environmental	Overseas
Some	Many	Strong	Volatile	Strong	Few	Environmental	Few
Severe	Few	Strong	Volatile	Strong	Pollution Control	Environmental	Few
Some	Several	Moderate	Volatile	Strong	Few	Environmental	Uncertain
Some	Tires	Weak	Stable	Strong	Pollution Control	Environmental	Others
Little	Filters	Strong	Stable	Little	Few	Environmental	Uncertain
Some	Many	Moderate	Stable	Strong	Capital Equip.	Health	Depressed
Little	Few	Frail	Discount	Strong	Few	Health	Depressed
Some	Many	Strong	Stable	Strong	Few	Health	Few
Some	Many	Moderate	Stable	Strong	Capital Equip.	Health	Few
Little	Few	Moderate	Discount	Strong	Few	Health	Depressed
Little	Few	Strong	Stable	Strong	Few	Health	Depressed
Severe	Few	Varied	Discount	Strong	Few	Health	Several
None	Few	Strong	Stable	Little	R&D	Food/Drug Adm.	Many
Little	Many	Frail	Volatile	Strong	Few	Food/Drug Adm.	Many
Little	All	Strong	Volatile	Strong	Few	Food/Drug Adm.	Many
None	Few	Moderate	Stable	Little	R&D	Food/Drug Adm.	Many
Little	Many	Moderate	Volatile	Strong	Few	Food/Drug Adm.	Many
Little	Few	Weak	Volatile	Strong	Few	Anti-Trust	Many
Little	Few	Moderate	Volatile	Strong	Few	Safety	Few
Little	Few	Moderate	Volatile	Strong	Few	Safety	Few
Little	Many	Strong	Volatile	Strong	Few	Safety	Few
Little	Few	Moderate	Stable	Strong	Capital Equip.	Safety	Some
Little	Few	Weak	Low	Strong	Few	Safety	None
Little	Few	Moderate	Stable	Strong	Few	Safety	Few
Little	Several	Strong	Volatile	Strong	Few	Safety	Few
Little	Several	Moderate	Volatile	Strong	Few	Safety	Few
Some	Many	Moderate	Stable	Little	Few	Imports	Few
Some	Many	Strong	Stable	Little	Capital Equip.	Imports	Few
Some	Many	Weak, but big	Stable	Little	Few	Imports	Few
Moderate	Few	Special	Discount	Moderate	Few	Imports	None
Some	Several	Weak	Stable	Little	Few	Imports	Few
None	Several	Moderate	Low	Moderate	Few	Safety	Depressed
None	Several	Weak, but big	Contract	None	Substantial	Safety	None
None	Internal	Moderate	Contract	None	Maintenance	Safety	None
None	Several	Strong	Low	Moderate	Maintenance	Safety	Depressed
None	Internal	Weak	Contract	None	Substantial	Safety	None
None	Few	Moderate	Contract	None	Maintenance	Safety	Few
None	Internal	Weak	Contract	None	Substantial	Safety	None
None	Internal	Strong	Contract	None	Maintenance	Safety	None
None	Internal	Moderate	Contract	None	Maintenance	Safety	Special
None	Internal	Moderate	Contract	None	Maintenance	Safety	None
None	Few	Weak, but big	Contract	None	Substantial	Safety	

Exhibit 1 (Continued)

Degree of Product Differentiation	Height of Exit Barriers	Degree of Concentration	Industries Studied	Firms Studied	Demand Uncertainty	Rapidity of Demand Decline	Pockets of Demand
		Concentrated	Synthetic soda ash	Allied Chemical	Little	Rapid	Few
				BASF Wyandotte	Little	Rapid	Few
				Diamond Shamrock	Little	Rapid	Few
				Dow Chemical	Little	Rapid	None
				Olin Corp.	Little	Rapid	Few
				PPG Industries	Little	Rapid	Few
Commodity	Low	Fragmented	U.S. leather tanning	A.C. Lawrence Leather	Moderate	Moderate	Few
				Allied Leather	Great	Moderate	Fashion
				Armira Corp.	Moderate	Moderate	Boots
				Brown Shoe	Moderate	Moderate	Shoe Uppers
				Garden State Tanning	Little	None	Upholstery
				Pfister & Vogel	Moderate	Slow	Military
				Seagrave Corp.	Moderate	Moderate	Fashion
				Spencer Foods	Moderate	Moderate	Few

clines induced by fashion or demographic changes produced great uncertainty about future industry prospects, while declines created by technological change were far more predictable, especially when the firms involved understood the substitute technology.

Some declining environments were also more favorable than others in terms of long-term sales volumes and profitability, lack of asset losses, and price stability. In general, the more favorable industries were ones where one or more firms could serve pockets of enduring demand even though the overall industry demand was declining rapidly. Such favorability was enhanced whenever the niches of demand that the firms served were protected from incursions by displaced competitors whose primary markets had dried up; when the niches were not inhabited by "maverick" firms who frequently instigated price wars; and when the firms could enjoy some benefits from their well-established brand names or corporate reputations. Other traits that increased the attractiveness of these declining industries were easy access to markets for the sale of the assets used in the industry, low reinvestment requirements for continued competition, and an absence of scale econ-

omies that would penalize firms for low plant utilization, as indicated in Exhibit 3.

The attractiveness of a particular declining environment also varied depending upon the viewpoint and strengths of each competitor. For example, if an enduring pocket of demand existed which a firm was not serving, that firm would prefer low mobility barriers in order to be able to enter that market segment relatively easily. Similarly, if a firm possessed the lowest cost position in the industry, it was normally much less averse to remaining in a declining market that was price-sensitive than its competitors.

In general, the less favorable declining industries had no niches of enduring demand, no mobility barriers to keep other competitors away, and little product differentiation. Other traits that decreased the attractiveness of declining industries included high reinvestment requirements, substantial diseconomies of scale, at least one "maverick" competitor who would cut prices below costs, the existence of customers who possessed and exerted strong bargaining power, and high exit barriers.

Within the more favorable declining industries examined, demand was highly price-sensitive

Import Competition	Number of Segments Served	Relative Competitive Strengths	Price Levels	Strength of Rivalry	Reinvestment Requirements	Government Regulations	Markets for Sale of Assets
None	All	Strong	Low	Strong	Few	Environmental	None
None	All	Moderate	Low	Strong	Few	Environmental	None
None	All	Moderate	Low	Strong	Few	Environmental	None
None	Internal	Moderate	Internal	None	Few	Environmental	None
None	All	Weak	Low	Strong	Pollution	Environmental	None
None	All	Moderate	Low	Strong	Few	Environmental	None
Severe	Many	Weak, but big	Rising	Strong	Pollution	Environ./Import	Several
Severe	Several	Weak	Rising	Bitter	Pollution	Environ./Import	Few
Heavy	Several	Moderate	Rising	Strong	Pollution	Environ./Import	Few
Severe	Few	Moderate	Rising	Strong	Pollution	Environ./Import	Several
Little	Few	Strong	Rising	Limited	Pollution	Environ./Import	Many
Severe	Several	Moderate	Rising	Moderate	Pollution	Environ./Import	Many
Severe	Few	Moderate	Volatile	Strong	Pollution	Environ./Import	Few
Severe	Several	Weak	Rising	Strong	Pollution	Environ./Import	Few

and often plummeted abruptly, creating sizeable write-off losses for firms that were forced to exit. Competitive price-cutting was rather severe, substantial reinvestment requirements often forced competitors to exit prematurely, and great uncertainty regarding the duration of demand frequently induced firms to reinvest in what was later revealed to be an unpromising industry. There was also substantial disorder in the patterns of firms' investments and exits, and quite often the need for major asset write-offs deterred some marginal competitors from making timely exits. (Note: Economic exit barriers also served as deterrents to the timely exits of some firms in several such industries. In each of these cases new investments in physical, but inflexible, assets had occurred near the time of the base year of the study.)

Industry Characteristics

Three demand characteristics in particular proved to be quite important in determining the broad contours of a declining industry's environment. Specifically, when there was relative certainty in the industry regarding (1) which pockets of demand would decline first, (2) how rapidly demand would decline for different market niches, and (3) whether demand would be likely to revitalize, the strategic behavior of most of the firms in the industry was relatively stable.

For instance, in these circumstances few firms suffered large write-off losses, and most of the firms that exited did so in a nondisruptive fashion about the time it was economically appropriate for them to do so. However, when there was substantial uncertainty concerning these three factors, chaos was more likely to ensue. Thus, discontinuities in the rate and pattern of decline were especially disastrous since these demand conditions could trap some firms that were unable to sell their underutilized assets quickly. This condition also increased the likelihood of price wars.

In general, declining industry environments were also relatively volatile when firms from significantly different (asymmetric) strategic groups[4] were forced — by shrinking demand — to compete against each other for the same customers. Other factors which exacerbated the volatility of competition, especially with respect to price levels, included the capital intensity (and excess capacity) of the industry, the presence of strong customer industries which controlled access to the ultimate

Exhibit 2. A Comparison of the Strategic Matrix's Predictions With the Observed Outcomes of Performance in Declining Industries*

	Relative Competitive			
	High		**Medium**	
	Recommended Strategies: "Increase" or "Hold"		Recommended Strategies: "Hold" or "Shrink"	
	Relatively Successful Outcomes	*Relatively Unsuccessful Outcomes*	*Relatively Successful Outcomes*	*Relatively Unsuccessful Outcomes*
Market Niches Favorable for Continued Competition	Dow Chemical . . . "Increase" + Chemetron . . . . . . "Increase" + Abbott Labs . . . . "Hold" + Tennessee Eastman . . "Hold" + Rohn & Haas . . . . "Hold" + GTE Sylvania . . . . "Increase" + Gerber Products . "Increase" + Monochem . . . . . . "Increase" + Regal Ware . . . . "Hold" + Garden State . . . . "Hold" + Pfister & Vogel . . . . . "Hold" +		Armira (leather) . . . . "Shrink" + General Electric . . . . "Shrink" + Mead-Johnson . . . . . "Shrink" + Air Products . . . . "Hold" + Raytheon. . . . ."Shrink" + Tampa Cigarmakers . . "Hold" +	

	Recommended Strategies: "Hold" or "Shrink"		Recommended Strategies: "Shrink" or "Milk"	
	Relatively Successful Outcomes	*Relatively Unsuccessful Outcomes*	*Relatively Successful Outcomes*	*Relatively Unsuccessful Outcomes*
Market Niches Intermediate for Continued Competition	Consoltd. Cigar . . . "Shrink" + Celanese. . . . ."Shrink" + Sunbeam . . . . "Shrink" + Brown Shoe . . . . "Hold" + Monsanto . . . . "Milk" − American Cyanamid . "Milk" −	Corning Glass . . "Milk" +	Mirro Aluminum . . . . . "Milk" + Union Carbide . . . . . "Shrink" + West Bend . . . ."Shrink" + Jno. Swisher . . . . "Milk" + H.J. Heinz . . . . "Milk" + General Electric . . . . . . "Milk" + American Enka . . . . "Shrink" + S.W. Farber . . . . "Milk" +	Havatampa Cigar . . "Hold" + Beech-Nut . . . . . "Increase" +

	Recommended Strategies: "Shrink" or "Milk"		Recommended Strategies: "Milk" or "Divest"	
	Relatively Successful Outcomes	*Relatively Unsuccessful Outcomes*	*Relatively Successful Outcomes*	*Relatively Unsuccessful Outcomes*
Market Niches Unfavorable for Continued Competition	Allied Chemical . . . "Shrink" + Courtaulds . . . . "Shrink" + DuPont (rayon) . . . . . "Milk" +		PPG Industries . . . . . . "Milk" + Diamond Shamrock . . "Milk" + BASF Wyandotte . . . . "Milk" + Dow Chemical . . . . "Milk" +	Culbro Corp. . . . . . "Shrink" +

American Cigar . . . . "Shrink" −

Advantages

Low

Recommended Strategies: "Shrink" or "Milk"

Relatively Successful Outcomes	*Relatively Unsuccessful Outcomes*
Westinghouse..."Milk"+	
RCA Corp......"Milk"+	

Recommended Strategies: "Milk" or "Divest"

Relatively Successful Outcomes	*Relatively Unsuccessful Outcomes*
	Swift & Co.............."Milk"+

Recommended Strategies: "Divest"

Relatively Successful Outcomes	*Relatively Unsuccessful Outcomes*
DuPont ......"Divest"+	AIRCO..............."Hold"+
	Proctor-Silex........."Shrink"+
	A.C. Lawrence........."Milk"+
	Spencer Leather........"Milk"+
	Industrial Rayon........"Milk"+
	Diamond Shamrock......"Milk"+
	Tenneco Chemical......."Milk"+
	Avtex Fibers..........."Shrink"+
	Beaunit.............."Shrink"+
	Olin Corp.............."Milk"+
	Allied Leather.........."Milk"+
	Bayuk Cigar ...."Milk"+
	El Paso Corp.........."Divest"+
	(Parent of Beaunit)
	FMC Corp............."Divest"+
	(Parent of Avtex)

+ Indicates an outcome consistent with the model, i.e., a firm that followed prescriptions and was successful or that did not follow them and failed.

− Indicates an outcome inconsistent with the model, i.e., a firm that followed prescriptions and failed or did not follow them and was successful.

*In addition to the sixty businesses studied, data on the parents of two of the surviving firms are included in this Exhibit. Both were forced to spin off their declining businesses after trying other, unsuccessful strategies. Since their treatments of the declining businesses differed from those of the surviving firms, it was felt their actions could and should be included in the study.

Exhibit 3. Structural Factors That Influence the Attractiveness of Declining Environments

Structural Factors	Environmental Attractiveness		
	Favorable	Intermediate	Unfavorable
Speed of decline	Very slow	Moderate	Rapid and/or erratic
Certainty of decline	100% certain predictable patterns	Fairly certain patterns	Great uncertainty, erratic patterns
Pockets of enduring demand	Several or major ones	Some niches	No niches
Price stability	Stable, price premiums attainable	Some volatility	Very unstable, pricing below costs
Reinvestment requirements	None	Some maintenance investments needed	High, often mandatory and involving capital assets
Diseconomies of scale	None	Slight	Substantial penalty
Excess capacity	Little	Some	Substantial
Asset age	Mostly old assets	Mostly undepreciated assets	Sizable new assets and old ones not retired
Resale markets for assets	Easy to convert or sell	Some outlets for disposal (overseas)	No markets available; substantial costs to retire
Product differentiability	Brand name loyalty	Corporate name recognition	Commodity-like products
Customer industries	Fragmented, weak	Long-term contracts	Strong bargaining power
Customer switching costs	High	Moderate	Minimal
"Single product" competitors	None	Very few large ones	Several large firms
Height of exit barriers	Low	Moderate	High
Shared facilities	Few—free-standing plants	Few—connected with weak products	Substantial and connected with important businesses
Vertical integration	None	Little	Substantial
Dissimilar strategic groups	Few	Some	Several in same target markets

consumers (usually shelf space), and/or a highly price-sensitive ultimate customer demand. On the other hand, high customer switching costs decreased the likelihood that competition would be volatile.

Of course, some declining industries contained both favorable and unfavorable structural traits, or were in intermediate positions with respect to the factors discussed above. These declining environments were classified as of "intermediate" attractiveness, as indicated in Exhibit 3, which summarizes the most important traits that affect the favorability of the declining environment.

Five Strategies to Use

Overall, five major types of strategic responses to declining environments were identified. They were as follows:

- Increasing the firm's investment (to dominate or get a good competitive position);
- Holding the firm's investment level until the uncertainties about the industry were resolved;
- Decreasing the firm's investment posture selectively, by sloughing off the unpromising models of customer groups, while simultaneously strengthening the firm's investment posture within the lucrative niches of enduring customer demand;
- Harvesting (or milking) the firm's investment to recover cash quickly, regardless of the resulting investment posture; and
- Divesting the business quickly by disposing of its assets as advantageously as possible.

Thus, Gerber Products and Dow Chemical increased their investments in baby food and acetylene, respectively, markets in which each faced excellent opportunities for profitability. On the other hand, Courtaulds and Havatampa Cigar maintained (held) their respective investment postures in rayon and cigars, where they were appropriately situated for the demand conditions they faced during the years of this study. However, Mead-Johnson and Sunbeam Appliance shrank their investment postures in baby foods and per-

colator coffee-makers, where their analyses of their industry's structural traits suggested they could not compete profitably in some portions of their declining businesses; and PPG Industries and DuPont milked their investments in synthetic soda ash and acetate, where their analyses of structural traits suggested there would be little profitability to be gained by fighting to stay in these businesses. Finally, Raytheon and DuPont divested their electronic receiving tube and acetylene businesses, respectively, when they saw an opportunity to cut their losses and recover a portion of their investments quickly.

Overall, six of the sixty firms studied increased their investment levels in response to decline. Eleven held their investment positions near historic levels. Fifteen firms selectively repositioned their investments in their declining industries by shrinking selectively. Twenty-five firms milked their investments, and three divested quickly.

In general, significant losses increased the likelihood that a firm would exit early from the end-game, but a variety of exit barriers decreased the likelihood of early exit. These included: strong brand loyalties, well-established distribution channels, goodwill generated by financial assistance provided to customers, customers who thwarted the firm's attempts to exit, a lack of markets for the disposal of undepreciated, special use assets, and the high strategic importance of the business to the firm. Also, the presence of dissimilar strategic groups in a firm's target market tended to increase the probability that firms would not retire their underutilized assets. Likewise, projections that demand will endure longest in the segments served by the firm made continued investments appear especially favorable for some competitors.

What Accounts for Success?

In growth industries, major strategic strengths involve factors such as economies of scale, vertical integration, technological leadership, brand loyalty, strong distribution systems, and so on. In declining industry situations, some of these factors are still key strengths, but others are not. In

Exhibit 4. Hypothesized Relationships Between Relative Industry Attractiveness and Competitive Strengths, and Decline Strategies

"Relative" Industry Attractiveness*	"Relative" Competitive Strengths*		
	High	Medium	Low
Favorable	"Increase the investment" or "Hold investment level"	"Hold investment level" or "Shrink selectively"	"Shrink selectively" or "Milk the investment"
Intermediate	"Hold investment level" or "Shrink selectively"	"Shrink selectively" or "Milk the investment"	"Milk the investment" or "Get out now!"
Unfavorable	"Shrink selectively" or "Milk the investment"	"Milk the investment" or "Get out now!"	"Get out now!"

*It should be remembered that both the Relative Industry Attractiveness and Relative Competitive Strengths assessments are for declining industries and the firms within them. Thus, favorability is measured vis-à-vis the options of continuing to compete or withdrawing from the industry. This is different than the more typical situation in which a favorable environment is one in which the firm would normally want to invest substantially for growth.

general, the major types of competitive strengths in such situations are directly related to the harsh reality that there are fewer customers to serve and smaller quantities of products to produce. Thus, factors such as established relationships with customers who comprise enduring (and lucrative) pockets of demand, a highly valued brand name, a plant that can operate efficiently when underutilized, a large market share (if one's product is commodity-like), strong and substantial distribution networks, a favorable location or raw materials contract, flexible assets (or highly depreciated ones that could be removed without substantial costs), and an advantageous posture of diversification are key strengths in such industries. However, other traditional strengths such as high vertical integration, shared facilities, and scale economies in production (where the firm did not possess a dominant market share in the base year) were frequently disadvantageous in declining environments.

Finding the Right Strategy

Exhibit 4 summarizes the relationships between relative industry attractiveness (i.e., favorability for continued investment), relative competitive strengths, and competitive investment strategies that would lead to the best economic results based on prior research and history. The actual pattern of performances of the firms studied is shown in Exhibit 2.

Performance of the Model

Overall, the hypothesized model proved quite good. Thus, while there were forty-two firms that were relatively successful and nineteen firms that were relatively unsuccessful, thirty-nine of the forty-two successful firms followed the prescriptions of the model, and sixteen of the nineteen unsuccessful firms violated its precepts. Stated somewhat differently, thirty-nine of the forty-two firms

Exhibit 5. Correlation Between the Model and Success

	Number of Relatively Successful Outcomes	Number of Relatively Unsuccessful Outcomes	
Number of Firms That Followed Recommendations	39	3	42
Number of Firms That Did Not Follow Recommendations	3	16	19
	42	19	

that followed the recommendations of the model were successful, while three failed. By contrast, sixteen of the nineteen firms that acted contrary to the recommendations of the model failed, and only three succeeded. In short, if you followed the recommendations of the model, your chances of success were better than 92 percent, while if you did not follow them, your chances of failure were almost 85 percent, as summarized in Exhibit 5.

The Exceptions

Two of the three firms that succeeded despite violating the prescriptions of the strategic matrix, milked their investments in industries where a more aggressive strategy was recommended. Both firms were pioneers in the technology of this declining industry and shut down their plants after milking them according to a depreciation schedule established in the 1950s. Both firms were out of time synch with the other competitors in their industry, which were still building plants when these firms had already decided to retire theirs.

More important, both firms served only internal markets (i.e., only other parts of their own firm). Consequently, they did not really have a "hold" or "shrink selectively" choice open to them since there were no excess customer groups to cast off. Instead, their real choice was between "hold" or "milk," and both chose the latter. In a sense, then, one could argue that these two firms also "followed the precepts." The other firm that violated precepts "shrunk" by focusing on a few of the market segments it already served, rather than by just milking its investment.

All three firms which suffered failures despite following the strategic matrix's precepts were in a very weak position relative to competitors and suffered large losses on their declining businesses which were almost inevitable. In two of these cases, the firms tried other strategies as noted in the footnote to Exhibit 2 before deciding to divest these businesses. Thus, these two firms really violated the precepts before they followed them. One could thus argue that they are not extreme contradictions to the model.

Factors Behind Firms' Decision Making

Firms did not always do what economic rationality would seem to indicate. In fact, in nineteen of sixty-two cases, firms chose actions inconsistent with the hypotheses. There were a number of possible reasons for this inconsistent behavior, including limited or inaccurate information, lack of funds, and poor management. One of the most important of these factors seemed to be the strategic importance of the business to the company involved. Such importance, whether assessed in terms of corporate image objectives, customer linkages, organizational reporting goals, or vertical integration constraints, created "strategic" exit barriers that retarded the withdrawal of several firms who should have abandoned the declining industry in which they were competing much sooner than they did. Exhibit 6 indicates the impact of such strategic exit barriers on the behavior of the firms in the study. Overall, among the businesses of high strategic importance, twenty-one of the thirty-one firms' strategies were consistent with the strategic matrix's prescriptions, while ten were inconsistent.

Among the businesses that were of relatively low strategic significance, nineteen of the thirty firms' strategies were consistent with the matrix's prescriptions, while eleven were inconsistent. However, whenever a business was of high strategic importance and the firm had a strong competitive position, or faced a favorable environment, the prescriptions of the strategic matrix were always followed (i.e., all firms either increased or held their investment levels in those businesses).

When the business was of high strategic importance with intermediate favorability and strength, most of the firms (six of seven) followed the prescriptions of the matrix (i.e., to shrink or milk such businesses). Those that did not tried to hold their positions more than the matrix recommended. The latter behavior was repeated by most of the firms (seven of ten) with businesses of high strategic importance that faced unfavorable environments or were in weak positions, or both. In these circumstances only three of the firms studied behaved in an economically rational fashion and either milked or divested these businesses as called for by the matrix, and two of these three were the parent firms that first tried incorrect strategies as noted above. All the rest attempted to hold on more strongly than they should have.

On the other hand, when the business was of low strategic importance, sixteen of the nineteen firms that faced intermediate or unfavorable environments, or which had strong or intermediate competitive positions, followed the recommendations of the model. Moreover, two of the three exceptions were the two firms noted earlier whose behavior was unusual because of the unusual characteristics and odd timing of their strategic positions and strategies. Thus, if these two firms are deleted from the sample (or adjustments made for their behavior) only one of the seventeen (or nineteen) businesses with low strategic importance and moderate or strong strengths and position followed a strategy inconsistent with the model. On the other hand, seven of the eight firms with businesses of low strategic importance that had weak positions in unfavorable markets attempted to hang on more than they should have.

Two broad generalizations that spring from this analysis of Exhibit 6 are seen even more clearly in Exhibit 7. First, almost all firms either adopt the strategies they should (72%) or put more resources into declining business than they should (26%). Almost none (2%) withdrew more rapidly or more strongly than they should. Second, all of the companies that have invested more in their declining businesses than they should have, had weak positions in unfavorable industries or have had intermediate (but not strong) positions in businesses of relatively high strategic importance to the firm. Taken together, these findings suggest that strategic exit barriers created by shared facilities, corporate identity, narrow diversification postures, etc., are often significant deterrents to timely exits from volatile, declining industries.

Effects of Competitor and Customer Behavior

One of the more important findings regarding the determinants and effectiveness of declining industry strategies relates to the power of competitor and customer expectations regarding future demand. Thus, some of the uncertainty which led to volatile price competition could have been reduced if better information about competitors and customers had been available. In this regard, better analytical tools and organizational procedures seem to be needed to help firms assess the potential evolutionary impact of technological, demographic, and cultural changes on their industry's competitive structure.

For example, if a firm faces a decline caused by changing technology and is not already producing the substitute products, or familiar with the economics, of the alternative technology, a strong argument can be made that it should make some investments in this new technology in order

Exhibit 6. A Comparison of the Strategic Model's Predictions of Competitor Behavior With the Actual Strategies Followed by the Various Firms in the Study

Relative Strategic Importance of the Business to the Corporate Portfolio	Relative Market Attractiveness	Relative Competitive Strengths		
		High	Medium	Low
High	Favorable	Recommended Strategy: "Hold" or "Increase"	Recommended Strategy: "Hold" or "Shrink"	Recommended Strategy: "Shrink" or "Milk"
		GTE Sylvania (tubes).........."Increase" + Gerber Products...."Increase" + Monochem (acetylene)......."Increase" + Garden State Tanning.........."Hold" + Regal Ware (percolator)........."Hold" + Pfister & Vogel (leather).........."Hold" +	Seagrave (leather)....."Shrink" + Tampa Cigarmakers..."Hold" +	RCA Corp. (tubes) ....."Milk" +
High	Intermediate	Recommended Strategy: "Hold" or "Shrink"	Recommended Strategy: "Shrink" or "Milk"	Recommended Strategy: "Milk" or "Divest"
		Consolidated Cigar ...."Shrink" + Celanese Corp. (acetate)........."Shrink" + Sunbeam Appliance (percolators) ....."Shrink" +	Beech-Nut Foods (baby food) ....."Increase" – S. W. Farber (percolators)......."Milk" + West Bend (percolators)......"Shrink" + Mirro Aluminum (percolators)......."Milk" + General Electric (percolators)......."Milk" + Jno. H. Swisher (cigars) ...."Milk" + Havatampa Cigar ....."Hold" – American Enka (rayon)........."Shrink" +	

Exhibit 6 (Continued)

Relative Strategic Importance of the Business to the Corporate Portfolio	Relative Market Attractiveness	Relative Competitive Strengths		
		High	*Medium*	*Low*
		Recommended Strategy: "Shrink" or "Milk"	*Recommended Strategy:* "Milk" or "Divest"	*Recommended Strategy:* "Divest"
High	Unfavorable	Courtaulds (rayon) . . . "Shrink" +	Diamond Shamrock (soda ash) . . . . "Milk" + American Cigar . . . . . "Shrink" − Culbro Corp. . . . . "Shrink" −	Avtex Fibers (rayon and acetate) . . "Milk" − Beaunit (rayon) . . . . . "Shrink" − Olin Corp. (soda ash) . . "Milk" − Allied Leather . . . . "Milk" − Bayuk Cigar . . . . "Milk" − El Paso Corp. . . . . "Divest" + (Parent of Beaunit) FMC Corp. . . . . "Divest" + (Parent of Avtex Fibers)
		Recommended Strategy: "Hold" or "Increase"	*Recommended Strategy:* "Hold" or "Shrink"	*Recommended Strategy:* "Shrink" or "Milk"
Low	Favorable	Dow Chemical (acetylene) . . . . "Increase" + Chemetron (acetylene) . . . . "Increase" + Abbott Laboratories . . "Hold" + Tennessee Eastman (acetate) . . . . . . "Hold" + Rohm & Haas (acetylene) . . . . "Hold" +	Armira (leather) . . . . . "Shrink" + General Electric (tubes) . . . . "Shrink" + Mead-Johnson (baby food) . . . . . . "Shrink" + Air Products and Chemicals . . . . "Hold" + Raytheon (tubes) . . . . "Shrink" +	Westinghouse Electric (tubes) . . . . "Milk" +

Relative Strategic Importance of the Business to the Corporate Portfolio	Relative Market Attractiveness	Relative Competitive Strengths		
		High	Medium	Low
Low	Intermediate	Recommended Strategy: "Hold" or "Shrink" — Brown Shoe (leather) .... "Hold" + / Corning Glass Works (percolators) .... "Milk" − / Monsanto (acetylene) .... "Milk" − / American Cyanamid (acetylene) .... "Milk" −	Recommended Strategy: "Shrink" or "Milk" — H.J. Heinz (baby food) .... "Milk" + / Union Carbide .... "Shrink" +	Recommended Strategy: "Milk" or "Divest" — Swift & Co. .... "Milk" +
Low	Unfavorable	Recommended Strategy "Shrink" or "Milk" — Allied Chemical (soda ash) .... "Milk" + / DuPont (rayon and acetate) .... "Milk" +	Recommended Strategy "Milk" or "Divest" — PPG Industries (soda ash) .... "Milk" + / Dow Chemical (soda ash) .... "Milk" +	Recommended Strategy "Divest" — A.C. Lawrence (leather) .... "Milk" − / DuPont (acetylene) .... "Divest" + / Air Reduction (AIRCO − acetylene) .... "Hold" − / Proctor-Silex (percolators) ...... "Shrink" − / Spencer Leather .... "Milk" − / Industrial Rayon ...... "Milk" − / Diamond Shamrock (acetylene) .... "Milk" − / Tenneco Chemical (acetylene) .... "Milk" −

+ Indicates an outcome consistent with the model.
− Indicates an outcome inconsistent with the model.

Exhibit 7. How the Model's Predictions of Competitor Behavior Compared with Actual Strategies Followed by Firms in the Study: A Synopsis

Relative Competitive Strength		*Relative Industry Attractiveness*		
		Favorable	*Intermediate*	*Unfavorable*
High	Strong	6 Match	3 Match	2 Match
	Average	2 Match	6 Match	1 Match
			2 Stronger	1 Stronger
	Weak	1 Match	—	2 Match*
				5 Stronger
Low	Strong	5 Match	1 Match	2 Match
			3 Weaker**	
	Average	5 Match	2 Match	2 Match
	Weak	1 Match	1 Match	1 Match
				7 Stronger

*Represents two corporate parents that initially tried stronger strategies.
**Includes two firms that "match" after allowance is made for their unique positions.

to monitor its rate of commercialization and control the speed of transition from the declining business to its substitute. Research indicated that those firms which invested in substitute technologies were able to judge when substitution would be complete, where substitution would occur most slowly, and when to shut down their plant (or plants) and procure the product externally (rather than produce it internally) much better than firms that did not make such investments. Moreover, this finding was true even for those firms that invested in these new technologies relatively late in the start-up period. There may also be some benefits to using scenario analysis and other qualitative forecasting tools which would help strategic managers to estimate:

- How quickly competitors are likely to exit,
- Which competitors would be most likely to remain, and
- What types of competitors would be potential entrants (by bringing a new technology to the industry, for example) when demand for a particular product declines.

At the same time, the study indicated that if a firm is not the lowest cost competitor in an industry where products are becoming commodity-like in nature, it will usually have to surrender market share during the decline. However, if the declining product is differentiated in some way, new investments in the business may be justified in order to secure a more favorable position. On the other hand, if the product does not service a demand which responds to differentiation—for example, if the product is developing commodity-like traits that make customers increasingly price-sensitive—such reinvestments may not be justified because no true customer "niche" is likely to exist. And without the protection of high mobility barriers, which product differentiation usually provides, such high-cost firms are vulnerable to market invasions by lower-cost competitors.

It would seem, therefore, that if a firm possesses a large share of the market but does not possess the lowest operating costs, a strong distribution system, or a loyal niche of customers, it should try to overcome its exit barriers early by selling the declining business to another competitor or even to a supplier. This is particularly true if it possesses a large proportion of undepreciated assets, since without these particular strengths, it will be increasingly difficult to retrieve the value of the firm's investments as the decline progresses. By contrast, if a firm possesses some strengths, and if it believes that demand for the products of the industry will endure (making continued participation in some niche desirable), it should probably look to purchase the assets of weaker firms that serve such enduring customer niches, particularly those of competitors who face high economic exit barriers or are indecisive regarding their expectations for demand. In this way it can reduce the presence of factors causing volatility during decline, particularly factors such as differing expectations concerning demand among competitors and excess capacity.

Such actions should, of course, keep the industry viable and profitable longer through orderly reductions in capacity that keep supply in line with demand. The execution of such maneuvers, however, requires that weaker competitors retire their plants in deference to more efficient competitors (or irrationally-committed competitors), a course of action they are sometimes reluctant to pursue because of the strategic exit barriers discussed earlier. One economic solution which the study suggests might work in such situations is the use of sourcing arrangements whereby the most efficient competitors (plants) would manufacture the declining product for several of their weaker competitors to sell under their own corporate or brand names.

Finally, the study indicated that certain external events could be particularly catastrophic for the vitality of a declining industry in the sense that investments might become necessary that were not likely to be recoverable. These events, which tended to encourage exits, included legislation concerning effluent standards, pollution controls, employee health work rules, import tariffs, export quotas, and a variety of other public policy decisions. In some instances, though, even these events can be used to the benefit of the firm. Thus,

if a firm wished to ease others out of a declining industry, it might make such investments in anticipation of such legislation and then actually encourage such laws to be enacted.

Implications for Management

Overall, the most significant finding of the research is that the strategy matrix model seems to be generally valid despite its limitations. This suggests that top management should carefully consider the types of strategies it selects for businesses facing decline since such choices can have a major impact on the performance of such a business. In addition, there was substantial evidence to suggest that firms with weak businesses in unattractive industries tend to hold on to these businesses too long. In this regard, there is a need for better ways to accurately project the future prospects of declining industries, as well as to help weaker firms to overcome the strategic barriers that might keep them invested in these areas.

In this respect, strategic exit barriers must also be better understood in order to recognize how the declining business units of competitors fit into their corporatewide plans. Thus, some firms faced significant exit barriers because the linkages and importance of their declining businesses to their overall corporate strategies deterred their exits from such industries. And, while other competitors frequently wished that these marginal firms would exit from the industry sooner because their presence exacerbated the industry's low profitability, most of these marginal competitors stayed and accepted returns that were lower than their corporatewide opportunity costs of capital in order not to disturb the strategic linkages and other relationships which they valued.

In sum, there was much evidence that many firms will not necessarily exit when an economic analysis, such as an abandonment calculation, would suggest they should do so. Also, it is useful to recognize that the stock market and other outsiders, who do not understand the complexities of managing declining businesses, will tend to overvalue companies that are willing to "bite the bullet" by divesting businesses when they first begin to sour. Consequently, while such early divestment behavior may actually short-change the firm of possible returns on such businesses, it still may be preferable because of the increased P/E ratio and bond ratings that outsiders may give to such firms because they believe them to be well managed.

Finally, since some types of uncontrollable external events can literally destroy entire industries, especially those facing decline already, and since many of these events are now of a governmental nature, it is essential that firms in such positions monitor governmental agencies closely. They should prepare factual forecasts of the likely economic impact of such legislation and regulations upon communities where the firm is operating in order to draw attention to the loss of jobs, tax revenues, and other benefits that the demise of the business would cause. Such analyses should include forecasts of the cost of exit in order to facilitate informed decision making by management. In addition, it may not be out of order for the firms which have performed such analyses to provide copies of their findings to the salient public policymakers and affected residents of the community.

Summary and Conclusions

Overall, the study has increased our understanding of the nature of environments with declining demand. More specifically, it has shown that not all declining environments are alike and that there are a variety of strategies that may be used to cope with decline. Each of these strategies will have different probabilities of success depending on the nature of the decline and the relative competitive strength of the firm involved. Since the cost of erring in such decisions is quite high, managers need to anticipate the problems of decline earlier in order to have more options in their portfolio of strategies and, also, to be able to divest sooner if that is their best strategic option.

Notes

1 Sometimes, for example, a stronger firm gave up early, leaving an opportunity for weaker firms where none previously existed.

2 To date, very little attention has been given to the problem of declining industries, and to the strategies appropriate for them. In general, the existing literature can be divided into four categories: (1) literature concerning declining brands of models of a product (Alexander, 1964; Talley, 1964; Kotler, 1965; Hutchinson, 1971; Hise and McGinnis, 1975); (2) literature concerning divestitures (Bettauer, 1967; Hayes, 1972; Davis, 1974); (3) "product life cycle" literature (Buzzell, 1966; Wasson, 1974; Clifford, 1976); and (4) strategic portfolio literature (Tilles, 1966; Boston Consulting Group, 1972; Carter and Cohen, 1972). Much of this literature is overgeneralized in several ways. First, except for cursory treatments of declining demand in the product life cycle materials, there was no attempt to sort out the factors that influence the strategic choices managers will face during such declines. Second, most of these writings looked at only one pattern of declining product or industry demand and espoused only one strategy alternative for coping with this problem. Unfortunately, such a simplified view of the strategies appropriate for declining industries is inadequate for the needs of managers running such businesses because differences in industry structures, in the reasons for such declines, and in the expectations regarding future demand, as well as in the strengths of different businesses, etc., may substantially alter the performance outcome that may be generated by the different strategies available to businesses in these circumstances.

3 Readers interested in the literature review, hypotheses, and the comparisons of observed and expected outcomes in the study may consult Harrigan, *Strategies for Declining Industries* (Lexington, MA: D.C. Heath & Company, 1980), for these details.

4 A strategic group consists of a group of firms serving the same market segment or niche with similar strategic postures (product line, cost structures, price levels, etc.). Usually during periods of industry growth, firms from different strategic groups compete on a nonprice basis because of their different approaches to and perceptions of the industry. During periods of decline, however, these same differences can often lead to severe price warfare as these firms fight for the declining volume because they misperceive each others' positions.

References

Alexander, R.S., "The Death and Burial of 'Sick' Products." *Journal of Marketing* 1–7 (April 1964).

Bettauer, A., "Strategy for Divestment," *Harvard Business Review* (March–April 1967).

Boston Consulting Group, *Perspectives on Experience* (Boston, MA: Boston Consulting Group, 1972).

Buzzell, Robert D., "Competitive Behavior and Product Life Cycles," in John S. Wright and Jac L. Goldstucker, eds., *New Ideas for Successful Marketing* (Chicago: American Marketing Association, 1966), pp. 46–68.

Carter, Eugene E. and Cohen, Kalman J., "Portfolio Aspects of Strategic Planning," *Journal of Business Policy* 8–30 (Summer 1972).

Clifford, Donald K., Jr., "Managing the Product Life Cycle," in Robert R. Rothberg, ed., *Corporate Strategy and Product Innovation* (New York: The Free Press, 1976), pp. 349–69.

Davis, J.W., "The Strategic Divestment Decision," *Long-Range Planning* (Feb. 1974).

Hayes, R., "New Emphasis on Divestment Opportunities," *Harvard Business Review* (July–Aug. 1972).

Hise, Richard T. and McGinnis, Michael A., "Product Elimination: Practice Policies and Ethics," *Business Horizons* 25–32 (June 1975).

Hutchinson, A.C., "Planned Euthanasia for Old Products," *Long-Range Planning* (Dec. 1971).

Kotler, Philip, "Phasing Out Weak Products," *Harvard Business Review* (March–April 1965).

Talley, Walter J., "Profiting from Declining Products," *Business Horizons* 7: 77–84 (Spring 1964).

Tilles, Seymour, "Strategies for Allocating Funds," *Harvard Business Review* (Jan.–Feb. 1966).

Wasson, Chester R., *Dynamic Competitive Strategy and Product Life Cycles* (St. Charles, Ill.: Challenge Books, 1974).

8

Sources, Responses, and Effects of Organizational Decline

David A. Whetten

Managing declining organizations and coping with the consequences of retrenchment are pressing societal problems. Evidence of decline is pervasive. Schools have cut back because of decreasing enrollments; industry has laid off record numbers in response to recessionary pressures; the military had to scale down its operations after the Vietnam War; many churches have been forced to close their doors due to lack of support; and municipal services have been curtailed as a result of declining revenues. The consequences of decline are far reaching. Families suffer the effects of unemployment, and the morale of the remaining workers deteriorates as they are forced to fight over smaller and smaller resource pools. When an entire industry retrenches, the effects are felt throughout society. For example, the displacement of thirty million farm workers due to increased mechanization in agriculture is claimed by some to represent the genesis of our contemporary urban problems (Boulding, 1974).

So alarming are the potential consequences of widespread organizational decline that several scholars have proposed radically new forms of government and commerce to meet this impending crisis (Benveniste, 1977; Heilbronner, 1976; Commoner, 1976). Whether or not these proposals will be adopted, it is clear that our society is ill prepared to cope with decline. Since the Second World War our country has enjoyed unprecedented growth, and, as Kenneth Boulding (1974) has noted, all our institutions have become adapted to survival under conditions of rapid growth. The need to adapt to emerging conditions of scarcity represents a significant challenge at the individual, organizational, and professional levels.

At the individual level, decline runs counter to our strong success ethic. During our golden era of abundance, the values of optimism and self-assurance have reigned unchallenged (Sutton and others, 1956). The ease with which people are able to live in an expanding economy encourages an ego-centered orientation (Fox, 1967). With few threats to collective interests, individuals are free to pursue personal accomplishment. However, under conditions of munificence, ease is confused

From John R. Kimberly and Robert H. Miles' *The Organizational Life Cycle.* © 1980 Josey-Bass. Reprinted with permission.

with effort, and success with accomplishment. During this age of "the power of positive thinking" (Peale, 1952), when we are instructed to "think and grow rich" (Hill, 1967), it is the norm to ascribe success to personal accomplishment. The dark side of this philosophy that success can be willed is its implication that failure reflects personal incompetence. This logical trap is also reflected in the tendency to treat organizational growth as evidence of youth and vitality; decline then becomes equated with old age and senility. So powerful is the association between growth and success and between decline and failure in our society that Scott (1976) has proposed that the chief issue in the management of declining organizations is not whether managers are capable of saving them but whether they are willing to make the attempt. The best hands are generally the first to abandon a sinking ship, and it is difficult to sign on a new crew for a ship that is taking on water (Argenti, 1976; Hirschman, 1970).

The success ethic is engrained in our culture to such an extent that, when individuals must discuss a failure experience, they tend to describe it as though it were a personal success. Personal credit is taken for being: perceptive enough to recognize that a marriage partner was ruining our life; capable enough to keep a business from losing any more than it did before we had sense enough to bail out; so ethical, smart, or experienced that our former boss felt threatened by our presence in the organization.

During a period of economic expansion, there are of course more organizational births than deaths, and there is more growth than decline. For example, between 1950 and 1975 there were 2.2 million business starts and only 100,000 deaths (Statistical Abstract . . . , 1976). In this kind of expansionary period, decline and death are discomforting anomalies that are explained away as examples of failure to implement properly fundamental management principles. Because growth has been the norm in our country for decades, the experiences of managers in declining organizations have not been widely documented (Smith, 1963). Thus, as we enter a period of economic

slowdown during which a larger number of organizations will experience decline, their managers will have relatively few precedents or guidelines to rely on (Bogue, 1972). Recognizing this problem, Boulding (1974) has called for the establishment of clearinghouses to facilitate the exchange of ideas and suggestions among managers coping with decline.

At the professional level, organizational behavior teachers and researchers are ill prepared to provide the necessary support services for administrators in declining organizations because the field is dominated by a growth paradigm (Scott, 1974; Whetten, 1979c). For example, few courses are taught on management in declining organizations or under crisis conditions. Further, many of the models used to teach administration assume conditions of expansion. A typical textbook discussion of conflict management instructs students to resolve conflicts over resource allocation by formulating a "win-win" alternative. When munificence prevails, this is a realistic prescription, since offers of side payments or promises of larger portions in the future can be made. However, when the total resource pie is shrinking, the "win-win" option becomes less plausible since current losses are not likely to be made up in future allocations.

Organizational research has also been dominated by studies on growth-related topics. The work of Blau and his associates (Blau, 1968, 1970; Blau and Schoenherr, 1971) dealt primarily with the problem of maintaining coordination in an expanding organization. This line of research spawned numerous studies on administrative ratios (Pondy, 1969; Rushing, 1967; Indik, 1964) and the relationship between control strategies and such other organizational properties as innovation (Hage and Aiken, 1967) and professionalization (Hall, 1968). While interest in this line of research has waned, the growth-oriented paradigm it represented remains strong (Benson, 1977; Kotter and Sathe, 1978).

A strong growth orientation is also reflected in the literature on organizational development (Greiner, 1972). One of the most frequently stated reasons for a so-called organizational development intervention is that workers have become alienated due to the negative effects of increasing organizational size. The use of profit centers, interdepartment integrators, team building, and humanistic leadership practices represent attempts to infuse an intimate, supportive, and tractable environment into large, complex organizations.

While our society as a whole is ill prepared to cope with widespread decline, we have few options (Boulding, 1973; Daly, 1973, 1977). The industrial complex has been forced to cut back in response to double-digit inflation and an aroused public's concern about the rapid depletion of our natural resources (Schumacher, 1973; Commoner, 1976; Meadows and others, 1972); educational institutions, as already noted, have been forced to retrench because of declining enrollments (Trow, 1975; Green, 1974; Cartter, 1970); and the legitimacy and resource base of government have been eroded by a taxpayers' revolt over poor services and high taxes (Smith and Hague, 1971; Dvorin and Simmons, 1972; Whetten, 1979b; Fenno, 1966). The purpose of this chapter is to call attention to the need for an intensive examination of organizational decline and to begin to sketch out the research domain involved.

Decline as a Concept

The word *decline* has two principal meanings in the organizational literature. First, it is used to denote a cutback in the size of an organization's work force, profits, budget, clients, and so forth. In this case, an organization's command over environmental resources has been reduced as the result of either decreased competitive advantage (the organization has a smaller share of the market) or decreased environmental munificence (the total market has shrunk). A decrease in market share might reflect poor management, but a shrinking market generally does not. The erosion of an inner city's tax base, a decrease in a school district's enrollment, or the scarcity of oil during an embargo all reflect drastic changes in environmental

munificence that are beyond the control of a city department head, school superintendent, or gasoline retailer. The best an organization can do under these conditions is to anticipate a downturn and buffer the production technology from its effects by stockpiling raw materials, diversifying services or product lines, or expanding into recession-resistant markets. The object is to reduce the element of crisis in decline through the use of forecasting techniques, diversification, and contingency plans for rationing (Thompson, 1967).

The term *decline* is also used to describe the general climate, or orientation, in an organization. Using a life cycle model, some authors speak of mature organizations that become stagnant, bureaucratic, and passive, as evidenced by their insensitivity to new product developments, workers' interests, and customers' preferences. This condition of deterioration may or may not result in a loss of revenues. One of the traditional arguments against monopolistic markets is that they allow firms to become stagnant without experiencing serious repercussions. Similar observations have been made about the consequences of a lack of competition in the public sector (Roessner, 1979). Kolarska and Aldrich (1978), Ansoff (1970), and Cyert and March (1963) argue that under competitive conditions a decline in revenues triggers a revitalization cycle in the organization.

It is important to note that decline-as-stagnation does not necessarily imply an absolute decrease in income, whereas decline-as-cutback does. Stagnation is more often reflected as a decrease in the rate of increase than as an actual decrease. This distinction is useful because it highlights the fact that it is decline-as-cutback, not decline-as-stagnation, that is the emerging crisis ushered in by an era of scarcity. The problem of stagnating organizations, which has been around for generations, is actually less likely to occur during periods of scarcity since the two forms of decline are activated by opposing environmental conditions. Stagnation is more likely to occur during periods of abundance, whereas cutbacks are more likely during times of scarcity. The focus of this paper will be primarily on decline-as-cutback.

Literature on Organizational Decline

The literature related to organizational decline is very broad and diverse. Unfortunately, very little of this material reports empirical research. Instead the literature is dominated by case-study descriptions of declining organizations, armchair analyses of the causes of decline based on reviews of published case studies, and prescriptive guidelines for preventing or coping with decline. In the literature, decline has been examined at two levels of analysis: (1) within a population of organizations and (2) in individual organizations. Conceptual and empirical work focused at each level will be discussed in turn.

Population Level

The dominant theoretical orientation in this area is the natural selection model (Aldrich, 1979; Aldrich and Pfeffer, 1976; Campbell, 1969; Hannan and Freeman, 1978). Its principal components are three ecological processes that proponents argue occur in all biological and sociological populations. These processes, or stages, are variation, selection, and retention. In a population of organizations variation in member characteristics occurs as a result of either planned or unplanned actions. Consequently, the model does not require the assumption of administrative rationality or intentionality. Applications of this model have tended to overlook the historical development of variations and have concentrated primarily on their effect on survival. The second stage, selection, reflects a differential rate of survival within a population. As certain variations are reinforced by the environment, some members develop a superior competitive advantage. The retention stage signifies that certain positively valued characteristics have been preserved, duplicated, or reproduced in the population. Thus, the focus of the natural selection model is primarily on the birthrate (rather than on the death rate as many suppose) of a mutant strain (Stebbins, 1965). The competitive advantage of a species does not appear suddenly in one generation; instead, it emerges gradually over several generations as the number of its members possessing a positively valued characteristic increases geometrically.

This model has been strongly advocated by Kaufman (1973, 1975). He argues that most models of organizational processes are overly rational: "Our pride in personal accomplishment seems exaggerated" (1975, p. 145). He reasons that the evolutionary model explains everything that can be treated by rational models, plus a great deal more. In reviewing rational models, Kaufman (1975) asks, "Why do some organizations adhere to practices that caused others to die? Why isn't the world filled with old organizations? Why don't organizations with the smartest people always survive the longest?" (pp. 144–45).

While several other authors have noted the difficulties of applying the natural selection model literally to the study of organizations (Aldrich and Pfeffer, 1976; Weick, 1969; Aldrich, 1979; Stebbins, 1965; Child, 1972), it is clearly a useful conceptual tool for analyzing changes in the composition of a population of organizations over time. Examples of research using this approach include Nielsen and Hannan (1977), Aldrich and Reiss (1976), Freeman and Hannan (1975), and Hannan and Freeman (1978).

There are several researchable questions emerging from this literature that warrant further investigation. We will examine two. First, "What organizational characteristics will enhance adaptability to the environmental conditions anticipated in the future?" This question represents the heart of the organizational growth and decline issue. But in order to understand the processes of growth and decline, one must first understand the conditions that determine the more fundamental states of survival and death.

There is an extensive body of literature that predicts future environmental conditions. Some futurists have argued that our pluralistic, decentralized, capitalistic system is doomed. As it becomes more and more evident that contemporary institutions are unable to respond adequately to the increasing turbulence and complexity of their environment, they will be replaced with centralized planning and a socialist economy that will foster a more equalitarian distribution of increasingly scarce resources (Heilbronner, 1976; Commoner, 1976). Other futurists, however, have proposed that the present trend toward increased complexity and centralization will eventually be checked because it is antithetical to the American spirit. As a result, there will be even greater emphasis placed on individualistic enterprise and mediating structures (Miles, 1976; Berger and Neuhaus, 1977). For the most part, however, it is assumed that organizations in the future will be located in turbulent, centralized, and highly complex environments (Bennis, 1966; Vacca, 1973; Kaufman, 1973; Chadwick, 1977; Ansoff, 1965).

There has been considerably more disagreement over the ideal organizational characteristics for these environmental conditions. There is clearly not unanimous agreement regarding the characteristics that will be selected out by the anticipated turbulent and complex environmental conditions of the future. The most widely discussed organizational characteristics are size, age, auspices, internal control, and structural complexity. Although these have been included in many cross-sectional organizational studies, they lend themselves to population ecology research. Some have argued that large size and old age are liabilities under turbulent environmental conditions. As an organization increases in size and grows older, it tends to become more bureaucratic and inefficient; it finds it more difficult to change quickly; it makes more enemies as it encroaches on a greater number of sacred domains; it becomes a larger target for militants and regulators alike; and it has fewer options for expansion as it reaches the maximum share of its markets allowed by law (Rubin, 1979; Bennis and Slater, 1968).

Others have argued that small, young organizations will have the greatest difficulty surviving because they are inexperienced. The consequences of a bad decision or a sudden downturn in the economy are intensified in a small organization due to a lack of slack resources; and the negative effects of interpersonal conflict are more difficult to contain than in a large organization (Stinch-

combe, 1965; Levine, 1978; Kaufman, 1975; Boswell, 1973; Perrow, 1979). There is also considerable disagreement over the advantages of centralization versus decentralization in turbulent environments. Burns and Stalker (1961), Aldrich (1978), and Porter and Olsen (1976) have argued in favor of decentralization. For example, Porter and Olsen maintain that a generalist in an outpost office is more responsive to changing environmental conditions than a specialist in a centralized headquarters. But Hawley and Rogers (1974), Yarmolinsky (1975), and Rubin (1979) have countered that decentralization can immobilize a system facing a turbulent environment. Yarmolinsky uses the term *institutional paralysis* to describe the inability of universities to change, because no one interest group has sufficient power to alter the organization's course.

There is considerably more agreement about the adaptive value of "loose coupling." This concept addresses the extent to which units in an organization must interact with one another in order to perform their systemic functions. While loose coupling is generally associated with decentralization, there is a difference between the two concepts. Generally, when we think in terms of centralization and decentralization, we are treating the organization as an integrated whole. The parts of the organization are assumed to be working in concert toward common objectives, and the extent to which power is delegated is an indication of the number of people involved in making strategic plans for reaching these objectives.

A decoupled system is quite different. Its components share a low level of dependence, as shown by Thompson's (1967) concept of pooled interdependence. A business conglomerate exemplifies this concept, as each subsidiary has considerable power to select product lines, adjust prices, and alter its operating structure, as long as these decisions do not adversely affect profits. Several authors have argued that this type of institutional structure facilitates long-term adaptability (Weick, 1976; Aldrich, 1979; Glassman, 1973). Not only is this structural configuration highly flexible and therefore responsive, but the freedom given each unit to respond to its unique environment also tends to produce a large pool of internal variety over time. This diversity makes the organization robust by preventing it from being adversely affected by changes in one sector of its environment (Ashby, 1956; Hedberg, Nystrom, and Starbuck, 1976; Rubin, 1979). The principal liability of this design is that it is extremely difficult for the organization as a whole to make purposive coordinated changes if those become necessary. The operating units strongly resist the usurpation of their autonomy, and their response to programs initiated by the central office varies from foot dragging to defiant opposition.

A loosely coupled structure is therefore best suited for organizations whose units do not need to respond to environmental changes in unison. The institutional paralysis in the face of massive environmental change, discussed by Yarmolinsky (1975), results when an organization that consists of sequentially or reciprocally interdependent parts (Thompson, 1967) adopts the structure of a holding company simply because this design is compatible with the institution's values of autonomy and self-governance.

There is also considerable agreement regarding the effect of auspices on organizational responsiveness. Many authors have noted the lack of incentives for innovation in the public sector, and Rainey, Backoff, and Levine (1976) have identified several key differences between public and private organizations. Compared to private organizations, public organizations have less market exposure, more environmental constraints, and are more subject to political influences that affect their internal operations. As a result, these organizations are marked by more complex and contradictory goals, less autonomy, less delegation of authority, more turnover, greater difficulty in linking individual performance with incentives, lower overall worker satisfaction and commitment, and greater variation in member characteristics and abilities. Drucker (1974) has proposed that the key difference between public and private organizations that influences their incentive to innovate is the "mode of payment." Public organizations are

rewarded by budget increases, while private organizations are rewarded by satisfied customers and repeat business. Roessner (1979) attributes the lower number of innovations in public organizations to the fact that innovations in the private sector are stimulated by production efficiency while innovations in the public sector are motivated by bureaucratic self-interest (Yin, 1978). The trend towards "third-sector" organizations, for example, the U.S. Postal Service, reflects efforts by the federal government to make key public service organizations more responsive to market conditions.

The fact that analysts in the field do not totally agree on the constellation of organizational characteristics that enhance adaptability in turbulent and complex environments signals a strong need for further research in this area. Although a number of empirical studies have tested various contingency theories of organizational design (Pennings, 1975; Dewar and Werbel, 1979), this line of research has been flawed by a lack of longitudinal data. While studies of business failures typically examine the performance of a large subject pool over time, these studies generally rely exclusively on secondary data (Brough in Argenti, 1976; Altman, 1971). Consequently, their analyses tend not to be very rich or insightful. It is true that these studies are nicely complemented by several published case studies of the collapse of notable business enterprises (Smith, 1963; Birchfield, 1972; Daughen and Binzen, 1971), but there remains a substantial need for more systematic research on the organizational characteristics that foster adaptability. Populations of organizations that vary according to the salient organizational characteristics identified by Hedberg, Nystrom, and Starbuck (1976), Argenti (1976), and others should be identified and studied over time to determine whether these characteristics indeed predict organizational performance. The alternative societal conditions predicted for the future could be identified on a small scale today, and a study of the survival rates of various organizational configurations under these conditions could be conducted. Another possibility for this type of research is to simulate various types of environmental conditions in a laboratory setting and thus to build on the work of Miles (1980) and McCaskey (1974).

A second research question focusing on populations of organizations is, "What effect does decline in one organization have on other members of a population?" While this is not an ecological question, it is related to populations. This question is prompted by the work of Aiken and Hage (1968), who proposed that organizations respond to scarcity by establishing joint programs to distribute the costs of innovation. In their model, staff members propose more innovations than an organization can fund. To make up the difference, other organizations are invited to cosponsor new ventures. It is logical to assume that when resources shrink this process will increase. One of the consequences of joint programs is that they increase the couplings among members of a population; if only a few members of a population have to retrench, the entire network becomes richly joined. As a result, the network becomes less stable, less flexible, and, hence, less adaptable (Weick, 1976, Aldrich, 1979). A study is currently underway to test whether this deductive model can be verified in populations that contain declining organizations (Whetten, 1979a).

Organizational Level

Organizational decline has, to some extent, been examined at the population level, but most of the literature has used the organization as the unit of analysis. While the intent of population ecology studies is to identify gross organizational characteristics that predict survival, the research focus at the organizational level is on internal processes. The research question shifts from "Which members of the organizational population present at Time 1 were also present at Time 2?" to "What is happening in these organizations as they experience and react to the changing conditions between Time 1 and Time 2?" While the first question is analogous to a biologist's study of changes in a gene pool over generations, the second question has no analogue in biology since it focuses on the purposive actions unique to social systems. The

first examines structural configurations, the second examines the structure-generating processes. The first is conducted by a diagnostician who, on the basis of surface conditions, makes inferences about what is inside; the second is conducted by an anatomist who examines internal conditions directly.

The theoretical perspective most commonly used in this type of organizational research is the resource dependence model (Yuchtman and Seashore, 1967; Pfeffer and Salancik, 1978; Aldrich and Pfeffer, 1976), which is closely related to the political economy model (Wamsley and Zald, 1973; Benson, 1975). These models assume that managers make strategic decisions based on their assessment of the political and economic conditions in their environment or, more specifically, that managers take actions to maintain adequate supplies of political legitimacy and economic resources.

Writers in this area tend to emphasize that organizations are either passive reactors or aggressive initiators in their dealings with the environment. This ideological split carries over to the study of decline. Some writers profess an organizational life cycle theory that includes an "inexorable and irreversible movement toward the equilibrium of death. Individual, family, firm, nation, and civilization all follow the same grim law, and the history of any organism is strikingly reminiscent of the rise and fall of populations on the road to extinction" (Boulding, 1950, p. 38). (See also Downs, 1967.) The "success breeds failure" and "failure stimulates further failure" organizational decline models that will be discussed later reflect this fatalistic philosophy (Starbuck, Greve, and Hedberg, 1978; Argenti, 1976).

A more optimistic view of decline is reflected in the work of Ansoff (1970) and Cyert and March (1963). These authors present a homeostatic model in which a decline in profits (or slack resources) triggers corrective actions to increase profits. While we are far from being able to make a definitive statement about the utility of these two models, the field is gradually accumulating enough case studies of decline to make possible a description of the contextual conditions under which each is likely to predominate. These studies tend to emphasize (1) the source of decline, (2) an organization's response to decline, or (3) the effects of decline on other organizational activities. Works addressing these three topics will be discussed in turn.

Sources of Decline

The kinds of crises that, if responded to improperly, precipitate organizational decline can originate within an organization (Greiner, 1972) or, more frequently, within the environment (Scott, 1976). Some authors have discussed the sources of crises as though they were objective phenomena (Balderston, 1972), while others have argued that the real source of a crisis is in the misperceptions of organizational members (Starbuck, Greve, and Hedberg, 1978). A useful typology must therefore accommodate both orientations. A typology proposed by Levine (1978) meets this requirement since it examines both internal and external causes of crises. His four sources of decline are organizational atrophy, political vulnerability, problem depletion, and environmental entropy. These labels must be modified to extend this typology beyond the public sector for which it was developed. A modified model appropriate for business organizations as well contains organizational atrophy, vulnerability, loss of legitimacy, and environmental entropy. Such a typology includes a much wider range of causes than those previously proposed in the business literature. For instance, Miller (1977) and Argenti (1976) identify such causes as impulsive decisions that overextend the organization's assets, not responding to change, an executive who is either too powerful or poorly informed (absentee owner), and taking unnecessary risks. A discussion of the literature related to the modified model's four causes of decline follows.

Organizational Atrophy

The consequences that result when organizations lose muscle tone are a recurring theme in the literature. A recent formulation of this argument has appeared in the work of Hedberg, Starbuck, Nystrom, and their associates as the "success breeds failure" syndrome. Following the logic of Cyert and March (1963), they argue that organizations formulate heuristic programs for dealing with recurring problems. Unfortunately, "because situations appear equivalent as long as they can be handled by the same programs, programs remain in use after the situations they fit have faded away" (Starbuck and Hedberg, 1977, p. 250). The result is the often maligned phenomenon of organizational inertia (Behn, 1977; Cyert, 1978). Organizations that habitually use programs based on their previous utility tend to become desensitized to environmental changes. As a result, organizations that were the most successful in the past become the most vulnerable to failure in the future.

While a decrease in responsiveness is generally associated with senility, this does not always hold true in organizations. The debilitating effects of success can occur at any age. Tornedon and Boddewyn (1974) in their study of divestiture found a common pattern: young, aggressive companies would generate high profits that then prompted the acquisition of overseas subsidiaries — often before the establishment of a policy for long-term overseas growth. Because of this topsy-turvy growth pattern produced by mercurial success, it would later become necessary for these companies to divest themselves of many of their acquisitions as changing business conditions made it apparent that the organizations had overextended themselves. This sawtooth cycle of rapid growth followed by drastic retrenchment is common, and it documents the fact that for organizations, as for human beings, the incidence of death is not perfectly correlated with poor health or old age. For example, Altman (1971) reports that in 1970 over 279 million-dollar firms went broke. Further, in terms of age, he reports that one third of bankrupt businesses were less than three years old, 53 percent were younger than five, and 23 percent were over ten. (Surprisingly, only 2 percent of the failures were less than one year old.)

Figure 1. Three Patterns of Organizational Decline

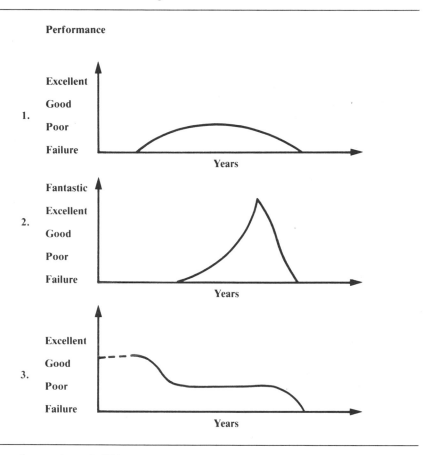

Source: Argenti, 1976.

Argenti (1976) has identified three patterns of organizational decline. These are shown in Figure 1. The second and third patterns illustrate the different varieties of the "success breeds failure" syndrome that we have discussed. An organization that follows the third pattern has established an excellent performance record. It is a major producer in its industry and is highly regarded as a solid ongoing business concern—examples would be Penn Central and Rolls-Royce. At the point of initial decline the company has lost touch "with [its] market or [its] customers or [its] employees. [Hence,] although a major change has occurred, no adequate response has been made. Perhaps two competitors have merged but the chief executive has decided 'it won't affect us.' Or the company has had its first strike, which the board dismisses as being 'one of those things' when in fact it is a sign that [it has] lost touch with the shop floor" (Argenti, 1976, p. 162). This pattern reflects the classic case of a large, old organization deluded by the myth of invulnerability. Such an organization confuses the achievement of age with immortality, that is, being immune to the travails of this life. As Argenti notes, this smugness precipitates a slow but very painful death.

The second trajectory of decline illustrates the risk of mercurial success. In this case, rapid growth is followed by a precipitous decline because managers, intoxicated with success, become careless. Typically this type of organization is formed by a charismatic entrepreneur afflicted with the Midas touch. Unfortunately, counsel to level off the organization onto a steady-state plateau is dismissed. This illustrates the extreme case of a growth-oriented business ideology, as reflected in the refrain, "Beyond the clouds lie the stars. Beyond the stars lies the Great Absurd" (Argenti, 1976, p. 159). This problem appears to be age-old. It is reflected in Jethro's counsel to Moses in the Book of Exodus and was discussed by Weber (1947) as the need to routinize charisma. In his study of an English public school, Pettigrew (1979) found that the most critical phase in the organization's life cycle was at the peak of its early growth curve. At this point it was necessary for the entrepreneur-founder to resign and appoint a "manager" who could solidify his gains and initiate the mundane rules and coordination mechanisms required for continued development. Pettigrew reports (personal correspondence) that if the entrepreneur had not been replaced at this point in the organization's development, precipitous decline would have followed.

Neither slow-growing nor fast-growing organizations are immune to decline, although the two types of organizations face different problems. The fast-growing organization is experienced in handling crises (Kotter and Sathe, 1978), so it has already established elaborate problem-solving routines. This organization's vulnerability to decline lies in its failure to identify sagging performance as a problem rather than in inadequate problem response. Having had little experience with this type of problem, the organization is likely to discount symptoms of impending decline. In contrast, slow-growing organizations tend to be very sensitive to changes in their vital signs. Hence, their vulnerability to decline is not in problem recognition but in problem response. These organizations have so little slack that they may not be able to survive long enough to respond to the problem.

Vulnerability

The second source of organizational decline is vulnerability. In his classic work on life cycles, Stinchcombe (1965) noted that organizations are particularly vulnerable in their infancy. During this time they must overcome the "liabilities of newness," some of which are temporary inefficiency due to inexperience, frequent interpersonal conflict resulting from distrust, and the lack of a stable set of ties to customers, suppliers, and regulators. The difficulty that young organizations have clearing these initial hurdles is reflected in the death-rate statistics for businesses reported earlier. From these it appears that "infant mortality is more common than senility" (Argenti, 1976, p. 7). The first decline trajectory in Figure 1 highlights the vulnerability of young organizations. The problems caused by the inexperience of youth illustrate the "failure breeds failure" form of decline. Argenti notes that business organizations that just never seem to get moving are typically formed by a person with a technical orientation, for example, an engineer, architect, or accountant.

In the public sector, political vulnerability is reflected in an agency's inability to resist budget decrements. Levine (1978) discusses some of the factors that contribute to vulnerability: "Small size, internal conflict, and changes in leadership, for example, seem less telling than the lack of a base of expertise or the absence of a positive self-image and history of excellence. However, an organization's age may be the most accurate predictor of bureaucratic vulnerability. Contrary to biological reasoning, aged organizations are more flexible than young organizations and therefore rarely die or even shrink very much" (p. 319). The postulated negative correlation between age and vulnerability is supported by Kaufman's (1976) study of turnover in federal agencies. He found that newly established agencies had the highest death rate of all federal agencies during the period from 1923 to 1973.

The fragility of a public institution's base of political support has been discussed by Mitnick

(1978) and Shefter (1977). Shefter outlines a three-stage model of municipal government fiscal crisis. First, a social group (such as the unions in New York City) gains considerable power and demands a larger share of the public benefits. Second, the government agrees to the demands either because the group is too powerful to fight or because it is a natural ally. Third, the government finds itself too weak to finance these new claims by cutting benefits to other groups or by raising taxes. This disparity between promise and reality then triggers a political crisis that typically results in new government leadership.

Loss of Legitimacy

Benson (1975) has stressed the importance of legitimacy as an organizational resource and noted the propensity in some organizations to overemphasize the acquisition of economic resources and to overlook the value of cultivating political acceptance. This legitimacy is especially salient in the public sector. Rothman (1972) has linked the rise and fall of various criminal justice programs with shifts in societal ideology. As the prevailing views shifted from incarceration to rehabilitation of criminals, for example, an organization gained or lost public funding support, depending on which value it embodied.

Levine (1978) has noted that problem depletion is a major cause of loss of legitimacy. Once the problem for which an agency was organized has been resolved, that agency should presumably be terminated. However, Behn (1977) provides several interesting examples of the unrealistic optimism of this conclusion. For instance, the Temporary Commission of Investigation of the state of New York has recently issued its sixteenth annual report. The Federal Metal and Non-Metallic Mine Safety Board of Review was abolished only after its executive secretary confessed in a front-page interview that he had no work to perform. The ability of an agency or program to establish a powerful constituency that allows it to function independently of its enabling constitution makes

it extremely difficult to terminate what appear to be anachronous organizations. This fact is reflected in the poor track record of American presidents who have attempted to overhaul the executive branch, despite the sage counsel of astute political and administrative advisers (Brown, 1977). Reflecting on this problem, Bardach (1976) and Biller (1976) lament that in general founders of new public programs do their job of institution building too well. As a result, it is most difficult to dismantle ineffective agencies. Behn (1976) argues that supporters of an existing organization have the upper hand in a debate over the fate of a facility because their examples of specific problems that would result from a termination order ("ten clients would have to travel 200 miles to receive comparable life-sustaining treatments") are more compelling than the opponents' vague complaints about inefficiency or ineffectiveness. Hence, while loss of legitimacy is a potential source of decline and termination, it is one of the environmental threats that many organizations are remarkably capable of deflecting.

Environmental Entropy

The fourth source of decline stems from the reduced capacity of the environment to support an organization. Cyert (1978) has proposed that organizations in this situation have basically two options: (1) they can find another ecological niche, or (2) they can scale down their operation. In the literature, the first (proactive) alternative has been emphasized by business authors, while the second (reactive) alternative has been discussed primarily in the public and educational administration fields. The second group views the management of a declining organization as the unfortunate victim of circumstances, while the first group regards a crisis-ridden management as having neither the vision nor the will to initiate the innovations necessary to reverse the downward spiral of decline. Exemplifying the business orientation, Starbuck and Hedberg (1977), Ross and Kami (1973), and Barmash (1973) all argue that an organization's presence in a stagnating environment says more about the organization's management than about the capacity or potential of the environment. Barmash (1973) concludes his study of fifteen corporate disasters with a clear statement of this orientation: "Corporations are managed by men; and men, never forget, manage corporations to suit themselves. Thus corporate calamities are calamities created by men" (p. 299). Hall's (1976) analysis of the demise of the *Saturday Evening Post* supports this position inasmuch as he noted that the egos of top administrators clouded their judgment at critical points in the magazine's life cycle.

In contrast, work done in municipal public finance (Muller, 1975; Clark and others, 1976) and university administration (Green, 1974; Furniss, 1974; Trow, 1975) tends to emphasize the passive retrenchment option. This literature assumes that public organizations are captives of their environments—tethered to declining enrollments and eroding tax bases. This orientation is reflected in Biller's (1976) recommendation that public organizations adopt a matrix design so that expendable programs can be cut back easily when retrenchment becomes necessary.

While this dichotomy between the public- and private-sector literatures certainly reflects the fact that businesses have considerably more flexibility than public organizations in changing their goals, product lines, and so on, it also appears to reflect a different orientation regarding organization-environment relations in public and private organizations. Glassberg (1978), Boulding (1975), Cyert (1978), Millett (1977), and Molotch (1976) have all argued that one of the greatest needs in the public sector is for a new cadre of leaders who will aggressively respond to declining resources. This suggests a promising topic for research. The need to construct explanations for events in one's immediate environment has been discussed by Weick (1969, 1977a) and Pondy (1977), but little research has been conducted on this topic. Recently Bougon, Weick, and Binkhorst (1977) have used a methodology called *causal mapping* to trace this "sense making" process. Organization members' beliefs regarding the sources of crises

provide a rich setting for extending this pioneering work. Since the definition of a problem influences the solutions considered, it would be interesting to explore the possibility of institutional paradigms (i.e., views in education, penology, city governments, business, etc.) that influence members in different types of organizations to construct highly predictable, but institutionally different, causal explanations for decline. The work reviewed here suggests that these paradigm-grounded causal maps do exist, but few attempts have been made to systematically study this phenomenon within a comparative perspective.

A related research topic involves the practice of denying that a crisis exists. Why do some administrators respond quickly to the first signs of decline while others explain them away? In his study of school districts with declining enrollments, Rodekohr (1974) found that several superintendents refused to accept the validity of data showing a decline in enrollment. In some cases this response was the result of the brief tenure of the administrator, but in other instances the superintendent was apparently simply not acknowledging this threatening information. "Creative accounting" is a related defense mechanism identified in several case studies of business failures (Argenti, 1976). In some cases business managers deliberately hide negative financial data so as not to alarm stockholders and bankers. In other cases, however, managers simply will not accept the implications of the negative information conveyed by doomsayers, and they juggle the accounting record until it gives what they are sure is a more accurate (and considerably more optimistic) reflection of the organization's health.

Responses to Decline

After managers have acknowledged that a crisis situation exists and have constructed a causal map for making sense out of it, a response is formulated. The literature on management responses to decline can be best organized around the central issue of attitude toward change. Figure 2 shows a continuum from "change positively valued" to

Figure 2. Management's Responses to Environmentally Induced Change

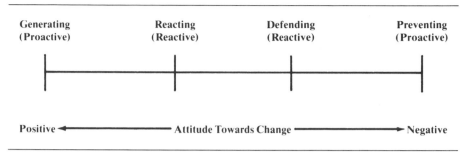

"change negatively valued." The categories "generating," "responding," "defending," and "preventing" highlight important benchmarks along this dimension. Unlike the usual typology for organization-environment relations, this one does not range from reactive to proactive (Thompson, 1967). Instead, the two extreme categories are proactive strategies, while the center two are reactive responses. [This typology is similar to a model of managerial response to stress developed by Burgoyne (1975). His categories are avoidance, defense mechanisms, and learning. It is also similar to one proposed by Miles, Snow, and Pfeffer (1974): domain defenders, reluctant reactors, anxious analyzers, enthusiastic prospectors.]

Defending

The defensive response to impending decline is typically found in highly bureaucratic settings or in ideologically based institutions. Merton's (1957) classic work on the bureaucratic mentality proposed that members of large (usually governmental) organizations tend to undergo a psychological means-end shift over time; that is, adhering to the organization's rules and procedures becomes more important to them than fulfilling the objectives for which the rules were originally created. Thus, members will likely respond to a proposed budget cut by defending the efficiency of the organization and the diligence of its members (Whetten, 1979b; Pfeffer and Salancik, 1978). In an ideologically based organization, such as a mental health facility, members are geared to defend the integrity

of the institution. Hence, they will likely react to a proposed budget cut by arguing that the government "ought" to maintain its commitment to the social values embodied in the mission of the threatened organization (Hirschman, 1970). This is illustrated in the case of a drug rehabilitation center in New York City that had a recidivism rate of 100 percent. When city officials attempted to close the facility, political supporters accused the city of dropping its commitment to drug rehabilitation. As a result the officials felt compelled to continue funding the program even though it was not fulfilling its intended purpose (Roessner, 1979). Thus, while the ideologist defends his or her organization by pointing out the symbolic political and social implications of a cutback, the bureaucrat uses facts and figures to demonstrate that his or her organization does not deserve to be cut back because its members have been both diligent and frugal.

Responding

The responding mode has been discussed extensively in the literature on public administration. Zald and Ash (1966) and Brouillette and Quarantilli (1971) have proposed models for predicting responses to decline. Levine (1978) has critiqued the common approaches to retrenchment, for example, across-the-board cuts, cuts based on performance, layoffs based on seniority. Mitnick (1978) outlined five steps for an agency responding to threatened termination. Furniss (1974), Smart and Vertinsky (1977), and Starbuck, Greve, and

Hedberg (1978) propose that a special decision-making task force be formed to address issues of decline. They recommended that this "crisis corps" rely primarily on informal power and informal communication channels. This group would determine the severity of the crisis, present alternative courses of action, and in general prepare the organization to "weather out the storm." Boulding (1975) has called for the establishment of an "invisible college" for administrative officials in educational institutions to facilitate the exchange of lessons learned in responding to declining revenues and enrollments. To complement this informal network, a cadre of consultants who specialize in the management of declining organizations would be extremely useful. These people would be called into organizations in shock much as Red Adair is called into oil fields on fire.

Outside observers are particularly helpful in times of stress since they can help management avoid the common mistakes of solving the wrong problem and attaching the wrong solution to the right problem (Cohen, March, and Olsen, 1972). The first error is exemplified by the tendency to solve symptoms rather than underlying problems. Under crisis conditions managers prefer quick responses. An agreeable solution, even for the wrong problem, relieves tension and gives management the satisfaction of achieving success in the face of failure. Unfortunately, the true problem may continue to grow and surface later as a calamity. A classic example of this management fallacy was depicted in the recent film *China Syndrome*. After a malfunction at a nuclear power generator, management thought that it had found the cause but overlooked evidence of more fundamental problems that nearly resulted in an ecological catastrophe.

The common error of attaching the wrong solution to the right problem in managing municipal financial crises and university decline has been noted by Glassberg (1978), Cyert (1978), Wildavsky (1964), and Cyert and March (1963). Their concern is based on theoretical work in the area of decision making. Wildavsky (1964) argues that decision makers tend to make incremental responses because "men cannot rationally choose between alternatives drastically different from present reality" (Dahl and Lindblom, 1953, p. 83). Cyert and March (1963) describe a similar tendency called "problemistic search"; that is, people tend to search for solutions in the area closest to the problem. It appears that this tendency increases as a function of stress (Smart and Vertinsky, 1977; Bozeman and Slusher, 1978). Glassberg (1978) argues that one of the most common mistakes in handling municipal fiscal crises is that public officials propose incremental solutions for quantum problems. In his study of the decline of the *Saturday Evening Post,* Hall (1976) found that problemistic search was one of the factors that precipitated that magazine's decline spiral. Between 1944 and 1946 the number of subscribers to the *Post* increased substantially. This in turn greatly increased production costs, and these led to a decline in the profit margin. Management's response was to increase the cost of a subscription, but this decision, which had the effect of drastically cutting back the number of subscribers, initiated a period of stagnation and eventual decline.

The defensive and responsive reactions described in this section have been discussed as though they were mutually exclusive decisions. In practice they are often linked together to form a more complex response pattern. In his analysis of the decline of civilizations, Toynbee (1947) noted that the initial response of a society to the threat of an invader is to retrench to traditional values. However, if the threat intensifies, then the victim tends to capitulate and embrace wholeheartedly the culture of the aggressors. This willingness to accept the bad aspects of the invaders' culture along with the good eventually leads to the degeneration of the host society. The same pattern of retrenchment and eventual capitulation can be found in threatened organizations.

Preventing

A great deal has been written about organizations' deliberate efforts to manipulate their environments to increase their competitive advantages and to remove potential threats (Hedberg, Nystrom, and Starbuck, 1976; Perrow, 1979; Penrose, 1952; Post, 1978; Galbraith, 1971). Tactics used include price fixing and other illegal practices (Staw and Szwajkowski, 1975), acquisitions (Pfeffer, 1972; Markham, 1973), buying political influence (Perrow, 1972), changing public opinion and influencing consumer preferences (Post, 1978), and shaping economic and social policy (Sethi, 1977; Post, 1978). The logic involved in describing these practices is that since organizations must act to avoid uncertainty, administrators must act to prevent the need for responsive change (as opposed to self-initiated change). The skill with which managers can use these tactics came out in an interview with one of John D. Rockefeller's sons. Asked if his father had ever broken any laws in building his immense oil empire, the son responded that he could not think of any laws broken by his father but that he could name several that were enacted because of him. The extent to which businesses should be restrained (either by self-regulation or by outside regulation) from engaging in practices that reduce the need for responsive change, while producing harmful side effects for others, is at the heart of the current debate over corporate social responsibility (Marris, 1974; Preston and Post, 1975; Walton, 1977).

Generating

The opposite attitude toward change is expressed by writers in the generating category. While the literature in the previous three categories was based on descriptions of current business practices, the writers in this category tend to be academics who encourage businessmen to turn about and embrace the enemy, that is, to make a virtue of responsive change. Relying on case studies of organizations that suffered substantial losses because they were too slow to respond, these authors argue in favor of "self-designing organizations." These organizations are characterized by experimentation, informal communication lines, slack resources, loose criteria for performance evaluation, tolerance for occasional failure, ad hoc jobs, frequent movement of personnel within and between organizations, and, most of all, a high incidence of innovation (Hedberg, Nystrom, and Starbuck,

1976, 1977; Starbuck, Greve, and Hedberg, 1978; Weick, 1977b; Staw, 1977; Bennis and Slater, 1968; Landau, 1973). Further, Hedberg, Nystrom, and Starbuck (1976) argue that these organizations should look more like collapsible tents than like stone palaces; that is, they should be characterized by minimal consensus, minimal contentment, minimal affluence, minimal faith, minimal consistency, and minimal rationality.

In reflecting on this literature, one is struck by the telling differences between the descriptive and prescriptive work. On the one hand, writers describe managers as being skilled at rigging the environment to prevent the need for change, slow in responding to unpredicted changes, inclined to select well-used solutions to problems, and disposed to think of innovation only in terms of incremental changes in current practices. On the other hand, the other writers warn managers that these practices will not be positively selected by the environments of tomorrow. This discrepancy reinforces the need for more ecological studies of organizations attempting to survive under different environmental conditions.

There is also a need for further theoretical development of the self-design orientation. The logical adequacy of this approach has been questioned by Wildavsky (1972) and Bozeman and Slusher (1978). In addition to responding to these criticisms, proponents need to give more consideration to the organizational and societal implications that widespread adoption of their self-design model would have. The prospect of managers, stockholders, workers, government regulators, and supporting social institutions all positively reinforcing frequent and significant innovations in production organizations suggests the possibility of a runaway innovation cycle that would have highly deleterious effects. There must be some negative loops built into the model to serve as a homeostatic mechanism, but thus far insufficient attention has been focused on this need. It is also questionable whether organizations have the capacity to become self-designing. This model suggests a level of rationality that organizations may simply not be capable of achieving, *especially during times of crisis when the need to self-design is greatest.* The work of March and Simon (1958), Cyert and March (1963), Cohen, March, and Olsen (1972), Rubin (1977), Benveniste (1977), and Smart and Vertinsky (1977) suggest that this is indeed the case. Forrester's (1971) "Counterintuitive Behavior of Social Systems" gives weight to this conclusion:

> Our first insights into complex social systems came from our corporate work. Time after time we have gone into a corporation which is having severe and well-known difficulties. The difficulties can be major and obvious, such as a falling market share, low profitability, or instability of employment. . . . Generally speaking we find that people perceive correctly their immediate environment. . . . In a troubled company, people are usually trying in good conscience and to the best of their abilities to solve the major difficulties. Policies are being followed at the various points in the organization on the presumption that they will alleviate the difficulties. One can combine these policies into a computer model to show the consequences of how the policies interact with one another. In many instances it then emerges that the known policies describe a system which actually causes the troubles. In other words, the known and intended practices of the organization are fully sufficient to create the difficulty, regardless of what happens outside the company or in the marketplace. In fact, a downward spiral develops in which the presumed solution makes the difficulty worse and thereby causes redoubling of the presumed solution [p. 55].

This observation underscores the need for the self-design proponents to reconcile the incongruity between their prescriptions and the natural tendency for administrators under stress to reflexively select responses contrary to the prescribed responses. The fact that this incongruity exists is not by itself problematic, but the fact that it is hardly mentioned in the self-design literature is troubling. If managers under stress need to behave contrary to their reflexive patterns, considerable thought and research will be required to discover methods for countering these natural tendencies. Hence, the self-design literature needs to move beyond its prescriptive mode and come to grips with the knotty issues of implementation, especially during periods of stress-inducing decline.

Effects of Decline

A declining resource base has widespread effects. It affects the state of mind and career patterns of the staff and the manner in which business is conducted in the organization. At the level of the individual organizational member, the most profound effect of decline is increased stress. As slack resources dwindle, the margin for error in an organization decreases. While the stakes for making good decisions increase, the penalties for making bad ones also increase. As the tension and pressure mount, morale tends to sag (Behn, 1978) and high turnover follows (Levine, 1979). To check turnover in declining organizations, Levine (1979) suggests new forms of compensation that make exit very costly (for example, deferred payment schedules for fringe benefits like profit sharing and retirement).

A related consequence is increased interpersonal conflict. In declining organizations more people find that they are losing more often with little prospect for making up current resource losses in future allocations (Levine, 1978; Starbuck, Greve, and Hedberg, 1978). To alleviate these negative consequences, Cyert (1978) proposes establishing new goals and evaluation criteria early in the decline process as a means of reducing uncertainty and increasing integration. Yetton (1975) has argued for new leadership models adjusted to the stress factor in crisis situations. In this vein, Glassberg (1978) has examined the leadership styles of mayors that are most effective during fiscal crises, and Yetton (1975) and Levine (1979) both note that, in order to avoid conflict, managers in decline conditions rely less on participative decision making than they normally would.

This literature points out the need for research on the ability of conventional theories about leadership, conflict resolution, decision making, and communication to explain behavior during the crisis of retrenchment. Since they were typically developed and verified by means of observations from expanding organizations, there are scarcely any organizational models or theories that do not require recalibration for conditions of decline.

One of the more disturbing effects of decline is that it tends to penalize most those who can least afford it—and in some cases least deserve it. This occurs both at the individual and organizational levels. Generally, the first to be dismissed during a period of retrenchment are the low-skilled, low-income, minority (including women), young, or very old staff members. These are the people who will have the most difficulty absorbing the loss of wages and finding new jobs (Levine, 1978). The organizational effect of this action is to decrease the internal pool of variability within the organization and increase the average age of the labor pool (Levine, 1979). When these effects of involuntary discharges are coupled with the fact that those who choose to leave the organization are those best qualified to formulate creative responses, the overall result of decline on personnel turnover is to produce a "regression to the mean" in labor pool qualifications.

A similar phenomenon occurs at the departmental level. The most common form of retrenchment is to distribute the cuts more or less evenly across all units. This option is politically more feasible than cutting off an entire program or department because it is less likely to be sharply contested. The consequence of this approach is that a cutback hurts those that deserve it the least, that is, the most efficient. A highly efficient unit has the greatest difficulty implementing a retrenchment order since it had operated with less fat in the past (Levine, 1979).

Another effect of decline is on the rate of organizational innovation. While the literature suggests a strong relationship between decline and innovation, the sign (plus or minus) of the correlation is disputed. On the one hand, some authors have argued that decline will hamper innovation. For example, Smart and Vertinsky (1977) and Bozeman and Slusher (1978) have proposed that during crises managers are paralyzed by a fear of failure. Hence, they become more conservative rather than more innovative. In the public sector this takes the form of trimming the fat from existing programs rather than exploring radically new service delivery alternatives (Whetten, 1979b). On the other hand, Wilson (1972) has argued that organizations are not likely to adopt significant innovations until they experience a major crisis. The regenerative benefits of crises have also been stressed by Lindblom (1968) and Glassberg (1978).

This lack of consensus regarding the effect of decline on innovation highlights again the incongruity between prescriptions for and descriptions of the management of stressful situations and underscores the pressing need for more research on decision making under conditions of stress. One hypothesis that warrants examination is that organizations follow the response pattern of threatened nations, as this pattern was described by Toynbee (1947). A small amount of stress may cause members to "clutch," that is, to have their creative faculties impaired by fear. However, as the threat increases in intensity, a threshold may be reached that triggers a desperate effort to generate creative alternatives. This proposition is consistent with Miller's "general theory for the behavioral sciences." Miller (1955) argues that all "living systems respond to continuously increasing stress first by a lag in response, then by an overcompensatory response, and finally by catastrophic collapse of the system" (p. 27). Miller's three-stage response model highlights a paradox of innovation. If we first assume that the overcompensatory response of an organization facing decline-induced stress is to initiate multiple innovations as an act of desperation, then we can conclude that under certain conditions innovation actually contributes to a system's collapse. Of course, not all innovations have this dysfunctional consequence, but when they are initiated under conditions of stress, it appears highly probable that this unintended consequence will result.

This conclusion points out the need for more research into the effect of innovation on decline. While it is implied in the self-design literature that a high level of innovation is associated with high organizational performance, others have argued that the relationship is curvilinear and that either too little or too much innovation leads to low performance (Smith, 1963; Argenti, 1976). This proposition is consistent with research on the effect of stress on individual performance that has shown performance to be highest at an optimal level of stress, that is, the highest point on an inverted U curve (Schuler, 1979).

The ultimate effect of decline is death—whether this is the outcome of a deliberate effort to terminate an ineffective public program or the consequence of poor management in a small business. While research on organizational death is beginning to emerge in the literature (Kaufman, 1976; Hall, 1976; Aldrich and Reiss, 1976; Behn, 1976), it is hampered by a lack of consensus on what organizational death represents. Does it occur when there is a change in the name of an organization? When all its members are replaced? When the facility is moved? Does it make a difference if these events are the result of a merger, as compared with a business failure? One of the most difficult situations to classify is the case in which a legal corporation ceases to exist but its organizational operation continues to function. In the business literature an organization is divided into three tiers. The enterprise controls the economic assets, the managerial level controls human resources, and the firm directs the production activity. In many mergers (and divestitures) there is no change at the firm or managerial levels—only the legal name of the enterprise is changed. Similarly, in a study of federal agencies, Kaufman (1976) found that the functions performed by a terminated agency are often transferred to another agency.

Some clarity can be achieved by distinguishing between the death and the failure of organizations. A study of death examines whether an organization still exists, a study of failure focuses on the causes of death. Organizational failure connotes total ineffectiveness due to managerial incompetence, political vulnerability, or environmental entropy (Pfeffer and Salancik, 1978). Hence, a failure would be considered a fatality in an organizational decline study even if its staff and programs (or products) are transferred to other organizations. In the business sector, organizational death due to failure is qualitatively very different from organizational death due to transformation, as in the case of a merger. An organization that is acquired must by definition have some marketable assets. The fact that it is purchased indicates that it is currently successful or has the potential to become successful. While both types of organizational death present interesting research issues, death due to failure is more closely related to our interest in the organizational consequences of the emerging era of scarcity.

Conclusion

The objectives of this chapter were to bring together a diverse body of literature relating to organizational decline and to identify some important research topics in the process. We have discussed the concept of decline and examined the conceptual and empirical work related to this topic at the population and organizational levels of analysis. At the organizational level we examined the causes, responses to, and effects of decline.

This review has identified two major disjunctions in the literature. First, authors addressing decline in the public sector tend to have a different orientation from those writing about crises in business organizations. In the business sector, organizational death is viewed as suicide, while in the public sector it is treated as homicide. In the private sector, declining profits are regarded as evidence of stagnating management rather than of environmental scarcity. Conversely, in the public sector, decline tends to be viewed as a characteristic of the environment rather than of the organization. Therefore, authors in this area speak of cutback management as though that were the only option. In the private sector this response is regarded as a last recourse—appropriate only after all proactive strategies have failed. This discrepant orientation reflects a difference in the level of autonomy in the two sectors. Public administrators generally have less freedom than private ones to relocate their organization to a new ecological niche. However, several authors have noted that this restriction is often more apparent than real; that is, public administrators may have more degrees of freedom than they choose to consider. Hence, the need for a more aggressive breed of public administrators has been stressed. To facilitate this process, the need for more dialogue between business and public administrators and for mechanisms for disseminating information about innovative options selected by public administrators have been noted.

Second, there is a significant discrepancy between descriptions of how managers actually react to decline-induced crises, and prescriptions for how they should react. Under pressure, managers tend to become more conservative rather than more innovative, more autocratic rather than more participative. Advocates of a self-design approach to organizational administration prescribe the opposite responses: in a crisis situation, managers should examine a wide range of alternatives, discredit past responses, and solicit extensive inputs from others. The fact that there is a discrepancy between ideal and actual behavior does not warrant concern. However, the fact that self-design proponents generally do not examine the feasibility of implementing their prescriptions does. Consequently, there is substantial need for research on organizational operations under crisis conditions to discover how innovative alternatives can be substituted for reflex actions. Further, to avoid the dysfunctional consequences of innovation suggested by Miller's (1955) three-stage model of response to stress, we need more information on how managers can use innovation as a strategy based on calculation rather than on desperation. In the former case it is analogous to a rifle shot aimed at a specific target; in the latter case it is like a shotgun blast searching for a target. In general, there is a significant need for more interdisciplinary research on responses to stress. Research previously conducted at the physiological level (Selye, 1976; Cooper and Marshall, 1976; Gal and Lazarus, 1975), psychological level (McGrath, 1970; Levi, 1967), and organizational level (Sales, 1969; Colligan, Smith, and Jurrell, 1977; House, 1974; Smart and Vertinsky, 1977) needs to be integrated and applied to decline as a special case of stress.

To complement this research on stress there is a considerable need for case studies of organizational responses to decline. Especially critical is information about the choice between alternative responses. It is obvious that different organizations choose different options, but we have little data on the factors influencing this process of choice. Information on this topic can be collected from historical records of organizations that have undergone retrenchment, as well as from longitudinal participant observations. Accounts of how single organizations and entire industries have managed these situations provide a rich data base for the development of inductive models (Rubin, 1977; Smith, 1963).

Interdisciplinary research is especially important in assessing the effects of decline. The decline of an organization can affect its members' emotional health and morale, family stability, interdepartmental relations, decision-making procedures, community labor market dynamics, and interorganizational relations. Research on the likely effects of widespread decline in an era of scarcity might produce radical reformulations of our theories of job design, employee compensation, organizational design, career development, and leadership. In addition, it might produce arguments for new forms of government, commerce, and society. These and other challenging research frontiers lie ahead.

References

Aiken, M., and Hage, J. 1968. "Organizational Interdependence and Interorganizational Structure." *American Sociological Review* 33: 912–30.

Aldrich, H.E. 1978. "Centralization Versus Decentralization in the Design of Human Service Delivery Systems: A Response to Gouldner's Lament." In R.C. Sarri and Y. Hasenfeld (Eds.), *The Management of Human Services.* New York: Columbia University Press.

Aldrich, H.E. 1979. *Organizations and Environments.* Englewood Cliffs, N.J.: Prentice-Hall.

Aldrich, H.E., and Pfeffer, J. 1976. "Environments of Organizations." *Annual Review of Sociology* 2: 79–105.

Aldrich, H.E., and Reiss, A. 1976. "Continuities in the Study of Ecological Succession: Changes in the Race Composition of Neighborhoods and Their Businesses." *American Journal of Sociology* 81: 846–66.

Altman, E.I. 1971. *Corporate Bankruptcy in America.* Lexington, Mass.: Heath.

Ansoff, I.H. 1965. "The Firm of the Future." *Harvard Business Review* 43: 162–78.

Ansoff, I.H. 1970. "Toward a Strategic Theory of the Firm." In I.H. Ansoff (Ed.), *Business Strategy.* New York: Penguin Books.

Argenti, J. 1976. *Corporate Collapse.* New York: Halstead Press.

Ashby, W.R. 1956. *An Introduction to Cybernetics.* New York: Wiley.

Balderston, F.E. 1972. "Varieties of Financial Crises." Ford Foundation Program for Research in University Administration, University of California, Berkeley.

Bardach, E. 1976. "Policy Termination as a Political Process." *Policy Sciences* 7: 123–31.

Barmash, I. 1973. *Great Business Disasters.* New York: Ballantine Books.

Behn, R.D. 1976. "Closing the Massachusetts Public Training Schools." *Policy Sciences* 7: 151–72.

Behn R.D. 1977. "Policy Termination: A Survey of the Current Literature and an Agenda for Future Research." Washington, D.C.: Ford Foundation.

Behn, R.D. 1978. "Closing a Government Facility." *Public Administration Review* 38: 332–38.

Bennis, W.G. 1966. *Changing Organizations.* New York: McGraw-Hill.

Bennis, W.G., and Slater, P.E. 1968. *The Temporary Society.* New York: Harper & Row.

Benson, J.K. 1975. "The Interorganizational Network as a Political Economy." *Administrative Science Quarterly* 20: 229–49.

Benson, J.K. 1977. "Innovation and Crisis in Organizational Analysis." *Sociological Quarterly* 18: 5–18.

Benveniste, G.B. 1977. *Bureaucracy.* San Francisco: Boyd and Fraser.

Berger, P.L., and Neuhaus, R.J. 1977. *To Empower People.* Washington, D.C.: American Enterprise Institute for Public Policy Research.

Biller, R.P. 1976. "On Tolerating Policy and Organizational Termination: Some Design Considerations." *Policy Sciences* 7: 133–49.

Birchfield, R. 1972. *The Rise and Fall of JBL.* NBR Books.

Blau, P.. 1968. "The Hierarchy of Authority in Organizations." *American Journal of Sociology* 73: 453–67.

Blau, P.M. 1970. "A Formal Theory of Differentiation in Organizations." *American Sociological Review* 35: 2101–18.

Blau, P.M., and Schoenherr, R.A. 1971. *The Structure of Organizations.* New York: Basic Books.

Bogue, E.G. 1972. "Alternatives to the Growth-Progress Syndrome." *Educational Forum* 37: 35–43.

Boswell, J. 1973. *The Rise and Decline of Small Firms.* London: Allen & Unwin.

Bougon, M., Weick, K., and Binkhorst, D. 1977. "Cognition in Organizations: An Analysis of the Utrecht Jazz Orchestra." *Administrative Science Quarterly* 22: 606–39.

Boulding, K.E. 1950. *A Reconstruction of Economics.* New York: Wiley.

Boulding K.E. 1973. "The Economics of the Coming Spaceship Earth." In H.E. Daly (Ed.), *Toward A Steady-State Economy.* San Francisco: W.H. Freeman.

Boulding, K.E. 1974. "The Management of Decline." Address to the Regents' Convocation of the State University of New York, Albany, September 20.

Boulding, K.E. 1975. "The Management of Decline." *Change* 64: 8–9.

Bozeman, B., and Slusher, E.A. 1978. "Scarcity and Environmental Stress in Public Organizations: A Conjectural Essay." Working Paper, Maxwell School, Syracuse University.

Brouillette, J., and Quarantilli, E.L. 1971. "Types of Patterned Variation in Bureaucratic Adaptations to Organizational Stress." *Sociological Inquiry* 41: 39–45.

Brown, D.S. 1977. "Reforming the Bureaucracy: Some Suggestions for the New President." *Public Administration Review* 37: 163–70.

Burgoyne, J.G. 1975. "Stress Motivation and Learning." In D. Gowler and K. Legge (Eds.), *Managerial Stress.* New York: Wiley.

Burns, T., and Stalker, G.M. 1961. *The Management of Innovation.* London: Tavistock.

Campbell, D.T. 1969. "Variation and Selective Retention in Sociocultural Evolution." *General Systems* 16: 69–85.

Cartter, A.M. 1970. "After Effects of Blind Eye to Telescope." *Educational Record* 51: 333–38.

Chadwick, G.F. 1977. "The Limits of the Plannable: Stability and Complexity in Planning and Planned Systems." *Environment and Planning* 9: 1189–92.

Child, J. 1972. "Organization Structure, Environment, and Performance: The Role of Strategic Choice." *Sociology* 6: 1–22.

Clark, T.N., and others. 1976. "How Many New Yorks? The New York Fiscal Crisis in Comparative Perspective." Report No. 72 of *Comparative Study of Community Decision Making,* University of Chicago, April.

Cohen, M.D., March, J.G., and Olsen, J.P. 1972. "A Garbage Can Model of Organizational Choice." *Administrative Science Quarterly* 17: 1–25.

Colligan, M.H., Smith, M.J., and Jurrell, J.J. 1977. "Occupational Incidence Rates of Mental Health." *Journal of Human Stress* 4: 34–39.

Commoner, B. 1976. *The Poverty of Power: Energy and the Economic Crisis.* New York: Knopf.

Cooper, C.L., and Marshall, J. 1976. "Occupational Sources of Stress: A Review of the Literature Relating to Coronary Heart Disease and Mental Ill Health." *Journal of Occupational Psychology* 49: 11–28.

Cyert, R.M. 1978. "The Management of Universities of Constant or Decreasing Size." *Public Administration Review* 38: 344–49.

Cyert, R.M., and March, J.G. 1963. *A Behavioral Theory of the Firm.* Englewood Cliffs, N.J.: Prentice-Hall.

Dahl, R., and Lindblom, C. 1953. *Politics, Economics, and Welfare.* New York: Harper & Row.

Daly, H.E. 1973. "Introduction." In H.E. Daly (Ed.), *Toward a Steady-State Economy.* San Francisco: W.H. Freeman.

Daly, H.E. 1977. *Steady-State Economics.* San Francisco: W.H. Freeman.

Daughen, J.R., and Binzen, P. 1971. *The Wreck of the Penn Central.* Boston: Little, Brown.

Dewar, R., and Werbel, J. 1979. "Morale and Conflict: Universalistic Versus Contingency Predictions." Paper presented at Academy of Management meetings in Atlanta, Ga.

Downs, A. 1967. *Inside Bureaucracy.* Boston: Little, Brown.

Drucker, P. 1974. *Management: Tasks, Responsibilities, and Practices.* New York: Harper & Row.

Dvorin, E.P., and Simmons, R.L. 1972. *From Amoral to Humane Bureaucracy.* San Francisco: Harper & Row.

Fenno, R. 1966. *Power of the Purse.* Boston: Little, Brown.

Forrester, J.W. 1971. "Counterintuitive Behavior of Social Systems." *Technological Review* 8: 53–68.

Fox, D.M. 1967. *The Discovery of Abundance.* Ithaca, N.Y.: Cornell University Press.

Freeman, J., and Hannan, M.T. 1975. "Growth and Decline Processes in Organizations." *American Sociological Review* 40: 215–28.

Furniss, T. 1974. "Retrenchment, Layoff, and Termination." *Educational Record* 55: 159–70.

Gal, R., and Lazarus, R.S. 1975. "The Role of Activity in Anticipating and Confronting Stressful Situations." *Journal of Human Stress* 2: 4–20.

Galbraith, J.K. 1971. *The Industrial State.* Boston: Houghton Mifflin.

Glassberg, A. 1978. "Organizational Responses to Municipal Budget Decreases." *Public Administration Review* 38: 325–32.

Glassman, R. 1973. "Persistence and Loose Coupling." *Behavioral Science* 18: 83–94.

Green, A.C. 1974. "Planning for Declining Environments." *School Review* 82: 595–600.

Greiner, L.E. 1972. "Evolution and Revolution as Organizations Grow." *Harvard Business Review* 50: 37–46.

Hage, J., and Aiken, M. 1967. "Program Change and Organizational Properties." *American Journal of Sociology* 72: 503–19.

Hall, R.H. 1968. "Professionalization and Bureaucracy." *American Sociological Review* 33: 92–104.

Hall, R.I. 1976. "A System Pathology of an Organization: The Rise and Fall of the Old *Saturday Evening Post.*" *Administrative Science Quarterly* 21: 185–211.

Hannan, M.T., and Freeman, J.H. 1978. "The Population Ecology of Organizations." In M.W. Meyer and Associates (Eds.), *Environments and Organizations: Theoretical and Empirical Perspectives.* San Francisco: Jossey-Bass.

Hawley, W.E., and Rogers, D. 1974. *Improving the Quality of Urban Management.* Beverly Hills, Calif.: Sage.

Hedberg, B.L.T., Nystrom, P.C., and Starbuck, W.H. 1976. "Camping on Seesaws: Prescriptions for a Self-Designing Organization." *Administrative Science Quarterly* 21: 41–65.

Hedberg, B.L.T., Nystrom, P.C., and Starbuck, W.H. 1977. "Designing Organizations to Match Tomorrow." In P.C. Nystrom and W.H. Starbuck (Eds.), *Perspective Models of Organizations.* North-Holland/TIMS Studies in the Management Sciences, Vol. 5. Amsterdam: North-Holland Publishing.

Heilbronner, R.L. 1976. *Business Civilization in Decline.* New York: Norton.

Hill, N. 1967. *Think and Grow Rich.* New York: Hawthorn Books.

Hirschman, A.O. 1970. *Exit, Voice, and Loyalty.* Cambridge, Mass.: Harvard University Press.

House, J.S. 1974. "Occupational Stress and Coronary Heart Disease: A Review and Theoretical Integration." *Journal of Health and Social Behavior* 15: 12–27.

Indik, B.P. 1964. "The Relationship Between Organization Size and Supervision Ratio." *Administrative Science Quarterly* 9: 301–12.

Kaufman, H. 1973. "The Direction of Organizational Evolution." *Public Administration Review* 33: 300–7.

Kaufman, H. 1975. "The Natural History of Human Organizations." *Administration and Society* 7: 131–49.

Kaufman, H. 1976. *Are Government Organizations Immortal?* Washington, D.C.: Brookings Institution.

Kolarska, L., and Aldrich, H. 1978. "Exit, Voice, and Silence: Consumers' and Managers' Responses to Organizational Decline." Working Paper, School of Industrial and Labor Relations, Cornell University.

Kotter, J., and Sathe, V. 1978. "Problems of Human Resource Management in Rapidly Growing Companies." *California Management Review* 21: 29–36.

Landau, M. 1973. "On the Concept of a Self-Correcting Organization." *Public Administration Review* 33: 533–42.

Levi, T. 1967. *Stress: Sources, Management, and Prevention.* New York: Liveright.

Levine, C.H. 1978. "Organizational Decline and Cutback Management." *Public Administration Review* 38: 316–25.

Levine, C.H. 1979. "More on Cutback Management: Hard Questions for Hard Times." *Public Administration Review* 39: 179–83.

Lindblom, C.E. 1968. *The Policy-Making Process.* Englewood Cliffs, N.J.: Prentice-Hall.

McCaskey, M.B. 1974. "Tolerance for Ambiguity and the Perception of Environmental Uncertainty in Organizational Design." Paper presented at the Management of Organization Design Conference, Pittsburgh, October.

McGrath, J.E. 1970. *Social and Psychological Factors in Stress.* New York: Holt, Rinehart and Winston.

March, J.G., and Simon, H.A. 1958. *Organizations.* New York: Wiley.

Markham, J.W. 1973. *Conglomerate Enterprise and Public Policy.* Boston: Graduate School of Business Administration, Harvard University.

Marris, R. 1974. *The Corporate Society.* New York: Macmillan.

Meadows, D.H., and others. 1972. *The Limits to Growth.* New York: Universe Books.

Merton, R.K. 1957. *Social Theory and Social Structure* (rev. ed.). New York: Free Press.

Miles, R.E., Snow, C.C., and Pfeffer, J. 1974. "Organization-Environment: Concepts and Issues." *Industrial Relations* 13: 244–64.

Miles, R.E., Jr. 1976. *Awakening from the American Dream.* New York: Universe Books.

Miles, R.H. 1980. "Findings and Implications of Organizational Life Cycle Research." In J.R. Kimberly and R.H. Miles (Eds.), *The Organizational Life Cycle.* San Francisco: Jossey-Bass.

Miller, D. 1977. "Common Syndromes of Business Failure." *Business Horizons* 20: 43–53.

Miller, J.G. 1955. "Toward a General Theory for the Behavioral Sciences." *American Psychologist* 10: 513–31.

Millett, J.D. 1977. "The Changed Climate of Planning." In J.D. Millett (Ed.), *New Directions for Higher Education: Managing Turbulence and Change,* no. 19. San Francisco: Jossey-Bass.

Mitnick, B. 1978. "Deregulation as a Process of Organizational Reduction." *Public Administration Review* 38: 350–57.

Molotch, H. 1976. "The City as a Growth Machine: Toward a Political Economy of Place." *American Journal of Sociology* 82: 309–32.

Muller, T. 1975. *Growing and Declining Urban Areas: A Fiscal Comparison.* Washington, D.C.: Urban Institute.

Nielsen, F., and Hannan, M.T. 1977. "The Expansion of National Education Systems: Tests of a Population Ecology Model." *American Sociological Review* 42: 479–90.

Peale, N.V. 1952. *The Power of Positive Thinking.* Englewood Cliffs, N.J.: Prentice-Hall.

Pennings, J.M. 1975. "The Relevance of the Structural-Contingency Model for Organizational Effectiveness." *Administrative Science Quarterly* 20: 393–410.

Penrose, E.T. 1952. "Biological Analogies in the Theory of the Firm." *American Economic Review* 42: 804–19.

Perrow, C. 1972. *The Radical Attack on Business: A Critical Analysis.* New York: Harcourt Brace Jovanovich.

Perrow, C. 1979. *Complex Organizations: A Critical Essay* (2nd ed.). Glenview, Ill.: Scott, Foresman.

Pettigrew, A.M. 1979. "On Studying Organizational Cultures." *Administrative Science Quarterly* 24: 570–81.

Pfeffer, J. 1972. "Merger as a Response to Organizational Interdependence." *Administrative Science Quarterly* 17: 382–94.

Pfeffer, J., and Salancik, G.R. 1978. *The External Control of Organizations: A Resource Dependence Perspective.* New York: Harper & Row.

Pondy, L.R. 1969. "Effects of Size, Complexity, and Ownership on Administrative Intensity." *Administrative Science Quarterly* 14: 47–61.

Pondy, L.R. 1977. "The Other Hand Clapping: An Information-Processing Approach to Organizational Power." In T.H. Hammer and S.B. Bacharach (Eds.), *Reward System and Power Distribution in Organizations: Search for Solutions.* Ithaca: New York State School of Industrial and Labor Relations.

Porter, D.O., and Olsen, E.A. 1976. "Some Critical Issues in Government Centralization and Decentralization." *Public Administration Review* 36: 72–84.

Post, J.E. 1978. *Corporate Behavior and Social Change*. Reston, Va.: Reston Press.

Preston, L.E., and Post, J.E. 1975. *Private Management and Public Policy*. Englewood Cliffs, N.J.: Prentice-Hall.

Rainey, H.G., Backoff, R.W., and Levine, C.H. 1976. "Comparing Public and Private Organizations." *Public Administration Review* 36: 223–34.

Rodekohr, M. 1974. "Adjustments of Colorado School Districts to Declining Enrollments." Unpublished doctoral dissertation, University of Colorado, Boulder.

Roessner, J.D. 1979. "Public Agencies' Capacity to Innovate." Paper presented at Coventuring in Public Issues Conference sponsored by the Charles F. Kettering Foundation, Montauk Point, N.Y.

Ross, J.E., and Kami, M.J. 1973. *Corporate Management in Crisis*. Englewood Cliffs, N.J.: Prentice-Hall.

Rothman, D.J. 1972. "Of Prisons, Asylums, and Other Decaying Institutions." *The Public Interest* 26: 3–17.

Rubin, I. 1977. "Universities in Stress: Decision Making Under Conditions of Reduced Resources." *Social Science Quarterly* 58: 242–54.

Rubin, I. 1979. "Loose Structure, Retrenchment, and Adaptability in the University." Paper presented at Midwest Sociological Society meetings, April.

Rushing, W.A. 1967. "The Effects of Industry Size and Division of Labor on Administration." *Administrative Science Quarterly* 12: 267–95.

Sales, S.M. 1969. "Organizational Roles as a Risk Factor in Coronary Heart Disease." *Administrative Science Quarterly* 14: 325–36.

Schumacher, E.F. 1973. *Small is Beautiful*. New York: Harper & Row.

Scott, W.G. 1974. "Organization Theory: A Reassessment." *Academy of Management Journal* 17: 242–54.

Scott, W.G. 1976. "The Management of Decline." *Conference Board Record* 8(6): 56–59.

Selye, H. 1976. *The Stress of Life* (rev. ed.). New York: McGraw-Hill.

Sethi, S.P. 1977. *Up Against the Corporate Wall: Modern Corporations and Social Issues of the Seventies*. Englewood Cliffs, N.J.: Prentice-Hall.

Shefter, M. 1977. "New York City's Fiscal Crisis: The Politics of Inflation and Retrenchment." *The Public Interest* 48: 98–127.

Smart, C., and Vertinsky, I. 1977. "Designs for Crisis Decision Units." *Administrative Science Quarterly* 22: 640–57.

Smith, B.L.R., and Hague, D.C. (Eds.). 1971. *The Dilemma of Accountability in Modern Government*. New York: St. Martin's.

Smith, R.A. 1963. *Corporations in Crisis*. New York: Doubleday.

Starbuck, W.H., and Hedberg, B. 1977. "Saving an Organization from a Stagnating Environment." In H. Thorelli (Ed.), *Strategy + Structure = Performance*. Bloomington: Indiana University Press.

Starbuck, W.H., Greve, A., and Hedberg, B.L.T. 1978. "Responding to Crises." *Journal of Business Administration* 9: 111–37.

Statistical Abstract of the United States. 1976. U.S. Department of Commerce, Bureau of the Census.

Staw, B.M. 1977. "The Experimenting Organization." *Organizational Dynamics* 6(1): 2–18.

Staw, B.M., and Szwajkowski, E. 1975. "The Scarcity-Munificence Component of Organizational Environments and the Commission of Illegal Acts." *Administrative Science Quarterly* 20: 345–54.

Stebbins, G.L. 1965. "Pitfalls and Guideposts in Comparing Organic and Social Evolution." *Pacific Sociological Review* 6: 3–10.

Stinchcombe, A.L. 1965. "Social Structure and Organizations." In J.G. March (Ed.), *Handbook of Organizations*. Chicago: Rand McNally.

Sutton, F.X., and others. 1956. *The American Business Creed*. Cambridge, Mass.: Harvard University Press.

Thompson, J.D. 1967. *Organizations in Action*. New York: McGraw-Hill.

Tornedon, R.J., and Boddewyn, J.J. 1974. "Foreign Divestments: Too Many Mistakes." *Columbia Journal of World Business* 9(3): 87–94.

Toynbee, A.J. 1947. *A Study of History*. Vols 1–4 (abridged by D.C. Somervell). New York: Oxford University Press.

Trow, M. 1975. "Notes on American Higher Education: Planning for Universal Access in the Context of Uncertainty." *Higher Education* 4: 1–11.

Vacca, R. 1973. *The Coming Dark Age*. New York: Doubleday.

Walton, C. 1977. *The Ethics of Corporate Conduct*. Englewood Cliffs, N.J.: Prentice-Hall.

Wamsley, G., and Zald, M.N. 1973. *The Political Economy of Public Organizations*. Lexington, Mass.: Heath.

Weber, M. 1947. *The Theory of Social and Economic Organization* (A.M. Henderson and T. Parsons, Trans.). New York: Oxford University Press.

Weick, K.E. 1969. *The Social Psychology of Organizing*. Reading, Mass.: Addison-Wesley.

Weick, K.E. 1976. "Educational Organizations as Loosely Coupled Systems." *Administrative Science Quarterly* 21: 1–19.

Weick, K.E. 1977a. "Enactment Processes in Organizations." In B.M. Staw and G.R. Salancik (Eds.), *New Directions in Organizational Behavior*. Chicago: St. Clair Press.

Weick, K.E. 1977b. "Organizational Design: Organizations as Self-Designing Systems." *Organizational Dynamics* 6(2): 30–46.

Whetten, D.A. 1979a. "Organizational Interdependence and Innovation." Presented at Coventuring in Public Issues Conference sponsored by Charles Kettering Foundation, Montauk Point, N.Y.

Whetten, D.A. 1979b. "Organizational Responses to Scarcity: Difficult Choices for Difficult Times." Working Paper, College of Commerce and Business Administration, University of Illinois.

Whetten, D.A. 1979c. "Organizational Decline: A Neglected Topic in Organizational Behavior." Working Paper, College of Commerce and Business Administration, University of Illinois.

Wildavsky, A. 1964. *Politics of Budgetary Process*. Boston: Little, Brown.

Wildavsky, A. 1972. "The Self-Evaluating Organization." *Public Administration Review* 32: 509–20.

Wilson, J.Q. 1972. "Innovation in Organization: Notes Toward a Theory." In J. Thomas and W. Bennis (Eds.), *The Management of Change and Conflict*. New York: Penguin Books.

Yarmolinsky, A. 1975. "Institutional Paralysis." *Daedalus* 104(1): 61–67.

Yetton, P.W. 1975. "Leadership Style in Stressful and Nonstressful Situations." In D. Gowler and K. Legge (Eds.), *Managerial Stress*. New York: Wiley.

Yin, R.K. 1978. *Changing Urban Bureaucracies: How New Practices Become Routinized*. Santa Monica, Calif.: Rand Corporation.

Yuchtman, E., and Seashore, S.E. 1967. "A System Resource Approach to Organizational Effectiveness." *American Sociological Review* 32: 891–903.

Zald, M.N., and Ash, R. 1966. "Social Movement Organizations: Growth, Decay, and Changes." *Social Forces* 44: 327–41.

PART III

Empirical Foundations: Macro and Micro Perspectives

This part contains seven chapters, all previously published articles that report empirical studies on the causes and consequences of organizational decline. As with other parts of this book, we chose papers that are of the highest quality and that represent an array of conceptual approaches to the study of decline. We also selected work that would demonstrate the broad range of methods that can be used to study organizational decline and its consequences.

These chapters illustrate that decline can be studied successfully by employing analysis of historical data with event-history methods, analysis of annual reports and of data from the *Census of Manufacturers,* and analysis of records data gathered by a state department of education. Other methods include combinations of archival- and survey-research methods, comparative case studies for the generation of grounded theory, and laboratory experimentation. Indeed, in reviewing the empirical literature on organizational decline, we were struck by how many different methods can and should be used to study this complex range of phenomena.

This part is divided into two sections, macro and micro. Following Pfeffer (1982), macrolevel studies focus on organizations as units and on populations of organizations. Conversely, microlevel studies center on the behavior of individuals, coalitions, and subunits within organizations.

The first three chapters are investigations conducted from a macro perspective. Glenn R. Carroll and Jacques Delacroix's "Organizational Mortality in the Newspaper Industries of Argentina and Ireland: An Ecological Approach" (Chapter 9) uses historical data from the nineteenth and twentieth century to show that newspapers from these two countries experience higher mortality rates during their early years, that organizational mortality rates are lower in mature industries and during periods of economic growth, and that newspapers born under conditions of political turmoil are outlived by newspapers born during politically stable periods. These data are viewed as supportive of the population-ecology perspective.

Kim S. Cameron, Myung U. Kim, and David A. Whetten's "Organizational Effects of Decline and Turbulence" (Chapter 10) develops conceptual and empirical distinctions between decline and turbulence. Their study of 331 colleges and universities suggests that turbulence has significant (and negative) effects on top leaders, but not on the responses of other organization members. Conversely, their results suggest that decline has significant (and negative) effects on organization members, but not on top leaders. They interpret these findings as evidence that the managerial subsystem of these loosely coupled structures may be less effective at absorbing the uncertainty of decline than the uncertainty of turbulence.

Danny Miller and Peter H. Friesen's "Successful and Unsuccessful Phases of the Corporate Life Cycle" (Chapter 11) reports a study that uses questionnaires, books, annual reports, and a series of magazine articles to construct histories of thirty-six corporations. They find that successful phases of the corporate life cycle are characterized by continual increases in the sophistication of information processing and decision-making methods. In contrast, such increases do not occur during unsuccessful phases. They also report that higher levels of innovation (e.g., product-market innovation) occur during successful phases, and that unsuccessful phases are characterized by alternating cycles of extreme innovation and extreme stagnation.

The remaining four chapters employ the micro perspective. They explore the psychological and behavioral consequences of decline for subunits, external stakeholder groups, top management, and individual organization members. Robert I. Sutton and Anita L. Callahan's "The Stigma of Bankruptcy: Spoiled Organizational Image and Its Management" (Chapter 12) describes a grounded theory of how Chapter 11 of the Federal Bankruptcy Code spoils the intertwined images of firms and their leaders. They propose that such stigma causes key organizational actors to have negative reactions that further reduce the viability of the troubled firms. They also identify strategies that leaders use to avert or repair such spoiled images.

James Krantz's "Group Process Under Conditions of Decline" (Chapter 13) uses two cases of action research to develop a theory about how the heightened individual anxieties evoked by organizational decline influence collective behavior. Drawing on work pioneered by the Tavistock Institute, Krantz proposes that powerful and primitive anxieties strain social defense systems beyond capacity, which leads to an increase in the dysfunctional fantasy-driven elements of group behavior.

Joel Brockner, Jeanette Davy, and Carolyn Carter's "Layoffs, Self-Esteem, and Survivor Guilt: Motivational, Affective, and Attitudinal Consequences" (Chapter 14) describes a laboratory study of the effect of layoffs on the subsequent productivity of "survivors." Their findings are consistent with equity theory: performance was greater among participants who had witnessed the lay-off of a coworker than among participants who had not witnessed a layoff. They also reported that this effect of "survivor guilt" was present entirely in the low–rather than the medium– and high–self-esteem participants.

The final chapter in Part III, by Leon Greenhalgh and Zehava Rosenblatt, "Job Insecurity: Toward Conceptual Clarity," (Chapter 15) integrates prior field research on employee reactions to job insecurity. They propose that perceptions of job insecurity cause individuals to decrease effort (in contrast to Brockner's laboratory study), to be more inclined to leave, and to resist change. Greenhalgh and Rosenblatt also propose that such individual reactions further reduce organizational effectiveness. Job insecurity is thus believed to be a key element on a vicious circle that accelerates organizational decline.

These chapters illustrate that decline can be studied from a variety of levels of analysis, from a number of conceptual perspectives, and with a wide range of research methods. But these seven chapters are similar in that each focuses on predicting and understanding — rather than controlling — organizational decline. Prescriptions for avoiding and managing decline are emphasized in the following part on normative foundations.

Reference

Pfeffer, J. 1982. *Organizations and Organization Theory.* Boston: Pitman.

9

Organizational Mortality in the Newspaper Industries of Argentina and Ireland: An Ecological Approach

Glenn R. Carroll

Jacques Delacroix

Introduction

Renewed interest in human ecology has shifted the problem of why organizations fail from policy studies to the center of basic organizational theory. Modern organizational ecologists have argued that environmental conditions interact with organizational forms to yield differential organiza-

tional mortality rates. These mortality differentials are considered the primary mechanism of temporal change in communities of organizations.[1] The ecological perspective has attracted considerable attention among organizational analysts, but its merits remain largely theoretical. We have yet to see much evidence of environmental variability in organizational failure rates.

We attempt in this paper to demonstrate empirically the effects of environmental conditions on mortality rates in organizations (see Hannan and Freeman, 1981, for another recent attempt). We study the history of a single industry in two locations and over a long period of time, exploring several general arguments that might account for the observed organizational mortality patterns in terms of historical, industrial, and environmental changes.

This research was supported by NIMH Grant #2T232MH-15149–03 to the Organizations Research Training Program at Stanford University and by NSF Grant #SOC78–12315 to Michael T. Hannan and Nancy Brandon Tuma. During part of the writing stage, Carroll was a guest professor at Zentrum für Umfragen, Methoden und Analysen in Mannheim, Federal Republic of Germany. We wish to thank Michael Hannan and John Meyer for comments on an earlier draft.

Reprinted with permission from *Administrative Science Quarterly,* Vol. 27, June 1982. © 1982 Cornell University.

We selected the newspaper industry because it has records going back very nearly to its beginnings. Although in one of the two locations selected we could not obtain information on the earliest beginnings of the industry, we still observed much of the initial phase of the industry's development. This early history is important because, in a new industry, organizations are forced to operate with few models and without specialized pools of labor. These conditions may well have important consequences for organizational mortality.

The availability of data and the rough comparability of the two countries led us to choose the newspaper industries of Argentina and Ireland. These countries historically have populations of similar magnitude, they are both within the European cultural orbit, and they share similar economic positions relative to the great industrial powers. In fact, for the main period of our observation, the nineteenth century, the two countries had a strikingly similar economic dependence on the United Kingdom.

We concentrate on two topics pertaining to organizational deaths. First, we model the relationship between organizational age and the probability of disappearance. Second, we explore how the social conditions at the time of an organization's founding affect its life chances. In particular, we examine the effects of industry age, economic transformations, and political turmoil on timings of death in individual newspaper organizations. We argue that in some instances environmental conditions affect individual organizations directly, but in others environmental effects are mediated by industry-level variables. At all times, we use the comparison between Argentina and Ireland to indicate the generality of the arguments we advance.

Our analysis is exploratory. It does not try to prove anything but rather probes the plausibility of a certain mode of explanation of organizational change: environmental selection within a population of organizations. We think that such an approach is a necessary precondition to the development of substantively informed ecological theory.

The Concept of Organizational Death

What is an organizational death? The question may seem trivial because all agree on the unproblematic case: an organizational death occurs when an organization fails, closes down its operations, and disbands its constituent elements. But what about mergers? When two organizations combine, at least one ceases to exist and this must be considered a death. If the merger involves a dominant partner that has absorbed the resources of the other partner, then the subordinate organization dies and the dominant organization experiences a change in structure. If, however, neither merger partner assumes a dominant position, it is difficult to assign a death to one organization and a structural alteration to the other. Instead, it is useful to consider the resulting organization as new and the two merger partners as dead.

Theorists tend to consider the disappearance of an organization as the endpoint on a scale of unsuccessful organizational performance (see the review by Whetten, 1980). This conceptualization is partly accurate; death is the ultimate manifestation of failure in organizational performance. However, as mergers often show, not all deaths are the result of performance failure. Many merger partners are highly successful—indeed, often their success makes these organizations attractive candidates for merger opportunities. Consequently, the death of a formal organization does not logically imply anything about its previous failure or success in performance.

Despite this theoretical distinction, our study of organizational deaths amounts to a study of organizational failure. We collected data on the timing of the births and deaths of all newspapers in Ireland from 1800 to 1975 and in Argentina from 1800 to 1900. We noted when the disappearance of a paper was associated with a merger and when it was not. Only in a small number of cases was the death the result of a merger, and these cases consisted almost totally of absorptions of subordinate partners. This leaves open the possibility for only a very small fraction of the sample to have experienced death by success. Since our data do not indicate how successful the papers were prior to the merger, we cannot separate the deaths by success from the deaths by failure. Our reading of the history of journalism suggests, however, that most of the absorbed papers were in a state of decline or of incipient failure. Thus, we assume that the organizational deaths in our study are the result of organizational failure.

Historical Description of Newspaper Deaths

The press is a rather recent industry. Its beginnings are fairly clearly defined; there was no imperceptible shading from an archaic craft to a modern industry as was the case in most manufacturing industries, such as shoemaking. Though we do not offer a formal definition of press organs, there is little debate as to what constitutes a newspaper in the widest sense of the word. This is particularly clear in Argentina. Prior to 1801, no organizations attempted to supply the general public with printed material aimed at influencing and informing on a regular basis. After this date, and except for an interlude of two and a half years between 1807 and 1810, one or more such organizations were always on the Argentinian scene.

The first newspaper, ambitiously titled *El telegrafo mercantil rural politico economico e historico (The Mercantile Rural, Political, Economic, and Historical Telegraph),* lasted less than one year. Even before its demise, the equally ambitious *Semanario de agricultura, industria y commercio (The Agricultural, Industrial, and Commerial Weekly)* had been launched. This publication lasted five years. During 1815, five newspapers were operating in Argentina; in 1820, there were eleven.

In Ireland, the press was not as clearly born with the nineteenth century. At least eleven periodicals appeared in the eighteenth century. Most survived one year or less. But one, the *Dublin Journal,* lasted one hundred years (1724–1825) and a second one, the *Waterford Chronicle,* fifty-one years (1771–1822). The first nineteenth-century Irish papers, established in 1800, unabashedly announced their political vocation: *The Constitu-*

tion or Anti-Union Evening Post; The Detector. General circulation informational media soon followed: *The Evening Herald, Irish Packet,* and *Freeman's Journal and Daily Commercial Advertiser,* all founded in 1807.

A lively provincial press soon was established in Ireland (*Connaught Journal, Kilkenny Chronicle, Westmeath Journal, Sligo Journal,* and *Kerry Evening Post,* all begun in 1813), and was established a little later in Argentina (*El tucumano imparcial [The Tucuman Impartial], La gaceta de Mendoza [The Mendoza Gazette],* and *El termometro del dia [Today's Thermometer]* in 1820, and *El correo ministerial del Parana [The Parana Ministerial Mail]* and *El restaurador tucumano [The Tucuman Restorer]* in 1821).

Even if many of these press organs were short-lived, the press had become a visible institution in both countries by 1810. From 1800 on, a new industry was irreversibly established, in Argentina as well as in Ireland. It is the pattern of disappearances in the populations of organizations that made up this industry that we study in this paper. (A discussion of the quality of our data is in Appendix A.)

Our analysis begins with an examination of the annual aggregate number of newspaper deaths in each of the two countries over time. Figure 1a presents these data for Argentina from 1800 to 1900, and Figure 1b shows similar data for Ireland from 1800 to 1975.

The number of newspaper deaths in Argentina is very low from 1800 to 1820. This reflects primarily the small number of newspapers present during this period. After 1820, the number of deaths rises considerably and remains high until 1835, despite periodic fluctuations. Between 1836 and 1851, the time of the successful Rosas dictatorship, there is a pronounced dip in the number of deaths. In 1851, immediately after the end of the dictatorship, the high death rate returns and continues throughout the century.

The pattern for Ireland (Figure 1b) is considerably different. The early period from 1800 to 1820 is similar to Argentina's and shows only a few newspaper deaths. From 1820 to the turn of

Figure 1a. Annual Newspaper Deaths in Argentina, 1800–1900

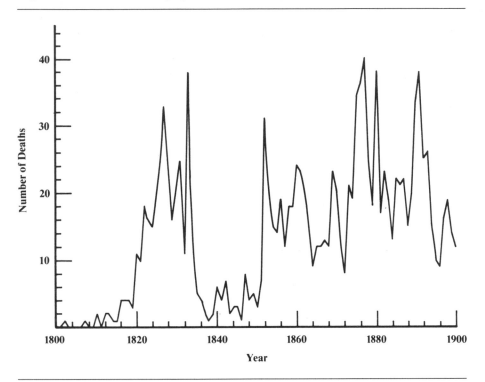

the century, the average number rises steadily. There is no sustained period of low mortality as there was during the Rosas period in Argentina. In the twentieth century, the average number of deaths declines after 1920. The mortality level at which the Irish industry stabilizes is considerably lower than that in Argentina: approximately five organizational deaths per year in Ireland, fifteen per year in Argentina.

There are several ways to look for plausible explanations for the variations in these death rates. One could aggregate the data on deaths and build time-series models of the process. This method might prove useful, but it wastes information. In particular, by aggregating the deaths annually at the country level, we lose information on the birth dates of individual organizations. Thus, we have no knowledge about the age distributions of those organizations that die in any single year. Since small organizations are believed to have high early failure rates, such information is critical. If

high mortality affected young organizations severely and uniformly and if the year of observation or the preceding years had witnessed a large number of births, we would expect high mortality. In such a case, an apparent bad year is in fact the direct consequence of previous good years for births.

When data are disaggregated, we can determine if a particular year's high mortality is simply due to intrinsic high infant mortality. If it is not, then either extrinsic events (an economic crunch, perhaps) or population dynamics of the press (overcrowding) are the root of the high mortality. If, however, the high mortality pertains to young organizations, it may simply express constant infant mortality, which is expectable irrespective of environmental change.

For these reasons, we renounce the time-series framework and analyze organizational event histories of the death process. An event history of an organizational death is simply a data record

Figure 1b. Annual Newspaper Deaths in Ireland, 1800–1975

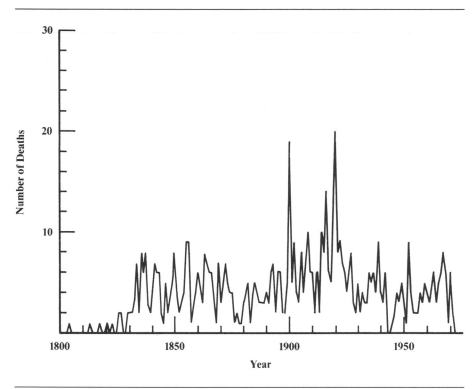

that contains information on the timing of an organization's birth and death. If the organization had not died by the last date of observation, then that case is said to be "censored." This means that observation of an event we expect to occur (death of a newspaper) has been interrupted before the event. A censored case is one for which we do not know if or when the event will occur. However, since censored cases contain information about the survival time during which an event does not occur, they are retained in the analysis. Other basics of event history methodology are explained as we proceed, but the reader interested in a more thorough treatment should consult Tuma, Hannan, and Groenveld (1979).

The Liability of Newness

New organizations are believed to have high failure rates. Stinchcombe (1965) has named this phe-

nomenon the "liability of newness." He distinguishes four major forms of liability. First, organizational newness often implies new roles for the firm as a social actor as well as for the individual participants in it. Since guidance in these new roles must come from resources outside the firm (if they can be obtained at all), the new firm operates somewhat blindly, and major blunders are easily committed. This argument implies that new organizations in new industries suffer from a double liability of newness: predecessors are rare and role information is hard to come by.

Second, the amount of time and effort required to learn and coordinate organizational roles is likely to be significant. During this learning period, behavior is decidedly nonroutine, and initiative is very important—without it the firm is threatened.

Stinchcombe's third explanation for the liability of newness focuses on the mutual socializa-

Figure 2a. Survivor Plot for Argentinian Newspapers

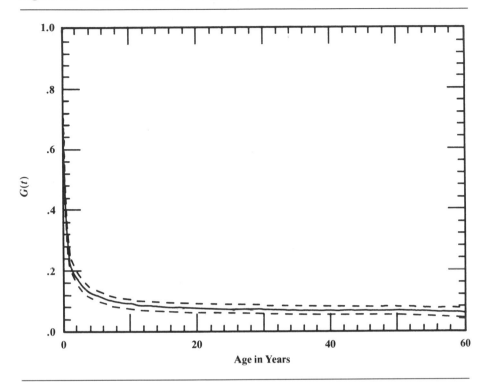

Note: N = 1457; *N* of deaths = 1346.

tion of the organizational participants. Because new firms are comprised mainly of strangers, he reasons, trust may not be readily forthcoming.

The fourth liability of newness concerns customers and other publics-in-contact. New firms usually compete with existing firms that have well-established clienteles, who are familiar with the existing firms' operating procedures and who are possibly resistant to change. New firms that cannot attract clients from existing firms are threatened by a lack of business. New organizations in new industries are spared the obligation of winning clients from established competitors. However, they may be required, as the first Argentinian and Irish newspapers were, to create clienteles from scratch.

We search for evidence of the liability of newness in the newspaper industries of Argentina and Ireland by examining the relationship between organizational age and the probability of death. Two stochastic functions can be used to describe this relationship in separate but equivalent ways.[2] The first of these is the hazard function, which describes the instantaneous rate of death, or more intuitively, the rate of death at each instant of a newspaper's age. The hazard function is the limit, as Δt goes to zero, of the probability of death between t and $t + \Delta t$ over Δt, given that the newspaper is alive at t:

$$h(t) = \lim_{\Delta t \to 0} \frac{\Pr(t, t + \Delta t \mid t)}{\Delta t}, \qquad (1)$$

where $h(t)$ is the hazard function, and (given that the unit is alive at t) $\Pr(t, t + \Delta t \mid t)$ is the probability of death between t and Δt.

When t is defined as age, the hazard function can be used to describe the rate of death in the population of newspapers at any given age. Using

Figure 2b.   Survivor Plot for Irish Newspapers

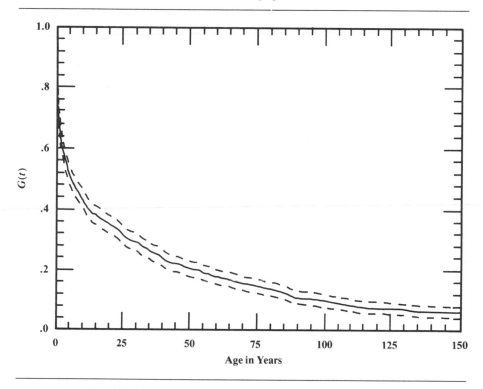

Note: N = 1017; N of deaths = 897.

this function, we can compare the instantaneous rate of death at different ages to determine if newspapers exhibit a liability of newness or any other form of age-dependence in the death rates.

The second stochastic function is the survivor function $G(t)$, which gives the probabilities of survival until all ages. In our analysis, we estimate the survivor function for populations of newspapers containing censored and uncensored cases (see Appendix B for a simple illustration of this technique). These estimates yield a general description of the survival probabilities to all ages for a newspaper.

Our starting point in this analysis is our estimation of the survivor function for newspapers at different ages. If the newness liability arguments are correct, then we will observe a rapid drop in the survival probabilities of young newspapers. We explore this issue by applying the Kaplan–

Meier non-parametric estimator to the newspaper event-history data. The estimates are shown in Figures 2a and 2b; dashed lines indicate 95-percent confidence intervals.

The estimates for the Argentinian data (Figure 2a) show a very steep early decline in the survival probabilities. The probability of survival to age two is below .20; after age eight, however, it remains relatively constant at approximately .10. Figure 2b shows a similar early decline in the survival probabilities of Irish newspapers, although it is less pronounced than in the Argentinian plot. In Ireland, newspapers have almost a 50-percent chance of surviving five years and the survival probability does not reach .10 until approximately 100 years of age.

These plots seemingly support the liability-of-newness hypothesis. A more appropriate test is to examine, as a function of age, not the survival

Figure 3a. Log Survivor Plot for Argentinian Newspapers

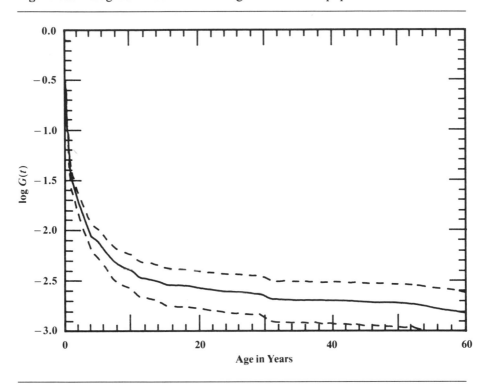

probabilities but the instantaneous rates of death. This change of method is particularly important because it is well known that when the rate of death is constant across age, the survival times will conform to an exponential distribution[3] (see Cox and Lewis, 1966). Since an exponential distribution of survival times implies a preponderance of short-lived newspapers, the "liability of newness" might be due not to changing life chances but instead to the illusion created by a constant rate. However, since the instantaneous rate of death is the negative of the slope of the natural log of the survivor function, we can test for a constant rate by plotting the log survivor function across age. With these plots, we can search for possible age dependence in the death rate: when the rate is constant across age, the log of $G(t)$ will be a straight line; when the rate changes across age, the line will bend. If Stinchcombe's liability-of-newness hypothesis is correct, then the log sur-

vivor plot will yield a curve showing declining age dependence.[4]

In Figure 3a, the log survivor plots are presented for all Argentinian newspapers. The instantaneous rate of deaths is not constant across the newspaper's lifetime but decreases with age. The rate of death is very high for the first two years of operation then slowly descends until at ten years it becomes nearly constant. This pattern suggests that death rates in these organizations are age dependent only until approximately the tenth year of operation. The pattern is consistent with the liability-of-newness hypothesis.

Figure 3b shows a similar plot for the Irish newspapers. Again, the early years are characterized by high rates of death, and these gradually diminish with age. In the Irish case, however, the age dependence in the rate of death disappears after only five years. The overall pattern is again consistent with Stinchcombe's hypothesis.

Figure 3b. Log Survivor Plot for Irish Newspapers

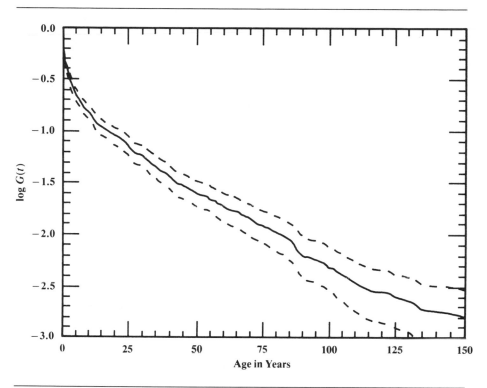

The difference between "infant" death rates in Argentina and Ireland is in line with Stinchcombe's first form of liability. Role borrowing must have been relatively easy for Irish newspapers, which were in close proximity and frequent intercourse with their English and Scottish predecessors. Argentinian newspapers, on the other hand, began in a nearly complete press vacuum.

From these survivor plots, we have established the plausibility of age dependence in the death rates of newspapers in Argentina and Ireland. Next we fit a parametric model to the data to describe parsimoniously the death process of newspapers. The parametric model is also the first step toward estimating the effects of exogenous variables on variations in age dependent death rates.

Since the rates of death are apparently age dependent for both countries, we use a stochastic model with an age dependent property, Makeham's (1859) extension of the Gompertz (1825) law:

$$h(t) = \alpha_0 + \beta_0 \exp(\gamma_0 t), \qquad (2)$$

where α_0, β_0, and γ_0 are the parameters describing the process by which the rate declines exponentially over time. Provided, as in our estimates below, that γ_0 is negative, the parameter β_0 gives that portion of the death rate due solely to infant mortality, α_0 gives the asymptotic rate that represents the value of the hazard function once age is no longer a factor, and γ_0 controls the speed with which the rate moves toward the asymptotic level α_0.

Using the maximum-likelihood program of Tuma (1980), we estimated the parameters of the Gompertz hazard function for newspaper deaths in Argentina and Ireland. The estimates for Argentina are:

$$h(t) = .035 + 1.08 \exp(-.484t) \qquad (3.1)$$

and for Ireland are:

$$h(t) = .020 + .276 \exp(-.429t) \qquad (3.2)$$

In both equations, all parameters are significant at the .01 probability level and chi-square likelihood ratio tests show the model to be a significant improvement over a constant rate model.

Comparing the estimates for the two countries leads to several observations. Despite slightly higher values for Argentina, the decline (γ_0) and asymptote (α_0) parameters are similar for the two equations. This suggests that the aging pattern and the death rate for older papers are similar in both countries. The estimates of the infant mortality (β_0) parameter, however, are considerably different. These observations are confirmed by the data in Table 1, which presents the predicted rates at different ages in a newspaper's life. These predictions show a higher rate of death in Argentina than in Ireland for newspapers at all ages. Nonetheless, the aging patterns are similar

Table 1. Predicted Rates of Death for Newspapers

Age of Newspaper (in years)	Predicted Rate of Death	
	Argentina	Ireland
0.0	1.115	.296
0.5	.883	.243
1.0	.701	.200
2.0	.445	.137
3.0	.288	.096
4.0	.191	.070
5.0	.131	.052
10.0	.044	.024
15.0	.036	.020
20.0	.035	.020
25.0	.035	.020
50.0	.035	.020
100.0	.035	.020

Note: The parameter estimates for these predictions are shown in Equations (3.1) and (3.2).

in the two countries: the rate is highest when newspapers are young, and gradually declines with age until the asymptote is approached at approximately age fifteen.

Observations from two countries do not supply a firm basis for generalizations. Yet the similarity in the ages of stabilization of the rates of death for these two countries is a remarkable coincidence worth further investigation. This coincidence might imply that two distinct processes account for the disappearance of organizations—one linked to what we have called infant mortality, the other based on different factors and seemingly operating randomly.

The estimates of the Gompertz hazard function describe a liability of newness for newspapers in both Argentina and Ireland. Perhaps more importantly, these estimates suggest that variation in the overall death rates between countries is due primarily to differential infant mortality. This observation suggests a refinement of the environmental-selection models of organizational change proposed by Hannan and Freeman (1977) and by Aldrich (1979). We suggest that environmental selection operates with greatest force on new organizations. If this is the case, then selection theory for organizations should focus on the variations in the liability of newness across organizational forms and environments, rather than on the differential death rates of established organizations. This focus would represent a significant shift in the current mode of characterizing selection and organizational mortality.

Our estimates of the death process also speak to critics of the ecological perspective like Scott (1981), who argued that, because large organizations rarely die, the selection model is plausible only for small organizations. To the extent that age and size coincide, our model leads one to expect that, relative to the total death rate in an organizational community, the death rates of large and old organizations will appear minuscule (see also the discussion in Starbuck and Nystrom, 1981). The critics of the ecological perspective appear to fail to consider the cross-sectional implications of aging in an organizational population.

Another serious criticism of selection perspectives on organizational change is that they assume a high degree of structural rigidity or inertia among organizations. Orthodox scholars point out that there exists a plethora of examples of organizations modifying both their behavior and their structure in response to environmental fluctuations. Indeed, it is the task of high-level corporate executives and other leaders to devise and implement such modifications. The proven adaptiveness of organizations seems to make selection theoretically superfluous. Our finding about the predominance of infant mortality allows us to relax dramatically the assumption of structural inertia. Organizations need be rigid for only a short initial period in their lives in order to become subject to severe environmental selection. Having passed this infancy test, survivors may indeed adapt to changing environments. Characterizing the process in such a way, we reconcile the selection perspective with the common-sense observations of organizational adaptation.[5]

Our characterization of inertia and the selection process also underscores Stinchcombe's (1965) suggestion to examine closely the social conditions at the time of an organization's founding. Since the greatest variations in the rates of death immediately follow the founding period, the environment is critical during this period both for organizations that live and for those that die. This focus also allows the methodological simplification of assuming the environmental variables are fixed, at least as a first approximation.[6]

These theoretical points have practical research implications. Organizations that disappear shortly after birth are the most likely to leave no records behind. Because of a natural paucity of the most appropriate data, it may be inherently difficult to establish that selection occurs in populations of organizations.

In the remainder of the paper, we examine the effects of several aspects of the environment on the mortality of Argentinian and Irish newspapers: the general period of their birth considered in relation to the history of the press industry; the actual moment of their birth in historical time and in economic time; the overall economic context during their birth; and the political stability of the period of their birth.

Cohort Dependence in the Death Rates

We have shown that a newspaper's mortality depends heavily on its age. Does this relationship vary with the historical timing of a newspaper's founding? To answer this question, we study the life chances of each successive twenty-year birth cohort.[7] We expect the life chances of individual papers to increase in successive cohorts for several reasons, all concerning the newness of the newspaper industry in the nineteenth century.

One intuitive reason is that new products often appear strange. They lack commercial and institutional legitimacy. Lack of commercial legitimacy makes it difficult to amass the initially required financial resources. Analysis of the titles of Argentinian newspapers suggests that the first newspapers were political organs and thus were probably supported by donations. Titles of Irish newspapers are more ambiguous but do not contradict this idea. Perhaps, like many new industries, the newspaper industry must first survive a critical early period and then gradually gain consumer acceptance until, finally, the newspaper becomes a normal household product.

Lack of political legitimacy for the press should have widely divergent consequences in different political environments. By the time the first newspapers appeared in British-controlled Ireland, a substantial and lively press existed in other parts of the British Isles. Newspaper issues may have been seized in politically oppressed nineteenth-century Ireland, but the publication of a newspaper was not generally sufficient cause for being thrown in jail.

The political legitimacy of the press in Argentina was more uncertain. The first newspapers were launched by the political elite. This de facto legitimacy was soon wrecked by the Rosas dictatorship. Rosas sponsored most of the existing press organs, with consequences that would appear paradoxical in the absence of an ecological explanation: newspapers started during his long rule, presumably with his approval, experienced a low level of infant mortality and hence enjoyed a long life expectancy. The experiences of the Argentinian press may be more typical in the industry than the Irish. For example, the first American newspaper editor, Benjamin Harris, was jailed in 1690 for the one-time publication of *Publick Occurrences, Both Foreign and Domestick*. Immediately subsequent American newspapers operated only with direct sponsorship of the governors (Mott, 1962; Emery and Emery, 1978).

The youth of the industry also implies an absence of accumulated technical knowledge. This must have decreased the life chances of newspapers in the early cohorts. In the early 1800s, most newspapers in both Argentina and Ireland must have been started and staffed by individuals with little or no previous press experience. By 1900, several hundred newspapers had seen the light of day. Presumably, a large pool of skilled personnel had accumulated from which press entrepreneurs could draw at will. An industry lore of some usefulness had also amassed.

In Figure 4, we present the log survivor plots for each successive twenty-year cohort of Argentinian newspapers. The early cohorts have extremely high rates of death for newspapers of all ages. The more recent cohorts continue to display an inverse relationship between age and the probability of death. The rate of death for any given age is lower for the more recent cohorts. As we expected, the force of mortality for Argentinian newspapers declines monotonically with cohort recency.

The cohort plots for Ireland (Figure 5) show little, if any, cohort dependence in the rates of death. At least as noteworthy, the mortality curve of the most recent Argentinian cohort closely resembles the mortality curve of all the Irish cohorts.

These findings beg our earlier arguments for qualification. Considering the cohort question in Ireland first, we argue that our failure to observe cohort dependence in the Irish press is an artifact of our observation period. By 1800, when we begin oberving the Irish industry, the periodical publishing industry had been in spotty existence for many years, publishing newsletters and pamphlets as well as newspapers. The commercial and political legitimacy of the press had been established. Skilled labor and industry lore likely had accumulated. Moreover, if the local Irish resources had ever reached an insufficient level, additional resources easily could have been imported from Great Britain, where they existed in substantial quantities.

In Argentina, by contrast, the beginning of our observation coincides with the actual birth of the industry. Also, Argentina was extremely distant from the existing resource pools, at least until the advent of the steamship during the middle of the century. Consequently, Argentina probably allows us a purer observation of the effect of the age of the industry on cohort mortality.

The stabilization of the cohort mortality rates at approximately the same level indicates there is a ceiling on the returns to industry of age and development. We argue that the newspaper industry—as distinct from the individual newspapers—reaches an age of maturity in which the process of legitimization has been completed, a stable labor pool of specialized skills has been developed, and the organizational members of the industry have been well integrated into the economy. At this point, additional industry growth does not provide additional resources to individual organizations, and, consequently, additional industry maturity does not affect the life chances of new individual press organizations.

The Economic Environment

Our analysis points to the existence of critical early years in the organizational life cycle. Stinchcombe (1965) has suggested that organizations tend to carry throughout their lives some of the traits they acquire at birth. Whatever the specific feature of this imprinting process hypothesized by Stinchcombe, it is likely to be influenced by the abundance of resources. We argue that for newspapers, capital availability and the financial contribution of the readership in the initial period will have a direct impact on structure and, subsequently, on life chances.

Figure 4. Log Survivor Plots for Argentinian Newspapers by Birth Cohort

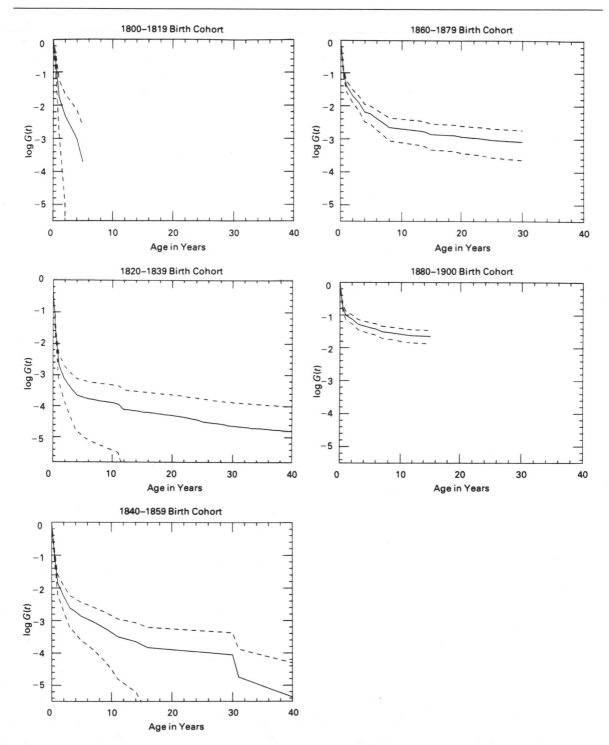

Figure 5.   Log Survivor Plots for Irish Newspapers by Birth Cohort

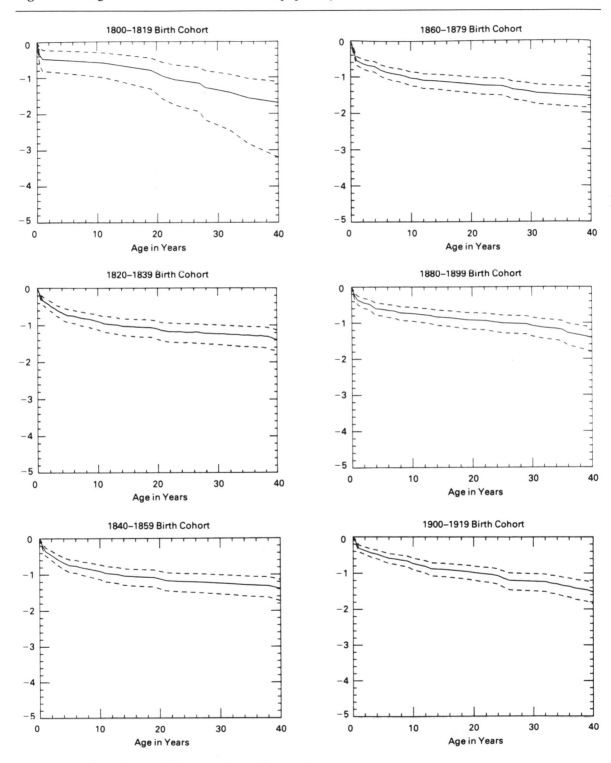

Figure 3 (Continued)

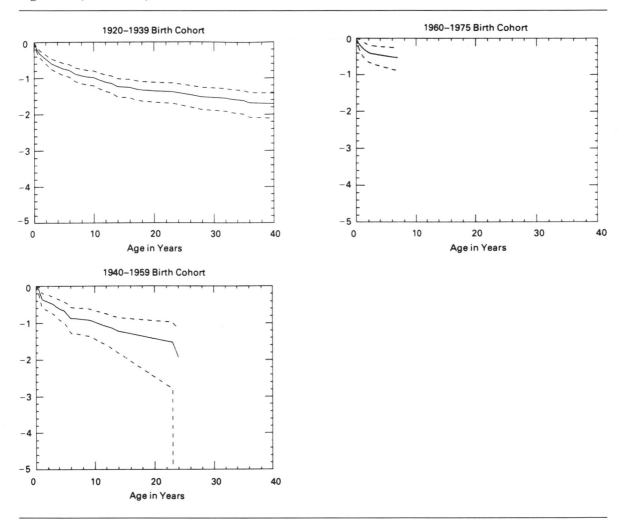

From the beginning of the nineteenth century onward, resource availability in the European and neo-European world has been subject to two distinct types of variations: short-term business cycles and an overall trend of tremendous expansion in the size of the economy. Given the imprinting process, both short-term cyclical fluctuations in the economy and long-term expansion of economic life should affect the life expectancy of newspapers. These economic factors should affect life chances in the phase of newspapers' lives where they are most vulnerable—that is, in their early years.

We explore these ideas by estimating hazard functions that specify the mortality rate as a parametric function of economic variables. We use models of the form:

$$h(t) = \alpha_0 + \exp[\beta_0 + \beta_1 X_1(t') + \cdots + \beta_K X_K(t')] \times \exp(\gamma_0 t), \qquad (4)$$

where $h(t)$ is the hazard, each $X(t')$ is an exogenous variable measured at time of birth t', and the β parameters measure the effects of the economic variables. The parameters are estimated using Tuma's (1980) maximum-likelihood program.

Table 2. Effects of Economic Variables on the Rates of Death of Newspapers in Nineteenth-Century Argentina

Exogenous Variable	Data Years	$\hat{\alpha}_0$	$\hat{\beta}_0$	$\hat{\beta}_1$	$\hat{\gamma}_0$
Dummy for peak year of industrial cycle	1800–1900	.035*	.052	.161*	−.480*
Dummy for trough year of industrial cycle	1800–1900	.035*	.091*	−.084	−.483*
Meat production	1831–1889	.033*	.418*	−.002*	−.418*
Grain production	1831–1889	.033*	.242*	−.046*	−.418*
Wool exports	1830–1889	.033*	.345*	−.002*	−.411*
Imports of fencing wire	1850–1899	.036*	.244*	−.008*	−.488*
Number of sheep	1857–1887	.032*	.182	−.032*	−.430*
Total value of export trade	1871–1900	.039*	.173	−.001*	−.539*
Total value of foreign trade	1800–1900	.034*	.377*	−.002*	−.436*
U.K. industrial production index	1800–1900	.034*	.600*	−.014*	−.433*
U.K. gross national product	1850–1900	.035*	.571*	−.001*	−.484*

*$p < .05$.

Note: The estimated models of the form $h(t) = \hat{\alpha}_0 = \exp[\hat{\beta}_0 + \hat{\beta}_1 X_1(t')] \exp(\hat{\gamma}_0 t)$. Parameter $\hat{\beta}_1$ is the estimate of the effect of the exogenous variable on the rate of death.

We explore first the effect of the business cycle on newspaper mortality. According to conventional wisdom, organizational demographics respond to the cyclical variations in the economy. When the economy is on the upswing, entrepreneurs are stimulated to establish new firms. Conversely, a downturn in the economy implies a contracting market and decreasing availability of capital. As the economic trough nears, bankruptcies and other organizational failures become more frequent. There is general agreement that it is more difficult to start a new business in times of recession and depression than during prosperity. We expect that newspapers launched near the trough should be in greater jeopardy than those founded near the peaks.

Business-cycle measures are generally difficult to find for the nineteenth century. For countries such as Ireland and Argentina, direct measures simply do not exist. Fortunately, it is possible to find good approximations of the business cycles of these two countries. Since both countries' economies are tightly linked to the United Kingdom's economy during the entire nineteenth century (Argentina's even more so than Ireland's), we simply use the United Kingdom's industrial-cycle measures from Aldcroft and Fearon (1972). Peak years and trough years in the industrial cycle are coded as separate dummy variables in which the value of unity is assigned to newspapers born in these years and the value zero is assigned to others.

The second type of economic variation we expect to influence the life chances of newspapers is expansion in the host country's economy. In the nineteenth century, both Argentina and Ireland moved from near subsistence and relatively autarkic economies to clearly capitalistic (though dependent) economies. As both countries began producing for a largely exterior market, the scale and complexity of their economic activities, as well as the intricateness of their social systems, expanded.

All measures of economic development available for nineteenth-century Argentina and Ireland are epistemologically imperfect and chronologically fragmented. We also do not have identical measures for the two countries. To compensate for these weaknesses, we use a variety of some-

Table 3. Effects of Economic Variables on the Rates of Death of Newspapers Founded in Nineteenth-Century Ireland

Exogenous Variable	Data Years	$\hat{\alpha}_0$	$\hat{\beta}_0$	$\hat{\beta}_1$	$\hat{\gamma}_0$
Dummy for peak year of industrial cycle	1800–1900	.020*	−1.19*	−.120	−.489*
Dummy for trough year of industrial cycle	1800–1900	.020*	−1.25*	.250	−.488*
Length of railway line open	1800–1900	.021*	−1.05*	−.00008*	−.483*
Number of agricultural employees**	1841–1900	.022*	−2.26*	.0009*	−.521*
Life expectancy	1871–1900	.022*	9.085	−.210	−.580*
U.K. industrial production index	1801–1900	.021*	−.983*	−.007*	−.485*
U.K. gross national product	1850–1900	.021*	−1.047*	−.0002*	−.485*

*$p < .05$.
**An inverse measure of industrialization.

Note: The estimated model is of the form $h(t) = \hat{\alpha}_0 + \exp[\hat{\beta}_0 + \hat{\beta}_1 X_1(t')]\exp(\hat{\gamma}_0 t)$. Thus the parameter $\hat{\beta}_1$ is the estimate of the effect of the exogenous variable on the rate of death.

what unusual, although historically justifiable, measures of economic development. For agriculturally exporting Argentina, we use production measures of the meat, grain, and wool industries. We also use the measures of the imports of fencing wire (used extensively in commercial ranching), the total value of export trade, and the total value of foreign trade in general. For Ireland, economic development is measured by length of the railway network, life expectancy, and, inversely, the number of agricultural employees. (Appendix C lists the sources for our data.)

We expect the estimates based on the several indicators of economic expansion to converge both within and between countries. As further check, we include for both countries estimates of the effects of economic expansion in the United Kingdom. This is justified by the tight dependence of both countries on the United Kingdom.

In Tables 2 and 3, we present the estimates of the effects of the economic indicators on newspaper mortality in the nineteenth century in Argentina and Ireland. In each table, α_0 represents the rates of death of newspapers once they reach the age at which infant mortality no longer has an impact. The parameter β_0 represents constant infant mortality, and γ_0 controls the decreases of the rate associated with age. The effect on the hazard function of each economic variable measured at the time of newspaper birth is given by the parameter β_1.

Our estimates of the effects of business cycles on the rates of death are paradoxical and unconvincing. An Argentinian newspaper born in a peak year has a significantly greater chance of disappearing earlier than a newspaper not born in a peak year. Birth in a trough year has a negative but insignificant effect for the Argentinian papers. In Ireland, the estimates of effects of the business-cycle measures are also inconclusive. The signs of the coefficients agree with the common-sense expectations, but the values fail to reach statistical significance.

It is possible that these tests are based on insufficiently sophisticated measures of economic cyclicality. The issue may deserve further study using more refined measures. However, Davis (1939) and Kinnard and Malinowski (1960) reported similar findings.

Economic expansion apparently lowers newspaper mortality in both countries. The estimates for all indicators converge and are significant at the .05 level except Irish life expectancy, which is a peculiar measure, given Ireland's idiosyncratic human demographic history. Although this finding appears strong, it does not establish the universality of the simpleminded idea that birth in a developed economy improves life chances. To understand the limitations of this idea, we need to detour and review the likely underlying mechanisms of the effects of economic development on organizational mortality.

There are few specific explanations of how organizations' life chances are affected by the level of development of the economy. One is that the greater abundance of resources (skilled labor and capital, in particular) in developed economies enhances the life chances of organizations (Stinchcombe, 1965). Hawley (1978) has argued that the ties among organizations in mature economies are primarily symbiotic. Since organizations in developed economies enjoy greater network integration, this symbiotic relationship should increase the ability of organizations to survive crises.

These arguments imply that each new industry begins in an environment that is poor relative to its specific needs. Elimination of this absolute poverty should improve the life chances of the individual members of the industry. However, this relationship is not likely to be forever self-perpetuating. There are two theoretical reasons to expect an attenuation of the relationship. First, resource availability and network support may easily have decreasing marginal utilities for individual organizations. Newspapers may need a minimum of resources and network support to survive; once this minimum is reached, other factors may cause newspaper mortality. The second reason is that an abundance of resources and network support may bring about a surfeit of newspapers, triggering mechanisms of concentration. Once the conditions of existence for the press have been defined through numerous separate and unrelated ventures, there develops a field of activity ready for capture by superior competitors.

By these views, the nineteenth century in both Argentina and Ireland is a period of deprivation for the whole press, in which scarcity and lack of network support are the main forces of mortality.

In the twentieth century or some fraction thereof, survival is assured for the newspaper industry, and competition within the industry predominates as the main source of mortality. If this is the case, then the economic variables should have a lesser impact in the twentieth century.

We attempted to test this idea with data for newspapers in twentieth-century Ireland. We do not report the estimates here, but our findings lend credibility to the preceding arguments. The economic variables cease to have statistically significant effects on newspapers born in the twentieth century. Although this issue certainly deserves further attention, it appears from our analysis that economic development increases the life expectancy of organizations at a decreasing rate.

Political Turmoil

Our unpublished analysis of organizational births shows that periods of political turmoil are especially fecund for the press. We argue that political turmoil is the visible expression of underlying social realignments that alter the resource environments for press organs. Tinker (1932: 282) illustrates this phenomenon by describing the impact of the Civil War in the United States on the French-language press of Louisiana:

> The Civil War in 1861 killed many papers, but New Orleans was captured the next year and the struggle which began between the carpet-baggers and Negroes on one side and ex-Confederates on the other, gave birth to eighteen partisan papers in New Orleans. Seventeen were started in the Parishes.

Such accounts raise the question, how long is the life of a newspaper born under tumultuous conditions? Newspapers created in a context of turmoil may be thought of as opportunistic organisms not genuinely fitted to the long-term variations of the wider social and economic environment.

We expect newspapers born in politically turbulent years to be short-lived. This expectation is based on two possibly additive but distinct theoretical ideas. First, newspapers founded during political crises are likely to be established for an explicit political purpose and, consequently, to become obsolete once the crisis is resolved. Second, political turbulence disrupts, or is a sign of disruption of, the previous social alignments; it often alters the ties between social groups and societal resources. When such realignment proceeds, resources are free for a short period. As ecologists have pointed out, the first groups to exploit these resources are those with the most flexible structures, labeled r-strategists by Lauwagie (1979) and Brittain and Freeman (1980). These first movers thrive in irregular resource spaces, but they are usually out-competed in stable conditions. Thus, we expect that when political disruption disturbs the newspaper market, opportunistic enterprises will thrive for a short period but eventually will be pushed out of the market by the more traditional press organs.

We tested these arguments by estimating the changes in the rates of death associated with birth in a politically turbulent year. To measure turbulence, we devised a dummy variable, POLIT. This variable has the value of unity in years when national political events occurred that historians generally agree provoked intense reactions in or involvement by contemporaries; it has the value of zero otherwise. This coding procedure does not involve a posteriori historical judgment on our part. For example, the year 1939, which marks the onset of World War II in Europe, is not a politically turbulent year for Ireland, but the year 1915 is turbulent because of the Easter Rising. The list of politically turbulent years and the events justifying their classification is presented for both countries in Appendix D.

We estimated the effect of POLIT in an equation similar to Equation (4). If it is true that newspapers born in politically turbulent years have shorter life spans, the parameters associated with POLIT will be positive. The estimated equations are

$$h(t) = 0.35 + \exp(-.010 + .289\text{POLIT})$$
$$\times \exp(-.472t) \qquad (5.1)$$

for Argentina and

$$h(t) = .020 + \exp(-1.36 + .190\text{POLIT})$$
$$\times \exp(-.431t) \qquad (5.2)$$

for Ireland. The parameters in both equations are in the expected directions. The POLIT parameter for Argentina is significant at the .01 level; the parameter for Ireland at the .10 level only.

Table 4 shows the predicted values of the hazard function from these parameter estimates. As expected, newspapers born in turbulent years exhibit higher infant-mortality rates in both countries. The effect continues until between the tenth and fifteenth years of existence.

Table 4 also shows that political turmoil at birth exerts a more severe effect in Argentina than in Ireland. This difference can be explained in several ways. It is probable that Argentinian political crises did not have the cumulative directionality of Irish political events, which culminated in a genuine independence movement. Unlike Irish newspapers, Argentinian newspapers created at times of crises quickly outlived their usefulness. But it is also likely that nineteenth-century political crises in Argentina corresponded to deeper social realignments than did those in Ireland, where political turbulence in the last two centuries represented only a portion of a larger political process. Such speculation implies that Argentinian newspapers born during politically turbulent years were more likely than their Irish counterparts to have r-strategy properties.

Since we used a dummy variable that did not measure the intensity of turmoil, we were unable to adjudicate between these two interpretations of the POLIT effect. We could, however, address this problem indirectly by estimating hazard-function differences of newspapers born in years characterized by political activity but not by an especially high level of turbulence.

We chose years of national elections and other regime changes. Since national elections must motivate partisans to establish newspapers with explicitly political purposes, newspapers born in such years must comprise large proportions of newspapers that run the risk of being instantly obsolete once the event is past.

The new variable ELECT was also a dummy variable, coded one if a newspaper was created in a year of election or other regime change, and zero otherwise. The estimated effects of ELECT are

Table 4. Predicted Effects of the POLIT Variable on the Rates of Death of Newspapers

Age of Newspaper (in years)	Predicted Rate of Death for Argentina (N=1454)		Predicted Rate of Death for Ireland (N=996)	
	Papers Established in Year without Political Turbulence	Papers Established in Year with Political Turbulence	Papers Established in Year without Political Turbulence	Papers Established in Year without Political Turbulence
0	1.024	1.355	.267	.467
.5	.816	1.078	.227	.270
1	.652	.859	.187	.222
2	.420	.549	.128	.151
3	.275	.355	.090	.105
4	.785	.235	.066	.075
5	.128	.160	.050	.056
10	.044	.047	.023	.024
15	.036	.036	.020	.020
20	.035	.035	.020	.020
25	.035	.035	.020	.020
50	.035	.035	.020	.020
100	.035	.035	.020	.020

Note: The parameter estimates used for these predictions are shown in Equations (5.1) and (5.2).

$$h(t) = .035 + \exp(-.027 + .159\text{ELECT})$$
$$\times \exp(-.472t) \quad (6.1)$$

for Argentina and

$$h(t) = .020 + \exp(-1.29 + .200\text{ELECT})$$
$$\times \exp(-.429t) \quad (6.2)$$

for Ireland.

In Ireland, ELECT had a negative effect, which suggests that newspapers born in election years live longer than average. The associated coefficient, however, is not statistically significant. In Argentina, the ELECT coefficient was positive and was significant at the .05 level. These estimates begin to move the weight of evidence in favor of the r-strategist interpretation; whereas the POLIT effect behaved in the expected direction for both countries, ELECT agreed with the prediction in only one country.

A third explanation for the positive POLIT effect derives from our earlier observation that politically turbulent years are characterized by high rates of newspaper founding. For example, in Ireland 36 percent of all newspapers were born in tumultuous years, which constitutes only 26 percent of the period; in Argentina, the proportions were 29 percent and 27 percent respectively. These facts imply that newspapers born in political years are members of larger birth cohorts and consequently are subjected to greater than average competition in their early, vulnerable years. This overcrowding, rather than the r-strategist process we hypothesize, might account for their initial high mortality.

In an attempt to test this alternative explanation, we reestimated the hazard functions, substituting for POLIT the variable FOUNDS, which measures the numbers of newspaper foundations in the year of a newspaper's first publication. The estimates with FOUNDS are

$$h(t) = .035 + \exp(-.001 + .004\text{FOUNDS})$$
$$\times \exp(-.431t) \quad (7.1)$$

for Argentina and

$$h(t) = .020 + \exp(-1.20 + .011\text{FOUNDS})$$
$$\times \exp(-.427t) \qquad (7.2)$$

for Ireland.

The effects of FOUNDS failed to reach statistical significance in either equation. However, it was positive for Argentina, leaving open the possibility that the previously adduced effect of POLIT was spurious.

As a stronger test of the POLIT effect, we reestimated the model with both variables included. The results were

$$h(t) = .035 + \exp(-.007 - .0002\text{FOUNDS}$$
$$+ .290\text{POLIT}) \exp(-.472t) \qquad (8.1)$$

for Argentina and

$$h(t) = .020 + \exp(-1.23 - .020\text{FOUNDS}$$
$$+ .236\text{POLIT}) \exp(-.424t) \qquad (8.2)$$

for Ireland. In both equations, the parameter for the POLIT variable was significant at least at the .05 probability level, and the FOUNDS parameter was insignificant.

These last findings lend more plausibility to the hypothesis that r-strategists spawned in large numbers by political turbulence account for the shorter life expectancy of newspapers born under such conditions. We argue that newspapers born during these social realignments have a high adaptive capacity for dynamic and irregular resource environments but a low adaptive capacity for more stable environments. Of course, greater confidence in the argument awaits a more direct test using more refined data.

Conclusion

We began this paper by arguing for the study of organizational mortality in an environmental context. Our research on newspapers has taken a first step in this direction. The analysis suggests strongly that the Makeham's Law hazard function is a good general model of the timing of organizational deaths. Moreover, our estimates of this model consistently show that the major variation in organizational death rates occurs in the early ages of organizational life. This observation, that en-

vironmental selection acts with greatest force on new organizations, should prove useful in future research on organizational mortality.

Our estimates of the effects of specific environmental conditions on newspaper death rates met with only limited success. On the one hand, our analysis clearly demonstrates that organizational mortality rates vary across a wide range of environmental dimensions, including industry age, economic development, and political turbulence. On the other hand, as in many historical explorations, data often did not allow us to choose among alternative interpretations of these findings. This situation is both frustrating and challenging. It is frustrating because it prevents us from immediately answering questions that we find genuinely interesting. It is challenging because we think the analysis has shown there is merit in our approach.

Notes

1   Hannan and Freeman (1977) argued persuasively that environmental selection operates on populations of organizations through differential mortality rates. Since birth rates can also vary across populations, selection processes at the population level do not necessarily imply similar or consistent processes at the individual level. Despite this theoretical possibility, the literature on organizational ecology often presumes that individual-level selection will parallel population-level selection. This does not seem totally unreasonable since inconsistency across the levels of analysis implies that entrepreneurs are founding large numbers of firms in conditions in which most of them will fail rather quickly. While we note this distinction, we refrain from taking a stance on the issue. Our approach is to study the demography of failure in individual organizations without arguing that a similar population-level process applies. We think that, given the current orientation of organizational ecology, the failure to find evidence of selection via mortality at the individual level would lead to a major rethinking of how to model selection processes in populations of organizations.

2   More thorough treatments of survival analysis can be found in Gross and Clark (1975) and in Kalbfleisch and Prentice (1980).

3   This can be seen by reviewing the relationship between the hazard function and the survivor function.

We can express this relationship in two ways. First, the hazard function is

$$h(t) = \frac{-d \log G(t)}{dt}.$$

We can also state the survivor function in terms of the hazard rate,

$$G(t) = \exp\left[-\int_0^t h(s)\,ds\right]$$

which shows the survivor function to be an exponential function of the rate integrated over time. These properties of the relationship are extremely important because they imply that when the log survivor function is plotted against time, the negative slope of that line or curve is the rate of death.

4 In many instances, population heterogeneity in the rates also implies a curve in the log survivor plots. The liability-of-newness arguments give us strong theoretical reasons to prefer the time-dependence argument.

5 This relaxation of the assumption, of course, still leaves open the problem of whether inertia applies to the first five years of operation. This is a substantive problem not addressed in this paper.

6 In certain instances, theoretical reasons prompt one to choose fixed environmental variables anyway. For example, in this paper we argue that the values of specific environmental variables at the time of organizational birth are the relevant selection conditions.

7 Our choice of twenty-year cohorts is somewhat arbitrarily based on the wish to observe a sequence of cohorts but to retain large enough samples to yield meaningful comparison.

References

Aldcroft, D.H., and P. Fearon. 1972. British Economic Fluctuations 1790–1939. London: McMillan.

Aldrich, Howard E. 1979. Organizations and Environments. Englewood Cliffs, NJ: Prentice-Hall.

British Library. 1975. Catalogue of the Newspaper Library (Ireland). London.

British Museum. 1905. Catalogue of Printed Books. Supplement—Newspapers Published in Great Britain and Ireland 1801–1900. London: William Clowes.

Brittain, Jack W., and John Freeman. 1980. "Organizational proliferation and density-dependence selection: Organizational evolution in the semiconductor industry." In J. Kimberly and R. Miles (eds.), Organizational Life Cycles: 291–338. San Francisco: Jossey-Bass.

Cortese, A. 1959. Historia economica argentina y americana. Buenos Aires: Macchi.

Cox, D.R., and P.A.W. Lewis. 1966. Statistical Analysis of Series of Events. London: Methuen.

Davis, Horace B. 1939. "Business mortality: The shoe manufacturing industry." Harvard Business Review, 17: 331–38.

Emery, Edwin, and Michael Emery. 1978. The Press and America, 4th ed. Englewood Cliffs, NJ: Prentice-Hall.

Fernandez, J.R. 1943. Historia del periodismo argentino. Buenos Aires: Perlado.

Fitzgibbon, Russell H., ed. 1974. Argentina: A Chronology and a Fact Book. Dobbs Ferry, NY: Oceana.

Galvan-Moreno, C. 1944. El periodismo argentino, amplia y documentada historia desde sus origenes hasta el presente. Buenos Aires: Editorial claridad.

Gompertz, Benjamin. 1825. "On the nature of the function expressive of the law of human mortality, and on a new mode of determining the value of life contingents." Philosophical Transactions of the Royal Society, 115: 513–80.

Gross, Alan J., and Virginia A. Clark. 1975. Survival Distributions: Reliability Applications in the Biomedical Sciences. New York: Wiley.

Hannan, Michael T., and John Freeman. 1977. "The population ecology of organizations." American Journal of Sociology, 82: 929–64.

———. 1981. "Dynamics of niche width in organizational populations." Technical Report No. 2, Institute for Mathematical Studies in the Social Sciences, Organization Studies Section, Stanford, CA: Stanford University.

Hanson, S.G. 1938. Argentine Meat and the British Market: Chapters on the Argentine Meat Industry. Stanford, CA: Stanford University Press.

Hawley, Amos. 1978. "Cumulative change in theory and history." American Sociological Review, 43: 787–96.

Ingenieros, Jose. 1937. La evolucion de las ideas argentinas, Vol 13, Book 1. Buenos Aires: Rosso.

Ireland Central Statistics Office. Various years. Census of Population of Ireland. Dublin: Stationery Office.

Irish Free State. Various years. Statistical Abstracts. Dublin.

Kalbfleisch, John D., and Ross L. Prentice. 1980. The Statistical Analysis of Failure Time Data. New York: Wiley.

Kaplan, E.L., and P. Meier. 1958. "Non-parametric estimation from incomplete observations." Journal of the American Statistical Association, 53: 457–81.

Kennedy, R.E. 1973. The Irish: Emigration, Marriage, and Fertility. Berkeley, CA: University of California Press.

Kinnard, William N., and Z. Malinowski. 1960. The Turnover and Mortality of Manufacturing Firms in the Hartford, Connecticut, Economic Area. Hartford, CT: University of Connecticut Management Research Program.

Lauwagie, Beverly. 1979. "Ethnic boundaries in modern states: Romano Lavo-Lil revisited." American Journal of Sociology, 85: 310–28.

Levene, R. 1937. A History of Argentina. Chapel Hill, NC: University of North Carolina Press.

Makeham, W.M. 1859. "On the law of mortality and construction of annuity tables." The Assu Magazine, 8: 301–10.

McCaffrey, L.J. 1979. Ireland from Colony to Nation State. Englewood Cliffs, NJ: Prentice-Hall.

McCartney, D. 1967. "From Parnell to Pearse (1891–1921)." In T.W. Moody and F.X. Martin (eds.), The Course of Irish History: 294–312. New York: Weybright and Talley.

McCracken, J.L. 1967. "Northern Ireland (1921–66)." In T.W. Moody and F.X. Martin (eds.), The Course of Irish History: 314–24. New York: Weybright and Talley.

Meenan, J. 1970. The Irish Economy since 1922. Liverpool, England: Liverpool University Press.

Mitchell, Brian R. 1976. Abstract of British Historical Statistics. Cambridge, England: Cambridge University Press.

———. 1978. European Historical Statistics, 1750–1970. New York: Columbia University Press.

Moody, T.W. 1967. "Fenianism, Home Rule, and the land war (1850–1891)." In T.W. Moody and F.X. Martin (eds.), The Course of Irish History: 275–93. New York: Weybright and Talley.

Mott, Frank Luther. 1962. American Journalism, 3rd. ed. New York: Macmillan.

Mulhall, M.G. 1903. The Dictionary of Statistics. London: Routledge.

Oddone, J. 1937. El factor economico en nuestras luchas civiles. Buenos Aires: La vanguardia.

O'Farrell, P. 1971. Ireland's English Question: Anglo-Irish Relations 1834–1970. New York: Shocken.

O'Thuataigh, G. 1972. Ireland before the Famine: 1798–1848. Dublin: Gill and McMillan.

Scobie, J.R. 1964. Argentina: A City and a Nation. New York: Oxford University Press.

Scott, W. Richard 1981. Organizations: Rational, Natural, and Open Systems. Englewood Cliffs, NJ: Prentice-Hall.

Starbuck, William H., and Paul C. Nystrom. 1981. "Designing and understanding organizations." In Paul C. Nystrom and William H. Starbuck (eds.), Handbook of Organizational Design, 1: ix–xxii. London: Oxford University Press.

Stinchcombe, Arthur L. 1965. "Organizations and social structure." In James G. March (ed.), Handbook of Organizations: 153–93. Chicago: Rand McNally.

Tinker, Edward L. 1932. "Bibliography of the French newspapers and periodicals of Louisiana." Proceedings of the American Antiquarian Society, 44: 247–370.

Tuma, Nancy Brandon. 1980. Invoking Rate. Menlo Park, CA: SRI International.

Tuma, Nancy Brandon, Michael T. Hannan, and Lyle P. Groenveld. 1979. "Dynamic analysis of event-histories." American Journal of Sociology, 84: 820–54.

U.S. Library of Congress. 1973. Newspapers in Microform (Foreign Countries). Washington, DC: Library of Congress.

Webb, A.D. 1911. The New Dictionary of Statistics, A Complement to the Fourth Edition of Mulhall's "Dictionary of Statistics." London: Routledge.

Whetten, David. 1980. "Sources, responses, and effects of organizational decline." In J. Kimberly and R. Miles (eds.), Organizational Life Cycles: 342–74. San Francisco: Jossey-Bass.

Whitaker, A.P. 1964. Argentina. Englewood Cliffs, NJ: Prentice-Hall.

Whyte, J. 1967. "The age of Daniel O'Connell (1800–1947)." In T.W. Moody and F.X. Martin (eds.), The Course of Irish History: 248–62. New York: Weybright and Talley.

Williams, N.C. 1966. Chronology of the Modern World: 1763 to the Present. London: Barrie and Roekliffe.

WORCO. 1940. Survey of Foreign Railways.

APPENDIX A
Argentinian and Irish Press Sources

Reliance on historical data is always fraught with risk. However, there are several reasons to believe the newspaper data used in this paper are not intolerably flawed.

(1) It is in the printed nature of a newspaper to leave an abundant record. Even short-lived newspapers tend to leave traces because they are often started by highly politically motivated individuals who treat their product with more respect than ordinary manufacturers. Nevertheless, we likely missed some very small, very short-lived early Argentinian publications. One ephemeral publication that *is* included in our data base, titled *Come here Portuguese for here it is,* must have been

little more than a pamphlet. Such short-lived pamphlets may have come and gone without entering the record.

(2) In poor, small countries such as Argentina and Ireland, the appearance of any publication is a rare event of great interest to the small, literate faction of the population. Such events are collected. This proposition becomes dubious in twentieth-century Argentina, where newspapers become very numerous without much improvement in their life expectancy. Accordingly, we refrained from using twentieth-century Argentinian data.

(3) For Irish data, we relied on the thorough collections of the British Museum (1905) and of the British Library (1975). The latter work completes the former and corrects it. These two sources are supplemented by the U.S. Library of Congress (1973).

Because of painstaking efforts of the British Museum to document precisely the periods of activity and latency of the listed journals, we believe that few journals could be missing.

Incidentally, the initial recording of Irish papers may have been more thorough than that of their British counterparts because of Irish papers' police value.

(4) For Argentinian sources, we benefited by a stroke of luck. In 1941, the Buenos Aires Press Club endowed a competition for the best book on the history of Argentinian journalism. The winning entry, *Historia del periodismo argentino* by J.R. Fernandez (1943) is little more than a glorified description and listing, hence presumably attentive to detail. A runner-up, C. Galvan-Moreno (in our opinion a much better scholar) published in 1944 *El periodismo argentino, amplia y documentada historia desde sus origenes hasta el presente,* prefaced with a bitter attack against Fernandez. We suppose that the late-arriving and choleric Galvan-Moreno would not have failed to criticize his rival's work on grounds of accuracy if this had seemed possible. In fact, we found that all of the nineteenth-century entries in Galvan-Moreno are found in Fernandez, but the reverse was not true. We are therefore inclined to believe that the Fernandez work we used as our source is not grossly defective.

The most likely bias, in general, is a slight underinclusion of very small and short-lived publications that might or might not be considered press organs, depending on the strictness of the definition adopted.

APPENDIX B
Estimating the Survivor Function

A simple example will show the ease with which the survivor function $G(t)$ is estimated. Suppose we follow a population of five newspapers and observe the deaths of three papers at 1.0 year, 3.0 years, and 4.0 years exactly. The remaining two newspapers are lost from observation before they die and thus are censored cases. Suppose they disappear at ages 3.5 years and 4.1 years exactly.

To calculate the survival probabilities, we use the Kaplan and Meier (1958) non-parametric estimator of the survivor function. For event-history data with censoring, this estimator is the multiplicative function:

$$\hat{G}(t) = \prod_{t_{(i)} < t} \frac{N_{(i)} - 1}{N_{(i)}}$$

where $t_{(1)} \leq \cdots \leq t_{(N^*)}$ are the ordered times of deaths from the earliest ($t_{(1)}$) to the latest ($t_{(N^*)}$) and $N_{(i)}$ is the number of papers alive immediately before the ith death.

To apply this estimator to the data in our example, we first order the papers according to ascending age at the time of last observation: 1.0, 3.0, 3.5, 4.0, 4.1. We next calculate $\hat{G}(t)$, the probability of survival, for each age at which a death is observed. That is,

$t_{(i)}$	$\hat{G}(t_{(i)})$
1.0	$4/5 = .80$
3.0	$4/5 \cdot 3/4 = .60$
4.0	$4/5 \cdot 3/4 \cdot 1/2 = .30$

As these calculations show, the probability of survival to 1.0 year is 0.80, to 3.0 years is 0.60, and to 4.0 years is 0.30.

If we had a larger population, we could plot these survival probabilities on a graph with $G(t)$ on the Y-axis and age on the X-axis. We could then draw a line connecting the plotted values and use this graph to estimate the survival probability for any age of interest.

APPENDIX C
Description of Variables and Data Sources

— ARGENTINA —

Description of Variable	*Data Years*	*Source*
ELECT; Dummy for national election and regime change years	1800–1900	Fitzgibbon (1974)

Description of Variable	Data Years	Source
Grain production, in tons	1831–1889	Mulhall (1903: 297)
Imports of fencing wire, in tons	1850–1899	Hanson (1938: 22)
Meat production, in tons	1831–1889	Mulhall (1903: 297)
Newspaper birth and death rates	1800–1900	Fernandez (1943)
Number of sheep, in millions	1857–1887	Hanson (1938: 6)
PEAK; Dummy for peak years of U.K. industrial cycle	1800–1900	Aldcroft and Fearon (1972)
POLIT; Dummy for political turmoil years	1800–1900	See Appendix D
Total value of export trade, in million pesos	1871–1900	Scobie (1964: 277)
Total value of foreign trade, in thousand sterling pounds	1800–1900	Mulhall (1903: 149); Webb (1911: 140)
TROUGH; Dummy for trough years of U.K. industrial cycle	1800–1900	Aldcroft and Fearon (1972)
U.K. industrial production index	1800–1900	Mitchell (1978: 355)
U.K. gross national product, in million pounds at constant market prices	1850–1900	Mitchell (1978: 782)
Wool exports, in millions of pounds	1830–1889	Mulhall (1903: 50)

— IRELAND —

Description of Variable	Data Years	Source
Agricultural employees	1841–1900	Ireland Central Statistics Office (Various years); Meenan (1970)
ELECT; Dummy for national election and regime change years	1800–1921	Mitchell (1976)
Exports of oats and oatmeal to U.K. in thousands of quarters	1800–1842	Mitchell (1976)
Industrial production index	1925–1969	Mitchell (1978: 356)
Length of railway line open, in kilometers	1848–1975	Mitchell (1978: 581–86); Irish Free State (Various years); WORCO (1940)
Life expectancy, in years	1870–1962	Ireland Central Statistics Office (Various years); Meenan (1970: 202)
Newspaper birth and death rates	1800–1900	British Museum (1905); British Library (1975)
PEAK; Dummy for peak years of U.K. industrial cycle	1800–1900	Aldcroft and Fearon (1972)
POLIT; Dummy for political turmoil years	1800–1975	See Appendix D
TROUGH; Dummy for trough years of U.K. industrial cycle	1800–1900	Aldcroft and Fearon (1972)
U.K. industrial production index	1800–1900	Mitchell (1978: 355)
U.K. gross national product, in million pounds at constant market prices	1850–1900	Mitchell (1978: 355)
Value of imports, in million pounds	1924–1969	Meenan (1970)
Value of exports, in million pounds	1924–1969	Meenan (1970)

APPENDIX D
Years and Events of Political Turbulence

— ARGENTINA —

1806 The British attacked and briefly occupied Buenos Aires. This event was of great political significance because the local inhabitants organized the resistance, forced the Spanish viceroy to flee, and appointed another viceroy (Fitzgibbon, 1974: 5). This, the first independent Argentinian political act, prepared the way for the first stirrings of a genuine independence movement. The 1806 British invasion gave the Argentinians their first concrete taste of autonomy.

1810 Responding to the Napoleonic invasion of Spain, the Buenos Aires city council, under popular pressure, set up a junta (Fitzgibbon, 1974: 5). The junta, the first independent governing body in Argentina, is said to have represented cattlemen's interests and to have been aided by British agents (Cortese, 1959: 264–65).

1816 A general congress of the Plata provinces formally declared independence from Spain under a republic. This decision was achieved after much vacillation (Fitzgibbon, 1974: 6) caused by Bourbon restoration in most of South America and in Spain itself. Political opinion was greatly divided (Ingenieros, 1937, 1.62: 152–53).

1820 This was "the terrible year" of considerable armed conflict between Buenos Aires and the interior provinces. A protracted struggle began between Buenos Aires "unitarians" or centralists inclined toward free trade and provincial "federalists," who were more or less protectionist (Fitzgibbon, 1974: 8; Whitaker, 1964: 27; Ingenieros, 1937).

1825 The Anglo-Argentinian trade treaty gave preferential treatment to Great Britain (Scobie, 1964: 102). This was a decisive victory for free trade, centralist forces.

1826 Centralist constitution was proclaimed against general opposition from the protectionist provinces (Fitzgibbon, 1974: 8; Whitaker, 1964: 27).

1827 The centralist head of state Rivadivia, faced by overwhelming resistance to the political centralization program, resigned under pressure (Ingenieros, 1937, 1.62: 333–39). This was a time of "civil war and near anarchy" (Fitzgibbon, 1974: 8) and of a deep reshuffling of the power structure (Oddone, 1937: 165–69).

1828–1829 (This is an example of events that *do not* lead to calling years as turbulent.) During these years, there was a war with Brazil over the independence of Uruguay. But Cortese (1959: 284) does not give this war much importance. Uruguay was declared independent under British pressure (Scobie, 1964: 90). Presumably, there was little favor for Uruguayan independence in the ranks of Argentina's masses.

1831 This year witnessed the "Federal Pact," by which the rising provincial star Rosas allied himself with another provincial leader and overtly promised to destroy the power of the leaders in Buenos Aires.

1833 In 1833 (in fact, late in 1832—Fitzgibbon, 1974: 8) Rosas refused to be reelected as governor of Buenos Aires province because he was refused dictatorial powers (Fitzgibbon, 1974: 9).

1839–1841 This was a very turbulent interlude in the otherwise quiet of Rosas' long and repressive dictatorship favoring the provinces (Cortese, 1959: 37). From the end of 1838 to 1841, the French occupied Argentina and intervened in Argentinian administration (Fitzgibbon, 1974: 9). Rosas faced political intellectual dissent in the capital (triggered by the French presence) and military risings against his dictatorial rule in some provinces (Levene, 1937: 416–20; Whitaker, 1964: 30; Scobie, 1964: 103; Oddone, 1937: 238).

1845–1848 (Another example of events *not* accompanied by turbulence.) The French-British naval blockade during this time was not accompanied by political dissidence.

1852–1853 Rosas was overthrown by a coalition of *littoral* provinces (one might think, free-trade oriented) helped by Uruguay and Brazil (Fitzgibbon, 1974: 10). A treaty with major powers opened Argentinian rivers to free navigation (Cortese, 1959: 386–87), undoubtedly a free-trade victory (Cortese, 1959: 382–83). However, conflict was renewed between Buenos Aires, unwilling to relinquish its privileged trade position, and the other provinces. A constitutional convention was held by the Argentinian provinces (Scobie, 1964: 104; Whitaker, 1964: 33–34; Cortese, 1959: 388–90), opposed by the province of Buenos Aires, which seceded.

1859–1862 The final game of musical chairs for ascendancy was played between Buenos Aires and the federalist provinces. This period includes the intermittent civil war between Buenos Aires and the united provinces. Militarily beaten, Buenos Aires joined the federation (Fitzgibbon, 1974: 10; Scobie, 1964: 104) but, in fact, ended up dominating it (Scobie, 1964: 105). The capital was again declared to be Buenos Aires (Fitzgibbon, 1974: 11). After a short-lived and defeated attempt to emasculate Buenos Aires by federalizing it (Fitzgibbon, 1974: 11), Argentina's modern institutions finally became stabilized under Buenos Aires hegemony. Whitaker (1964: 36) described the ongoing squabbles of this period as a "tame affair." The terms "Argentine nation" and Argentine "Republic" were first used (Whitaker, 1964: 37).

1880 Federalization of the city of Buenos Aires was accomplished despite resistance by the inhabitants of Buenos Aires province (Fitzgibbon, 1974: 12). The military hero Roca conducted the last military campaign against the Indians and then became president (Fitzgibbon, 1974: 12; Scobie, 1964: 114).

1890 The "Revolution of 1890" was an unsuccessful popular class revolt (Whitaker, 1964: 44), apparently the first Argentinian political movement clearly established along class lines. The first middle-class (anti-oligarchy) mass political organization entered the political scene (Fitzgibbon, 1974: 12). This Radical Civil Union was to win the election in 1916 after a long uphill struggle (Whitaker, 1964: 42). Militarily insignificant, the 1890 revolt was politically important as the perceived starting date of middle-class political power. The deputies forced the incumbent president to resign (Levene, 1937: 492–93).

1898 A national convention was held to amend electoral dispositions of the constitution. Members of all parties united (unsuccessfully) to oppose a second presidential term for Roca (Levene, 1937: 495–96).

— IRELAND —

1801 Act of Union. Ireland was formally annexed by Great Britain. Elimination of Irish representative organs generated aftereffects.

1802 De facto failure of Protestant Ascendency. There was agitation among literate, wealthy Protestants (O'Farrell, 1971: 67–71).

1803 This was the year of Emmet's rebellion and execution. He was the first of a long series of nationalist martyrs. The rebellion had little substantive significance, according to McCaffrey (1979: 39–40), but did briefly excite popular indignation.

1813 The Catholic Relief Bill was introduced in the British Commons and was rejected by main nationalist leader O'Connell. There was a massive split within Catholic ranks (O'Thuataigh, 1972: 54–55). Peace Preservation Act: installation of repressive machinery in Ireland (McCaffrey, 1979: 38).

1826 This was the year of the first election in which there was an organized Catholic partcipation (Whyte, 1967: 250–52).

1828 Catholic leader O'Connell won a seat, though he was by law barred from occupying it (Whyte, 1967: 253–55). This was a year of great popular enthusiasm.

1829 The Catholic Emancipation Act was strongly opposed by Irish Protestant elites (Whyte, 1967: 255).

1830–1831 The anti-tithes (anti-Anglican) campaign began. There was considerable cross-class and cross-country agitation (O'Thuataigh, 1972: 91, 157).

1845–1851 These were easily the most eventful six years in Ireland in the nineteenth century. Events run into one another so that it is impossible to separate years. We treat the whole period as one, which includes famine, epidemics, and massive emigration; more or less successful remedial measures to the above were adopted in the midst of great controversy (O'Thuataigh, 1972: 204). The period also includes the Maynooth Bill, endowing the Irish Catholic church despite popular opposition coming from both Protestants and Catholics (O'Farrell, 1971: 91). In 1848, the Young Ireland rising, one of the first nationalist insurrections, was suppressed (Kennedy, 1973: 43).

1858 The Irish Republic Brotherhood (Fenial) was simultaneously founded in Dublin and New York (Moody, 1967: 278).

1867 This was the year of the unsuccessful Fenian rising (Moody, 1967: 278).

1874 First general elections with secret ballot were held. A Home-Rule advocate was elected (Moody, 1967: 282).

1879–1882 "Land Wars" began between tenants and landlords (Moody, 1967: 275, 287–88). The 1881 Land Act was passed (O'Farrell, 1971: 185). In the general election, there was an overwhelming nationalist victory in Ireland for Parnell (called the "uncrowned King of Ireland" by O'Farrell, 1971: 180, 186). This was a landmark in Anglo-Irish relations (Moody, 1967: 291).

1891–1892 Parnell fell after public revelations of moral turpitude in divorce courts. Nationalist movement was split (Moody, 1967: 292; McCaffrey, 1979: 114–15; O'Farrell, 1971: 269).

1893 The second Home-Rule bill was introduced by Gladstone and defeated.

1905–1906 Sinn Fein (nationalist) party was founded in Dublin (Moody, 1967: 304). The "decisive Liberal victory" (McCaffrey, 1979: 128) in Parliament was accompanied by the Irish nationalists' winning 83 seats in Parliament (Williams, 1966).

1913 Labor struggles of great magnitude were supported by main Irish nationalist organizations (McCartney, 1967: 303; McCaffrey, 1979: 125; O'Farrell, 1971: 269).

1914 Home Rule agitation: "five armies in presence" (McCartney, 1967: 305–6). Rising in Dublin (Williams, 1966: 446).

1916 The "Easter Rebellion" (McCartney, 1967: 307) was followed by executions and the imposition of martial law.

1919–1921 "Anglo-Irish War" (McCartney, 1967: 311).

1922–1923 Civil war in South Ireland (O'Farrell, 1971: 295) ended with the execution of seventy-eight Republicans by the Irish Free State (McCaffrey, 1979: 153).

1927 General election in Ireland in which "Republican" (radical) leader DeValera, de facto joined the government's side (McCaffrey, 1979: 1965).

1932–1933 A campaign was begun for the first real Irish general elections. The first DeValera government brought together mainstreams of several nationalist movements (McCracken, 1967: 327). First manifestations of welfare-style social reforms (McCaffrey, 1979: 165). Some fascist agitation. Oath of allegiance to British Crown was formally removed from Irish Constitution.

1936–1937 External Relations Act, de facto independence with new Irish Constitution (McCracken, 1967: 321, 329) followed by the formal abolition of the Office of the (British) Governor General (O'Farrell, 1971: 281).

1948 General elections resulted in the ouster of the Conservative party–left coalition (McCaffrey, 1979: 140).

1949 The Irish Republic was formally declared a relatively minor event confirming "fait-accompli" (O'Farrell, 1971: 299).

1969–1970 Protestant violence in Ulster revived the Irish Republican Army (McCaffrey, 1979: 180–81) and the actuality of the partition issue (O'Farrell, 1971: 292).

10

Organizational Effects of Decline and Turbulence

Kim S. Cameron
Myung U. Kim
David A. Whetten

The increasing emphasis on the temporal aspects of organizations represents a significant trend in the organizational sciences (Miller & Friesen 1980; Cameron & Whetten 1981; Whetten 1987). Evidence of this emphasis is reflected in the extensive use of the life-cycles metaphor to describe organizational changes (Kimberly & Miles 1980). Several authors writing on this topic have argued that more attention should be given to the nongrowth periods of organizational development and evolution (Whetten 1980; Greenhalgh 1983; Cameron & Zammuto 1984) inasmuch as the large majority of life-cycles models consider only patterns of growth, while ignoring decline (Cameron & Whetten 1983). In response, an extensive litera-

ture on the management of decline has emerged within the last several years, in business administration (Starbuck, Greve & Hedberg 1978; Taber, Walsh & Cook 1979) as well as in such related fields as public administration (Levine 1978; Biller 1980), hospital administration (Jick & Murray 1982), and educational administration (Cyert 1978; Petrie & Alpert 1983; Berger 1983; Cameron 1983).

However, typical of most new research areas, this literature is uneven and, to a large extent, noncumulative. The development of a systematic body of knowledge on this subject is hindered not only by the confused status of the theoretical literature but also by the paucity of empirical research, especially comparative investigations. Few studies have appeared that compare organizational differences in large samples of growing, stable, and declining organizations within the same population.

To assist in establishing a more solid theoretical and empirical foundation for this field, the

Financial support for this study was provided by The National Institute of Education and by the Graduate School of Business Administration and the Center for the Study of Higher and Postsecondary Education at the University of Michigan.

Reprinted with permission from *Administrative Science Quarterly,* Vol. 32, June 1987. © 1987 Cornell University.

current study has two purposes: (1) to clarify the appropriate meaning and conceptual domain of organizational decline by delimiting it from related constructs; and (2) to investigate propositions about organizational attributes commonly associated in the literature with organizational decline. These propositions will be compared with a similar set of propositions historically associated with a related theoretical concept, organizational turbulence.

Conceptual Domain of Organizational Decline

The meaning of organizational decline has been neither consistent nor clear in the literature. As has been the case with other organizational constructs (e.g., effectiveness, size), this lack of precise definition has often led to confused and contradictory research findings (Cameron & Whetten 1983; Kimberly 1976). It is important at the outset of this study, therefore, to specify precisely the conceptual domain of organizational decline.

The literature on organizational decline has derived most of its conceptual foundations from three theoretical traditions. One is the organization-environment literature (Lawrence & Lorsch 1967; Meyer 1978; Aldrich 1979) and, in particular, the resource dependence perspective (Pfeffer & Salancik 1978). A second is the crisis-management literature (Smart & Vertinsky 1977; Starbuck, Greve & Hedberg 1978; Milburn, Schuler & Watman 1983), and a third is the uncertainty literature (Simon 1962; Thompson 1967; Cohen & March 1972).

The organization-environment tradition emphasizes the strategic importance to organizations of controlling critical environmental resources. The crisis management literature has examined the impact of major environmental discontinuities on organizations. A theme common in these studies is that organizations place a premium on predictability and stability in transactions with the environment (Hermann 1963; Billings, Milburn & Schaalman 1980; Nystrom & Starbuck 1984; Perrow 1984). Similarly, Thompson (1967: 13) iden-

tified the "essence of the administrative process" as the management of uncertainty. The prescriptions that have emerged from this literature emphasize eliminating ambiguity, buffering the technical core, and designing systems that can scan the environment so as to process needed information. A contributing theme in this research is that organizational attributes vary according to the amount of uncertainty encountered.

This brief overview of the theoretical context of the organizational decline concept helps highlight three main sources of confusion in this emerging literature, and it suggests possible avenues for clarifying empirically the conceptual boundaries of this construct. These sources of confusion form the basis for this investigation.

First, although the core dimensions of resource munificence and turbulence have been carefully delineated in the research on environmental characteristics (Dess & Beard 1984), that distinction has broken down in much of the decline literature. Empirically, most investigations have not separated turbulence or fluctuation from absolute decline. The most common measurement is to subtract levels of resources at Time 1 from levels at Time 2 without considering the patterns of fluctuation in between. The effects of turbulence and decline, therefore, have not been clearly differentiated from one another in research.

This is related to a second source of confusion. In studies in which decline is defined as a significant decrease in the level of resources, it has sometimes been treated as a property of the environment (Starbuck & Hedberg 1977; Harrigan 1980; Zammuto & Cameron 1985) and at other times as a characteristic of the organization (Manns & March 1978; Greenhalgh 1982). In principle, environmental decline refers to changes in either the size (e.g., shrinkage in consumer demand) or the shape (e.g., shift in consumer demand) of an environmental niche. Organizations may or may not be affected by these changes. Organizational decline, on the other hand, refers to reduction in resources within the organization itself. The environment may or may not have changed.

A third source of confusion in the decline literature is the failure to distinguish between decline and stagnation (Bozeman & Slusher 1979; Whetten 1980). Stagnation and decline both focus on the resource concerns of an organization, and they have been used interchangeably. However, stagnation as a concept may be associated with either growth or decline. A slowdown in growth patterns, for example, may lead to perceptions of stagnation, whereas decline refers to an absolute (and substantial) reduction in resource levels (i.e., a negative slope). Because differences between organizational decline and these three related concepts—turbulence, environmental decline, and stagnation—have not been explicated in the literature, the referent of research findings is often unclear.

To assist in bringing more conceptual precision to the decline literature, we propose the following simple definition. Organizational decline is a condition in which a substantial, absolute decrease in an organization's resource base occurs over a specified period of time. Although brief, this definition contains several critical features. It distinguishes between turbulence and munificence, stating that decline's conceptual roots are linked to the latter, not the former. It also differentiates between declining environmental resources and declining organizational resources. This relationship is far from determinate, being mediated by a variety of internal organizational factors. The definition also differentiates between stagnation and decline by proposing that decline involves a substantial negative slope in a resource curve over a specified period of time, not just a slight depression in upward or downward trends. The term "substantial" may be operationalized in different ways in different studies (e.g., significant difference from industry averages or past trends), so it must be clearly delineated in each investigation. Finally, this definition avoids defining decline in terms of its consequences. Much of the literature on decline has focused on the negative effects of shrinkage and has equated decline and ineffectiveness. Our view of decline is a neutral one: whether it results in positive or negative consequences depends on how it is managed.

Presumed Consequences of Decline

The lack of conceptual clarity we have described is typical of emerging research areas. A related characteristic of a new field is lack of perspective, in the sense that advocates of the new viewpoint tend both to exaggerate its uniqueness as a cause and overstate the breadth of its consequences. While this intellectual zealousness is understandable, if left unvalidated it can eventually undermine even the legitimate claims of the new perspective.

These traits are evident in the decline literature. Although virtual consensus exists regarding certain proposed dysfunctional consequences of decline, little empirical research has investigated the individual and organizational factors characteristic of declining organizations.[1] Seldom has empirical research been conducted to determine the antecedents or consequences of decline in organizations or how to manage them. Writers generally have agreed that in conditions of organizational decline, conflict, secrecy, rigidity, centralization, formalization, scapegoating, and conservatism increase. Morale, innovativeness, participation, leader influence, and long-term planning decrease (e.g., Hall & Mansfield 1971; Starbuck, Greve & Hedberg 1978; Dunbar & Goldberg 1978; Levine 1978, 1979; Whetten 1980; Jick & Murray 1982; Petrie & Alpert 1983; Bourgeois 1985). The logic of these "outcomes of decline" is explained in detail elsewhere (Cameron, Whetten & Kim 1987).

Thus, despite the lack of empirical verification, general consensus exists in the literature that declining organizations are characterized by a wide range of organizational processes that erode organizational effectiveness and undermine member satisfaction and commitment. The management of decline is characterized, therefore, as both operationally difficult and politically hazardous.

Thurow (1981: 1106) summarized this point: "There may be no solution to the problem of how to manage decline well. It may simply be impossible."

Presumed Consequences of Turbulence

Environmental turbulence has often been identified as the major challenge facing modern organizations (Drucker 1980; Cameron 1984; Huber 1984). Turbulence exists when changes faced by an organization are nontrivial, rapid, and discontinuous. Following Burns and Stalker (1961), writers have frequently used turbulence and uncertainty synonymously. But a clear conceptual distinction must be made between the rate of change and the unpredictability of change (Miles, Snow & Pfeffer 1974). Turbulence usually creates uncertainty, so that uncertainty is best thought of as an outcome of turbulence rather than a synonym for it. That is, the rapid and hard-to-predict change that is characteristic of turbulence may lead to uncertainty and, indeed, studies have consistently shown that turbulence is the best predictor of perceived environmental uncertainty (Bourgeois 1980; Duncan 1973).

Turbulence has figured prominently in most models of environmental characteristics. Emery and Trist (1965), Terreberry (1968), Aldrich (1979) and McCann and Selsky (1984), for example, examined the interconnectedness among environmental elements as a major source of turbulence. Pfeffer and Salancik (1978: 68) argued that this high degree of interdependence between organizations creates uncertain and unstable environments and that "changes can come from anywhere without notice and produce consequences unanticipated by those initiating the changes and those experiencing the consequences." Aldrich (1979: 69) underscored the difficulty of coping with turbulence by characterizing these types of changes as "obscure to administrators and difficult to plan for."

Research on the impact of turbulence and its resultant uncertainty on individuals and organizations suggests that feelings of crisis, anxiety, and stress, along with "a narrowing of the perceptual field and limitation of information that can

be received, . . . rigidity of response, and primitive forms of reaction" (Withey 1962: 118) occur (Menninger 1952; Janis 1962). Organizations experiencing turbulence have been shown to increase centralization and place greater emphasis on efficiency, standardization, and routinization (Zajonc 1965; Khandwalla 1978; Starbuck, Greve & Hedberg 1978). Bourgeois, McAllister, and Mitchell (1978: 508) found that students acting as managers preferred mechanistic over organic structures when facing turbulent environments and that "most managers respond to turbulent environments in a manner opposite to that which is predicted to lead to greater effectiveness."

The consequences of turbulence described in these and other studies are strikingly similar to claims made in the decline literature. When turbulence is encountered, centralization, conservatism, conflict, rigidity, secrecy, and scapegoating of leaders increase, and information sharing, participativeness, long-term planning, morale, innovativeness, and credibility of leaders decrease (Fleishman, Harris & Burtt 1955; Hall & Mansfield 1971; Pfeffer & Leblebici 1973; Zaltman & Duncan 1977; Smart & Vertinsky 1977; Bourgeois, McAllister & Mitchell 1978; Bozeman & Slusher 1979; Staw, Sandelands & Dutton 1981).

Because previous studies have not empirically differentiated conditions of decline from conditions of turbulence in studies of organizations, however, the enthusiasm with which authors claim that these attributes are unique consequences of decline or turbulence is still without foundation. The intent of this study, therefore, is twofold: (1) to differentiate operationally the concept of organizational decline from turbulence, environmental decline, and stagnation, and (2) to investigate the extent to which negative attributes that are presumed to emerge in organizations under conditions of organizational decline and turbulence are actually found.

Method

Here, we investigated the relationship between conditions of decline and turbulence and twelve commonly predicted negative attributes that are expected to emerge in organizations when decline or turbulence is present. They are listed and described in Table 1, along with the questionnaire items used to measure them. Whereas some previous studies have investigated one or a few of these attributes, they have never been investigated all together in one study, nor has organizational decline—as differentiated from environmental decline, stagnation, and turbulence—been investigated in multiple, comparable organizations. No attempt is made here to link organizational decline

Table 1. Organizational Attributes Associated with Decline and Turbulence

Attribute	Description	Questionnaire Item
Centralization	Decisions are passed upward, participation decreases, control is emphasized.	Major decisions are very centralized.
No long-term planning	Crises and short-term needs drive out strategic planning.	Long-term planning is neglected.
No innovation	No experimentation, risk-aversion, and skepticism about noncore activities.	Innovative activity is increasing [reverse-scored item].
Scapegoating	Leaders are blamed for the pain and uncertainty.	Top administrators are often scapegoats.
Resistance to change	Conservatism and turf protection lead to rejection of new alternatives.	There is lots of resistance to change in this school.
Turnover	The most competent leaders tend to leave first, causing leadership anemia.	There is a great deal of turnover in administrative positions.
Low morale	Few needs are met and infighting is predominant.	Morale is increasing at this institution [reverse-scored item].
No slack	Uncommitted resources are used to cover operating expenses.	We have no place that we could cut expenditures without severely damaging the school.
Fragmented pluralism	Special-interest groups organize and become more vocal.	Special-interest groups within the school are becoming more vocal.
Loss of credibility	Leaders lose the confidence of their subordinates.	Top administrators have high credibility [reverse-scored item].
Nonprioritized cuts	Attempts to ameliorate conflict lead to attempts to equalize cutbacks.	When cutbacks occur, they are done on a prioritized basis [reverse-scored item].
Conflict	Competition and infighting for control predominate when resources are scarce.	Conflict is increasing within this institution.

and turbulence causally with the twelve attributes, because the cross-sectional data we collected do not permit it. The individual, group, and organizational level literature underpinning this study clearly attribute causal directionality, however (e.g., Staw, Sandelands & Dutton 1981; Whetten 1981; Krantz 1985), and we have used that assumption to guide this investigation.

Investigating organizations faced with decline and turbulence requires that growing, stable, and declining organizations as well as turbulent and non-turbulent organizations be included in the study for comparison purposes. Moreover, assessing decline and turbulence over a narrow time span (e.g., a year or two) raises the possibility that these conditions are temporary aberrations from normal conditions and that they would be ignored in organizations. It was necessary, therefore, to include organizations in this study for which data about growth, decline, stability, and turbulence could be acquired over several years and for which data were available about the predicted negative organizational consequences.

The organizations selected for study were colleges and universities in the United States, because they met the data requirements (i.e., a substantial number of institutions that are similar in most other respects have experienced conditions of decline, growth, stability, and turbulence over the past several years; revenue and enrollment data were available over a multi-year period; the associated attributes could be assessed as part of a larger study of organizational performance), and because a great deal of the decline literature has focused on these kinds of organizations (see Zammuto 1983).

Sample

A stratified, random sample representative of all four-year colleges and universities in the United States was selected on the basis of size (200–20,000 FTE), control (public–private), enrollment and revenue change (growth, decline, stability), and degrees offered, (bachelor's, master's, doctorate). Of the 331 institutions studied, 38 percent were public and 62 percent private; 54 percent were small (200–2,500 FTE), 36 percent were medium-sized (2,500–10,000 FTE), and 10 percent were large (10,000–20,000 FTE). This is very close to the demographics of the population of four-year institutions in the United States. Enrollments and revenues were tracked from 1977 to 1982 using the Higher Education General Information Survey data base.[2]

Four hundred institutions were contacted initially by means of a letter to the president asking permission for the institution to be included in the study. No systematic bias among nonparticipating institutions was detected, and the remaining sample of schools ($N = 334$) matched the population demographics as well as the originally intended sample. Information on organizational characteristics was gathered in February and March 1983 as part of a larger study of organizational performance, using data from dominant coalition members: presidents; chief academic, financial, student affairs, institutional research, and external affairs officers; faculty department heads; and trustees. Names of administrators, faculty, and trustees were obtained from each institution, and a questionnaire was mailed personally to respondents, promising anonymity for themselves and their organizations. Faculty department head and trustee respondents were selected randomly within each institution, but special attention was given to assuring heterogeneity in disciplines (among faculty) and locations and titles (among trustees).

The number of respondents contacted at each institution ranged from 12 to 20 (approximately 6 administrators, 6 faculty, and 6 trustees). In all, 55 percent (3,406 individuals) of those receiving questionnaires responded. Administrators constituted 39 percent of that group; faculty, 34 percent; and trustees, 27 percent. Three institutions were eliminated from the analyses because they did not have at least one respondent in each of these three job categories, leaving a sample of 331. Response rates for single institutions ranged from 25 percent to 95 percent. Comparisons among respondents holding different job classifications using

ANOVA revealed no systematic biases (i.e., the responses to questionnaire items by trustees were not systematically different from the responses to questionnaire items by faculty or administrators).

Concepts and Operationalizations

Questions asked respondents to rate the extent to which certain attributes were present at their school. Using a five-point Likert response format, the questions centered on the twelve commonly predicted consequences of decline and turbulence described in Table 1. Because the questionnaire also assessed a variety of other attributes, length constraints made possible the use of only single-item scales to assess the decline and turbulence attributes. Special statistical analyses, described below, were conducted in order to determine reliability for these single-item measures.

A variety of alternative operationalizations exist for measuring decline and turbulence. Focusing on organizational (not environmental) decline, however, suggests that critical resources inside the organization be considered, not externally-based resources such as demographic trends, availability of federal funding, political support, and so on. In this study, therefore, we used changes in enrollments and revenues as well as respondents' perceptions of these changes. Respondents rated the extent to which they thought the institution had experienced decline in revenues or enrollments in any or all of the past four years. One reason for using multiple measures of organizational decline was to determine if the results using decline and turbulence measured one way were different from the results measured another way. As it turned out, results were largely the same whether we used enrollment trends, revenue trends, or respondents' perceptions of them. Consequently, we report here only the results using revenue changes over a six-year period, the 1976–1977 academic year through the 1981–1982 academic year.

This time period was chosen in order to guarantee a time span long enough to map trends, not just short aberrations, but short enough to identify responses to the phenomena. Revenues were used not only because they are likely to have the most impact on organizational functioning (Cameron, Whetten & Kim 1987) but also because it is not unusual for institutions to constrain enrollment growth artificially. This condition of capped enrollments does not represent a true condition of decline. On the other hand, we know of no circumstance in which institutions have voluntarily capped revenue acquisition. In addition, using revenue trends instead of perceptions of them as a measure of decline avoids the problems created by correlating perceptions with perceptions.

Confusion and ambiguity characterize the measurement of decline in the literature. In fact, at least four different measures exist for decline, but no comparison of their appropriateness has ever occurred in the literature. After careful analysis of the strengths and weaknesses of the four measures, we selected a regression-slope operationalization as most appropriate in this study.[3] The regression coefficient was obtained by regressing each year's percent revenue change on each time point (using 1977 as a base year). A positive slope indicated growth, while a negative slope indicated decline.

A decision was made to categorize institutions into groups according to their patterns of decline and turbulence. This was done in order to remain most consistent with the predictions made in the literature that the attributes associated with decline are discontinuous in their relationships with it—that is, present under conditions of decline but not present in stable or growth conditions. Moreover, grouping the institutions was intended to distinguish stagnation from absolute decline and determine the extent to which those two conditions may differ (as predicted by Whetten 1980; and Cameron, Whetten & Kim 1987). Cutoff points for identifying the groups were determined from interviews with administrators to determine the level at which organization members actually experience decline.

By dividing the sample into groups instead of using interval data, some variance was lost. However, in this study maximum variance in the variables was not so important as was conceptual clarity and consistency with the predictions of past literature. We feel that grouping institutions was appropriate for at least three reasons. (1) The literature does not predict a linear relationship between attributes associated with decline and revenue change. Rather, these attributes are assumed to be a product of decline alone. The relationship is discontinuous. (2) An important, unanswered question in the literature is whether stability is similar to decline (stagnation) or similar to growth in its organizational consequences. Cameron, Whetten, and Kim (1987), for example, found stability to be similar to decline in its organizational consequences, but other authors (Levine, Rubin & Wolohojian 1981) have argued the reverse. Grouping institutions makes a comparison possible. (3) Considerable effort went into establishing accurate cutoff points by interviewing approximately forty administrators regarding what level of decline was greater than the "just-noticeable-difference threshold." Our intent was to determine with some degree of confidence when an organization actually experienced conditions of decline, stability, or growth. We assumed that attributes associated with decline would more likely be present under conditions where members of the organization were aware of decline. In the interviews (lasting from thirty minutes to two hours), questions were asked such as: "How much revenue (or enrollment) decrease occurred before people began defining your institution as being in a condition of decline?" and "What organizational factors do you think were associated with. . . [for example, increased conflict in this institution]?" While quite a lot of variance in responses was obtained, the cutoff points we identified represent the modal percentage response and are near the median. In sum, the cutoff points were selected to try to represent actual organizational experience as well as to create groups that were somewhat similar in size.

As a result of the interviews, institutions that experienced more than a 5 percent drop in revenues (adjusted for inflation) over the time period were classified as declining, those experiencing an increase of more than 5 percent were classified as growing, and all others were classified as stable. Operationally, this 5 percent cutoff point for defining decline and growth dictated that slopes of -1 and $+1$ were used as the decline/growth cutoff points. Using this definition, 60 schools were declining, 72 were stable, and 199 were growing.

A great deal of obscurity and diversity also exists in the literature regarding the appropriate measure of turbulence. The best operationalization is clearly neither simple nor straightforward. In order to assess this construct accurately, its measurement must be separated from conditions of growth or decline. Simply measuring relative variation from the mean or summative change, as has been done in almost all studies that have tried to assess turbulence and volatility objectively (e.g., Tosi, Aldag & Storey 1973; Downey, Hellriegel & Slocum 1975; Snyder & Glueck 1982; Salancik & Meindl 1984), confounds turbulence with decline and growth. For example, continuous growth over a six-year period may result in large absolute change, but it is doubtful that this change would be experienced as turbulence.

A variety of alternative procedures were considered for assessing turbulence. Because no guidance was uncovered in the existing literature for determining which might be best, we carefully analyzed the strengths and weaknesses of five different measures in the context of a decline study.[4] We chose to measure this construct across the six years with the *coefficient of alienation* (Cohen & Cohen 1983), using the same variables as for measuring decline—the percent change in revenues and the time points. The coefficient of alienation is defined as $1 - r^2$, or $(Sd_{y-\hat{y}}/Sd_y)$ and has the advantage of a straightforward interpretation, that is, the coefficient varies between 0 and 1.0; the higher the coefficient, the greater the degree of turbulence; it is uncorrelated with either the mean revenues or the trend to increase or decrease revenues year by year; and it can separate conditions of decline from conditions of turbulence. The higher the regression coefficient for turbulence, the more the institution would experience nontrivial, rapid, and discontinuous changes, and if the slope is negative, the institution would also be in a state of decline.

This study is the first to use such a measure of turbulence, which distinguishes it from patterns of decline. Low levels of turbulence were defined as coefficients of .44 or lower, medium turbulence was between .44 and .75, and high turbulence was defined as coefficients of .76 and higher. These cutoff points divided the sample equally on the three levels (i.e., low = 110 schools, medium = 110 schools, high = 111 schools).[5]

Analyses

To ascertain the reliability of each of the single-item measures of the twelve attributes of decline, a repeated-measures approach was taken. The amount of agreement among respondents within each institution was examined using one-way ANOVA. If more agreement existed in the ratings of the item among respondents within an institution than among respondents outside the institution, one could have confidence in the reliability of the single-item measures. The assumption is that the item is being measured multiple times (across multiple respondents) in a consistent fashion. A significant main effect for the institution resulted from each item (F's ranged from 1.41 to 1.84, d.f. = 329,3070, $p < .000$), suggesting that each item was reliable in terms of repeated measures.

Multivariate analysis of variance was then performed with the twelve attributes to determine if conditions of decline-stability-growth and of high-medium-low turbulence had significant effects. Next, data-reduction techniques were applied to the twelve organizational attributes so that they could be more easily reported. Therefore, factor analysis was performed resulting in two interpretable factors that included all the attributes but one. Univariate analyses of variance were performed comparing conditions of growth, stability, and decline on the two factors, and comparing conditions of high, medium, and low tur-

bulence on the two factors. As a check for biased results due to grouping institutions, partial correlations (using the interval, not the categorical, data) also were computed between decline (after controlling for the effects of turbulence) and turbulence (after controlling for the effects of decline) and the two dependent variable factors.

Results

Factor analysis (oblique rotation) produced two interpretable factors from the twelve organizational attributes, as shown in Table 2. One factor seemed to consist mainly of attributes characterizing top-management actions taken in response to decline and turbulence (i.e., centralizing decision-making, neglecting long-term planning, instituting across-the-board cuts, and top-management turnover). These items all focus on the top administrators in the institutions. The other factor appeared to represent attributes characterizing organization members' (other than the top managers') reactions to decline and turbulence (i.e., scapegoating leaders, resisting change, decreas-

Table 2. Factor Analysis of Twelve Attributes* Associated with Decline and Turbulence

Factor Name and Attributes	Factor 1	Factor 2
Top-Management Responses		
Centralization	−.045	.316
No long-term planning	.319	.419
Nonselective cuts	.290	.454
Turnover	.035	.418
Organization-Member Responses		
Scapegoating leaders	.658	.044
Resistance to change	.573	.191
Low morale	.724	.078
Fragmented pluralism	.794	−.165
Lost leader credibility	.549	.440
Conflict	.862	.058
No innovation	.450	.113

*"Loss of slack" did not load on either factor.

Table 3. Multivariate Analysis of Variance for Decline and Turbulence, Using Associated Organizational Attributes

MANOVA Source*	d.f.	F	P
Decline (D)	24,624	1.86	.01
Turbulence (T)	24,624	1.72	.02
Decline × turbulence	48,1256	1.00	.46

*The most robust and conservative test, Phillais trace, was used to test the MANOVA results.

ing morale, organizing special-interest groups, increasing conflict, curtailing innovation, and losing confidence in top management). Although this distinction between top management and organization-member reactions may not be precise, the attributes associated with decline do intuitively seem to characterize one of these group's activities more than the other. One of the attributes (loss of slack) did not load on either factor.

Each factor score was generated by summing the items that have the highest loadings on the factor (Kim & Mueller 1979). Reliability coefficients were computed for each factor (Factor 1, $r = .88$; Factor 2, $r = .53$). The coefficient for Factor 2 is not high, but Nunnally (1979) treats .50 as marginally acceptable in exploratory research such as this. These two factors, therefore, serve as the dependent variables for the rest of the analyses.

Tables 3 and 4 report the results of the multivariate and univariate analyses of variance for decline and for turbulence. No significant interaction effect occurs between the two main conditions — decline and turbulence. However, a significant main effect does occur for decline ($p < .01$), and for turbulence ($p < .02$) in the MANOVA. This suggests that the presence of negative organizational attributes is significantly more likely under conditions of decline than in conditions of growth and that the same is true for high turbulence, as opposed to low turbulence.

To determine more precisely and parsimoniously the meaning of these main effects, univariate analyses of variance were computed. Under conditions of decline, significant differences appeared in the organization-member response factor but not on the top-management response factor. Under turbulent conditions, the opposite was the case — significant differences occurred on the top-management response factor but not on the organization-member response factor. Again, no significant interaction effect exists between decline and turbulence.[6]

These results suggest that top managers tend to respond differently under conditions of high turbulence than under conditions of low or medium turbulence. However, they do not respond differently when faced with decline than with growth or stability. Turbulence has an important association with top-management responses, decline does

Table 4. Univariate Analyses of Variance, Using Two Factors

ANOVA Source	Organization-Member Responses				Top-Management Responses			
	Mean square	d.f.	F	p	Mean square	d.f.	F	p
D	410,053	2	2.94	.05	123,278	2	1.03	.36
T	75,445	2	.54	.58	885,260	2	7.37	.00
D × T	76,394	4	.55	.70	192,590	4	1.60	.17
Residual	139,268	322			120,168	322		

not. On the other hand, the results suggest the opposite for organization members. Organization-member responses are most powerfully associated with decline, not turbulence. The best predictor of negative organizational attributes being associated with organization-member responses is the presence of decline. Turbulence has no significant association with organization-member responses.[7]

Because some readers may question whether or not biased results were produced by clustering the institutions into growth, stability, and decline groups as well as into three levels of turbulence (thus losing variance), partial correlational analysis was also computed using the interval data on decline and turbulence. Table 5 shows that the relationship of decline (partialling out the effect of turbulence) and turbulence (partialling out the effect of decline) with the two organizational attribute factors is similar to the results produced by the ANOVAs. A significant correlation exists between decline and organization-member responses but not top-management responses. The reverse relationship occurs in the case of turbulence. These results lend support to the proposition that when turbulence is held constant, top managerial actions appear to be similar whether decline or growth is faced. It is the presence of turbulence that most affects managers' responses. Positive responses of organization members, on the other hand, are associated with conditions of growth, and negative

responses are associated with decline. Conditions of turbulence have little effect.

Conclusions and Implications

In this study, a variety of organizational attributes were investigated to determine their association with conditions of decline and with turbulence. These attributes have been identified in the literature as products of both organizational decline and turbulence. When rated by observers as to their occurrence in colleges and universities, they form two main factors: attributes associated with the reactions of organization members and attributes associated with top-management responses. Analysis of variance, as well as partial correlational analysis, revealed that organization-member responses are affected by the presence of decline, but not turbulence. When decline is present, organization-member responses are characterized by significantly more scapegoating of leaders, resistance to change, low morale, fragmented pluralism, withdrawal of leader credibility, conflict, and curtailment of innovation than under conditions of growth. The opposites of these attributes are present to a significant degree in conditions of growth. The presence of high or low turbulence, however, does not affect these attributes one way or the other.

On the other hand, attributes characteristic of top-manager responses are significantly affected by turbulence but not by decline. That is, significantly more centralized decision making, absence of long-term planning, nonselective cuts in resources, top-administrator turnover, and loss of leader credibility occur when high turbulence is experienced. The opposite of these attributes is present under conditions of low turbulence. The presence of decline, however, does not affect these top management attributes significantly.

We can only speculate at this point on an explanation for these findings. However, the differential effects of turbulence and decline reported in this study appear to reflect the division of responsibility in colleges and universities in who

Table 5. Partial Correlations between Organizational Decline and Turbulence and Organization-Member and Top-Management Responses

Organizational Condition	Organization-Member Responses		Top-Management Responses	
	Partial r	p	Partial r	p
Decline	.11	.03	.02	.36
Turbulence	.06	.12	.15	.00

bears the costs of different forms of uncertainty. Previous research by Hannan and Freeman (1975), for example, found that under conditions of decline, administrators in schools tended to respond by cutting back nonadministrative positions. If dynamics are similar in this study's organizations, this implies that the responsibility for absorbing the costs of decline falls disproportionately on organization members. It might be expected that this group, feeling more vulnerable to and threatened by the effects of decline, would be characterized by behaviors dysfunctional for the organization. This argument also is consistent with recent discussions by Greenhalgh and Rosenblatt (1984), Brockner, Davy, and Carter (1985), and others in which they demonstrated the dysfunctional psychological consequences of job layoffs. Specifically, they described the negative impact of decline-induced employment insecurity on the contentment and commitment of organization members.

Top-management responses may not be differentially affected by decline because the primary response mandated by conditions of decline, resource-acquisition activities, is a continuing challenge for top managers no matter what the pattern of resource change experienced by the institution. The central role of top managers in colleges and universities is tied very closely to this resource-acquisition responsibility in times of growth as well as decline (Cameron 1986). Decline, therefore, may be experienced as less ambiguous and less threatening than high turbulence.

During times of turbulence, however, the brunt of the consequences of uncertainty falls on the top-management cadre. Unlike conditions of decline, in which top management may react by projecting the consequences onto organization members (e.g., Hannan & Freeman 1975), turbulent conditions activate the buffering function of management (Thompson 1967). That is, the information-processing role of management requires that uncertainty be reduced and that managerial decision processes provide continuity in organizations (Galbraith 1977; Leblebici & Salancik 1981). Organization members are thus buffered from turbulence by top-management action, as well as by the loosely coupled design of higher-education institutions (Meyer & Rowan 1978).

For top managers, who must deal with these conditions, turbulence reduces their ability to make long-term projections regarding future resource levels, yet managers in colleges and universities still need to make decisions that have long-term consequences (e.g., tenure, curriculum, and staffing decisions). Moreover, the vagaries of a fickle resource base multiply the pressure on managers to accentuate even more their planning and resource-acquisition activities, thus increasing stress and turbulence. In the presence of these conditions, it is quite understandable that top managers would tend to centralize control over decisionmaking, truncate long-term planning, apply conservative cutback strategies, and leave the institution when less stressful opportunities become available.

Despite the somewhat speculative nature of the findings' interpretations, these results do suggest three important implications for organizational theory. *First, the presumed advantages of loosely coupled structures in turbulent conditions may not be universal throughout the organization.* Colleges and universities are often described as having loosely coupled structures (Weick 1976; Meyer & Rowan 1978). Simon (1962), Thompson (1967), Aldrich (1971), Glassman (1973), Cohen and March (1972), and others have espoused the advantages of loose coupling for buffering the technical core and producing adaptability in organizations. The basic assumption is that environmental jolts and encroachments can be easily absorbed by individual units without negatively affecting the whole system, and coordination and information processing are more efficient. Rubin (1979: 220) found in a study of five universities, however, that "the hypothesized benefits of loose structure did not generally occur [in universities experiencing decline]." Loose coupling was not as adaptive as expected. In our study, the loosely coupled structure of these institutions seemed to help buffer organization members (non-top managers) from the negative attributes associated with turbulence, but it did not buffer them from the attributes induced by decline. The structural advantages of looseness were mixed.

One possible inference from this finding is consistent with Brinton's (1938) early theories of revolution in organizations (adopted by others such as Miller 1960; Stein 1960; Scott 1972; Scott & Hart 1979; and Durham & Smith 1982). Brinton's theory suggested that decline and deterioration in organizations inspire revolution, which ultimately terminates the tyranny of inefficiency. Bloated bureaucracies require insurrection as a prerequisite to turnaround. This study's results may imply that the negative attributes associated with organization-member responses (e.g., conflict, scapegoating) may be akin to pre-insurrection reactions, but they are not experienced by the institutions' top management. Thus, organizational decline may paradoxically be both functional and dysfunctional at the same time—fraught with conflict, resistance, and recalcitrance, while simultaneously sowing the seeds of effective long-term adaptation and survival.

A second implication of this study relates to the implicit association that exists in the literature between organizational decline and turbulence and organizational uncertainty (Bourgeois 1985). *These results may suggest that the uncertainty assumed to result from decline and turbulence in organizations reflects itself differently depending on which condition produces it.* Even though decline and turbulence have not been differentiated operationally in the literature, and predictions of organizational consequences are universalistic, this study implies that the source of uncertainty may be an important moderator. Uncertainty created by turbulence may have significant effects on organizational attributes associated with top-management responses but not with organization-member responses. Uncertainty created by decline may have significant effects on organizational attributes associated with organization-member responses but not with top-management responses.

One possible inference from this finding is that, in order to capture the main source of variance, studies of decline should focus more on the factors in organizations associated with organization member (non-top manager) processes and outcomes. Studies of turbulence should focus more on organizational attributes associated with top-manager actions. Most studies of organizational uncertainty up to now have limited themselves to the top-management perspective. In studies where organizational decline produces the uncertainty, this may not be the appropriate area of focus.

Another possible inference is that future research should be sensitive to a more fine-grained conceptualization of uncertainty, based on its sources. One reason for the continued marginal support for contingency theories linking environmental uncertainty and organizational designs may be that the source of uncertainty can have differential effects on different parts of the organization. Focusing on the wrong organizational attributes may produce spurious results.

A third implication entails an opposite point of view from the first two. Up to now, we have followed the dominant perspective in the literature, namely that the presence of organizational decline leads to dysfunctional organizational attributes. However, the opposite perspective is also viable, inasmuch as we have not tested for temporal precedence in our data. That perspective suggests that *organizations typified by dysfunctional attributes—scapegoating of leaders, resistance to change, low morale, fragmented pluralism, conflict, and no innovation—may perpetuate decline.* Organizations simply may not be able to maintain a growth pattern while harboring these dysfunctional conditions. Moreover, when centralization is high, planning ceases, nonselective cutbacks occur, turnover is high, and leader credibility is low; turbulence (marked fluctuation in both growth and decline) may also be perpetuated.

This reversed perspective has theoretical implications as well, inasmuch as many of these dysfunctional attributes represent Likert's (1967) System 1 characteristics and are predicted to be ineffective. A mismatch between positive organizational attributes and the demands of the environment is also consistent with the congruence theories espoused by Nadler and Tushman (1983),

Galbraith and Kazanjian (1986), and others. Lack of fit produces decline and ineffectiveness; therefore, the presence of dysfunctional attributes may be nonadaptive.

Of course, without longitudinal data it is impossible to determine which theoretical explanation is valid—whether decline causes dysfunctional attributes or dysfunctional attributes cause decline. Most likely, both are at least partially true. By clarifying the concept of decline, however, and separating it from related concepts, this study makes possible the investigation of this causal directionality. Moreover, because organizational decline and death are occurring at a record pace in the United States, because the popular press is filled with descriptions of a hyperturbulent post-industrial environment, and because decline, downsizing, and retrenchment are the most frequent organizational changes in large organizations today, such studies of causality will be requisite for practical as well as theoretical reasons. Practicing managers as well as organizational theorists will benefit from attention being paid by researchers to issues of causality between organizational attributes and organizational decline.

Notes

1   This is not to say that decline cannot stimulate organizational renewal through increased productivity, prioritization of organizational commitments, and renewed personal dedication. A sizeable literature has emerged during the past decade codifying the procedures for turning around declining organizations (Hofer 1980; Schendel, Patton & Riggs 1976; Bibeault 1982; Chaffee 1984). However, it is evident from these writings that, as its name implies, "turnaround management" involves taking an organization that has been buffeted by the vagaries of diminished resources and setting it on a new course. With rare exceptions, organizations are turned around only after the internal organizational and personal consequences of decline are so pervasive and severe that a consensus around the need for drastic action grudgingly emerges.

2   The year 1982 was selected because it was the most recent year for which financial information was available when the questionnaire data were collected. Five or six months probably elapsed for most institutions between the end of the 1982 fiscal year and the reporting of the organizational attribute data used in our study.

3   Four measures of decline are (1) Time 1 subtracted from Time n, (2) a mean ratio of yearly changes, (3) regressing yearly resource changes on the previous year's resource level, and (4) regressing yearly resource changes on the previous year's resource level. The disadvantage of the first measure $[100 * (T_n - T_1/T_1)]$ is that it relies on the absolute level of the first year's resources (which may not be typical), and it ignores variation between year 1 and year n. The second measure [(Year 2/Year 1 + Year 3/Year 2 + $\cdots$ + Year n/Year $n-1$)/Year $n-1$/Number of years minus 1] is insensitive to turbulence during the time period and, by defining decline as statistical significant difference from 1.0, relatively few organizations are included (only 10 of 331 in this study). The third measure is appropriate only when the intercept is zero or clearly interpretable. However, the interpretation of the intercept is seldom clear in regression equations, and misclassification may occur because of insensitivity to differences in resources patterns. For example, a yearly change of 2, 3, 4, 5, 6, 7 and the pattern 7, 6, 5, 4, 3, 2 would be classified the same based on the regression coefficients (as stagnating). Yet the intercept for the first pattern is +1 and the second −1, and they should be classified differently. The fourth measure—the one used in this study—makes adjustments for different resource levels, takes into account temporal ordering, presents a more accurate picture of the regression slope, allows for trichotomization of the organizations based on cutoff points, and permits direct comparison with a measure of turbulence. A more detailed comparison of these four measures is available from the senior author.

4   Five measures of turbulence considered were (1) the sum of percent change from year to year, (2) standard deviation, (3) coefficient of variation, (4) coefficient of fluctuation, and (5) coefficient of alienation. The first measure $[\Sigma \% \Delta]$ may be difficult to interpret since no upper limit exists, may deflate the amount of actual turbulence present when the change occurs from positive to negative and, more importantly, may mask actual turbulence when a large change that occurs in one year inflates the base for the next year's change. The second measure assesses average variation of yearly change, but actual variation may be misinterpreted because the larger the base rate (e.g., size) the larger the variation. Large organizations may have larger variance but not necessarily more turbulence. The third measure

$[\sigma/\bar{x}]$ is the approach used most frequently, but misinterpretation may result because a constantly growing pattern (e.g., +5, +5, +5, +5, +5, +5) would be interpreted as more turbulent than a constantly flat pattern (e.g., 0, 0, 0, 0, 0, 0), and an outlier year (e.g., +2, +2, +2, +44, +2, +2) masks turbulence by increasing both the variance (numerator) and the mean (denominator). The fourth measure (Kim 1987) $[\Sigma|\%\Delta| - |\Sigma\%\Delta|]$ is the absolute values of the percent change from year to year minus the absolute value of the sum of the yearly change for the period. The disadvantages are that no upper limit exists, the measure is insensitive to fluctuation in a continuously growing or declining pattern even though yearly changes are different (e.g., +2, +22, +3, +3, +33, +4, +44 would not be interpreted as fluctuating), and a large change in a single year inflates the base rate for the succeeding year. The fifth measure, and the one selected for use in this study, $[(1 - r^2)^{1/2}]$ identified an upper limit to the amount of turbulence possible (the range is 0 to 1.0). It is statistically uncorrelated with the mean resource level or the trend to grow or decline, and several ways can be used to obtain the Pearson correlation coefficient (e.g., the correlation between each year and the previous year's resource change, or between time points and yearly change, the first year, or the mean resource level). Unfortunately, no rule of thumb exists for deciding what level of coefficient represents true turbulence for a particular organization using any of these measures, so we addressed this problem using interviews with administrators. A more detailed comparative analysis of each of these measures of turbulence can be obtained from the first author.

5 In order to examine whether this procedure of dividing the sample into equal-sized institutional groups biased the results, analyses were conducted with institutions representing the lowest 10 percent of the turbulence scores and the highest 10 percent of the turbulence scores. The results were consistent, indicating that no significant bias characterizes these groupings.

6 Analyses of variance also were conducted in which the interaction effects of organizational size (total FTE) and organizational control (public-private) were examined. Past literature has suggested that these might be important moderators of main effects in colleges and universities. However, no significant interaction effects result in any of the fourteen analyses; hence, these variables are not discussed further in this study.

7 Multivariate and univariate analyses of variance do not produce information about differences in the cell means for decline or for turbulence. Moreover, with no significant interaction effects present, cell contrasts are not called for. However, an examination of cell means for the two factors found that significant differences exist between conditions of growth and decline but not between growth and stability. This supports the argument that conditions of stability are responded to by organization members more as decline-as-stagnation than as slow growth (Whetten 1980; Cameron, Whetten & Kim 1987).

References

Aldrich, Howard E. 1971. "Organizational Boundaries and Interorganizational Conflict." *Human Relations* 24: 279–87.

———. 1979. *Organizations and Environments.* Englewood Cliffs, N.J.: Prentice-Hall.

Berger, Michael A. 1983. "Retrenchment Policies and Their Organizational Consequences." *Peabody Journal of Education* 6: 49–63.

Bibeault, D.B. 1982. *Corporate Turnaround.* New York: McGraw-Hill.

Biller, R.P. 1980. "Leadership Tactics for Retrenchment." *Public Administration Review* 40: 604–9.

Billings, R.S., T.W. Milburn, and M.L. Schaalman. 1980. "A Model of Crisis Perception: A Theoretical and Empirical Analysis." *Administrative Science Quarterly* 25: 300–16.

Bourgeois, L. Jay. 1980. "Strategy and Environment: A Conceptual Integration." *Academy of Management Review* 1: 25–39.

———. 1985. "Strategic Goals, Perceived Uncertainty, and Economic Performance in Volatile Environments." *Academy of Management Journal* 28: 548–73.

Bourgeois, L. Jay, D.W. McAllister, and Terrence R. Mitchell. 1978. "The Effects of Different Organizational Environments upon Decisions about Organizational Structure." *Academy of Management Journal* 21: 508–14.

Bozeman, Barry, and E.A. Slusher. 1979. "Scarcity and Environmental Stress in Public Organizations." *Administration and Society* 11: 335–56.

Brinton, C. 1938. *The Anatomy of Revolution.* New York: W.W. Norton.

Brockner, Joel, J. Davy, and C. Carter. 1985. "Layoffs, Self-esteem, and Survivor Guilt: Motivational, Affective, and Attitudinal Consequences." *Organizational Behavior and Human Decision Processes* 36: 229–44.

Burns, Tom, and G.M. Stalker. 1961. *The Management of Innovation.* London: Tavistock.

Cameron, Kim S. 1983. "Strategic Responses to Conditions of Decline." *Journal of Higher Education* 54: 359–80.

———. 1984. "Organizational Adaptation and Higher Education." *Journal of Higher Education* 55: 122–44.

———. 1986. "A Study of Organizational Effectiveness and Its Predictors." *Management Science* 32: 87–112.

Cameron, Kim S., and David A. Whetten. 1981. "Perceptions of Effectiveness over Organizational Life Cycles." *Administrative Science Quarterly* 26: 525–44.

———. 1983. *Organizational Effectiveness: A Comparison of Multiple Models.* New York: Academic Press.

Cameron, Kim S., David A. Whetten, and Myung U. Kim. 1987. "Organizational Dysfunctions of Decline." *Academy of Management Journal* 30: 126–38.

Cameron, Kim S., and Raymond F. Zammuto. 1984. "Matching Managerial Strategies to Conditions of Decline." *Human Resource Management Journal* 22: 359–76.

Chaffee, Ellen E. 1984. "Successful Strategic Management in Small Private Colleges." *Journal of Higher Education* 55: 212–41.

Cohen, Jacob, and Patricia Cohen. 1983. *Applied Multiple Regression/Correlation Analysis for the Behavioral Sciences.* Hillsdale, N.J.: Lawrence Erlbaum.

Cohen, Michael, and James G. March. 1972. "A Garbage Can Model of Organizational Choice." *Administrative Science Quarterly* 17: 1–25.

Cyert, Richard M. 1978. "The Management of Universities of Constant or Decreasing Size." *Public Administration Review* 38: 344–49.

Dess, Gregory G., and Donald W. Beard. 1984. "Dimensions of Organizational Task Environments." *Administrative Science Quarterly* 29: 52–73.

Downey, H. Kirk, Don Hellriegel, and John W. Slocum. 1975. "Environmental Uncertainty: The Construct and its Application." *Administrative Science Quarterly* 20: 613–29.

Drucker, Peter F. 1980. *Managing in Turbulent Times.* New York: Harper & Row.

Dunbar, R.L.M., and W.H. Goldberg. 1978. "Crisis Development and Strategic Response in European Corporations." In *Studies on Crisis Management,* edited by C.F. Smart and W.T. Stanbury, pp. 135–49. Toronto: Butterworths.

Duncan, Robert B. 1973. "Multiple Decision Making Structures in Adapting to Environmental Uncertainty." *Human Relations* 26: 273–91.

Durham, J.W., and H.L. Smith. 1982. "Toward a General Theory of Organizational Deterioration." *Administration and Society* 14: 373–400.

Emery, F.E., and E.L. Trist. 1965. "The Causal Texture of Organizational Environments." *Human Relations* 18: 21–31.

Fleishman, Edwin A., E.F. Harris, and H.E. Burtt. 1955. "Leadership and Supervision in Industry." Research Monograph No. 33. Ohio State University, Bureau of Educational Research, Columbus, Ohio.

Galbraith, Jay R. 1977. *Organizational Design.* Reading, Mass.: Addison-Wesley.

Galbraith, Jay R., and Robert K. Kazanjian. 1986. *Strategy Implementation: Structure, Systems, and Process.* St. Paul, Minn.: West Publishing.

Glassman, R. 1973. "Persistence and Loose Coupling in Living Systems." *Behavioral Science* 18: 83–98.

Greenhalgh, Leonard. 1982. "Maintaining Organizational Effectiveness During Organizational Retrenchment." *Journal of Applied Behavioral Science* 18: 155–70.

———. 1983. "Organizational Decline." In *Research in the Sociology of Organizations,* Vol. 2, edited by Samuel B. Bacharach, pp. 231–76. Greenwich, Conn.: JAI Press.

Greenhalgh, Leonard, and Z. Rosenblatt. 1984. "Job Insecurity: Toward Conceptual Clarity." *Academy of Management Review* 9: 438–48.

Hall, Douglas T., and Roger Mansfield. 1971. "Organizational and Individual Response to External Stress." *Administrative Science Quarterly* 16: 533–47.

Hannan, Michael, and John Freeman. 1975. "Growth and Decline Processes in Organizations." *American Sociological Review* 40: 215–28.

Harrigan, Kathleen. 1980. *Strategies for Declining Businesses.* Lexington, Mass.: Lexington Books.

Hermann, C.F. 1963. "Some Consequences of Crisis which Limit the Viability of Organizations." *Administrative Science Quarterly* 8: 61–82.

Hofer, Charles W. 1980. "Turnaround Strategies." *Journal of Business Strategy* 1: 19–31.

Huber, George P. 1984. "The Nature and Design of Post-Industrial Environments." *Management Science* 30: 928–51.

Janis, Irving L. 1962. "Psychological Effects of Warnings." In *Man and Society in Disaster,* edited by G.W. Baker and D.W. Chapman, pp. 55–92. New York: Basic Books.

Jick, Todd D., and Victor V. Murray. 1982. "The Management of Hard Times: Budget Cutbacks in Public Sector Organizations." *Organization Studies* 3: 141–70.

Khandwalla, Pradip N. 1978. "Crisis Response of Competing Versus Noncompeting Organizations." In *Studies on Crisis Management,* edited by C.F. Smart and W.T. Stanbury, pp. 158–78. Toronto: Butterworths.

Kim, Myung U. 1987. "On the Measurement of Organizational Decline and Turbulence: Criticisms and Suggestions." Working paper. Institute for Social Research, University of Michigan, Ann Arbor, Michigan.

Kim, Jae-On, and Charles W. Mueller. 1979. *Introduction to Factor Analysis.* Beverly Hills, Calif.: Sage.

Kimberly, John R. 1976. "Organizational Size and the Structuralist Perspective: A Review, Critique and Proposal." *Administrative Science Quarterly* 21: 571–97.

Kimberly, John R., and Robert H. Miles. 1980. *The Organizational Life Cycle.* San Francisco: Jossey-Bass.

Krantz, J. 1985. "Group Processes Under Conditions of Organizational Decline." *Journal of Applied Behavioral Science* 21: 1–17.

Lawrence, Paul R., and Jay Lorsch. 1967. *Organization and Environment.* Cambridge, Mass.: Harvard University Press.

Leblebici, Huseyin, and Gerald R. Salancik. 1981. "Effects of Uncertainty on Information and Decision Processes in Banks." *Administrative Science Quarterly* 26: 578–96.

Levine, Charles H. 1978. "Organizational Decline and Cutback Management." *Public Administration Review* 38: 316–25.

———. 1979. "More on Cutback Management." *Public Administration Review* 39: 179–83.

Levine, Charles H., Irene S. Rubin, and G.G. Wolohojian. 1981. *The Politics of Retrenchment.* Beverly Hills, Calif.: Sage.

Likert, Rensis. 1967. *The Human Organization: Its Managment and Value.* New York: McGraw-Hill.

Manns, Charles, and James G. March. 1978. "Financial Adversity, Internal Competition, and Curriculum Change in a University." *Administrative Science Quarterly* 23: 541–52.

McCann, J.E., and J. Selsky. 1984. "Hyperturbulence and the Emergence of Type 5 Environments." *Academy of Management Review* 3: 460–70.

Menninger, W.C. 1952. "Psychological Reactions in an Emergency Flood." *American Journal of Psychiatry* 109: 128–30.

Meyer, John, and Brian Rowan. 1978. "The Structure of Educational Organizations." In *Environment and Organization,* edited by Marshall Meyer, pp. 78–109. San Francisco: Jossey-Bass.

Meyer, Marshall. 1978. *Environment and Organization.* San Francisco: Jossey-Bass.

Milburn, T.W., R.S. Schuler, and K.H. Watman. 1983. "Organizational Crisis, Part I and Part II." *Human Relations* 36: 1141–80.

Miles, Raymond E., Charles C. Snow, and Jeffrey Pfeffer. 1974. "Organization-Environment: Concepts and Issues." *Industrial Relations* 13: 244–64.

Miller, Danny, and Peter Friesen. 1980. "Archetypes of Organizational Transition." *Administrative Science Quarterly* 25: 268–99.

Miller, James G. 1960. *Living Systems.* New York: McGraw-Hill.

Nadler, David, and Michael Tushman. 1983. "A General Diagnostic Model for Organizational Behavior: Applying a Congruence Perspective." In *Perspectives on Behavior in Organizations,* edited by J.R. Hackman, E.E. Lawler III, and L.W. Porter, pp. 112–24. New York: McGraw-Hill.

Nunnally, Jim. 1979. *Psychometric Theory.* New York: McGraw-Hill.

Nystrom, Paul C., and William Starbuck. 1984. "To Avoid Organizational Crises, Unlearn." *Organizational Dynamics* (Spring): 53–65.

Perrow, Charles. 1984. *Normal Accidents: Living with High-Risk Technologies.* New York: Basic Books.

Petrie, Hugh G., and Daniel Alpert. 1983. "What is the Problem of Retrenchment in Higher Education?" *Journal of Management Studies* 20: 97–119.

Pfeffer, Jeffrey, and Huseyin Leblebici. 1973. "The Effects of Competition on Some Dimensions of Organizational Structure." *Social Forces* 52: 268–79.

Pfeffer, Jeffrey, and Gerald R. Salancik. 1978. *The External Control of Organizations.* New York: Harper & Row.

Rubin, Irene S. 1979. "Retrenchment, Loose Structure, and Adaptability in Universities." *Sociology of Education* 52: 211–22.

Salancik, Gerald R., and James R. Meindl. 1984. "Corporate Attributions as Strategic Illusions of Management Control." *Administrative Science Quarterly* 29: 238–54.

Schendel, D., G.R. Patton, and J. Riggs. 1976. "Corporate Turnaround Strategies: A Study of Profit Decline and Recovery." *Journal of General Management* 3: 3–11.

Scott, J.C. 1972. *Comparative Corruption.* Englewood Cliffs, N.J.: Prentice-Hall.

Scott, William G., and David K. Hart. 1979. *Organizational America.* Boston: Houghton Mifflin.

Simon, Herbert A. 1962. "The Architecture of Complexity." *Proceedings of the American Philosophical Society* 106: 467–82.

Smart, Carolyne F., and Ilan Vertinsky. 1977. "Designs for Crisis Decision Units." *Administrative Science Quarterly* 22: 640–57.

Snyder, N.H., and William F. Glueck. 1982. "Can Environmental Volatility Be Measured Objectively?" *Academy of Management Journal* 25: 185–92.

Starbuck, William G., A. Greve, and Bo L.T. Hedberg. 1978. "Responding to Crisis." *Journal of Business Administration* 9: 111–37.

Starbuck, William G., and Bo L.T. Hedberg. 1977. "Saving an Organization from Stagnating Environments. In *Strategy + Structure = Performance,* edited by H. Thorelli, pp. 249–58. Bloomington: Indiana University Press.

Staw, Barry M., Lance E. Sandelands, and Jane E. Dutton. 1981. "Threat-Rigidity Effects on Organizational Behavior." *Administrative Science Quarterly* 26: 501–24.

Stein, M. 1960. *The Eclipse of Community.* Princeton, N.J.: Princeton University Press.

Taber, Tom, J.T. Walsh, and R.A. Cook. 1979. "Developing a Community-Based Program for Reducing the Social Impact of a Plant Closing." *Journal of Applied Behavioral Science* 5: 133–55.

Terreberry, Shirley. 1968. "The Evolution of Organizational Environments." *Administrative Science Quarterly* 12: 590–613.

Thompson, James D. 1967. *Organizations in Action.* New York: McGraw-Hill.

Thurow, Lester. 1981. Review of Charles H. Levine, ed., *Managing Fiscal Stress. Journal of Economic Literature* 81: 1105–6.

Tosi, Henry, Ramon Aldag, and Ralph Storey. 1973. "On the Measurement of the Environment." *Administrative Science Quarterly* 18: 27–36.

Weick, Karl E. 1976. "Educational Organizations as Loosely Coupled Systems." *Administrative Science Quarterly* 21: 1–19.

Whetten, David A. 1980. "Sources, Responses, and Effects of Organizational Decline." In *The Organizational Life Cycle,* edited by John R. Kimberly and Robert H. Miles, pp. 342–74. San Francisco: Jossey-Bass.

———. 1981. "Organizational Responses to Scarcity." *Educational Administration Quarterly* 27: 80–97.

———. 1987. "Growth and Decline Processes in Organizations." *Annual Review of Sociology.* Palo Alto, Calif.: Annual Reviews (in press).

Withey, S.B. 1962. "Reaction to Uncertain Threat." In *Man and Society in Disaster,* edited by G.W. Baker and D.W. Chapman, pp. 93–123. New York: Basic Books.

Zajonc, Robert B. 1965. "Social Facilitation." *Science* 149: 269–74.

Zaltman, Gerald, and Robert B. Duncan. 1977. *Strategies for Planned Change.* New York: Wiley.

Zammuto, Raymond F. 1983. "Bibliography on Decline and Retrenchment." Working paper. National Center for Higher Education Management Systems, Boulder, Colorado.

Zammuto, Raymond F., and Kim S. Cameron. 1985. "Environmental Decline and Organizational Response." In *Research in Organizational Behavior,* edited by L.L. Cummings and B.M. Staw, pp. 223–62. Greenwich, Conn.: JAI Press.

11

Successful and Unsuccessful Phases of the Corporate Life Cycle

Danny Miller

Peter H. Friesen

Introduction

Recent years have witnessed a dramatic increase in research into corporate and organizational life cycles. Much of this research has been theoretical; very little of it empirical. Interesting perspectives on the life cycle have been given by Adizes (1979), Scott (1971), Torbert (1974), Kimberly and Miles (1980), and Quinn and Cameron (1983).

The theme that one takes away from this work is that organizations progress through an orderly succession of stages as they grow, age and change their strategies. In their recent study of the corporate life cycle, Miller and Friesen (1982a) have largely borne out the distinctiveness of five life-cycle stages suggested by the literature, show-

ing how firms varied significantly in their strategies, environments, structures and decision making styles from one phase to another. They also demonstrated a common but by no means universal tendency for firms to move through the phases of the corporate life cycle in the following sequence: the *birth* phase led to a *growth* phase which in turn resulted in a period of *maturity*. Eventually product-market diversification and divisionalization could move the firm from *maturity* to the *revival* phase, while sometimes a *decline* phase followed maturity or revival. The major characteristics of each of these phases (as reported by Miller and Friesen, 1982a) as well as their sources in the literature are given in Table 1.

The objective of the research reported here was to determine whether there were significant differences between successful and unsuccessful phases of the life cycle. For example, how would

Table 1. Review of Characteristics of Phases of the Life Cycle

	Context	Organization	Innovation and Strategy
Birth Phase [cf. Scott's (1971) Stage One, Greiner's (1972) Creativity Stage, and Quinn and Cameron's (1983) Entrepreneurial Stage]	– Small firm – Young – Dominated by owner manager – Homogeneous, placid environment	– Informal structure – Undifferentiated – Power highly centralized – Crude information processing and decision making methods	– Considerable innovation in product lines – Niche strategy – Substantial risk taking
Growth Phase [cf. Downs' (1967) Rapid Growth Stage, Adizes' (1979) Go-go Stage, and Lyden's (1975) Second Stage]	– Medium sized – Older – Multiple shareholders – More heterogeneous and competitive environment	– Some formalization of structure – Functional basis of organization – Moderate differentiation – Somewhat less centralized – Initial development of formal information processing and decision making methods	– Broadening of product-market scope into closely related areas – Incremental innovation in product lines – Rapid growth
Maturity Phase [cf. Scott's (1971) Stage 2, Greiner's (1972) Direction Stage, and Adizes' (1979) Maturity Stage]	– Larger – Still older – Dispersed ownership – Competitive and still more heterogeneous environment	– Formal, bureaucratic structure – Functional basis of organization – Moderate differentiation – Moderate centralization – Information processing and decision making as in growth phase	– Consolidation of product-market strategy – Focus on efficiently supplying a well-defined market – Conservatism – Slower growth
Revival Phase [cf. Scott's (1971) Stage 3, Greiner's (1972) Coordination Stage, and Quinn and Cameron's (1983) Elaboration of Structure Stage]	– Very large – Environment very heterogeneous, competitive, and dynamic	– Divisional basis of organization – High differentiation – Sophisticated controls, scanning, and communications in information processing; more formal analysis in decision making	– Strategy of product-market diversification, movement into some unrelated markets – Higher level of risk taking and planning – Substantial innovation – Rapid growth
Decline Phase [cf. Downs' (1967) Deceleration Phase, Lyden's (1975) and Kimberly's (1979) Fourth Stages, and Adizes' (1979) Prime Organization Stage]	– Medium size – Homogeneous and competitive environment	– Formal, bureaucratic structure – Mostly functional basis for organization – Moderate differentiation and centralization – Less sophisticated information processing systems and decision making methods	– Low level of innovation – Price cutting – Consolidation of product-markets – Liquidation of subsidiaries – Risk aversion and conservatism – Slow growth

successful vs. unsuccessful phases of birth, growth, etc. differ in their information processing, decision making and innovation characteristics? A 'successful phase' is simply a period of the life cycle in which a given firm performs well. Poor performance characterizes unsuccessful phases. All five phases show good and poor performers. When we compare phases we are really comparing the attributes of the successful and unsuccessful firms within each. We do not use the terms 'successful firms' or 'unsuccessful firms', however, since the same firms can perform quite differently over time. Although this is in every respect an exploratory study, previous research suggests two general hypotheses about potential differences between successful and unsuccessful phases of the life cycle.

Hypotheses

H_1: The Life Cycle, Information Processing and Decision Making Sophistication

As firms progress through the first four phases of the life cycle, it is generally accepted that the environment becomes more complex and challenging (Chandler 1962; Scott 1971; Channon 1973; Miller and Friesen 1982a). Market heterogeneity increases, as might the level of competition or 'hostility'. Firms also become much larger. This makes the administrative task more complex, creating the need for more effective organizational intelligence systems (Galbraith 1973) and a more sophisticated decision making approach. We therefore hypothesize the following (the names of the variables are italicized).

H_1a. Over the Life Cycle Firms Must Increase Their Use of Intelligence Systems. They must: (i) *scan* the environment more for information concerning threats and challenges (Aguilar 1967; Tushman 1977); (ii) make more use of *controls* such as employee performance appraisals, quality controls, cost and profit centres, budgeting and cost accounting (Galbraith 1973; Chandler 1962; Channon 1973); and (iii) increase cross-functional and interdivisional *communications* to improve

coordination and facilitate collaboration (Chandler 1962; Channon 1973; Galbraith 1973). The increased information processing activity will provide managers with a better understanding of environments which are becoming too complex for a few top executives to analyse by themselves. It also allows increasingly differentiated departments and subunits to be appraised, monitored and controlled. Finally, it enables a growing variety of experts and decision makers to collaborate more effectively.

H_1b. Over the Life Cycle Firms Must Increase the Sophistication of Their Decision Making Methods. They must do so in order that managers can handle a broader array of information. This can involve, first, more detailed and systematic *analyses* of decisions (Mintzberg 1973; Porter 1980), second, a greater attempt to bring together and take into account multiple points of view in decision making (*multiplexity*) (Khandwalla 1972), and third, assurance of consistency and complementarity among decisions over time and across departments (*integration*) (Ansoff 1965; Andrews 1980).

As firms progress through the life cycle, we hypothesize that successful phases will exhibit a steady and significant (linear) increase in information processing and decision making variables in order to adapt to the increasing levels of administrative complexity. In contrast, we expect that unsuccessful phases will not demonstrate so orderly a progression and may only reveal nonlinear fluctuations. They are also expected to have a lower level of information processing activity and decision making sophistication than successful phases, especially *after* the simple birth phase which involves the lowest information handling burden.

H_2: The Life Cycle and Innovation

Organizations must constantly make certain that their product lines are more or less up to date. The life cycle literature has shown that certain phases such as birth, growth and revival place more emphasis on innovation, product-market renewal, risk taking and surpassing the competition, while other phases, notably maturity and decline, are more stable and conservative (Kimberly 1979; Scott 1971; Greiner 1972; Quinn and Cameron 1983; Miller and Friesen 1982a). We hypothesized that firms in successful phases would devote regular attention to product-market renewal, avoiding extremes of conservatism, reactiveness, stagnation and insularity, as well as those of *risk taking, proactiveness* and *innovation*. They will also avoid extremely short or very lengthy time horizons (*futurity*), focusing on the most relevant intermediate range. We anticipated that firms in unsuccessful phases would be more likely to fall victim to excesses, alternating between extremely innovative phases of the life cycle, which badly tax resources, and extremely stagnant phases which allow product lines to become anachronistic.

The literature on organizations has often pointed to the lack of innovation or inadequate product-market renewal as the causes of failure (Hedberg 1972; Thompson 1961; Schon 1971). But it has also pointed out the dangers of excessive innovation, in which resources are squandered in developing too many new products or designs (Miller and Friesen 1982b; Hedberg et al. 1976). We expected these excesses of stagnation and innovation to be more common in unsuccessful than in successful phases, and that this would be reflected by a more jagged and variable profile of innovation across the life cycle.

Together, our hypotheses examine two potential obstacles to success: the failure to boost the level of information processing and decision making sophistication to cope with the increased complexity of the administrative task, and the dangers caused by very high or very low levels of innovation as firms progress through the life cycle.

Method

The need to study numerous organizations over long periods of time required us to use a rather unorthodox data base. A series of histories was constructed on 36 corporations each of which has been in existence for at least 20 years. These were developed from books, corporate annual reports, series of *Fortune* articles going back many years and numerous magazine articles written about the firms. The information was verified using questionnaires sent to top executives or past top executives. Appendix II lists the firms and industries included in the study.

Scoring of the histories proceeded in three stages. The first involved a complex heuristic for splitting the histories into representative 'snapshots' or periods. Scoring of the variables occurred at the tranquil boundaries of crucial organizational transitions—that is, before and after any significant changes in environment, organization structure, strategy making or leadership. This scoring procedure captured the 'extremes' of strategy making, structure and environment during a firm's history. For example, if a firm moved, say, from being a conservative bureaucracy to an entrepreneurial 'ad-hocracy', we scored it at its most conservative and its most entrepreneurial times, ignoring the parts in between. The same held true for all of our variables. As soon as a variable began to reverse its direction of change (moving, perhaps, from an increasing trend to a decreasing one), the variables were scored at the point of inflection in order to capture the extreme. As a result, we recorded the most interesting multivariate profiles of the firms as they developed over time. The authors independently isolated 171 such profiles, or 'periods' as we call them, using the heuristic discussed by Miller and Friesen (1980b: 596-7). Scoring points were six years apart on average, the shortest interval being 18 months, the longest, 20 years. Miller and Friesen (1980a, 1980b) describe the methods used to identify the scoring points, and report the high level of reliability that was achieved among the raters.

The second task was to rate the 24 variables of environment, structure and strategy making at each of the 171 points. This research examines only 10 of these variables: scanning, controls, communication systems, analysis, multiplexity and integration of decisions, product-market innovation, proactiveness, risk taking, and futurity. These are defined in Appendix I. Variables were scored on 7-point scales for a 'period', really a specific point in time. Raters assigned scores according to whether the variables for this period in question were much higher (7), much lower (1), or about the same as for all the other periods in their total experience. The exercise resulted in 171 profiles scored along 24 variables. The scoring was done several years ago by the authors, two policy professors at Mc-Gill University, and a graduate student who was well acquainted with the case method of analysis. All raters had read a large number of histories of very different companies so as to have a sufficiently broad basis of comparison in assigning the ratings. Interrater reliability was tested by having 50 periods spanning 26 organizations rated in double-blind fashion. The Spearman coefficient for this exercise was .86. Only in 3 percent of the cases did scores differ among raters by more than 2 points on the 7-point scales.

The validity of the scores was established by approaching top executives of 12 firms who had presided over a particular period of analysis. As reported in Miller and Friesen (1980b: 597–8), there was a very high level of agreement between rater scores and executive scores for the 24 variables. Readers are referred to Miller and Friesen (1980a, 1980b) for a more detailed discussion of the samples, period boundary definition rules, and reliability and validity of the data. Miller and Friesen (1977) give a detailed account of the strengths and weaknesses of published data bases and discuss the manner in which they can be scored.

A third scoring procedure was necessary. This involved assigning the 171 periods to the five phases of the life cycle that were identified from the literature. Both authors independently assigned these to one of the phases according to the classification criteria listed in the following table (top of next column). Using these criteria, raters agreed on their classifications of the periods 94 percent of the time. Where there was disagreement, it usually involved the maturity and decline phases. In the 6 percent of the cases where no unanimous

Phase	Criteria
Birth	Firm is less than 10 years old, has informal structure and is dominated by owner-manager.
Growth	Sales growth greater than 15%, functionally organized structure, early formalization of policies.
Maturity	Sales growth less than 15%, bureaucratic organization.
Revival	Sales growth greater than 15%, diversification of product lines, divisionalization, use of sophisticated controls and planning systems.
Decline	Demand for products levels off, low rate of product innovation, profitability starts to drop off.

assignment could be made, periods were dropped from the sample. We were left with 161 periods classified into our five stages. These are shown in Appendix II.

Note that we went through two stages in classifying the published histories into the phases of the life cycle. The first divided the histories into 171 brief slices that were quite different from one another. The second classified these periods into the phases. We could not directly identify phases of the life cycle from the published histories because each phase is quite long and therefore encompasses a great deal of variation along the 10 variables of our hypotheses. We wished to record all of this variation since it is most germane to our research postulates. For example, a firm in the maturity phase may undergo great transitions in information processing and innovation variables. Rather than taking some rough average of these variables over a diverse and lengthy phase, we used a period definition heuristic that allowed all of the extremes of the variable scores to be reflected individually (from the highest score to the lowest score). This sometimes produced two or more periods of analysis within the same life cycle phase (as we can see from Appendix II).

Having classified periods into their life cycle phases, we wished to split the sample into its successful and unsuccessful components. A success score was obtained for each period by rating annual growth in profits and sales, normalizing, converting to 7-point scales, and averaging the two scales. Scores of 5 or more caused periods to be assigned to the successful groups; all other periods were said to be unsuccessful. For the older firms, it was sometimes impossible to obtain information on performance for the early years. In this case, we reread the published histories to obtain a rough estimate of performance for assigning a success score directly. The published accounts would often contain references to increased orders, a boom in sales, an increase in margins, the landing of a large account, the hiring of more employees to meet increased production requirements and other indicators of success. Failure might be indicated by plant closures, layoffs, economic recession, declines in market share or the loss of a major client. Raters' subjective scores

correlated at .89, differing by more than 2 points only 4 percent of the time. In all cases, estimates were made relative to the other periods in the sample. Had we avoided this method of approximation, our birth and growth phases would have been reduced in sample size by about 50 percent and 35 percent respectively, making it impossible to reliably test our hypotheses. Because corporate performance does seem to vary over the life cycle, the proportion of periods classified into the maturity and decline phases was higher in the unsuccessful than in the successful subsample. Note that the very same firm was often successful in some periods and unsuccessful in others. Our successful subsample contained 7 periods of birth, 53 of growth, 23 of maturity, 22 of revival and 2 of decline. The unsuccessful subsample contained 5 periods of birth, 8 of growth, 22 of maturity, 5 of revival and 14 of decline. Appendix II provides the names of our firms, their industries, the number of periods for each, the phases to which periods were assigned and their performance.

Table 2. Means and Standard Deviations of Information Processing and Decision Making Variables

	Successful Group N = 107		Unsuccessful Group N = 54			
	M.	S.D.	M.	S.D.	t-statistic*	p-value (two-tailed)
Information Processing						
Scanning	4.34	1.90	2.87	1.95	4.52	.005
Controls	3.62	2.32	2.61	1.61	2.22	.025
Communication	3.63	2.23	2.35	1.75	3.96	.005
Decision Making						
Analysis	3.85	1.93	3.09	1.64	2.59	.01
Multiplexity	4.41	1.46	2.89	1.27	6.76	.005
Integration	4.58	1.46	3.41	1.45	4.79	.005

*Since we did not wish to assume that the unknown population variances were equal, we used an adjusted *t*-statistic. The adjustment lowered the degrees of freedom from 159 to 103 and *t* was calculated as

$$t = (m_1 - m_2)\left(\frac{s_1^2}{n_1} + \frac{s_2^2}{n_2}\right)^{-1/2}$$

where m_1 and m_2 are the respective sample means, s_1^2 and s_2^2 the variances, and n_1 and n_2 the sample sizes 107 and 54 respectively. The same *t*-statistic was used in Table 4.

Strictly speaking, we cannot say that our periods represent independent observations since they sometimes describe the same firm, which may preserve certain characteristics from one period to the next. There is no way of avoiding this potential drawback as it is inherent in all longitudinal studies of organizations. The dependence applies to successful and unsuccessful samples alike, these being the principal objects of comparison. It is therefore hard to see how it could systematically bias our results, except perhaps to reduce the effective sample size of our research. We ascertained that a random 30 percent reduction in our sample influenced none of our major findings.[1] Such a reduction might be considered to be conservative since the possible interdependence of periods is very often broken by dramatic organizational transitions, and by alternating intervals of success and failure which often place

sequential periods into different subsamples. Indeed only 27 percent (44) of the adjacent periods were in the same life cycle phase and the same performance subgroup.

Findings

Our analysis attempted to test our two principal hypotheses in a variety of ways. An analysis of variance was performed as was a comparison of means for all variables in successful and unsuccessful subgroups.

H_1: Information Processing and Decision-Making Style

Tables 2 and 3 show that there are very significant differences among successful and unsuccessful phases of the life cycle. This is true of all information processing and decision making style

Table 3. Analysis of Variance of Information Processing and Decision Making Variables

	Means					p-values		
	Birth (1)	Growth (2)	Maturity (3)	Revival (4)	Decline (5)	Total (6)	Linear (7)	Nonlinear (8)
Successful Firms								
N = 7		53	23	22	2	107		
Information Processing								
Scanning	2.7	3.9	4.8	5.5	5.0	.001	.0000	.71
Controls	1.3	3.1	4.2	5.0	4.5	.0005	.0000	.57
Communication	3.0	3.0	4.0	4.9	3.0	.015	.0025	.34
Decision Making								
Analysis	2.7	3.5	3.8	5.0	5.5	.006	.0003	.84
Multiplexity	2.7	4.1	5.0	5.0	5.0	.0004	.0000	.20
Integration	2.9	4.5	5.1	4.9	4.5	.005	.009	.05
Unsuccessful Firms								
N = 5		8	22	5	14	54		
Information Processing								
Scanning	3.4	2.1	3.0	3.8	2.6	.56	.86	.40
Controls	1.2	2.5	3.1	3.8	2.0	.025	.78	.01
Communication	2.4	2.1	2.5	3.6	1.9	.43	.70	.31
Decision Making								
Analysis	2.4	2.6	3.1	5.6	2.7	.004	.35	.002
Multiplexity	2.4	2.8	3.0	4.6	2.4	.009	.98	.004
Integration	3.6	2.9	3.5	4.6	3.1	.25	.93	.15

Figure 1. Average Mean Scores for Variable Categories Across the Life Cycle

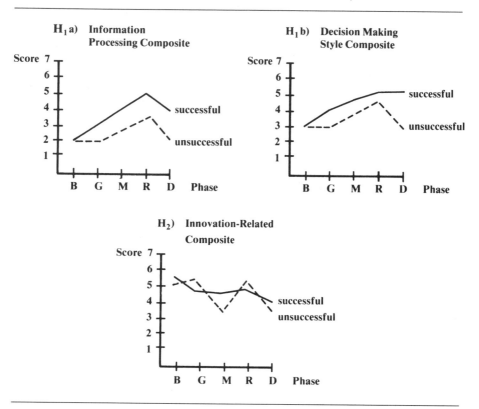

variables. Table 2 shows that in general, there are higher scores along these variables in successful than in unsuccessful groups of periods. The average variable scores for scanning, controls and communication (information processing), and for analysis, multiplexity and integration (decision making) are significantly greater in the successful than in the unsuccessful groups. But these scores have been aggregated across all the life cycle phases. Table 3 shows the mean scores for all variables in each phase of the life cycle. There are no significant differences in the birth phase between successful and unsuccessful subsamples. These differences only materialize later on. This is rather dramatically illustrated in graphs H_1a and H_1b of Figure 1 where the figures plotted represent the average variable scores for each category of variables. The divergences between sub-

groups for the information processing and decision making style variables only become noticeable in the growth phase of the life cycle.

Our hypotheses H_1a and H_1b proposed that successful phases would show a linear progression in these variables, increasing over the life cycle to match administrative challenges, especially during the first four stages. The analysis of variance presented in Table 3 confirms this. For the information processing variables, the successful group shows important differences among the phases of the life cycle (column 6), while, in general, the unsuccessful group does not. Perhaps even more supportive of our H_1a is the fact that the linear component of the ANOVA is very significant for the successful group, while the nonlinear one is not (columns 7 and 8). In the unsuccessful sample the reverse is true in the one case, that of controls, where the total p-value is significant. In other words, instead of showing progressive increases in the capacity to cope with administrative complexity over the life cycle, unsuccessful phases retain a primitive information processing apparatus. An even cruder information processing system is manifested in the decline phase. The successful phases show a consistent and gradual build-up of information processing efforts, which do *not* fall all that much in the decline phase.

The same findings hold for decision making style (H_1b). Table 2 shows that successful phases have a more sophisticated decision making approach; performing more analysis, systematically considering more factors and points of view (multiplexity), and taking greater pains to integrate the decision making effort. Differences between successful and unsuccessful groups again arise only *after* the birth phase, as we can see from Figure 1. Finally, the ANOVA of Table 3 shows that the differences among the mean variable scores across the five phases are due to a linear component (column 7) in the successful group and a nonlinear component (column 8) in the unsuccessful group.

To conclude our discussion of H_1a and H_1b, it seems the hypotheses are strongly borne out. Successful groups show gradual and steady increases in information processing and decision making sophistication over successively more complex phases of the life cycle, at least up until and including the revival phase. Unsuccessful groups show no such tendency. In the latter, intelligence and decision making sophistication often *decline* from the simple birth phase to the more complex growth phase. In fact, the only real increase in these variables comes during the very complex revival phase. Perhaps, then, it is wise to gradually build up capacity for coping with administrative complexity and to avoid a strategy that retains a primitive information system until rather late in the life cycle.

H_2: Innovation-Related Variables and the Life Cycle

We hypothesized that there would be a tendency for all successful phases to have a moderately high rate of innovation, and that these would *not* differ a great deal in their innovation levels. In contrast, we expected unsuccessful phases to show important differences in their levels of innovation. More specifically, birth, growth, and revival phases might be extremely innovative, while maturity and decline phases might be quite stagnant. Our variables measured four aspects of innovation: product-market innovation, the amount of risk taking, the tendency to react vs. beating competitors to the punch (proactiveness), and the length of planning time horizons (futurity).

Table 4 shows that in general, there is significantly more innovation-related activity in successful than in unsuccessful phases (columns 5 and 6). However, this difference is probably caused by the predominance of conservative phases (e.g. maturity) in the unsuccessful sample and the predomi-

Table 4. Means and Standard Deviations of Innovation-Related Variables

	Successful Group N=107		Unsuccessful Group N=54		t-statistic	$\bar{p}$	F-ratio	$\bar{p}$
	M. (1)	S.D. (2)	M. (3)	S.D. (4)	(5)	(6)	(7)	(8)
Innovation	4.86	1.28	3.91	1.59	3.78	.01	1.53	.06
Proactiveness	4.96	1.47	3.98	1.85	3.36	.01	1.58	.05
Risk Taking	4.44	1.43	4.20	2.02	.77	NS	2.00	.01
Futurity	4.62	1.40	3.76	1.65	3.25	.01	1.39	.10

Table 5. Analysis of Variance of Innovation-Related Variables

	Means					p-values		
	Birth (1)	Growth (2)	Maturity (3)	Revival (4)	Decline (5)	Total (6)	Linear (7)	Nonlinear (8)
Successful Firms								
N = 7		53	23	22	2	107		
Innovation	5.7	4.8	4.9	4.8	3.5	.24	.21	.28
Risk Taking	5.9	4.4	4.0	4.7	3.0	.01	.21	.01
Proactiveness	6.1	4.9	4.7	5.1	4.0	.17	.31	.15
Futurity	4.4	4.6	4.3	5.1	4.5	.36	.23	.40
Unsuccessful Firms								
N = 5		8	22	5	14	54		
Innovation	5.0	4.9	3.5	5.6	3.0	.0007	.007	.004
Risk Taking	5.0	5.5	3.6	5.0	3.9	.118	.19	.13
Proactiveness	5.2	5.6	3.4	5.2	3.1	.001	.004	.011
Futurity	4.8	5.0	3.4	5.8	2.6	.0000	.0007	.0002

nance of innovative phases (e.g. revival) in the successful group. A more interesting finding is that there is significantly more variability in the level of innovation across the life cycle among unsuccessful phases (cf. columns 7 and 8). This is consistent with the notion of extremes in innovation for the unsuccessful phases. Such a tendency is demonstrated graphically in Figure 1 (H_2). It is also supported by the ANOVA results shown in Table 5. Except for the variable of risk taking, the successful phases show no significant differences in innovation-related variables across the stages of the life cycle (column 6), while the unsuccessful phases are very significantly different. In addition, the significant differences in the latter group are caused by both a linear and a nonlinear component. The former might be due to the rather high level of innovation at the beginning of the life cycle, and the rather low level in the last decline phase. The significance of the nonlinear component is caused by the important fluctuations (in opposite directions) among adjacent phases.

Risk taking does not seem to fit into the above pattern. The successful periods show a rather high level of risk taking in the birth phase, when the unsuccessful group is more conservative. The opposite is true for the decline phase where the successful group is more conservative than the unsuccessful one. Perhaps newborn companies are forced to take risks as they attempt to establish distinctive competences for the first time. The high levels of innovation and proactiveness allow firms to take the lead. But this entails risks, especially since firms are small and resources scarce. In the decline phase, some of the firms in our sample took some rather bold refinancing and new market-entry steps. These firms raised the level of risk taking for the unsuccessful group, making a traditionally conservative phase appear much less so. It is noteworthy that these risks had very little to do with innovation. But they did reduce the interphase differences in risk taking for the unsuccessful group of firms. In other words, the anomalous findings for the risk taking variable might be due to our failure to differentiate between product-market innovation related risk taking and other kinds of risk taking. But more research is needed on this question.

Conclusions

There seem to be very significant contrasts between successful and unsuccessful phases of the life cycle. There are differences both in the levels and in the progression of information processing, decision making, and innovation-related variables. More specifically, we noticed three major distinguishing features between our high and low performance groups. First, the information processing varibles of scanning, controls and communications had, on average, higher scores in the successful group than in the unsuccessful group. We believe these differences stem from the need for firms to escalate their information processing efforts as they encounter increasing levels of administrative complexity. Our second main finding was that the same differences between the subgroups held true for the variables of decision making, namely, analysis, multiplexity and integration. We believe the explanation for this to be the same as that underlying the first finding.

Our third finding concerned the innovation-related variables. Successful phases in general had a higher level of innovation-related activity (except in the case of risk taking). They also showed fewer differences along the life cycle. Unsuccessful phases on the other hand showed significantly greater variation along the life cycle in innovation-related variables, having more of a tendency to move from one extreme to another (again, the risk taking variable was an exception to the rule). Perhaps, unsuccessful firms innovate too little in some phases and too much in others.

Though our results are tentative, they do point to significant differences among successful and unsuccessful phases of the life cycle. While the direction of causality is very much in doubt, it seems reasonable to postulate that evolutionary patterns and levels of information processing, decision making and innovation-related variables will influence performance. However, further longitudinal research, perhaps in a field setting, will be needed to confirm our findings.

APPENDIX I
Definitions of the Variables

Information Processing

Scanning involves the search for problems and opportunities in the external environment of the firm. Firms are to be scored in terms of the amount of scanning performed on consumer tastes, competition, technological and administrative developments, etc. Scanning may be done by staff departments, executives, the sales force, etc. The greater the number of factors tracked and the more widespread the participation in scanning activity, the higher the score.

Controls monitor the internal trends and incidents relevant to organizational performance. M.I.S., employee performance appraisals, quality controls, cost and profit centres, budgeting, and cost accounting are types of control devices. Score high if there is much emphasis on such controls.

Internal Communication Systems reflect the openness and fidelity of information channels in the organization. A high score is given when information reaches decision makers quickly, when it is relevant and undistorted, and when communication flows readily in top-down, bottom-up, and lateral directions.

Decision Making

Analysis of Major Decisions. Do decision makers devote much reflective thought and deliberation to a problem and the array of proposed responses? Time spent on correlating symptoms to get at the root cause of problems and effort spent on generating solutions (good or bad) are examples of analysis. A low score is given when there is a rapid intuitive response to an issue (this response may be ideal or the worst possible). Evidence of analysis includes time delays, frequent meetings and discussions, the use of staff specialists, and the writing of lengthy reports.

Multiplexity of Decisions. Do top managers address a broad or narrow range of factors in making strategic decisions? For example, in deciding whether to acquire a company, a multiplex strategist would consider marketing, financial, production, demographic, administrative, and other problems, whereas low multiplexity would be evidenced by a focus, say, on marketing factors alone.

Integration of Decisions. Are actions in one area of the firm complementary to or supportive of those in other areas, or are they conflicting and mutually inhibiting? High integration would result in (or from) a concerted and well-coordinated strategy while low integration might be manifested by fragmented or clashing tactics (e.g., acquiring new companies when there is inadequate ability to finance or run them or selling products that compete against each other).

Innovation Related

Product Market Innovation. Does the firm seem particularly innovative in terms of number or novelty of new products and services introduced and new markets entered?

Proactiveness of Decisions is determined by whether or not a firm shapes its environment by introducing new products, technologies, administrative techniques, etc. A reactive firm follows the leader while a proactive firm is the first to act.

Risk Taking. Is there evidence that top managers are risk averse (score low), or does the firm frequently make large and risky resource commitments, commitments that have a reasonable chance of costly failure?

Futurity of Decisions concerns the extent to which the firm looks into the future in planning its strategies and operations. A distant time horizon (5 years) warrants a high score. A focus on crisis decision making warrants a low score.

APPENDIX II
Firms, Periods, Phases and Performance

	Period #										
	1	*2*	*3*	*4*	*5*	*6*	*7*	*8*	*9*	*10*	*11*
Armstrong Cork (Flooring)	M S	R S									
Ayer (Advertising)	B F	G S	G F	G S	G S	M F	G S	G S	R S	D F	R S
Berenschot (Consulting)	M S	M F									
Boise Cascade (Paper, lumber)	G S	G S									
Burlington Ind. (Textiles)	R S	M S									
Cdn. Pacific (Transport'n)	B S	M S	M F								
Caterpillar (Constr. Equip.)	G S	G S	M F								
Consol. Edison (Utility)	D F	M F									

APPENDIX II (Continued)

| | Period # | | | | | | | | | | |
	1	2	3	4	5	6	7	8	9	10	11
Control Data (Computers)	G S	G S									
Du Pont (Chemical)	M S	M S	R S	R F	R F						
Ford (Auto)	D F	R S	M S								
Franklin Bank (Banking)	M F	D F									
General Motors (Auto)	B S	B S	G F	G F	G F	G S					
General Dynamics (Defense)	G S	G S									
W. R. Grace (Chemical)	M F	R F	R S								
H. J. Heinz (Food)	M S	M F	R S								
I.B.M. (Computer)	M S	G S	M S	G S	M S						
Int'l. Paper (Pulp & Paper)	G F	M Γ	M F	R F							
I.T.T. (Divers)	D F	G S	M F	R S	R S	R S					
Litton (Divers)	G S	G S	G S								
Macy's (Dept. Store)	B S	G S	G S	G S	D F	M S	M S	G S	G S		
Melville (Shoe Retailing)	M F	R S									
Polaroid (Photog.)	G S	M S	M S	R S							
Procter & Gamble (Cons. Prod.)	M S	M S	M S								
R.C.A. (Elect.; Broadcast.)	G S	G F	G S	M F							
Sears (Retailing)	G S	G S	M F	G S	D S	G S	G S	R S			
Singer (Sewing; Elect.)	G S	M F	R S	M F							

APPENDIX II (Continued)

	Period #										
	1	2	3	4	5	6	7	8	9	10	11
Std. Oil (N.J.) (Oil)	G	M	M	R	R						
	S	F	F	S	S						
Unilever (Chem.)	B	G	G	R	G	G	M	M			
	S	S	S	S	S	F	F	S			
United Airlines (Airline)	D	R									
	F	S									
Volkswagenwerk (Auto)	B	G	G	G	D	R	R				
	S	S	S	S	F	F	S				
Waltham (Watches)	B	B	G	G	G	M	M	D	D	M	D
	F	F	S	S	S	F	F	F	F	S	S
Wheeling Steel (Steel)	D	D									
	F	F									
Whitin (Textile machinery)	B	G	G	G	G	D	M	M	M	M	
	S	S	F	S	S	F	F	S	S	S	
Xerox (Office Equip.)	B	G	G	G							
	F	S	S	S							
Yellow Freight (Trucking)	B	G	G	G	D	R	R				
	F	S	S	S	F	S	S				

Key: B, G, M, R, D stand for birth, growth, maturity, revival, and decline phases (respectively) of the life cycle. S and F indicate that the period of analysis is successful or unsuccessful (failing) respectively.

Note

1 We chose a random 70 percent of the sample, reran all of our analyses, and found that all of the principal findings were borne out for the smaller sample. The results of this analysis are available from the authors.

References

Adizes, I. 1979. 'Organizational passages: diagnosing and treating life-cycle problems in organizations'. *Organizational Dynamics,* Summer, 3–27.

Aguilar, F. 1967. *Scanning the business environment.* New York: Macmillan.

Andrews, K. 1980. *The concept of corporate strategy.* Homewood, Ill.: Irwin.

Ansoff, H.I. 1965. *Corporate strategy.* New York: McGraw-Hill.

Chandler, A. 1962. *Strategy and structure.* Cambridge, Mass.: MIT Press.

Channon, D. 1973. *The strategy and structure of British enterprise.* Boston: Harvard Business School.

Downs, A. 1967. 'The life-cycle of bureaus' in *Inside bureaucracy.* A. Downs (ed.), 296–309. San Francisco: Little, Brown.

Galbraith, J. 1973. *Designing complex organizations.* Reading, Mass.: Addison-Wesley.

Greiner, L. 1972. 'Evolution and revolution as organizations grow'. *Harvard Business Review,* July–August, 37–46.

Hedberg, B. 1972. 'Organization stagnation and choice of strategy', *Working paper,* International Institute of Management, West Berlin.

Hedberg, B., P. Nystrom, and W. Starbuck. 1976. 'Camping on seesaws: prescriptions for a self-designing organization'. *Administrative Science Quarterly* 21: 41–65.

Khandwalla, P. 1972. 'Environment and its impact on the organization'. *International Studies of Management Organization* 2: 297–313.

Kimberly, J. 1979. 'Issues in the creation of organizations: initiation, innovation, and institutionalization'. *Academy of Management Journal* 22: 437–57.

Kimberly, J., and R. Miles. 1980. *The organizational life cycle*. San Francisco: Jossey-Bass.

Lyden, F. 1975. 'Using Parsons' functional analysis in the study of public organizations'. *Administrative Science Quarterly* 20: 59–70.

Miller, D., and P. Friesen. 1977. 'Strategy-making in context: ten empirical archetypes'. *Journal of Management Studies* 14: 258–80.

Miller, D., and P. Friesen. 1980a. 'Archetypes of organizational transition'. *Administrative Science Quarterly* 25: 268–99.

Miller, D., and P. Friesen. 1980b. 'Momentum and revolution in organizational adaptation'. *Academy of Management Journal* 23: 591–614.

Miller, D., and P. Friesen. 1982a. 'A longitudinal study of the corporate life cycle'. *Working paper,* Montreal: McGill University.

Miller, D., and P. Friesen. 1982b. 'Innovation in conservative and entrepreneurial firms: two models of strategic momentum'. *Strategic Management Journal* 3: 1–25.

Mintzberg, H. 1973. 'Strategy-making in three modes'. *California Management Review* 16: 44–53.

Porter, M. 1980. *Competitive strategy.* New York: Free Press.

Quinn, R., and K. Cameron. 1983. 'Organizational life cycles and shifting criteria of effectiveness: some preliminary evidence'. *Management Science* 29: 33–51.

Schon, D. 1971. *Beyond the stable state.* New York: Norton.

Scott, B. 1971. *Stages of corporate development—part 1, case No. 9-371-294.* Boston: Intercollegiate Case Clearing House, Harvard Business School.

Thompson, V. 1961. *Modern organization.* New York: Knopf.

Torbert, W. 1974. 'Pre-bureaucratic and post-bureaucratic stages of organization development'. *Interpersonal Development* 5: 1–25.

Tushman, M. 1977. 'Special boundary roles in the innovation process'. *Administrative Science Quarterly* 22: 587–605.

12

The Stigma of Bankruptcy: Spoiled Organizational Image and Its Management

Robert I. Sutton

Anita L. Callahan

My reputation was smirched. It was as if I had committed some sort of sin. I felt guilty. I will never be able to get [venture capital] funding again. I will never get another chance to be CEO.
— From an interview with a former chief executive officer of a bankrupt computer firm.

Top management's image can be spoiled by a variety of organizational problems, including poor financial performance, fatal industrial accidents, and defective products. Both popular writings (Kanter, 1983; Peters & Waterman, 1982) and academic perspectives (Hambrick & Mason, 1984; Pfeffer, 1981; Salancik & Meindl, 1984) emphasize that competent leaders are expected to exercise control over their organizations and that such control is expected to lead to organizational success. Thus, when a firm is in a serious predicament, observers may wonder: if top management is in control, why is the firm in so much trouble?

We wish to acknowledge the exceptional personal and institutional support that enabled us to write this paper. A pair of colleagues deserve special mention. Sim Sitkin served as a first-rate devil's advocate during the early stages of theoretical development. Leonard Greenhalgh provided literally hundreds of useful comments on an early draft of the paper. We also wish to acknowledge contributions by Paul Adler, Tamara Bryant, John Callahan, Stewart Friedman, Paul Goldman, Cherly Householder, James Jucker, Barbara Lawrence, Peter Nitze, Marina Park, Anat Rafaeli, Cheryl Ray, John Van Maanen, Steven Vargas, Margaret Whiffler, and Mayer Zald.

Financial support for gathering these data was provided by Stanford University's Center for Teaching and Research in Integrated Manufacturing Systems. Portions of this paper were prepared while Robert Sutton was a fellow at the Center for Advanced Study in the Behavioral Sciences. He is grateful for financial support provided by the Carnegie Corporation of New York and the William and Flora Hewlett Foundation.

Reprinted with permission from *Academy of Management Journal,* Vol. 30, No. 3, © 1987 *Academy of Management Journal.*

Even if no one explicitly raises that question, the idea is in the air and is deeply discrediting to leaders.

The images of organizations and their leaders are intertwined. Indeed, Hambrick and Mason (1984) argued that an organization is a reflection of its top managers. If the members of an organization and its external constituencies do not perceive top management as credible, their faith in the organization erodes. Such spoiled images can cause those individuals, who constitute the *organizational audience* for whom top management must perform, to withdraw their support for the organization (Salancik & Meindl, 1984). Such withdrawal deepens the predicament, for the effectiveness of any organization depends on the continued participation and support of its organizational audiences (Cameron & Whetten, 1983).

Discrediting predicaments like poor financial performance or deadly industrial accidents also create difficulties for leaders as individuals. In Goffman's (1967) terms, such signs of poor leadership make it difficult for top managers to maintain "face," or to present an image that enables them to claim the status associated with their role. Discredited leaders may feel embarrassed. They may be fired. And their careers may sustain long-term damage.

The present research considers one such discrediting predicament. We used case studies of four computer firms to develop a grounded theory about the stigma that results when a company files for protection under Chapter 11 of the Federal Bankruptcy Code. The bankrupt firms we studied were often shunned by members of their organizational audiences. The leaders we interviewed were hurt and embarrassed. Even though we were careful not to mention the word "stigma" during interviews, informants used it often in describing their predicament.[1]

Indeed, our research revealed that the spoiled images resulting from the Chapter 11 label are analogous to those described by Goffman (1963) in his classic book *Stigma: Notes on the Management of Spoiled Identity* and in more recent writings by Page (1984) and by Jones, Farina, Hastorf, Markus, Miller, and Scott (1984). These writings indicate that a stigma refers to an attribute that is deeply discrediting. A stigma reduces "a whole and usual person to a tainted, discounted one" (Goffman, 1963: 3).

Evidence from the four cases we investigated indicated that both internal organizational audiences like lower-level employees and members of middle management and external audiences like customers, creditors, and suppliers viewed leaders of bankrupt firms as tainted and incompetent people; such unfavorable images even extended to leaders who joined a firm after Chapter 11 had been filed. In the framework presented here, we propose that the spoiled image of top management and the associated spoiled image of a firm lead key organizational audiences to change both enacted relationships with a firm and espoused evaluations of the firm and its leaders. We hypothesize that those negative reactions, or "sent stigmas," further reduce the viability of bankrupt firms. We also propose that such sent stigmas damage the careers of top managers and cause them to feel the embarrassment, anger, and loss of self-esteem experienced by stigmatized people.

The literature on stigma also guided theory building about the techniques used to manage the spoiled images of bankrupt firms and their leaders. Writings on stigma management (Goffman, 1963; Jones et al., 1984) and related literature on the impression management strategies used by individuals in identity-threatening predicaments (Schenkler, 1980) provided useful points of departure for understanding and sorting the strategies used by leaders in their efforts to avert or reduce damage to individual and organizational images. We propose a hierarchy of five strategies for managing stigma that is based on the extent to which top managers acknowledge the stigma of bankruptcy when addressing a given organizational audience. The five strategies are concealing, defining, denying responsibility, accepting responsibility, and withdrawing.

The remainder of this paper describes the four case studies and elaborates a conceptual perspective grounded in those data. Following the logic of induction, we present the method first and the theory second.

Methods

Organizations and Informants

Each organization selected for this research met three criteria: (1) it had filed for reorganization under Chapter 11 of the Federal Bankruptcy Code, (2) it was still operating, and (3) it was in the computer industry. Table 1 gives pseudonyms and some descriptive statistics for the core group of four Silicon Valley computer firms: Visionary Computers, Enoch Computers, Perfect Peripherals, and Mega Peripherals. In addition to those firms, we attempted to interview the leaders of two other bankrupt firms, but they refused to participate in our study. As we explain later, however, some data were gathered during these initial phone conversations with potential informants.

Each firm in the core group sought protection under Chapter 11 of the Federal Bankruptcy Code because it lacked the assets to pay major creditors. Under Chapter 11, creditors' claims against a firm are stayed pending a bankruptcy court's approval of plans for restructuring all debts. Restructuring debts means determining (1) the order in which creditors will be paid according to legal rules of priority—for example, whether the creditors made secured or unsecured loans; (2) how much creditors will be paid—typically, less than 100 cents on the dollar; and (3) the time over which payments will be stretched out. A bankrupt firm's major creditors usually form a committee that hires and pays a bankruptcy lawyer. The debts of each of the four firms studied had been or were being restructured through negotiations between the firm's top management and a creditors' committee.[2]

The number of informants interviewed for each case (see Table 1) was determined by Glaser and Strauss's (1967) concept of "theoretical saturation"—we stopped interviewing additional informants when we began hearing the same stories repeated again and again. More specifically, for each organization, we tried to interview the president at the time of the Chapter 11 filing, at least one other member of top management, a major creditor, and a lawyer who was involved. We also interviewed other people who were nominated by informants as key actors.

We were able to interview the president who was in place at the time of the Chapter 11 filing in

Table 1. Core Cases of Bankrupt Firms

Firms[a]	Numbers of Employees[b]	Ages of Organizations in Years	Numbers of Informants Interviewed	Unsecured Debts at Time of Filing Chapter 11[c]
Visionary Computers	175 30	6.25	7	$1,266,000 116,000
Enoch Computers	200? 25	12.00	5	1,175,000 80,000
Perfect Peripherals	225 50	3.50	4	6,894,000 939,000
Mega Peripherals	525 95	3.50	6	11,500,000 2,700,000

a. Pseudonyms are used to protect the confidentiality of these firms and their members.

b. The first number is the number of employees when the company was at its largest. The second is the number of employees the day the company filed for Chapter 11. A question mark appears for Enoch Computers because the first number is based on an informant's estimate.

c. The first figure represents the total unsecured debt rounded to the nearest $1,000; the second represents the largest individual unsecured debt. Data are from court records.

each firm except Enoch Computers. In the case of Enoch, however, we were able to observe the president during a meeting of the creditors' committee at which he did much of the talking. We were able to interview at least one other member of top management, a major creditor, and a lawyer for all but one bankruptcy—Visionary Computers' two major creditors declined to be interviewed.

Data Sources

This research relied primarily on four data sources: (1) initial observations, (2) semistructured interviews, (3) records data, and (4) observation of a creditors' committee meeting.

Initial observations. A form was used to summarize the telephone conversations in which we introduced the research and ourselves to potential informants and their gatekeepers. It was a modified version of an instrument used by Sutton (1984) to record the reactions of informants in a study of organizational death. We viewed initial conversations as "field stimulations" (Salancik, 1979: 638) that tickled, tempted, and perturbed prospective informants and their gatekeepers.

The instrument included open- and closed-ended items. Although this source yielded both quantitative and qualitative evidence, our theory-building effort relied primarily on the qualitative evidence. The items concerned behavioral reactions, such as shielding by gatekeepers, and emotional reactions, including anger, denial, avoidance, sadness, and joking. The form also had space for recording miscellaneous data that emerged during the initial conversations.

Potential informants we spoke to who would not, or could not, participate in a face-to-face interview were asked if they "would mind answering a brief question about the bankruptcy." The question was, "What is the most important bit of advice that you would give to someone who faced the prospect of managing a company that had filed for reorganization under Chapter 11?" A 45-minute answer provided by the president of one bankrupt computer company to which we failed to gain

entry was especially enlightening. When we were unable to reach a potential informant, initial observations were still made about the behavior of the gatekeeper or gatekeepers we encountered.

The telephone instrument was completed for the 34 individuals we chose as informants. Three informants associated with the two organizations in which failure at entry occurred and nine individuals involved in the core cases did not participate further. Twenty-two informants granted face-to-face interviews. Thus, the response rate for complete participation was 65 percent.

Semistructured interview. An interview was developed for the present study; its content was based on a rough working framework developed prior to data collection and on pilot studies[3] of three bankrupt firms. It consisted of 72 open-ended questions. In addition, since this was an inductive study, we pursued unexpected but interesting lines of discussion. Twenty of the 22 interviews were tape recorded and then transcribed. The typical interview was 90 minutes; the length varied from 30 minutes to three hours.

The interview began with questions about the history and structure of an organization. We then asked about the onset of financial difficulties and the filing of bankruptcy. Next, informants were given a list of key individuals and groups that may have participated in the bankruptcy. These were customers, consumers, suppliers, top management, middle management, lower level employees, founders, venture capitalists, stockholders, employees' families, lawyers, banks, community, journalists, user groups, associates in other computer firms, and creditors. We asked informants to list key participants who had been left out and to cross out individuals and groups that were not involved in the bankruptcy. We then asked them to tell us: (1) how each individual or group responded to the bankruptcy, (2) how leaders of the bankrupt company were managing relations with that individual or group, and (3) the informant's own role in the relationship.

The interview concluded with questions about the anticipated fate of a firm and ways in which the bankruptcy had been managed well and managed badly. The final question was a request for the names of other people involved, both people who agreed and those who disagreed with the informant's perspective.[4]

Records data. We obtained copies of court records for each case. Companies that file for Chapter 11 in the United States Bankruptcy Court must submit lists of all creditors, and lawsuits pending against the company must be identified. Reorganization plans must also be filed with the court and approved by a judge. We gathered other records data, including newspaper and magazine articles and correspondence between the company and creditors. The correspondence did not provide any new information, but it was useful for confirming data obtained from other sources. At least one article was written about each bankruptcy, including feature-length articles about Visionary Computers and Mega Peripherals.

Observation of a creditors' committee meeting. We were invited to observe a creditors' committee meeting, which lasted for three hours. We observed about 90 minutes of heated negotiation between the creditors and management of Enoch Computers. We also were allowed to observe discussions between the creditors and their lawyer that occurred before and after the confrontation with Enoch's management. This observation was an essential part of the data collection because both the audiences' negative reactions and the managers' emotional responses were highly explicit.

Qualitative Analysis

The method of qualitative analysis used here draws on descriptions of how to generate grounded theory written by Glaser and Strauss (1967), Mintzberg (1979), and Miles and Huberman (1984). The method entailed constantly comparing data and theory until we developed adequate conceptual categories.

An important assumption which underlies the method is that data do not develop theory; human

creativity and intuition are required (Mintzberg, 1979). Yet the method requires theory builders to compare their ideas to empirical evidence. As an investigator travels back and forth between theory and data, some initial ideas can be grounded in the evidence, others may be modified considerably on the basis of evidence, and still others may be abandoned for lack of evidence.

Some variation of this method was used at all stages in the research. Before, during, and after data collection, we had frequent meetings to discuss the emerging theory. Early meetings focused on developing a rough working framework. The framework was based on the pilot studies of three bankrupt organizations and on a review of pertinent literature. Meetings during the data collection phase entailed adjusting the framework to allow for new facts and ideas and planning to collect new evidence. Several of those meetings were enriched by a third researcher, who served as devil's advocate. His primary assignment was to discover and describe flaws in data collection methods and in the rough working framework.

Qualitative analysis after the data had been gathered entailed systematic comparison of data and theory. The emerging theory reflected Van Maanen's observation that "qualitative work is more concerned with commonality and things shared in the social world than it is with differentiation and things not so shared" (1983: 257). Our analysis of the data thus focused on identifying theoretical elements that remained constant across the four cases. Some concepts suggested by the literature on stigma and by our initial intuitions were ultimately deleted from the framework because they could not be grounded in evidence. Other elements were not included because, even though they appeared across the cases, there were too many other examples that were inconsistent with the proposed element. Still other initial ideas had to be modified considerably. A few of the theoretical elements we proposed initially could be grounded firmly in the evidence and required no modification.

Our methods of comparing and reporting the evidence across the four cases built on Miles and

Huberman's (1984) suggestions for cross-site analysis with qualitative data and on the methods used by Harris and Sutton (1986) for identifying constant elements across cases. We completed cross-site display tables about audience responses (see Table 2) and stigma-management strategies (see Table 3). Constructing the tables entailed reviewing the four sources of evidence for each case. The tables indicate how strongly each proposed theoretical element can be grounded in evidence from the initial observation form, semistructured interview, records data, and observation of the creditors' committee meeting. The model of how the stigma of Chapter 11 affects organizations and leaders (Figure 1) was also developed through continuous comparison of data from the four cases and the emerging theory.

Finally, it is important to make explicit our assumptions about the strength of the match between the proposed theoretical elements and the evidence. The conceptual perspective advanced here emphasizes ways in which bankrupt organizations are similar rather than different. Yet some of the proposed constant elements were not observed in every case. In quantitative research, one does not expect a set of independent variables, for example, to explain 100 percent of the variation in a set of dependent variables (Mintzberg, 1979). Similarly, the conceptual perspective proposed here fits well with the qualitative evidence — but it does not fit perfectly.

The Set of Spoiled Relationships Between Bankrupt Firms and Organizational Audiences

Our central argument is that filing for Chapter 11 can spoil the image of top management and, by extension, the image of a firm as a whole. Representatives of key organizational audiences who perceive that top management is not credible will withdraw support from a firm (Salancik & Meindl, 1984). Thus, the survival of the troubled companies we studied depended heavily on the ability of top management to maintain — both in terms of quality and quantity — the participation and support of key members of the organizational audiences for whom they performed. In each bankruptcy studied, key relationships existed between top management and each of the following organizational audiences: (1) customers, (2) lawyers, (3) journalists, (4) stockholders, (5) venture capitalists, (6) middle managers, (7) lower level employees, (8) competitors, (9) creditors, (10) suppliers, (11) government officials, (12) peers in other computer firms, and (13) members of employees' families. Other participants, such as "head hunters" and bankers, were key actors in some, but not all, of the firms.

Chapter 11 does not automatically spoil the image of a firm or its leaders. The stigma literature distinguishes between "markable" and "marked" relationships. Markable relationships are those that have the potential to be spoiled by a discrediting label; marked relationships are those that have been spoiled (Jones et al., 1984: 6–9).

Relationships between a firm and each audience are not automatically marked by the fact of Chapter 11 because, like many other stigmas (Page, 1984; Jones et al., 1984), bankruptcy can sometimes be concealed from some audiences — at least for a time. The top managements of all four firms hid the planned legal action as long as possible. Moreover, firms that have filed for Chapter 11 are required to notify all creditors, but not other people like customers or new suppliers.

Further, from the perspective of some organizational audiences, Chapter 11 may not spoil the image of a firm or its leaders. For example, some bankruptcy lawyers argued that they did not believe that there was, or should be, a stigma associated with Chapter 11.

Nevertheless, the stigma literature suggests that when a potentially discrediting predicament arises, people who are viewed as blameworthy will be most likely to suffer from spoiled identity (Goffman, 1963; Page, 1984). There is universal agreement that top management will receive most of the blame for poor organizational performance (Argenti, 1976; Peters & Waterman, 1982; Pfeffer, 1977; Pfeffer & Salancik, 1978; Salancik & Meindl, 1984). Moreover, research by Meindl, Ehrlich, and Dukerich (1985) suggests that observers will attribute the strongest responsibility to leaders when organizational performance is very good or very poor. Bankruptcy is an unambiguous case of very poor organizational performance.

Our analysis of the qualitative data is congruent with the view that bankruptcy poses a profound threat to the credibility of top management. Not every relationship between individual top managers and individual audience members was spoiled. But in each firm studied, at least one representative of each key organizational audience perceived that the image of the firm and its top management was spoiled. The next section details the negative reactions of audience members to such spoiled images and the hypothesized effects of those negative reactions on firms and their leaders.

A Model of How the Stigma Process Unfolds in Bankrupt Firms

Goffman (1963) and Jones and his colleagues (1984) proposed that encountering a stigmatized person will lead "markers" (exchange partners and other observers) to have negative reactions like withdrawal, irrational beliefs about the peril posed by the stigma, and negative attitudes. Those negative reactions are "sent stigmas"; the perception of such negative reactions by a marked person leads to emotional reactions (e.g., guilt, anger, embarrassment) that are "felt stigmas" (Page, 1984). A sent stigma can also cause difficulties for a marked person that go beyond internal feelings, such as trouble finding a job.

This conceptual perspective served as our point of departure in developing an empirically grounded model of how the stigma process unfolds in bankrupt firms. Figure 1 indicates that the discovery of Chapter 11 leads some organizational audiences to perceive that a firm and its top management are discredited. Such spoiled images cause key audiences to change enacted relationships and espoused evaluations associated with a firm and its top managers. We propose that these negative reactions have undesirable effects on an organization as a whole, with increased probabil-

Figure 1. A Model of How the Stigma of Chapter 11 Affects Organizations and Top Management

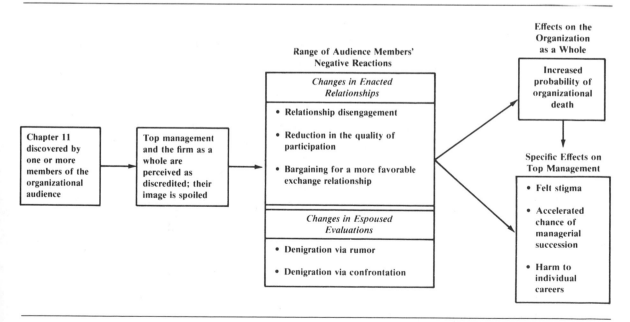

ity of organizational death the principal negative outcome, and on the members of top management specifically. Felt stigma, accelerated chance of managerial succession, and harm to individual careers are salient negative effects on managers.

The Range of Audiences' Negative Reactions

Table 2 is a summary of our efforts to ground a set of five negative reactions in data from the interviews, initial phone conversations, records, and observations of the creditors' committee meeting. The table also provides an example of each negative reaction.

The first three reactions are changes in the enacted relationship between an organizational audience and a firm: (1) disengagement, (2) reduction in the quality of participation, and (3) bargaining for more favorable exchange relationships. The remaining two reactions are changes in the espoused evaluation of the firm and leaders: (4) denigration via rumor and (5) denigration via confrontation.

Disengagement. The stigma literature indicates that people who are engaged in a long-standing relationship with a recently stigmatized person may react with overt or subtle rejection (Jones et al., 1984). Similarly, relationship disengagement after the Chapter 11 label had been discovered was among the most frequent negative reactions observed across the four cases.

Some suppliers refused to send parts, even though they would have received cash on delivery. In all four firms, customers stopped buying products because they did not want an "orphan" computer or computer peripheral.[5] Some customers even disengaged in ways that caused the bankrupt firms to lose money on goods that had already been sold. For example, a newspaper article on Visionary Computers reported the following customer reactions to the bankruptcy:

> As word of the troubles spread, customers may refuse to pay bills or even ship back, marked "defective," perfectly functioning equipment.

There was much variation in the means by which disengagement occurred. The last example suggests that some customers simply began treating the firms as if they did not exist. Our interviews suggested that suppliers usually severed relationships through formal communication. Other forms of relationship disengagement appeared to be more personal. The president of one company joked that "my neighbors treat me as if I have AIDS." He explained that neighbors had been avoiding him since news had spread that his firm had filed for Chapter 11.

Reduction in the quality of participation. This second negative reaction was observed in all cases except Enoch Computers. Some audiences are unable or unwilling to disengage from their relationship with a bankrupt firm. Landlords and suppliers may have binding contracts, and old friends may feel guilty about deserting the troubled firm.

Reducing the quality of participation is an implicit way to withdraw partially from a marked relationship. Individuals or groups that use this tactic often think that a bankrupt firm should not be treated as well as a healthy organization. Moreover, some audiences may reduce the quality of their participation because they can get away with it. Stigmas tend to reduce the power of those who are marked (Jones et al., 1984). Similarly, leaders of the troubled firms we studied often did not have the funds, personnel, or legitimacy required to entice or force participants to maintain high quality participation. To illustrate, informants from three of the four firms reported that suppliers began sending "junk" to the firm after Chapter 11 had been announced. A manager at Mega Peripherals, for example, complained that the quality of disks sent by one supplier had deteriorated since they had filed for bankruptcy:

> When 30 percent of the disks that come in are obviously defective, you know that you are in trouble. That's our big killer right now. Right now we're spending a lot of time using disks as frisbees basically because they're not any good. Almost all the vendors are trying to [use the bankrupt firm to] clean out their stock.

Table 2. Organizational Audiences' Negative Reactions to Chapter 11 [a]

Audience Responses	Visionary Computers [b]	Perfect Peripherals	Enoch Computers	Mega Peripherals	Examples
(a) Changes in Enacted Relationships					
Disengagement	I, p	I, p	I, O	I	The attitude of the members of the creditors' committee when they first get started is "Those SOB's burned me for a bunch of money, I'll never do anything for them now!" (Creditor)
Reduction in the quality of participation	I	i	I	I	It's been a problem getting good disks all along because we have a very tight criterion. . . . It's gotten worse in the last month. . . . They're trying to dump some material on us. (Manager of product testing)
Bargaining for more favorable exchange relationships	I, C	I, C	I, O, C	I	Finally we agreed to continue supplying them based on cash in advance on all material and the rest on a COD basis. (Creditor)
(b) Changes in Espoused Evaluations					
Denigration via rumor	I	i	O	I	You know that when they [competitors] can they're gonna try to go after your customers. And if they're really unscrupulous, they will say, "Ah, but they're in bankruptcy." (President)
Denigration via confrontation	I, C	A, p	O, C	i	Oh, there was one letter he wrote to the board of directors: "We believe that certain officers of the company are methodically carrying the company towards bankruptcy for their own personal enrichment." (President)

a. Observation of creditors' committee meeting was available only for Enoch Computers. We defined strong evidence as multiple and unambiguous examples from multiple sources, and modest evidence as a single and unambiguous example from a single source.

b. *Key:* I = strong evidence from interviews
    i = modest evidence from interviews
    A = strong evidence from articles
    a = modest evidence from articles
    C = strong evidence from court records
    c = modest evidence from court records
    O = strong evidence from observation of creditors' committee meeting
    o = modest evidence from observation of creditors' committee meeting
    P = strong evidence from initial phone contact
    p = modest evidence from initial phone contact

Bargaining for a more favorable exchange relationship. This third negative reaction occurs because individuals or organizations that participate in relationships with bankrupt firms can often negotiate more favorable terms of exchange than previously existed; the fact of Chapter 11 increases their bargaining power. Creditors who have not received promised payments often do not trust the leaders of bankrupt firms, nor do customers who are concerned about continued support for their purchases. Thus, audience members who maintain relationships with a bankrupt firm can argue for a better deal because they face some objective peril.

But more subtle forces may also affect such bargaining. We noted that the Chapter 11 label encourages some audiences to disengage from relationships with a firm. Since the pool of exchange partners shrinks, a bankrupt firm is more dependent — and thus less powerful — in its relationships with remaining exchange partners (Pfeffer & Salancik, 1978). Furthermore, just as those associated with a marked person suffer a "courtesy stigma" (Page, 1984: 9), employees, customers, lawyers, suppliers, and venture capitalists who engage in such relationships may suffer reduced status because they are linked to a firm that has a spoiled image.

We encountered much evidence that suppliers were able to negotiate for higher prices and for cash on delivery. Customers were able to negotiate for lower prices. New executives hired by bankrupt firms were able to negotiate for higher salaries. The president of Visionary Computers argued that high pay was essential to his career because he could give future employers a good reason for accepting a job in a bankrupt firm.

Denigration via rumor. We also encountered persistent evidence that key organizational audiences cast aspersions on firms after bankruptcy had been announced. As is often the case with a stigmatizing label (Jones et al., 1984), much of this denigration exaggerated the peril associated with participating in a firm that has filed for Chapter 11. Denigration via rumor was the most common change in the espoused evaluation of firms

(see Table 2). Former managers, current employees, journalists, suppliers, interested observers in other computer firms, and competitors would spread nasty rumors about a troubled firm. Although we encountered occasional evidence of complimentary rumors, most rumors reflected badly on the bankrupt firms and their leaders. To illustrate:

> I think Montgomery [the current president] deserves most of the credit for Perfect Peripheral's demise. More than anyone else, he is responsible. . . . [He] did everything possible to snatch defeat from the jaws of victory. (Former president, Perfect Peripherals, in a letter to a newspaper concerning a previously published article.)

The function of rumor is to "restructure ambiguous situations by explaining what has happened, by reporting what is happening, and by predicting what will happen" (Smelser, 1962: 82). Chapter 11 creates much ambiguity — organizational audiences typically have little knowledge about the legal meaning of the term, management is often secretive, and events may happen so quickly that current information is inadequate. Thus, perhaps it was inevitable that rumors were a persistent theme in the four bankruptcies.

Leaders of bankrupt firms were the most visible employees of such firms and, as mentioned earlier, were viewed by audiences as most blameworthy. Thus, the bulk of the rumors focused on their incompetence and likely departure. One chief executive described a phone call from a journalist:

> He was absolutely irresponsible in putting in gossip bits. He called me up one day and said, "I understand there's somebody waiting to invest 10 million in Mega Peripherals if you'll leave."

Other rumors reflected badly on a firm as a whole. At least two of the companies faced persistent and false rumors that a closing was to occur any day. In one case, representatives of a competitor urged customers to stop buying products from a bankrupt firm because it was "dead."

Denigration via confrontation. Direct insults were encountered less frequently than rumors, but

Table 2 reveals that they did occur in all four cases. Such denigration may be especially damaging to its targets because it is so embarrassing. Insults make it difficult for any person to maintain face, or to claim the status associated with a role (Goffman, 1967).

The company presidents we studied appeared to be the most frequent targets of denigration via confrontation. There were, for example, many nasty insults during the creditors' committee meeting. One creditor (a big fellow, with a red and angry face) told the president to "quit making excuses for your incompetence." We encountered a case of a former president casting aspersions on the entire top management team. Court records revealed that he wrote a series of letters in which he accused the company of poor management and stated that a closing was inevitable. The former president tried, unsuccessfully, to purchase the assets of the company. The new president believed that such denigration was intended to reduce the value of the firm, thus dropping the price the former president would have to pay.

Effects of Negative Reactions on Organizations and Top Managements

Survival is unlikely for most firms that have filed for Chapter 11 because of their objective financial condition (Nelson, 1981; Platt, 1985). We propose, however, that stigma further damages the viability of a bankrupt firm. As Figure 1 shows, we propose that negative audience reactions increase a bankrupt firm's already high probability of organizational death. Chances of demise increase because the loss of valuable relationships, lower quality participation, and less favorable exchange relationships directly reduce the quality and the quantity of inputs to organizational systems. Further, denigration via rumor and via confrontation further encourage organizational actors to withdraw from a firm and discourage new actors from participating in relationships with it.

Moreover, independent of any denigration, the stigma of Chapter 11 makes it difficult to establish new relationships that can help save a firm.

The presidents of Perfect Peripherals and Mega Peripherals tried to save those firms through acquisition by a larger corporation. Both presidents reported that, although they were willing to settle for very low prices, the stain caused by the words "Chapter 11" severely hampered such efforts.

In Katz and Kahn's (1978) terminology, organizational systems begin to run down because they cannot import sufficient energy from the world around them; such systems are characterized by positive entropy. Imperfect laws and judges certainly hamper firms that file for Chapter 11 (Nelson, 1981), and some of our informants blamed greedy lawyers for the demise of such firms. But the model advanced here may help explain why—in addition to financial troubles experienced before filing for Chapter 11—so few firms survive bankruptcy proceedings.

Figure 1 also indicates that the five negative reactions and the associated increased probability of organizational death are proposed to have ill effects on top management. First, managers feel a strong stigma. Like members of other stigmatized groups, they suffer from loss of self-esteem, guilt, anxiety, and anger (Goffman, 1963; Jones et al., 1984). Figure 1, combined with Goffman's (1959, 1967) writings on "face-work," help us understand the spoiled image felt by the leaders of the four companies. Goffman contends that a person can claim the status associated with a role by presenting a self that is consistent with the "face" that observers believe is acceptable for the role. Goffman asserts that embarrassment occurs when aspects of the presented self are discrepant from the claimed self.

One of top management's primary functions is to maintain exchange relationships between an organization and key individuals and groups (Pfeffer & Salancik, 1978; Salancik & Meindl, 1984). Moreover, leaders are expected to keep others from denigrating their companies. Top managers are also expected to be able to keep their companies alive. The stigma of bankruptcy increases the chances that leaders will fail at those tasks. Thus, members of organizational audiences interpret firms' problems as personal attributes of their leaders (Meindl et al., 1985; Pfeffer, 1977). As a result, suppliers, employees, customers, and others may expect leaders of bankrupt firms to feel shame and guilt. Moreover, since managers are socialized to believe that they should be able to control the fate of an organization, they may view their firm's financial troubles as a personal failure regardless of the expectations of audience members.

Nonetheless, we were surprised by how frequently—and how intensely—leaders of bankrupt firms acknowledged felt stigma. Consider the following quotes from presidents of the bankrupt firms studied:

> I feel as if I committed some kind of sin.

> I think it is the equivalent of having accidently killed your spouse and then having to live with it the rest of your life.

Felt stigma was also evident from observing top managers. Our field notes from the creditors' committee meeting describe the president of Enoch Computers:

> Tom was extremely nervous. He cleared his throat over and over again. He chain-smoked. He was hunched over. His hands and voice trembled. And he made an odd sort of hissing noise over and over. He looked psychologically beaten. I felt like a voyeur, spying on Willy Loman.

Moreover, at least two of the managers we interviewed reported feeling stigmatized in part because their families felt a courtesy stigma. A courtesy stigma is guilt by association suffered by the colleagues, friends, and family of a tainted individual (Page, 1984). The president of one company reported that his wife felt shunned by friends because of the bankruptcy. Similarly, the president of another bankrupt firm had been a manager at IBM for many years and lived in a neighborhood populated primarily by his former coworkers who still had secure, unstigmatized, positions at "Big Blue." He was upset because his children were being teased by other children in the neighborhood about the bankruptcy.

Second, we propose that the negative effects listed in Figure 1 increase the probability of managerial succession because powerful organizational audiences view the changes in enacted relationships and espoused evaluations presented in Table 2 as evidence that top managers have lost control of a firm. The proposal is consistent with evidence that leaders of poorly performing organizations are more likely to be replaced than leaders of healthy organizations (Gamson & Scotch, 1964; McEachern, 1975; Pfeffer & Salancik, 1978).

There was much managerial succession in firms we studied; the top-ranking financial officer had left shortly before or after the Chapter 11 filing in all four firms, and three of the four presidents had been replaced shortly before or after the filing. The hypothesis is also consistent with Schwartz and Menon's (1985) statistical study of executive succession in 140 bankrupt firms. They found that leaders of bankrupt firms were replaced significantly more often than leaders of comparison firms that were not bankrupt.

Succession in bankrupt firms is often involuntary. But the embarrassment of being associated with a bankrupt firm may also encourage leaders to voluntarily seek employment with successful organizations. A controller who had acquired his job after the Chapter 11 filing told us that family and friends kept asking him: "Why do you want to be part of it?" He also reported that people viewed him as a "loser."

Finally, Figure 1 proposes that members of top management face harm to their individual careers. We offer that hypothesis because association with failure is contrary to expectations held for managers. Managers will have difficulty finding new jobs, or jobs with equal prestige and pay, if they have demonstrated that they are unable to stop a firm from going bankrupt, unable to maintain the organizational participation of key groups and individuals, and unable to stop others from denigrating the firm.

Our review of the literature indicated no published research on that topic. But informants we interviewed told us about the subsequent career progress of former members of top management for all firms except Enoch Computers. There was a consistent pattern: former members of top management were having trouble finding new jobs and were often forced to accept new jobs with lower status and pay. As the quotation that introduces this paper indicates, one ex-president told us that his association with a bankrupt firm meant that he could never be a CEO again and could never get venture capital.

Stigma-Management Strategies

Once an organization files for Chapter 11, it is incumbent on top management to avert or repair spoiled relationships with key organizational audiences. We used the stigma literature (Berk, 1977; Goffman, 1963; Jones et al., 1984) and related writings about impression management techniques used by individuals in identity-threatening predicaments (Schenkler, 1980; Tedeschi, 1981) as points of departure for developing theory about the stigma-management strategies used by the leaders of bankrupt firms. Evidence from the bankrupt firms enabled us to propose five stigma-management strategies that leaders may use: concealing, defining, denying responsibility, accepting responsibility, and withdrawing. Table 3 presents examples and information regarding the prevalence of each strategy across the four cases.

Departing from the practice of much social science research (Trice, 1985), we considered both the functional and the dysfunctional aspects of the strategies. We drew on evidence from the qualitative study to illustrate key hazards and opportunities associated with each strategy but made no predictions about the relative effectiveness of those strategies; our aim was to propose a set of strategies that top managers are *likely* to use, rather than should use, in their struggle to attenuate the stigma of Chapter 11.

The strategies presented in Table 3 can be viewed as a continuum reflecting the extent to which top management acknowledges the stigma of bankruptcy to organizational audiences. At one extreme, concealing entails avoiding any acknowledgement that Chapter 11 has occurred or will occur. Defining and denying responsibilty both entail acknowledging that a potentially stigmatizing event has occurred. Those two strategies also convey, however, that top management and the firm are not, or should not be, discredited. Leaders who accept responsibility for a bankruptcy are admitting some blame for their organization's spoiled image and thus acknowledging that their own image may be somewhat tarnished. But, as will be discussed, accepting blame is a strategy that is sometimes used to convince organizational audiences that top management deserves only secondary, rather than primary, blame for a bankruptcy. In contrast, although the message is implicit, withdrawing or hiding from organizational audiences who are reacting negatively is often interpreted as a strong acknowledgment of the stigma of Chapter 11. Audience members often construe withdrawal as an indication that leaders are unable to develop any strategy to improve spoiled individual and organizational images.

Concealing

The strategy of concealing a bankruptcy from an organizational audience can be passive, as when an organization does nothing to change an audience's ignorance of the fact of Chapter 11, or active, as when management makes deceptive public statements. We encountered examples of both variations of concealing (see Table 3).

The strategy of "passing," or pretending to be something other than what one really is (Goffman, 1963), may require both covert and overt concealing of the facts. Leaders may avoid situations in which they must reveal the fact of bankruptcy. By not revealing the bankruptcy, they have passively reinforced their firm's unstained image without having to make a deceptive statement (Page, 1984). Enoch Computers' lawyer recommended this technique, saying "We have no duty or any inclination to tell them that we're under the protection of bankruptcy." Similarly, the director of

Table 3. Stigma-Management Strategies in Four Cases of Bankruptcy[a]

Strategies	Visionary Computers[b]	Perfect Peripherals	Enoch Computers	Mega Peripherals	Examples
Concealing					
Passive	i	I	I, o	I, p	We have no duty or any inclination to tell them [potential customers] that we're under the protection of bankruptcy. (Lawyer)
Active	i	i, a	I, C	I	I made a personal visit to sit in front of Sue and look her in the eye because a lot of business is done on good faith in this world. . . . She assured me that the firm was in sound financial condition. (Creditor)
Defining					
Explaining the Chapter 11 label	I, p	I	I, P	I	And Charlie explained what Chapter 11 really means that there quote, unquote, there still is hope, you know. That it's not the final answer, the final word. (Vice-president of engineering)
Invoking uniqueness	I	I	I, O, p	I	They told everybody that the only reason they filed Chapter 11 was because of the dispute they had with the landlord over their right to sublease. (Creditor)
Denying responsibility					
Blaming the environment	I	I	I, O, p	I, a	The marketplace went away and the Japanese competition came on board. (President) / The negative financial situation was completely because of external situations. (Founder and ex-president)
Blaming others in the firm who are no longer employed	I	I, A	I	I	The [former] president was unable or unwilling to recognize that and do anything about it. (President)
Accepting responsibility	I		O	i	If I had been a little more experienced, perhaps I may have been able to cope with it better. (President) / Well, I guess I hold the board responsible, of whom I was a member . . . yes, I admit that I was responsible for the problems we had with the [product]. . . . I'm really sorry that it happened. It didn't need to happen. (Founder and ex-president)
Withdrawing	I, P	p, A	p	i, p	I just don't want to talk about it. (Founder and ex-president) / And there are times when I won't answer the phone. (President)

a. Observation of creditors' committee meeting was available only for Enoch Computers. We defined strong evidence as multiple and unambiguous examples from multiple sources, and modest evidence as a single and unambiguous example from a single source.

b. *Key:* see notes to Table 2.

software of Visionary Computers reported that "unless one of our potential customers asks, we won't tell them."

Persistent evidence of active concealing (Berk, 1977; Page, 1984) was also encountered; creditors and other audience members often contended that members of a bankrupt firm's management had lied to them. In an attempt to present an organization as an unsoiled entity, managers would seemingly misrepresent their firm's financial condition. Leaders told us and told audience members that such deception was occasionally necessary so as not to prejudice court cases or to reveal company secrets. Managers and their lawyers also concealed bankruptcy because they believed that organizational audiences would back out of relationships if the severity of their firm's predicament was discovered. The vice-president of human resources for Perfect Peripherals stated:

> Perfect's management and board chose to take a very secretive approach all the way up to the end. The position that the board had taken was "if we're going to make it at all we need to retain the employees who are left." Therefore we encouraged people to stay even though I knew we were going out of business.

Concealing strategies have at least two major functions. If the concealing strategy is successful, then an organization and its members do not have to cope with a sent stigma since it has been eliminated before it can occur. Of course, many audiences will eventually discover that a firm is bankrupt, unless the bankruptcy is somehow avoided. But concealing can be effective as a temporary measure, even if bankruptcy cannot be kept secret permanently. Temporary secrecy may allow top managers enough time to regain composure and to present a coherent story to their key audiences (Schenkler, 1980). Comments by the president of Mega Peripherals about his attempts to find a buyer for the company reflect that idea:

> I felt that I would have had a stronger case in doing that or at least in negotiating the deal outside of an 11, even though an 11 may have had to be the

vehicle through which such a transaction was carried out.

There are also dysfunctions associated with concealing strategies. A primary drawback is that concealing is often unethical and sometimes unlawful. Further, if key audiences perceive that top management is attempting to conceal vital information, the strategy may cause loss of trust. Top management may find it impossible to convince deceived audiences to continue their relationship with a firm (Schenkler, 1980). A member of the creditors' committee for Enoch Computers summed up such feelings as follows:

> The attitude of the members of the creditors' committee when they first got started was "They lied to me! Those SOB's burned me for a bunch of money, I'll never do anything for them again!"

Defining

The strategy of defining allows top management to acknowledge that something has happened without having to admit that the predicament is discrediting. In effect, the leaders convey to organizational audiences that something has happened that appears to be discrediting but is really misunderstood.

This strategy may take one of two forms. First, leaders may take the approach that there is a general misunderstanding among audience members about the meaning of bankruptcy and Chapter 11. Managers may use an attempt to neutralize the label of Chapter 11, or stigma disavowal (Page, 1984), to correct either the label or the situation. Such an attempt is analogous to the "disconfirmation of stereotypes" described in the literature on stigma management (Goffman, 1963; Jones et al., 1984: 180–84).

An attempt to educate organizational audiences about the so-called true nature of bankruptcy occurred in each of the four organizations studied. The examples in Table 3, along with the following quote from a lawyer for Enoch Computers, illustrate that strategy:

Most people have an aversion to the word bankruptcy...so I go in and I tell them, "There's nothing to be ashamed of. Financial distress doesn't mean that you're guilty of misconduct or mismanagement. Financial distress strikes Chrysler and Lockheed and you name 'em. That doesn't mean those companies are guilty of mismanagement."

Claims of uniqueness (Martin et al., 1983) are the second variation of defining the situation that management may use. It can be viewed as a form of the "defense of nonoccurrence" described by Schenkler: "the actor tries to show that the event under consideration did not occur" (1980: 138). Specifically, top management tries to show that although their organization has filed for Chapter 11, the firm is unique, or at least unusual, because it was *not* forced into Chapter 11 by the occurrence of financial problems.

Statements like "Our company is different; we didn't file Chapter 11 because of financial disaster but because..." were frequent; various explanations of how the company was unique would follow. Rather than acknowledging that Chapter 11 was evidence of poor financial control on the part of top management, top managers tried to transform the bankruptcy into an event that permitted their organization to proceed in a direction that would have been impossible otherwise. Table 3 indicates that such claims were present in all four firms and that several members of each organization made them. The following quotes further illustrate claims of uniqueness:

We analyzed state law for eviction in those circumstances with bankruptcy law in eviction and concluded that there were additional protections available for the debtor under federal bankruptcy law that improved his chances of success against the landlord...so the precipitating factor that triggered the bankruptcy in the case was that circumstance. (A lawyer for Enoch Computers.)

The bankruptcy laws provide that you can't resurrect terminated leases and the issue is pending right before the bankruptcy court. They say that's why they filed a Chapter 11 petition. (A lawyer for Enoch Computers' creditors' committee.)

Because both varieties of defining permit management to acknowledge the situation, the risk of alienating the remaining audiences is less than it is with concealing. Management can demonstrate to key audiences that—despite appearances—a discrediting event has not occurred.

A dysfunction also exists. As with concealing, if an audience construes that top management has misrepresented the situation, it feels that its trust has been violated, and it is difficult for an organization to continue the relationship. The cost may not be as high as when an organization unsuccessfully attempts to conceal its predicament, but loss of trust can occur.

Denying Responsibility

Denying is another strategy that was present in each of the four bankruptcies. In this strategy, top management acknowledges that something discrediting has occurred but denies responsibility for the occurrence. One strategy that was prevalent throughout the study (see Table 3) is the "defense of noncausation" (Schenkler, 1980: 138), in which top management states that a bankruptcy is the fault of the environment. Organizational research on self-serving attributions indicates that leaders of troubled firms use that strategy frequently (Bettman & Weitz, 1983; Staw, McKechnie, & Puffer, 1983). Along those lines, the president of Mega Peripherals justified the organization's filing for Chapter 11 by arguing that "The marketplace went away and the Japanese competition came right on board."

There are other sources that can be blamed. Scapegoating of past leaders was present in all four organizations. As did a previous case study of layoffs at the Atari Corporation (Sutton, Eisenhardt, & Jucker, 1986), the present research indicated that blame was often placed on people no longer associated with the organization and therefore unable to defend themselves against accusations (see Table 3). To illustrate:

Vladmir (the former president) had no real management skill. He had lost touch with the product and refused to believe that the product had serious problems. Because of that he began to dismiss key people, and that led to the demise of Visionary. (President, Visionary Computers.)

The remaining members of top management teams did much of the finger-pointing at former leaders. One function of blaming former leaders is that it allows current leaders to appear to organizational audiences as unsullied by the stain of bankruptcy, a variation of the instrumental scapegoating described by Bonazzi (1983). Once again, top managers used Schenkler's (1980) defense of noncausation in attempts to repair the spoiled images of the organizations and their leaders.

Denying responsibility can also be dysfunctional for members of top management. Leaders who claim that Chapter 11 was caused by uncontrollable events may be spoiling their image further. As was noted, people expect competent leaders to exercise effective control of their organizations (Pfeffer, 1981; Salancik & Meindl, 1984). Blaming external forces may backfire because members of top management are presenting an image that makes it difficult to claim the status associated with the managerial role.

Another reason denying responsibility may be dysfunctional for leaders is because organizational audiences may see it as merely making excuses. Schenkler (1980) proposed that excuses do not have the effect of eliminating responsibility, but only of mitigating it. When leaders deny all responsibility for a predicament, but audience members perceive that they are at least partly to blame, any sympathy that existed for a bankrupt firm may disappear, and further damage to already tarnished images may result (Jones et al., 1984). To illustrate:

Everybody knew they had been very slow in paying. But they told everybody that the only reason they filed Chapter 11 was because of the dispute with the landlord over their right to sublease. I mean anybody who leases property in business knows you don't just make an alteration to the property without the landlord's consent. It's incredibly poor management, incredibly poor. I'm

sure that the creditors' committee is going to try and pierce the corporate veil and basically say that we cannot allow that to go on. (A supplier for Enoch Computers.)

Accepting Responsibility

The strategy of admitting that something discrediting had happened and accepting responsibility for it was observed less frequently than concealing, defining, or denying responsibility (see Table 3). The strategy, which we encountered in investigating three of the four firms, was the only stigma-management strategy not encountered in all four. Nonetheless, top managers accepted blame more frequently than social-psychological studies on self-serving attributions might suggest (Nisbett & Ross, 1980; Weiner, 1971).

In the case of Visionary Computers, the founder was at first willing to accept complete responsibility in his discussions with creditors, board members, and fellow top managers. He told us during our first interview:

I can't blame anyone else for the failure of my company. It was my fault and I am completely responsible for what happened. I'm sorry that it happened.

By the second interview, six months later, he had modified his thinking (see Table 3). Although still accepting some responsibility for the bankruptcy, he no longer felt completely at fault. The strategy of accepting partial responsibility and conveying such acceptance to key organizational audiences was used at Visionary Computers, Enoch Computers, and Mega Peripherals. To illustrate, the current president of Visionary attributed most of the blame to the previous president. But he did admit one mistake:

Visionary was unique. Ninety percent of the time I force the issue so that I have absolute control of the corporation—of the board of directors. If I tell somebody I don't want them on the board, they're off the board. In this case I didn't do it. That was a mistake on my part.

Schenkler (1980) proposed that the partial acceptance of responsibility is functional for at least two reasons. First, it allows the members of top management to garner sympathy from other participants. By admitting responsibility for a portion of the problem, managers present themselves as good people who have tried their best. Organizational actors may continue dealing with the bankrupt firm for emotional reasons, like feeling sorry for management, rather than economic reasons.

Perhaps a more important function of accepting some of the responsibility for an organizational predicament is the legitimation of other claims (Jones et al., 1984; Schenkler, 1980; Sutton, 1983, 1984). Accepting partial responsibility also has the advantage of increasing top management's credibility (Schenkler, 1980). Credibility with respect to specific incidents may then be extended to related circumstances.

If members of top management deny all responsibility for a bankruptcy, then the face they present will be inconsistent with audience expectations of a strong link between managerial action and organizational performance. But accepting all responsibility implies incompetence. Accepting partial responsibility, however, may enable leaders to cope with that nasty dilemma. By accepting blame for *secondary* causes of the bankruptcy, leaders' claims that they do not deserve blame for the *primary* causes are more likely to be accepted.

Salancik and Meindl (1984) presented an alternative explanation for the strategy of acceptance. By accepting responsibility for the fate of a firm, top management may be enhancing the illusion of management control. Statements of informants that take the form "If I had to do it all over again..." reinforce the concept that managerial action determines the course of an organization and confirm that managers are indeed necessary.

Such statements also imply that a manager has learned from past mistakes. The acceptance of responsibility with an added "but I learned something and would never make that mistake again" may be an attempt on the part of a manager to present him or herself in an enhanced light when seeking future employment:

> The more you push me, the more I stick. I get calls from headhunters all the time. This place is a better education than college. (A service manager, Visionary Computers.)

Nonetheless, even partial acceptance of responsibility can be dysfunctional for members of top management. Building on Schenkler (1980), we suggest that an audience may believe an admission of self-blame but may not believe that managers have learned from their mistakes and will now be able to turn a troubled firm around. For example, creditors of Enoch Computers believed the president when he said "Look, we have made some mistakes." But the creditors did not believe him when he introduced plans for a new product that was "going to make millions."

Withdrawing

The last stigma-management strategy identified during this study was withdrawing. Withdrawing from an organizational audience whose members know of the predicament can be interpreted as an admission by top management that something discrediting has occurred. By refusing to participate in any activity that might reduce the stain of bankruptcy, management may unintentionally convey to organizational audiences that the stigma is indeed applicable (Berk, 1977; Goffman, 1963; Jones et al., 1984; Page, 1984; Schenkler, 1980).

Periods of withdrawing range from brief to extended. If a retreat from an organizational audience is brief, it is similar to temporary, passive concealing because it may allow top management a chance to marshal forces and develop plans for managing a predicament (Schenkler, 1980). It differs from temporary concealing because audience members know that top management is hiding from them. Audience members may assume that only those who have something to be ashamed of will hide (Schenkler, 1980). Thus, brief withdrawal can anger members of an organizational audience. An executive who told us that "some-times I won't answer the phone" admitted that after avoiding creditors "you really have to go out of your way to placate them."

Extended withdrawal was encountered less frequently than brief withdrawal. One executive did state that he "categorically refused to be a part of that situation in any way." His refusal to talk to us bore that out; he also refused to talk with other members of his company about the firm's predicament, and later he declined to be interviewed for a feature article on the closing of the company.

Although an extended period of withdrawal may reduce unpleasant interactions with organizational audiences, it does not eliminate the predicament. Even more so than a brief withdrawal, it may cause a situation to worsen (Schenkler, 1980). If members of top management are eventually confronted by audience members after refusing to deal with them, they may discover that any hope of repairing damaged relationships will have vanished, and only hard feelings remain. The following quote illustrates that dysfunction of withdrawal:

> They dragged it out indefinitely and nobody was ever willing to sit down and speak frankly about what it would take, I don't mean to be melodramatic but, to save the company. And as a result, they had to liquidate. (Vice-president of human resources, Perfect Peripherals.)

Discussion

A qualitative and inductive study of four firms led us to describe Chapter 11 of the Federal Bankruptcy Code as a label that can spoil the intertwined images of organizations and their top managements. The stigma of Chapter 11 is proposed to cause key organizational audiences to respond with a set of five negative reactions: disengagement, reduction in the quality of participation, bargaining for more favorable exchange relationships, denigration via rumor, and denigration via confrontation. We also proposed a hierarchy of five techniques that leaders will use to avert or reduce the stigma of Chapter 11: concealing, defining, denying responsibility, accepting responsibility, and withdrawing.

This conceptual perspective should be viewed with some caution, however, because of methodological limitations of the present study. If this were a deductive study, its most serious limitation would be the small, homogeneous group of firms studied. Because the purpose of the present study was to develop, rather than test, theory, we drew on detailed descriptions of a small number of organizations or individuals — an approach thought to be best for inspiring and guiding development of new theories (Glaser & Strauss, 1967; Mintzberg, 1979).

The most troublesome methodological drawback for theory building was that we could not spend enough time at each firm observing the interactions between top management and other organizational audience members. We learned this lesson at the creditors' committee meeting, which provided some of the most important data gathered. But we were not invited to other meetings, despite our polite requests. Perhaps participant observation is the best approach for future inductive research.

As for potential conceptual drawbacks, the use of the stigma metaphor may have led us to exaggerate the perils of Chapter 11 and to underestimate the benefits. The legal and financial benefits of Chapter 11 have been discussed widely (Nelson, 1981; Platt, 1985). Moreover, although we focused on the negative aspects of stigma, being discredited can be functional (Goffman, 1963). We observed that top management used Chapter 11 as a reason to ignore tasks and to garner sympathy from stakeholders. One manager was called about joining the local chamber of commerce; he angrily told the caller that the firm was in Chapter 11 and could not be expected to donate money. One president almost begged creditors not to put him out of business, and they were hesitant to close the company partly because he looked physically and psychologically beaten.

Despite limitations, the present study suggests at least four important topics for future research. First, Chapter 11 is not the only predicament that can spoil the intertwined images of organizations and leaders. Events that cause mass deaths and illnesses, such as the chemical spill at Union Carbide's plant in Bhophal, India (Lueck, 1984) and Jalisco Cheese's selling a tainted product (Soble, 1985) may evoke stigma. Allegedly criminal acts like E.F. Hutton's check-kiting scheme and General Dynamics' unsavory practices (Kleinfield, 1985) may also evoke stigma. The present study proposed a middle-range theory (Merton, 1957; Weick, 1974). But the five negative reactions and their effects on firms and leaders proposed in Figure 1 could help guide efforts to build a general theory about discrediting organizational predicaments. And the stigma-management strategies proposed in Table 3 may be useful points of departure for building a general theory of image or impression management during an organizational predicament.

Second, this study focused on similarities across the reactions of organizational audiences and top management when firms filed for Chapter 11. Yet as occurs with theories proposed to explain differences across firms, the match between the proposed constant elements and the case data was imperfect. Those mismatches may provide clues about important differences among bankruptcies.

Enoch Computers, for example, was the only case in which no reduction in the quality of participation was observed. A resource-dependence perspective (Pfeffer & Salancik, 1978) may help explain why that firm differed from the others. Enoch was the primary customer for the parts produced by two major suppliers. Moreover, employees at all hierarchical levels had only firm-specific skills that were of little value to other organizations. Since suppliers and employees had few options outside the firm, the quality of their participation remained high because their financial well-being depended on the survival of the firm. In contrast, the suppliers of the three firms in which the quality of participation decreased had

many customers, and most of their employees had adequate external employment options.

Third, we proposed five strategies that leaders of bankrupt companies may use to avert or reduce the stigma of Chapter 11 but offered no propositions about the relative effectiveness of those strategies. Hypotheses could be advanced about the contingencies under which each strategy is most and least effective. For example, the limited evidence from this study suggests that although concealing is a poor—and perhaps unethical—long-term strategy, it is a useful short-term strategy. Concealing gives leaders time to regain their composure and develop more sophisticated defining, denying, and accepting strategies.

We are especially interested in the conditions under which accepting blame for a bankruptcy is effective. Salancik and Meindl's (1984) work suggested that accepting blame for poor organizational performance helps create the illusion that leaders can control organizational environments that are objectively uncontrollable. But accepting responsibility may also be effective under other conditions. For example, leaders and their organizations may benefit from offering apologies. Although such a technique appears to be more common in Japan than the United States, Schenkler's (1980) writings on impression management suggest that if audience members are convinced of the sincerity of an apology, they will be unlikely to punish an actor further—unless they want revenge.

Fourth and finally, the evidence we gathered suggests that future work should consider the role of humor in bankrupt firms. No matter how effective managers are at implementing stigma-management strategies, Chapter 11 creates tensions between top managers and organizational audiences. Anthropologists, including Radcliffe-Brown (1952), have argued that joking relationships, or permitted disrespect, serve the function of maintaining a satisfactory relationship between people who have social ties that might generate hostility. Similarly, Freud (1960) contended that jokes release tension about issues that make people uncomfortable, and writings on stigma have indicated that those who convey and feel stigma use humor in order to ease tension (Goffman, 1963).

The need to ease unavoidable tensions may explain the persistent joking and laughing that occurred during interviews, casual conversations among members of bankrupt firms, and the creditors' committee meeting that we observed. One president, a bald and wrinkled fellow who was about 50 years old, joked: "I'm a turnaround expert. I'm 28 years old." The president of Mega Peripherals told us several nasty jokes about lawyers, including: "My definition of waste is a busload of attorneys going off a cliff with two empty seats."[6]

The role of humor in Chapter 11 and in other organizational predicaments may be a useful subject for future theory building. Humor may be an effective means for implementing some of the stigma-management strategies described above, especially denying responsibility. And humor may stand alone as a separate stigma-management strategy.

In closing, it is important to recall that we have proposed, rather than tested, a conceptual perspective. We assert that conducting a systematic qualitative study—rather than relying exclusively on imagination and published works—is a sound means for theory building (Glaser & Strauss, 1967). However, hypothesis-testing research should be conducted to assess whether organizational audiences perceive bankruptcy as discrediting and whether that stigma leads to negative reactions that further damage bankrupt organizations and their leaders. Deductive research could also help determine if the five stigma-management strategies are constant elements across all bankruptcies.

Notes

1 This study focused on firms that have filed for Chapter 11 because they are financially insolvent and are seeking protection from their creditors. Our theory is not intended to extend to firms that have filed for Chapter 11 for other reasons. Thus, the present analysis might not apply to Continental Airlines, which may have filed for Chapter 11 in an effort to break a union. Nor does it extend to the Manville Corporation, a profitable firm that is alleged to have filed in anticipation of costly personal injury lawsuits. Such organizational predicaments may also discredit management, but we prefer not to stretch our analysis to those atypical cases.

2 For further information about Chapter 11, see Nelson (1981), Herzog and King (1983), and Platt (1985).

3 The three pilot studies were conducted by student groups in the senior author's course on Managing Organizational Transitions. Approximately 12 interviews were conducted with the top managers of three computer firms that had filed for Chapter 11. These pilot studies addressed three primary questions: (1) is a stigma cast by Chapter 11 of the Federal Bankruptcy Code? (2) if there is a stigma, how is it managed? and (3) is it possible to gain interviews with leaders of bankrupt firms? The success of these pilot studies encouraged us to conduct the present research. The pilot studies influenced the content of semistructured interviews directly because students told us about which questions had worked well and which had not. The pilot studies also influenced the content of the interview indirectly because these preliminary data helped us refine our rough working framework.

4 Copies of the initial observation form and the structured interview can be obtained by writing the first author.

5 An orphaned computer product is one that is no longer manufactured or supported by any company.

6 Bankruptcy lawyers are paid before all creditors, and they typically demand payment in advance. Creditors and members of top management often became angry about how much lawyers gained from this system. The president of Mega Peripherals ranted: "They're vultures. They're just around to pick bones. [They are only concerned with questions such as:] How soon can I liquidate that sucker? How can I maximize the billable hours?" Even relatively neutral observers have questioned the large financial gains that lawyers enjoy under the current system of bankruptcy laws (Aaron, 1979).

References

Aaron, R. 1979. The Bankruptcy Reform Act of 1978: The full-employment-for-lawyers bill—Part I. *Utah Law Review* 1979(1): 1–28.

Argenti, J. 1976. *Corporate collapse.* New York: Halstead Press.

Berk, B. 1977. Face-saving at the singles dance. *Social Problems* 24: 530–44.

Bettman, J.R., & Weitz, B.A. 1983. Attributions in the boardroom: Causal reasoning in corporate annual reports. *Administrative Science Quarterly* 28: 165–83.

Bonazzi, G. 1983. Scapegoating in complex organizations: The results of a comparative study of symbolic blame-giving in Italian and French public administration. *Organization Studies* 4(1): 1–18.

Cameron, K.S., & Whetten, D.A. 1983. *Organizational effectiveness: A comparison of multiple models.* New York: Academic Press.

Freud, S. 1960. *Jokes and their relation to the unconscious.* London: Pergamon Press.

Gamson, W., & Scotch, N. 1964. Scapegoating in baseball. *American Journal of Sociology* 70: 6–29.

Glaser, B., & Strauss, A. 1967. *The discovery of grounded theory: Strategies for qualitative research.* London: Wiedenfeld and Nicholson.

Goffman, E. 1959. *The presentation of self in everyday life.* New York: Doubleday Co.

Goffman, E. 1963. *Stigma: Notes on the management of spoiled identity.* Englewood Cliffs, N.J.: Prentice-Hall.

Goffman, E. 1967. *Interaction ritual.* Garden City, N.Y.: Anchor Books.

Hambrick, D.C., & Mason, P.A. 1984. Upper echelons: The organization as a reflection of its top managers. *Academy of Management Review* 9: 193–206.

Harris, S.C., & Sutton, R.I. 1986. Functions of parting ceremonies in dying organizations. *Academy of Management Journal* 29: 5–30.

Herzog, A.S., & King, L.P. 1983. *1983 bankruptcy code.* New York: Matthew Bender.

Jones, E.E., Farina, A., Hastorf, A.H., Markus, H., Miller, D.T., & Scott, R.A. 1984. *Social stigma: The psychology of marked relationships.* New York: W.H. Freeman & Co.

Kanter, R.M. 1983. *The change masters: How people and companies succeed through innovation in the new corporate era.* New York: Simon & Schuster.

Katz, D., & Kahn, R.L. 1978. *The social psychology of organizations* (2d ed.). New York: John Wiley & Sons.

Kleinfield, N.R. 1985. Job shame: Corporate scandals take toll on workers. *San Jose Mercury News,* July 21: 1F, 4F, 5F, 6F

Lueck, T.J. 1984. Crisis management at Carbide. *New York Times,* December 14: D1–D2.

McEachern, W.A. 1975. *Managerial control and performance.* Lexington, Mass.: D.C. Heath Co.

Martin, J., Feldman, M.S., Hatch, M.J., & Sitkin, S.B. 1983. The uniqueness paradox in organizational studies. *Administrative Science Quarterly* 28: 438–53.

Meindl, J.R., Ehrlich, S.B., & Dukerich, J.M. 1985. The romance of leadership. *Administrative Science Quarterly* 30: 78–102.

Merton, R. 1957. *Social theory and social structure.* Glencoe, Ill.: Free Press.

Miles, M.B., & Huberman, A.M. 1984. *Qualitative data analysis.* Beverly Hills, Calif.: Sage Publications.

Mintzberg, H. 1979. An emerging strategy of "direct" research. *Administrative Science Quarterly* 24: 580–89.

Nelson, P.B. 1981. *Organizations in crisis: Behavioral observations for bankruptcy policy.* New York: Praeger.

Nisbett, R., & Ross, L. 1980. *Human inference: Strategies and shortcomings of social judgment.* Englewood Cliffs, N.J.: Prentice-Hall.

Page, R.M. 1984. *Stigma.* London: Routledge & Kegan Paul.

Peters, T.J., & Waterman, R.H., Jr. 1982. *In search of excellence.* New York: Harper & Row Publishers.

Pfeffer, J. 1977. The ambiguity of leadership. *Academy of Management Review* 2: 104–12.

Pfeffer, J. 1981. Management as symbolic action. In L.L. Cummings and B.M. Staw (Eds.), *Research in organizational behavior:* 1–52. Greenwich, Conn.: JAI Press.

Pfeffer, J., & Salancik, G.R. 1978. *The external control of organizations: A resource dependence perspective.* New York: Harper & Row Publishers.

Platt, H.D. 1985. *Why companies fail.* Lexington, Mass.: Lexington Books.

Radcliffe-Brown, A.R. 1952. *Structure and function in primitive society.* New York: Free Press.

Salancik, G.R. 1979. Field stimulations for organizational behavior research. *Administrative Science Quarterly* 24: 638–49.

Salancik, G.R., & Meindl, J.R. 1984. Corporate attributions as strategic illusions of management control. *Administrative Science Quarterly* 29: 238–54.

Schenkler, B.R. 1980. *Impression management.* Monterey, Calif.: Brooks-Cole.

Schwartz, K.B., & Menon, K. 1985. Executive succession in failing firms. *Academy of Management Journal* 28: 680–86.

Smelser, N.J. 1962. *Theory of collective behavior.* New York: Free Press.

Soble, R.L. 1985. Sources of contamination elusive in Jalisco probe. *Los Angeles Times,* September 1: 1, 4, 5.

Staw, B.M., McKechnie, P.I., & Puffer, S.M. 1983. The justification of organizational performance. *Administrative Science Quarterly* 28: 582–600.

Sutton, R.I. 1983. Managing organizational death. *Human Resource Management* 22(4): 391–412.

Sutton, R.I. 1984. *Organizational death.* Unpublished doctoral dissertation, University of Michigan, Ann Arbor.

Sutton, R.I., Eisenhardt, K.M., & Jucker, J.V. 1986. Managing organizational decline: Lessons from Atari. *Organizational Dynamics* 14(Spring): 17–29.

Tedeschi, J.T. (Ed.). 1981. *Impression management theory and social psychological research.* New York: Academic Press.

Trice, H.M. 1985. Rites and ceremonials in organizational culture. In S.B. Bacharach & S.M. Mitchell (Eds.), *Research in the sociology of organizations* 4: 221–70. Greenwich, Conn.: JAI Press.

Van Maanen, J. 1983. Epilogue: Qualitative methods reclaimed. In J. Van Maanen (Ed.), *Qualitative methodology:* 247–68. Beverly Hills, Calif.: Sage Publications.

Weick, K.E. 1974. Middle range theories of social systems. *Behavioral Science* 19: 356–67.

Weiner, B. 1971. *Perceiving the causes of success and failure.* Morristown, N.J.: General Learning Press.

13

Group Process Under Conditions
of Organizational Decline

James Krantz

A massive shift is occurring in the environment of social service organizations. One can safely predict that major alterations in models of provision, and in the organizational forms they will take, will come about. Understanding the effects of this will take years. While the possibilities for alternative forms of service delivery and for innovative community development schemes are being discussed by stakeholders on all sides of the debate, the present shifts in funding will inevitably entail major cutbacks — and frequent failure — for many service organizations.

The management of this process of retrenchment, which in many cases leads to demise, is a relatively unexplored area. The lack of relevant models is complicated by our looking at the management of decline in a declining sector, because failure in this context often results not from management mistakes or organizational dysfunction, but is symptomatic of a larger, more inclusive structural change. Better tactics simply will not

Reprinted with permission from NTL Institute, *The Journal of Applied Behavioral Science,* Vol. 21, No. 1, pp. 1–17, © 1985.

suffice. The successfully managed decline in this sense is not the turned-around situation, but a well-managed cutback and in many cases a dismantling of the organization.

The literature related to issues of decline and retrenchment is vast and wide-ranging. Considerable attention has been given to the arrival of a period of scarcity (Heilbroner, 1976; Hirsch, 1976) and to the fact that our organizations are adapted to conditions of continued growth (Boulding, 1975). Similarly, others have noted the extent to which organizational research and theory is dominated by organic growth metaphors that are less helpful in trying to illuminate conditions of decline (Scott, 1974; Snow, 1983; Whetten, 1980a, b).

Most attention given to the specific impact of retrenchment itself can be sorted into two categories. One group of researchers has studied the impact of retrenchment on the climate and behavior of organizations, finding decreases in morale (Behn, 1978), increased turnover (Levine, 1978) and conflict (Starbuck, Greve, & Hedberg, 1978), and threats to organizational effectiveness (Greenhalgh, 1982; Hirschhorn & Gilmore, 1983). The second group has explored various approaches to implementing retrenchment policies so as to minimize the dysfunctional aspects of decline and failure (Greenhalgh, 1982; Levine, 1978). Some of these writers have examined methods of promoting careful strategic choice under such conditions so as to take advantage of whatever opportunities exist (Hirschhorn, 1983), and the sort of leadership best suited to managing in such difficult conditions (Glassberg, 1978; Yetton, 1975).

While a general consensus holds that decline and retrenchment call for reorientation and change, little work has focused on understanding the conditions required for making successful adjustments. Whetten (1980b) suggests that an innovative, proactive response requires a level of rationality that may be impossible to achieve during times of crisis. He also points out in his exhaustive literature review that "if managers under stress need to behave contrary to their reflexive patterns, considerable thought and research will be required to discover the methods for countering these natural tendencies" (p. 368).

Relatively little research, however, has examined the social and psychological dynamics of organizational decline, one element needed to fill the gap identified by Whetten. While the impact of retrenchment is undoubtedly profound, we know little about the conditions within which managers must think and act and the conditions that influence their capacity to do so effectively. This article attempts to address that question by examining the dynamic impact of the stress of major cutbacks on the capacity of work groups to function and the implications of this for managing these painful situations.

On a note of qualification, I must underscore that this article discusses a degree of decline involving significant diseconomies of scale in which ordinary cost-saving measures cannot forestall major organizational changes. Such cuts require a basic rethinking of organizational structure, functions, and role constellations—if any funds are available at all.

My comments grow largely out of two action research projects. In one, a team of consultants

that I belonged to worked for several years with a large nonprofit organization in the United States. Funded at the national level, this organization, which I will call Direct Services, has a grantee relationship with several hundred local service delivery organizations. Its funding has been severely cut, and the organization continues to face the threat of far more massive cuts. The other organization—called the Green Lodge in this article—is a therapeutic community for adolescents. A colleague and I were providing management consulting to Green Lodge when rather suddenly their referral source of children was completely cut off, forcing the institution to close within five to eight months.

Theoretical Framework

My analytic focus stems largely from the work pioneered at the Tavistock Institute since World War II. Social scientists there have explored ways to apply the insights of a psychoanalytic theory to the social field, thereby relating individual and collective levels of analysis. Working first with Bion's (1961) well-known theory of group process and later with the discovery of how social systems can function as defenses against painful anxieties (Jacques, 1955; Menzies, 1970), the Tavistock theorists and researchers established an approach that powerfully illuminates some of the central issues of retrenchment and organizational decline.

Their work yields a theory useful for understanding organizational functioning because its focus renders the impact of individually experienced anxieties and stress visible in the collective behavior of task groups. By relating different levels of abstraction, the framework enables us to see the way the intrapsychic process manifests itself at the group level, the interaction between intrapsychic process and the social structure and culture of an institution, and how different features of the social system in turn penetrate individual experience and group process. The framework is particularly useful and important for understanding the phenomena and management of decline because of the emotional turbulence characteristic of such processes.

Bion (1961) posits two levels of group functioning, both existing simultaneously. The "work group" engages in mature, reality-oriented behaviors aimed seriously at whatever task the particular group faces. The other group, labeled the "basic assumption" group, functions to relieve members' anxieties. Such anxieties arise from a variety of factors, including the various intrapsychic conflicts stemming from the confrontation between the task itself and the existence of unconscious fantasies, the interpersonal politics involved when people cooperate with each other and with authority figures, and any unusual stress that might result from the impact of external events. The various individual behavior changes provoked by these anxieties interact with one another to form a collective response.

Increased anxieties may cause individual members to revert to less-mature forms of behavior that function as more primitive defenses against anxiety. These include the splitting apart of good and bad, projection of unpleasant feelings and ideas onto others, and the denial of the unwanted experience, all of which characterize earlier levels of mental functioning and which distort perception and undermine competence. These responses are manifested *collectively* in an increase in what Bion calls the group's "basic assumption" functioning, which he categorizes into three modes, following the basic fantasy assumptions guiding the group's behavior (as the name implies). "Dependency groups" unconsciously presume the existence of an omnipotent, idealized leader who will protect and nourish them. This leader inevitably disappoints the hopeful followers, who then search for a new hero. "Fight or flight groups" are bound together by the imagined presence of an external enemy who they believe wants to destroy the all-important unity and safety of the group. Such groups choose leaders to do battle against this threat, which may come from outside the group altogether or consist of a deviant subgroup. The third type of group, which Bion labels a "pairing group," hopes to preserve its identity and unity through the intimacy of two members, leading to the fantasized reproduction of the group and its magical salvation from the aggression, conflicts, and threats to its present existence. Work groups acting on basic assumptions do so to increase the comforts and security threatened by anxiety-producing situations.

While this strata of fantasy-governed motivation always underlies group experience, it becomes more apparent—and perhaps even predominates work-oriented behaviors—under conditions in which anxieties cannot be contained or modified by higher-level defenses used against them. Powerful feelings are associated with each of these basic assumptions. Different affective states accompany the existence of these modes, which is why under certain conditions—such as war—one would hope for the emotional tone of certain basic assumption states, such as fight or flight.

Bion's observation that the two levels of group functioning always exist simultaneously, with an oscillating predominance of one over the other, is often forgotten. The motions associated with the operative basic assumption can either be congruent with the task demands or antagonistic to them. Bion offers the dramatic examples of how the Army benefits from being suffused by fight or flight mentality and how hospitals benefit from dependency cultures, and the more questionable example of the aristocracy's use of pairing motivations. But the emergence and use of these emotional states must always be channeled or work will come to a halt. Fight or flight at the wrong moment will be disastrous. When a seriously ill patient improves and starts to think for her- or himself, the institution—in terms of pure task considerations—should be able to accommodate a changed relationship with the patient. But hospitals are often unable to do so, and insist on keeping the patient helpless long after this sort of dependency ceases to contribute to the person's health or recovery.

One can expect to find inappropriate, maladaptive, or destructive forms of basic assumption functioning when members experience anxieties arising either directly from task activity or external sources of stress that they cannot manage or contain in a mature way. Organizations' styles of defending against anxiety become institutionalized in stable and persistent organizational structures and cultures (Menzies, 1970). This process develops a self-reinforcing quality in that these patterns create a contingency framework of reward and punishment for members' behavior. Patterns of expectation, managerial decision making, reward systems, and other normative features of the organization come to express these postures. The modes of administrative leadership, organizational culture, and structure in turn create the context to which members' behavior and functioning become immediately adaptive. This context will then select and reinforce patterns of functioning in members that converge with the way in which they face or avoid anxieties in that setting.

While individual defenses are well understood, group and organizational level defenses remain relatively unused in organization analysis. Yet as a construct to describe certain features of social institutions, the concept of social defenses provides a powerfully illuminating way to characterize the manner in which psychic defense systems become institutionalized. Individuals unconsciously collude to externalize their defenses in the culture, structure, and mode of functioning in the organization. Menzies (1970, p. 10) states that the "needs of the members of the organization to use it in the struggle against anxiety leads to [the] development of socially structured defense mechanisms." Thus, various features of the organization can serve the defensive needs of members as well as task accomplishment. The extent to which these aspects of the organization reinforce internal defenses against anxiety may help explain why members resist change so (Jacques, 1955).

The key here is to appreciate the reciprocal relationship between individual psychic process and the social systems created by their members. Individuals alone operate defenses. Nevertheless, they do so in ways that reify their unconscious strategies to contain anxiety and doubt.[1] Over time, these strategies become objectified as formal structures and informal traditions, thus conferring added authority on them. The construct of social defense is used to account for this property of organizational life.

As Menzies's hospital research shows, anxieties associated with particular tasks are common to all those sharing the work, such as the nurses in her example. The need for these nurses to bind the deep anxieties associated with close contact with sick and dying patients was aided by the creation of schedules, patterns of delegation, and cultural norms that minimized the development of ongoing relationships with individual patients. While effective in helping nurses evade their anxieties, however, the particular collective strategies—or social defenses—were implemented at considerable cost to patient care, the education of student nurses, and the quality of the staff nurses' work lives. Other social defenses might yield different results.

Ineffective social defense systems will manifest themselves as patterns of interaction, beliefs, and norms that help people avoid confronting the anxieties involved in working. This leads to a heightened enactment of these anxieties in the form of basic assumption functioning. More sophisticated social defense systems, however, will provide the time, space, encouragement, and authority for members to talk about anxieties and openly address difficult interpersonal situations.

Changing circumstances call for the capacity for flexibility. Under conditions of retrenchment, people must make new decisions, devise novel plans, and complete unfamiliar transactions with the environment. A major problem with social defenses—at least those that reinforce less mature responses to anxiety—is that they are rigid and unable to accommodate flexible demands of task performance. More sophisticated defense systems provide for structures and cultures that enable members to think realistically about, confront, and modify whatever anxieties arise, thereby conferring substantial flexibility on an institution.

With decline and retrenchment, the most severe anxieties stem not from the primary tasks of the organization, but chiefly from threats to its existence and stability. The social defenses established to handle task-induced anxieties are called upon to "contain" the newer and extraordinary stress. An effective response to these pressures requires members to face the enormous anxieties arising from the wide variety of pressures, including the sense of failure and possible loss of employment. My experience suggests that these pressures are so intense and volatile that the capacity of virtually any social defense system to contain and modify anxiety in a mature fashion becomes stretched to its limits. As a result, in such a situation one can predict an increase in the amount and potency of basic assumption functioning within the system. Established ways of dealing with anxiety will be challenged far beyond ordinary circumstances.

While powerful emotions accompanying the activation of these states can either support and further the tasks at hand or interfere with them, experience predicts that the likelihood that the destructive sides will emerge forcefully under these conditions is great. The combined effect of the uncertainties involved, the senses of loss and failure, and the impact of massive change tends to evoke very primitive states and corresponding regression in organizational performance. Leadership has the difficult job of helping to moderate those affective states that are detrimental to the group's capacities to work and channeling the potentially constructive ones (Rice, 1965). Decline can be a time of emotional turbulence in which the oscillation between work and basic assumption functioning may be violent and rapid. Nevertheless, when the future of the institution is in doubt, one also has reason to expect that some groups will be able to mobilize powerful fight-assumption feelings in the service of sophisticated work toward preserving their organization.

Case Illustrations

This section describes some of the ways in which the enormous fears and anxieties brought about

by a severe cutback—and the defenses employed to contain them—often appear in the form of dysfunctional, basic assumption functioning.

Green Lodge

A colleague and I worked as management consultants with the staff of this school for disturbed adolescents. At that time, a new upper-management group had been trying to incorporate therapeutic community principles into its pattern of organization. Previously, the school had been run along the lines of a traditional reform school. Our work had been to assist them in this developmental effort. Over the year, some real progress had been made when suddenly the school staff was informed that a revised regional plan meant that no more children would be sent there. The school would have to close in five to eight months because it depended entirely upon social service placements for its clients.

This change required reconceptualizing priorities and plans at all levels. Starting with our own work, we saw our new objective as helping management plan realistically for closing the institution, confront critical issues head-on, and minimize the acting out by clients that we anticipated in the face of such an unsettling situation. Our task thus shifted from development to support.

Our first regularly scheduled meeting came the day after the decision had been announced to the staff. The director and his two assistant directors had known of the impending closing for three days when a leak of the news forced them into announcing it to the staff, and then to the children, earlier than they wanted. The day after the decision was made final, when it was supposedly still a secret, the director, Bob, called the director of another home. The conversation started with Bob's counterpart saying, "I hear you're closing soon." Being forced into premature action—for fear that the children, their parents, and their social workers would hear the rumor—created bitterness in upper management. Negotiations regarding possible future scenarios for the school, which had been underway with various agencies and stakeholders, were now viewed as decoy moves on the others' parts, designed to bring about the closing of Green Lodge rather than to forestall it. Upper management felt their suspicion of the planners, trustees, and councilors was confirmed, and they ascribed purely political motives to these persons' recent behavior. The emergence of this basic assumption fight stance, though understandable, inhibited the cooperation and negotiation needed with outside agencies to relocate the children.

The sense of persecution and failure, so obviously felt by upper management and reflected in their adversarial, suspicious attitude, was equally present in the initial responses of the middle managers. A strong tendency to take the closing personally, as a sort of punishment, persisted in spite of discussions on how the field was crowded with similar situations. Their despair over finding new employment revealed the injury many felt to their self-esteem. One very competent, highly experienced manager spoke of taking any entry-level job he could find, doubting that he had much to offer.

The mixture of shock, sadness, and anger took its toll on the group's capacity to work soon after the final decision was announced. Nevertheless, the staff seemed to pull together with a kind of collective bonding reminiscent of the responses people make to natural disaster (Wallace, 1975). Early discussions, though rather disjointed and rambling, covered a range of important topics, roughly divided into three related areas: concern about the personal futures of the staff, working through the loss with the children, and making plans for the children.

Discussions about the children and future arrangements for them proved less ruminating and more purposeful than those about the staff's personal dilemmas. The staff accomplished a considerable amount of sophisticated work, and managers identified key tasks and revised plans in light of present circumstances. A plan to restructure the community into two units rather than three would still have to go ahead, though now in the context of a gradual dispersal of the community

rather than as a permanent shift. While the specifics of the former plan were built around making the best use of facilities, the plan would now proceed on the basis of protecting the ongoing relationships between the staff and the children as long as possible while both groups disbanded.

The most pressing decision was whether to tell the children that afternoon rather than the next day, as Bob had planned. He and the other staff members feared the childrens' reactions and wanted time to prepare themselves. Given the leak of information, however, they worried that the children might discover the news anyway. So the staff decided to make the announcement and to do it as a community group rather than as separate units. The staff feared that the children would be unable to control themselves in a large group, but the children responded calmly, with much the same tendency to pull together as the staff group experienced.

Two important themes emerged from this first day's discussion with the staff. One was the strain they felt in keeping the news a secret from the children. The sense of being false and in having to "wallow" alone made them feel out of contact with their charges when they particularly needed to be in contact with them. We worried that the presence of unexplained, vague anxieties emanating from a dispirited staff might affect the children, and we argued for putting the children in the picture sooner rather than later. One unit manager explicitly expressed his concern by saying, "I will work better with the kids knowing." The other theme that emerged was the need for Bob to communicate that, within the constraints imposed by the decision, he would be in charge of this process. An early role-play of the announcement showed how his own anxieties were in danger of being transferred to the children if he made the announcement in an uncertain, hesitant way. The children, who had been shuffled around their entire lives—with several having been in other places that had closed—needed reassurance that the staff would manage this process and make certain that the children's appropriate dependency needs were met to the extent possible.

Two weeks later there seemed to be a lot of denial. Basic assumption life was more in evidence. People in our meeting spoke of anger and mourning, but they seemed to speak about it as if from a distance rather than as people truly expressing these emotions. The staffs' behavior also had a manic quality. For example, during the week when I had spoken to the director, he reported in an excited way about the "Dunkirk" mentality that was keeping them all working together and spoke about his hopes that it would keep up until the end.

The impression of high-level functioning was contradicted in a meeting of the auxiliary staff of persons responsible for maintenance, housekeeping, and cooking. Among the variety of topics discussed, they reported noticing the staff was "slipping." Care staff weren't picking up food supplies from the central store, no entries had been made in the maintenance request book since the announcement, and so forth. They also expressed great concern that the children were building up for an "explosion," and connected this to what they perceived as growing inattention to them by the care staff.

More evidence of the denial came from discussions among care staff later about family issues. Several people mentioned that they were not discussing their concerns with their spouses, feeling they had to put on a show of strength. We later confirmed this in a meeting with the staff's spouses, at which we discovered, to our surprise, how little they knew about what was going on. The staff had not even shared information that affected their living arrangements. Spouses expressed considerable anger about their sense of isolation and were grateful for at least having had this meeting.

We encouraged the staff to talk with each other about what was going on, as avoidance of discussions about the closing was having an isolating effect. In this regard two important points emerged. Many clearly felt it impossible to open new channels of support and communication with those with whom relations had been previously strained. Second, failed working and personal relationships seemed to loom large. For the staff to accomplish its mourning, people needed to acknowledge and address their personal failures. Often, when pressed to talk about their working relationships, the staff talked about relationships that had failed even during good times. The implication seemed to be that we should not expect more openness and sincere dialogue now than had been achieved before. That Green Lodge's closing did not result from collective failure was being used defensively to avoid the important issues of personal failure. This, in turn, was helping staff members block their ability to mourn the loss of Green Lodge, which interfered with their capacity to work during the final months.

When we returned for a final meeting shortly before the last operating day of the institution, our discussion focused on two similar incidents. One had to do with a staff member who was found mismanaging some of the children's money. He had been generally resistant and irresponsible, and at times insubordinate; for example, he refused to be on duty at night. The director expressed a sense of helplessness, feeling unable to control the staff member or really address the issues with him. Attempts to raise the issue with this person proved fruitless.

The other incident involved one of the children who had become violent one night. He did considerable damage to his room and hurt a staff member who had been trying to restrain him. Again the director felt helpless. He understood the boy's anxiety at losing his strong bond to Green Lodge and the child's fears about not yet having another place to go. At the time, the director was concerned that responding only with therapeutic concern would ultimately reinforce the behavior and possibly lead to its repetition or escalation. Sending the boy away on account of his violence, however, meant sending him to an undesirable institution.

In discussing both incidents, the managers were reluctant to consider any authoritative action. Some sort of disciplinary action in the first instance, and setting and holding a limit in the second, would certainly have been the typical response under ordinary conditions. The message conveyed by the powerless responses highlighted the perceived deterioration of the director's authority in the system. The director described the resistant staff member's attitude as if that person were saying, "This place is closing down any day, so there's nothing you can do."

Direct Services

Direct Services is one of the most successful antipoverty programs to emerge out of the social reforms of the 1960s. It has grown to include several hundred local offices, coordinated and funded by a private national corporation that includes 10 regional offices through which the relationship with local programs is administered. These offices provide both direct service to underprivileged people and public advocacy on related issues.

As with so many social service organizations, Direct Services has strong dependency themes in its functioning. The primary task of the organization is to respond to the needs of its clients, and research has suggested that the affective qualities of an organization's primary task will influence, and often suffuse, its culture (Menzies, 1970; Rice, 1965). Many features of the dependency orientation were reflected throughout the organization and its social defenses. Leadership at all levels has often taken the form of a "cult of the hero" with an all-powerful, individualistic leader model. Other reflections of basic assumption dependency culture include the organization's hiring practices and management development efforts, which both seemed shaped by a vague fear of the outside world as being an empty, unenlightened place. Members often acted as though "outsiders" would not manage programs, or that others' experiences were not useful in shedding light on Direct Services' special organizational concerns.

Unlike most social services, however, the organization also engaged in advocacy work, for which elements of the "fight" culture were needed. This task involved designing and orchestrating battles with local, country, and state govern-

ments. The organization drew a lot of its strength in this area from its highly ideological roots, which stem from the social-action movement of the sixties. At times the fight emotions, so necessary for achieving important organizational tasks, were accompanied by a predominance of basic assumption fight-or-flight functioning and petty bickering, unrealistic accusations about the central office, or an excessively adversarial relationship with other organizations.

The culture is suffused primarily, then, with dependency and fight emotions. Expressed maturely, dependency appears as care and concern for clients and strong support for fellow staff members. Fight emotions appear in conjunction with the strong commitment to social change and the ability to mobilize effective advocacy campaigns. Both of these features are also potentially valuable to a maturely handled process of decline. While the capacity for concern for colleagues is fairly typical of social service organizations, the capacity to mobilize and fight effectively for survival was an unusual source of strength for this kind of institution.

One could also see less task-oriented expressions of these emotional qualities in the organization. We often encountered passive, withdrawn, lethargic staff groups. The less mature expression of both dependency and fight often appeared together as a counterdependent relationship of the staff with authorities at all levels and in field-headquarters relations. The close association of serious efforts for social change and the sixties-flavored rebellion against authority was reflected in the organization's oscillating between dominant work and basic-assumption modes.

A great deal of this struggle focused on the increasingly bureaucratic features of the organization and the growing emphasis on management concerns as expressed by the central office organization. Expansion had come rapidly—to a budget of several hundred million dollars in less than two decades. Many staff members felt they were becoming part of what they had set out to change in the first place. This feeling was coupled with a widespread sense of disappointment and disillusionment. Great hopes of making significant inroads into poverty conditions had given way to a more realistic assessment of the difficulties of change. With this loss of inspiration, the organization was less bound together by its sense of mission, and the staff became increasingly concerned about other, more self-enriching rewards—such as pay, benefits, and working conditions.

Both of these trends became manifested in strong doubts as to whether management was a legitimate activity and in suspicion of the collective tasks of the organization. Functions associated with management or planning were, at the field level, frequently denigrated or considered dishonest or false in some way. Staff members often experienced denial that collective elements established better or worse conditions for professionals to work in; the lone gunfighter image loomed large in this culture. As a result, coordinating mechanisms were generally underdeveloped. The long-standing mistrust of coordination and planning was an important aspect of Direct Services' social defense system.

I have given considerable attention to this aspect of Direct Services because the need for collective planning, effective management, and concerted effort is exactly what comes to the fore in times of cutback. While resources for dealing with the challenge were considerable—including a highly developed capacity to fight—the constraints embedded in Direct Services' culture also proved formidable. Many of its social defenses rendered it difficult to undertake thoughtful cutback.

In the political climate of the first year of the Reagan administration, the organization clearly needed to make a shift in its planning orientation from an operational to a strategic one. On the local level, for instance, the emergence of state agencies as the critical decision mechanisms for social programs required a major reorientation of program activity. This change accompanied the need to make major policy decisions regarding layoffs and organizational structure. At the regional level, offices needed to redirect their own work in a way appropriate for the possibility that their existence might be limited.

For a long time, staff members avoided these painful and difficult issues. Almost complete denial of the upcoming changes occurred in some sectors for nearly a year after the new U.S. president was elected. During this period a variety of developmental projects were considered and research funded at the national level assumed a "business-as-usual" posture.

The hope that Direct Services would not be affected, or at least not much, guided the selection of issues addressed during that period. The organization had fended off attacks by another administration, and images of that successful struggle were often evoked during this period. Once awareness came that it might very much be affected, the next stage of response was to mount a massive survival fight.

The first stages of this fight again contained some denial of the situation at hand. Staff members put enormous energy into this struggle, assigning roles and issues as if they were not cognizant of the enormous ideological shift taking place in the country. In the context of this shift, Direct Services could hardly expect to be totally protected from the massive wave of reform. A good deal of the work and energy harnessed during this fight-or-flight activity, however, was put to more effective use during the next, more realistic period of political maneuvering that occurred when the staff accepted the inevitability of major cuts.

Once serious planning for cutbacks got under way—though with many sectors of the organization still clinging to the most optimistic scenario possible—many efforts revealed enormous anxieties in the situation. For example, many staff members looked to quite fantastic ideas for profit-making initiatives in order to generate alternative sources of funding and to "make up for the cuts." Little consideration was given to the ways in which administrative structures and organizational values would have to be profoundly transformed for Direct Services to incorporate for-profit operations, and the staff gave even less thought to how these profits might specifically be used. While some potentially successful schemes were devised at the local level, the massive interest, time, and energy expended at the regional and national levels often constituted a defensive avoiding of the more painful realities.

Other attempts at planning had a lethargic, hopeless quality. Often a great deal of the capacity for dealing with retrenchment issues was projected outside of the organization onto the group of consultants working with Direct Services on these issues, who traveled around the country giving seminars and workshops on the issues and wrote a variety of papers on the topics. Many managers and staff seemed to see themselves as inadequate and incompetent to perform such tasks.

Further illustration of the dysfunctional basic assumption dependency can be seen in the way one of the consultants on our team became perceived as an idealized, almost messianic leader whose research was accorded something of a magical quality. For example, a senior executive asked this consultant to give a workshop on his learnings "on life and retrenchment." The power of this projective process sometimes drew our team into distorted roles, particularly the consultant who had become so lionized. He felt so authorized by this process that he began to reinterpret his role as being far more interventive and directive than appropriate. At times, we all believed our stated rationale for this, which was that crisis intervention literature from the psychotherapy field suggests that during crises patients need direct intervention and guidance (Weakland, Fisch, Watzlawick, & Boden, 1974). This rationale expresses the basic assumption dependency functioning that had so affected us, for it reduces the client system to the status of a mental patient undergoing acute crisis and causes the consultant to become a therapist/savior. The projection onto a perceived leader is one hallmark of the basic assumption dependency group, and, as with all such instances, this served to diminish the organization's capacity to work on the situation.

We observed additional defensive processes at the same conference mentioned above. For various reasons, some of the regional offices experienced more cutbacks during this first round of layoffs than did others. The offices were sorted in-

to three categories, each of which would end up with different staffing levels, with the specifics left to the regional groups to work out. The participants immediately sorted themselves into "winners" and "losers," depending on the category their regional office fell in. This splitting denied the central element of the situation—that all Direct Services offices faced enormous loss. Even the details of the plan could not establish a more balanced distribution of feelings; several of the so-called "winning" offices would end up with only one more staff member than the so-called "losers," and, again, this was only the first round of cuts. But the division of the group into these two subgroups enabled members to simplify their emotional response to this extremely difficult situation. Many could feel sorry for the "losers" and glad for or envious of the "winners" and, by attending to that, avoid struggling with the very painful decisions *each* regional group had to make in the upcoming period concerning its staffing and its work. Those whose jobs were temporarily saved could project their feelings of loss and helplessness onto those being immediately laid off.

While this split persisted, little real dialogue was established. The staff ridiculed attempts to establish forums for discussion. Yet the most primitive behavior that I observed in this system also occurred at this conference. Two days after the cutbacks were announced, several staff members from one of the regions most reduced in size and a group identified as "losers" started a food fight at the dinner buffet. This had the effect of infuriating the leadership of the organization, provoking a great deal of hostility and criticism from the hotel management, and gaining the disapproval of many peers. On one level it suggests the sense of persecution felt by some staff, who enacted childish behavior and created substantial disapproval. On another it reveals the depth of the pain that people could not address in that culture at the time. The group that started the food fight left the conference early. The experience underscores the difficulties of dealing with increased, primitive aggression during such stressful periods.

Throughout the organization, layoff policies provided a focal point for heightened emotional responses. Task considerations suggest that layoff decisions express the new structural and strategic orientation. This means members must be differentiated according to their strengths and weaknesses and their potential contributions to the new organizational form. Doing so, of course, completely upsets established social relations, because organization structure and its role distribution are inextricably linked with the dynamics of informal social interaction. Major redesign efforts of this sort disrupt sentient boundaries. As with many organizations under threat, this rigid organization, characterized by prescribed role distribution and a structure of fixed authority, congealed and emerged to overwhelm redesign efforts in many local programs. Staff clung to existing patterns, thereby diminishing their organization's capacity to adapt to a radically changing environment.

Implications for the Management of Decline

Managing the process of decline — whether it is partial, as with Direct Services, or complete, as with Green Lodge — is extraordinarily difficult. The conditions are perilous: An increased need for careful thought and collaborative planning is undermined by the volatility of the situation and the anxieties inherent in failure and mourning. Enormous stress inevitably leads to an increase in the fantasy-driven elements of group behavior. Powerful and primitive emotions strain social defense systems beyond the group's capacity to contain and modify them. This section reviews some of the practical implications of the framework used here for managing decline.

Behavioral scientists have compared the psychosocial process of organizational decline to the way in which people react to death or serious impairment. Lieberman (1980) describes several stages of the response, beginning with denial, leading through anger and depression, and ending with forms of acceptance. The parallel has its merits: Massive denial certainly seems to be a frequent starting point when a major cutback is threatened, and other stages occur in response to

decline. The analogy is limited, however, in that imminent death or a lost limb cannot be altered, but strategic and programmatic decisions often do affect the future of an organization. Unstable environments make it harder to know when activity is mobilized for realistic work and when it has lost its reality orientation. The uncertainty inherent in the situation removes some of the most accessible criteria for discerning the degree of reality orientation and makes collusion with fantastic planning far easier. This makes it extremely difficult for the manager to sort the fantasy-filled elements of the planning process from those grounded in reality.

For example, several of the local programs in the Direct Services system had already developed alternative local funding sources. By the time cutbacks impinged on so many programs' ability to operate at all, those programs that developed attractive funding sources showed far greater robustness. Other programs that only later began scurrying to do the same, when massive numbers of other organizations were chasing the same scarce funds, found the task impossible.

The chief danger to the manager is succumbing to the same regressive pressures affecting the work group, thereby providing leadership in unrealistic or destructive directions (Glassberg, 1978; Whetten, 1980b). While certain leaders are more vulnerable than others to these pressures, the additional anxieties of retrenchment lead to a greater tendency for all to enact their unresolved personal conflicts in the social field.

Managers frequently say that their ability to lead effectively is eroded by difficult external conditions. Turbulence surrounding their units does indeed make coherent decision making and systematic planning all the more difficult. But in my experience, a far greater source of the managers' sense of becoming incompetent and undermined is the erosion of their internally conferred authority to lead and represent the organization.

Leaders frequently serve as the focus for the hostility and aggression ever present in organizational life. Ordinary decisions inevitably favor some and not others, and the person of the leader often "catches" a response more appropriately directed at the role. An increase in the acrimony can be expected when such serious and threatening decisions are made. Far more difficult, however, is the diffuse, undifferentiated aggression and anger that accompanies individual and group regression as task structure is threatened with dissolution and the role structures upon which members rely for part of their identity disintegrate. Their sense of persecution and punishment will often be projected into the leadership. This more primitive anger isolates leaders from their staff at a time when they most need to work together. Much of this emotionality also fuels rumors that become increasingly unsettling for managers (Greenhalgh, 1982). Long-standing conflicts emerge, interest-based subgroups coalesce, and staff members become envious of people in higher positions who are thought to be more secure. All of this adds to the turmoil and further undermines the manager's ability to lead.

While an increase in paranoid thinking probably cannot be avoided, organizations can moderate it. Managers have often asked how much to disclose and when. Experience suggests that disclosure of as much as possible is helpful (Hirschhorn & Gilmore, 1983). While a manager may understandably respond to the increased isolation and acrimony with more concealment, this will probably escalate the paranoid fantasies and aggravate the projection of punitive feelings onto the leadership, who are then likely to complete the vicious cycle by withholding even more information. Once rumors are discussed openly and their content subjected to the light of day, the vehicle loses its power to co-mingle shared fantasy and suppressed antipathy.

One important response to primitive fantasy systems is to allow for the mourning process. The inevitable losses involved in decline will be far better integrated, and in a more mature way, if the leadership provides the opportunity for mourning (Krantz, 1981). Both the angry and depressive phases of the mourning process must be encouraged and acknowledged (Trist, 1980).

A particularly damaging and pervasive process is the tendency for groups to isolate emotionally those losing their jobs from those staying with the organization. A sort of "survivors syndrome" develops, causing those who are staying to feel guilty and ambivalent about keeping their posts. Alternatively, those employees made redundant can feel contaminated in some way, as the split-off, fragile, impotent parts of the "survivors" become projected into those losing their jobs. Under these conditions, little authentic dialogue can occur, and the mourning process will be seriously blocked.

A comparable splitting process projects all security and certainty onto upper levels. In Direct Services, people believed that "they"—meaning managers the next level up, or perhaps top executives—had a blueprint they weren't telling the others about. At Green Lodge, middle managers asking, "How long have you known?" or "What will they do with the staff lodging?" seemed to convey the feeling that more certainty existed at higher levels than was the case.

In my experience, uncertainty was distributed equally; no one knew what was going to happen, and major decisions at all levels had quite rapidly been made public. But the belief that some answers or certainty were being secretly retained by leaders conveys the fantasy notion that part of the uncertainty and discomfort was a form of punishment from above, with mobilization of corresponding feeling states. Protestations to the contrary were often quickly incorporated into conspirational frameworks.

Accepting the prevalence of individual needs in uncertain times enables the staff to consider legitimately their personal futures, perhaps by providing some resources such as an office with a phone or even career counseling. Career anxieties will be at a peak, and such moves help the staff contain the anxieties and directly confront the challenges ahead. Personal concerns, which inevitably diverge from the organizations' interests to a degree, will draw an increasingly greater part of the staff's attentions during decline. Fighting or denying this fact alienates the staff members and further undermines their capacity to work while they are still there.

No matter how well managed the situation is, one must anticipate increased organization dysfunction. Expecting a "Dunkirk spirit" to exist much beyond the initial phase following announcements, or expecting a new esprit de corps to enable the organization to end with a flurry of competence and effectiveness, denies important realities. The managers I have known who tried to accomplish tasks in the last six months or year that they were unable to achieve in the previous three years have been deeply disappointed and behaved in self-defeating ways. Organizations in decline accomplish less, not more, as much of their members' energy becomes directed to personal and fantasy-driven activities.

In helping staff members meet the dual demands of personal planning and working effectively, the manager faces enormous odds. One important contribution she or he can make is to understand the particular system's social defenses and to protect its strengths. This amounts to observing where and under what conditions real dialogue can occur and protecting that time and space as one of the most valuable resources available for addressing the painful issues of decline or cutback.

Note

1 For a detailed discussion of the psychodynamic processes by which this occurs, see Heimann (1952).

References

Behn, R. 1978. Closing a government facility. *Public Administration Review* 38: 332–38.

Bion, W.R. 1961. *Experiences in groups and other papers*. London: Tavistock.

Boulding, K. 1975. The management of decline. *Change* 64: 8–9.

Glassberg, A. 1978. Organizational responses to municipal budget decreases. *Public Administration Review* 38: 325–42.

Greenhalgh, L. 1982. Maintaining organizational effectiveness during organizational retrenchment. *Journal of Applied Behavioral Science* 18(2): 155–70.

Heilbroner, R. 1976. *Business civilization in decline*. New York: Norton.

Heimann, P. 1952. Certain functions of introjection and projection in earliest infancy. In M. Klein, P. Heimann, & R. Money-Kyrle (Eds.), *Developments in psycho-analysis*. London: Hogarth Press.

Hirsch, F. 1976. *Social limits to growth*. Cambridge, MA: Harvard University Press.

Hirschhorn, L. 1983. Managing retrenchment in uncertain times. In L. Hirschhorn & Associates (Eds.), *Cutting back: Retrenchment and redevelopment in human and community services*. San Francisco: Jossey-Bass.

Hirschhorn, L., & Gilmore, T.M. 1983. Management challenges under conditions of retrenchment. *Journal of Human Resources* 22(3): 5–17.

Jacques, E. 1955. Social systems as a defense against persecutory and depressive anxiety. In M. Klein, P. Herman, & R. Money-Kyrle (Eds.), *New directions in psychoanalysis*. London: Tavistock.

Krantz, J. 1981. *Constructive outplacement: Moderating the trauma lay-off* (Unpublished Working Paper). Philadelphia, PA: Management and Behavioral Science Center, The Wharton School, The University of Pennsylvania.

Levine, C.H. 1978. Organizational decline and cutback management. *Public Administration Review* 38: 316–25.

Lieberman, J. 1980. *Mourning and organizational decline*. Unpublished notes.

Menzies, I.E.P. 1970. *The functioning of social systems as a defense against anxiety*. London: Tavistock Institute of Human Relations.

Rice, A.K. 1965. *The enterprise and its environment: A system theory of management organization*. London: Tavistock.

Scott, W. 1974. Organization theory: A reassessment. *Academy of Management Journal* 17: 242–54.

Snow, R. 1983. *The biological view of organizations: From a descriptive to a prescriptive model*. Unpublished paper.

Starbuck, W., Greve, A., & Hedberg, B. 1978. Responding to crisis. *Journal of Business Administration* 9: 111–37.

Trist, E. 1980. *The evolution of socio-technical systems*. Ontario: Ontario Quality of Working Life Centre.

Wallace, A.F.C. 1975. *Human behavior in extreme situations* (Disaster Study No. 1: Division of Anthropology and Psychology, Publication 390). Washington, DC: Committee on Disaster Studies.

Weakland, J., Fisch, R., Watzlawick, P., & Boden, A. 1974. Brief therapy: Focused problem resolution. *Family Process* 13(2): 141–67.

Whetten, D. 1980a. Organizational decline: A neglected topic in organizational behavior. *Academy of Management Review* 5: 57–58.

Whetten, D. 1980b. Sources, responses and effects of organizational decline. In J. Kimberly, R. Miles, & Associates (Eds.), *The organizational life cycle.* San Francisco: Jossey-Bass.

Yetton, P. 1975. Leadership style in stressful and nonstressful situations. In D. Gowler & K. Legge (Eds.), *Managerial stress.* New York: Wiley.

14

Layoffs, Self-Esteem, and Survivor Guilt: Motivational, Affective, and Attitudinal Consequences

Joel Brockner

Jeanette Davy

Carolyn Carter

The study of layoffs has long been a topic of interest to organizational behaviorists and labor relations theorists. This topic has met with renewed interest in the past few years, in view of the large number of business organizations which have resorted to involuntary dismissals as a cost-cutting procedure. Both the antecedents (Cornfield, 1983) and consequences (Jahoda, 1979) of work layoffs have received empirical and theoretical scrutiny.

The authors thank Jenny Bortz and Tom Laase for their competent assistance collecting the data. In addition, the first author is indebted to the University of Arizona for its research support.

Reprinted with permission from *Organizational Behavior and Human Decision Processes,* Vol. 36, © 1985 by Academic Press, Inc.

Much of the research on the consequences of work layoffs has looked at the psychological impact of unemployment on the dismissed parties (e.g., Eisenberg & Lazarsfeld, 1938).

An intriguing possibility which has received far less attention is that layoffs may also affect the work attitudes and behaviors of those who are not laid off (i.e., the "survivors"). Several theoretical perspectives suggest that the survivors' affective states and levels of productivity may be systematically altered. For example, their co-workers' dismissal may engender perceived job insecurity (i.e., anxiety) in the survivors. Consequently, the survivors may work harder in order to avoid meeting a similar fate. In addition, anecdotal evidence suggests that survivors experience considerable remorse or, more extremely, "survivor guilt." A recent article in *The Wall Street Journal* (January 20, 1984) described employees' reactions to compulsory overtime in the automobile industry. Among the sources of psychological distress mentioned was the discomfort associated with receiving such high wages when so many of their fellow employees had yet to be recalled for work. The article described the attitude of one employee as follows: "She is grateful to be working when unemployment is still high. But she feels guilty about how much she is working—nine or 10 hours a day, sometimes six days a week." The employee's own words were, "It makes you feel bad that you're working overtime and others are desperate. I wish that (other) people could come in and work my overtime hours. If they could work a few hours a day, they could save their homes."

It is not intuitively obvious that survivors should feel guilty about their co-workers' dismissal. In fact, it could be plausibly argued that survivors should *not* feel guilty, in that they are typically not responsible for making the decision to dismiss their peers. Why, then, might they feel guilty? According to equity theory (Adams, 1965), workers are very concerned with being treated fairly. That is, their ratio of work outcomes to work inputs should be commensurate with those of relevant others. Deviations from perceived equity (in either direction), according to the theory, will produce behavior and/or belief change designed to restore perceived fairness.

Much of the equity theory research in the industrial/organizational psychology literature has explored the effect of positive inequity (i.e., the perception that one's outcome to input ratio is greater than that of relevant others) on work motivation (Mowday, 1979). In several studies Adams and his associates (e.g., Adams & Rosenbaum, 1962) have shown that positive inequity (or overpayment) caused workers to work harder, presumably in order to redress the positive inequity. Whether this enhanced effort resulted in increased quantity (productivity) or quality of work was shown to depend upon a host of factors (e.g., hourly vs piece rate pay).

Most positive inequity inductions employed in experimental research have led workers to believe that they were being compensated by an unreasonably large amount for their efforts. However, in actual work organizations employees may experience positive inequity through a number of mechanisms (e.g., Greenberg & Ornstein, 1983). More succinctly, it may well be that co-worker layoffs can induce a state of positive inequity in the survivors. For example, survivors may feel that they, rather than their co-workers, could have just as easily been dismissed. Thus, unlike in the typical overpayment study, in which positive inequity is created by *increasing the worker's outcomes* in relation to the comparison other, layoff survival may produce positive inequity by *decreasing the comparison other's outcomes* relative to the worker's. It is in this sense that the worker's survival of the layoff, while hedonically desirable, may also seem "unfair."

The present study was designed to explore the hypothesis that layoffs cause survivors to experience positive inequity, which in turn will have motivational consequences. In order to reduce the sense of remorse or guilt over their co-workers' dismissal, workers should increase their level of output (just as they would in response to other, more traditional inductions of positive inequity). In a simulated work environment, subjects completed a series of tasks in the presence of another presumed subject. (In reality, the other "subject" was an accomplice of the experimenter.) Halfway through the proceedings the subject and confederate were given a "rest period," at which time the Layoff manipulation took place. In the Layoff condition the subject and confederate were told (for reasons that seemed somewhat unfair) that one of them would not be able to complete the final experimental task. Instead, that person would have to leave and would not receive remuneration for participating. In all instances the subject was allowed to stay while the confederate was forced to leave. In this manner subjects witnessed the layoff of another worker. In the No-Layoff condition the subject and confederate merely waited to complete the final experimental task. The dependent variable was the degree of productivity on the final experimental task. It was expected that subjects would be more productive in the Layoff than in the No-Layoff condition.

It should be emphasized that the layoff manipulation was intended to isolate the effect of perceived inequity from any possible influence due to job-insecurity-produced anxiety. Accordingly, the layoff induction was implemented in such a way that subjects in the Layoff condition had no reason to believe that they, like the confederate, might be dismissed from the experiment.

An additional purpose of the experiment was to study the effect of an individual difference variable—the worker's self-esteem—on reactions to the Layoff manipulation. As Mowday (1979) has pointed out, "one area of research on equity theory that has received little attention is the impact of individual differences on employee perceptions of and reactions to inequity." Indeed, apart from a few experiments (Tornow, 1971; Vecchio, 1981) there has been very little research exploring the effects of individual difference variables.

Prior research clearly suggests that self-esteem may be a relevant moderator variable in this context. However, it is far less certain whether higher or lower self-esteem participants will show a greater increase in productivity in the Layoff than in the No-Layoff condition. On the one hand, it could be predicted that the high self-esteem workers (high SEs) will be more apt to increase their output in the Layoff than in the No-Layoff condition. Why? In a previous study (Brockner, in press) subjects were either overpaid (Positive Inequity condition) on an hourly basis or equitably paid (Equity condition) for working on a proofreading task. High SEs and medium self-esteem participants (medium SEs), in accordance with equity theory, were more productive in the Positive Inequity than in the Equity condition. High and medium SEs were also more productive than low SEs *in the Positive Inequity condition*. By contrast, low SEs violated the basic equity theory prediction, by being less productive in the Positive Inequity than Equity condition. On the assumption that the Layoff manipulation will simi-

larly serve as a positive inequity induction, it may be that the high and medium SEs will be more motivated in the Layoff than in the No-Layoff condition, relative to the low SEs.

On the other hand, much research has shown that the work motivation of low SEs is more susceptible to influence by external or social cues (Brockner, 1983; Brockner & Guare, 1983) than is that of high or medium SEs. More specifically, low SEs may feel especially guilty or remorseful about their co-workers' dismissal; low SEs may reason that they (i.e., the low SEs) were unworthy of remaining, if it were the case that someone had to leave. This analysis would suggest that the low SEs would be especially motivated to redress the positive inequity, and lead to the alternative prediction that it would be this group who would show the greatest boost in motivation in the Layoff relative to the No-Layoff condition. The present study allowed us to evaluate these alternative possibilities.

Method

Participants

A total of 78 undergraduates at a large state university completed the experiment. Subjects were drawn from an introductory psychology class with the understanding that they would receive extra course credit for taking part.

Procedure

Upon their arrival at the laboratory for a "Test Validation" experiment, subjects were led into a large research room and seated at a desk. They were told that they would have to wait for the other subject to arrive before the experiment would begin. Approximately 30 s later a female confederate, posing as the other subject, arrived and was asked to sit at the desk diagonally opposite to the subject. Both subject and confederate were informed that the study would consist of a number of parts. In the "first part" they completed the Revised Janis–Field Self-Esteem Scale (Eagly, 1967).

In a review of the psychometric properties of self-esteem scales Robinson and Shaver (1973) provided considerable evidence for the reliability of the measure (e.g., split half reliability = .83). Robinson and Shaver also reported that the scale correlates significantly with other standardized self-esteem measures. Perhaps the most compelling evidence of the measure's construct validity stems from the results of 10 experiments conducted by the first author and his colleagues, in which the Janis–Field scale was the operational measure of self-esteem. Five of these studies have been published elsewhere (Brockner, Gardner et al., 1983, two experiments; Brockner & Guare, 1983; Brockner & Swap, 1983; Lloyd, Paulsen, & Brockner, 1983). The remaining five are currently in press or under editorial review (Brockner, in press; Brockner & Elkind, in press, two experiments; Brockner, Hjelle, & Plant, in press; Lloyd & Brockner, 1985). This series of studies explored the relationship between self-esteem and a wide variety of dependent measures (e.g., task performance, affect, cognition). In each of the experiments low SEs (defined as those scoring in the bottom half or bottom third of the overall distribution) differed from the higher SEs (defined as those scoring in the top half or top two-thirds of the overall distribution) on the dependent variable(s) of interest in the theoretically expected direction. Such results lend considerable construct validity to the measure. A tertiary split was used in this study to classify subjects as high, medium, or low in self-esteem.

After completing the self-esteem measure the subject and confederate were told that they would now proceed to the "next part of the experiment." More specifically, subjects were told that they would (1) work on a proofreading task, (2) have a short break, and (3) work on a second proofreading task. The alleged purpose of the proofreading was to "develop some standardized tests of cognitive performance. These standardized tests will be very useful in the future. Not only will we be able to use them in educational and research settings, but we will also be able to apply them to working situations to measure the aptitude and performance of paid employees." To minimize competition, the subject and confederate were told that they would not be proofreading the same material. Furthermore, "to minimize any possible distractions we are going to have you do the proofreading in separate, private rooms."

At this point the confederate and subject were ushered into separate research cubicles to perform the proofreading task that has been used in previous research (Reis & Burns, 1982). They were given an eight-page booklet of a passage taken from Jane Jacobs' book, *The Death and Life of Great American Cities*. There were numerous spelling, grammatical, and punctuation errors throughout, which subjects were required to underline (but not correct). Subjects were given 10 min to read the passage. *Both speed (i.e., quantity) and accuracy (i.e., quality) in performance were stressed.*

The experimenter then left the subjects alone in their research cubicles for 10 min to perform the proofreading. After 10 min had elapsed the experimenter reentered the subjects' cubicle and asked them to underline the last line that they had proofread. The subject was asked to follow the experimenter back to the large research room. They were joined there several seconds later by the confederate, who was similarly fetched by the experimenter. During this "rest period" the Layoff manipulation was introduced. In the Layoff condition the experimenter mentioned that because of a "room scheduling problem" only one person would be allowed to finish the experiment and thus receive the extra course credit for taking part. On a seemingly impromptu basis the experimenter said that the subject and confederate would have to draw lots to determine which one of them would get to stay. The lottery was rigged such that the subject always was able to stay. To buttress the manipulation the confederate said as she was exiting that it was unfair to make her leave and deprive her of the extra credit. The experimenter verbally "agreed" that it was a tough break, but said nothing else. After the confederate exited the experimenter turned to the subject and said, "Well, I guess you're the lucky one who gets to finish today and receive credit. Let's get started."

In the No-Layoff condition the experimenter asked subjects not to speak with one another during the "rest period." In the interim the experimenter made busy work for himself, in order to allow a period of time to lapse that was comparable to the time needed to complete the layoff in the Layoff condition (approximately 45 s).

In all conditions subjects were led back to their private research cubicles, in which they worked on another (different) eight-page proofreading task. This task was taken from the same book as the one used for the first task. (In the No-Layoff condition the confederate was led back to her cubicle first, in full view of the subject.) The instructions, as well as the length of time allotted for the second proofreading were the same as in the first proofreading task. After 10 min the experimenter reentered the subjects' cubicle and asked them to underline the last line that they had proofread.

Dependent variables.   The behavioral dependent measures were quantitative and qualitative measures of proofreading performance on each task. The former was assessed by counting the number of lines that subjects had proofread during the 10-min reading periods. The latter was determined by computing the percentage of errors that subjects had correctly identified in those lines that they had finished reading.

After completing the second proofreading task all participants responded to a final questionnaire, which included a manipulation check, as well as a number of measures of subjects' affective states while working on the second proofreading task (i.e., after the Layoff manipulation had been introduced). The two manipulation check questions required subjects to rate (1) how fairly they were treated by the experimenter and (2) how fairly the "other subject" was treated by the experimenter. Responses could range from *not at all* (1) to *very fairly* (7). In addition, subjects indicated the extent to which each of the following emotional states applied to the way that they felt while proofreading the second task: frustrated, lucky, confident, guilty, glad, angry, lonely, and

sorry for the other person. Responses to each of these measures could range from *not at all* (1) to *a great deal* (7).

In addition, subjects' attitudes toward their "co-worker" and the experimenter were assessed. For the former, subjects were asked, "Based upon your brief interaction, how would you characterize your feelings toward the other subject?" (endpoints: *very negative* (1) and *very positive* (7)) and "Based upon your brief interaction how much do you think you and the other subject are *similar* to one another?" (endpoints: *not at all similar* (1) and *very similar* (7)). Subjects' attitudes toward the experimenter were assessed with the following question: "Based upon your brief interaction, how would you characterize your feelings toward the experimenter" (endpoints: *very negative* (1) and *very positive* (7)). All subjects were then thoroughly debriefed and thanked for their participation.

Results

Manipulation Check

A three-factor (Self-Esteem × Layoff × Self–Other) analysis of variance with repeated measures on the last factor was employed on the manipulation check data. The relevant effect is the Layoff × Self–Other interaction, which was highly significant, $F(1, 72) = 40.17$, $p < .001$. Subjects reported that they had been treated much more fairly than the "other subject" in the Layoff condition (M's = 6.31 vs 4.14, respectively), but not in the No-Layoff condition (M's = 6.32 vs 6.29, respectively). The Layoff induction thus appeared to have been successfully implemented.

Behavioral Measures

Quantitative assessment of performance.   A three-factor (Self-Esteem × Layoff × Task) analysis of variance with repeated measures on the last factor was performed on the number of lines which subjects had proofread. The Task main effect was highly significant, $F(1, 72) = 112.76$, $p < .001$. Across conditions, subjects proofread much more of the second than the first task. This effect (which was not of primary importance) may have been due to a practice or warm-up effect, or to the possibility that the second task was somehow easier than the first. The Task main effect was moderated by several higher-order interactions, however. First, and as predicted, the Layoff × Task interaction effect was significant, $F(1, 72) = 4.39$, $p < .05$. Whereas all groups were more productive (i.e., proofread more lines) on the second task than on the first, this was considerably more true in the Layoff than in the No-Layoff condition.

The Self-Esteem × Layoff × Task interaction was also significant, $F(2, 72) = 4.87$, $p < .01$. As can be seen in Table 1, the Layoff × Task interaction was entirely attributable to the low SEs. Simple effect analyses elucidated the significant triple

interaction. Low SEs showed a much greater increase in productivity from the first to the second task in the Layoff condition (average increase = 52.10 lines) than in the No-Layoff condition ($M = 17.07$ lines; $F(1, 72) = 13.65$, $p < .001$). The corresponding increase for the medium SEs did not differ in the Layoff and the No-Layoff condition (M's = 25.69 lines and 30.60 lines, respectively; $F < 1$). Similarly, the high SEs exhibited no difference in increased productivity in the Layoff and No-Layoff conditions (M's = 26.62 and 22.31 lines, respectively; $F < 1$).

To state the triple interaction effect differently (according to simple effect analyses), within the No-Layoff condition the increase in productivity from the first to the second task did not differ as a function of the workers' self-esteem, $F(2, 72) = 1.04$, n.s. Within the Layoff condition, however, the increase exhibited by the low SEs ($M = 52.10$

Table 1. Number of Lines Proofread

| Self-Esteem | Layoff Condition | Proofreading Task | | Increase from First to Second |
		First	Second	
High	Layoff	$N = 13$ $M = 97.31$ $SD = 21.33$	$N = 13$ $M = 123.92$ $SD = 32.01$	26.61
	No Layoff	$N = 13$ $M = 106.38$ $SD = 39.20$	$N = 13$ $M = 128.69$ $SD = 51.98$	22.31
Medium	Layoff	$N = 13$ $M = 92.54$ $SD = 42.45$	$N = 13$ $M = 118.23$ $SD = 47.91$	25.69
	No Layoff	$N = 15$ $M = 109.67$ $SD = 39.13$	$N = 15$ $M = 140.27$ $SD = 49.80$	30.60
Low	Layoff	$N = 10$ $M = 111.40$ $SD = 25.15$	$N = 10$ $M = 163.50$ $SD = 35.99$	52.10
	No Layoff	$N = 14$ $M = 80.29$ $SD = 29.25$	$N = 14$ $M = 97.36$ $SD = 42.05$	17.07

Note: Maximum score on each task = 218 lines. Higher scores reflect greater productivity. The Layoff manipulation took place between the first and second tasks.

lines) was significantly greater than that shown by the medium SEs ($M = 25.69$ lines) and the high SEs ($M = 26.62$ lines; $F(2, 72) = 4.99$, $p < .01$).

The only other significant finding was the Self-Esteem × Layoff interaction, $F(2, 72) = 5.23$, $p < .01$. Across both tasks, low SEs were considerably more productive in the Layoff than in the No-Layoff condition; medium and high SEs were slightly more productive in the No-Layoff than in the Layoff condition. It should be emphasized that this interaction was in turn moderated by the Self-Esteem × Layoff × Task interaction reported above. That is, the Self-Esteem × Layoff interaction was much more pronounced on the second proofreading task (i.e., after the Layoff manipulation occurred) than on the first task (before it occurred).

Although the Self-Esteem × Layoff interaction was moderated by the triple interaction, it may be worthwhile to discuss the Self-Esteem × Layoff interaction that emerged on the first proofreading task. First, it should be mentioned that this initial task difference was in all likelihood due to error in random assignment. The experimenters were unaware of the subjects' self-esteem level, and subjects were randomly assigned to the Layoff and No-Layoff conditions. Second, as can be seen in Table 1, the interaction on the first proofreading task was attributable to two facts: (a) low SEs were more productive in the (still to come) Layoff than No-Layoff condition, and (b) medium SEs, and to a lesser extent high SEs, were more productive in the (still to come) No-Layoff than Layoff condition. What interpretational difficulties might be posed by initial task differences? Regression toward the mean is *not* a problem in this instance. Note that a regression effect would cause the low SEs in the No-Layoff condition (who proofread an average of 80.29 lines on the first task) to increase their productivity to a greater extent on the second task than (1) medium and high SEs in the No-Layoff condition, who had proofread 109.67 and 106.38 lines on the first task, respectively, and (2) low SEs in the Layoff condition, who had proofread 111.40 lines on the initial task. However, neither of these possibilities material-

ized. In short, regression effects due to differences on the initial task would have worked *against* finding the Self-Esteem × Layoff × Task interaction that did emerge.

The fact that low SEs in the Layoff condition proofread more lines ($M = 111.40$ lines) than their counterparts in the No-Layoff condition ($M = 80.29$ lines) still lends itself to a different alternative explanation of the low SEs' data. It could be argued that the low SEs in the Layoff condition showed a greater increase from the first to the second task ($M = 52.10$ lines) than the low SEs in the No-Layoff condition ($M = 17.07$ lines), but not because of the Layoff. Instead, it could have been that faster proofreaders (as measured by initial task performance) are simply likely to become even faster than slower proofreaders with repeated administrations of the task. This explanation cannot be completely eliminated, but other evidence suggests that it is not particularly compelling. If it were correct, then medium and high SEs in the No-Layoff condition should have shown a greater increase in productivity than their medium and high self-esteem counterparts in the Layoff condition. Why? Because the former groups proofread more on the initial task than the latter two groups. This did not occur, however, as an inspection of Table 1 reveals.

Finally, we performed a two-factor (Self-Esteem × Layoff) analysis of covariance of productivity on the second task, with initial task productivity serving as the covariate. This procedure statistically controls for differences on the initial task. If the Layoff × Task interaction and the Self-Esteem × Layoff × Task interaction reported in Table 1 are not artifactual, then the Layoff main effect and the Self-Esteem × Layoff interaction should still be significant in the analysis of covariance. In fact, this is exactly what occurred. For the layoff main effect, $F(1, 71) = 4.00$, $p < .05$; for the Self-Esteem × Layoff interaction, $F(2, 71) = 3.62$, $p < .03$.

Clearly, it would have been preferable if no differences emerged on the initial proofreading task. However, the differences that did occur do not appear to lend themselves readily to a damaging alternative interpretation. If anything, the Self-Esteem × Layoff × Task interaction reported in Table 1 may underestimate the "true" effect, because any effect due to regression would have produced results contrary to those obtained.

Qualitative assessment of performance. A three-factor analysis of variance of performance quality (percentage of errors found) yielded no significant effects involving the Layoff and Self-Esteem variables (all p values > .20). The only significant finding was the Task main effect, $F(1, 72) = 47.92$, $p < .001$. Across conditions, performance quality was higher on the first than on the second task (M's = 59.56 and 48.65%, respectively).

Within-task correlational analyses revealed that the performance quantity and quality were inversely related, $r(75) = -.24$, $p < .05$ on the first task, $r(75) = -.55$, $p < .001$ on the second. Apparently, however, the decline in quality which accompanied increased productivity and vice versa (across conditions) was not pronounced enough to yield between-groups differences in performance quality (see the preceding paragraph).

Affective States

Several patterns emerged in the two-factor (Self-Esteem × Layoff) analyses of the affective state responses. First, there were a handful of significant Layoff main effects. Subjects reported feeling significantly more lucky ($p < .001$), sorry for the other person ($p < .001$), glad ($p < .01$), and marginally more guilty ($p < .06$) in the Layoff than in the No-Layoff condition. These findings seem conceptually related to one another, and consistent with equity theory. Subjects' reported feeling states seem to indicate that they perceived that they had been treated much more favorably than the other person in the Layoff than in the No-Layoff condition. Second, the Layoff variable affected some mood states (i.e., those just reported), but not others. There were no differences in perceived frustration, confidence, anger, or loneliness as a function of the Layoff variable (all F's < 1).

Third, did any of the results on the affective state measures shed light on the Self-Esteem × Layoff × Task interaction effect observed on the productivity data reported in Table 1? That is, were any of the Self-Esteem × Layoff interaction effects significant in the analyses of the affective state measures? The only significant effect emerged on the guilt measure, $F(2, 72) = 3.29$, $p < .05$. High SEs reported feeling more guilty in the Layoff than in the No-Layoff condition (M's = 2.38 and 1.58, respectively), as did the medium SEs (M's = 3.54 and 1.40, respectively). Interestingly enough, low SEs reported feeling slightly *less* guilty in the Lay-off than in the No-Layoff condition (M's = 2.00 and 2.57, respectively).

At first glance the nature of this interaction seems inconsistent with the observed productivity results. How can the interaction effect on the guilt measure be explained? Recall that subjects completed the affective state measures *after* they had performed the second proofreading task. It is possible that the layoff engendered much higher levels of perceived positive inequity (guilt) in the low SEs than in the other two groups. To redress this inequity, low SEs may have worked much harder on the second task; in so doing, they may have either eliminated, or been distracted from, their relatively high guilt levels. This reasoning is, of course, purely speculative. It is, however, consistent with the results of a study by Kenrick, Reich, and Cialdini (1976). In that study all subjects witnessed an injustice, and their perceptions of this inequitable event were assessed. Before perceived inequity was measured, half of the subjects were able to take action which restored equity whereas half were not. The former group, who had been able to redress the injustice behaviorally, perceived the injustice as less inequitable than the latter group. In order to evaluate whether in the present study the low SEs' behavioral equity restoration (i.e., working harder) eliminated their (stronger) feelings of guilt, it would be necessary to measure affect after the positive inequity has taken place, but before they have been given any opportunity to redress the inequity behaviorally.

If this analysis is correct, low SEs should report feeling more guilty than medium and high SEs at this point in time.

Attitudes toward Others

Co-worker. Two-factor (Self-Esteem × Layoff) analyses of the measures of subjects' feelings about their "co-worker" indicated highly significant main effects for the Layoff variable, and no other significant findings. Participants rated their feelings about the co-worker as much more negative in the Layoff condition ($M = 4.24$) than in the No-Layoff condition ($M = 5.19$; $F(1, 72) = 8.65$, $p < .01$). Furthermore, subjects perceived their co-worker as less similar to themselves in the Layoff than in the No-Layoff condition (M's $= 2.99$ and 4.17, respectively; $F(1, 72) = 11.24$, $p < .01$).

Such findings — indicative of a "victim-blaming" response — are consistent with equity theory. The "just world" literature (e.g., Lerner, 1975) assumes that workers need to believe that people get what they deserve, and deserve what they get. This need may cause them to derogate their laid-off co-worker, rather than to respond with unadulterated sympathy.

At first blush, these findings seem inconsistent with the affective state results showing that subjects felt more guilty and sorry for the other person in the Layoff than No-Layoff condition. One possible interpretation for this apparent paradox is that layoffs do, in fact, instill ambivalent feelings in survivors about their laid-off co-workers. On the one hand, the survivors' "altruistic" motives may cause them to experience sympathy; on the other hand, their need to believe in a just world may elicit more negative feelings. Said differently, the apparent inconsistency may "simply" reflect the complexity of emotions that are engendered by layoff survival.

The "just world" interpretation should be accepted with caution, however, in that an alternative account is possible. Specifically, the confederate mildly protested about her dismissal in the Layoff condition. By contrast, no such displea-

sure was exhibited by her in the No-Layoff condition. It could have been that her protestations per se, independent of the fact that she was laid off, caused subjects to evaluate her more negatively in the Layoff than in the No-Layoff condition. This is an important question to be addressed by further research. In any event, the whole notion that workers' attitudes toward their fellow employees may be negatively affected by the latters' dismissal may have important implications — especially if the laid-off employees are subsequently recalled to work in that organization.

Experimenter. Subjects' attitudes toward the "authority figure" — the experimenter — did not differ as a function of the Self-Esteem and Layoff variables (all F's < 1). In spite of this nonsignificant result, it may be worthwhile to explore further the effects of layoffs on the survivors' attitudes toward management.

Discussion

In summary, the quantity (but not the quality) of the workers' task performance was enhanced by the dismissal of their fellow subject, as predicted. In addition, the participants' level of self-esteem proved to be an important moderator variable in that only the productivity of the low SEs was significantly affected by the Layoff manipulation. Such findings have a variety of practical and theoretical implications.

Practical Implications

The results of the present study suggest that co-worker layoffs can have a dramatic effect on the subsequent productivity of the "survivors." This finding can serve as the impetus for much future research. For example, will *all* layoffs yield results similar to those observed in the present study? We suspect not. Rather, it may well be that workers' causal attributions for the dismissal of their co-workers are of critical importance in affecting subsequent task performance. More specifically, let us suppose that the organization has developed clear rules about whom to lay off in times of scarcity. (Such decisions can be based on seniority, and/or on the merit of the worker's prior performance, for instance.) If these rules are followed, then the survivors may either (1) feel less remorseful or guilty about their co-workers' dismissal and/or (2) rationalize away such feelings by concluding that the dismissals were, after all, consistent with company policy. It is the whimsical or arbitrary layoff (much like the one in the present study, in which the layoff decision was based on the results of a lottery) that appears to elicit strong feelings of positive inequity and thus spur them on to increased productivity. It could be argued that the method by which the layoff was enacted in this study has no external referent. After all, layoff decisions are rarely decided by a lottery. However, we suspect that many layoff decisions are *perceived* (by those laid off and/or by the survivors) to be the result of a chance or otherwise inexplicable process. To that extent the present findings may have greater external validity than that suggested by a cursory reading of how the layoff was introduced.

Further research should also explore the motivational consequences of other layoff-induced affective states. In real-life layoff situations survivors probably experience a variety of emotions, only one category of which are those produced by positive inequity (remorse, guilt). Layoffs may also produce a sense of job insecurity (i.e., anxiety), which could affect the survivors' task effort and performance (but for reasons having little to do with equity theory). This theoretical ambiguity was probably minimal in the present study, because the experimental procedure had been intentionally structured so that subjects would not have to worry about their own "job security." That is, there was no threat that they, like the confederate before them, might have to leave the experiment without receiving credit. However, in eliminating the job insecurity issue from this situation, we may have stripped away an important consequence of layoffs in actual organizational settings. Future research should determine the joint (and possibly interactive) effects of a variety of layoff-induced

affective states on productivity. It may be, for example, that layoffs which arouse job insecurity in the survivors reduce the potential impact of positive-inequity-produced guilt. Said differently, if the survivors are worried about being able to keep their own jobs, they may not be able to "indulge" themselves in feeling guilty about their co-workers' dismissal.

More generally, the external validity of the present findings to "real-life" layoff situations is questionable, of course, given the laboratory methodology employed in this study. Field research on this topic is sorely needed. We speculate, however, that laboratory experiments that investigate the impact of layoffs on survivors probably do so conservatively. That is, laboratory simulations of layoffs are apt to have far less impact than layoffs that occur in actual organizational settings. The fact that the simulated layoff had a significant impact on motivation and attitude in the present study, therefore, may be all the more compelling.

Theoretical Implications

Many studies have shown that positive inequity increases workers' level of motivation, at least on a short-term basis (Adams, 1965). Most of the positive inequity manipulations have consisted of telling workers that they are being paid an amount that is much more than they deserve (e.g., greater than the remuneration given to similar others). The present results suggest that layoffs may also produce a similar state of positive inequity, which in turn will have its typical motivational consequences. The key difference between previous manipulations of positive inequity and the one employed in the present study is the following: in the earlier studies positive inequity was induced by increasing subjects' outcomes, relative to those of appropriate targets for social comparison. In this study positive inequity was induced by decreasing the target's outcomes, relative to the subject's.

Finally, further theory and research is needed to explore the joint effects of workers' self-esteem and positive inequity on task performance.

In a previous study (Brockner, in press) the overpayment-produced positive inequity increased the motivation level of high and medium SEs, but not the low SEs. In the present study the layoff-produced positive inequity increased the low SEs' degree of striving but had no impact on that of the medium and high SEs. We speculate that these apparently contradictory results are related to differences in the salient psychological event produced by the positive inequity induction. In the previous study the overpayment may have been viewed as an implicit challenge to exhibit a large increase in productivity. High and medium SEs, who had the confidence to meet the challenge, may have responded by redoubling their efforts. Low SEs, who presumably lacked the necessary confidence, may have withdrawn from the task at hand. In the present study the positive inequity may have aroused remorse or guilt feelings to a greater extent than challenging the workers' ability to achieve a difficult goal. It is precisely under such circumstances that low SEs may feel especially guilty, because they are apt to view themselves as being less worthy to be chosen as the "survivor." Accordingly, low self-esteem survivors should be most productive following this type of layoff. Research is currently in progress to test these hypotheses.

References

Adams, J.S. 1965. Inequity in social exchange. In L. Berkowitz (Ed.), *Advances in experimental social psychology* (Vol. 2, pp. 267–69). New York: Academic Press.

Adams, J.S., & Rosenbaum, W.B. 1962. The relationship of worker productivity to cognitive dissonance about wage inequities. *Journal of Applied Psychology* 46: 161–64.

Brockner, J. 1983. Low self-esteem and behavioral plasticity. In L. Wheeler & P.R. Shaver (Eds.), *Review of personality and social psychology* (Vol. 4, pp. 237–71). Beverly Hills, CA: Sage.

Brockner, J. In press. The effects of trait self-esteem and positive inequity on productivity. *Journal of Personality.*

Brockner, J., & Elkind, M. In press. Self-esteem and reactance: Further evidence of attitudinal and motivational consequences. *Journal of Experimental Social Psychology.*

Brockner, J., Gardner, M., Bierman, J., Mahan, T., Thomas, B., Weiss, W., Winters, L., & Mitchell, A. 1983. The roles of self-esteem and self-consciousness in the Wortman–Brehm model of reactance and learned helplessness. *Journal of Personality and Social Psychology* 45: 199–209.

Brockner, J., & Guare, J. 1983. Improving the performance of low self-esteem individuals: An attributional approach. *Academy of Management Journal* 26: 642–56.

Brockner, J., Hjelle, L., & Plant, R. In press. Self-focused attention, self-esteem, and the experience of state depression. *Journal of Personality.*

Brockner, J., & Swap, W.C. 1983. Resolving the relationships between placebos, misattribution, and insomnia: An individual differences perspective. *Journal of Personality and Social Psychology* 45: 32–42.

Cornfield, D.B. 1983. Chances of layoff in a corporation: A case study. *Administrative Science Quarterly* 28: 503–20.

Eagly, A.H. 1967. Involvement as a determinant of response to favorable and unfavorable information. *Journal of Personality and Social Psychology,* Monograph Suppl., 7: 1–15.

Eisenberg, P., & Lazarsfeld, P.F. 1938. The psychological effects of unemployment. *Psychological Bulletin* 35: 358–90.

Greenberg, J., & Ornstein, S. 1983. High status job title as compensation for underpayment: A test of equity theory. *Journal of Applied Psychology* 68: 285–97.

Jahoda, M. 1979. The impact of unemployment in the 1930s and the 1970s. *Bulletin of the British Psychological Society* 32: 309–14.

Kenrick, D.T., Reich, J.W., & Cialdini, R.B. 1976. Justification and compensation: Rosier skies for the devalued victim. *Journal of Personality and Social Psychology* 34: 654–57.

Lerner, M.J. 1975. The justice motive in social behavior: Introduction. *Journal of Social Issues* 31: 1–20.

Lloyd, K., & Brockner, J. 1985. *Self-esteem and self-perceived attractiveness: Separating fact from fantasy.* Manuscript submitted for publication.

Lloyd, K., Paulsen, J., & Brockner, J. 1983. The effects of self-esteem and self-consciousness on interpersonal attraction. *Personality and Social Psychology Bulletin* 9: 397–404.

Mowday, R.T. 1979. Equity theory predictions of behavior in organizations. In R.M. Steers & L.W. Porter (Eds.), *Motivation and work behavior* (pp. 124–46). New York: McGraw-Hill.

Reis, H.T., & Burns, L.B. 1982. The salience of the self in response to inequity. *Journal of Experimental Social Psychology* 18: 464–75.

Robinson, J.R., & Shaver, P.R. 1973. *Measures of social psychological attitudes.* Ann Arbor, MI: Institute for Social Research.

Tornow, W.W. 1971. The development and application of an input–outcome moderator test on the perception and reduction of inequity. *Organizational Behavior and Human Performance* 6: 614–38.

Vecchio, R.P. 1981. An individual differences interpretation of the conflicting predictions generated by equity theory and expectancy theory. *Journal of Applied Psychology* 66: 470–81.

15

Job Insecurity: Toward Conceptual Clarity

Leonard Greenhalgh

Zehava Rosenblatt

Four recent phenomena in the United States have made job insecurity a particularly important variable for organizational scholars to understand. First, the prolonged economic downturn beginning in the mid-1970s resulted in the highest rates of job loss since the Great Depression of the 1930s. Second, there has been an upsurge of mergers and acquisitions since the mid-1960s. These events often result in job loss or a curtailment in the privileges and expectations of job incumbents. Third, the rapidly changing industrial structure — from a predominantly manufacturing economy to a service economy and from the predominance of basic industries to the rise of high-technology industries — has changed many people's assumptions about the stability of their employers. Fourth, the trend toward decreasing union representation of the U.S. workforce means that an increasing number of workers are vulnerable to the effects of unilateral decisions from which they have little recourse.

These phenomena can be threatening to workers. The threat is experienced as some degree of job insecurity, which is defined as perceived powerlessness to maintain desired continuity in a threatened job situation. Furthermore, workers react to job insecurity, and their reactions have consequences for organizational effectiveness.

Despite its increasing importance, job insecurity has yet to receive significant attention from organizational researchers. The variable has been included as a facet of job satisfaction in numerous studies — for example, Hackman and Oldham (1974) — but few scales have been specifically developed to investigate the importance of the construct per se. Perhaps the best attempt to measure the construct is the Caplan scale (Caplan, Cobb, French, Van Harrison, & Pinneau, 1975). This scale spans only a small portion of the content do-

Reprinted with permission from *Academy of Management Review*, Vol. 9, © 1984 *Academy of Management Review*.

main, has undergone almost no psychometric development, and has seen little use. In addition to the limitations of the available measurement techniques, there have been limitations in the range of organizational conditions under which the impact of job insecurity has been measured. Specifically, because of ease of access there has been a tendency to conduct research in well-managed, healthy organizations in which the job-insecurity construct would have been of limited concern to employees and would have shown limited variability. Thus it is not surprising that job insecurity has never become adequately recognized as an important construct in organizational psychology.

This paper takes a step toward increasing knowledge about individuals' responses to organizational situations in which continuity is threatened. The paper has four purposes: (1) to correct conceptual inadequacies evident in past research involving the job insecurity construct, (2) to specify the content domain of the construct, (3) to show how individual differences moderate how people experience and react to job insecurity, and (4) to identify those reactions. A model is presented (see Figure 1) to help organize existing knowledge and to suggest a research agenda for systematically investigating this important but neglected topic.

Although job insecurity per se has received little attention, the more generic concept of security has been a prominent concern of organizational behaviorists and psychologists. Theorists have focused on security either as part of a press/need duality (Murray, 1938), as part of a personality theory (Blatz, 1966; Sullivan, 1964) or as a motivation theory (Maslow, 1954). Not surprisingly, there has been little consistency in what the construct denotes in the literature. For instance, Maslow uses the terms safety and security interchangeably. He defines safety as "security, stability, dependency, protection, freedom from fear...need for structure, order..." (1954, p. 39). Whereas Blatz (1966) contrasts safety and security, he views security in terms of independence and describes it as the antithesis of safety.

Lines of Inquiry

Amid this conceptual diversity, three lines of inquiry have emerged that have been particularly influential in shaping theory and research relevant to security in organizations. These lines of inquiry can be identified with the works of Maslow, Herzberg, and Super. Maslow's need hierarchy was not conceived as a theory of behavior in an organizational context, but Maslow himself suggested its applicability to organizational settings: "We can perceive the expressions of safety needs...in such phenomena as...the common preference for a job with tenure and protection" (1954, p. 87). Maslow's theory proved appealing to scholars of the human relations school and was widely adopted. Most applications of the need hierarchy appearing the literature, however, have been normative rather than empirical. The most widely used operationalization of the need hierarchy is that of Porter (1961), which accommodates both the need and the experience dimensions. Others have expanded on Porter's operationalization of job security to include variables such as interference with one's personal life and obsolescence of skills (Mitchell & Moudgill, 1976).

Another body of literature, reflecting a different approach, involves Herzberg's two-factor theory (Herzberg, Mausner, & Snyderman, 1959). In contrast to Maslow's view of security as a motivator, Herzberg considers security an extrinsic hygiene factor (along with such job properties as salary and working conditions). Herzberg also incorporates the dual need-experience dimensions, referring to job security as both a first level factor (an objective aspect of the situation that can be experienced) and a second level factor (the meaning of events for the individual, with meaning partly determined by needs). He defines job security "to include those features of the job situation which lead to assurance for continued employment, either within the same company or within the same type of work or profession" (Herzberg et al., 1959, p. 41). This definition focuses on continuity of employment as the main core of job security. It also suggests a useful distinction between organizational security and occupational or professional security. Herzberg's content analysis of interview data showed that job security was the most important extrinsic factor, but his approach has since been discredited (House & Wigdor, 1967; Vroom, 1964).

Borgatta's (1967) notion of the "play-safe and security complex" was directly inspired by Herzberg. A secure job was defined as something "easy and pleasant to do, that would provide a good life for. . . family, and sufficient comfort and leisure" (Borgatta, Ford, & Bohrnstedt, 1973). Borgatta's conceptualization contrasts job security with work orientation. His theory is somewhat normative. For example, he claims "it is questionable that the person is operating properly from the point of view of organized society. . . if he deliberately and methodically calculates all his actions to maximize playing safe and being secure" (1967, p. 3).

Super viewed security as ". . . one of the dominant needs and one of the principal reasons for working" (1957, p. 13). He incorporated the construct into his occupational development theory. He observed that the subjective meaning attributed to security varies but the main components of job security are always the same, namely, seniority and a stable company.

Rosenberg (1957) studied the occupational values of college students and concluded that job security is based on a broader economic orientation. His view is consistent with Super's (1970) work values inventory in which security concerns economic returns. It is also consistent with Herzberg's two-factor theory.

Blum (1960) continued this line of inquiry, identifying job security as a major factor in occupational choice. He constructed a security scale based on 19 theoretically derived subdomains of job security such as a preference for physical safety, dependence on rules, and adequate job training. This scale was validated against two subscales of the Edwards (1957) personal preference schedule: desire for order and avoidance of change. Blum's (1975) subsequent findings support Super's

theory in that they demonstrate the relationship between security tendencies and occupational orientations.

Beyond these major lines of inquiry, numerous studies have related job security to different organizational phenomena. These include organizational climate (Boss, Allhiser, & Voorhis, 1979), job enrichment (Fein, 1974), risk taking (Williams, 1965), job satisfaction (Schaffer, 1953), and unionization and politicization of professionals (Greenwald, 1978). The diversity of these studies reflects a body of knowledge that is slowly proliferating rather than systematically building. To achieve orderly progress, the meaning and content of this concept must be clarified.

This paper seeks to clarify the meaning of the job insecurity construct and to specify its content domain. A model of the nature, causes and consequences of job insecurity is presented. It is based on the results of a program of research in declining organizations and a review of the relevant literature. The model (Figure 1) attempts to reconcile and integrate the diversity in the existing literature. It focuses on job insecurity as an environmental *press* — an experienced characteristic of the individual's work environment. The *need* for security is explicitly included as an individual difference dimension moderating individuals' perceptions of threat and their reactions to it. Although the model is explained as it pertains to a declining organization in which employees may anticipate shrinkage of the work force, it is equally applicable to individual's experience of job insecurity when there is no group-wide threat. This might include a young executive in a selective retention system or a junior faculty member facing a tenure decision.

Individual's Experience of Job Insecurity

What the individual perceives as potential loss of continuity in a job situation can span the range from permanent loss of the job itself to loss of some subjectively important feature of the job.

Figure 1. Summary of the Causes, Nature, Effects, and Organizational Consequences of Job Insecurity

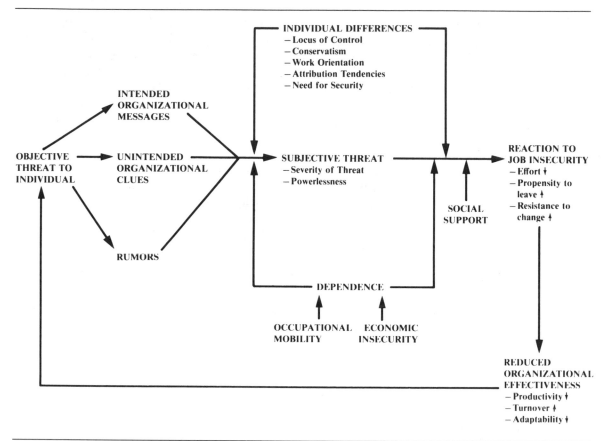

Job insecurity occurs only in the case of involuntary loss. For example, having left a job by choice, an individual might have given up valued job features and might consequently experience a sense of loss. However, this individual would not be powerless to maintain continuity, and therefore would not experience job insecurity as it is presently defined.

Figure 1 shows that subjective threat is derived from objective threat by means of the individual's perceptual processes, which transform environmental data into information used in thought processes (Thayer, 1967). Employees have three basic sources of data, each of which requires interpretation. The first source is official organiza-

tional announcements. These typically are minimal during times of change (Jick & Greenhalgh, 1981) and tend to be viewed by employees as rhetorical rather than factual. They are designed to shape employees' perceptions in a way that serves organizational interests. The second source—unintended organizational clues evident to employees—includes data that are not mediated by power elites. For example, the reduction of a plant maintenance budget may be interpreted as evidence of an impending plant closing. Rumors are the third data source. They abound during times of threat, especially when official messages are scarce. Given the scope of the objective data to which employees might attend, it is not surprising that employees vary widely in their assessment of subjective threat.

Little research attention has been given to the process of threat perception or to the nature of the threat perceived. Instead, job insecurity usually has been conceptualized and measured as a simple global variable. For example, in the Job Diagnostic Survey (Hackman & Oldham, 1974) respondents are asked, "How satisfied are you with . . .the amount of job security [you] have?" The danger of using only a global measure of a complex variable is that different respondents may use the same response to refer to quite different aspects of the phenomenon. The threats to the scientific and organizational usefulness of data thus obtained are obvious and serious.

A search of the literature and the authors' field research reveal that the subjective threat involved in job insecurity is multifaceted. It cannot be captured by a global variable. The facets can be grouped into two basic dimensions: the severity of the threat to one's job and powerlessness to counteract the threat.

Severity of Threat

The severity of the threat to continuity in a work situation depends on the scope and importance of the potential loss and the subjective probability of the loss occurring. The scope of potential loss is shown in Table 1. Important distinctions to jobholders include: (1) whether the anticipated loss is temporary or permanent; (2) whether the action causing the loss is layoff or firing (these are subjectively different forms of job loss in that they probably involve different patterns of attribution); and (3) whether the change represents loss of the job itself or loss of job features.

Loss of valued job features is an important but often overlooked aspect of job insecurity. The phenomenon is experienced as a type of job loss inasmuch as it involves losing the job as the affected employee currently knows it. The threat is less severe because organizational membership — and all that such membership means to the individual — is not lost. The job features principally

associated with job insecurity are listed in the second subsection of Table 1.

Career progress is perceived to be in jeopardy when the jobholder anticipates that organizational changes will impose new ceilings on intraorganizational mobility. This, in turn, may represent to the jobholder an abrogation of the psychological contract (Schein, 1965) whereby the expected organizational career (Milkovich, Anderson, & Greenhalgh, 1976) appears suddenly to become limited; or it may represent a frustrating barrier to pursuing a personal career (Martin & Schermerhorn, 1983). An anticipated curtailment of income expectations also may violate the psychological contract. The visualized loss may be an actual pay cut, or it may be a shrinking of expected future raises. Sometimes the employee's focus is on the potential loss of less tangible properties of jobs. An anticipated organizational change could involve a loss of status for the individual, less autonomy, or fewer resources. The severity of the anticipated loss experience would be proportional to the valence of each to the individual. Finally, employees may worry about the loss of community occurring when their work groups are fragmented or traumatized.

The subjective probability of the loss occurring depends on the nature and number of sources of threats to continuity. The principal sources of threat are identified in Table 1. The most important source of threat is organizational decline. Employees usually know when an organization is in decline, that is, when it has become maladapted to its niche (Greenhalgh, 1983). They also know that maladaptation often leads to organizational shrinkage and other adjustments that are likely to affect the continuity of their current job situations.

Similar fears can be evoked by the anticipation of a reorganization. Most employees are familiar with instances (real and fictitious) of the elimination of positions during organization-wide or subunit reorganizations, or with the elimination of job features existing prior to the reorganization. Changes in the organization's technology that are perceived as reducing the demand for the employee's skills also produce subjective threat, especially

Table 1. Dimensions of Job Insecurity and Their Inclusion in Reported Studies

						Studies					
			1	2	3	4	5	6	7	8	9
Nature of loss	Lose present job	Indefinite job loss		X	X						
		Temporary job loss		X	X						
		Demotion to another job within organization									
	Keep present job but lose job features	Career progress		X			X	X	X	X	
		Income stream	X	X			X		X	X	
		Status/self-esteem			X				X	X	
		Autonomy									
		Resources									
		Community		X			X		X		
	Sources of threat	Decline/shrinkage		X	X			X	X		
		Reorganization				X		X			
		Technological change									
		Physical danger		X			X				X
	Powerlessness	Lack of protection		X					X		
		Unclear expectancies				X	X				
		Authoritarian environment		X		X	X			X	
		Dismissal.standard operating procedures		X		X	X	X			X

Key: 1 = Schaffer (1953)
2 = Thompson & Davis (1956)
3 = Herzberg et al. (1957)
4 = Harrison (1960)
5 = Blum (1960)
6 = Goldthorpe et al. (1968)
7 = Borgatta et al. (1968); see also Miskel & Heller (1973)
8 = Caplan et al. (1975)
9 = Mitchell & Moudgill (1976)

Severity of threat

Nature of loss

in the absence of retraining opportunities. The threat usually involves loss of the job itself. Finally, some jobs are dangerous, and the threat of injury jeopardizes the continuity of a job situation. Physical danger is not a concern in all job situations. But if it is of concern, physical danger can be an important aspect of job insecurity and therefore needs to be included in the model.

Powerlessness to Counteract the Threat

The sense of powerlessness is an important element of job insecurity because it exacerbates the experienced threat. Powerlessness can take four basic forms, as noted in Table 1. The first form is lack of protection. Unions, seniority systems, and employment contracts are forms of protection serving to boost the individual's power to resist threats to continuity.

The second factor contributing to a sense of powerlessness is unclear expectancies (Porter & Lawler, 1968). For example, the employee may perceive a threat to continuity but may not know what achieved performance is necessary to maintain status in a job. The perceived lack of an adequate performance appraisal system is often the specific cause of unclear expectancies. The sense of powerlessness arises because the employee does not know what corrective action to take to avert the perceived threat.

The culture of the organization also is likely to influence the employee's sense of powerlessness to maintain desired continuity. An authoritarian culture, for instance, would provide little comfort. The employee's sense of powerlessness would be exacerbated if: (1) the organization had no strong norms of fairness; (2) the employee had no input into decisions and no right of appeal; and (3) superiors were seen as arbitrary in their evaluations and even capricious in their decisions affecting employees.

The fourth factor affecting powerlessness is the employee's beliefs about the organization's standard operating procedures for dismissing employees. In the case of firing, the absence of policies such as progressive discipline and automatic review of a decision to fire makes the employee feel very much at the mercy of the superior. In the case of work force reductions, many organizations resort to layoff as a standard operating procedure without seriously considering such alternatives as attrition, early retirement, and work sharing (Greenhalgh & McKersie, 1980; Shultz & Weber, 1966). Employees' beliefs are derived from knowledge of actual policies, inference from practice, and observation of events in other organizations.

Operationalizing Job Insecurity

To possess adequate content validity, a measure of job insecurity would have to encompass both the severity of the threat and the employee's sense of powerlessness to avert the anticipated loss. Table 1 summarizes the content domain of the construct and shows that no existing measure even approaches operational adequacy. As a result, the current potential for scientifically conclusive or organizationally useful research is limited.

The two basic dimensions of job insecurity are related multiplicatively, as follows: felt job insecurity = perceived severity of threat × perceived powerlessness to resist threats. The relationship is multiplicative in the sense that if either of the two factors is insignificant, the degree of experienced job insecurity also is insignificant. In practical terms, this relationship implies that separate scores have to be calculated for each dimension.

Assessment of threat severity ideally would encompass: (1) the range of work situation features that could be in jeopardy; (2) the valence of each such feature; (3) the subjective probability of losing each feature; and (4) the number of sources of threat. Assessment of powerlessness would encompass the number of areas in which the respondent experienced a power deficit.

The ideal operationalization suggested by the model would not be as simple as researchers might prefer. But its content validity would be adequate, which is not true of currently available operational definitions. The construct and face validity of such a measure also would be high. This is because the operationalization would correspond closely to the job security concerns expressed in interviews with workers. Existing measures are suspect particularly because they solicit summary judgments using a complex construct, as noted earlier. Two employees reporting their jobs to be insecure may visualize vastly different contingencies.

Reactions to Job Insecurity

Job insecurity has not been extensively researched as an independent variable. Nevertheless, even with the use of fairly crude job insecurity scales, relationships have been documented between job insecurity and reduced work effort, propensity to leave, and resistance to change. Table 2 summarizes these findings. The findings involving propen-

Table 2. Reactions to Job Insecurity Reported in the Literature

Type of Reaction to Job Insecurity	Study
Effort	Beynon, 1973
	Greenhalgh, 1979; 1982
	Guest & Fatchett, 1974
	Hackman & Lawler, 1971[a]
	Hall & Mansfield, 1971[b]
	Hershey, 1972[c]
	Roethlisberger & Dickson, 1946
Propensity to Leave	Gow, Clark, & Dossett, 1974
	Greenhalgh, 1979; 1982
	Jick, 1979
	Ronan, 1967
	Smith & Kerr, 1953
	Stogdill, 1965
Resistance to Change	Fox & Staw, 1979
	Greenhalgh, 1979
	Rothman, Schwartzbaum, & McGrath, 1971

a. Did not reach significance.
b. No relationship found.
c. No relationship found, but study flawed; see Greenhalgh (1983).

sity to leave and resistance to change are consistent across studies. But the investigations involving work effort have shown mixed results (Greenhalgh, 1983). Further research is needed to identify the conditions under which work effort is reduced as a result of felt job insecurity.

These empirical findings are both interesting and important. The negative correlation found in some studies between job insecurity and work effort is interesting because it contradicts expectations. First, there is a widely held assumption that security and complacency are related. Second, it would be rational for employees who feel insecure to exert more effort in order to become more valuable to the organization and thereby reduce their objective job insecurity. The positive correlation between job insecurity and resistance to change also is of interest because it, too, appears to contradict rational behavior. Specifically, one would expect insecure employees to welcome adaptive change because it should make their jobs more secure by counteracting organizational decline (Greenhalgh, 1983). The positive correlation between job insecurity and propensity to leave is not unexpected. It would be rational for employees worried about continuity of employment to seek more secure career opportunities. However, this relationship is important because exits are not randomly distributed across employees. Rather, the most valuable employees tend to be the first to leave (Greenhalgh & Jick, 1979).

Such predispositions have behavioral manifestations. These in turn have organizational consequences in the form of impaired productivity, increased turnover, and barriers to adaptation. All of these reduce organizational effectiveness. This phenomenon is shown as a positive feedback loop in Figure 1; reduced organizational effectiveness increases objective job insecurity.

Three investigators have conducted empirical research that helps explain the mechanism underlying reactions to job security. The three go beyond noting the association of anxiety with nonrational behavior and focus on psychological withdrawal reactions to loss. Katcher (1978) found similar reactions to leaving a job, divorce, termination from psychotherapy, and terminal illness. His study did not differentiate voluntary and involuntary job leavers. Strange (1977) studied involuntary job loss resulting from a plant shutdown in a company town and reported that reactions to job loss were similar to reactions to death and dismemberment. Greenhalgh (1979) studied workers who had kept their jobs in a declining and shrinking organization in which others had been laid off. The anticipation of job loss produced the same reaction as an anticipated death. Workers begin the grieving process in anticipation of the loss and psychologically withdraw from the to-be-lost object, in this case the job.

The unconscious tendencies of anticipatory grieving may operate in conjunction with—or instead of—conscious rational tendencies that might explain the same behavior. The March and Simon (1958) framework, for instance, would categorize job insecurity as a reduced organizational inducement. Under their schema decreased effort and increased resistance to change would be categorized as reduced employee contributions. Increased propensity to leave would be considered reduced motivation to participate. However, the grief reaction has been shown to be a better predictor than the rational model (Greenhalgh, 1979).

Moderator Variables

Individual Differences

It is likely that individual differences moderate the relationship between experienced job insecurity and individuals' reactions to it. Specifically, people with personality characteristics that give them an aversion to job insecurity would react more strongly to encountering it. Five personality traits are hypothesized to be moderators.

First, job insecurity is defined in terms of powerlessness. Powerlessness is likely to bother individuals whose locus of control (Rotter, 1966) is internal rather than external. Second, the referent of powerlessness is the maintenance of situational continuity. Conservative individuals are more likely to be averse to loss of continuity than

are their less conservative counterparts. Third, the referent of continuity is the work situation. Individuals differ in the importance they attribute to their work situations. It is logical to hypothesize that job insecurity would evoke stronger reactions in individuals for whom the work situation is more important. The differential importance could arise from work values. For some individuals work ranks high among their central life interests (Dubin & Champoux, 1977); for others work does not. Fourth, individuals differ in their attribution tendencies. Those who tend to blame themselves for their perceived vulnerability to organizational career discontinuity are hypothesized to have stronger reactions than are those who tend to place the blame external to themselves. The fifth personality dimension is the most obvious. Some individuals have a high need for security (Blum, 1960; Murray, 1938) and therefore would be the most averse to any form of impaired security.

The discussion thus far has focused on the obvious moderating effect of individual differences whereby insecurity-averse individuals have the stronger reactions to perceived threats (Bhagat, 1983). The less obvious moderating effect is in the arousal of perceptual defenses. Insecurity-averse individuals are the more likely to block out threatening objective data (see Figure 1). The dual moderating effects tend to be mutually exclusive. If insecurity aversion leads to perceptual defense, there will be little perceived threat to which to react. If insecurity aversion leads to stronger reactions, threat must have been perceived. A theory of job insecurity needs to specify when one moderating effect is likely to predominate over the other. It is hypothesized that the greater the equivocality in the objective data, the greater the tendency to favor perceptual defense.

No studies were located in the literature investigating these hypotheses per se. However, one study conducted in a declining and shrinking organization shows the dual effects of individual differences. Greenhalgh and Jick (1983) studied individuals' experiences of and reactions to role ambiguity and ambiguity concerning the organization's future. There was objective ambiguity in both because the organization was declining and the process of retrenchment had caused widespread role upheaval. Individual differences in tolerance for ambiguity were measured. The aversion to ambiguity did produce stronger reactions to perceived ambiguity. It also apparently aroused perceptual defenses whereby ambiguity-averse individuals proved to be less likely to perceive objective ambiguity.

Dependence

The experience and impact of job insecurity should similarly be moderated by demographic characteristics, particularly individuals' dependencies on their current jobs. Dependence in this context is a function of occupational mobility and economic insecurity. Individuals who have an occupation offering mobility are less concerned with the stability of a particular job than are employees who have fewer alternatives. Economic insecurity is the inability to meet living expenses without the income from the current job. Operationally, dependence arises when: (1) individuals' skills are in low demand in the labor market (for example, because of changing technology or high relative supply); (2) the current job yields a high proportion of the family income; (3) individuals face high fixed obligations; and (4) supplementary sources of income—such as unemployment compensation, continued health insurance, and pension benefits—are unavailable or uncertain. Individuals who are highly dependent on their current job are more likely to engage in defensive sensemaking and to react more strongly to perceived threat.

Social Support

Social support also is hypothesized as a moderator variable. It is likely to affect only individuals' reactions to perceived threat. Considerable evidence of the moderating effect of social support in coping with adversity is reported (Beehr, 1976; Blau, 1981; LaRocco, House, & French, 1980; Seers, McGee, Serey, & Graen, 1983). Specifically, social support somehow increases the individual's ability to cope with stressful organizational situations by buffering the individual's life outside the organization.

A Research Agenda

Due to recent environmental events, U.S. workers are and will continue to be less complacent about job security. The nature, effects, and moderators of job insecurity are not well understood. But the consequences of job security for organizations are known to be considerable. Thus it is time to embark on a systematic investigation of the phenomenon. The investigation, in its exploratory phase, should be guided by the model summarized in Figure 1. Five components should receive high priority.

Development of a Job Insecurity Scale

A comprehensive instrument needs to be developed that spans the domain of the construct. This instrument would have to encompass the dimensions listed in Table 1 to have adequate content validity. Less comprehensive measures during the exploratory stage of research might miss important aspects of job insecurity.

Mapping of the Causes

Little is understood about the linkage between job insecurity and subjectively experienced job insecurity. In essence, this linkage involves perceptual processes that could be addressed from the perspective of communication theory (Thayer, 1967) or of classical social psychology. The perceptual processes are complicated by the effects of grieving on information processing (for example, denial) that attend the loss of any important object. The perceptual processes also are complicated by differential attention given to official organizational messages, evidence not deliberately communicated to organizational members, and rumors. Finally, they are complicated by individual differences in tolerance for security-threatening data.

Identification of the Reactions

Table 2 shows that very little research has been undertaken to identify relationships between job insecurity and individual reactions. Development of an adequate job insecurity scale obviously will foster such research. Much of this research will have to be conducted in organizations in which there is high objective threat of job loss. These organizations tend to be reluctant to grant research access, but they must be studied to ensure adequate variance in objective job insecurity.

Investigation of Individual Differences

The five individual difference variables included in Figure 1 are obvious first targets for investigation. Other organizationally important personality traits, such as cognitive abilities and need for achievement, also are worth investigating. The same individual difference variable can have a moderating effect at more than one point in the causal chain. Thus, complex statistical analysis such as multiple moderator regression may be necessary to identify the nature of moderating effects with accuracy.

Understanding the Positive Feedback Loop

Individual reactions have consequences for organizational effectiveness. Reduced organizational effectiveness further increases the objective threat of job loss. This, in turn, tends to increase job insecurity. This relationship (see Figure 1) is only one of several positive feedback loops accelerating organizational decline (Greenhalgh, 1983). It is essential that organizational researchers and managers understand feedback relationships. This is because intervention to arrest the decline of an organization requires cutting these feedback loops. In most organizations the positive feedback loop involving job insecurity and workers' reactions to it is the most important one.

References

Beehr, T.A. 1976. Perceived situational moderators of the relationship between subjective role ambiguity and strain. *Journal of Applied Psychology* 61: 35–40.

Beynon, H. 1973. *Working for Ford.* London: Allen Lane.

Bhagat, R.S. 1983. Effects of stressful life events on individual performance effectiveness and work adjustment processes within organizational settings: A research model. *Academy of Management Review* 8: 660–71.

Blatz, W.E. 1966. *Human security,* Toronto: University of Toronto Press.

Blau, G. 1981. An empirical investigation of job stress, social support, service length, and job strain. *Organizational Behavior and Human Performance* 27: 279–302.

Blum, S.H. 1960. *Security in vocational choice: A study of male college upper-classmen.* Unpublished doctoral dissertation, Columbia University.

Blum, S.H. 1975. The desire for security in vocational choice: A comparison of men and women. *Journal of Psychology* 94: 87–91.

Borgatta, E.F. 1967. The work components study: A set of measures for work motivation. *Journal of Psychological Studies* 15: 1–11.

Borgatta, E.F., Ford, R.N., & Bohrnstedt, G.W. 1968. The work components study (WCS): A revised set of measures for work motivation. *Multivariate Behavioral Research* 3: 403–14.

Borgatta, E.F., Ford, R.N., & Bohrnstedt, G.W. 1973. Work orientation vs. hygienic orientation: A bipolar approach to the study of work motivation. *Journal of Vocational Behavior* 3: 253–68.

Boss, R.W., Allhiser, G.W., & Voorhis, D.J. 1979. The impact of pay and job security on organizational climate. *Journal of Police Science and Administration* 7: 361–67.

Caplan, R.D., Cobb, S., French, J.R.P., Jr., Van Harrison, R., & Pinneau, S.R., Jr. 1975. *Job demands and worker health.* Washington, D.C.: U.S. Department of Health, Education, and Welfare, National Institute for Occupational Safety and Health.

Dubin, R.L., & Champoux, J.E. 1977. Central life interests and job satisfaction. *Organizational Behavior and Human Performance* 18: 366–77.

Edwards, A.L. 1957. *Manual of the Edwards Personal Preference Schedule.* New York: Psychological Corporation.

Fein, M. 1974. Job enrichment: A reevaluation. *Sloan Management Review* 15(2): 69–88.

Fox, F.V., & Staw, B.M. 1979. The trapped administrator: Effects of job insecurity and policy resistance upon commitment to a course of action. *Administrative Science Quarterly* 24: 449–71.

Goldthorpe, J.H., Lockwood, D., Bechhofer, F., & Platt, J. 1968. *The affluent worker: Industrial attitudes and behavior.* Cambridge, England: Cambridge University Press.

Gow, J.S., Clark, A.W., & Dossett, G.S. 1974. A path analysis of variables influencing labor turnover. *Human Relations* 27: 703–19.

Greenhalgh, L. 1979. *Job security and the disinvolvement syndrome: An exploration of patterns of worker behavior under conditions of anticipatory grieving over job loss.* Unpublished doctoral dissertation, Cornell University.

Greenhalgh, L. 1982. Maintaining organizational effectiveness during organizational retrenchment. *Journal of Applied Behavioral Science* 18: 155–70.

Greenhalgh, L. 1983. Organizational decline. In S.B. Bacharach (Ed.), *Research in the sociology of organizations* (Vol. 2), pp. 231–76. Greenwich, Conn.: JAI Press.

Greenhalgh, L., & Jick, T.D. 1979. The relationship between job insecurity and turnover, and its differential effects on employee quality level. Paper presented at the Annual Meeting of the Academy of Management, Atlanta.

Greenhalgh, L., & Jick, T.D. 1983. The phenomenology of sensemaking in a declining organization: Effects of individual differences. Paper presented at the Annual Meeting of the Academy of Management, Dallas.

Greenhalgh, L., & McKersie, R.B. 1980. Cost effectiveness of alternative strategies for cutback management. *Public Administration Review* 40: 299–303.

Greenwald, H.P. 1978. Politics and the new insecurity: Ideological changes of professionals in a recession. *Social Forces* 57: 103–18.

Guest, D., & Fatchett, D. 1974. *Worker participation: Individual control and performance.* London: Institute of Personnel Management.

Hackman, J.R., & Lawler, E.E., III. 1971. Employee reactions to job characteristics. *Journal of Applied Psychology* 55: 259–86.

Hackman, J.R., & Oldham, G.R. 1974. The Job Diagnostic Survey: An instrument for the diagnosis of jobs and the evaluation of job redesign projects. Technical Report No. 4, Department of Administrative Sciences, Yale University.

Hall, D.T., & Mansfield, R. 1971. Organizational and individual response to external stress. *Administrative Science Quarterly* 16: 533–47.

Harrison, R. 1960. Sources of variation in managers' job attitudes. *Personnel Psychology* 13: 425–34.

Hershey, R. 1972. Effects of anticipated job loss on employee behavior. *Journal of Applied Psychology* 56: 273–75.

Herzberg, F., Mausner, B., & Snyderman, B.B. 1959. *The motivation to work.* New York: Wiley.

Herzberg, F., Mausner, B., Peterson, R.O., & Capwell, D.F. 1957. *Job attitudes: Review of research and opinion.* Pittsburgh: Psychological Service of Pittsburgh.

House, R.J., & Wigdor, L.A. 1967. Herzberg's dual-factor theory of job satisfaction and motivation: A review of the evidence and a criticism. *Personnel Psychology* 20: 369–90.

Jick, T.D. 1979. *Process and impacts of a merger: Individual and organizational perspectives.* Unpublished doctoral dissertation, Cornell University.

Jick, T.D., & Greenhalgh, L. 1981. Information processing of new recruits in a declining organization. Paper presented at the Annual Meeting of the Academy of Management, San Diego.

Katcher, B.L. 1978. An analysis and review of three literatures relevant to the study of the psychological experiences of individuals leaving jobs: Marital separation and divorce; termination from psychotherapy; and the experience of the terminally ill patient. Working paper, University of Maryland, Department of Psychology.

LaRocco, J.M., House, S., & French, J.R.P, Jr. 1980. Social support, occupational stress, and health. *Journal of Health and Social Behavior* 21: 202–18.

March, J.G., & Simon, H.A. 1958. *Organizations.* New York: Wiley.

Martin, T.N., & Schermerhorn, J.R., Jr. 1983. Work and nonwork influences on health: A research agenda using inability to leave as a crucial variable. *Academy of Management Review* 8: 650–59.

Maslow, A.H. 1954. *Motivation and personality.* New York: Harper.

Milkovich, G.T., Anderson, J.C., & Greenhalgh, L. 1976. Organizational careers: Environmental, organizational, and individual determinants. In L. Dyer (Ed.), *Careers in organizations: Individual planning and organizational development,* pp. 17–30. Ithaca, N.Y.: N.Y. State School of Industrial & Labor Relations, Cornell University.

Miskel, C., & Heller, L. 1973. The educational work components study: An adapted set of measures for work motivation. *Journal of Experimental Education* 42: 45–50.

Mitchell, V.F., & Moudgill, P. 1976. Measurement of Maslow's need hierarchy. *Organizational Behavior and Human Performance* 16: 334–49.

Murray, H.A., Barret, W.G., Homburger, E., et al. 1938. *Explorations in personality: Clinical and experimental study of fifty men of college age, by workers at the Harvard psychological clinic.* New York: Oxford Press.

Porter, L.W. 1961. A study of perceived need satisfactions in bottom and middle management jobs. *Journal of Applied Psychology* 45: 1–10.

Porter, L.W., & Lawler, E.E., III. 1968. *Managerial attitudes and performance.* Homewood, Ill.: Irwin.

Roethlisberger, F.J., & Dickson, W.J. 1946. *Management and the worker.* Cambridge, Mass.: Harvard University Press.

Ronan, W.W. 1967. A study of and some concepts concerning labor turnover. *Occupational Psychology* 41: 193–202.

Rosenberg, M. 1957. *Occupations and values.* Glencoe, Ill.: Free Press.

Rothman, R.A., Schwartzbaum, A.M., & McGrath, J.H., III. 1971. Physicians and a hospital merger: Patterns of resistance to organizational change. *Journal of Health and Social Behavior* 12: 46–55.

Rotter, J.B. 1966. Generalized expectancies for internal versus external control of reinforcement. *Psychological Monographs* 80: 1–28.

Schaffer, R.H. 1953. Job satisfaction as related to need satisfaction in work. *Psychological Monographs* 67: 1–29.

Schein, E.H. 1965. *Organizational psychology.* Englewood Cliffs, N.J.: Prentice-Hall.

Seers, A., McGee, G.W., Serey, T.T., & Graen, G.B. 1983. The interaction of job stress and social support: A strong inference investigation. *Academy of Management Journal* 26: 273–84.

Shultz, G.P., & Weber, A.R. 1966. *Strategies for the displaced worker.* Westport, Conn.: Greenwood Press.

Smith, F.J., & Kerr, W.A. 1953. Turnover factors as assessed by the exit interview. *Journal of Applied Psychology* 37: 352–55.

Stogdill, R.M. 1965. *Managers, employees, organizations.* Columbus, Ohio: Ohio State University Press.

Strange, W.G. 1977. *Job loss: A psychological study of worker reactions to a plant-closing in a company town in southern Appalachia.* Unpublished doctoral dissertation, Cornell University.

Sullivan, H.S. 1964. *The fusion of psychiatry and social science.* New York: Norton.

Super, D.E. 1957. *The psychology of careers.* New York: Harper & Brothers.

Super, D.E. 1970. *Work values inventory manual.* Boston: Houghton Mifflin.

Thayer, L. 1967. Communication and organization theory. In F.E.X. Dance (Ed.), *Human communication theory,* pp. 70–115. New York: Holt, Rinehart & Winston.

Thompson, A.S., & Davis, J.A. 1956. What workers mean by security. *Personnel Psychology* 9: 229–41.

Vroom, V.H. 1964. *Work and motivation.* New York: Wiley.

Williams, L.K. 1965. Some correlates of risk taking. *Personnel Psychology* 18: 297–310.

PART IV

Normative Foundations: Adaptation to Decline

The order of the parts of this book accurately represents the evolution of work on the topic of organizational decline. Early theoretical work was followed by empirical research, and only recently have suggestions on how to manage decline appeared in the literature. Indeed, there is such a paucity of normative articles written on this subject that we have included several research and theory pieces in this part. They are distinguished from similar works in the previous parts of the book by their focus on specific responses to decline.

The chapters emphasizing managerial responses to decline fall roughly into two categories. Section A focuses on recovery and turnaround strategies. The assumption is that declining resources have created a mandate for organizational change, and counsel for how to capitalize on that support is offered. These chapters tend to focus on the private sector, since business managers operating in a market environment have both the incentive and latitude to adapt to changing external conditions.

Section B concentrates on downsizing and retrenchment strategies as well as on the management of organizational death. Here we see a much stronger public-sector orientation, since administrators in these organizations have fewer strategic options, but also less chance of going out of business. Consequently, it is important for them to know how to adjust their manpower levels to fluctuations in funding. However, retrenchment is certainly not peculiar to the public sector. With large manufacturing firms announcing layoffs numbering in the tens of thousands at a time, it is critical that business managers understand the tradeoffs associated with various downsizing strategies.

Despite their best efforts to cut costs, many organizations do not survive severe financial crises. Therefore, the last chapter in this part addresses the effective management of organizational death. The assumption here is that the strategies outlined previously have not worked, so the organization must be shut down or sold. This can happen through divestiture, involving the sale of a piece of an organization, bankruptcy, or a plant or program closeout. Shutting down an operation might seem deceptively straightforward and simple, but for those managers who are concerned about the impact of their actions on terminated employees and their families, the fortunes of the host community, and the image of the parent organization, the effective management of organizational death is both extremely important and very difficult.

In Section A, the three chapters represent very different perspectives. The first chapter by Donald C. Hambrick and Steven M. Schecter is a large-scale research study of the short-term turnaround attempts of 260 business units in mature industrial-product corporations. Using the PIMS database, they found that efficiency-oriented moves were more successful than entrepreneurial initiatives, for example, developing new products. The authors isolated three types of successful turnaround gestalts: asset/cost surgery, selective product/market pruning, and piecemeal moves. Further, they found that asset/cost reductions were generally utilized by businesses with low levels of capacity utilization; selective product/market pruning was undertaken primarily by businesses with high levels of capacity utilization; and the piecemeal strategy was followed primarily by businesses with high market share. Although this study does not focus on normative prescriptions, it is an important extension of the line of thinking begun by Hofer and Schendel. In early articles these authors argued that successful turnaround strategies were closely linked to the causes of organizational decline. That is, a strategic response is most appropriate when dealing with strategic problems, and operational approaches are best suited for falling profits stemming from internal inefficiencies. This line of thought serves as the foundation for a widely held view of how *not* to effectively manage decline, namely, do not respond to an effectiveness problem with an efficiency solution.

The second chapter in this section is the most normative. It reports the condensed experiences the authors, Paul C. Nystrom and William H. Starbuck, have had examining a multitude of declining firms. The pattern they observed in these studies was so consistent that they labeled it the "success-breeds-failure syndrome," characterized by overconfidence following an era of substantial organizational prosperity. The organization has done so well that management feels it is no longer necessary to closely monitor environmental changes. The tendency to discount evidence of impending, serious problems leaves the organization vulnerable to new competition or technological revolutions. To avoid this cycle, mature organizations are encouraged to "unlearn," or in other words, not rely on tradition and precedent as standards for problemsolving.

The last chapter in Section A urges public administrators to shift their thinking from decrementalism to strategic thinking. Instead of accepting a passive response to declining revenues, program leaders are urged to become more aggressive in their strategic planning. Charles H. Levine notes the serious consequences that occur in organizations accepting cuts year after year, and draws upon the strategic planning literature in business administration for several recommendations to counter this process of accelerating decline. In particular, Levine argues in this chapter that managers should examine the match between their organizational strategy and key organizational and environmental contingencies. Next, the organization must develop a strategic capacity by considering innovative approaches to internal operations and the delivery of services. To do this, managers must avoid the trap of fiscal constrictions driving out innovative planning in the organization. The key ingredient in this approach is aggressive, innovative, global-thinking leadership.

The first chapter of Section B, by Robert D. Behn, continues this theme. He argues that managers have certain responsibilities during a period of retrenchment, including: deciding what to cut, maintaining morale, attracting and keeping quality people, and creating opportunities for innovation. He goes on to argue that these management initiatives will be successful only if management also exercises strong leadership during an organizational crisis. This includes forthrightly acknowledging and explaining the problem, seizing upon the short-term crisis to formulate a long-term strategy for organizational improvement, creating incentives for cooperation through the transition period, and finally, demonstrating compassion and concern for those adversely affected by the changing policies and priorities. One of the interesting features of this chapter is that Behn examines one of the challenging dilemmas embedded in the retrenchment process. This involves how soon managers should publicly acknowledge a serious financial problem. If they go public too soon they may unnecessarily erode internal, as well as public, confidence, and thus research on bankruptcy has consistently noted that a contributing factor to organizational failure is the reluctance of top management to acknowledge serious difficulties. By postponing public acknowledgment, they dissipated precious organizational slack, and found that by the time they could mobilize a concerted, systematic response, the problem had become unmanageable.

The next chapter, by Lee Tom Perry, focuses on a specific retrenchment management challenge: selecting a reduction-in-force strategy. Perry examines several alternatives. The first set of approaches is used in cases where management is convinced their business will turn around. These "survival" strategies include job sharing, leaves of absence, and pay cuts. A different set of strategies must be considered when the organization shifts directions, moving from one niche to another. In these cases management should consider "realignment" strategies, including early retirement incentives, intrafirm transfers, and rehiring selected individuals as consultants. After considering the pros and cons of various strategies, Perry concludes with a discussion of lifetime-employment programs. He argues that these are best suited for rapidly growing, rather than declining, industries. For businesses in the latter category, the best form of job security is firm-specific skills.

Cynthia Hardy's chapter expands the concept of retrenchment program costs. Whereas Perry examined the costs of alternative retrenchment strategies, Hardy proposes that any form of retrenchment can encounter inherent hidden costs if the retrenchment process is not managed effectively. Specifically, she argues that retrenchment as a piecemeal, one-shot response to cash-flow problems runs the risk of setting debilitating, long-term problems in motion. These include lower employee morale, union grievances, unfavorable publicity, and the loss of vital skills and experience. Consequently, this chapter argues that retrenchment strategies should be considered as an investment in the future, not as a knee-jerk reaction to past problems. To accomplish this, the organization must manage several key aspects of the retrenchment process, including awareness, involvement, equity, disclosure, and support.

Very little has been written about the effective management of organizational death and, consequently, myths about the topic abound. In his chapter, Robert I. Sutton debunks many common management beliefs about the reactions of employees once the plans to close down an operation are announced. These include: a drop in productivity, an increase in employee sabotage, the swift resignation of quality employees, and an increase in conflict. He also examines eight tasks that must be performed by management during the organizational-death process. These include disbanding, informing, blaming, inventing, and coping. He further points out that, when considered together, several of these steps create dilemmas for management. For example, should a manager accept or deflect blame for the events leading to organizational death? To what extent should a manager give hope versus take it away? How much information should be shared with the rest of the organization, as opposed to shielding them from the bad news? This chapter highlights the challenges faced by managers who must perform the unpleasant task of shutting down an organization.

16

Turnaround Strategies for Mature Industrial-Product Business Units

Donald C. Hambrick
Steven M. Schecter

There is an abundant folklore on how to revive poorly performing businesses, but systematic evidence about turnarounds is scant. Turnarounds are of increasing relevance. Global competition, technological turbulence, high costs of capital, and other nettlesome factors will cause more and more businesses to face occasional hard times. Businesses in mature industries face particularly difficult turnaround situations. Demand is flat, customer loyalties are relatively strong, and competition generally is zero-sum.

The purpose of this study is to examine the short term turnaround attempts of a sample of poorly performing mature business units. (The short term limitation is imposed by the data.) There are three primary research questions:

1. In general, which strategic moves are associated with turnaround success?
2. Are there any combinations of strategic moves, that is, strategics, that arc cspccially common routes back to profitability?
3. How do the operating and market positions of the business affect its choice of a turnaround strategy?

Naturally, the study does not address all facets of these questions. It is limited in its scope, on the premise that some systematic evidence — even if narrow — is what is needed now.

Theoretical Foundation

Three important pilot studies on turnarounds served as the key antecedents of this project: Schendel, Patten, and Riggs (1975); Hofer (1980); and Bibeault (1982). Some of the specific points in these studies will be drawn on below, but it is useful to summarize the three here.

The authors wish to acknowledge support from the Strategy Research Center at Columbia University's Graduate School of Business and the Strategic Planning Institute, Cambridge, Mass.

Reprinted with permission from *Academy of Management Journal,* Vol. 26, No. 2, © 1983 *Academy of Management Journal.*

Schendel et al. (1975) studied 54 firms that, based on Compustat data, had suffered four consecutive years of earnings decline and then four consecutive years of earnings improvement. Using business periodicals, the authors subjectively rated the causes of the declines and the actions accounting for the upturns and classified each as either "strategic" or "operating" in nature. On the basis of their admittedly "soft data," the authors generally found support for their theory: that declines caused by operating problems (e.g., production bottlenecks, labor strife) tend to be followed by operating cures (e.g., new cost controls, plant modernization) and that declines caused by strategic factors (e.g., obsolete products, intense price competition) tend to be followed by strategic cures (e.g., new products, redefining the business).

Hofer (1980) similarly classified turnarounds as "strategic" or "operating": "strategic" basically was defined as a major redefinition of the firm and/or attempts to increase market share dramatically. By analyzing written cases on 12 poorly performing firms, he found support for his theory that the appropriateness of a strategic or operating turnaround depends on whether the firm's "illness" stems from poor strategy or poor operations. He also laid out a framework for choosing among different operating turnarounds according to the firm's closeness to breakeven, and here again he found some support. In particular, he found that firms operating close to breakeven tended to turn around successfully if they pursued cost-cutting strategies and that firms operating far below breakeven required more ambitious revenue-increasing or asset reduction strategies.

Bibeault (1982) conducted a survey of 81 chief executives who had faced turnaround situations. He coupled the data with anecdotes to discuss why failures occur, characteristics of successful and unsuccessful turnarounds, and leadership aspects of turnarounds. His book, written primarily for practitioners, emphasizes organizational and human issues, but it also provides some insight on formulating turnaround strategies. Some of these will be discussed in the theoretical subsections that follow.

Problems with "Strategic" Turnarounds

Schendel et al. and Hofer stressed the distinction between strategic and operating turnarounds. Roughly speaking, the difference is between "doing different things" and "doing things differently." As examples, Schendel et al. indicated plant expenditures, new emphasis on functional areas, and efficiency actions as operating cures; and diversification, vertical integration, and divestment as strategic cures. This dichotomy is not used in this paper for two reasons. First, many of the specific actions considered as strategic by previous research (e.g., diversification, divestment, vertical integration) have only limited applicability at the business level—the focus of this study. One, of course, can conceive of strategic versus operating moves at the business level, but most available data would cause the dichotomy to be blurred. For example, improved cost controls and the purchase of new automated equipment might easily be taken as operational moves, but these could be the major actions taken by a firm to move more toward a "cost leadership" (Porter, 1980) or "defender" strategy (Miles & Snow, 1978).

The second misgiving with the strategic/operating dichotomy is that, as defined by Hofer, the strategic turnaround seems unrealistic for most mature businesses. For Hofer, there are three variations of a strategic turnaround. One is product/market refocusing, a realistic option that will be retained in the analysis below. The other two strategies are "one-level" (100 percent) and "two-level" (200 percent or more) increases in market share. These rather ambitious figures are at odds with a finding by Hambrick, MacMillan, and Day (1982) that among a large sample of mature businesses in the PIMS data base, 90 percent of all year-to-year market share changes were less than five share points. Presumably, weak businesses would exhibit even a more negative distribution. As Henderson (1979), Porter (1980), and others have noted, market shares in mature industries are relatively fixed. Perhaps this accounts for Hofer's own finding that 10 of the 12 firms he studied pursued operating turnarounds rather than strategic turnarounds. The present authors' pessimism about so-called strategic turnarounds also is consistent with Bibeault's finding that only 4 percent of the firms he studied were revived by "new product breakthroughs." None of this is to say that expansionary turnaround strategies are not possible, only that the ambitious criteria set by Hofer to define "strategic" turnarounds probably preclude observing them in numbers sufficient for systematic study. "Revenue generating" strategies will be noted here, however, but criteria for classifying them as strategic or nonstrategic will not be set.

Tentative Classification of Turnarounds

Hofer's various operating turnarounds, plus his product/market refocusing strategy, provide a reasonable typology of turnarounds about which one can theorize. Hofer's types, which are not inconsistent with the views of Schendel et al. or Bibeault, have the attraction of being holistic patterns, that is, genuine "strategies," rather than isolated moves. This distinction between isolated "moves" and "strategies" is of central importance here in developing hypotheses and selecting data analytic techniques.

The first two strategies can be considered "entrepreneurial" in nature. A *revenue-generating* strategy is an attempt to increase sales by some combination of product (re-)introductions, increased advertising, increased selling effort, and lower prices. A *product/market refocusing strategy* (retained from among Hofer's "strategic" turnarounds) involves a shifting of emphasis into defensible or lucrative niches. The remaining two strategies can be considered of an "efficiency" nature. A *cost-cutting* strategy typically involves cutbacks in administrative, R&D, marketing, and other seemingly discretionary expenses. Improved management of receivables and inventories also could be considered within the spirit of a cost-cutting strategy. An *asset reduction* strategy involves disposal of assets — primarily fixed assets. Of course, as Hofer noted, combinations of these four strategies also can be pursued.

A Contingency View

Hofer argued that the selection of a turnaround strategy should depend on the situation — in particular the business's closeness to breakeven. According to Hofer, if a business is far below breakeven, an asset reduction strategy is warranted. Such a business must recognize that it should be smaller than it once hoped it would be. If a business is moderately below breakeven, a revenue-generating strategy is called for, according to Hofer. In such a situation, the business probably does not have enough idle capacity to allow major asset disposal, nor is it close enough to breakeven to prosper simply by cutting costs. The business must make a concerted push to increase volume. If a business is very close to breakeven, a cost-cutting strategy is appropriate. Such a strategy often will be sufficient to push the business to acceptable profit levels without exposing it to undue risks. One of the aims of this study was to test Hofer's contingency argument.

It would seem that the market share of a business might be another factor affecting its choice of a turnaround strategy. Specifically, it could be reasoned that businesses with high market share tend to avoid the unpleasant retrenchment strategies — asset reduction and cost-cutting. They typically involve firings (often of close associates) or a dismantling of earlier visions of the scale of the business. Instead, high-share businesses might rely on attempts to exert their relative market power (Porter, 1980) by following the more offensive strategies — revenue generation and product/market refocusing. Their generally strong channels of distribution, brand recognitions, already low costs, and economies of marketing could allow them to solve their problems at less human and organizational cost than can their low-share competitors.

Turnaround Timetables and Magnitudes

Unfortunately, previous researchers of turnarounds have not been very precise about what constitutes poor performance (warranting a turnaround) or good performance (a successful turnaround). Schendel et al. stand alone in providing a concrete definition of a downturn (four consecutive years of declining profits) and of an upturn (four consecutive years of increasing profits). A weakness of their measure is that it lacks an absolute anchor. A firm whose ROI declines from 30 percent to 20 percent is said to need a turnaround. Conversely, a firm that steadily raises its ROI from −20 percent to zero over four years is said to have successfully turned around. Neither Hofer nor Bibeault specified criteria for "decline" or "success." Part of the problem in establishing criteria is that there exists no universal performance measure or threshold level (Goodman & Pennings, 1977). Still, a systematic study of turnarounds should articulate criteria for decline and upturn, even though they may not suit all circumstances.

The amount of time required for a turnaround is of interest both for its practical significance and in developing a research design. None of the previous turnaround researchers have stressed the temporal aspects of their findings, but some patterns are evident. Among Hofer's successful turnarounds, the average elapsed time from trough to peak was three years. The range was one to four years. Among Bibeault's successful turnarounds, the average elapsed time from trough to peak was four years. No data on the range were provided. Bibeault noted that the time required for a turnaround is a function of the size of the organization: "Altogether, we are talking about anywhere between one and three years, with a $20 million company taking one year and a company the size of Memorex taking three years" (1982, p. 93). Because his study was for entire corporations, presumably the average for business units is less than three years.

Associated with the turnaround timetable is the issue of stages or sequence of moves. Bibeault concluded that most turnarounds involve five stages. First is the *management change* stage (Hofer agrees that a change in top management almost always is required). Second is the *evaluation* stage (generally a matter of several weeks). Third is the *emergency* stage ("stop the bleeding"; "unloading"). Fourth is the *stabilization* stage (with

emphasis on organizational rebuilding). Fifth is the *return-to-normal growth* stage (new products and other entrepreneurial activity). This sequence is somewhat at odds with Hofer. It implies that cost cutting and/or asset reduction is done before any entrepreneurial activity is undertaken. Hofer indirectly expressed some agreement saying that, in general, efficiency-oriented moves tend to produce the quickest, most dramatic results. Thus, from the standpoint of Bibeault's sequence and Hofer's point about relative effectiveness, one could expect that in the short run the most prevalent and effective turnaround moves are of an efficiency nature.

Propositions

The literature summarized above suggests several propositions that were tested in this study of short-run turnaround success:

1. Among mature businesses, short-run turnaround success is associated primarily with retrenchment and efficiency moves, not with entrepreneurial moves (Hofer, 1980; Bibeault, 1982).
2. Still, a variety of successful turnaround "gestalts," or "set of moves," can be observed. These include four gestalts that Hofer distilled from his case studies:
   —asset reduction;
   —cost cutting;
   —revenue generation;
   —product/market refocusing.

   Some expected indicators of these four strategies are presented in Table 1. (The list of strategic change variables in Table 1 is the actual set used in the study and is discussed in the section on method.)

3. The tendency to pursue any of the above four strategies is partly a function of the position of the business during its decline:
   —businesses with low capacity utilization (a surrogate for closeness to breakeven) will tend to pursue an asset reduction strategy;

Table 1. Expected Indicators of Hofer's Four Turnaround Strategies[a]

	Strategy			
Strategic Move	*Revenue Generation*	*Product/ Market Refocusing*	*Cost Cutting*	*Asset Reduction*
Product/market initiatives				
Sales from new products	+ +[a]			
Product R&D	+ +		−	
Marketing	+ +		−	
Product quality	− −	+		
Price	− −			
Market share	+ +	−		−
Efficiency				
Employee productivity		+	+ +	
Relative direct costs		+	− −	
Asset levels and use				
Receivables/revenue	+		−	− −
Inventories/revenue	+	−	−	− −
Plant and equipment newness				− −
Capacity utilization	+	−		+ +

a. Two signs suggest a primary indicator (stressed by Hofer as integral to the strategy); one sign suggests a secondary indicator (an expected by-product or lesser component of the strategy).

— businesses with relatively high capacity utilization will tend to pursue a cost cutting strategy;

— businesses with relatively high market share will tend to pursue entrepreneurial strategies, that is, revenue generation and product/market refocusing.

This study also examined some recurring unsuccessful turnaround gestalts, although no theory was available for establishing propositions.

Method

PIMS Data Base

The data used in this study were drawn from the Profit Impact of Market Strategies project (PIMS), an on-going, large scale statistical study of environmental, strategic, and performance variables of individual business units. About 200 cor-

porations submit data annually on a total of 2,000 of their business units. Each business — often a division — is a distinct product–market unit. (For a technical summary of the PIMS data base, see Schoeffler, 1977).

Anderson and Paine (1978) provided a comprehensive critical review of the PIMS data base. Most of their concerns were about the ways in which PIMS data had been statistically analyzed and presented in previous studies. Although they raised limited concerns about the quality of the data, they more generally acknowledged the data base to be of high quality and reliability. Hambrick et al. (1982) also concluded that the data base seems reliable, given its questionnaire methodology.

The Turnaround Sample

The sample used in this study was drawn from the last four years of available data on all mature industrial-product businesses in the data base ($n=$ 770). A mature business is defined by PIMS as one in an industry whose real growth is less than 10 percent annually, in which most potential buyers understand the product, and whose set of competitors is well known. Growth and decline businesses, as well as consumer-product businesses, were excluded so as to achieve some homogeneity.

A business was included in the turnaround study if its average pretax return on investment (ROI) for the first two years under study was below 10 percent. This equates with roughly a 5 percent after-tax ROI, which would be well below the cost of capital for firms in the mid-to-late seventies, the period covered by the study. (The average pretax ROI for all mature industrial-product businesses in the PIMS data base was 25 percent.) A total of 260 businesses met the criterion for low performance and so were included in the study. The 260 businesses included both those that subsequently made performance improvements and those that did not.

Four years' data were available in the data base used. Given Hofer's (1980) and Bibeault's (1982) findings, this time frame should be sufficient to observe many business-level turnaround attempts. Still, the short timeframe will not allow all the turnaround attempts (or their aftermaths) to be seen in their entirety and hence limits the study.

Variables

A total of 12 strategic change variables were included in the study (Table 1). (Definitions of the variables may be obtained from the authors.) The list was based on three considerations. First, only variables that are annually reported to PIMS, and hence can exhibit change, were included. This ruled out some interesting possibilities such as product line breadth and number of customers. Second, the available variables were screened for their redundancy (e.g., capacity/market size and market share) and for their statistical properties (e.g., process R&D/revenues has a very restricted range). As a result, all correlations among the 12

variables were less than ±.30. Third, variables with a strong mathematical link to ROI (the performance measure) were excluded. Examples are investment/revenue and value added/revenue. The problem with such variables is that their statistical association with ROI is due in great part to their arithmetic link. (See MacMillan, Hambrick, and Day, 1982, for a fuller description of this problem.)

The change in a strategic variable for a business was calculated using the difference between the average for the first two years (the period when ROI was less than 10 percent) and the average for the last two years. This approach closely mirrored results obtained using a four-year least squares trend line.

ROI was the primary performance measure of interest because for mature businesses it is a common, often dominant, goal. It has the weaknesses of any accounting measure, for example, varying depreciation and inventory valuation methods. However, it is the most suitable available in the PIMS data base. Market share figures also will be reported to provide a broader picture of each turnaround strategy observed.

In order to identify successful turnaround gestalts, "success" was defined as a business that achieved an average ending ROI (years three and four) of at least 20 percent ($n=53$). An unsuccessful turnaround was a business whose ending ROI was still less than 10 percent (even though it might have improved significantly, say from -20 percent) ($n=153$). Thus, absolute criteria rather than relative criteria were used for defining success. There are weaknesses in this approach that other of the statistical analyses attempt to overcome. (There were 54 businesses with ending ROIs between 10 and 20 percent that were omitted from certain of the analyses.)

Data Analysis

Least-squares regression was used for identifying the strategic changes most strongly associated with improved performance. Cluster analysis (Euclidean distances, minimum squared-error grouping technique) was used for identifying successful strategic gestalts. Cross-tables and chi-square analysis were used for identifying relationships between position factors and selection of different turnaround strategies.

Results and Discussion

Strategic "Moves" Associated with Turnaround

It was hypothesized that short-run turnaround success among mature businesses would be associated primarily with improved efficiency and retrenchment, rather than with product/market initiatives. This reasoning led to the hypothesized signs presented in Table 2. Multiple regression was used to test the effects of these isolated strategic moves (as distinguished from the examination

Table 2. Regression of Strategic Moves on Change in ROI ($N = 260$)

Strategic Move	Hypoth-esized Sign	Standardized Beta (Actual)
Product/market initiatives		
Sales from new products		.01
Product R&D/sales	−	−.06*
Marketing/sales	−	−.19***
Relative product quality		.03
Relative price		.03
Relative market share		.16***
Efficiency		
Employee productivity	+	.43***
Relative direct costs	−	.00
Asset levels and use		
Receivables/revenue	−	−.09**
Inventories/revenue	−	−.14***
Plant and equipment newness	−	.08**
Capacity utilization		.01
Served market growth		.12***
R^2		.53***

*$p < .10$.   **$p < .05$.   ***$p < .01$.

of strategic gestalts, to be discussed below). The dependent variable was ROI change (ending ROI minus beginning ROI; mean = +4 percent; s.d. = 8). For this particular analysis it seemed more satisfactory to retain interval-quality data on all 260 observations rather than to use discriminant analysis between successful and unsuccessful turnarounds. The regression results presented are similar to patterns yielded by alternative analyses.

The hypotheses received mixed support. Cutbacks in R&D, marketing, receivables, and inventories all were associated with improved ROI, as expected. Improved employee productivity also was a significant factor in raising ROI. Improved employee productivity can stem from a variety of submoves that are impossible to isolate from the data available. The business could be increasing its value added. This seems unlikely, given the apparent negative effects of value-creating initiatives (e.g., marketing, R&D). Alternatively, and more likely, the business could be getting more output from its employees through some combination of relaxed union work rules, motivation, and layoffs of marginal or semiproductive employees. In general, though, there were indications that "belt tightening" was a key aid to short-term turnarounds.

The expectation that reductions in relative direct costs would help ROI was not observed. No persuasive explanation comes to mind as to why this indicator of improved efficiency was not found to be significant.

It was expected that increased plant and equipment newness would impair the ability to raise ROI. The rationale was that plant and equipment newness (net book value/gross book value) has a minor mathematical link to ROI, tending to depress it. The positive beta actually observed is especially notable because it includes an offsetting of the downward mathematical link. Apparently the efficiency that can be derived from disposing of old assets and/or adding new state-of-the-art assets is, on average, a significant aid to ROI for poorly performing businesses.

Unexpectedly, increases in market share were positively related to increases in ROI. Recall that the logic was that product/market initiatives were not likely to be successful short-term turnaround avenues. The finding seems to square with theories about the payoffs from market share, stemming from experience, scale, and market power (Henderson, 1979; Porter, 1980; Schoeffler, Buzzell, & Heany, 1974). But because both the independent and dependent variables were expressed in terms of change (rather than static), the finding casts doubt on the common supposition that market share and profitability cannot be pursued in tandem (Biggadike, 1979; Henderson, 1979). For this sample, increases in market share helped, not hurt, *current* profitability. This finding may be frustrating for the strategist, because various ways of building market share (product R&D, marketing, product quality, and new products) were not encouraged by the regression results. Through the gestalts reported below, some insight can come as to how some businesses profitably gained market share.

One of the weaknesses of the research design was lack of data on the origin of the business's trouble, or on how long the business had been in trouble. Of particular interest was the possibility that some of the businesses were suffering as part of a short-term malaise in their industry, and that the most reasonable response would be to be patient and wait for an industry upturn. In this vein, Bibeault (1982) found that 5 percent of the turnarounds he studied were "competitive environment turnarounds." A straightforward way to test for this phenomenon was to include served market growth (change in primary demand over the four years) in the regression. As might be expected, this variable was a significant, though not dominating, predictor of ROI change. A more complete test of the effects of industry "munificence" (Porter, 1980; Staw & Szwajkowski, 1975) was not possible with the available data, but it is apparent that short-term business fates are tied somewhat to industry characteristics. For some businesses, the appropriate response may be to wait for an industrywide improvement. For others, it may be to set a course that steers clear of fluctuating market sectors, powerful customers, or cutthroat competitors that can make an overall industry appear unattractive (Porter, 1980).

In sum, the regression analysis indicated that various forms of belt-tightening and productivity improvements were associated with ROI improvements. A shift to a newer mix of fixed assets also helped ROI for this sample. This is an especially noteworthy finding. New fixed assets place a downward pressure on ROI, strictly because of arithmetic. Gains in market share also were associated with gains in ROI. This finding suggests that market share and profitability at times can be pursued in tandem, even in the short term. For the strategist, the apparent payoff from market share begs the question, "How do I gain market share at the same time I am belt-tightening?" This is a question that the cluster analysis addresses to some extent.

Successful Turnaround Gestalts

A major aim of the study was to identify common "packages" of strategic moves or turnaround "gestalts" (Miller, 1981; Miller & Friesen, 1977). Hofer's four types of turnarounds were set up as straw men against which the results of cluster analysis could be compared. Included in the clustering were 53 businesses whose ending ROIs were over 20 percent. The researcher faces a difficult decision as to how many clusters to report. A discussion of the decision to report three clusters will benefit from a description of those three clusters.

Three Successful Gestalts. Table 3 presents the profiles of three successful turnaround strategies, as well as the profile of all 260 poorly performing businesses. For the sake of the clustering algorithm, all variables were standardized (mean = 0; s.d. = 1) using as norms data from all mature industrial-products businesses. Thus, the means for the 260 poorly performing businesses are not necessarily zero, and they may be of interest themselves.

The first cluster, consisting of six businesses, has several distinguishing features: significant reductions in R&D, marketing, receivables, and in-

Table 3. Profiles of Three Successful Turnaround Gestalts[a]

Strategic Move	All Low Performers (N = 260)	Asset and Cost Surgery (N = 6)	Selective Product/Market Pruning (N = 19)	Piecemeal Productivity (N = 28)
1. New products	.02 (1.03)	.21 (.61)	−.13 (.65)	.06 (.35)
2. Price	−.05 (.86)	−.19 (.21)	.33** (.62)	.05 (.77)
3. Product R&D	−.16 (1.18)	−3.30*** (2.05)	−.00 (.80)	−.09 (.40)
4. Plant and equipment newness	−.32 (.84)	−1.27*** (1.06)	−.30 (.79)	−.26 (.72)
5. Marketing	−.17 (1.00)	−.72*** (1.29)	−.60** (1.00)	−.26 (.39)
6. Receivables	−.20 (1.09)	−.59*** (.49)	−1.92*** (1.09)	.13 (.56)
7. Inventories	−.32 (1.03)	−1.10*** (.77)	−1.09*** (.93)	−.31 (.72)
8. Capacity utilization	.12 (1.03)	2.06*** (.96)	−.39** (1.24)	.71*** (.70)
9. Employee productivity	.27 (1.23)	3.69*** (3.19)	.97*** (1.23)	.60*** (.74)
10. Product quality	.16 (1.30)	.00 (.47)	.46** (.76)	.18 (.91)
11. Relative direct cost	−.06 (1.10)	−.37 (.90)	.40* (1.16)	.02 (.52)
12. Market Share	−.03 (1.04)	.49 (.90)	.38 (.80)	.13 (.69)

a. Means reported. Standard deviations in parentheses.
*$p < .10$.   **$p < .05$.   ***$p < .01$.

ventories; significant declines in plant and equipment newness, suggesting disposal of newer (i.e., most saleable) facilities. This leads, in turn, to much higher capacity utilization levels and significantly increased employee productivity levels.

This asset/cost surgery strategy represents a combination of Hofer's asset reduction and cost-cutting strategies. Basically, every type of excisive move possible was taken by the businesses in this cluster. This strategy, to a great extent, represents the moves one would make if adhering to the regression results presented earlier, with the added emphasis here on asset reduction (or, perhaps in some cases, nonreplacement of assets). A skeptic of this strategy would say that it is short-sighted and enfeebling. Such a view pales in light of the steady market shares reported by these businesses. Apparently there are some businesses that have surplus assets and high costs that can be substantially cut back, with a result of immediate profit improvement but no damage to the market position of the business.

The second cluster, consisting of 19 businesses, suggests a *selective product/market pruning* strategy. It can be inferred that these businesses refocused toward those sectors that were most profitable or in which they had a distinctive strength. Manifestations of this strategy were: increases in relative prices, direct costs, and product quality (signaling a tendency to focus on those niches in which the business had a quality edge rather than a cost edge); decreased marketing expenses and inventory expenses (possibly stemming from a narrower, more homogeneous set of products and markets); reduced receivables (abandoned marginal customers or those who exert great power over credit terms); decline in capacity utilization because the emphasis was not on volume but on selective high-profit opportunities; increase in employee productivity, possibly as a result of the enhanced value added (higher quality) of the average product or as a result of fewer product lines (lower changeover costs, etc.).

This strategy is a variant of Hofer's product/market refocusing strategy. Here again, even though the strategy is one of caution (this time selectivity instead of retrenchment) rather than entrepreneurial boldness, market shares remained stable.

This cluster highlights the advantage of cluster analysis for strategy research. On the basis of the more traditional econometric technique of regression, one would conclude that capacity utilization is not an important predictor of improved performance, and common sense would indicate that, if anything, high capacity utilization is desirable. But when viewed as part of a gestalt — a set of internally consistent strategic moves — it is seen that a decrease in capacity utilization can be a logical accompaniment of a rather powerful strategy for turning a mature business around.

The third cluster consists of 28 businesses and has only 2 distinguishing features: increased capacity utilization and increased employee productivity. These characteristics do not paint a very specific picture of what these businesses actually did. The standard deviations of all the changes are moderate in magnitude, indicating that a number of substrategies, or tactics, were employed. This might be considered a piecemeal strategy; it does not involve a comprehensive set of moves. Rather, each business in this cluster perhaps made as few as one or two modifications — these differing from one business to another — that tended to accompany increased capacity utilization and employee productivity and, in turn, a successful turnaround. It also may be that a number of these businesses were in industries whose overall sales improved, thus raising their capacity utilization and employee productivity figures.

Alternative Cluster Solutions. The choice to report three clusters was not arbitrary. In fact, insight can come from the factors leading to the decision.

The clustering algorithm begins by considering each object — in this case a turnaround business — as a distinct cluster. Reflecting the 12 strategic moves being studied, 12-dimensional distances are calculated for each pair of clusters. The two closest clusters are combined into a new cluster. This process, which is a form of a "hierarchical" clustering procedure, continues until all objects are combined into one cluster.

Then the researcher has the problem of deciding how many clusters (between 1 and *n*) provide the most meaningful portrayal of the data. The rule of thumb is to look for a pronounced increase in the "tightness" (mean squared error) of the clusters as the algorithm moves from, say, a 5-cluster to a 4-cluster solution. In this study, the data yielded only steady increments for all solutions below the 10-cluster level. This is a common problem when clustering social science data: "natural" species or genera simply do not exist. In such a case, the researcher must use judgment as to which cluster-level solution to report.

One could legitimately ask whether a 4- or 5- or 6-cluster solution wouldn't portray a richer array of turnaround gestalts than was portrayed with the 3-cluster solution. One would especially hope that the biggest cluster ("piecemeal" strategy"), which provides scant insight, might yield two or three more interesting clusters when it splits in the clustering hierarchy. Unfortunately, it does not split until the 8-cluster solution is reached and, even then, the two resulting clusters are no more suggestive than what has been presented. Rather, up until the 8-cluster solution, it is the two already rich strategies—"asset/cost surgery" and "selective product/market pruning"—that split into smaller and smaller "substrategy" clusters.

This pattern should not be taken as a detraction from the study. Rather, it suggests at least three interesting possibilities. First, it appears that the dominant turnaround strategy is not a gestalt, but rather piecemeal moves that vary from business to business and hence are difficult to generalize about. A business that is in only marginally poor condition might pursue a piecemeal approach, as might a business that is simply waiting for its industry as a whole to improve. Second, it appears that the two "fundamental" turnaround gestalts are the two reported here: asset/cost surgery and selective product/market pruning. As the clustering algorithm moved from a 3-cluster to an 8-cluster solution, only new variations of these two strategies were observed. No other basic gestalts emerged. This raises the third conclusion: Hofer's revenue generation strategy was not found in the cluster analysis. Granted, some businesses significantly raised their market shares or revenues, but no recurring combination of revenue-generating tactics was observed. On the one hand, this raises questions about the efficacy of a

revenue-generating strategy in a mature industry. After all, market shares are relatively fixed, brand loyalties relatively solid, and technology stable. Can an aggressive, entrepreneurial strategy work under such conditions? On the other hand, it may be that a revenue-generating strategy requires highly situational moves (certainly more so than does the asset/cost surgery strategy) that are difficult to observe in their myriad combinations, especially in a heterogeneous sample.

Situations Affecting Strategic Choice

It was theorized that the choice of a particular turnaround strategy would be a function of the business's situation, particularly its market share and its capacity utilization. To test this, the successful businesses were divided into high- and low-market share (cutpoint = 29 percent) categories, and further subdivided according to which of the three successful strategies they had pursued. The results, presented in Table 4, indicate significant associations between the business's situation and strategy selected.

All of the six businesses that used an asset/cost surgery strategy had low capacity utilization. This generally conforms to Hofer's supposition that businesses that are far below breakeven will tend to (or should) retrench. Such businesses have only a slim likelihood of reaching profitability through less dramatic moves.

Table 4. Situational Factors and Choice of Turnaround Strategy[a]

Situational Factors	Strategy Selected			
	Asset/ Cost Surgery	Product/ Market Pruning	Piece- meal	Over- all
Low market share—low capacity utilization	3	3	4	10
Low market share—high capacity utilization	0	7	5	12
High market share—low capacity utilization	3	4	11	18
High market share—high capacity utilization	0	5	8	13
	6	19	28	53

a. Significance by χ^2 test = < .05.

The 19 businesses that used the product/market pruning strategy came from all situational categories, but there was a marked tendency for them to have high capacity utilization (12 out of 19). Presumably, these were businesses that were operating at "healthy" volumes, but they simply had a poor product mix. Their response was to shift to higher-margin products or markets, even if it meant reduced capacity utilization (as indicated by the earlier cluster profiles).

The 28 businesses that used the piecemeal strategy were primarily high-market share businesses (19 out of 28). Presumably, these businesses were strategically healthy and felt that they had to make only minor or selective changes in order to become profitable. They did not have to undergo the major, comprehensive changes that some of the other businesses felt compelled to make.

In summary, it appears that businesses do select a turnaround strategy partly on the basis of their market share and capacity utilization. Hofer's scenarios were basically confirmed, particularly as regards the selection of retrenchment strategies by businesses operating at low capacity utilization levels. These findings should stimulate more systematic inquiry into the inevitable array of contingent factors entering into the turnaround decision, much as was done by Harrigan (1980) in looking at strategies for declining industries.

Unsuccessful Turnarounds

A legitimate question is whether the successful turnaround gestalts differed from the most common unsuccessful gestalts. Space limitations prevent a detailed analysis of unsuccessful turnarounds, but a brief discussion of the findings may be instructive. This description relies on a 4-cluster solution for the 153 businesses whose ROIs did not rise above 10 percent during the period under study.

The first cluster consisted of six businesses that undertook significant entrepreneurial initiatives (increased R&D and marketing) but whose efficiencies dropped precipitously (increased inventories, decreased employee productivity, and decreased capacity utilization). It could be argued that this is a far-sighted strategy that cannot be expected to yield fast profits. Such an argument is weakened by the substantial drop of the average market share of these businesses during the change period. These businesses appear not to have improved their fitness for the future. Five of the six members of this cluster had high beginning market share, suggesting that high market share might inject a blind sense of optimism or market power that causes bold entrepreneurial attempts with no attention to efficiency.

The second cluster consisted of 13 businesses that had only one distinguishing feature: dramatically reduced R&D expenditures. R&D may be seen as the first "discretionary" budget item to cut, especially by mature businesses that face relatively calm technological environments. As part of a broader cost-cutting effort, as was waged by the successful asset/cost surgery businesses, cutbacks in R&D can help bring about an early turnaround. By itself, though, a cut in R&D is not a big contributor to a turnaround, and it may have the unfortunate side effect of making the business feel that it is doing something momentous to bring about a turnaround when, in fact, relatively little has been done. Of the 13 businesses in this unsuccessful cluster, 10 had high market share. Here again may be another form of optimism on the part of high share businesses. In this case, perhaps they think that they simply do not have to do much to turnaround—that a mere cutting of R&D will be sufficient.

The third cluster consisted of 12 businesses that had only 2 distinguishing features: a significant increase in new products and a significant decrease in marketing expenses. This obvious inconsistency may point to an over-reliance on the new products as a way out of trouble. Just as the businesses in the previous cluster may have thought that cutting R&D would be sufficient, these businesses may have thought that new products would be sufficient for turning the business around. Unfortunately, new products tend to put sharp pressure on current profits (Hambrick, 1983), such that the best hope from such a strategy is that it will improve the business for the future. Such logic pales in view of a lack of any significant market share changes by businesses in this cluster. Of the 12 businesses in this cluster, 9 had low beginning market shares.

The fourth cluster consisted of 122 businesses and had no distinguishing characteristics, hence qualifying as another piecemeal approach. Obviously, if more clusters were examined, this large cluster could split into more interpretable, interesting subclusters. Businesses in this cluster were very evenly distributed in terms of their beginning market shares and capacity utilization.

The purpose here has not been to document all the possible ways in which a business can fail in a turnaround attempt. Rather, the primary aim has been to confirm that the most common failure gestalts are quite different from the primary success gestalts. This appears to be the case, although ambiguity remains about the nondescript piecemeal strategies that emerge in both groups. A secondary aim has been to present some gestalts that can suggest the kinds of unsuccessful turnaround strategies that may occur. Brought to light have been strategies that are unduly bold and strategies that are unduly conservative. Obviously, much more research is needed into failure gestalts in general.

Summary

This study of turnaround attempts by businesses in mature industries has produced a variety of significant findings. On the basis of regression analysis, it was found that efficiency measures are major avenues toward improved profits. It also was found that market share increases are associated with increased profits, although the regressions gave no indications of how market share increases might come about—an especially frustrating shortcoming in light of the apparent payoff from "belt-tightening" moves. Some doubt has been cast on the notion that profits cannot increase at the same time market share is being increased. Finally, the regressions confirmed that improvement in ROI is partly a function of increased industry sales.

The cluster analysis indicated three primary successful turnaround gestalts: asset/cost surgery, selective product/market pruning, and a piecemeal strategy. These bear a fair resemblance to the turnaround strategies that Hofer proposed on the basis of case evidence. It was found that the choice among these three strategies was associated with certain characteristics of the business, again basically in line with Hofer's suppositions. Asset/cost surgery was pursued primarily by businesses with low levels of capacity utilization; selective product/market pruning was undertaken primarily by businesses with high levels of capacity utilization; and the piecemeal strategy was followed primarily by businesses with high market share.

With the exception of a heavily-populated piecemeal strategy, the unsuccessful gestalts bore little resemblance to the successful gestalts and further provided some sketchy insight into some common types of ill-conceived (or ill-executed) turnaround attempts.

The study has several important limitations that bear noting. First, no data on causes of downturns were available, hence ruling out a direct test of the theory offered by Schendel et al. (1975) that turnaround attempts must address the source of the problem. Second, the lack of a long time-series of data hurt in another way. It prevented examination of the aftermath of the short-term moves actually observed. Do certain types of "quick fixes" lead to ultimate failure? Or, conversely, does quick success tend to be a sign of resilience and strong management? No light was shed here. A third, and related, problem is the reliance on ROI as the performance measure. ROI is a very limited, manipulable figure, even though it is a common indicator of effectiveness of mature businesses. A multidimensional view of performance would have been desirable but was not possible with the data available. A fourth limitation is that no organizational or managerial characteristics were studied. This reflects a shortcoming of the PIMS data base in general. Bibeault placed major emphasis on leadership, style, teamwork, and other "soft" factors in turnarounds. Such factors should be strongly considered for inclusion in future turnaround studies. Finally, the sample studied is narrow — only mature industrial-product businesses. Would entrepreneurial endeavors have greater apparent payoff in consumer businesses? In growth-stage businesses? What would the successful gestalts look like if service businesses were observed? These are sectors in which turnaround evidence should be gathered and analyzed.

Overall, the study has added to a sparse literature but leaves open many questions for future study. Both theoreticians and practitioners need frameworks and evidence for thinking about responses to poor organizational performance.

References

Anderson, C.R., & Paine. F.T. 1978. PIMS: A re-examination. *Academy of Management Review* 3: 602–12.

Bibeault, D.G. 1982. *Corporate turnaround: How managers turn losers into winners*. New York: McGraw-Hill.

Biggadike, R. 1979. The risky business of diversification. *Harvard Business Review* 59(4): 131–37.

Goodman, P.S., & Pennings, J.M. 1977. *New perspectives on organizational effectiveness*. San Francisco: Jossey-Bass.

Hambrick, D.C. 1983. Some tests of the effectiveness and functional attributes of Miles and Snow's strategic types. *Academy of Management Journal* 26: 5–26.

Hambrick, D.C., MacMillan, I.C., & Day, D.L. 1982. Strategic attributes and performance in the four cells of the BCG matrix — A PIMS-based analysis of industrial-product businesses. *Academy of Management Journal* 25: 510–31.

Harrigan, K.R. 1980. *Strategies for declining businesses*. Lexington, Mass.: Heath.

Henderson, B.D. 1979. *Henderson on corporate strategy*. Cambridge, Mass.: Abt Books.

Hofer, C.W. 1980. Turnaround strategies. *Journal of Business Strategy* 1(1): 19–31.

MacMillan, I.C., Hambrick, D.C., & Day, D.L. 1982. The product portfolio and profitability: A PIMS-based analysis of industrial-product businesses. *Academy of Management Journal* 25: 733–55.

Miles, R.E., & Snow, C.C. 1978. *Organizational strategy, structure and process*. New York: McGraw-Hill.

Miller, D. 1981. Toward a new contingency approach: The search for organizational gestalts. *Journal of Management Studies* 18: 1–26.

Miller, D., & Friesen, P. 1977. Strategy making in context: Ten empirical archetypes. *Journal of Management Studies* 14: 251–80.

Porter, M.E. 1980. *Competitive strategy*. New York: Free Press.

Schendel, D.E., Patten, R., & Riggs, J. 1975. Corporate turnaround strategies. Working Paper 486, Krannert Graduate School of Industrial Administration, Purdue University.

Schoeffler, S. 1977. Cross-sectional study of strategy, structure and performance: Aspects of the PIMS program. In H. Thorelli (Ed.), *Strategy + structure = performance*, pp. 108–21. Bloomington, Ind.: Indiana University Press.

Schoeffler, S., Buzzell, R.D., & Heany, D.F. 1974. Impact of strategic planning on profit performance. *Harvard Business Review* 52(1): 137–45.

Staw, B.M., & Szwajkowski, E. 1975. The scarcity-munificence component of organizational environments and the commission of illegal acts. *Administrative Science Quarterly* 20: 345–54.

17

To Avoid Organizational Crises, Unlearn

Paul C. Nystrom

William H. Starbuck

Organizations learn. Then they encase their learning in programs and standard operating procedures that members execute routinely. These programs and procedures generate inertia, and the inertia increases when organizations socialize new members and reward conformity to prescribed roles. As their successes accumulate, organizations emphasize efficiency, grow complacent, and learn too little. To survive, organizations must also unlearn.

Top managers' ideas dominate organizational learning, but they also prevent unlearning. Encased learning produces blindness and rigidity that may breed full-blown crises. Our studies of organizations facing crises show that past learning inhibits new learning: Before organizations will try new ideas, they must unlearn old ones by discovering their inadequacies and then discarding them.

Organizations in serious crises often remove their top managers as a way to erase the dominating ideas, to disconfirm past programs, to become receptive to new ideas, and to symbolize change.

This article begins by describing some organizational crises and the ways in which top managers' past learning only made the crises worse. The following section shows how clever managers have executed remarkable turnarounds by changing their organizations' beliefs and values. After considering why organizations unlearn by the drastic step of replacing top managers en masse, the article urges top managers to accept dissents, to interpret events as learning opportunities, and to characterize actions as experiments.

Learning from Crises

Many managers and scholars think that organizational survival indicates effectiveness. Survival is an insufficient measure of effectiveness, but the organizational survival rates are so low that there

Exhibit 1. Survivals by U.S. Corporations

Ages in Years	Percentages Surviving to Various Ages	Percentages Surviving at Least Five Years After Various Ages
5	38	55
10	21	65
15	14	70
20	10	73
25	7	76
50	2	83
75	1	86
100	0.5	88

is clearly much room for improvement. Exhibit 1 gives some approximate statistics for American corporations: Only 10 percent survive 20 years. Moreover, of those that do survive 20 years, more than a fourth disappear during the ensuing five years. The statistics for U.S. federal agencies look much like those for corporations.

A crisis is a situation that seriously threatens an organization's survival. We have spent several years studying organizations in crises — why crises arise, and how organizations react. Our studies suggest that most organizational failures are quite unnecessary. The following two cases illustrate typical patterns.

Company H successfully published a prestigious daily newspaper for more than 100 years. Circulation reached a new peak in 1966, and the managers invested in modern printing equipment. The following year, circulation leveled off and advertising income dropped, while costs increased. Despite altered accounting procedures, the next year brought losses and a severe cash shortage. The board reacted by focusing even more intensely on cost control; a proposal to change the product a bit was rejected with laughter. Another bad year led the managers to raise prices radically and to form a task force to study corrective actions. Of five alternatives proposed by the task force, the board chose the only one that avoided all strategic reorientation. That is, the board decided to concentrate on those things the organization had always done best and to cut peripheral activities. Many key staff departed. Financial losses escalated. In 1972, the managers sold the printing equipment to pay operating costs, and Company H disappeared altogether a year later.

In the late 1960s, Company F made and sold mechanical calculators as well as typewriters and office furnishings. The company had succeeded consistently for nearly 50 years, and its top managers believed that no other company in the world could produce such good mechanical calculators at such low costs. These beliefs may have been accurate, but they soon proved irrelevant, for an electronic revolution had begun. Although some of the company's engineers had designed electronic calculators and computers, the board decided against their production and sale. The board understood how to succeed with mechanical calculators, the company had invested heavily in new plants designed specifically to manufacture mechanical calculators, this industry had always evolved slowly, and the board believed that customers would switch to electronic calculators only gradually. However, sales began a dramatic decline in 1970, and profits turned into losses. The board retrenched by closing the factories that manufactured typewriters and office furnishings in order to concentrate on the company's key product line: mechanical calculators. After three years of losses, bankruptcy loomed and the board sold Company F to a larger company. What happened next is reported later in this article.

These cases illustrate that top managers may fail to perceive that crises are developing. Other people see the looming problems, but either their warnings do not reach the top, or the top managers discount the warnings as erroneous. When top managers eventually do notice trouble, they initially attribute the problems to temporary environmental disturbances, and they adopt weathering-the-storm strategies: Postpone investments, reduce maintenance, halt training, centralize decision making, liquidate assets, deny credit to customers, raise prices, leave positions vacant, and so forth. During this initial phase of crises, top managers rely on and respond to routine formal reports, particularly accounting statements, that present only superficial symptoms of the real problems. A major activity becomes changing the accounting procedures in order to conceal the symptoms.

In real crises, weathering-the-storm strategies work only briefly. Then the symptoms of trouble reappear; only this time, the organizations start with fewer resources and less time in which to act. The second phase in organizations' reactions to crises involves unlearning yesterday's ideas. People in organizations rarely abandon their current beliefs and procedures merely because alternatives might offer better results: They know that their current beliefs and procedures have arisen from rational analyses and successful experiences, so they have to see evidence that these beliefs and procedures are seriously deficient before they will even think about major changes. Continuing crises provide this evidence. People start to question the conceptual foundations of their organizations, and they lose confidence in the leaders who advocated and perpetuated these concepts. Conflicts escalate as dissenters, voicing new ideas, challenge the ideas of top managers.

Reorienting by Changing Cognitive Structures

Some people see potential crises arising and others do not; some understand technological and social changes and others do not. What people can see, predict, and understand depends on their cognitive structures — by which we mean logically integrated and mutually reinforcing systems of beliefs and values. Cognitive structures manifest themselves in perceptual frameworks, expectations, world views, plans, goals, sagas, stories, myths, rituals, symbols, jokes, and jargon.

Not only do top managers' cognitive structures shape their own actions, they strongly influence their organizations' actions. Albert King conducted a field experiment that reveals the power of a top manager's expectations. A top manager of Company J told the managers of plants 1 and 2 that he expected job redesigns would raise productivity; and he told the managers of plants 3 and 4 that he expected job redesigns would im-

prove industrial relations but would not change productivity. What actually happened matched the top manager's initial statements. In plants 3 and 4, productivity remained about the same, and absenteeism declined. In plants 1 and 2, productivity increased significantly, while absenteeism remained the same. What makes the experiment even more interesting is that different types of job redesign were used in plants 1 and 3 than in plants 2 and 4. Plants 1 and 3 implemented job enlargement whereas plants 2 and 4 implemented job rotation, yet both types of job redesign produced the same levels of productivity and absenteeism. Thus, differences in actual job activities produced no differences in productivity and absenteeism, whereas different expectations did produce different outcomes.

Expectations and other manifestations of cognitive structures play powerful roles in organizational crises, both as causes and as possible cures. The Chinese exhibited great wisdom when they formed the symbol for crisis by combining the symbols for danger and opportunity: Top managers' ideas strongly influence whether they and their organizations see opportunities as well as dangers. For example, Company F, one of the companies described earlier in this article, surmounted its crisis primarily because a change in its top managers introduced different beliefs and perceptions.

Its top managers and board saw Company F as being designed to adapt to slow, predictable changes in technologies and markets. They initially predicted that electronic calculators would have slow, predictable effects, and the sudden electronic revolution both bewildered and terrified them. They decided that, for their company, the electronic revolution posed an insurmountable challenge. As it floundered at the brink of disaster, Company F was acquired by Company E, which promptly fired all of F's former top managers.

The top managers of Company E soon discovered opportunities that seemed obvious to them: Demands for typewriters and office furnishings were two to three times production capacities; sales staff had been turning down orders because the plants could not fill them! Also, the company's engineers had designed good electronic calculators and computers that the previous board had refused to put into production. The new top managers talked optimistically about opportunities rather than dangers, challenges rather than threats. They borrowed a small amount of money from the parent company with which to experiment, they converted plants producing mechanical calculators into ones making typewriters and office furnishings, and they authorized production and energetic marketing of electronic products. Within a year of acquisition, losses converted into profits, production and employment began rising, and optimism prevailed again.

Top managers' cognitive structures also block recoveries from crises. In Company H, the newspaper described earlier, the top managers' beliefs intensified their commitment to a faulty strategy, generating actions and inactions that sealed the company's fate.

Top managers who clung steadfastly to incorrect ideas also undermined the success of Company T, which made and sold consumer electronics equipment such as television receivers, tape recorders, loudspeakers, and radios. Sales had doubled about every three years over its 40 years' existence. The top managers invested in two new plants in order to replace labor with capital because they thought that labor costs were rising too rapidly relative to sales revenues. Sales growth slowed substantially while these new plants were being constructed. The top managers attributed this deceleration to various environmental factors even though available evidence contradicted each of their attributions. The top managers asserted that these problems would be solved by the new plants with low labor costs that would enable lower prices. In the fourth year of this crisis, the national government lent Company T many millions of dollars to save it from collapse. But the loan only postponed the collapse for two years...and increased its cost.

A Harsh Way to Unlearn

Organizations succumb to crises largely because their top managers, bolstered by recollections of past successes, live in worlds circumscribed by their cognitive structures. Top managers misperceive events and rationalize their organizations' failures. Some top managers, like those in Company F, admit privately that they do not understand what is happening and do not know what to do, while publicly they maintain facades of self-assurance and conviction. Other top managers, like those in Company T, never doubt that their beliefs and perceptions have more validity than anyone else's.

Because top managers adamantly cling to their beliefs and perceptions, few turnaround options exist. And because organizations first respond to crises with superficial remedies and delays, they later must take severe actions to escape demise. They must replace constricting, hopeless cognitive structures. But if only one or a few new managers join an ongoing group, either they adopt the prevailing cognitive structure or the other managers regard them as deviants with foolish ideas. Crises intensify these social processes by creating a wagon-train-surrounded-by-Indians atmosphere. So the top managers must be removed as a group, except for the rare individuals who dissented from the prevailing beliefs and perceptions. Moreover, revitalizing a crisis-ridden organization requires enthusiasm and energy...these from people who have grown cynical after hearing their top managers make failed promises and hollow excuses for several years. Before they will replace their cynicism with effort and vision, the people will have to be convinced that this time, at last, someone is serious about making real changes. One way to do this, usually the only way, is to turn the former top managers into scapegoats.

Cognitive reorientations spark corporate turnarounds. Some enterprising people take over ailing corporations and successfully convert losses into profits by seeing opportunities that the former managers overlooked. Conversely, William Hall reported that turnaround efforts generally fail when firms in stagnating industries get subsidies from their parent corporations or from governments. The difference in outcomes seems to spring from infusions of new ideas, not solely infusions of financial resources. Indeed, the finanɔlal lifusluns aɪe usually small lii successful tuɪn-arounds. Strategic reorientations are rooted in cognitive shifts, and turnarounds almost always involve both significant changes in top management and changes in overall strategies.

Company S, which made ferrous screws, lapsed into persistent losses caused by aging machinery and brisk competition. A new president and vice-president for marketing embarked on a strategic reorientation: shifting from large orders of ferrous screws to small orders of nonferrous screws. But two years of persuasion failed to loosen the other top managers' adherence to old modes of acting and thinking. Because the two new managers could not afford to waste more time, they replaced their colleagues. Company S subsequently achieved substantial success.

Removing people is a quick, effective way of erasing memories. Our colleague, Bo Hedberg, reviewed the psychological literature and concluded that unlearning must precede the learning of new behaviors. But top managers show a quite understandable lack of enthusiasm for the idea that organizations have to replace their top managers en masse in order to escape from serious crises. This reluctance partially explains why so few organizations survive crises.

Unlearning Continuously

Top managers might try to keep emerging crises from becoming serious, by reacting promptly to early symptoms of trouble and by avoiding weathering-the-storm strategies and superficial cover-ups. But not all symptoms warrant prompt reactions, and weathering-the-storm strategies can be useful. The top managers we studied all believed that they were acting wisely (at least when they took the actions), but they were misled by their faulty beliefs and perceptions. Faulty cognitive structures do not always plunge organizations into crises, but they do always keep managers from controlling their organizations' destinies.

To stay in control of their futures, top managers have to combat the inevitable errors in their own beliefs and perceptions. This is, of course, very difficult. It demands exceptional objectivity

and humility as well as enough self confidence to face errors within oneself. But it is easier to keep managers' cognitive structures continuously realistic and up-to-date than to try abruptly to correct errors that have added up and reinforced each other. And it is easier to correct cognitive structures while things are going well than to do so after troubles develop.

Top managers can stimulate their own unlearning and new learning in at least three ways: They can listen to dissents, convert events into learning opportunities, and adopt experimental frames of reference. The next three sections give examples of ways in which top managers can use these methods to benefit themselves and their organizations. However, we intentionally stop short of offering how-to-do-it prescriptions. Managers often get into trouble by trying to follow prescriptions that have been formulated by someone else in a different situation. For one thing, obeying someone else's prescriptions requires a partial substitution for one's best judgment. The simpler and more practical prescriptions sound, the more trust one puts in them, and so the more danger they pose. For another thing, effective methods of getting things done respect the constraints and exploit the opportunities that distinguish specific situations. We also question the view that "If managers knew how to do it, they would already be doing it." Many managers exhibit great skill at creating pragmatic techniques and procedures to achieve the goals they are pursuing. Top managers who want to unlearn will likely find ways to do it, ways that mesh with the other aspects of their jobs. But the top managers we studied never looked upon their past learning as impediments and they never tried to unlearn.

Listening to Dissents

Complaints, warnings, and policy disagreements should cause reflection that sometimes leads to unlearning. Because such messages assert that something is wrong, top managers ought to respond by reconsidering their beliefs and practices. However, well-meaning colleagues and subordinates normally distort or silence warnings and dissents.

So top managers receive only some of the messages sent, and even these messages arrive in watered-down forms, often accompanied by defensive rationalizations.

Moreover, research shows that people (including top managers) tend to ignore warnings of trouble and interpret nearly all messages as confirming the rightness of their beliefs. They blame dissents on ignorance or bad intentions—the dissenting subordinates or outsiders lack a top manager's perspective, or they're just promoting their self-interests, or they're the kind of people who would bellyache about almost anything. Quite often, dissenters and bearers of ill tidings are forced to leave organizations or they quit in disgust, thus ending the dissonance. For example, after Company F had struggled with its crisis for two years, the head of the typewriter division quit in protest over his colleagues' decisions to sell typewriter plants in order to get funds to subsidize the production of mechanical calculators. His division was the only division earning a profit.

Lyman Porter and Karlene Roberts reviewed research showing that top managers do not listen carefully to their subordinates. People in hierarchies talk upward and listen upward: They send more messages upward than downward, they pay more attention to messages from their superiors than to ones from their subordinates, and they try harder to establish rapport with superiors than with subordinates. People also bias their upward messages to enhance good news and to suppress bad news, yet they overestimate how much real information they transmit upward. Although these communication patterns are understandable, they are also harmful. In every crisis we studied, the top managers received accurate warnings and diagnoses from some of their subordinates, but they paid no attention to them. Indeed, they sometimes laughed at them.

After studying 20 corporations enmeshed in crises, Roger Dunbar and Walter Goldberg concluded that the chief executives generally surrounded themselves with yes-sayers who voiced no criticisms. Worse yet, the yes-sayers deliberately filtered out warnings from middle managers who saw correctly that their corporations were out of touch with market realities. Many of these middle managers resigned and others were fired for disloyalty.

Top managers might maintain more realistic cognitive structures if they would personally interview some of the people leaving their organizations. But why wait until people exhaust their loyalty and decide to leave? Top managers should listen to and learn from dissenters, doubters, and bearers of warnings. Not all dissents are valid, and warnings are often wrong, but dissents and warnings should remind one that diverse world views exist, that one's own beliefs and perceptions may well be wrong. Indeed, top managers should worry if they hear no such messages: Long silences signal distortion, not consensus. Although consensus sometimes occurs within top-management groups, we have found no organizations in which strong consensus pervaded the managerial ranks. Furthermore, Peter Grinyer and David Norburn conducted careful research that found no benefits from strategic consensus: Firms in which managers disagree about goals, policies, and strategies earn just as much profit as firms in which managers agree.

How are top managers to know which dissents and warnings to consider seriously? They certainly dare not rely on their own judgments about ideas' validity because everyone's beliefs and perceptions contain errors. Messages that sound obviously correct add little to knowledge. On the other hand, messages that sound fanciful can highlight defects in one's knowledge, because they arise from premises quite different from one's own.

We recommend this screening procedure: First, assume that all dissents and warnings are at least partially valid. Second, evaluate the costs or benefits that would accrue if messages turn out to be correct: Fanciful messages typically entail high costs or benefits; realistic messages likely entail low costs or benefits. Third, try to find some evidence, other than the messages' content, about the probabilities that messages might prove to be correct. For instance, have the messages' sources acted as if they truly believe what they are saying? Are the sources speaking about their areas of special expertise? Fourth, find ways to test in practice those dissents and warnings that might yield significant costs or benefits. Launch experimental probes that will confirm, disconfirm, or modify the ideas.

Exploiting Opportunities

Changes induce people to question their world views. One very successful organization, Company G, actually appointed a vice-president for revolutions, who stepped in approximately every four years and shook up operations by transferring managers and reorganizing responsibilities. When asked how he decided what changes to make, he answered that it made little difference so long as the changes were large enough to introduce new perceptions. Statistics show that productivity rose for about two years after each shakeup, then declined for the next two years, until another shakeup initiated another productivity increase.

Company G's practice should be imitated widely. The vice-president for revolutions injected unexpected and somewhat random question marks into operations that, otherwise, would have grown smug and complacent through success and would have lost opportunities and alertness through planning. Indeed, Company G itself might have benefited from more frequent doses of its own medicine: Shouldn't the shakeups have happened every two years, when productivity had peaked and before it began to decline?

However, managers would not have to generate so many question marks if they turned spontaneous events into question marks. Managers can create unlearning opportunities by analyzing the consequences of such events as new laws, technological innovations, natural disasters, disrupted supplies, fluctuating demands for outputs, and recessions. Our colleague, Alan Meyer, learned a lot about the dynamics of hospital organizations because he happened to be studying some hospitals when they were jolted by a doctors' strike. To his surprise, he found that ideologies were more powerful than structures as forces guiding organizational responses. The hospitals that took best advantage of the strike were ones with ideologies that cherish dispersed influence in decision making, frequent strategic reorientations, and responsiveness to environmental events. Such hospitals both anticipated the effects of the strike and used the strike as a stimulus for long-run improvements.

One of the most successful adaptations to the doctors' strike was made by Hospital C. This hospital's culture values innovation, professional autonomy, and pluralism; its administrator urges the subunits to act entrepreneurially and to maintain bonds with the community. The administrator himself devotes 70 percent of his time to outside relationships, and he predicted the strike two months before it began—well before other hospitals anticipated it. Because he purposely avoids codifying procedures and formalizing relationships, he subtly encouraged the (overtly spontaneous) coalescing of an informal group to consider the strike's impacts. This group sent all supervisors a scenario of what might happen and asked them to write up plans for response. When the strike occurred, Hospital C cut costs and reallocated resources so quickly that it continued to earn a profit; and after the strike ended, the hospital easily adapted back. The administrator said, "We learned that we could adapt to almost anything—including a drastic drop in our patient load—and, in the process, we discovered some new techniques for cutting our operating costs."

Experimenting

Experimentation offers many benefits as a central frame of reference for top managers. People who see themselves as experimenting are willing to deviate temporarily from practices they consider optimal in order to test the validity of their assumptions. When they try out other people's ideas that they themselves expect to be suboptimal or foolish, they create opportunities to surprise themselves. They also manage experiments in ways that cut down the losses that failures would produce; for instance, they attend carefully to feedback.

Because they place fewer personal stakes on outcomes looking successful, they evaluate outcomes more objectively. They find it easier to modify their beliefs to accommodate new observations. And they keep on trying for improvements because they know experiments never turn out perfectly.

A team from McKinsey & Company studied ten companies that executives think are unusually well run. Experimenting tops the list of characteristics they have in common. To quote Thomas Peters' conclusion from *Business Week* (July 21, 1980):

> Controlled experiments abound in these companies. The attitude of management is to "get some data, do it, then adjust it," rather than wait for a perfect overall plan.

Managers can program some searches for better ideas. For example, evolutionary operation (EVOP) is a well thought-out method for continual experimentation. The basic idea is to run experiments that entail little risk because they deviate only incrementally from what the experimenters believe to be optimal operation. The experiments should be planned and interpreted by committees that are carefully designed to meld technical expertise and political clout. Although George Box and Norman Draper created EVOP as a way to improve manufacturing processes, the basic ideas generalize to repetitive activities in finance, marketing, personnel management, and office procedures.

Experiments need not be carefully designed in order to be revealing, and they need not be revealing in order to stimulate unlearning, but it is better to use experiments fruitfully. Company K's experience suggests some of the differences between fruitful and unfruitful experiments.

Company K had successfully made and repaired railroad rolling stock for almost 90 years; then, in 1963, the nation's major railroad announced that it would buy no more new rolling stock from anyone for the foreseeable future. Company K's managers saw the railroad industry collapsing about them, so they studied several possibilities

and chose three new product lines for development. After two years, however, the company had achieved no sales whatever in two of these lines. The managers launched two more experimental product lines, but they concentrated their efforts on the one new product line that looked most promising: a small automobile. Sales multiplied two and a half times over the next five years, but profits were only 0.8 percent of sales! Despite frequently repeated dire predictions, railroad rolling stock was accounting for 95 percent of sales; and despite frequent hopeful predictions, the automobile had not yet gotten into production and was generating high costs. When the automobile finally did come into production in 1970 the result was horrendous losses in both 1970 and 1971—so horrendous that the directors decided to close the company.

Why did Company K's experiments turn out so badly? One reason was too many eggs in one basket. The managers poured all their energies and most of their company's money into the automobile; their experiments with other new product lines were half-hearted and ritualistic. A second reason was an absence of feedback. The managers ignored evidence that the automobile project was developing badly and evidence that the rolling-stock business was doing well. Nor did they learn from their failures. Recall that two of their experimental product lines yielded zero sales: Might this have occurred because Company K had no sales personnel, not even a sales manager? Might it have forewarned what would happen when the automobile came into production? Company K did add a sales department to promote the automobile: a sales manager and one salesman!

Shortly after the directors decided to close Company K, five of the six top managers and half of the lower-level employees departed voluntarily. The board appointed the remaining senior manager president, with orders to continue shutting the company down. Instead, the new president (who had nothing to lose) launched some new experiments. These disclosed substantial foreign demand for railroad rolling stock—the previous managers had ignored foreign markets. The experiments also showed that the blue-collar workers could run the factory themselves with very little assistance from managers—the previous managers had created a competitive game in which managers and workers were trying to outsmart each other. In fact, after they took charge, the blue-collar workers doubled productivity: By 1974, production was 36 percent higher than in 1963 even though employment was only 69 percent of the earlier figure. Two new product lines were tried, and one of these became as important as rolling stock. By then, the directors had decided to keep the company in business. Profits in 1975 were six times the highest profits the company had ever earned previously, and they have continued upward since.

Why did the second wave of experiments turn out so differently? The directors' decision to close Company K initiated unlearning: The people who departed took with them their convictions about how the company should operate and what opportunities the environment offered; the people who remained became ready to abandon their past beliefs. No longer sure they knew what to do, people tried some experiments that they would previously have rejected as outrageous or silly. The company had no resources to squander on experiments that were turning out badly, so everyone paid close attention to how the experiments were turning out: Feedback quickly had real effects. Not least, the new president was an unusually wise man who knew how to engender enthusiasm, entrepreneurship, and a team spirit.

Conclusion

Our studies underline top managers' dominance of their organizations' survival and success. Top managers are the villains who get blamed for steering organizations into crises, and they are the heroes who get the credit for rescuing organizations from crises. Such blaming and crediting are partly ritualistic, but also partly earned. Top managers do in fact guide organizations into crises and intensify crises; they also halt crises by disclosing opportunities, arousing courage, and stirring up enthusiasm.

The top managers who instigate dramatic turnarounds deserve admiration, for they have accomplished very difficult tasks of emotional and conceptual leadership. Even greater heroes, however, are the top managers who keep their organizations from blundering into trouble in the first place. To do this, they have had to meet the still more difficult challenge of conquering the errors in their own beliefs and perceptions.

Selected Bibliography

For more detailed descriptions of our studies about organizational crises, see Paul Nystrom, Bo Hedberg, and William Starbuck's "Interacting Processes as Organization Designs" in Ralph Kilmann, Louis Pondy, and Dennis Slevin's (eds.) *The Management of Organization Design,* Vol. 1 (Elsevier North-Holland, 1976); William Starbuck and Bo Hedberg's "Saving an Organization from a Stagnating Environment" in Hans Thorelli's (ed.) *Strategy + Structure = Performance* (Indiana University Press, 1977); William Starbuck, Arent Greve, and Bo Hedberg's "Responding to Crises" (*Journal of Business Administration,* Spring 1978); William Starbuck and Paul Nystrom's "Designing and Understanding Organizations" in Paul Nystrom and William Starbuck's (eds.) *Handbook of Organizational Design,* Vol. 1 (Oxford University Press, 1981); and in Bo Hedberg's "How Organizations Learn and Unlearn" in Paul Nystrom and William Starbuck's (eds.) *Handbook of Organizational Design,* Vol. 1 (Oxford University Press, 1981).

Related studies of organizational crises appear in Roger Dunbar and Walter Goldberg's "Crisis Development and Strategic Response in European Corporations" in Carolyne Smart and William Stanbury's (eds.) *Studies on Crisis Management* (Toronto's Institute for Research on Public Policy, 1978); also see William Hall's "Survival Strategies in a Hostile Environment" (*Harvard Business Review,* September–October 1980).

More information on Albert King's study of job redesigns appears in "Expectation Effects in Organizational Change" (*Administrative Science Quarterly,* June 1974).

Research concerning communications between people in superior and subordinate roles is reviewed in Lyman Porter and Karlene Roberts' "Communication in Organizations" in Marvin Dunnette's (ed.) *Handbook of Industrial and Organizational Psychology* (Rand McNally, 1976).

Alan Meyer's study of hospitals' reactions to the physicians' strike are reported in his article, "How Ideologies Supplant Formal Structures and Shape Responses to Environments" (*Journal of Management Studies,* January 1982).

A detailed study of 21 companies' planning systems appears in Peter Grinyer and David Norburn's "Planning for Existing Markets: Perceptions of Executives and Financial Peformance" (*Journal of the Royal Statistical Society,* Series A, Vol. 138, Part 1, 1975).

Readers interested in EVOP philosophy and procedures should refer to George Box and Norman Draper's *Evolutionary Operation* (Wiley, 1969).

18

Police Management in the 1980s: From Decrementalism to Strategic Thinking

Charles H. Levine

If the early 1980s was not an easy time for local governments, it was an especially sobering time for their police and sheriff departments. After a decade or more of unprecedented federal aid and budgetary growth, funding growth came to a halt and in many places actually declined. In the mid-1980s, the growing gap between rising demand for service and scarce resources has forced many top police managers to rethink their role and the role of their departments in local affairs.

This article is intended to address many of the problems that fiscal stress has posed for police managers and their departments. It presents models for understanding the typical choices most police departments have made to cope with the resource-demand gap, that is, by "decrementalism," the consequences of these choices, and what some departments are doing, and more could do, to overcome the most negative impacts. In doing so, it argues that problems stemming from fiscal stress require creative and innovative solutions and advocates a strategic management approach to organizational revitalization. Such strategic responses require: (1) a multiyear time frame, usually three to five years; (2) a significant reallocation and reconfiguration of resources; (3) substantial changes in organizational structure and work force activity; and (4) a comprehensive as opposed to an *ad hoc* re-examination of the organization's problems, mission, and structure. Changes of this scope suggest that strategic management involves political as well as financial and technical considerations.

To partially substantiate this argument, several sources will be used, including the results of a national mail survey to which 92 cities with populations over 50,000 responded. In addition, sev-

Material for this article was drawn from the author's report, *Fiscal Stress and Police Services: A Strategic Perspective* (Washington, D.C.: National Institute of Justice, U.S. Department of Justice, 1985).

Reprinted with permission from *Public Administration Review,* © 1985 The American Society for Public Administration, Washington, D.C. All rights reserved.

333

eral of the cities were examined in greater depth through field interviews.[1]

Fiscal Stress, Police Services, and "Decrementalism"

Police departments in the United States have undergone many changes as a result of fiscal stress. For example:

1. Of the 92 police departments surveyed, 73 indicated that there was a perception of fiscal stress within their cities.
2. Thirty-eight percent of the departments reported having made budget cuts, and 72 percent indicated that they had made other changes due to fiscal stress during the 1976–81 period.
3. About one-quarter of the departments laid off employees, decreased overtime use, or slowed promotion rates.
4. Fifty-two percent of the departments terminated programs in the 1976–81 period. Most of these terminations were in new services whose funding came largely from federal sources.
5. About one-third of the departments decreased in size.
6. Thirty percent of the departments made major changes in their budget formats and processes.
7. Eighty-eight percent of the departments reported that in 1981 they used call prioritization procedures to ration immediate dispatch as a response to calls for service, up from 56 percent in 1976.
8. Fifty-six percent of the departments reported that they used vehicles that exceeded their ideal replacement point, and 53 percent reported having other equipment that needed replacement.

While not all of the items were exclusively results of nor responses to fiscal stress, taken together they present a picture of agencies grappling with serious resource and cutback problems.

Decremental Responses

There is a marked pattern in the way police departments have been coping with fiscal stress. For the most part, they have been balancing their budgets by making marginal adjustments in their operating procedures and expenditures. In doing so, they have been essentially pursuing a strategy of "decrementalism"; that is, they have made small short-term adjustments in their operating arrangements that have yielded some cost savings without a corresponding loss of visible operating effectiveness. Examples of such tactics include stretching the use of patrol cars an extra year, marginally thinning out manpower on patrol, and targeting patrol activity more carefully through the use of patrol allocation models.

But many departments have arrived at the point where any additional revenue cuts likely will produce a more than proportional decline in services. The problem now for many police managers is how to live with long-term resource scarcity while protecting their department's capacity to fulfill its core mission. This is no easy problem because there is a strong preference among policy makers for familiar, short-run, incremental, and piecemeal problem-solving methods and an aversion toward viewing retrenchment as a long-term problem requiring large-scale strategic choices.

Furthermore, although decremental strategies usually include some productivity improvement devices that have potential long-term value to a department, other tactics for stretching resources —such as across-the-board budget reductions, hiring freezes, reduction-by-attrition, deferred maintenance, and freezing and rationing operating expenses—cause problems to accumulate that may eventually catch up with the organization if funding is not restored or increased. Over time these problems may become compounded, producing long-run costs that eventually may cause the need for additional expenditures to improve services or serious erosion in the levels and quality of public services. These problems occur especially when the length and depth of fiscal stress is underesti-

ⅱⅾⅾ or when policy makers act as if resources can be stretched indefinitely. These consequences include:

- *Human resource erosion:* A decline in the aggregate skill levels of an agency's work force, a decline in its energy, commitment, and physical and mental health, and a concomitant decline in its performance and responsiveness.
- *Overcentralization:* Increased control and clearances at higher and higher levels for smaller and smaller expenditures. If in place too long, such overhead control discourages initiative and stifles innovation throughout the organization.
- *Allocation shifts:* Resources gradually shift to the more powerful service delivering units in the department (e.g., patrol) and away from the less powerful staff units (e.g., planning and analysis) irrespective of their importance to the long-term effectiveness of the organization.
- *Decisional paralysis:* The inability of policy makers to make hard decisions about the long-term mission and priorities of the agency because of their disinclination to confront public employees and interest groups with new work rules, service cutbacks, or organizational arrangements. Decisional paralysis is marked by across-the-board cuts and delay-and-denial strategies—i.e., to deny that there is a crisis and delay making any major changes.[2]

In the most fiscally stressed jurisdictions, these problems tend to cluster together threatening to produce a condition called "general service default"; that is, when the government is no longer capable of delivering services that either enhance or protect the quality of life of its residents. Such a condition is a particularly critical concern for law enforcement agencies because if they are no longer seen as an effective and benign institution of government that provides security and safety, alienation, with all its attendant problems of grudging compliance, vigilantism, and middle-class flight is likely to result.

The purpose of describing these consequences of decremental adjustments to long-term fiscal stress is to underscore the point that short-sighted responses eventually produce departments that are not only smaller and cheaper but also weaker and less vital and, as a consequence, less able to cope with problems of crime and public order. The next section describes an attractive alternative to decrementalism—strategic management—which is beginning to be used, at least in part, by some police departments. It is an approach to managing resource scarcity that is fundamentally different from decrementalism but one that is within the reach of most law enforcement agencies. Above all, a strategic management perspective recognizes that decrementalism at the margins of units and programs does not reflect a realistic assessment of public needs and preferences for services. Instead, a strategic perspective requires top law enforcement managers to develop a clear understanding of what their departments' mission and core services are, to prioritize accordingly, and to create administrative arrangements to finance and deliver these services.

The Strategic Management of Police Services

The city of Oakland, California, was confronted with the triple bind of an increasing dependent population, rising crime rates, and Proposition 13 which limited the revenues that could be derived from taxes on property built before 1978. But hope is literally in sight as several large new buildings have been constructed to reshape Oakland's skyline. The problem the city faced was how to provide the perception of a secure environment in the area of new construction within the constraints of a declining budget for the police department. The answer came in the form of a 10-year agreement with developers to provide a fund to pay for a highly visible horse patrol in the downtown area, a stable, trained police dogs, and additional officers. The initial contribution was for $400,000 and in the second year they provided $350,000 to continue these activities. The program calls for the fund to reach approximately one-half million dollars in 1986 and then decrease to zero in 1990.

The assumption behind this funding scheme is that by the end of the decade the new economic activity will have increased the tax base enough to absorb program costs.

Unemployment and unpaid property taxes (about 16 percent of the total owed the city) forced the city of Eugene, Oregon, to cope with fiscal stress in two ways: enhancement of economic development and cutback of expenditures by laying off city employees. In the police department actual layoffs were minimal, but unfilled vacancies meant that the complement of sworn officers had declined significantly. To make up for this shrinkage, the department recruited, trained, and extensively used (up to 80 hours per month) reserve police officers in a wide variety of roles, including patrol work. The result was the maintenance of departmental effectiveness while allowing the city to capture appreciable savings.

The city of South Bend, Indiana, was experiencing extreme economic hardship. The population of the city declined from 130,000 to around 100,000 during the 1970s and unemployment exceeded 15 percent. To facilitate the active involvement of neighborhood groups in crime prevention, the police department decentralized into a neighborhood team policing mode, thereby cutting central administrative staff and strengthening the effectiveness of the neighborhood watch program.

These jurisdictions were among the nation's most financially hard hit by the recession of the late 1970s and early 1980s. But in coping with fiscal scarcity, their responses and those of their police departments moved beyond balancing budgets through short-term incremental means. Instead, they made strategic management choices that affected the services they deliver and the way they are organized to deliver them. In each case, fundamental trade-offs in police management were considered and eventually made. To date, the result of these changes has been to maintain and enhance the capacity of these departments to serve their constituents despite resource declines.

These examples have been characterized as strategic because they realign resources and skills

with the environmental opportunities and risks the organizations face and the purposes they wish to accomplish.[3] By encouraging the examination of linkages between governmental and non-governmental actors, a strategic management perspective encourages police managers to look beyond their departments as their focus of analysis and to view the direct provision of police services by the department and its sworn officers as only one of several options for designing law enforcement and crime prevention service delivery systems.

Key Assumptions Behind Strategic Management

The idea of a strategic approach to managing fiscal stress in policing depends on four key assumptions:

- The effectiveness of a management plan depends on "contingency relationships" between the strategy and the situation. For example, deep, long-term resource declines must be met by extensive restructuring of police operations while shallow, short-run declines can be managed by decremental tactics.
- Strategic choices require that a department have an appropriate "strategic capacity." For example, a police department cannot develop long-term plans for reallocating its budget without financial forecasting and cost accounting systems.
- Strategic choices require an examination of a full array of alternative service delivery options. Major cost adjustments are likely to require significant changes in the way police departments deliver services. Options such as shifting service responsibility, contracting for services, user fees, and service coproduction need to be given full consideration in designing long-term departmental strategies.
- Fiscal stress will close some windows of opportunity for innovative ideas, but will open others. For example, proposals that promise to save money or generate revenue are likely to be more feasible than proposals that promise to improve service but may cost more.

Each of these ideas has direct applicability to the management of police departments under conditions of fiscal stress, especially to the effectiveness of strategies that departments choose. To illustrate this point further, the remainder of this section will explore each of the four assumptions in greater detail.

Contingency Relationships

In the cities studied, fiscal stress created a crisis for local government and its departments or was managed like a routine budgeting problem. The difference was in whether coping with fiscal stress required radical changes in a department's decision-making processes, and eventually in its operations, or whether the problems that arose from fiscal stress were well within the existing decision-making and operational capacity of the department to handle them.

The cutting edge of what constituted a fiscal crisis differed from city to city and from agency to agency. A number of factors intervened in the relationship between revenue shortfalls and the perception of crisis. Of these, several were especially significant, including: (1) the authority and desire of the top administrative and political officials to cut expenditures; (2) the power of interest groups to protect agencies and services against cuts; and (3) the ability of departments to absorb budget cuts without having to make major downward adjustments in services delivered.[4] In addition to these political and administrative factors, the size of the cut and the time available for planning and adjustment were key factors in determining whether or not fiscal stress produced a fiscal crisis. For example, one-year budget cuts of 7 percent or less, in non-inflated dollars, were much less likely to produce a crisis than a cut of greater magnitude. Likewise, the longer the duration of fiscal stress, the more time and experience managers had to create appropriate responses to it. For example, fiscal stress episodes of three years or longer allowed police managers to install new techniques for improving operations, such as improved budgeting and cost accounting procedures,

prioritization arrangements to screen calls for service, and beat and shift realignments to improve resource targeting. In addition, there was time to change technologies, such as downscaling the vehicle fleet, and to adjust the size of the work force through the absorption of attrition vacancies. More important, in many communities long periods of fiscal stress provided evidence to the political forces in the community that a serious problem had arisen and that no outside bail out was likely. As a consequence, a consensus was built about the objective characteristics of the problem and the appropriate means for dealing with it.

The duration of fiscal stress combines with severity to creat four types of problems which are presented in Figure 1.[5] The four types are simplifications of many possible combinations. They are presented as "ideal types" so that the range of crisis types and responses can be categorized and narrowed to a few common properties. Of the four, the situation of low fiscal stress and short duration was the most familiar and the most easily dealt with by police managers. It occurred when a reduction in revenues relative to demands and costs was not especially severe, but it happened with little forewarning. Such a *fiscal crunch* may have been caused when a jurisdiction changed its program priorities; when revenues dropped deeper than expected due to a sudden change in tax laws, such as taxing and spending limits; or when tax revenues declined because of factors such as slumping retail sales, payrolls, or simply because of large amounts of unpaid taxes. In most cases revenue reductions were less than 7 percent over one fiscal year and were often met with budget balancing mechanisms, such as the issuing of short-term revenue anticipation notes, or with decremental strategies like freezing unfilled vacancies, reducing overtime, deferring maintenance, and other cost control devices, such as increased clearances for equipment replacement, that stalled expenditures until the next fiscal year.

The second type of fiscal stress situation — high severity but short duration — usually was preceded by danger signals, such as falling tax collec-

Figure 1. Types of Fiscal Stress and Some Tactics for Coping with Them

Duration of Fiscal Stress

	SHORT TERM	LONG TERM
LOW	**I. FISCAL CRUNCH** (a) Absorb attrition (b) Hiring and expenditure freezes (c) Defer maintenance (d) Stall payments	**III. FISCAL SQUEEZE** (a) Improve operations management (b) Target overtime (c) Trade-off raises and benefits for staff reductions (d) Downscale fleet and contract out peripheral programs
Severity of Fiscal Stress	**III. FISCAL CRISIS** (a) Layoff civilians (b) Cancel equipment replacement (c) Close some peripheral programs (d) Reorganize desk-to-field ratio	**IV. FISCAL CRUSH** (a) Use more reserves and volunteers (b) Shed functions (c) Use citizen watches and patrols (d) Extensive contracting out and cooperation with the business community and civic associations
HIGH		

tions, inflation, rising short-term debt, and year-end budget deficits. However, the signals were either ignored or met by delaying tactics for at least one or two fiscal years so that when the fiscal situation had to be dealt with, it had become very severe, requiring cuts in excess of 7 percent in one fiscal year.

In these cases the inability of top political leaders to come to terms with the growing *fiscal crisis* eventually forced their successors to take drastic action to restore fiscal solvency. In addition to all the tactics employed in minor stress situations, short-term fiscal stress required police departments to lay off employees, both sworn and civilian, but especially civilian; cancel equipment replacement; eliminate overtime; terminate some peripheral programs; renegotiate work rules; and reassign headquarters personnel to patrol work — reorganize the desk-to-field ratio.

The third type of stress situation — low severity but long duration — evolved over a period of at least three to five years. This type of situation occurred in slowly declining communities and also in slow-growing communities where budgets did not keep up to the rate of inflation or increases in demand for service. The effect was a slow *fiscal squeeze* on agency budgets.

In communities that experienced this type of fiscal stress, the opportunity existed to anticipate budget cuts and to plan some appropriate action. For the most part, this involved changes in operations and management systems, but some changes also occurred in the size and mission of the local government and its agencies. In police departments such slow squeezes prompted a more managerial approach to administration at all levels. This involved training, upgrading records management and fleet management, and improving budgeting, financial management, and cost accounting systems. Finally, time allowed factor substitution and other innovations to be implemented. For example, the number of police employees frequently was reduced in order to provide raises that at least approximated increases in the cost of living; some user fees for copying reports or for answering false burglar alarms were initiated; vehicle fleets were reduced and downscaled (four- and six-cylinder engines instead of six- and eight-cylinder vehicles); overtime was allocated with greater care; and some minor functions were contracted out or reorganized on a regional basis. In short, the long time frame and relatively minor level of stress at any one time allowed many departments to adjust gradually to lower levels of resource consumption without causing a decision-making crisis or major declines in services delivered.

Finally, the fourth type of fiscal stress — deep cuts over a long period of time — was the most difficult to cope with and required the greatest change in organization and services. It occurred in cities that experienced a series of major economic shocks like the closing of a large plant with a deep drop in jobs, sales, or population and therefore the tax base, or contrariwise, a rapid rise in demand for services without a concomitant rise in tax revenues, as in the case of some Sunbelt cities or some jurisdictions with restrictive taxing ceilings. In these cases of *fiscal crush,* cuts of more than 15 percent of revenue relative to inflation or rising demand over three to five years created the need for police departments to: (1) redefine their mission; (2) realign their service mix; (3) reallocate resources internally; (4) reorganize their internal structure; and (5) redesign means for delivering services, including the creation of new service delivery arrangements with other organizations in the community.

Under these conditions, law enforcement services were significantly affected. Changes included: police encouragement of greater citizen involvement in crime prevention through such means as increasing the responsibilities of neighborhood watches and patrols, and crime-stopper programs; greater use of reserves and auxiliaries; shedding of functions to the private sector (privatization) and to other units of government (for example, jails and courts transferred from cities to counties and from counties to states); the use of business and civic groups to fund some services and to purchase equipment; and the regional consolidation of some functions. Clearly, extended fiscal stress required major changes in police services and the way they were organized.

The contingency relationships outlined in Figure 1 suggest that some tactics fit some situations better than others. It should be recognized, however, that fiscally troubled departments used tactics that were appropriate to more than one of the four situations simultaneously. In general, however, departments chose tactics that were more extreme in impact as their fiscal problems deepened. In other words, departments moved their choice of tactics from the upper left corner of the typology in Figure 1 toward the lower right corner in order to meet the full range of contingencies produced by deep and expanded episodes of fiscal stress.[6]

It is important to note that as fiscal stress deepened, many solutions to long-term fiscal stress that at first appeared to officials to be too radical, later proved to be workable. For example, local governments and police departments began to give greater attention to the mix of services they delivered. Such analysis enhanced the possibility of finding services that were amenable to termination or "load shedding" onto the private and nonprofit sectors or other units of government. The consequence of these changes has been to create governments of narrower scope that perhaps will be more fiscally solvent in the future.

Strategic Capacity

One of the most significant issues confronting police departments trying to cope with fiscal stress concerns the capacity of their management systems to design and implement strategies. The strategic capacity of a department also has a contingency quality; that is, departments do not build sophisticated management systems unless they expect to confront complex problems. It makes little sense to set up an exhaustive checklist of ideal management tools for a department with few problems, where citizens demand little in the way of services, or where resources are ample. The tools must fit the task. If a rudimentary set of management systems serves a community now and in the foreseeable future, spending time, money, energy, and political capital upgrading them simply may not pay off. If, however, problems arise that cannot be handled by the old machinery, a reassessment and redesign of the department's problem-solving capacity is in order. In short, the key question for determining the appropriate strategic capacity for a police department is: What is the ability of this department to meet its current problems and what additional capacity will it require to meet probable future contingencies?[7]

This definition of "appropriate strategic capacity" relates directly to the problem of coping with fiscal stress and, if need be, retrenchment. Earlier research found that given equal levels of fiscal stress, some cities and agencies managed their stress and retrenchment far better than others.[8] The cities and agencies that adjusted best to deep and protracted levels of fiscal stress were able to:

- formulate and stick to a strategic plan with a multiyear time frame of three to five years; in other words, had a strategic management capacity
- develop a political and administrative climate conducive to the creation of an "experimenting polity"; that is, they created a governmental situation where citizens, clients, public employees, and political officials were willing to try new methods for delivering traditional services.

Without the capacity to plan and implement strategic responses and to engage in experiments and innovations with methods of service delivery, cities and police departments are likely to fall victim to all the short-term hazards and pitfalls of decrementalism, and consequently, service quality and quantity are bound to deteriorate as budgets contract.

What are the attributes (functional components) of a strategic management capacity that police departments will need to meet the problems of fiscal stress successfully? Based on recent empirical studies of cities confronting fiscal stress, the following nine functions appear to be preconditions for managing fiscal stress successfully:

- forecasting and planning capacity
- decision-making authority
- a management philosophy to define the department's future
- rapid and accurate feedback

- budgetary flexibility
- performance incentives
- ability to identify core services
- ability to target resources to high priority programs and cuts to low priority programs
- ability to link service and expenditure decisions to economic development strategies.[9]

Without these elements, the process of adaptation to problems of fiscal stress will likely be confused and painful. To underscore this point, two of these preconditions will be explored in greater depth: management philosophy and the linkage between services, expenditures, and economic development.

Management Philosophy. A management philosophy is an indispensable aspect of strategic management. In the case of law enforcement it involves a way of thinking about local crime problems, citizen expectations, and the future development of the community. Such a philosophy supports consistency and multiyear strategies so that a retrenchment plan can unfold over several budget cycles without confusion, backtracking, and changes of direction. Lack of such a philosophy, in contrast, breeds uncertainty among middle managers and employees who are needed to carry out the strategy. When there is rapid turnover of police chiefs, elected officials, or other top managers or vacillation in management philosophy, there is always the possibility that subordinates will delay implementing the plan in order to be sure that the new managers support the intent and the content of the strategy. These delays can accumulate into a period of general immobility, creating a financial or service delivery crisis of major proportions.

Linking Services and Expenditures to Economic Development. Some services have a greater effect on attracting and retaining taxpayers than others, and some types of taxation will have different effects for encouraging or discouraging the inward and outward mobility of taxpayers from a community.[10] All agencies of local government must have at least a rough idea of these relationships in order to protect and enhance their community's economic base. Without an understanding of these linkages, a local government may make policy choices that are self-defeating, that is, the net effect is to worsen the fiscal situation of the community.

One clear example of this linkage has already been cited in the case of the Oakland Police Department working with local developers to provide a highly visible mounted patrol in a downtown redevelopment area. By providing such a patrol, the department directly enhanced the likelihood that the redevelopment project would be successful or at least would not fail because potential patrons were fearful of their safety. This shows that some cities and police departments have been able to develop their strategic capacity well enough to allow the planning of integrated strategic responses to fiscal stress on a multiyear basis that unfolds over time.

Service Delivery Alternatives

From a strategic perspective, the main task of police management is thinking through the mission of the police department and designing an organizational system to accomplish that mission. Part of this strategic planning activity is the systematic identification of opportunities and risks that lie in the future as well as the tools to exploit these opportunities and avoid these risks. What strategic management means in this context is the activity of designing a desirable future for a community and identifying methods of accomplishing it.

In police management there has been a tendency to put too much emphasis on daily operations by maximizing patrol and investigations with not nearly enough concern devoted to defining the appropriate scope, quality, and levels of police services. In short, too much attention has been devoted to tactics and the fine tuning of police operations within the traditional framework of police management. The questions of grand strategy—mission, design, and service delivery options—have largely been ignored.

Perhaps the most important message to be derived from a strategic management perspective on policing is that *there is a variety of institutional arrangements that can be used to provide police services*. This is the case even though in most cities law enforcement functions are commonly provided by a municipal police department organized into a closed system of complex rules, procedures, and positions. This form of organization, called direct service provision, is taken as a given in most jurisdictions. It implicitly accepts as fact that: (1) the advantages of a bureaucratic form of organization—such as reliability, political neutrality, fiscal integrity, and technical rationality—outweigh the advantages of alternative arrangements; and (2) the proper way to organize public services is for public employees to be seen as the producers of public services and the citizens to be viewed as consumers of these services. However, in the past few years local government officials have begun to question both of these assumptions. As a consequence, changes in the way services are organized and delivered are taking place in many localities and others have begun the process of reassessing their service delivery systems.[11]

These activities recognize that outside of the decision of whether to provide a service at all, the most important strategic choice in urban management involves methods of service provision. Shulman observes: "To *provide* service is to decide that a service shall be made available and to arrange for its delivery. . . . To *deliver* a service, on the other hand, is to actually produce the service. Although a local government may decide to provide a service, it does not necessarily have to be directly involved in its delivery."[12] Furthermore, service can be provided in communities in several other ways even if the local government does not provide it. A particular service may be provided by another local government, such as a special district or a county, by a non-profit agency such as United Way, or simply by the private sector, thus eliminating the need for local government to get involved at all. Even though these choices may have significant political and equity effects, for now, it is appropriate to point out that the major options to direct service provision used in the United States by police departments—such as shedding service responsibility to other service providers, contracting for service, franchising, intergovernmental agreements, voluntary service, and individual and neighborhood self-help or coproduction—are gaining increasing popularity as solutions to some of the problems caused by scarce resources.

It is important to note that most police services are unlikely to be shed totally. Their long tradition, strong constituency, and the legal monopoly position of police departments in law enforcement assure that most police services will continue to be considered central to city government.[13] This helps to explain why the services that police departments have shed or privatized so far can generally be classified as peripheral to the department's core mission.

Innovation Opportunities

The final key attribute of a strategic management approach concerns the feasibility of innovation. The previous sections have argued that when confronting fiscal stress most public managers, including police chiefs, have been either passive or reactive, preferring decremental tactics to large-scale innovative solutions. But if fiscal stress deepens, passive or reactive responses and decremental tactics eventually will lead to declines in service levels and quality. In short, to avoid such outcomes, managers must search beyond conventional policy options (methods of stretching resources) to explore non-traditional service delivery approaches. Such a search forces managers to view service delivery in a new light because relying on traditional methods may be no longer possible without incurring a loss of service. Managers searching for new ways to provide services are likely to be cross-pressured by the demand from citizens and elected officials to do something and by the high risks (job, career, lost opportunities) of carving out very scarce resources to try something new. At a minimum the search for a resolution to these pressures is likely to push police

managers toward innovations that strengthen the management system. In their review of the effects of fiscal contraction on innovation in the public sector, Walker and Chaiken identify five types of management innovations that appear relatively likely to succeed in time of fiscal constraint.[14] They include:

- *Low-Cost Innovations:* Innovations with high initial costs are unlikely to be tried no matter how persuasive advocates of cost savings projects might be. "Innovations that have low continuing cost and yield substantial improvements in inefficiency will. . . be likely to gain sufficient support for implementation."

- *Revenue Generation:* Innovations that promise to generate revenues are likely to gain ready acceptance. Such innovations include computer software packages that facilitate collecting revenue such as fines, parking tickets, and user fees, as well as "imaginative legal or institutional restructuring that allows for collection of new fees."

- *Effective Budgeting Tools:* Innovations likely to be implemented give clear answers to questions like: How much will be saved by a specific budget cut? Who will be affected? What will the consequences be? Such budgetary tools will likely conform more or less to the principles of zero-base budgeting.

- *Resource Allocation Packages:* Innovations that rationally allocate resources by need or demand, such as patrol allocation models and call screening schemes, are likely to be found attractive during periods of resource contraction. Such models are especially attractive to departments and jurisdictions attempting to minimize the negative consequences of budget cuts. Such departments and jurisdictions want to have scientific-looking documentation (i.e., computer printouts) showing that they did the best they could under the circumstances.

- *Innovations That Confer Relative Advantage on an Agency:* Innovations that convey advantage to an agency in budget battles and other turf struggles are likely to meet acceptance.

Such innovations provide meaningful management information about productivity, work loads, and priorities that allow a department with well-documented charts and graphs to fare better in relative budget allocations than agencies whose demands are undocumented.

Clearly, the opportunity available for innovation during fiscal contraction is not large, but it does not disappear altogether. The need to stabilize funding and staffing levels, unfreeze position and promotion freezes, replace equipment, and reward good performance in order to improve morale, productivity, and effectiveness induces top managers to search for innovations in organizational and management structures suitable for both smaller size and revitalization.

Conclusion

The main challenge confronting police managers who must cope with the squeeze between rising demand and costs and stable or declining budgets and work forces is how to maintain organizational effectiveness. As we have seen in the preceding sections, in the long run their response likely will have to include changing the way things are done, including the way they think about problems and solutions.

Another way to illustrate this point is presented in Table 1, which breaks the structure of police departments into four levels of analysis: operations, programs, intraorganizational structure, and organization-environment relations. Traditional, primarily internal approaches to managing fiscal stress are categorized in the center column of the table and non-traditional, primarily external responses are listed in the right-hand column. Throughout, it has been argued that as episodes of fiscal stress deepen, strategies must shift from the traditional to the non-traditional and from operational tactics in the upper left-hand corner toward environmental tactics in the lower right-hand corner.

The movement of strategies from traditional (primarily internal) to non-traditional (primarily external) responses is hardly automatic.[15] It depends on a combination of leadership and political factors and, most important, on learning how to ask the right questions about a department's environment, mission, and administrative capacity.

The central task for many police chiefs in the 1980s will be to adapt their departments to diminishing resources and to revitalize them when the initial shock of cutbacks has ended. To do this, it will be necessary to develop a new "strategic image" that defines what the organization will look

Table 1. Traditional and Non-Traditional Approaches to Managing Fiscal Stress

Levels of Analysis	Traditional Approaches	Non-Traditional Approaches
Operations	Case management (tightening productivity)	Case prioritization (differential response)
Programs	Program prioritization (core vs. periphery)	Alternative service delivery arrangements (contracts, interjurisdictional agreements, volunteers, coproduction)
Intraorganizational Structure	Emphasize cost control (audits and clearances)	Emphasize capacity building (financial analysis and human resource development)
Organization-Environment Relations	Minimize interdependencies (reduce cooperative arrangements)	Network leadership (arranging combinations of interorganizational agreements)

like in the near-term future, what it will be doing, and how it will be doing it. Such an image specifies the department's purposes, plans, programs, size, and resources. It fixes the balance between resources and programs into the future and describes how to reach this new arrangement. Thus, the strategic management process will involve an iterative analysis; that is, a series of comparisons between the resources required to operate proposed programs and a realistic assessment of what political and managerial actions will be necessary to fund and implement them.[16] In doing so, top managers are bound to address one of the key questions of strategic management: Is there another way of delivering this service that is better or costs less than the way we have been doing it?

In communities that have grappled with this question, new ideas have come forward that have resulted in entirely new public and private linkages requiring a substantial modification of relationships between line command arrangements within the department and the service delivery outside the department. As this process has developed, the structure of public organizations, including police departments, has begun to be transformed from a tightly controlled hierarchy into a much more complex structure of networks of cooperative relationships.[17] Examples of such networks in policing are numerous. In addition to neighborhood watch groups, police departments are increasingly involved in working with other government agencies and non-profit organizations in arranging for services such as victim assistance and rape crisis centers and spouse abuse programs and shelters. Also, many departments are moving toward better and more integrated relationships with private security firms that provide guard, patrol, and burglar alarm services in their jurisdictions.

This cooperative approach is a departure from past practices in which many police managers either ignored these other agencies and private firms, regarded them as peripheral, or tried to control them by legally circumscribing their activities. In many places these responses will no longer suffice. Departmental effectiveness will increasingly depend on the ability of top managers to build networks that link service provision and delivery functions. In such a system, police chiefs, sheriffs, and other top managers will have to build cooperative relationships with public and private organizations across their communities and regions. In doing so their role will have to change from that of a commander of a closed hierarchy to that of an arranger of interorganizational networks.

Notes

1   This data will be presented in greater detail in Charles H. Levine, *Fiscal Stress and Police Services: A Strategic Perspective* (Washington, D.C.: National Institute of Justice, forthcoming 1985). Because police departments have only recently begun to experiment with the idea of strategic management, some of the points made in this article are admittedly impressionistic and may seem somewhat at odds with the way police chiefs, sheriffs, and other police managers have traditionally thought about their jobs, but they should be more persuasive when considered within the framework of the trends of the past decade.

2   These hidden costs of retrenchment are explained at greater length in Charles H. Levine, "Retrenchment, Human Resource Erosion, and the Role of the Personnel Manager," *Public Personnel Management,* vol. 13 (Fall 1984), pp. 249–63.

3   See Robert W. Backoff and Barton Wechsler, "Integrating Tools and Networks: A Strategic Management Approach," prepared for the Annual Meeting of the American Political Science Association, Denver, Colorado, September 2–6, 1982, pp. 15–16.

4   For similar findings, see Charles H. Levine, Irene S. Rubin, and George G. Wolohojian, *The Politics of Retrenchment* (Beverly Hills, Calif.: Sage Publications, 1981).

5   For a similar approach, see Todd D. Jick and Victor V. Murray, "The Management of Hard Times: Budget Cutbacks in Public Sector Organizations," prepared for the Annual Meeting of the Academy of Management, San Diego, California, August 15–17, 1980, pp. 15–16.

6   The process involved in changing strategies as fiscal stress episodes deepen and extend over time suggests that the choice of strategies followed a development sequence; that is, old strategies were abandoned, but not necessarily all the old tactics, and new strategies were formed to better deal with the new, more difficult situation. In general, each new set of decision rules and strategies built upon the previous set and allowed for consequences that were broader and more extensive in scope than the previous set.

7 See John Gargan, "Consideration of Local Government Capacity," *Public Administration Review,* vol. 41 (November–December 1981), p. 652.

8 See Levine, Rubin, and Wolohojian, *op. cit.*

9 *Ibid.,* ch. 8.

10 See Paul E. Peterson, *City Limits* (Chicago, Ill.: University of Chicago Press, 1981), p. 34; also Stephen L. Garman, "The Terminal City," *State and Local Government Review,* vol. 15 (Winter 1983), pp. 32–37.

11 See, for example, Harry P. Hatry, *A Review of Private Approaches for Delivery of Public Services* (Washington, D.C.: The Urban Institute Press, 1983); E.S. Savas, *Privatizing the Public Sector* (Chatham, N.J.: Chatham House, 1982); and Robert W. Poole, Jr., *Cutting Back City Hall* (New York: Universe Books, 1980).

12 Martha A. Shulman, *Alternative Approaches for Delivering Public Services,* Urban Data Reports, vol. 14 (Washington, D.C.: International City Management Association, October 1982), p. 1.

13 See Mark H. Moore and George L. Kelling, "To Serve and Protect: Learning from Police History," *The Public Interest,* No. 70 (Winter 1983), p. 64.

14 Warren E. Walker and Jan M. Chaiken, "The Effects of Fiscal Contraction on Innovation in the Public Sector," *Policy Sciences,* vol. 15 (1982), pp. 157–60.

15 For more on this problem, see Robert P. McGowan and John M. Stevens, "Local Government Initiatives in a Climate of Uncertainty," *Public Administration Review,* vol. 43 (March–April 1983), p. 134.

16 See Robert D. Behn, "Leadership for Cutback Management: The Use of Corporate Strategy," *Public Administration Review,* vol. 40 (November–December 1980), pp. 613–20.

17 See Ted Kolderie, "Rethinking Public Service Delivery," *Public Management,* vol. 64 (October 1982), pp. 7–9.

19

The Fundamentals of Cutback Management

Robert D. Behn

In the history of human organizations, retrenchment is a modern problem. Many organizations have contracted and disappeared over the centuries, but the idea of managing an organization so as to make it smaller but still effective is quite contemporary. In the past, the inevitability of growth — economic, population, and technological growth — made the task of cutback management unimportant. If an organization lost its market or its clientele, it simply shrank or disappeared while other, expanding organizations absorbed those functions for which some private or public demand still existed. Moreover, for most organizations, growth itself was a primary goal. In business, the imperative of market share motivated this quest. To obtain economies of scale and

to move further along the learning curve, firms sought greater market share. Their reward for this growth was increased profit.

Governments have different motivations and rewards, yet they also pursue growth. Organizations whose funds come from budgets rather than markets have no criterion like profit — a simple ratio that specifies how effectively the organization is using its resources to achieve its objectives — to measure success. For several reasons, governments have a difficult time measuring the impact of their actions and thus cannot easily compare resources used with results produced. Consequently, size itself becomes a surrogate measure of success and a key to power. The bigger an agency and its budget, and the more rapid its growth, the more successful it is considered to be.

But growth, in government and business, is no longer inevitable. Business is learning to cope with stable or declining markets. And government can no longer assume that it will be permitted to allocate an increasing (or even a constant) share of the nation's resources. That does not mean that all organizational growth will cease. It does mean,

---

This essay draws freely upon the ideas developed by a small community of scholars who have investigated the problems of policy termination and cutback management: Eugene Bardach, Garry D. Brewer, Robert P. Biller, Richard M. Cyert, Andrew Glassberg, Charles H. Levine, and Irene Rubin.

Reprinted with permission from *What Role for Government: Lessons from Policy Research,* ed. by Richard Zeckhauser and Derek Leebaert, pp. 310–22. © 1983 Duke University Press.

however, that some organization will have to stop growing and that others will have to contract. And the more successfully public and private managers handle the process of retrenchment, the more resources they will free up for growth—both by other organizations and by their own—to meet new demands, new opportunities, and new needs.

In government, the contraction of resources is forcing retrenchment at all levels. President Reagan's budget, public referenda, and continued inflation without economic growth are creating new fiscal realities for NASA and the Department of Agriculture, for New York City and Cleveland, for state highway departments and local school systems (which also face a drop in demand due to declining enrollments). In such an environment, public managers can create opportunities for growth, for expanding existing activities and starting new ones, only if they can cut back on some of their existing programs.

Thus, public managers may have several reasons to learn about cutback management: the current clamor for smaller government, the competing demands for limited resources in a barely expanding economy, a drop in the demand for particular public services, or simply the desire to expand some other components of the organization. Being able to take an agency and make it smaller, while still maintaining morale and productivity and fulfilling the agency's most basic purposes, will be an important, and perhaps essential, responsibility of public managers during the coming decade.

The Fact of Retrenchment

The Assumption of Real Retrenchment

The analysis of any managerial problem depends upon assumptions about its severity. Indeed, worrying about cutback management is worthwhile only if the required retrenchment is major. If the following three conditions are met, it is safe to assume that the problem is real and significant—that it cannot be solved with some simple economies or by a technological fix.

Retrenchment is necessary. Real resources are declining, for whatever reason (tax cut, shifting priorities, a steady budget combined with inflation). Moreover, the agency cannot easily expand by creating new programs with new clients who will supply new resources. The agency will simply have to get along with less.

The problem is serious. It cannot be solved simply by cutting out the fat. The required retrenchment is greater than whatever organizational slack the manager has been able to accumulate. Representative Delbert L. Latta (R-OH) observed, "If I were President, I'd say cut back spending without cutting back services" (Leman, 1980). This second assumption precludes such a miracle, since the retrenchment necessitates some real cuts in services.

The manager's responsibility is to make the retrenchment work. Naturally, the temptation is to resist—to make cuts in such a way that the natural forces of politics will restore them. (This has been called "the Washington Monument strategy" after a success by the National Park Service: Forced to make budget cuts, NPS eliminated elevator service at the Washington Monument and suggested to out-of-town tourists that their representatives just down the Mall were reponsible for this unfortunate cutback in service. Soon the funds and the elevator service were restored.) But the other two assumptions preclude this possibility; there will be fewer resources and the manager will simply have to make the agency function as well as possible under this constraint.

Still, the public manager does not have to manage. Confronted by contradictory demands—for contractions and cuts, but also for services and performance—he or she can simply resign. Or, without officially resigning, the manager can abdicate responsibility, surrendering control to superiors, to the legislature, the public employee unions, to the banks, or to the most powerful interest groups. Some managers, however, will accept the challenge. Recognizing the reality of retrenchment, they will seek to lead their organizations through the process and to create a smaller, more efficient (and perhaps more effective) organization. To such managers—Andrew Glassbcrg (1978: 328) calls them "revitalizing entrepreneurs"—this chapter is addressed.

The Basic Responsibilities of Cutback Management

The necessity of retrenchment presents the leaders of an organization with a number of tasks. Their ability to handle these basic responsibilities of cutback management will determine how productive the organization is when it emerges from the retrenchment process.

Decide what to cut. This is, of course, the fundamental dilemma of retrenchment: Which functions should be abandoned and which continued? Which organizational subunits should be eliminated and which maintained? Which employees should be laid off and which retrained? How intelligent the manager is in choosing—and how effective he or she is in obtaining the necessary support for the decisions—will determine how well the organization copes with retrenchment.

In choosing what to cut, the basic issue—for it applies to all organizations—is whether to favor equity or efficiency. Equity considerations suggest a share-the-burden strategy. Across-the-board cuts are attractive, for not only can they be defended as equitable but they also avoid the necessity of making real choices about priorities. If the required cuts are large, however, across-the-board retrenchment does not make sense. It is silly to require every unit, regardless of the importance of its mission or the effectiveness of its work, to absorb, for example, a 30 percent cut. Such a decision could well destroy the effectiveness of all the subunits. Since some units may require a critical mass of personnel and equipment to function effectively, a 30 percent cut may result in more than a 30 percent loss of effectiveness. Moreover, across-the-board cuts punish the most efficient units, for they have little of the fat that the sloppily managed units can use to absorb the cuts.

Further, what principle of ethics states that organizational subunits deserve equal protection? Ethical considerations should concern people, not organizations; and in human terms, retrenchment is inherently unfair. Some people will lose their jobs; others will not. To the people who are laid off, it hardly matters whether the layoffs come proportionately from every subunit of the organization or from just a few. True equity would require that everyone make an equal sacrifice: instead of a 30 percent cut in the workforce, everyone would take a 30 percent cut in pay. (This approach has been employed in some industries, with union acceptance and support.)

An effective manager of an organization undergoing retrenchment must consciously decide whether to target the cuts. Yet this decision will not be easy. The targets will naturally complain, and with all the political force they can mobilize. Further, a variety of legal constraints—seniority, veteran's preferences, bumping rights, entitlements, mandated programs—will limit a manager's ability to focus the cuts. But if the organization must undergo a 30 percent cut in resources, the manager will have to decide what 70 percent is the most essential and the most productive, and concentrate the cuts so as to maximize the organization's post-retrenchment effectiveness.

Maintain morale. Since growth has been the traditional measure of performance, retrenchment can have a devastating impact upon morale. Employees, constituents, legislators, and journalists see the organization becoming smaller and conclude that it is becoming less important and less successful as well. Such an inference can easily destroy morale and affect the motivation of employees to work, of legislators to appropriate funds, of constituents to provide support, and of journalists to provide attention. The result can be what Richard Cyert (1978: 345) calls the "vicious circle of disintegration": a first set of cutbacks leads to declining morale, which leads to poorer performance, which leads to a second round of cutbacks, which leads to a further decline in morale, and so on. To keep the agency productive, the manager will have to find some way to turn retrenchment into a positive force that actually boosts morale.

Attract and keep quality people. As morale begins to decline, the best people, who are by definition the most mobile, will begin to leave. This trend can be further aggravated by across-the-board cuts, which fail to distinguish between productive and unproductive people and subunits. Indeed, the consequence (if not the intent) of across-the-board cuts may well be to lay off the organization's best workers. Cutback management requires the ability to recognize good performance and reward it. Otherwise, the most productive workers will simply leave—Charles Levine (1979: 180) calls this the "Free Exiter" problem—contributing still more torque to Cyert's vicious circle of disintegration.

Develop the support of key constituencies (and legislators). Any agency needs outside support. Yet how can it continue to attract such support when it has less to offer? Which constituencies should the agency's managers continue to court? Which should it risk alienating, perhaps turning into enemies? These decisions are obviously related to the choices about where to make the required cuts. The functions and units that the managers wish to retain, emphasize, and strengthen will need constituent and legislative support. Mangers must concentrate remaining resources so that these target constituencies will have something worth supporting.

Create opportunities for innovation. Even in retrenchment, an organization can improve if it increases productivity. This requires flexibility, the ability to experiment with innovations. When cutbacks are required, however, such experiments seem like a luxury; how can we think of funding new activities which will (implicitly) necessitate cutting back further on existing units and laying off even more personnel? Still, the organization faced with retrenchment cannot survive unless it learns to do new things, or to do old things better.

For a growing organization, innovation is desirable and occurs automatically as the agency experiments to find the best use of each increment of resources. For a contracting organization, innovation is essential; yet it will not occur unless the manager makes a conscious effort to create the opportunities (and find the resources) for it.

Avoid mistakes. While stimulating innovation, however, the manager must be careful to avoid any disastrous mistakes. In the middle of retrenchment, the organization is vulnerable enough. One serious error can twist the circle of disintegration into a cyclone of destruction.

The desire to avoid mistakes will come naturally—too naturally, perhaps. Even managers of stable or growing agencies are conservative in their style, seeking (at all costs, it often appears) to avoid mistakes that could create reasons for budget cuts. When cuts are already occurring, the natural tendency is to be even more conservative. Thus, public managers faced with retrenchment must find a balance between encouraging innovation and avoiding mistakes. They must not make the one error that can end the organization's chances for recovery and success. At the same time, however, they need to experiment with innovations that might increase productivity, improve morale, and recapture stability.

The (Marginal) Economies of Retrenchment

These six responsibilities are not unique to cutback management. Deciding what to cut is really just the traditional chore of allocating resources; in retrenchment, however, this means deciding who must absorb the decrements rather than who will be awarded the increases. And all managers must maintain morale, attract and keep quality people, develop the support of key constituencies (and legislators), create opportunities for innovation, and avoid mistakes. Whether resources are growing or shrinking, the challenge of management is to organize the productive activities of individuals into a coherent enterprise so that they can accomplish more working together than they could separately. Consequently, whether the organization is growing or contracting, the basic responsibilities of the manager remain the same.

In retrenchment, however, these responsibilities are much more difficult to carry out. For example, the task of allocating growing resources is relatively simple. The manager need only decide who will get how much of this year's increase. He or she will, of course, make some mistakes in allocating resources, but these can be easily rectified. For example, the manager may have overestimated the ability of subunit A to make productive use of additional resources and underestimated the ability of subunit B to do so. As a result, the manager allocates to A some resources that would have better been given to B, and the entire organization is less productive than it could be. Still, both B and A are alive and functioning, and the mistake can easily be corrected with the next round of increases by allocating more of the increase to B and less to A. Thus, the manager's mistake is not disastrous in the short run (both A and B continue to function quite well) and can be corrected in the long run (by allocating the next round of increases differently).

In retrenchment, however, the managerial responsibility of allocating resources is qualitatively different. Now the manager must decide which units will absorb the greatest portion of the losses, and the consequences of any error can be significant, indeed disastrous. For example, suppose that more cuts should be made in A than in B, but the manager decides wrong and cuts more from B than from A. In the short run, A will continue to function more or less as it has, but B may be significantly wounded. Moreover, the manager may not be able to correct the problem in the next round of cuts. Subunit B may already have been permanently damaged; even if extra cuts are made in other subunits to give B a real increase, the loss of key personnel may make recovery an extremely expensive process. In retrenchment, a mistake in allocating resources can be much more disastrous than in growth.

Indeed, growing resources facilitate all of the basic managerial chores. More money can help resolve the inevitable conflicts between subunits over resources or policy. Morale is much easier to maintain when funds exist to reward productive subunits and individuals; even if there are limitations on salary increases, quality personnel can be recruited and retained by using the growing resources to provide perquisites, staff, equipment, and promotions. And just as such resources can win support inside the organization, they can also be used to develop support from key constituencies, for there will be programs and benefits to offer them.

Moreover, managers blessed with growing resources will find it easier to avoid mistakes. Not only will their mistakes be less serious and more easily corrected, managers of growing organizations can afford the analytical capability to make better decisions. In retrenchment, however, the analytical staffs are often the first to be cut. In an effort to maintain the line units—the productive components of the organization—as close to full strength as possible, the organization sacrifices some of its ability to avoid mistakes. The decrease in resources makes all of the tasks of management more difficult.

The Two Stages of Retrenchment

Who has the motivation to declare that the reality of retrenchment has arrived and to initiate the cutbacks? Unfortunately, very few public officials do. Indeed, they have a strong incentive to avoid the immediate abuse they will receive for even suggesting that retrenchment is coming. Who will cheer the announcement of impending cutbacks? Very few. Who will boo? All of us. Most public managers have very short time horizons (compared, at least, with managers in the private sector) and will see little benefit in making unnecessary enemies. After all, the discrepancy between revenues and expenditures can always be disguised for a little longer with "creative financing" or deferred maintenance.

The process of retrenchment can be divided into two stages: before and after the organization's leaders publicly recognize the cutbacks are necessary. Both before and after this milestone, the organization is coping with the mismatch between revenues and expenditures. In the first stage, however, the tactic is to borrow against the future, to make the future pay for the deficits of the present. Yet unless some future miracle increases revenues significantly, this approach only exacerbates the problem. The longer the organization's managers delay making cutbacks, the worse the problem becomes — the greater the operating debt that is accumulated (no matter how "creative" the financing) and the longer the maintenance will be deferred. The sooner the reality of retrenchment is recognized, the sooner the organization moves to the second stage of retrenchment and the easier it will be to solve the problem.

The rub is that other people — employees, constituents, legislators, even journalists — often will not believe the reality. They, too, have little incentive to believe it or to do anything about it. They have experienced the growth of the past and want it to continue. Any momentary imbalance between revenues and expenditures, they hope, will surely correct itself; some miracle will happen to make everything better again. Levine (1979: 181) calls this the "Tooth Fairy Syndrome." Eventually, however, reality will arrive, either because the bridges fall down or because the banks refuse to lend any more money. If retrenchment is required, it will come. The only question is who will announce its approach: the organization's leaders, who recognize the reality and are willing to take the risk of doing something about it, or some outsiders, who — in return for their continued, essential cooperation — insist that something be done. For example, in the cases of Cleveland, New York City, and Antioch College these outsiders were the banks, who as a condition for their continued support demanded that revenues and expenditures be brought into balance.

It is, unfortunately, in most people's collective interest but in few people's individual interest that the second stage come quickly. The debilitating impact of remaining in the first retrenchment stage for too long is dramatically illustrated by the plight of Cleveland. During the eight years

under mayors Ralph Perk and Dennis Kucinich (November 1971 to November 1979), the city's budget was never in balance. In Ohio, no city can increase taxes without a voter referendum, and in 1970 and 1971 Cleveland Mayor Carl Stokes failed in three attempts to increase the city's income tax. Both Perk and Kucinich campaigned on promises not to increase taxes. Both followed the example of New York City and used debt to cover operating expenses. Only in December 1978, after the city defaulted on $15 million in short-term notes, did Mayor Kucinich agree that more taxes were needed; the city's citizens then voted to increase the income tax (Humphrey, Peterson, and Wilson, 1979).

The failure to advance quickly from the first to the second stage of retrenchment has been particularly destructive to Cleveland's fiscal and physical condition. A study by the Urban Institute examined the city's capital plant (its street, sewer, bridge, water and transit systems) and found that "Cleveland now faces a backlog of some $700 million in basic improvements to its infrastructure systems. . . . Many facilities have outlived their expected service lives or have become functionally obsolete" (Humphrey, Peterson, and Wilson, 1979: 75). Specifically, the report concluded:

> The city-owned water system, which serves most of the metropolitan area, needs $250 to $500 million in replacements and renovation. One treatment plant is in hazardous condition, and clogged and corroded pipes have reduced the system's capacity to deliver water at acceptable pressures. The condition of 30 percent of the city-owned bridges has been rated as unsatisfactory or intolerable, and in need of more than $150 million in major repairs. The city's sewer collection system is plagued with frequent overflows and basement floodings; an estimated $340 million would be needed to alleviate floodings alone. (Humphrey, Peterson, and Wilson, 1979: xv)

Cleveland's capital plant has clearly been a primary victim of its financial plight; deferred maintenance and the use of debt for operating expenses were the chief means of handling declining resources during the 1970s. The Urban Institute team found that "maintenance spending has borne more than a proportionate share of Cleveland's budget retrenchment, primarily because of its lesser urgency or less visibility" (Humphrey, Peterson, and Wilson, 1979: 42–43). Cleveland delayed, for nearly a decade, moving from the first stage of retrenchment to the second, and that delay has proved extremely costly to the city and its residents.

The Role of Leadership

Leadership Fundamentals

In this type of environment, how can public managers carry out their basic responsibilities? How can they lead their organizations into the second stage of retrenchment and take them through the necessary cutbacks so as to rejuvenate and not demolish them? Five fundamentals of retrenchment leadership are important.

Explain the reality. Unless the manager is willing to let the banks (or whoever is covering the deficit) decide when the organization should enter the second stage of retrenchment, he or she must educate the organization to this reality. This educational process takes time and ideally should be initiated long before the first cuts are even suggested. Before people can begin the painful process of actually making cuts, they need time to adjust their thinking from growth to contraction. In retrenchment the chief difficulty, both emotional and intellectual, lies not in deciding what must be done to close the gap, but in accepting the fact that a problem exists—that there exists a gap that must be closed.

In addition to recognizing the imbalance between resources and expenditures, people must also realize that there are significant costs to not cutting back. The costs of cutting back will be very clear; they are direct, out-of-pocket costs imposed on particular individuals and groups. In contrast, the costs of not cutting back will be much more obscure; they are indirect, opportunity costs imposed on larger, less well-identified and less well-

organized groups. As leader and thus as educator, the manager needs to explain who will bear what costs if the organization does not cut back.

Take a long-term view. Retrenchment cannot be managed on an ad hoc basis. The leaders of an organization must have a long-term perspective on the problem. They must understand where they are going and how they can get there. And they must recognize the subtle steps that need to be taken today to ease the more difficult cutback decisions that must be made tomorrow. For example, the Department of Defense has had for nearly 20 years an ongoing and very successful program of closing military bases across the country. And when the Pentagon announces that it is closing a base, the base is usually closed. Part of the reason for such success lies in the characteristics of the department—its budgeting process and the nature of its military mission—and part in the inability or unwillingness of Congress to overturn its decisions. But part of the secret also lies in the department's long-term approach to its program of cutback management. The Department of Defense is consciously shrinking its base structure. Consequently, it can plan ahead. If it believes that it may want to phase out a base in five years, it begins now by not putting any new facilities on the base, by not modernizing existing equipment, by letting the base become slightly obsolete. Then, when the time comes for some base to be closed, any unbiased individual can see that this base is the best choice for closing, and that the other alternatives are simply in much better shape. The department's willingness to take a long-term approach to this program—to act ahead as well as think ahead—is one of the keys to its success (Behn and Lambert, 1979).

For two important reasons, cutback management requires a long-term view. First, retrenchment can produce few short-term gains. Unless layoffs are massive, the costs of any cutbacks may well exceed the gains during the first year. Closed facilities must be put in mothballs. Individuals who are fired or "retired" must be given severance payments. Consolidating units involves transitional costs. Most of the sensible tactics for reducing the scale of an organization produce benefits only in the long run. One observer of cutback management in school systems observed, "The gurus of decline say it takes about 10 years for a district to realize any substantial saving from retirement after enrollment decline" (Divoky, 1979: 87).

The second reason for taking a long-term perspective is that decisions based on short-term considerations may only exacerbate the problem. Ad hoc decisionmaking does little to fulfill any of the six basic responsibilities of cutback management. A promise that "this is the last set of layoffs" will be viewed skeptically. A second such promise (after a first round of layoffs) will be taken as a deliberate lie. Yet if managers do not know where their organizations are going, they will be sorely tempted to make such promises in an attempt to mitigate the consequences of any cutback.

Ad hoc decisionmaking, which is responsive to the crises and pressures of the moment rather than to an overall plan, is the easiest way to enter Cyert's vicious circle and to make it spin faster. The organization's leaders need to know where the cutbacks can stop, where the retrenchment can level off, and how they can get the organization to stop there. Only then can they take actions and make commitments that will be realistic, not just expedient. Everyone in the organization will be suspicious of deals that involve present sacrifices for future benefits; everyone will believe that the deal will be forgotten. The managers need to convince employees, clients, supporters, and observers that they know where they are going and that they can and will honor their commitments to get there.

Develop a new "corporate strategy." To provide the basis for such long-term thinking, the organization needs a new plan of its basic purposes, programs, and resources. Such a comprehensive plan makes clear what the new equilibrium of the organization will be (i.e., at what point the organization will be able to establish a new balance between resources and programs) and how it will get there. Such a plan provides a basis for sustaining

employee morale by emphasizing the positive aspects of the organization's future—the things it *will* be doing. It clarifies the types of innovations the organization should most enthusiastically promote, and the types of people it needs to retain and recruit. Finally, it provides the criteria for deciding what should be cut and what should not.

In the business world, such a comprehensive plan is called a "corporate strategy" (Andrews, 1971). Unfortunately, governments rarely develop explicitly corporate, organizational, or agency strategies. As a result, government agencies tend to expand in a disorganized, incoherent manner, responding to the pressures of the moment. Without an explicit overall statement of purposes, programs, and resources, agencies become a menagerie of programs which have little in common other than the fact that they are funded with taxpayer dollars.

In a period of growth, the lack of an organizational strategy is merely costly. Without a clear statement of purpose, there can exist no criteria for allocating resources between competing interests. Resources cannot be concentrated on the agency's most fundamental purposes, for these have not been defined. As long as the agency is expanding, however, each year's growth in resources can be allocated so as to minimize conflicts between competing interests. Everyone can have a little more, and so no one feels neglected.

In retrenchment, however, the absence of an explicit corporate strategy upon which to base key decisions is disastrous. For without a clear purpose, the debate over where to make cuts quickly deteriorates into a childish squabble with everyone making demands on the basis of personal selfishness. (Little wonder that across-the-board cuts are so attractive; without any clear purpose, there is no justification for any other mode of decision, and the equity argument can dampen the whines.) A healthy, productive organization must have a purpose; otherwise, how can it be said to be productive? Further, to lead an organization through a retrenchment process and have it emerge healthy and productive, a manager must be able to articulate a clear, specific mission for the organization. The manager who tries to muddle through without such an explicit corporate strategy cannot lead but can only react (Behn, 1980).

Develop measures of performance. In deciding which functions to emphasize in the corporate plan and which to cut during retrenchment, the performance of different units is important. Yet how does the manager know which units are performing well? How can he or she know which units are sustaining productivity while cutting back and which units are deteriorating rapidly? How can the manager recognize and reward those who are performing well? To carry out all these basic functions, the manager needs to be able to measure performance.

During retrenchment, people and subunits will have obvious and credible explanations for why performance is deteriorating. The manager needs to know what is really happening and where the major weaknesses lie, and to be able to compare various subunits to each other and to reasonable standards. Moreover, he or she needs to determine who is performing well despite the cutbacks; morale will be bad enough anyway during retrenchment, and the manager needs to be able to recognize and reward those who are still performing well.

Create incentives for cooperation. Few people believe that retrenchment is in their self-interest. Indeed, many members of the organization will have both the incentive and the ability to resist the cutbacks, if not to sabotage the process and the manager too. People can hide resources, complain to higher authorities about cutback priorities, create rumors, and purposefully underperform to prove the evils of the cutback process. In retrenchment, the members of the organization see only the prospect for punishment; they perceive no chance for reward and thus have little reason to cooperate. Yet without cooperation the manager cannot manage.

As Robert P. Biller (1980) has emphasized, managers need to create incentives for cooperation and participation in the retrenchment process. This will not, of course, be easy. People see clearly why they should cooperate in increasing

their budget; it is not at all obvious, however, what they have to gain by decreasing it. A clear corporate strategy can provide one reason, for this plan will state which units will remain stable (and perhaps even expand) as well as which units will be cut or disappear. Those whose relative or absolute importance will be enhanced by the retrenchment will have a reason to cooperate.

Moreover, the budget process can be redesigned to create incentives for managers of subunits to make their own cuts. Permitting managers to carry forward some fixed fraction of unused funds from one fiscal year to the next would encourage savings. Under present rules, all unspent funds revert to the treasury at the end of the fiscal year. Official commandments not to spend unused funds at the end of the fiscal year have little impact when compared with the incentives which the rules create for managers: not to spend the money is to lose it. Yet if managers were rewarded rather than punished for not spending money, they might not engage in traditional end-of-the-year spending sprees. If they could keep some unspent money to be used as they saw fit during the coming year, the incentive to spend could be turned into an incentive to save.

Governments have traditionally relied upon commands rather than incentives to achieve their purposes. The results are often unsatisfactory and sometimes counter-productive. When the natural incentives are clear and work against cooperation, as is the case in retrenchment, managers need to think carefully and creatively about how they can establish positive incentives for cooperation. For example, Irene Rubin (1980) has discussed how the budgetary process in cities could be redesigned to curtail the ability of the city council and others to hide operating deficits. Hidden deficits prevent the city from moving into the second stage of retrenchment; consequently, creating incentives to expose deficits can help the city cope with its unfortunate fiscal realities in a realistic manner.

At the University of Southern California, reports Biller (1980: 607), a system of across-the-board cuts has been used to create extra funds for which departments can compete. Every department might be required to take, for example, a

5 percent cut, with some of these funds put into a special pool. Departments submit proposals for new undertakings to a committee that then awards funds from the pool. The outcome is a system of targeted, not across-the-board, cuts, but the process itself creates the incentive for departments to cooperate, since they all have a chance to win some of the awards from the special pool.

Be compassionate.   Retrenchment is not a happy time. People are losing their jobs, their benefits, their expectations. Their world is changing suddenly and drastically, and they have trouble coping with the uncertainty. Managers who want to sustain the support of key constituencies will have to demonstrate that they understand the hardships retrenchment imposes on people. As one observer of cutback management in school systems has concluded, "A cold-blooded approach won't work. The [school] board and administration must make it clear that this is an extremely unpleasant decision. The number one concern must be people" (Mazzarella & Barber, 1978: 32). Managers who seek the cooperation of individuals, although they have been deprived of the resources usually available to promote such cooperation, must demonstrate that they recognize the human problems caused by retrenchment and that they truly sympathize with the plight of the members of their organizations.

The Necessity of Leadership

Public agencies with declining resources require conscious and effective management. An organization cannot simply drift through retrenchment. Centralized decisionmaking and centralized leadership are essential. A public manager who is responsible for an organization when it is forced to cut back faces a particularly demanding assignment. Nevertheless, such a task is not impossible. But unless a manager is able to think ahead and to learn from similar managerial endeavors (and

records now exist of a variety of such experiences), he or she may overlook some of the fundamentals of cutback management and thus lose the opportunity to convert a declining organization into a smaller but more stable and effective one.

References

Andrews, Kenneth R. 1971. *The Concept of Corporate Strategy.* Homewood, Ill.: Dow Jones-Irwin.

Behn, Robert D. 1980. "Leadership for Cut-Back Management: The Use of Corporate Strategy." *Public Administrative Review* 40 (November/December): 613–20.

Behn, Robert D., and David P. Lambert. 1979. "Cutback Management at the Pentagon: The Closing of Military Bases." Paper presented at the Research Conference on Public Policy and Management, Chicago, Ill., October 19.

Biller, Robert P. 1980. "Leadership Tactics for Retrenchment." *Public Administration Review* 40 (November/December): 604–9.

Cyert, Richard M. 1978. "The Management of Universities of Constant or Decreasing Size." *Public Administration Review* 38 (July/August): 344–49.

Divoky, Diane. 1979. "Burden of the Seventies: The Management of Decline." *Phi Delta Kappan* 61 (October): 87–91.

Glassberg, Andrew. 1978. "Organizational Responses to Municipal Budget Decreases." *Public Administration Review* 38 (July/August): 325–32.

Humphrey, Nancy, George E. Peterson, and Peter Wilson. 1979. *The Future of Cleveland's Capital Plant.* Washington, D.C.: The Urban Institute.

Leman, Nicholas. 1980. "Fiscal Conservative's District: A Lot of Bucks Stop Here." *Washington Post* (January 29).

Levine, Charles, 1979. "More on Cutback Management: Hard Questions for Hard Times." *Public Administration Review* 39 (March/April): 179–83.

Mazzarella, Jo Ann, and Larry Barber. 1978. "Facing Declining Enrollment: Considerations and Procedures." School District No. 4J, Eugene Public Schools, Eugene, Ore. Mimeographed.

Rubin, Irene. 1980. "Preventing or Eliminating Planned Deficits: Restructuring Political Incentives." *Public Administration Review* 40 (November/December): 621–26.

20

Least-Cost Alternatives To Layoffs In Declining Industries

Lee Tom Perry

Consider the following two capsule histories of response to industry decline:

> The demand for services provided by a telecommunications firm dropped sharply during the 1979 recession. The company had no history of layoffs. Because it was in a regulated industry and its rate-of-return was guaranteed, the firm was buffered from many of the usual uncertainties associated with declining demand. In spite of its secure position, history, and reputation, top management made a decision to respond quickly to the downturn and lay off 100 employees. Perhaps the layoffs were intended to be a symbolic gesture, since the number of people affected was very small relative to the total number of employees. If this was the company's intention, the impact was grossly miscalculated. Because of the unwise timing of the layoffs, they caused widespread disaffection. Employee morale and confidence in top manage-

ment plummeted. The event gained in infamy, and in the corridors and washrooms of corporate headquarters it became known as the "Christmas Eve Massacre."

> In the early 1970s the entire electronics industry suffered a drop in orders, and most companies were laying off people in significant numbers. At Hewlett-Packard estimates indicated that it was necessary to cut back 10% in both output and payroll to match the decline in orders. In this company the obvious solution was to follow its competitors and lay off 10% of the work force. Top management, however, was committed to avoiding layoffs. After considerable discussion, a novel solution surfaced. Management decided to require everyone from the president to the lowest-paid employee to take a 10% cut in pay and to stay home every other Friday. By distributing the "pain" across organizational levels, Hewlett-Packard avoided both the human resources loss and the human costs associated with layoffs. What is especially interesting about this story is that when Hewlett-Packard was again faced with a similar drop in orders in 1974, it redeployed the "nine-day fortnight" strategy.

These two responses to industry decline are, of course, very different from each other. Although

I am particularly grateful to Gene Dalton, Robert Pitts, Paul Thompson, Daniel Brass, and James Dean for their helpful comments on earlier drafts of this paper.

Reprinted, by permission of the publisher, from *Organizational Dynamics,* Spring 1986, © 1986 American Management Association, New York. All rights reserved.

it could be argued that the conditions facing these two companies were different, it would be difficult to contend that the telecommunications firm's situation was any more severe than Hewlett-Packard's (H-P). So why did the telecommunications firm have to lay people off while H-P was able to find an alternative solution?

What's very interesting about the "nine-day fortnight" is that employees' and top management's interpretations of this event were generally different. Employees assumed that they would not be laid off under any circumstances, while top management did not want H-P to be a "hire-and-fire company." This difference is subtle but revealing. H-P's executives were committed to avoiding layoffs whenever possible. Nevertheless, they did concede that if alternatives could not be found, employees would be laid off to preserve the viability of the firm. The fact that these two different interpretations of the "nine-day fortnight" could coexist at H-P for so long without discovery of the inconsistency suggests that (1) a no-layoffs policy seldom is in conflict with management's concern about a firm's viability because (2) alternatives to layoffs can usually be found when compelling reasons to find alternatives exist.

Unfortunately, responses of firms facing industry decline usually resemble the "Christmas Eve Massacre," not the "nine-day fortnight," and employees are laid off. Most of the arguments against layoffs focus on morale and moral issues. Those concerned about morale know that layoffs create a rift between those who made the decision and those who fear they may be in future lines of fire. Although employees who are afraid of losing their jobs might respond initially with a flurry of panicked activity—that is, they may temporarily become more productive—the long-term effects of this fear are negative. Realizing this, many companies ask: What will layoffs do to worker productivity? What about worker commitment? Will some of our better people leave?

The critics of corporate America say that management never questions the morality of layoffs. Our experience, however, tells us that laying off employees is a painful experience for execu-

tives. They question their motives very carefully and are very concerned about moral implications. They ask: Are we really being fair? Don't our people have a right to work? What will be the consequences for these workers and their families? If the public looks unfavorably on our actions, how will our firm's image be affected?

These questions all lead to compelling reasons to avoid layoffs. But apparently, many cases exist in which these reasons are not compelling enough. The discussion that follows argues against layoffs—for some very practical reasons. We propose that in most cases layoffs do not make sense because they are inefficient. Layoffs, when compared with other options available to the management of firms in declining industries, are high-cost rather than least-cost strategies. Once we have made this case, we will review organizational responses to industry decline and examine alternatives to layoffs consistent with each type of response.

Identifying a Least-Cost Human Resources Strategy

Oliver Williamson, in his path-breaking book, *Markets and Hierarchies,* broadened our understanding of how to make the most efficient use of human resources. His most significant contribution was the identification of some of the hidden costs associated with the voluntary or involuntary movement of employees between firms. Basic to Williamson's argument is the distinction between firm-specific and firm-nonspecific employee skills.

Firm-specific skills are acquired in a learning-by-doing fashion. Both technological expertise and organizational experience unique to a firm qualify as firm-specific employee skills. Williamson proposes that when employees with firm-specific skills leave an organization either voluntarily or involuntarily, a loss of productive value occurs. This is because firm-specific skills are not transferable to other organizations. Loss of productive value adversely affects both the organization and the former employees. When the organization hires replacement employees it must train them to acquire firm-specific skills; thus the firm incurs training costs that would have been unnecessary if the former employees had stayed. Similarly, when employees leave an organization, their firm-specific skills do not qualify them for work in other organizations. Therefore, changing organizational membership carries significant costs.

Williamson concluded that the costs of losing and replacing firm-specific skills usually are greater than is recognized. Nevertheless, they are acknowledged to some extent, and organizations and employees devise policies and procedures that discourage both voluntary and involuntary exit. Thus companies have procedural safeguards to limit arbitrary dismissal and nonvested pension and other benefits that accrue in ways that discourage employees from quitting their jobs.

Williamson's reasoning, however, does not apply to employees with firm-nonspecific skills. Unless skills are specialized to a particular organization, neither organizations nor employees have built-in incentives to maintain employment relationships. In these instances, organizations can easily hire replacement employees, and employees can move to other organizations without losing productive value.

It is easy to differentiate between firm-specific and firm-nonspecific employee skills. It is unusual, however, for employees who spend even a short time in an organization not to acquire firm-specific skills. Thus some loss of productive value nearly always occurs when employees move to other organizations.

Secretaries, for example, have typing and stenographic skills when they join a company—firm-nonspecific skills, of course. Secretaries may enhance these skills with practice but, as with all firm-nonspecific skills, they will be equally valued by present and potential employers. As soon as secretaries learn their firm's filing system, however, they acquire firm-specific skills. If they choose to leave, this knowledge does not qualify them for work as a secretary in another organization. If the firm were to dismiss them and replace them with new secretaries, it would be necessary to duplicate their filing-system training.

Even professional employees and experienced managers, who bring with them more firm-nonspecific skills when they join new companies, soon acquire many firm-specific skills. They learn, for example, about the data-processing system, the performance-appraisal system, and the unique values, culture, and mission of the firm. They become acquainted with other staff members and learn their personalities, styles, and expectations. Gradually they become aware of the political subtleties that are crucial to getting anything done. Moreover, they acquire skills that are unique to a firm's products and/or services. When professional employees and experienced managers are dismissed or decide to move elsewhere, this firm-specific training is forfeited—with negative consequences to both themselves and the firm.

An important oversight in Williamson's thinking is that he fails to consider that the costs associated with employees' acquiring firm-specific skills are sunk. When incremental analysis of markets confirms that a business unit is no longer viable, sunk costs should not enter into a decision about whether to continue or discontinue operations. This reasoning applies to all sunk costs, including those related to employees with firm-specific skills. When the decision is made to discontinue operations, employees' firm-specific skills become unnecessary. Therefore, it is important to consider the inefficiency (that is, replacement costs) associated with laying off employees only when their skills are both firm-specific and necessary.

The matter of which firm-specific skills remain necessary and which become unnecessary depends on an organization's response to industry decline. A finer breakdown of firm-specific skills is needed to make such determinations; such a breakdown would consider differences between industry-specific and industry-nonspecific and unit-nonspecific and unit-specific skills.

For example, salespeople acquire firm-specific knowledge of company ordering and billing procedures. They also learn company policies concerning expense accounts, reimbursement for mileage, and so forth. If a salesperson were transferred to another division that operated in a different industry, much of this knowledge would be useful; these are industry-nonspecific skills. But salespeople also acquire knowledge and expertise about industry technology that is not transferable across divisions operating in different industries. These are industry-specific skills.

Moreover, when firms have multiple business units, industry-specific skills are both unit-specific and nonspecific. Salespeople also gain knowledge of the products they sell. Their knowledge and expertise about industry technologies, then, is both general (unit-nonspecific) and specific (unit-specific). Usually the longer salespeople sell the same products, the more they can offer knowledge-based service to their customers. When they move, product knowledge is no longer of value to the firm and is not transferable. This finer breakdown of firm-specific employee skills can be used to show how the choice of a least-cost human resources strategy depends on a firm's response to industry decline.

Linking Least-Cost Human Resources Strategies with Organizational Responses to Industry Decline

When firms pursue a wide product line within a declining industry, an understanding of (1) which pockets of demand are declining, (2) whether demand is likely to revitalize, and (3) how rapidly demand will decline for different market niches is critical to formulating appropriate strategic responses. Information pertinent to the first question shows where operating leverage and associated costs should be cut. The second question suggests whether these cuts should be permanent or temporary. These two questions are important to the typology of organizational responses to industry decline presented in Exhibit 1. The third question pertains to the expediency and degree of response that conditions warrant and focuses attention on how each organizational response to industry decline is implemented.

The typology in Exhibit 1, which we have used to organize the discussion that follows, allows us

Exhibit 1. Organizational Responses to Industry Decline

Extensiveness of Declining Market Demand	Expected Duration of Industry Decline	
	Short-term	Long-term
Widespread decline	Survival	Divestiture/ disinvestment
Isolated decline	Maintenance	Realignment

to explore least-cost human resources strategies that can be coupled with each organizational response to industry decline.

Survival Strategies

Survival strategies are implemented when industry decline is widespread, and supply-and-demand imbalances are soon expected to resolve themselves. Because market demand is expected to revitalize, all firm-specific employee skills retain their productive value (that is, they continue to be necessary). The primary reason to avoid layoffs is that a firm can gear up quickly for a recovery because it does not need to rehire and train skilled workers.

During the 1981–82 recession, conventional wisdom encouraged executives to take actions — including laying off significant numbers of employees — that would lower their firms' breakeven points. For the short-term, this seemed to be a good idea. With economic recovery, however, came a resurgence in market demand. What had been excess capacity in the trough of recession quickly became needed capacity. Companies that had laid off workers found that it was now necessary to hire new employees and train them before the benefits of economic recovery could be reaped. Delays were costly and put these firms at a competitive disadvantage. Moreover, they incurred duplicate training costs. The inefficiencies resulting from their decision to lay people off added up very quickly.

The key to choosing a least-cost human resources strategy when survival strategies are implemented is to lower human resources costs without permanently losing firm-specific skills. Polaroid Corporation, for example, instituted a job-sharing program with 100 hourly employees. Some employees at Polaroid worked half-days; others worked every other month. Pacific Northwest Bell Telephone encouraged workers to take unpaid leaves of absence with their jobs being guaranteed on their return. H-P's nine-day fortnight was another way to weather the storm. The nine-day fortnight is an example of a work-sharing program involving reductions in both employee hours and pay. In some states, like California, employees participating in work-sharing programs are even eligible for partial unemployment benefits.

All the above options are appropriate when the effect of industry decline is less work to be done. Industry decline also can result in a situation in which the same amount of work still has to be done, but less money is available to pay people to do it. This usually occurs when firms lower prices to restimulate demand for their products. As long as firms can avoid cutthroat price cutting, this approach offers a good survival strategy. What becomes necessary is a means of cutting the cost of operating without cutting back on operations. Again, several options are open to management.

Probably the least disruptive approach is for firms to reduce their financial leverage by restructuring debt. Specifically, they can replace short-term debt with more stable bond and stock financing. Moreover, firms can swap debt for equity by selling future tax benefits. These are one-shot fixes, but they can help a struggling company ride out the storm. The whole idea is to improve a firm's balance sheet so that other cost-cutting measures that would be potentially more disruptive become unnecessary.

Certain hazards are associated with cuts in benefits and wages—but, even so, they should not be ignored as ways to reduce operating costs. Some companies, for example, have negotiated with employees to give up some of their paid time off.

Mountain Bell saved 92,130 workdays with this program in 1982 alone. Experiences at Natomas, where top executives took a 10% salary cut, and other large companies have shown that when pay cuts are reasonable and used as a short-term solution to conditions in a declining industry, they offer significant relief and seldom lead to the exodus of key personnel. Generally, the potential hazards of pay cuts can be avoided when management signals that it will "make it up" to employees and keeps its word once conditions improve.

A cautionary note, however, is in order. Charles Levine suggests "exploiting the exploitable" as a strategic response to industry decline. He proposes gaining concessions from labor unions as an example of such a strategy. This is a very dangerous approach. If the exploitable were to feel exploited, their cooperation would be lost. Recent events at Continental Airlines illustrate this concern. Continental's management demanded $150 million in annual wage, benefits, and work-rule concessions. When it was discovered that the airline still had $60 million in the bank, however, union resistance to these company demands hardened. The resulting distrust between workers and management gradually snowballed into a no-win stalemate.

Another way for managers to reduce human resources costs more naturally and, therefore, with less risk, is to realize that businesses are cyclical in nature; thus compelling reasons exist to tie a substantial portion of employee salaries to company performance. With such a pay plan in place, human resources costs naturally follow the ebb and flow of company decline and growth. In Japan it has been shown that such programs are not met with employee resistance and that they provide substantial protection against layoffs.

These alternatives to layoffs are least-cost human resources strategies for firms implementing survival responses to industry decline. They are summarized in Exhibit 2 along with examples and some of the potential problems associated with them. It is also possible that any of these alternatives alone will provide inadequate relief from industry decline. In such cases, managers should

Exhibit 2. Survival Alternatives to Layoffs

Alternatives	Descriptions	Potential Problems	Examples of Use
Job sharing	Two employees reduced to half time who essentially share one full-time job, pay, and benefits.	Division of benefits is difficult. Only for employees with specialized skills.	Polaroid: 100 hourly workers shared jobs. Worked half-days one month on, one month off.
Leave of absence	Encourage workers to take unpaid leaves with jobs guaranteed on return.	Few takers.	Pacific Northwest Bell Telephone.
Work sharing	Reduction made in both hours and pay.	Most acceptable to workers in two income families.	Hewlett-Packard's "nine-day fort-night" policy.
Less paid time off	Reductions in paid vacation time or decreases in long holiday weekends.	Effect is small unless company is large.	Mountain Bell saved 92,150 work days during 1982.
Pay cuts	Salaries reduced by certain percentage.	Resistance from workers who feel exploited.	Natomas: Top executives took a 10% pay cut.
Performance-based pay	Link high percentage of salary to company performance.	Prevents problems.	Common practice of large corporations in Japan.

consider putting together a package of layoff alternatives with adequate cost-cutting leverage to weather the storm.

Divestiture/Disinvestment Strategies

When industry decline is pervasive and expected to continue indefinitely, no future exists for industry businesses. Sooner or later market demand will dry up or in some cases be absorbed by foreign competitors who have substantial cost and/ or technological advantages. When an industry declines rapidly, companies can sometimes recoup at least some of their losses by selling early. Firms may even give up assets to avoid sustaining chronic losses and to free working capital for more promising uses. Both selling and abandonment are divestiture strategies.

Divesting firms will sell a business intact when a prospective buyer can be found. Often the acquiring firm sees opportunities that the selling firm either does not see or is not in a position to exploit. This kind of acquisition is often viewed favorably by employees because it breathes new life into their failing company. Several cases of potential layoffs have been avoided because divesting firms have carefully selected the right buyer.

Although such transactions often require that new firm-specific skills be learned and old ones be unlearned, significant efficiencies can be gained by retaining industry-specific employee skills. Of course, the gains associated with the careful sale of a business unit accrue mostly to the economy and employees of the acquired firm. Nevertheless, such a divesting company has acted in a socially responsible manner and very often has struck the best possible deal.

When firms abandon their holdings in an industry, layoffs generally are more economically justified than when firms choose any other strategy for handling decline. This is so primarily because divestiture makes most firm-specific skills unnecessary. Only industry-nonspecific employee skills retain productive value for the firm.

Layoffs, however, are not an inevitable outcome of abandonment. There is still good reason to retain people when their industry-nonspecific skills have productive value and lateral movement outside the industry is possible. Motorola's sale of its color-television picture-tube manufacturing facilities (which were losing money) to General Telephone and Electronics International in 1970 affected more than 600 employees. Even though some of these people were eventually laid off, Motorola tried to integrate them into other operations outside the picture-tube industry. Management believed that it was efficient to keep these employees even when it was necessary to move them to other business units within the firm.

When industry decline is more gradual, firms do not necessarily have to divest affected businesses. This suggests other least-cost human resources strategies. Milking an investment in a declining industry is usually thought of in terms of capital assets: Machines keep producing revenues until they break. Milking an investment, however, can be applied to human assets. Disinvestment in a business can be coupled with a decision not to replace employees who voluntarily leave the organization. When a firm's exit from an industry is drawn out, attrition provides a natural, concomitant reduction of employees. Gradual disinvestment also provides the opportunity for the gradual assimilation of some workers into businesses outside the declining industry. Because a milking strategy implies that a firm is investing elsewhere, there should be ample opportunity for intrafirm transfers. Again, the incentive is to retain industry-nonspecific employee skills.

Realignment Strategies

While the intent of firms deploying divestiture/ disinvestment strategies is to get out of an industry, firms that adopt realignment strategies intend to stay put. Because demand appears to endure in some market niches, firms find it advantageous to realign themselves to serve the most desirable customer groups. When such a realignment strategy is adopted, unit-specific skills become less valuable while all other firm-specific skills retain their productive value. Because realignment both closes and opens opportunities, intrafirm transfers of employees within the same industry have obvious advantages. These efficiencies, however, often go undervalued because they are neither obvious nor immediate. IBM's long-term use of realignment strategy, for example, suggests how very effective it can be and how it offers tangible benefits.

When shifts within an industry cannot assimilate all displaced personnel, other alternatives to layoffs are available. Although strategic realignment usually affects only a small percentage of a firm's total work force, it has permanent consequences. Because business units are being phased out, either a new home is found for affected employees inside the firm or they are forced out. Moreover, usually fewer exit barriers are associated with divestiture of isolated business units within a troubled industry than with across-the-board industry exit. Accordingly, quick divestiture is often preferable to milking strategies, since attrition works slowly, and is therefore less useful. Attrition, however, should not be written off too quickly. When combined with survival alternatives (for example, job sharing, leaves of absence, work sharing) as stop-gap measures, attrition can gain renewed viability.

In addition, there are ways to hasten attrition and thus make it a more viable realignment strategy. Many firms are using early-retirement incentives to trim burdensome payrolls. The logic here is that employees who are either obsolescent or disenchanted (and considering retirement anyway) will choose to leave the firm when enticed to do so. 3M recently offered early retirement with full pension credit to all of its 20-year employees who were at least 55 years old; 950 employees signed up.

A problem with early retirement incentives, however, is that outcomes are unpredictable. Logic does not always prevail, because an employee's decision to leave a firm is complex. Firms almost always will lose some of their "stars" when they offer early retirement. Manville Corporation, for example, actually lost its president through such an incentive program.

Something that firms can do when indispensable employees retire early is to rehire them as consultants. When Union Bank lost a vice-president who specialized in personal service to blue-chip customers, it awarded her a part-time consulting contract. Rank Xerox has taken this idea further, in what is perhaps the shape of things to come, as new technology redefines employment relationships. Rank Xerox encouraged middle-managers in such support functions as purchasing, personnel, pensions, and planning to quit and sign on as outside consultants for up to two days a week on renewable two-year contracts. Managers were offered separation bonuses and consultant fees that were up to 95% of their former salaries. Rank also offered them free use of a microcomputer that links up with company databases. By doing this, Rank was able to cut such costs as office space, support workers, fringe benefits, and national payroll taxes; these had accounted for two-thirds of its costs of employing a worker. (Exhibit 3 summarizes the realignment alternatives discussed above.)

Maintenance Strategies

Firms implement maintenance strategies in response to temporary and isolated industry decline. Because they expect market demand to be revitalized—and they know market share will be difficult to recover once industry conditions improve—they do not consolidate their positions.

When maintenance strategies are appropriate, there is little justification for layoffs. When industry decline is isolated, firms with wide product lines usually will have more profitable business units than unprofitable ones. The overall position of the firm, therefore, is favorable. Because conditions are expected to improve in units where industry decline is having its affect, little incentive

Exhibit 3. Realignment Alternatives to Layoffs

Alternatives	Descriptions	Potential Problems	Examples of Use
Intrafirm (within industry) transfers.	Movement of employees from unhealthy to healthy units within same industry.	Loss of unit-specific skills.	Used widely.
Survival alternatives (job sharing, leaves of absence) and attrition.	Any of the alternatives used in Exhibit 2 are deployed as stopgap measures. Then staff vacancies resulting from retirement, death, or resignation are left unfilled.	Important jobs sometimes go unattended. Lots of unplanned shuffling of personnel required.	
Early retirement incentives.	Offering full pension benefits, cash bonuses, or additional payments to supplement income until Social Security benefits start at age 62, when employees retire early.	Employers have no control over who accepts or rejects them.	3M offered early retirement with full pension credit to all of its 20-year employees who were at least 55 years old; 950 employees signed up.
Early retirement incentives and rehiring selected retirees as consultants.	Same as above, but awarding part-time consulting contracts to critical personnel who decide to retire.		Union Bank lost vice-president who specialized in personal service to blue-chip customers. Awarded her a part-time consulting contract.
Resignation and rehiring selected persons as part-time consultants.	Encourage middle managers in areas such as purchasing, personnel, pensions, and planning to quit and sign on as outside consultants.	Limited to middle managers in support functions.	Rank Xerox expects program to apply to 25% of corporate management staff. Offers separation bonuses and consultant fees that are 95% of salary. Fringe benefits are discontinued. Employees linked via microcomputers.

exists to make the kinds of strategic adjustments that would displace workers. Moreover, all firm-specific employee skills retain their productive value when firms maintain present operations.

Mild pressures may be exerted to keep costs down when firms are deploying maintenance strategies. Accordingly, declining business units may use pay freezes or hiring freezes to hold the line on human resources costs until performance improves. However, management needs to look at the possible ripple effects of such seemingly minor policy decisions. Several years ago, one of three divisions of a firm in the electronics industry imposed a hiring freeze immediately after the report of a minor drop in revenues. The year before the hiring freeze, just over 100 moves had occurred within the division—either promotions or lateral assignments. The year after, only 20 moves occurred. Because the firm's overall profitability remained solid and the effect of the hiring freeze on employee careers was so severe, the overwhelming consensus among division employees was that management had overreacted. This perception led to all kinds of second-guessing and questions about management's competency. In this case the marginal advantages gained from the hiring freeze were not worth what it cost the division in terms of lost management credibility and lowered employee morale.

When Layoffs Are Unavoidable

A least-cost approach does not offer an organization guarantees against layoffs. Situations will inevitably arise in which layoffs are the only alternative available to a firm. At such times, it is important that management consider the moral and morale consequences of its actions. Arguments against layoffs based on moral and morale considerations are weaker than a least-cost rationale, but such arguments can guide a firm's treatment of employees once they are laid off. The key point is that these considerations are crucial to the continued productivity of employees who survive the layoffs.

Survivors of layoffs will feel sympathy for their co-workers who were laid off, but these emotions often will be tempered by relief over not having been laid off themselves. Survivors' principal concern is their own job security: Will there be further cutbacks? How will they affect me? There is no way to alleviate these concerns completely. Firms can bolster the morale of survivors only by taking steps to do everything they possibly can to help the victims of layoffs.

When Honeywell acquired General Electric's computer equipment line several years ago, a decision to consolidate overlapping product lines made it necessary to lay off large numbers of employees. The efforts of Honeywell's management after these layoffs, however, should serve as a model of how much firms can do to help displaced employees. Honeywell initially set up a placement center for laid-off employees. Later it created another center that provided free phone, clerical, and mail services. It also distributed "resumé books" to 100 companies and contacted more than 200 companies and employment agencies in New England. More than 70% of Honeywell's former employees who used these services found new jobs within three months.

The positive effects of these programs on former General Electric employees retained by Honeywell are inestimable. They knew that their new employer cared about them. Honeywell was able to build employee loyalty from the outset, which resulted in increased cooperative efforts and higher productivity.

Conclusion: A Comparison of Benefits

A common scenario repeats itself time and time again when the firms in an industry decline: Management lays employees off because it sees no other alternatives and claims its hands are tied. The principal counterargument presented here is that company and employee interests are interconnected. Because a merging of concerns occurs when employees acquire firm-specific skills, a close scrutiny of the special conditions surrounding industry decline is in order to identify human resources strategies that are more efficient than layoffs.

Before we can claim that we have untied managers' hands, however, we must be certain that a least-cost approach offers benefits to firms in declining industries — benefits that are better than those offered by other human resources management practices. To make our case, we will compare a least-cost approach with two human resources practices that recently have received a great deal of attention across industries: lifetime employment guarantees and human resources planning.

Lifetime-Employment Guarantees

At least on the surface, the cold, calculated rationale of a least-cost approach seems to be no competition for lifetime-employment guarantees, which imply a holistic concern for employees, a partnership between the individual and the firm, and the kind of security that can be counted on. On the other hand, a least-cost approach puts human resources in the same category as that of other capital assets. The value of employees' firm-specific skills depends on whether costs are sunk and on alternative uses and replacement costs.

When we compare these two approaches more carefully, however, we gain a somewhat different perspective. Most of the support for lifetime-employment guarantees comes from our recent admiration of the Japanese economic system. What too often goes unconsidered, however, are those aspects of the Japanese lifetime employment guarantees that most Americans would find unacceptable.

Even in Japan, lifetime employment does not apply to everyone. Only full-time employees of "elite" Japanese firms are protected. The army of part-time employees, mostly women, and the employees of "satellite" firms form a buffer for the privileged, and they are laid off whenever conditions warrant it. So, as William Ouchi observes, the Japanese system distributes social costs in ways that most Americans would find unacceptable. When lifetime-employment guarantees are made in the United States, they seldom apply to all employees in the firm. Usually the workforce is divided into two classes: one protected and the other unprotected. If we examine this issue carefully we quickly realize that it is probably unrealistic to expect such guarantees to work otherwise. Guarantees for some workers can be made only if other workers are in place to absorb the inevitable economic shocks.

The bottom line appears to be that lifetime-employment guarantees are better suited to rapidly growing than to declining industries. Even Japan's system of lifetime employment is being severely challenged as that nation moves into a period of slowed economic growth. Guarantees made to older workers have limited the numbers of younger workers being hired by the "elite" companies. Accordingly, serious concerns are being raised about the fairness and future viability of lifetime-employment guarantees in Japan. Several Japanese firms already have begun to experiment with systems that provide management with wider discretion in making decisions about human resources costs. As challenges continue to be raised, the fragility of Japan's lifetime employment system is becoming increasingly apparent.

On the other side of the ledger, a least-cost strategy is extremely flexible. The real beauty of this approach to managing human resources is that it is never in conflict with what makes good business sense. Management and workers are in the same boat, and in most cases they will discover that they want the same things. Of course, a least-cost approach does not guarantee lifetime employment, but its ultimate aim is long-term employment because it focuses on firm-specific employee skills. Because management is increasingly aware of the efficiencies associated with keeping employees with firm-specific skills, these employees are highly valued by firms. Thus management is guided by incentives that directly affect profit-and-loss to find ways to avoid layoffs.

A least-cost approach offers employees a different kind of security than does a lifetime-employment guarantee. Security comes primarily through the acquisition of firm-specific skills. The more firm-specific skills employees have the greater is their value to a firm and the less likely management is to view layoffs as an acceptable response to industry decline.

The recent interest in quality of work life also has a favorable impact on employee security. Work is being redesigned to be more complex and to require more learning-by-doing. As a result, employees are acquiring more firm-specific skills. It takes a long time for employees to become effective in organizations because there is so much to figure out. This supports a view of employees as organizational treasures—they increase in value with time. Management realizes that it should hold on to valuable employees—not at all costs, but within reasonable cost, because often greater costs are associated with losing them. Again, this provides employees with some degree of job security.

Human Resources Planning

Recently, a great deal of interest has been shown in human resources planning as a way to prevent layoffs. Preventive approaches, of course, are to be encouraged. Organizations should be forward-looking as they assess human resources needs. When, for example, we consider the potential displacement of workers that can occur with the introduction of automated manufacturing technologies, careful human resources planning is essential.

The application of human resources planning to declining industries, however, hinges on the question of predictability. When the human resources needs of firms in declining industries are highly predictable then heavy reliance on human resources planning makes perfect sense. But when human resources needs are less predictable (for example, when economic conditions bring wild, unanticipated shifts in market demand for a firm's products) planning can offer only ballpark estimates. It is impossible to be accurate, and it can't

be assumed once conditions settle that they will remain settled. What is required is an ability to shoot from the hip, to respond to present conditions that are not what was expected. At times like these, a least-cost approach to managing human resources can offer management a clear rationale for making decisions that are in the firm's and in the employees' best interests.

Nevertheless, there probably is no reason to replace human resources planning with a least-cost approach to managing human resources. Because they involve different functions, these two approaches work better in tandem rather than separately. They seem to complement each other: Human resources planning offers a general direction, and a least-cost approach provides adjustments when unpredictable shifts in human resources needs arise. This synergy is especially powerful when a major concern of human resources planning is the systematic development in employees of those firm-specific skills that are critical to the organization's future success.

Selected Bibliography

The work of Oliver Williamson has been integral to the development of a least-cost approach to managing human resources, and a deep intellectual debt is owed. Although Williamson's discussion of firm-specific employee skills appears in many places, one of the clearer presentations is "The Economics of Organization: The Transaction of Cost Approach" (*American Journal of Sociology,* November 1981).

One of the more insightful discussions of organizational strategies in response to industry decline is an article by Kathryn R. Harrigan, "Strategy Formulation in Declining Industries" (*Academy of Management Journal,* October 1980). The four strategic responses presented in this article are very similar to Harrigan's.

Finally, William G. Ouchi's *Theory Z: How American Business Can Meet the Japanese Challenge* (Addison-Wesley, 1981) has been helpful in two respects. First, it offers one of the better accounts of the "nine-day fortnight" story and second, it provides a description of lifetime-employment guarantees in Japan.

21

Investing in Retrenchment: Avoiding the Hidden Costs

Cynthia Hardy

- In 1976, the managers of Northville Area Health Authority (AHA) put forward a plan to close Maine Road Maternity Hospital. The AHA is part of the British National Health Service (NHS), responsible for the administration of all hospitals in Northville, a city in the north of England. Senior management is responsible for making recommendations to the AHA, whose members include medical representatives, interested lay people, and members of the local council. The AHA has decision making power and can choose to accept or reject managerial recommendations.[1]

Maine Road has been a candidate for closure since the 1960s, simply because it was an old hospital. A fall in the birth rate and a move of people out of the inner city area in the 1970s made it clear that Northville had an overprovision of maternity beds and the proposal to close Maine Road was made.

A number of groups immediately expressed concern. Staff at the hospital set up an action committee to stop the closure. They appeared on TV and radio, received sympathetic press coverage, lobbied Members of Parliament (MPs), and presented the AHA with a petition opposing the closure that contained more than 10,000 signatures. A consultant obstetrician at the hospital criticized the closure on TV and radio, in the local newspapers, and at public meetings. A national TV program on the issue was aired. The two Community Health Councils (CHCs), representing patient interests, and the National Union of Public Employees also opposed the proposal.

Bowing to this pressure, the AHA voted against management's recommendation, retaining the hospital and closing maternity wards in other hospitals. Had the AHA not taken this action, the union was ready and willing to make plans for the occupation of the hospital in an attempt to force a change of heart, even though they agreed in principle with the fact that the city had too many maternity beds.

The handling of this and other cuts resulted in increasing criticism of management by unions, CHCs, employees, politicians, and the public. The uproar culminated in a massive protest in May 1977. A delegation was sent to the minister of health, who, as a result, set up a committee of inquiry into the health area. The committee, in turn, was very critical of management's actions.

- In 1975, Imperial Chemical Industries (ICI) announced that Mountside works could look forward to a life expectancy of only five to ten years. The following year, it announced that the closure was to start immediately. Mountside was a chemical factory in the north of England, employing over 1,000 individuals. Competitive pressures from European producers with large integrated sites and low overheads had prompted the division to reduce the number of manufacturing sites. Mountside was one of those scheduled for closure. The bulk of the rundown was carried out between 1976 and 1978, although the works did not close completely until 1980. The rundown was a long and tightly scheduled process since some products were being transferred to other plants, and facilities had to be built up.

  Local stewards raised the issue with national officials, who saw no reason not to accept the closure. Discussions about how the process was to be carried out and how employees were to be protected were carried out successfully at the local level, without resorting to grievance procedure. There was no industrial action or loss of production; productivity remained stable over the first three years of the rundown; absenteeism fell; the rundown schedule was adhered to; local press coverage was low-key and generally supportive of the company, while national exposure was nonexistent; and, perhaps most importantly, of all the stewards, union officials, and employees interviewed, none criticized the company's actions.

What differentiates these two organizations is clear — ICI was able to implement its plans while Northville was not. However, Northville managers lost more than the opportunity to save £500,000 a year by closing a hospital: they also incurred many of the "hidden" costs associated with retrenchment, while ICI incurred virtually none. Northville managers provoked union action, alienated employees, damaged their own credibility, evoked government intervention, and generated public criticism. They also jeopardized the larger retrenchment strategy designed to reduce their annual deficit of £1 million and accommodate government spending cuts.

The Hidden Costs of Retrenchment

All too often, costs such as those incurred at Northville are neglected — many companies view retrenchment as an isolated and unpleasant incident, best carried out and forgotten as quickly as possible. This attitude ignores the fact that retrenchment is not purely about disbanding operations: it is often part of a strategy designed to sustain the larger organization. When the global picture is taken into consideration, it becomes clear that the hidden costs are significant and can jeopardize the future survival of the organization. There are a number of factors which give rise to these hidden costs.

Union resistance, regardless of the form it takes, causes major problems for management. A strike weakens the larger organization. Occupations, in which employees take over the factory or hospital in question to prevent the sale of assets or transfer of production, are expensive. Even in North America where such overt resistance is less common, unions can withdraw cooperation, make contract negotiations difficult, initiate grievances, and prevent the smooth transfer of production, all of which represent additional costs to managers wishing to make effective cost savings.

Employers often dismiss the impact retrenchment has on continuing employees, seeing the problem purely in terms of those who leave. Yet the survivors are crucial to the future success of the organization and if they are alienated, productivity will fall; commitment will be reduced and may result in people leaving the organization as soon as the opportunity arises; creativity and innovation will be difficult to foster; and employees will be reluctant to make the concessions and sacrifices integral to future competitiveness. Companies which change policies of job security are particularly vulnerable if employees feel management is reneging on past promises and compromising managerial credibility over the handling of cutbacks. This makes it difficult to foster a creative and effective team spirit at a time when it is most needed.

Unfavorable publicity is another cost. If detailed reports of cutbacks are published, customers may start to worry that the firm is going out of business. Potential new recruits will look elsewhere for jobs if they feel that the organization has a poor record. Union officials and employees in other plants may become interested—and anxious. Community officials will start to question decisions and actions.

Organizations linked to the public sector will want to avoid political intervention. Government officials may have the ability to revoke cutback decisions if they feel that they have been handled in a way that is politically embarrassing. Even where intervention is less direct, the clumsy handling of retrenchment can lead to a series of difficult questions for senior managers. Private organizations are not exempt from political interference: contracts are awarded, subsidies granted, and payments made from government sources—and all of these can be jeopardized by retrenchment actions that meet with government disapproval.

Plant closures, cutbacks, and the rationalization of operations have been and will continue to be one of the major challenges facing contemporary managers. Increasing economic uncertainty and tough foreign competition are making such decisions imperative. Managing them in a way that incurs the costs described above will be expensive—particularly in the long term, as the struggle to restore viability unfolds. For these reasons, *retrenchment must be considered to be an investment in the future,* since contraction is the price paid for future success. Retrenchment deserves the same creative analysis as any other investment decision; otherwise, downgrading—rather than downsizing—will be the result.

Despite the emphasis on the global view in this and other articles,[2] managers continue to adopt a short-term perspective. This is particularly true of the U.S., where "the right to close a business down has long been regarded as a management prerogative."[3] As a result, legislation is minimal, owing to concerted resistance; and, even where it does exist, it is often not complied with.[4] Despite some claims that a consensus is developing around the need for severance, notice, extended health care, and outplacement, there is little evidence to support the view that such practices constitute a widespread phenomenon. In fact in 1985, a bill requiring 90-days notice of plant closure was defeated in the House of Representatives, while only three states have advance warning legislation in place.[5] Moreover, there continue to be examples of plants closed with no notice or outplacement aid, particularly when companies relocate plants in areas of nonunionized labor.[6] It would seem then that many American employers require convincing of, and information about, the need to view retrenchment as an investment.

The U.S. can look to both Canada and Europe on these matters. Both are far in advance of the U.S. in terms of legislation and practice and, as has been pointed out, initiatives in these countries often precede action in the U.S.[7] This article, by examining ten Canadian and British organizations (including Northville and ICI), identifies the tasks associated with the successful management of retrenchment. These organizations were part of a study carried out since 1978 in both public and private sectors. ICI and Northville represent the extremes; the remaining organizations incurred some costs, and avoided others, during their experience with retrenchment (see Table 1).

Avoiding the Costs

Many of the costs associated with downsizing can be avoided with the implementation of a retrenchment program that takes into account the needs of both the departing and continuing employees, as well as the unions and other interest groups which are involved. This would allay many of the fears associated with cutbacks and would help employees to view retrenchment as a challenge rather than a threat, enabling them to respond positively to the increased demands and changes required of them. Individuals must be convinced that the cutbacks are a step towards increased profitability and efficiency, that there are opportunities associated with a more streamlined operation, that their increased effort will be rewarded,

Table 1. The Organizations

The ten organizations referred to in the article are described below. At the request of their respective organizations, the names "Andersons," "Whitefields," "Midville," and "Northville" have been substituted to conceal their identity.

- Between 1975 and 1980, Imperial Chemical Industries (ICI), the British chemical manufacturer, closed **Mountside** works. The factory, situated in the northwest of England, employed more than 1,000 people.

- ICI closed another plant at **Brookside** in Scotland during the mid-seventies. In this case, local union officials put up considerable resistance, involving the press and political leaders in an effort to prevent the closure. They eventually accepted the decision, but only after national union leaders and the headquarters level of the company had been drawn into the negotiations, despite the fact that there was no enforced redundancy and all employees were given the option of working in another plant on the site.

- **"Andersons"** is an engineering multinational. In 1978, it announced the loss of 1,000 jobs in a Scottish factory. Attempts to bring in a new product to save the remaining 500 jobs failed, and the factory was closed in 1980. The company helped employees to set up a small engineering factory on the site of the old one to save 200 jobs.

- In June 1983, **CIL**, a divisionalized Canadian manufacturer and distributor of chemical and allied products, announced the partial closure of an explosives factory in an isolated community in Northern Ontario. There were 176 people involved, of whom 53 continued to work in the ongoing part of the operation. This, however, was closed in 1985.

- **"Whitefields,"** a manufacturing multinational offered, in 1983, an early retirement option to all employees with 25 years service in its Canadian operations. Of more than 1,200 eligible employees, 432 accepted.

- **Air Canada**, the stateowned airline, offered a voluntary severance program to all of its managerial staff in August 1982. Nearly 18 percent, more than 600 people, took advantage of the program.

- **Atomic Energy of Canada Ltd. (AECL)**, the state-owned nuclear power agency, laid off over 500 people in its manufacturing operations in 1983.

- **"Midville"** and **"Northville"** AHAs both proposed hospital closures in the mid-seventies in response to funding cuts. At Midville, the proposed closure was implemented. At Northville, however, unions, employees and patient groups united in their opposition to the closure and the recommendation was overruled, forcing management to retain the hospital.

- **Ville Marie** is a social service agency in Montreal. In 1981, an 11 percent funding cut was announced by the provincial government of Quebec.

Nearly 200 interviews were carried out with managers, union officials, employees, and representatives of other interest groups in each organization. Documentation—in the form of managerial and union reports, correspondence and memoranda, and newspaper articles—was also analyzed.

---

and that their concerns will not be ignored. The remainder of this article addresses the tasks required of management in this respect.

The Task: Managing Awareness

> "We were able to say: let's do it, we have the time to do it; let's not wait until the crisis is so great all we can do is swing the axe. We have the time to do it in a more socially responsible way; in a way that minimizes the hurt on people, so let's do it before it is forced upon us in a more unpleasant way."
>
> — *a human resource executive*

Once the costs of retrenchment have been ascertained and the larger picture established, the situation of the individual organization can be assessed in terms of whether there is a need to adopt a broader and longer-term view of downsizing. Awareness of this need must be created among the senior level of management for two reasons: to ensure that the necessary cuts are made in a timely and logical model, avoiding a crisis and allowing for a more humane approach to be put into place; and to secure a commitment among decision makers to a more enlightened approach and the investment which that entails.

A lack of awareness of the need for downsizing will result in counterproductive decisions that worsen an already difficult situation. At Atomic Energy of Canada Ltd. (AECL), where more than 500 individuals were laid off in 1983, previously full order-books in the late seventies and early eighties had obscured management's perceptions. Senior management was unwilling to face up to the prospect of layoffs even though the numbers showed that something was "definitely wrong." As a result, AECL was hiring new graduates up until 1981 (to arrive in 1982). Before the end of 1981, however, the corporation had been forced to do an about-turn with a hiring freeze, followed by an announcement of layoffs in November 1982. This not only compromised managers' credibility, it left them with the difficulties of laying off additional staff and dealing with a disaffected group of people who had turned down other jobs to work

for AECL. As a result, future graduates will look a little more critically at AECL's hiring promises.

Human resource managers at Air Canada, which has undergone a series of cost-cutting measures in recent years, took steps to persuade senior executives of the need for action. The experience of the American airline industry with recession and deregulation was "powerful ammunition" in this respect. It enabled them to convince senior management that cost cutting should begin as soon as possible while there was still time to plan a more humane program than had been the case in most of the American companies.

Difficulties in predicting the future with any degree of certainty can be overcome. Managers at Ville Marie, a Montreal social service agency, knew the government planned to cut their budget in 1981, but not by how much. They responded by planning three scenarios representing cuts of 8 percent, 10 percent, and 12 percent. The knowledge accumulated in the process put them in a good position to effect the 11 percent cut they ultimately received.

Senior managers will provide the funds necessary to protect and support employees only if they consider it worthwhile. As a result, there is a need to impress upon them the hidden costs of retrenchment. The explosives division at CIL (the Canadian chemical manufacturer) effected the partial closure of a factory in a small town in Ontario. Divisional and human resource managers presented the executive committee with nine reasons why they should handle the closure carefully, ranging from the possibility of sabotage and other potential union problems to the difficulties of finding alternative employment in such an isolated area. The result was that a retrenchment program was approved, as were the funds (nearly $1 million for 123 employees) required to carry it out.

The Task: Managing the Alternatives

> "We were prepared to seriously look at [alternative ways of reducing costs] if there was an emotion out there that wanted it." — *a manager*

The aim of creating awareness is to buy time and commitment, both of which allow a more flexible approach to downsizing, including the opportunity to consider some of the alternative methods of reducing costs. If action is taken early enough, attrition can be used to reduce personnel. Work-sharing, early retirement, and voluntary severance as well as leaves of absence, pay freezes, and redeployments to other locations are other options for cost cutting. Since these methods involve an additional cost to the employer or take longer to have an effect, employers need to be well prepared to be able to make use of them.

Of particular interest to managers wishing to reduce the effect of retrenchment on employees is the question of whether severance can be conducted on a purely voluntary basis. Air Canada, ICI, and Whitefields (a manufacturing multinational which offered an early retirement option to all its Canadian operations staff with 25-years service) all used voluntary programs.

Voluntary severance has been criticized as an expensive method of cutback: employees have to be paid to leave. However, even at AECL—where more than 500 had already been laid off at the height of the recession, and the incentive offer "was not a rich package"—80 people took advantage of it.

The concern that the best people leave is not borne out in practice, since people have loyalties which bind them to the organization "regardless of the job market." Managers felt it was often the marginal performers who left; perhaps because they were disillusioned with their jobs and voluntary severance provided an opportunity to leave, or perhaps because they feared a less honorable discharge later. Even when experience is lost, the opening up of promotion opportunities more than compensates.

> "A lot of people say nobody's indispensable and it seems to be true because [although] I was afraid when I saw the number of people leaving and the quality of those people, it turned out we could do without them...[and it] certainly hasn't crippled us because what it's done has provided opportunities for people who were waiting. So we haven't

really suffered even though we've lost a lost of experience." — *a manager*

The company can always protect itself by stating formal conditions. Air Canada reserved the right of refusal in cases where scarce skills would be lost to the competition. Informal persuasion can be used to ease out some of the more marginal performers. However, voluntary programs must be *seen* to be voluntary to be effective. Managers must not be perceived as "leaning" on people. Nor must there be too many denials: even at Air Canada there was pressure from the CEO down to let everyone go unless there were some "really dire circumstances." A "voluntary program" also means accepting the numbers who apply, be they above or below expectations. Managers at Whitefields were willing to cut expenses or carry the extra overhead rather than fire anyone, in the event that an insufficient number of people volunteered.

Voluntary severance provides both the company and the employee with benefits. Employees are given a choice and there is no stigma attached to their dismissal. The company gains credibility by being seen to accommodate employee needs, which translates into commitment and productivity from continuing employees.

The Task: Managing Involvement

> "[The joint committee] worked well because what it did was keep the company and the union working together, solving the problems. By making them participants I think it was much more successful." — *a manager*

Employees will be worried about the impact the cutbacks will have. Involving representatives in at least part of the decision-making process helps to reduce feelings of powerlessness and provides a forum in which employee interests can be protected.

Companies that restricted involvement have met with criticism. Andersons, a multinational which had set up a feasibility study to investigate the closure of a Scottish engineering factory with 1500 employees, refused to allow union participation or to release the figures on which the recommendation for closure was based. The result was a great deal of suspicion concerning the company's motives and an unwillingness to believe that the closure was necessary.

> "Andersons has a traditional position—they make a decision and the union agrees...I think they made a mistake. If they'd come to the same decision with union involvement it would have been easier to accept."—*a union official*

Beliefs that effective involvement cannot be created around the issue of cutbacks are unfounded. Mechanisms were established to facilitate employee involvement in most of the organizations. At Mountside, a special committee was set up with union and management representation to secure the cooperation of the senior stewards. It brought together the two sides as a problem-solving group, avoiding the need to resort to the formal negotiating procedure. It made recommendations concerning employee needs to the works manager, who was then able to make decisions fully aware of the likely consequences. He sometimes made concessions, for example, allowing people to leave before their termination date (with full severance pay) if they found another job. This helped win the goodwill of the stewards. They felt they were an active part of the process, able to safeguard their own interests rather than having to watch helplessly from the sidelines. The committee acted as a safety valve, achieving a "remarkable degree of trust on both sides" and preventing any industrial unrest.

At CIL, placement committees were established with managers and union representatives to consider the issues of retraining, counselling, and outplacement. Federal legislation dictated the establishment of a Joint Planning Committee at AECL with union/employee and management membership and an independent chair. For each of the four employee groups, the corporation also set up Joint Manpower Adjustment Committees (JMACs), with a similar format, to handle the grievances and outplacement needs of the particular group.

The Task: Managing Fair Play

> "[It's important that the] employee group perceives there's been a lot of fairness, a lot of trust and the selection process is done fairly objectively; because if it isn't, the more you upset people."
> —*a manager*

Employees were reassured by a sense of fairness in how the process was handled, particularly when managers were forced to undertake dismissals involving some sort of selection process. A perception of fairness prevents the initiation of grievances and provides some security to continuing employees.

Three common selection criteria are seniority, required skills, and performance. Seniority has the advantage of being a criterion that workers "relate to," helping them to view dismissals "in a rational fashion" and accept the choices that are made. Some critics argue that it robs the organization of its young blood. However, the problem with the other two criteria is that they are more subjective and decisions may be contested. Unions at AECL disagreed with the selection criteria that were used to protect critical skills, initiating over 100 grievances, some of which they won in arbitration.

On another issue, AECL's sense of fair play was commended: its willingness to handle unionized and nonunionized groups in the same way. Of the four employee groups at the corporation, only two were represented by unions. However, JMACs were set up on the same basis for all these groups, and management established grievance procedures for the nonunionized employees who were not protected by collective agreements.

Discrimination between management and nonmanagement employees creates a sense of injustice. Air Canada ran into this problem: voluntary severance was offered only to managers on the basis that their jobs were being terminated permanently. Other employees were laid off on a temporary basis according to union contracts and did not qualify for the same severance pay. Despite the difference in the nature of the layoffs, union representatives felt that their members were being discriminated against and management had a difficult time explaining the position to them.

The Task: Managing Support

> "It's marvellous how it's been done. Every help one could imagine was there." — *a manual worker*

A variety of support mechanisms can prove valuable in helping employees deal with job loss, which enhances managerial credibility in the eyes of both departing and continuing employees and provides a firm foundation for future employee relations. Of particular importance here are attempts to reduce the insecurity of employees, such as with severance pay and help in finding new jobs.

All the firms provided some sort of severance pay. Both Andersons and ICI exceeded the state minimum.[8] Air Canada offered one month per year of service (up to 18 months). Whitefields offered two years' salary over the following four years. CIL instituted a minimum of $4,000 and paid between one and two weeks' pay per year of service. AECL offered one week's pay per year of service with a variety of supplements providing up to an additional 55 days' pay for some employees.

Outplacement also helps employees. ICI advertised on behalf of its employees, appointed a redeployment manager, set up a "job shop" in which vacancies were posted, provided training in interview skills, and allowed paid time off to attend interviews. CIL provided job search seminars, moving expenses, job search expenses, paid time off, retirement counselling, and financial planning. AECL undertook "ad tracking" on behalf of employees, posted vacancies, advertised, provided seminars on job search techniques, offered secretarial support, staffed an outplacement center, and organized a job fair in which potential employers were invited on site. This type of aid has a positive impact at a relatively low cost.

> "There's no denying that providing that sort of [outplacement] aid helps the acceptance of the pain of workforce reduction. . . . It really doesn't cost you that much. It costs a lot in time and effort

in the organizing, but it doesn't cost you in terms of dollars in cash outlay, and in some respects it's more appreciated." — *a manager*

Managers at Andersons took a somewhat different approach. First, they tried to save some jobs by transferring a substitute product to the Scottish factory. When that failed, they hired a consultant to conduct an international search for a buyer for the factory and equipment. When this proved unsuccessful, a local search, instigated by the company and its employees, uncovered a demand for the engineering skills of the workforce. As a result, a small subcontracting engineering firm was set up, with the company's help, employing around 200 of the original employees.

The Task: Managing Disclosure

> "The worst thing is the insecurity of not knowing."
> — *an employee*

Empirical studies agree that it is in the employees' interests if managers disclose as much information as they can, as soon as they can, as often as they can. Advance notice improves morale and enhances the chances of finding another job. The absence of information, on the other hand, leads to rumor, which is usually more pessimistic than reality.

Some managers at Ville Marie withheld information, believing it would add to anxiety to say too much about impending cuts. Employees, however, found that the resulting rumors increased uncertainty and tension.

> "It was mostly rumor. That's what we found so maddening — that there was nothing we could grasp. It was just rumor and it was very tense. Everyone was concerned that they might be cut and they didn't know whether it was going to be [on] seniority or not." — *an employee*

CIL sent specially trained counsellors to the closing plant on the day of the announcement "to get as much information to all the employees as quickly as possible." Even though they were not legally required to do so, AECL managers informed individuals of their future at the same time as the announcement of group dismissals (sixteen weeks in advance) to avoid having the entire corporation worry and thus having a detrimental effect on production.

Advance notice does not necessarily result in conflict, sabotage, or declining productivity, as is sometimes charged. The percentage of hours lost due to industrial action fell at Andersons from 18 percent in 1977 to less than 1 percent in the first nine months of 1979, after the announcement of redundancies. Absenteeism fell during the rundown process at Mountside, as did the number of customer complaints, while the output per man-week remained stable. Productivity actually rose at CIL.

It is not enough simply to inform employees at the beginning of the exercise; information should be updated as the retrenchment program progresses. A weekly bulletin at Mountside was issued both in a newssheet and via the internal telephone. It ran for more than two years and was revised weekly to ensure that employees were aware of what was happening.

Information should be realistic—raising false hopes can backfire. At another closure in ICI, three statements were made shortly before the closure was announced, indicating that there was no threat to jobs. The actual announcement took employees by surprise and they started to question the company's motives, blaming the closure on ineffective planning and accusing it of hiding the real situation from them.

The Task: Managing Understanding

"We spent so much time and effort in trying to get understanding of why it happened and how we were going to close it [the factory], and what help we were going to give, that acceptance became rather inevitable." — *a manager*

From the effective disclosure of information should come an understanding of why retrenchment is occurring, which is important if union officials and employees are to accept the cuts. Opposition arose at Northville because medical reasons for the cuts were disputed by medical staff, while the financial rationale was considered an unacceptable basis on which to cut health services.

Air Canada took a number of steps to create an understanding of the corporation's position throughout the organization. An audio-visual program was created called "The Air Canada Challenge," which included a film, articles in the company magazine, and meetings between managers and employees. It was used to explain what was happening in the industry in terms of costs, declining markets, and deregulation. Individuals were informed of the steps being taken to deal with these problems—the marketing efforts to attract new business, the measures to save gasoline, the steps to increase efficiency. Finally, it impressed upon employees the need for sacrifices, cost cutting, and increased productivity.

The Task: Managing Blame

"There has to be a very well argued case for closure—people need convincing. They are going to have to be satisfied that the reasons for closure are credible." — *a manager*

One issue that will arise from trying to create an understanding of the reasons behind the cutbacks is the question of who is responsible. Managers have to choose between accepting responsibility for the current situation and directing the blame elsewhere. The latter can be a very risky strategy: if employees find out the reasons for cutbacks are not valid, they will start to question the entire retrenchment exercise, and management will find itself the subject of a great deal of suspicion.

Andersons's attempt to blame the closure on falling world demand was contested by the unions who felt it was a "cosmetic exercise" designed to placate financial institutions worried about their investments. The closure was interpreted as a political move rather than a financial necessity and the unions felt that they could pressure the company into changing its decision.

Managers can sometimes take advantage of an external scapegoat. Although the Mountside closure was part of a rationalization plan, managers tended to blame it on the old age of the plant and the proximity of the potentially dangerous chemical plant to a hospital and residential area. These reasons were visible, comprehensible, and had the added advantage of absolving management from all blame. In this case, the "scapegoating" worked, as did a similar situation at Midville AHA where a proposed hospital closure was blamed on government spending cuts, even though:

> "I know darn well that had we had the money we still would have closed it. They [the unions] don't realize that. We were using the financial argument but what we were really after was rationalization."
> — *a manager*

If a clearly visible scapegoat exists, one that does not implicate management and that is easy to understand, managers may choose to use it. If, however, the explanation is complicated or contentious, this strategy may well backfire.

Conclusion: The Task is Managing Survival

> "It's like most dollars ahead of people decisions. They are short term in their good effect, and long term in their bad effect; if indeed there is any good effect." — *a manager*

Retrenchment should not be viewed as an unpleasant but short-lived affair, to be put to one side and forgotten as soon as possible. It is an investment in the future, the basis on which success depends. Layoffs are the price that a company or institution is prepared to pay. That price will only produce benefits if retrenchment does not hamper the return to viability. For retrenchment to play its part in the performance of the organization, it should be part of an integrated strategy to restore competitiveness, with a focus on all the necessary ingredients for success.

While this article finishes with the larger picture, managers ideally should *start* with it. Managers and employees need to know where the organization is going and how it intends to get there — and whether more cuts are part of that picture. Only in this way can managers assess the hidden

costs and design a program accordingly. Moreover, it is only by knowing that retrenchment lies ahead that managers can take timely action, use alternative measures, prevent hiring mistakes, and demonstrate to employees that their sacrifices will indeed produce a more viable organization. The earlier the recognition that retrenchment is part of a survival strategy, the more likely it is to be viewed as an investment rather than a crisis. With this type of forward thinking and proactive planning, managers should be thinking of how to manage *survival,* rather than how to manage retrenchment. They can then carry out the necessary tasks to successfully implement the program, which include:

- extending *awareness* of the situation to all senior management;
- considering *alternatives* and less disruptive ways of downsizing;
- *involving* employee representatives;
- maintaining a sense of *fair play;*
- providing the necessary *support;*
- *disclosing* information to employees;
- ensuring that they *understand* the need for cutbacks; and
- dealing with the issue of *blame.*

This article has used the experiences of some Canadian and British organizations to illustrate some of the reasons why managers should view retrenchment decisions like any other kind of investment. This is not to say that retrenchment is easy, or that those employees affected by it will not suffer from the loss of their jobs and from uncertainty, financial insecurity, and stress. Under any circumstances, retrenchment means less for some people — that makes it difficult to manage, and it transforms a business problem into an acute personal problem for many people. What the experiences of these organizations does show, however, is that there are more and less effective ways of managing retrenchment and, for the most part, the more commercially effective methods also provide benefits for the employees. Retrenchment will never be painless, but it most certainly can be made less painful.

Notes

1 The NHS structure described in the article refers to the situation following the 1974 Reorganization.

2 See, for example, J.P. Gordus, P. Jarley, and L.A. Ferman, *Plant Closings and Economic Dislocation* (Kalamazoo, MI: W.E. Upjohn Institute for Employment Research, 1981); L. Greenhalgh, "Managing the Job Insecurity Crisis," *Human Resources Management,* 22/4 (1983): 431-44; S. Luce, *Retrenchment and Beyond* (Ottawa: The Conference Board, 1983); B. Portis and M. Suys, *A Study of the Closing of the Kelvinator Plant in London, Ontario* (London, Ontario: University of Western Ontario, 1970); R.I. Sutton, "Managing Organizational Death," *Human Resources Management,* 22/4 (1983): 390-412.

3 A.B. Carroll, "When Business Closes Down: Social Responsibilities and Management Actions," *California Management Review,* 26/2 (Winter 1984): 129. Also, see R.B. McKenzie, *Plant Closings: Public or Private Choices?* (Washington, D.C.: The Cato Institute, 1982).

4 Carroll, op. cit., pp. 125-40; B. Bluestone and B. Harrison, *The Deindustrialization of America* (New York, NY: Basic Books, 1982); N.R. Folbre, J.L. Leighton, and M.R. Roderick, "Plant Closings and Their Regulation in Maine, 1971-82," *Industrial & Labor Relations Review,* 37/2 (1984): 185-96.

5 The Conference Board, *Company Programs to Ease the Impact of Shutdowns* (New York, NY: The Conference Board, 1986).

6 T.F. Buss and F.S. Redburn, *Shutdown at Youngstown: Public Policy and Unemployment* (New York, NY: State University of New York Press, 1983); B. Harrison, "Plant Closures: Efforts to Cushion the Blow," *Monthly Labor Review,* 87/6 (1984): 41-43; T.A. Kochan, R.B. McKersie, and P. Cappelli, "Strategic Choice and Industrial Relations Theory," *Industrial Relations,* 23/1 (1984): 16-39.

7 Carroll, op. cit., pp. 125-40; William L. Batt, "Canada's Good Example with Displaced Workers," *Harvard Business Review,* 6/22 (July/August 1983).

8 In Britain, redundancy compensation is mandatory. Minimum requirements are ½ week's pay per year of service while age 18-21; one week's pay per year of service while age 22-41; 1½ week's pay while age 42-65. This is for employees with more than 2 years of service up to a maximum of 20 years of service. The state reimburses 41% of this amount.

APPENDIX
The Tasks for Retrenchment:
The Issues to Consider

Managing Survival

What is the organization's strategy for the future and what role does retrenchment play in it?

What are the hidden costs associated with mishandling retrenchment?

Managing Awareness

What is the view of senior managers to retrenchment?

Are they prepared to invest money in it?

Are they aware of the hidden costs?

Are they aware of the need for timely action?

Managing the Alternatives

Have alternative ways of making cuts been considered?

Can measures that will reduce the need for enforced dismissals be used?

Managing Involvement

Will there be employee involvement in the process?

Who is to be involved in the process and how are they to be selected?

What committee should be set up with what terms of reference?

Managing Fair Play

What criteria are being used to select dismissals?

What is the effect of these criteria on the organization?

Are unionized and nonunionized employees being treated the same?

Are managerial and nonmanagerial ranks being treated the same?

Is the process perceived as fair?

Managing Support

Have the various forms of outplacement aid and other support mechanisms been considered?

Managing Disclosure

What information is going to be disclosed?
When and how is it to be disclosed?
Is the information accurate, realistic and up to date?

Managing Understanding

Has the need for cutbacks and sacrifices been explained?

Have the benefits of the cutbacks been explained?
Do employees have some idea of the larger picture, where and how the cuts fit in, and where the organization is going?

Managing Blame

Who is responsible for the current situation?
What are the risks associated with accepting responsibility?
Is there a convincing and visible external scapegoat?
What are the risks associated with unsuccessful scapegoating?

22

Managing Organizational Death

Robert I. Sutton

The recent surge of scholarly thought on organizational decline may reflect a change from the view that only organizational growth is natural and expected and that organizational decline is unnatural and unexpected (see bibliographies by Whetten, 1981 and Zammuto, 1982). Writings by scholars including Adizes (1979), Whetten (1980a, 1980b), Greenhalgh (1982, in press), and Hirschhorn (Hirschhorn & Associates, 1983) all imply that organizational decline is a predictable phase of the organizational life cycle. Moreover, the deep recession of the late 1970s and early 1980s forced many managers to change their view that organizational growth is normal and expected. It also created an immediate need for practical knowledge on the subject.

Most writings produced in response to this need concern two related aspects of organizational decline: strategies for transforming unsuccessful organizations to successful ones (e.g., Cameron, 1983; Harrigan, 1980; Harrigan and Porter, 1983; Hambrick and Schecter, 1983), and strategies for reducing the work force in ways that are humane, and ultimately enhance (or at least do not hamper) organizational effectiveness (e.g., Greenhalgh and McKersie, 1980a, 1980b; Hirschhorn & Associates, 1983; Greenhalgh, 1982; Jick and Murray, 1983).

This article explores a third transition that often occurs in combination with turnaround strategies and work force reductions: organizational death. Much has been written about how to avoid this outcome, but the transition itself is described only occasionally (e.g., Slote, 1969; Loving, 1979; Whitestone, 1981; Stotland and Kobler, 1965). And, with few exceptions (Nicoll, 1982; Taber, Walsh, and Cooke, 1979), little is known about how it is best managed. Yet thousands of decision-makers faced management of organizational death during the last recession. Business failures were at the highest rate since the Great Depression. Federal and state budget cuts caused many government facilities to close. And, as children from the "baby boom" era completed their education, de-

I wish to thank James Jucker and Marina Park for their helpful comments, and Reginald Bruce, Stanley Harris, and Susan Schurman for assistance with collecting these data. Most of all I would like to thank Robert Kahn for supporting this research since its inception.

Reprinted with permission from *Human Resource Management,* Vol. 22, No. 4, Winter 1983 © 1984 John Wiley & Sons, Inc.

clining student enrollment caused the closing of many schools.

Moreover, enormous numbers of organizational deaths occur even during good economic times. In the 1960s, for example, almost 9% of the companies registered in America were removed from the list each year (Argenti, 1976). There were also numerous plant closings in the years prior to the last recession. In a sample of 12,449 American manufacturing plants that existed in 1969, for example, fully 30% were closed by 1976 (Bluestone and Harrison, 1982). Thus, chances are substantial that, regardless of economic conditions, a manager will help orchestrate an organizational death during his or her career.

Given that a closing will occur, poor management can have disastrous effects for employees, the parent organization (if one exists), and careers of managers, administrators, and union leaders. While some distress among displaced employees is probably impossible to avoid, management can take steps that are of considerable help to threatened employees (Taber, Walsh, and Cook, 1979; Gordus, Jarley, and Ferman, 1981; Cobb and Kasl, 1977). Managers who ignore employee well-being not only risk harm to employees, they also risk poor publicity that can hurt the parent organization. Poor publicity is most damaging to service industries that rely on their good reputation to attract customers. However, any parent organization that treats members poorly during a closing may have subsequent problems in recruiting quality employees.

Mistakes can also lead to lengthy litigation. The threat of legal entanglements may increase since the U.S. Congress (1980) and a variety of states are considering legislation to regulate plant closings (Cipparone, 1981). Finally, mere association with a closing can hurt the careers of managers, administrators, and even union leaders. The success-oriented American society profoundly rewards success and punishes indications of failure (Whetten, 1980b). Association with an expensive and widely criticized closing can be especially devastating to managerial careers.

I became interested in studying organizational death, in part, because of these high stakes for employees, parent organizations, and participating decision-makers. I recently directed eight detailed case studies of organizational death. My colleagues and I gathered information about these cases by using questionnaires, organizational records, and most important, 44 interviews with decision-makers and other key participants in the closings. These 44 people included managers and administrators from the defunct organizations and from their parent organizations, as well as a number of union leaders. The study included five closings from the private sector: a small independent automobile plant, a large automobile plant owned by a major corporation, a large department store owned by a national chain, a small retail store, and a nonprofit hospital. Also included were three public sector closings: a center for the disabled, an academic unit, and a research organization. Finally, all organizations were about to close or had been closed for less than a year.

Rather than collecting data to test a preconceived theory about organizational death, my aim was to use these eight cases to help generate a theory about this organizational transition and discover techniques for its management. The cases and theory are described elsewhere (Sutton, forthcoming). This article focuses on the lessons from this research most relevant to the management of organizational death. Specifically, findings pertaining to seven common managerial beliefs about employee reactions during organizational closings are presented first. Next, eight managerial tasks required in most organizational deaths are described. These eight tasks do not capture the complexity of managing this transition, however. Following the discussion of the tasks, four dilemmas in the management of organizational death are proposed along with steps that can be taken to balance these competing demands.

Employee Reactions During Organizational Death

The interviews revealed that managers had many prior expectations about how employees would respond during the organizational closing. Some of these expectations were confirmed, others were

Table 1. Employee Reactions During Organizational Death

Common Managerial Beliefs	Evidence
(1) Productivity and quality plummet.	1. Not supported in most cases; more common are cases of increased productivity and quality.
(2) Employee sabotage and stealing increase.	2. No support for increased sabotage; some cases do support increased thefts, but these appear to be the exception rather than the rule.
(3) The best employees "jump ship."	3. Supported, except in cases where employees are extremely loyal or are assured equal or better positions in the parent organization.
(4) Rumors abound.	4. Supported; many rumors are more bleak than the truth, particularly when information is poor.
(5) Anger toward management is the dominant emotion.	5. Limited support; while hostility is often observed, fear and sorrow appear to be the most dominant emotions.
(6) Conflict increases.	6. Little support; conflict actually appears to decrease after the announcement *except* in special cases.
(7) Employees have trouble accepting that a closing is actually going to occur.	7. Supported, but lack of acceptance is often not "irrational."

refuted, and still others received partial support. A summary of seven common managerial beliefs, and the evidence garnered about each belief, are presented in Table 1. Each belief is explored below.

Productivity and Quality Plummet

Productivity and quality did not plummet in six of the eight closings studied. They decreased in two: the academic unit and the research organization. These two organizations experienced long periods of uncertainty about their fate and members devoted much time to losing battles for organizational survival. Resources were inadequate for both fighting for the organization's life and completing routine tasks. In several of the other closings, however, productivity and quality increased. To illustrate, the institution for the disabled and the hospital we studied received their best quality-of-care evaluations in memory *after* closing was certain. Similarly, the auto plant had lower absenteeism and higher quality after the closing was announced. Thus, my research, along with another case study (Slote, 1969), suggests that quality and productivity will not plummet if sufficient resources are present, and chances are substantial that they will increase. These outcomes may be due to employee pride, a struggle to save the organization, or, as one administrator asserted, because employees need good recommendations to get another job.

Sabotage and Stealing Increase

A common argument for closing with little advance warning is that empolyee sabotage and thefts will rise after the announcement. No cases of sabotage were reported in my research, and I have never read of a confirmed instance in other writings on organizational death. With respect to stealing, there was evidence of increased thefts by employees in two of the eight closings we studied. There was near chaos in the large department store because a closing sale brought in hordes of customers. A few part-time employees were caught stealing during this time. Similarly, employee thefts increased in a case study of a paint plant closing (Slote, 1969). There is also evidence that equipment, books, and supplies disappeared in the research organization, but it is unclear how much was taken by employees of the dying organization and how much by "scavengers" from the parent organization.

Thefts did not rise in the other six closings we studied, although this might be attributed to increased security in several of the organizations. An alternative explanation was offered by one manager we interviewed, however. He asserted that thefts will decrease after the first major round of layoffs because new or marginal employees with little loyalty are the first to go. In sum, there is evidence that employee thefts will increase, but the weight of evidence suggests increased thefts are the exception rather than the rule.

The Best Employees "Jump Ship"

The eight case studies do reveal that employees with the most marketable skills are among the first to leave dying organizations. In the closing of the facility for the disabled, for example, four of the most respected administrators began searching for, and obtained, positions in other organizations at the first strong indication that a closing was likely. There are at least two major exceptions to this pattern, however. First, high-quality employees who are extremely loyal may remain to the end. In the closing of a small auto plant, for example, a skilled craftsman was offered a good job but turned it down because the new work was less interesting and the management of the auto plant had treated him fairly. Second, the best employees are sometimes retained through promises of equal or better positions in the parent organi-

zation. The large auto plant used this tactic to keep many managers and engineers.

Rumors Abound

This managerial belief received strong support in six of the closings studied, and is confirmed by research on organizational decline (see Hirschhorn & Associates, 1983) and plant closings (e.g., Taber, Walsh, and Cooke, 1979; Cobb and Kasl, 1977). Rumors were less prevalent (though not absent) in the small retail store and small auto plant, probably because the few employees in these organizations had frequent direct communication with management.

I offer two observations about rumors in dying organizations. First, the less information employees have, the greater the number of rumors, particularly rumors that paint a bleaker picture than the (unavailable) information warrants. Second, the content of rumors changes as the organizational death proceeds. Four phases can be identified:

(a) *Prior to the announcement:* Rumors concerning the fate of the organization are most common. False rumors that a definite decision to close the center for the disabled were rampant, for example. As a result, management installed a "hot line" to give employees current information.

(b) *Just after the announcement:* Rumors concerning who is to blame for the closing are prevalent. In the research organization, for example, rumors about mistakes the director had made were most common.

(c) *When the movement of employees begins:* Rumors concern *who* is going *where*. In the large department store, for example, local stores in the parent organization competed for the best salespersons. Rumors about who was going to which store changed by the minute and dominated many conversations.

(d) *After the closing:* Former members typically gossip about what will happen (or has happened) to the old facility, equipment, or other former employees. Also common are rumors that the organization will reopen. Former employees of the large auto plant and the facility for the disabled report that they still hear rumors that a reopening will occur.

Note that these phases illustrate general tendencies; they may overlap since rumors about almost anything can appear at any time!

Anger Toward Management Is the Dominant Emotion -No

Many decision-makers whom we interviewed worried that employees would be hostile toward them; some even feared for their well-being. Verbal hostility toward decision-makers who closed the organization is evident in most closings. Yet anger does *not* appear to be the dominant emotion in organizational death. Rather, our research suggests that fear and sorrow are the dominant emotions. Employees fear an uncertain future: They may have no job, or may be taking a new job with many unknown qualities. They also may fear what others will think of their new and often lower status.

Sorrow is perhaps the single dominant emotion, however. Employees often experience a profound sense of loss when their organization closes. This is illustrated by questionnaire responses of twenty-three interviewees who had been members of the eight defunct organizations. These managers, administrators, and union leaders were asked to compare the closing experience with five increasingly threatening life events: (1) receiving a parking ticket; (2) an argument with a friend or relative; (3) a serious illness; (4) a divorce; (5) the death of a spouse.

On the average, the twenty-three former members reported that involvement in the closing was similar to having a serious illness. That organizational death can entail a profound sense of loss is accentuated by the responses of nine of the twenty-three former members. These nine people revealed that the closing caused distress equal to divorce or the death of a spouse. This sense of loss was equally profound among lower-level employees. It was particularly acute among long-standing em-

ployees at the center for the disabled and the large auto plant. People from these organizations often spoke of "missing the old place," and how much they "loved" it.

Conflict Increases

The *opposite* pattern held in most of the dying organizations. Conflict among members usually waned after the announcement of the closing. In the large auto plant, for example, union–management bargaining became less adversarial. The research organization is the exception to this finding. There was conflict before the announcement of the closing, but it was suppressed because members were trying to work together to save the organization. After the announcement, however, there was no longer a common enemy and reports suggest that infighting increased.

Employees Have Trouble Accepting That a Closing Is Actually Going to Occur

This is a consistent pattern in all eight closings. In particular, employees at the hospital, the large auto plant, and the center for the disabled had difficulty believing that the closing would occur. These three cases illustrate, however, that lack of acceptance should not always be passed off as an "irrational" form of denial. For twenty years hospital employees had heard administrators threaten to close the facility. It was difficult for them to know that the final "announcement" was not just another idle threat. The center for the disabled was a member of a larger organization in which many closings had been announced in recent years, but other "dying" facilities had remained open for years after the target date. They expected a similar pattern in their own case. Finally, the auto workers who—to this day—spread rumors that the plant will reopen do so because the parent organization has made a rapid economic recovery. Is it unreasonable to infer that their old plant may be needed again soon? Labeling these examples of human hope as "denial" may shield the complexity and rationality of such beliefs.

In sum, evidence about organizational death is consistent with common managerial beliefs that the best employees "jump ship" first, that rumors are rampant, and that many employees have trouble accepting the organizational closing. In contrast, beliefs that productivity and quality decrease, that the rate of employee thefts increase, that the dominant emotion among employees is anger toward management, and that conflict increases were generally not confirmed, although there were significant exceptions. Finally, the managerial belief that sabotage increases was not confirmed in any of the cases.

Evidence about these seven common beliefs may help decision-makers better understand the ways in which employees respond during an organizational closing. Yet this evidence does not directly address which actions organizational death typically demands of managers. The next section describes eight managerial tasks identified in our research.

Tasks Required for Managing Organizational Deaths

Certainly, each organizational death makes unique demands on decision-makers. The eight case studies of organizational death, however, reveal that managing this transition typically requires a predictable set of tasks. These are (1) disbanding, (2) sustaining, (3) shielding, (4) informing, (5) blaming, (6) delegating, (7) inventing, and (8) coping. These tasks are listed and defined in Table 2, and are discussed below.

Disbanding

Managing organizational death entails breaking the psychological and physical links that bind people and things in the organization, and breaking links between the organization and its environment. The layoff and transfer of employees is the aspect of disbanding most people think of first.

The managers we interviewed, however, reported that while the movement of employees was usually the most emotionally trying task, it was not the most time-consuming. Literally thousands of routine tasks must be performed to "disband" an organization of significant size and age. Contracts with suppliers and customers must be terminated gracefully. Machines, books, and office equipment must be cataloged and removed. In the center for the disabled, for example, a public auction was held and hundreds of people attended. Organizational records must be cataloged, disposed of, or kept. In the hospital, several employees remained in the building for months after the doors closed trying to organize almost fifty years of poorly maintained patient records. Thus, in addition to symbolic and sensitive tasks, managers should be aware that most of their time in a closing is likely to be spent performing the routine (and often boring) tasks required for moving people and materials.

Sustaining

Ironically, how well an organization does its work is a useful indicator of how well its demise is managed. Maintaining productivity and quality is important when there is a significant period between the announcement of the closing and the final day. And this often appears to be the case. In our research we found, for example, that the automobile plants had to fill orders until almost the very last days and that the retail stores were flooded with customers seeking bargains until the final minutes.

Thus, while managers must move people and things out of the organization, they must also maintain standard operating procedures for accomplishing the work of the organization. This challenge will be discussed later since it is a conspicuous dilemma.

Shielding

It is not socially acceptable in America to admit that one has been secretive. Yet, there are at least

Table 2. Eight Tasks Typically Required for the Management of Organizational Death

Task	Definition
(1) Disbanding	1. Movement of people and things out of the organization
(2) Sustaining	2. Accomplishing the primary tasks of the organization
(3) Shielding	3. Hiding factual or symbolic information from employees, customers, suppliers, the community, or the parent organization
(4) Informing	4. Providing factual or symbolic information to employees, customers, suppliers, the community, or the parent organization
(5) Blaming	5. Placing blame for the closing
(6) Delegating	6. Giving employees down the hierarchy the opportunity to participate in decisions, or to make them
(7) Inventing	7. Constructing new ways of doing things
(8) Coping	8. Finding ways that individual decision-makers and groups of decision-makers can manage the inevitable stress

two instances in which secrecy, or perhaps even deception, might be justified from the dying organization's perspective, or that of its parent organization. First, in the *very early* stages of deciding if an organization should be closed, it appears useful to hold discussions away from employees, the community, and other stakeholders. Public discussions are more formal and entail intense scrutiny of decision-makers. These characteristics of open discussions make it difficult for those in the spotlight to think freely and offer suggestions without fear of critical response. Secret or private meetings help managers feel more free to explore unusual ideas about how to save the organization, or how it should be closed. Secret discussions should be used sparingly, however; secrecy causes employees to mistrust management and it is a symptom of groups that make poor decisions (Janis, 1972; Smart and Vertinsky, 1977). It appears that about the right amount of secrecy was used in the hospital closing; the board of directors held long and secretive meetings in which they discussed ways to save the institution, and, later, ways it should be closed. They announced major decisions, however, immediately after the meetings.

Second, secret discussions about whether an organization should be closed may be justified when news that an organization *might* close will guarantee its demise. Clients, creditors, or suppliers may lose confidence in the organization, assuring organizational death. For example, many clients in the research organization we studied stopped using its services because they heard the organization *might* close. A similar threat was faced by Pan American Airlines when it was suffering severe financial troubles. Braniff Airlines had halted service recently without notice and left many passengers stranded. As a result, some customers avoided flying Pan American for fear that they too would be stranded. An announcement that Pan American's management was *considering* closing might have guaranteed the airline's demise.

Informing

There are a few instances in which secrecy appears warranted. Our research reveals, however, that providing valid information about when and why events occur is among the most essential tasks. Small, seemingly innocent, events can cause employees to start rumors and become distraught if left unexplained. In one closing, a woman associated with a committee considering the survival of the organization had a role that was unclear to those being reviewed. She appeared to "turn the tape recorder on and off and to make faces." Rumors began about how her role was a devious one in the demise of the organization and hostility by the members of the closed organization is still expressed toward her. It is expressed, I believe, primarily because her role was never adequately explained.

It is impossible to stop rumors. Yet, when decision-makers provide information of sufficient quantity and quality it helps people understand why events occur and to know when they occur; this appears to have the effect of keeping rumors down to a dull roar and reducing anxiety among members. In the closing of the center for the disabled, for example, a hotline was installed to answer employee questions about the fate of the organization. Moreover, the head of the facility sent frequent memos and met with employees to discuss rumors.

Blaming

While attributing blame for an organizational death can be viewed as a subset of "informing," it is such a persistent issue that it requires separate discussion. In writing about *Corporate Collapse,* Argenti (1976) observed: "If success brings acclaim, surely failure should bring blame." Our interviews revealed that managers, administrators, and union leaders expected themselves, and were expected by others, to spend enormous portions of time explaining *why* the organization closed. This appears to occur because all humans have a strong, and sometimes dysfunctional, need to understand why things happen (Nisbett and Ross, 1980).

The management of blame is less difficult for decision-makers when there is an unambiguous outside cause, or causes, for the closing. In the hospital, for example, external causes including lack of demand and the recession were easy to identify, and these explanations were accepted by most employees and other stakeholders. In contrast, those closings in which the leaders of the organization were blamed proved to be difficult for all concerned.

Yet, regardless of the cause of the closing, the placing of blame is an essential task in the management of organizational death and decision-makers would do well to develop a "blame-placing" strategy. Still, it is not always wise to blame outside factors exclusively. The dilemma of blaming managerial errors versus other causes is a complex one that is explored below.

Delegating

The case studies reveal that the management of organizational death places a severe workload on decision-makers. One strategy for coping with overload is to delegate tasks to other employees. This does not mean simply keeping employees well informed of managerial actions. Rather, it means either seeking opinions about how the organization's demise should be implemented, or giving employees responsibility for making such decisions.

The eight case studies suggest that delegation is common in better-managed organizational deaths. The hospital was managed successfully, and then closed successfully, by its parent hospital because members of the larger hospital were delegated new responsibilities: The head of surgical intensive care was made head of nursing and the vice-president for personnel was made acting president of the smaller hospital, for example. The president of the larger hospital could only effectively manage efforts to save the smaller hospital, and later efforts to close, by delegating responsibilities. Similar kinds of delegation took place in the center for the disabled. The director reported that many middle-level managers went far beyond (and above) their job descriptions to help the closing go smoothly.

Inventing

The management of organizational death was a novel task for most decision-makers who participated in our research. Most organizations did not have standard operating procedures for closings, although an exception was the large department store. Store management used a manual provided by the parent company that listed many technical details. Yet even in this closing, none of the managers had participated in a closing before and they had to invent new ways of doing things.

The case studies teach us that managers spent much of their time searching for ways to close the organization and developing their own techniques. A common story (in the hospital and center for the disabled, for example) was that managers first searched for writings on the subject, gave up when they saw that little was available, and began developing their own way of doing things. The most important message for those who manage an organizational closing is that the development of these new methods takes enormous amounts of time. Moreover, decision-makers should expect that initial plans will change since perfect information is rarely available.

Decision-makers should also be aware that the stress of closing is likely to increase the chances that they will rely on old ways of doing things instead of spending time inventing new ways. This is because the perception of threat usually causes people to become rigid and use available responses rather than develop new, more appropriate responses (Staw, Sandelands, and Dutton, 1981). Ways of managing these and other outcomes of stress are explored in the following subsection on coping.

Coping

Anger, guilt, and worries about future employment prospects plague decision-makers as well as lower-level employees. When a group of decision-makers develop and choose options for managing an organizational death, this stress can reduce the quality of decision outcomes. Several of the case studies of organizational death reveal a pattern that is common in dysfunctional groups under stress. As a result of time pressures, inexperience with managing organizational decline or death, concern about bad publicity, and a variety of other sources of distress, the decision unit design and

decision processes chosen in many closings resulted in problems described by Smart and Vertinsky (1977). These included arriving at decisions before evaluating enough alternatives, distorting information, group pathologies (Janis, 1972) such as the illusion of invulnerability and suppression of personal doubts, and the use of rigid, programmed responses inappropriate for the novel tasks associated with organizational death.

As predicted by Smart and Vertinsky, stress had less negative impact on the quality of the decisions when certain measures were taken. Among the most critical for decision-makers facing organizational death were encouraging critical evaluation of all points of view, inviting outside experts to give their opinions, focusing on the long-term consequences of all decisions, and encouraging discussion of the worst possible outcome when evaluating an alternative. Another tactic that could have been used was appointing a member of the group to play "devil's advocate."

Managing organizational death requires careful attention to the eight tasks described above. Yet, the completion of these tasks is complicated by some sticky dilemmas. The most common and most troublesome of these dilemmas are described in the following section.

Dilemmas in the Management of Organizational Death

The four managerial dilemmas most prominent in the management of organizational death are:

(1) Accepting vs. Deflecting Blame
(2) Disbanding vs. Sustaining
(3) Informing vs. Shielding
(4) Giving Hope vs. Taking It Away

Each dilemma is defined and described below. I also present some steps that decision-makers can take to balance these competing demands.

Accepting vs. Deflecting Blame

It may seem to always be best for the dying organization, its parent organization, and the careers of managers if responsibility for the closing is denied by decision-makers and other people and events are blamed. Deflecting blame is effective when there are clear external reasons for closing and few observable internal reasons. All blame was *not* easily attributable to external forces in many of the organizational deaths we studied, however.

A dilemma emerges for management in such cases. If decision-makers choose to accept blame for the closing, employees may be less helpful during the closing, the reputation of the parent organization may suffer, and managerial careers may be harmed. In contrast, blaming "uncontrollable" forces can also be a troublesome strategy. Customers, employees, and other stakeholders may perceive that decision-makers are lying. Stakeholders may also view deflection of blame as evidence that managers were not competent enough to influence, or even notice, outside forces that could have been controlled. A formidable dilemma emerges. Accepting blame for the closing is likely to be viewed as *direct* evidence of management incompetence. Conversely, deflecting blame is often interpreted as *indirect* evidence of incompetence, and even dishonesty.

This dilemma comes about, and can be managed, because the symbolic acts of leaders help people make sense of events within the organization and its environment (Pfeffer, 1981). The decision-makers in our research used three kinds of symbolic acts to manage the placing of blame.

The first tactic was *scapegoating*. Baseball teams replace managers and blame them for poor performance (Gamson and Scotch, 1964). Similarly, top level decision-makers from parent organizations blamed the leader in two of the organizational deaths we studied. These decision-makers acknowledged that poor management was a cause of the closings, yet the scapegoating tactic deflected blame from them. Members of the two organizations, the press, and clients generally agreed with the blame-placing in the cases of scapegoating we observed. The arrival of a new leader was concurrent with the onset of each organization's troubles. Scapegoating was effective because it made sense given available information.

The second tactic entails a *qualified acceptance of blame*. Some decision-makers acknowledged that, "with the benefit of 20/20 hindsight," some actions could have been taken that *might* have saved the organization. This tactic was used in the hospital. A decision-maker revealed that, in looking back, bringing in physicians from other cities to set up new practices might have been easier than trying to convince local physicians to use a hospital that had an historically poor reputation. This tactic of accepting some blame for closing can be useful because it signals to stakeholders that decision-makers are not lying, are human, and that they learn from their mistakes. This tactic is especially important for decision-makers when they have made many widely recognized errors. If they do not accept some blame, their efforts to deflect blame to other persons and events will be ineffective. Again, a blame-placing strategy must be chosen that makes sense given available information.

The third tactic is *changing the subject*. Distracting the press, employees, and even clients from the placement of blame was particularly effective in the large department store that we studied. Statements to the press would focus on how hard management was working to get jobs for all full-time employees and many part-time employees. Questions about the closing would be answered briefly, or not at all, before shifting the discussion to the great things being done for employees. This tactic is only effective, however, when management has a powerful distraction.

Disbanding vs. Sustaining

Those who manage dying organizations often face the challenge of maintaining high productivity and quality while, at the same time, moving out people and equipment. Many decision-makers reported they were evaluated by superiors for the effectiveness of simultaneously disbanding and sustaining. The director of the center for the disabled was expected to lay off employees, move residents, and maintain quality of care at the same time. Conflicting demands such as these were present in all closings and were always burdensome. There are, however, some guidelines that appear to be helpful.

The most important general guideline is that more resources are needed than usually imagined. If resources can be scraped up, then four specific tactics can be used to balance the tension between disbanding and sustaining. First, many people, particularly middle managers, will be required to go beyond their usual tasks. If these people can be paid more, even a small amount, it may substantially increase motivation. Second, among the most common mistakes in the management of organizational death is moving out the administrative staff too soon. Managers are needed to complete traditional tasks, work on disbanding, and oversee these processes. Moreover, it is also a mistake to remove secretaries too soon. Most secretaries were let go very early in one closing and managers had to stay longer than expected, primarily because they had so many clerical tasks to perform. A third tactic used (where a parent organization existed) was the promise of employment in an equal or better position to those who stayed and helped with the closing. Fourth, and finally, when in doubt, equipment should be moved out more slowly. Some closings dragged on because key equipment, especially typewriters and copy machines, were removed too early. Such equipment is essential for the enormous number of clerical tasks required in most closings. Retention of equipment is facilitated if plans are made about where they will go as early as possible. If no plans are made, chances are higher that aggressive "scavengers" from other units in the parent organization will claim equipment and remove it too early.

There are also other tactics that cost little or no money. Managers were given honorific titles during several closings. Typically, they were promoted to vice presidents. This may seem to be a silly strategy. In fact, one person joked that it was "like being promoted to assistant captain of the Titanic." Yet it does appear to motivate people. Moreover, it helped at least one person get a better job. Another tactic entails appealing to employee pride. The closing of the large department store went smoothly partly because key employees wished to implement the best closing in the history of the national chain.

Informing vs. Shielding

This dilemma has been discussed as the problem of "revealing vs. concealing" in writings by Hirschhorn & Associates (1983) on the management of retrenchment. How much to tell employees and other stakeholders during the implementation of a closing is also challenging. Perhaps the most common dilemma is whether to give employees substantial advance notice of a closing or to close the organization suddenly and without warning. Managers may perceive that advance notice will make future dealings with the union easier and be helpful in maintaining good community relations, and is more humane. Yet, they often prefer to give little advance notice because of fears that productivity and quality will plummet, employees will become hostile, and the like. While our research indicates that such fears are often unjustified, the decision-makers whom we interviewed almost always engaged in some secrecy about if and when the organization would be closed. As suggested here earlier, a modest amount of "secret" time is needed to plan how the closing will be announced and implemented. These decisions, however, are often extremely difficult to conceal for significant periods of time. For example, it was difficult for the owner of the small retail store to hide the fact of the closing because she had stopped ordering new merchandise and employees noticed that the shelves were becoming empty.

While the dilemma between informing and shielding creates some problems *after* the decision to close has been made, this dilemma poses the greatest challenge prior to the decision. Decision-makers struggling to save an organization may consider warning customers, employees, and creditors that they are in trouble. News that a favorite store is in trouble may encourage loyal customers to shop there. Employees may work harder, take pay cuts, and even consider buying the company.

Creditors may be convinced to wait longer for payment. All of these actions were observed in our research and they did help some organizations stay open longer. Thus, secrecy about troubles can actually hurt an organization's chances for survival.

There are other cases, however, when secrecy about the organization's troubles seem to be justified. Informing customers, employees, and creditors that a closing may happen and that help is needed to avert the threat can create severe problems. Customers may prefer to avoid patronizing a struggling organization for fear of poor service, or no service. As mentioned above, those travelers who bought tickets from Braniff were left stranded. Employees, particulary the best ones, may jump ship at the first sign of trouble. Finally creditors, particularly unsecured creditors, may demand payment at the first sign of trouble, thus hastening the demise of the organization.

A cruel dilemma emerges: asking for help may hasten death, and not asking for help may also hasten it. This complex dilemma cannot be addressed completely in this short space, but I will describe some tactics for dealing with clients or customers, employees, and creditors.

Generally, if clients or customers can be convinced to rally behind the organization, they must be informed and recruited. Loyal customers may be drawn to a store, low prices may increase sales, or clients may be convinced to write letters and speak out for the organization. If such tactics are feasible, then sales, open pleas, or other strategies might be used to inform clients or customers of the organization's plight. Nonetheless, if efforts to gain support will not be dramatically successful, then this technique can backfire. If sale prices do not cause an increase in product volume, then organizational survival will be threatened further. In service organizations, particularly in the public sector, a *lack* of outcry among clients can hasten organizational death. This was, in fact, one of the justifications for closing the research organization we studied.

A persistent theme here has been that it is better to err on the side of informing employees

rather than shielding. Knowledge about the organization's troubles is generally better for employees, as well as for the survival of the company. Employees can increase chances for organizational survival by agreeing to lower wages, as was done in both auto plants and the hospital. They can buy the plant, a method that is becoming more common (Stern, Wood, and Hammer, 1979). They may also work harder to increase productivity and quality to help save the organization, as happened in the hospital. If they perceive it is a bluff, they may become angry and work *less* hard. Moreover, as reported above, news that the organization faces trouble can prompt the best employees to "jump ship," which can reduce chances of survival.

Fear of creditors is a common reason for being secretive in private sector organizations. Bad news can convince banks and suppliers to stop extending credit for goods—which causes certain death in retail businesses. Creditors may also seize assets. Fear of having assets seized, for example, drove executives of Braniff to close secretly and swiftly so they could get every airplane back to Dallas, their home base. They lied about mechanical problems and poor weather to get their planes back because they feared creditors would seize their planes. This would eliminate any hope that the firm could reorganize under federal bankruptcy laws (*Detroit Free Press,* 1982).

In contrast, the manager of the small automobile plant in our study used an open approach with his creditors to prolong the life of his firm. The firm had about 250 creditors, all of whom were invited to a meeting with the company president. The president explained that steps were being taken to save the company. He asked the creditors to give him a few months before they sued for their money; they agreed this was a good idea and made some useful suggestions about ways that the company might be saved. This prolonged the life of the company for several months. Thus, it may be helpful to be open with creditors at times. I must observe, however, that the assets of the small auto company were far less marketable than the airplanes owned by Braniff. As a result, a tactic of openness may not have been effective for the airline.

These tactics for balancing or choosing between informing and shielding may be useful for struggling organizations. The complexity of managing this dilemma, however, is oversimplified in the above discussion. Choosing to inform one group will almost always cause all other groups to be informed. It is impossible to inform clients and not employees, for instance. The overall benefits and costs of informing or shielding all groups must be weighed for each case.

Giving Employees Hope vs. Taking It Away

Employees at all levels need hope to help them fight for the life of the organization. After the decision to close the organization is made, employees need hope about the significance of the work they have done over the years and hope about their chances of getting a good job. Yet, they also need realistic, perhaps even pessimistic, evaluations to help them plan for the future. If chances are small that the organization will survive, it is better for employees if they are informed of this news, and that they accept the news. Yet, it may be better from management's perspective if unrealistic hope is given to employees so that the best do not "jump ship." After the announcement of the closing, employees need to have hope taken away if prospects for gaining employment in the parent organization or another organization are not high. False hope about employment opportunities can hurt people because they may not try hard enough to find another job, are shocked they can't find one, and may harbor massive hostility against the decision-makers who gave the false hope. Moreover, when false hope has been given by decision-makers, it can ultimately hurt the parent company's reputation and lead to lawsuits when people are promised but not given positions in the parent organization.

Thus, the dilemma that arises for management is that giving employees too much hope makes things easier in the short term but more difficult in the long term. The other choice is to give employees realistic, or somewhat pessimistic, data. This makes life more difficult in the short term and easier in the long term. Neither choice is pleasant, but our research suggests that managers err on the side of optimism. This unwarranted optimism is apparently expressed because managers do not want to lose quality employees. Moreover, they do not wish to confront sad or angry people; no one likes giving bad news. There were also a number of the managers in our research who became inappropriately optimistic in an effort to help themselves cope with a difficult time. One company president found it much easier to tell others, and to believe himself, that a sudden rise in business would occur any day rather than to accept the demise of the company.

Our research did not reveal any panaceas for managing hope, but we did uncover some useful tactics. We found that, prior to the formal decision to close the organization, it was best if employees were given realistic information about the organization's chances for survival combined with information about steps that they could take to help save the organization. The realism often took away hope, but the action steps helped people get through each day and increased chances for organizational survival. This tactic was perhaps used most effectively in the hospital. Employees knew that it would be a tough battle to save the institution, and were told as much. They could maintain hope, however, by participating in management's program to save the hospital. Note that this tactic is effective only when specific actions are outlined; vague directions such as "work harder" or "improve your attitude" are likely to be useless.

After the closing is certain, a similar strategy of giving employees realistic data combined with action steps they can take is the best way to manage hope about future employment. It was better for employees when they were warned that many would have trouble finding jobs and might have to accept unemployment insurance. Yet, hope must also be provided. Again, it is best to provide hope in terms of specific action steps. The hospital and the center for the disabled ran workshops on resume writing, on how to interview for a job, and on other aspects of searching for a job. This provided employees with hope that there were some steps they could take to help themselves.

The above tactics concern managing hope about the future, and the balance between optimism and pessimism is a difficult one to maintain. Our research also suggests that decision-makers should manage hope about the past. The case studies suggest consistently that formal occasions honoring past accomplishments are especially important for maintaining hopes throughout the process of organizational death. Moreover, the final days of an organization are usually marked by a final get-together of employees. These events, which are labeled variously as "wakes," "the last supper," and the "final hurrah," are likely to be generated by employees even if they are not supported by management. These final gatherings give employees hope about their years with the organization, provide a final chance to see old friends, and make it a bit less depressing to leave the organization. They also help all organization members understand that the organization is truly dead, which helps avoid unhealthy hope that the organization will reopen.

Conclusion

This article on managing organizational death presented lessons from eight case studies. This evidence was used to evaluate seven commonly held managerial beliefs about how employees react during a closing and to identify eight managerial tasks required to close most organizations. Finally, four dilemmas in the management of organizational death were explored. Since this is one of the few efforts to develop guidelines for the management of this transition, this single article cannot reveal the full range of managerial assumptions, tasks, and dilemmas associated with organizational death. I am certain that each of the 44 people whom we interviewed could identify key lessons that I have omitted.

Perhaps the most important omissions concern differences among closings; the focus here has been on similarities among all, or almost all,

organizational deaths. I have implied above that managing the closing of an organization that is dependent on a parent organization is a different task than managing the closing of an independent organization. I have not, however, explicitly developed different sets of guidelines for managing these two types of closings. Similarly, contingent recommendations should be developed for organizational deaths in which resources are scarce versus plentiful, closings in the private sector versus the public sector, and for closings that occur quickly versus those that occur slowly.

How quickly to shut an organization is, in fact, another critical issue that has not been dealt with in this article. Certainly, announcing the closing one day and shutting the next is a questionable practice because it gives employees no time to plan for their futures or to adjust to the psychological shock. Conversely, waiting too long can be troublesome because employees will begin to cling to false hopes that the organization isn't going to die and it places decision-makers in the position of managing this difficult transition for a long period of time. The present study, however, does not provide sufficient data about the speed at which organizations should be closed; thus, no recommendations can be made.

Furthermore, only a small amount of space has been devoted to the distress experienced by managers and how this influences the closing process. As indicated above, the stress of managing one of these transitions can be profound. The managers whom we interviewed often expressed much sadness, anger, and embarrassment. It is in the interest of managers, workers, and academics to learn about the effects of this distress on the quality of decisions made and the well-being of those reporting this discomfort. Related research suggests that the inability to cope with stress during an organizational crisis can have a profound negative impact on the quality of decision outcomes (Anderson, Hellriegal, and Slocum, 1977).

These and other strides must be made in research and practice for those concerned about organizational death. I was impressed throughout this investigation by the steps that most decision-makers took to seek knowledge about managing organizational death, by how carefully they thought about the lessons they had learned, and by the amount of effort they took to share these lessons with us. As a result, I am optimistic that scholarly and applied knowledge about organizational death will continue to be generated.

References

Adizes, I. 1979. Organizational passages: Diagnosing and treating life cycle problems in organizations. *Organizational Dynamics* 86: 3–25.

Anderson, C.R., Hellriegel, D., and Slocum, J. 1977. Managerial response to environmentally induced stress. *Academy of Management Journal* 20: 260–72.

Argenti, J. 1976. *Corporate Collapse.* New York: Halsted Press.

Bluestone, B., and Harrison, H. 1982. *The deindustrialization of American Industry.* New York: Basic Books.

Cameron, K.S. 1983. Strategic responses to conditions of decline: Higher education and the private sector. *Journal of Higher Education* 54: 359–80.

Cipparone, J.A. 1981. Advance notice of plant closings: Toward national legislation. *Journal of Law Reform* 14: 283–319.

Cobb, S., and Kasl, S.V. 1977. *Termination: The consequences of job loss* [HEW Publication No. (NIOSH) 77-224]. Washington, DC: U.S. Department of Health, Education and Welfare.

Countdown to end of an airline. *Detroit Free Press,* May 19, 1982, p. 113.

Gamson, W.A., and Scotch, N.R. 1964. Scapegoating in baseball. *American Journal of Sociology* 70: 69–76.

Gordus, J.P., Jarley, P., and Ferman, L.A. 1981. *Plant closings and economic dislocation.* Kalamazoo, MI: Upjohn Institute for Employment Research.

Greenhalgh, L. 1982. Managing organizational effectiveness during organizational retrenchment. *Journal of Applied Behavioral Science* 18(2): 155–70.

Greenhalgh, L. In press. Organizational decline. In S.B. Bacharach (Ed.), *Research in the Sociology of Organizations.* Greenwich, CT: JAI Press.

Greenhalgh, L., and McKersie, R.B. 1980a. Cost effectiveness of alternative strategies for cutback management. *Public Administration Review* 40: 575–84.

Greenhalgh, L., and McKersie, R.B. 1980b. Reduction in force: Cost effectiveness of alternative strategies. In C.H. Levine (Ed.), *Managing fiscal stress.* Chatham, NJ: Chatham House Publishers.

Hambrick, D.C., and Schecter, S.M. 1983. Turnaround strategies for mature industrial-product environments. *Academy of Management Journal* 26: 231–48.

Harrigan, K.R. 1980. *Strategies for declining businesses.* Lexington, MA: D.C. Heath.

Harrigan, K.R., and Porter, M.E. 1983. End-game strategies for declining industries. *Harvard Business Review* 61: 111–20.

Hirschhorn, L., & Associates. 1983. *Cutting back: Retrenchment and redevelopment in human and community services.* San Francisco: Jossey-Bass.

Janis, I.L. 1972. *Victims of groupthink.* Boston: Houghton Mifflin.

Jick, T.D., and Murray, V.V. 1982. The management of hard times: Budget cutbacks in public sector organizations. *Organization Studies* 3: 141–71.

Loving, R., Jr. 1979. Grant's last days. In R.M. Kanter and B.A. Stein (Eds.), *Life in organizations.* New York: Basic Books.

Nicoll, D. 1982. Organizational termination as an organizational development issue. *Group and Organization Studies* 7: 165–78.

Nisbett, R., and Ross. L. 1980. *Human inference: Strategies and shortcomings of social judgment.* Englewood Cliffs, NJ: Prentice-Hall.

Pfeffer, J. 1981. Management as symbolic action. In L.L. Cummings and B.M. Staw (Eds.), *Research in organizational behavior.* Greenwich, CT: JAI Press.

Slote, A. 1969. *Termination: The closing at Baker plant.* Indianapolis, IN: Bobbs-Merrill.

Smart, C.F., and Vertinsky, I. 1977. Designs for crisis decision units. *Administrative Science Quarterly* 22: 640–57.

Staw, B.M., Sandelands, L.E., and Dutton, J.E. 1981. Threat-rigidity effects in organizational behavior: A multilevel analysis. *Administrative Science Quarterly* 26: 501–24.

Stern, R.N., Wood, K.H., and Hammer, T.M. 1979. *Employee ownership in plant shutdowns: Prospects for employment stability.* Kalamazoo, MI: Upjohn Institute for Employment Research.

Stotland, E., and Kobler, L.K. 1965. *Life and death of a mental hospital.* Seattle: University of Washington Press.

Sutton, R.I. 1984. *Organizational death.* Doctoral dissertation, The University of Michigan, Department of Psychology.

Taber, T.D., Walsh, J.T., and Cooke, R.A. 1979. Developing a community-based program for reducing the social impact of a plant closing. *Journal of Applied Behavioral Science* 15: 133–35.

U.S. Congress, House, Committee on Education and Labor. 1980. Joint hearing before the Subcommittee on Employment Opportunities and the Subcommittee on Labor–Management Relations on H.R. 5040, 96th Cong., 2nd Sess., January 18.

Whetten, D.A. 1980a. Organizational decline: A neglected topic in organizational behavior. *Academy of Management Review* 5: 577–88.

Whetten, D.A. 1980b. Organizational decline: Sources, responses, and effects. In J. Kimberly and R. Miles (Eds.), *Organizational life cycles.* San Francisco: Jossey-Bass.

Whetten, D.A. 1981. *Managing organizational retrenchment: A bibliography* (No. P-754). Monticello, IL: Vance Bibliographies, Public Administration Series.

Whitestone, D. 1981. *Management of innovation in a complex organization.* Doctoral dissertation, Harvard Graduate School of Education.

Zammuto, R.F. 1982. *Bibliography on decline and retrenchment.* Boulder, CO: National Center for Higher Education Management Systems.

PART V

Commentaries

23

Organizational Decline from the Population Perspective

Bill McKelvey

If the editors of this volume have done their job well, as I believe they have, the articles they have collected represent the best literature on salient issues in organizational decline. My chapter follows from two problems I observe in this literature. First, most authors writing about organizational decline tend to approach it from a perspective akin to that of relatives coping with the terminal illness of a loved one. The key questions are: Can the illness be overcome? Can the pain and misery be eased? How can one best take care of those who are dependent on the dying person? Impending mortality is a tough, heartrending, and uncertain time in the life cycle of both the dying person and those close to him or her. The same is true for a dying organization. Emotions run high.

People can't achieve immortality. But Lee Iacocca has achieved celebrity status and has become a folk hero to many people because he rescued Chrysler Corporation from certain death. Forgotten is the $200 million bailout by the federal government. Forgotten is the import quota on Japanese automobiles that reduced competition. Ignored is the likelihood that a quick Chrys-

ler death would have speeded up the importation of new technology into the U.S. automobile industry, forcing the remaining American automobile manufacturers into a more rapid and constructive adoption of the imported technology. Forgotten are questions such as: Why should companies live forever? Why should society pay the cost of keeping dying companies alive in spite of their inefficiencies? Why are corporate raiders who go in and break up large, inefficient companies perceived as "bad guys?" No one seems to consider all the benefits of letting Chrysler and similar firms die.

The second problem I observe in the current organizational decline literature concerns the paucity of quality theories explaining organizational decline, especially theories that differentiate between autogenic (endogenous) and allogenic (exogenous) causes of decline. In fairness, I should hasten to add that many papers in this book draw on implicit theories, and the ecological papers by Hannan and Freeman and Carroll and Delacroix contain elements of a more explicit theory. Still, I venture to say that the ecology of organizational decline looks more like a desert than a horticultural showplace. For example, a student recently presented me with a proposal to study the relationship between environmental attributes and the evolution of the insurance industry in the latter part of the 19th century. His proposed theory included seventeen environmental attributes, only two of which he thought would produce decline (he thought the rest would induce growth). Missing were all the competitive effects from other insurance companies and other competing populations of organizations. I asked him, "If your theory is correct, why isn't the world covered with insurance companies?"

Why *isn't* the world covered by General Motors, General Electric, AT&T, or the thousands of companies using Theory Y, achievement motivation, human relations, the two-factor theory of motivation, or sociotechnical systems? Starting with Moonie and Riley and Barnard, these organizations have had the benefit of over fifty years of consulting on effectiveness and growth, not to mention their tremendous assets, research budgets, talented management and staffs, large size, and so forth. Why isn't there an incredible proliferation of companies run by one-minute managers, Theory Z managers, or managers following Tom Peters' mania? The obvious answer, of course, is competition and decline. The other answer is that organizational behavior and management consultants don't have much effect.

I think these two answers are related. The causes of organizational growth, regulation, and decline and the reasons why consulting theories about how to cause improvements don't seem to work are more ecological than heretofore recognized.

Unfortunately, most organizational scientists seem to have a rather thin understanding of ecological theory. It is hard to believe that a decade has passed since the first Hannan and Freeman (1977) paper was published. Since then, there has been almost no elaboration of basic organizational ecological theory in the literature. Most of the emphasis has been on testing the twenty year old "liability of newness" idea posed by Stinchcombe (1965).

Consequently, my comment on the literature will really be a presentation of some patently ecological explanations of organizational decline that researchers could study. I will also comment on causes of organization decline in an effort to convey some sense of the importance of ecological theory for better understanding and possibly reversing organizational decline.

Population Effects on Organizational Decline

Intrapopulation Effects on Decline

Populations are sets of organizations that draw on the same pools of knowledge and skills in developing competencies (what McKelvey (1982) termed "comps") useful in drawing the resources from their environment that are necessary for survival and growth. In light of this definition of a population, two forces affect the growth or decline of the members of a population: (1) the diffusion and retention of survival-enhancing comps, and (2) the competition of members over the resources available from the environment. Given a supply of alternative comps (variations), ecologists believe that competition and natural selection create the process by which survival-enhancing comps are identified. The more successful members of a population are those who most quickly and effectively take advantage of a newly identified survival-enhancing comp.

Comps. The relationship between the general level of competence and the number of organizations in a population holding the competence is interesting. In the case of the U.S. textile machinery manufacturers, Sabel and his colleagues (1987) argue that the reduction of the population down to two members and the captivity of the textile mills by the machinery manufacturers was the cause of the decline of this industry in the United States. This case suggests that a viable and stable population may require both consolidation to a few dominant, low-cost producers accompanied by a peripheral set of more innovative "custom" producers. There seem to be conditions in which the natural trend toward consolidation, which seems unavoidable due to the effects of competition, may undermine the natural ability of a population to continue its life-sustaining innovations of new competencies. Thus, the traditional argument among industrial organization economists about whether consolidation leads to monopoly pricing (and, implicitly, hegemony and riches for the few) may be off target—at least in today's world economy. Nation-based monopolies contain the seeds of their own decline. Worldwide monopolies seem unlikely to exist since currency exchange rates, quotas, and tariffs are never subject to their control. If desired, national governments can always give local monopolies or oligopolies preferred treatment over a multinational monopoly.

Populations that, for various reasons, retain large numbers of members may also be prone to decline. Decline will be due in part to the natural emergence of a few dominant, low-cost producers at the expense of many smaller, less competitive firms. Attempts by various interests, particularly government entities, to maintain an artificially high number of small producers (for example, small farms and the U.S. active-passive solar industry) may invariably be misguided. In the latter case, government research subsidies and tax credits thwarted the natural development of larger lower-cost, more reliable firms by unnaturally supporting small, uncompetitive firms.

It is also important to point out that in organizational populations, growth or decline in the number of members is not always an indication of the health of the population. A decline in the number of members may be an indication of health during the consolidation transition from numerous birth forms to fewer low-cost producers. A population's health might improve as the result of increases in comps even though growth in the number of members is stable or declining. It is also possible to infer that a population is healthy because of growth in the number of members. In reality, it may be that the health of the population is marginal or declining as new entrants take away resources from a finite pool, thus lowering the health of each individual member. Such a misperception is akin to believing that the population

of Ethiopians is healthy because their birth rate is increasing, even though there is not enough food to feed them properly.

Life cycles. Another set of issues concerns age and life-cycle distributions of, and within, a population. I am not sure we know what a healthy population looks like at various times in its evolution. Before being able to better understand the dynamics leading to the growth or decline of comps or population members, we need to know more about the evolution and demographics of industry populations. Is there a ratio between the number of dominant low-cost producers and small custom producers that is optimal for enhancing the survival of a population under competitive conditions? Is it possible for a few large firms to play the role of both low-cost (competitive) producer and competence innovator? Are there different life expectancies for large and small organizations in various populations? In some populations, decline may be a sign of good health. In others, it may indicate the decline of the population as a whole.

The evolution of a population of organizations seems to follow a life cycle of stages not unlike the birth, growth, maturity, revival, and decline stages suggested for individual organizations (Cameron & Whetten, Chapter 2). A population emerging due to a dramatic technical innovation, such as microcomputers, may pass through the life-cycle stages in synchrony with its member organizations; this is an example of a *synchronous* population. In other populations (restaurants, for example), the life cycles of the members fall into all stages, with most members' stages not coinciding with the life-cycle stage of the population; such a case involves an *asynchronous* population. I think the field would benefit by more careful mapping of the life-cycle stages of populations relative to the stages of their members. There may be identifiable life-cycle mixes in healthy populations. Clearly, explanations of decline, and responses to it, would depend on the life stage of the population and the particular organization within it.

What is important, then, is to critically and cautiously assess studies that focus only on births, deaths, and population growth without also taking into account changes in competence and the health of individual members: an increase in the hazard function is not necessarily an indication of deteriorating population health! Organizational populations clearly differ from biological populations in the effect of number of members, improvements in competence, and the health of individual members on population health. Hence, equations used by theoretical ecologists to describe population increase and density are even more problematic for organizational ecologists than they are for biological ecologists. Unfortunately, we are far from achieving a mathematics of organizational decline, and I am not aware of much activity that would bring us significantly closer to reaching that goal.

Density dependence.   Assuming that the demographic states of populations differ and fluctuate across time, the question arises, "Why?" Factors affecting the decline (and growth) of populations come in two forms: *density dependent* and *density independent*. As a population becomes denser relative to the resource pool available to it, density-dependent factors have more impact; for example high density may lead to decreasing births and fewer resources. Generally, density-dependent factors tend to stabilize a population at a certain size. (Presumably, this holds for competence and other aspects of health as well, although size is usually the only demographic variable considered.) Density-independent factors, typically elements of the environment, do not alter the intensity of their impact on a population as its size varies. In the various studies of decline available, I have not seen any attention given to distinguishing between the effects of density dependence and independence. Until this distinction is made clearer, both explanations for and normative approaches to dealing with decline have to be considered suspect.

Density-dependent factors have their strongest effect when the *carry capacity* (K) of the environment is reached. Carrying capacity is typically defined as that point in the growth of a population

when its intrinsic rate of increase (r) equals zero. Competitive conditions in a population's niche emerge only after the carrying capacity of its environment is reached. Organizations that thrive under the competitive conditions in such niches are called K strategists. Sometimes a niche becomes subject to drastic environmental changes or shocks such as the energy crisis or a new technology such as microchips. Some members of the population may become opportunistic in trying to take advantage of the new situation. These kinds of (entrepreneurial) organizations are termed r strategists because their proliferation is governed more by the rate at which they multiply rather than by the limits of environmental resources. Clearly, circumstances leading to, and theories explaining, the decline of r types must be quite different than theories about K types. Yet I do not see any attention to these issues in the decline literature.

Interpopulation Effects on Decline

Biologists have developed a fairly standard language for describing interactions between populations. Of the eight kinds of interactions that can occur (Pianka 1978: 174), biologists tend to emphasize competition and predation. Whether organizational scientists should emphasize these interactions as well remains to be seen. In any case, these two varieties of interaction do seem to be fruitful points of departure for the study of organizational decline.

Competition.   Theoretical ecologists have used the Lotka–Volterra equations to model the dynamics of competition between two populations (Pianka 1978). The equations describe the interplay of four forces:

1. Population A's inhibition of itself;
2. Population A's inhibition of population B;
3. Population B's inhibition of itself; and
4. Population B's inhibition of population A.

Four cases of competitive interaction emerge from the interplay of these forces:

Case I: Population A inhibits B more than itself; thus B declines.

Case II: Population B inhibits A more than itself; thus A declines.

Case III: Each population inhibits the other more than itself; the outcome depends on which population was largest to begin with.

Case IV: Each population inhibits itself more than the other; the outcome is stable equilibrium.

Biological and organizational ecologists place most emphasis on the fourth case. In this situation, while there might be increases and decreases in the sizes of the two populations at various times, the populations remain in long-term equilibrium.

Industrial economists developed their field on the premise that forces existed that inevitably pushed industrial populations into situations of monopoly or oligopoly and found their primary field of application in the antitrust activities of the federal government. In assuming that monopoly or oligopoly are the inevitable outcomes, industrial economists place themselves in the same camp as the ecologists, in principle. However, organizational ecologists (e.g., Freeman & Hannan 1983; Freeman, Carroll & Hannan 1983; Carroll & Delacroix (Chapter 9); Singh, House & Tucker 1986) have studied populations that clearly have not moved toward monopoly or oligopoly. The implication of their work is that stable equilibrium exists in populations, but not at monopolistic or oligopolistic states. Competitive strategies, on the other hand, have discovered that a variety of forces exist in industry populations that do not seem to lead inevitably toward monopoly or oligopoly, or even stable equilibrium. Instead, changes in the four forces mentioned above continually undermine whatever tendencies toward homeostasis might exist in a population.

Those studying the ecology of organizational decline should acknowledge that all four cases are provocative. At this time, it does not seem to be an incontrovertible fact that organizational populations are all in stable equilibrium. I question whether much is to be gained by applying the competition equations to study only equilibrium if we are not sure that equilibrium conditions prevail. Perhaps it is understating it to say that most organizational scholars hold the view that organizations are much better able to alter inhibitions to growth, both their own and their competitors', than are biological organisms.

The examples from the literature included in this book focus on individual organizational approaches to coping with declining industries rather than population effects. Once we realize that the activities that inhibit growth, discussed below, are brought on or accentuated because the organizations in the populations are experiencing K conditions, we can see that all of these activities combine to form the basis of self-inhibition.

As supply outpaces demand, populations clearly inhibit their own growth because they approach the carrying capacity of their environments. But non-supply-and-demand factors also come into play as populations approach K conditions and the attendant increase of threats to their survival stemming from stiffer competition. Harrigan (Chapter 7) points out that populations inhibit themselves by not minding costs and operational improvements, by ignoring technological developments, by panicky behavior, by product obsolescence, and so forth. She also discusses more strategic actions members of a population may use to counter inhibition such as: investing in some niches, divesting units in other (less promising) niches, harvesting an investment rapidly, or disposing of unproductive assets quickly. Hambrick and Schecter (Chapter 16) discuss entrepreneurial strategies (revenue-generating and product/market refocusing) and efficiency strategies (cost-cutting and asset reduction). Staw, Sandelands, and Dutton (Chapter 5) point out that threat-rigidity effects undermine information processing and control. Thus, bold leadership and formalization, which can lead to growth, can also lead to stagnation. These strategies all pertain to altering self-inhibition. If all, or even some, members of a population could raise the inhibition level, they could stave off non-case IV declines and bring the population back into a case IV situation.

There has been much interest in changes within firms that move them in or out of equilibrium positions into growth or decline states. These dynamics are, perhaps, even more interesting to study at the population level. As a population moves in and out of a case IV state, observers can see member organizations in states of decline. Paradoxically, the population could be healthy, getting stronger, or recovering from difficulty. Furthermore, which case a population is classified in should help determine how one might advise a member organization to attempt a recovery—or exit. Decline therapy is very much dependent on the state of the population, a firm's microniche within the population macroniche, and the relationship of the population niche to the niches of adjacent populations.

Predation.   Intrapopulation predation in the biological world is rare but, among organizations, both intrapopulation and interpopulation predation abound. Consider the relationship between predation and decline. So far, strategists and ecologists seem to treat acquisition or merger as the death of the target organization. But predation via merger or acquisition may or may not feel like decline to the target organization. In terms of niche occupancy, many target firms are both financially and technologically stronger after merger than before. The firm as a separate identity may disappear, but the niche pressure against intrapopulation competitors may increase. Frequently an infusion of new managerial personnel negates active self-inhibition processes, leading the target firm to a stronger position, even if financial or technological aids are not forthcoming. Generally, the merger and acquisition process, its aftermath, and its effects on growth and decline are not yet well understood; however, it remains an important phenomenon. Because of secrecy beforehand, and sensitivity afterward, research sites are difficult to obtain.

Whether predatory behavior increases or decreases the overall decline or growth of a population is not entirely clear. Free-market advocates would argue that corporate raiders do us all a favor by taking over and breaking up large, ungainly, and uncompetitive organizations. Presumably the population in which a division of a large firm competes is better off with the division freed from an incompetent owner. If the division is strong, it may gain from autonomy and strengthen the competitive level within its population. If it is weak, it no longer is propped up by the corporation, and when it declines the population is probably better off.

A prevailing logic is that corporations should settle on about three basic businesses for purposes of risk aversion via diversification. Any additional unrelated businesses seem to complicate attempts to master appropriate strategies and operational excellence in the face of widely varying niches and strong competitors. Corporate pruning, either before or after raiding activity, may at first resemble decline, but, in the long run, better health may follow. The newest organizations seem patterned after firms in the construction industry. There is ever increasing whittling away at permanent employees balanced by increasing reliance on outside vendors, subcontractors, consultants, and other kinds of temporary employees. Depending on the nature of an emergent project, players are assembled from a relevant competence pool, rather than being moved around within the firm. Theory Z and lifetime employment notwithstanding, the U.S. corporate world seems to be moving toward fewer rather than more lifetime employees.

Niche Effects on Organizational Decline

In Figure 1, I offer a preliminary delineation of causes of organizational decline. These causes may be classified as external or internal. Externally caused decline may fall into one of two categories: (1) decline due to a reduction in the number of resources available to an organization and (2) decline due to the nature of structural or contextual changes in the niche that then impinge on the organization. The importance of this distinction is well illuminated in the work of Cameron, Kim, and Whetten (Chapter 10), which shows that effective organizations differ markedly from inef-

Figure 1. Causes of Organizational Decline

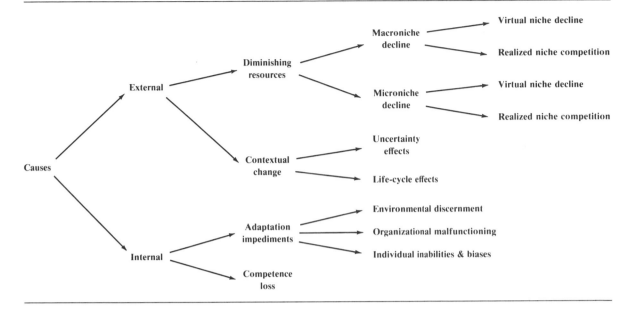

fective ones in their response to decline and turbulence.

Internally caused decline generally arises either (1) from conscious attempts by managers to adapt an organization to changing external conditions or (2) from the systematic loss of survival competence, that is, the loss of those knowledge and skill elements necessary both for responding to environmental change and for survival under new circumstances.

Diminishing resources. Organizations, as members of a population, exist in microniches that are subsets of the macroniche in which the population exists. Niches develop as a population develops its proficiency for garnering resources from its targeted resource pool. While it is important to keep in mind that both micro- and macroniches exist and are different, my discussion of resource decline applies to both.

Building on basic conceptual developments by Hutchinson (1957), ecologists define the fundamental or virtual niche as the hypothetical or idealized niche containing the resources an organ-

ization is able to draw on for its survival, without the interference of competition or predation. In reality, no organization ever exists in a virtual niche. Instead, organizations exist in realized or actual niches in which they suffer the full effect of competition and predation and other activities within and between populations.

Taking into account both virtual and realized niches, organizational decline may be caused by two kinds of resource contractions. On the one hand, the realized niche might be diminishing. In this situation, the contraction in resources is due to the increasing strength of an organization or population's competitors, or a decline in its commensal host. (For example, the decline of a prime contractor may affect its subcontractors.) On the other hand, the virtual niche might be declining because the pool of resources upon which a population or organization depends for its survival is declining.

Recognizing the difference is important. If the decline is in the realized niche, the logical survival strategy is to focus on gaining strength relative to the competitors or otherwise deal with the inter- or intrapopulation interactions. But, if the decline is in the virtual niche, other kinds of adaptation may prove more productive than simply contending with competitors.

Contextual change. Much has been written about the difficulties organizations face as a result of uncertainties and environmental shocks. The maladaptive and decline potential from misaligned structure and process due to progressive developmental stages and the evolution of the business environment is much more destructive. Why? Because life-cycle changes and industry evolution are so insidious.

In most development theories, organizations seem to progress through birth, high growth, maturity, and revitalization as they become larger and older (for example, Greiner 1972; Flamholtz 1986) until they hit a decline phase (Miller and Friesen, Chapter 11). In reality, decline is hovering at every stage. Singh, House, and Tucker (1986) and Carroll and Delacroix (Chapter 9), for example, show that decline may be more likely during the birthing stage than at any other time. Decline may result, in fact, from several ecological states related to life-cycle development, and it is probable in all stages. First, the liability of newness is due to poor choice of niche. The identified resource pool simply does not sustain the organization. For example, if an entrepreneur opens a gourmet sandwich shop in an area where there is no demand for such a product, no amount of organizational expertise is going to save the would-be entrepreneur from disaster.

Second, liability of decline is as much a danger to a firm lucky enough to hit upon a much sought-after product. Ironically, as detailed by Flamholtz (1986), very rapidly growing companies may actually decline and go bankrupt (or become highly vulnerable to competitors) from being too successful because their managerial infrastructure cannot keep pace with the organizing demands of rapid growth.

Third, even if a firm manages to organize for conditions of high growth (r conditions), the onslaught of competitors and K conditions may rather quickly bring on the requirement of advancing into the subsequent stage of development. Ecologists think of this as changing from an r strategist to a K strategist. This is the period of time in the evolution of an industry known vernacularly as a "shakeout." Failure to make this transition is generally regarded as the prime reason for the decline of firms in a new industry.

Fourth, an implication I can draw from the quantum view of organizational development taken by Miller and Friesen (1984) and Tushman, Newman, and Romanelli (Chapter 3) is that decline is more likely during punctuations (really metamorphic changes) between life-cycle stages than during them. I realize that these theorists believe that their quantum or punctuated equilibrium theories apply to organizational evolution, but my understanding of their work suggests that their ideas apply more to the life-cycle change and development of individual organizations than to the evolution of form within a population. In any event the point is that, for the study of the ecology of decline, the effects during transitions between stages may be more important than what happens during a particular stage.

Fifth, the incidence of failure of relatively mature, functionally designed firms is less recognized in the business literature than is failure during the shakeout time, but many firms decline because of a delayed transition to the multidivisional form. Textbooks are full of examples of functional firms not recognizing the need to move toward a product or matrix form.

Even when firms do adopt a multidivisional form, top managements seem capable of fully understanding only a few unlike niches at any one time, which results in their failure to aggressively respond to contextual changes in one or more of these niches. Individual decisions may, therefore, become maladaptive and wayward, followed by their decline and that of the corporation. Consequently people in general, and the corporate raiders in particular, have discovered that diversified firms, like stolen Porsches, are often worth more stripped than intact. Whether stripping divisions slows or hastens corporate decline seems moot at this time.

Adaptation impediments. At the heart of most theories of how organizations achieve effectiveness lies the assumption that managers first view the external environment and then interpret it, develop strategies about how to respond, develop structural and process improvements, develop change approaches, and then implement the adaptations. (See, for example: classical management theory, Weber's (1947) bureaucratic model, the rational goal model (Georgiou 1973), March & Simon's (1958) administrative behavior model, the market failures model (Williamson 1975; Williamson & Ouchi 1981), the resource dependency model (Pfeffer & Salancik 1978), and so forth.) However, there is substantial reason to believe that the joint probability that all the required elements necessary for this model to produce successful adaptation to environmental novelties are ever present in any given organization is very low.

First, consider the problem of accurately identifying what to adapt to in an organizational environment. Except in the situations where environments are well understood, and where an organization is essentially copying adaptations already performed by its competitors or conforming to the external institutional structure (DiMaggio & Powell 1983), environments are typically seen as multidimensional, complex, and changeable (Jurkovich 1974; McKelvey 1982 chap. 4). In addition there is a causal texture imposed by the actions of other firms and broader events that creates an inescapable uncertainty (Emery & Trist 1965). Finally, external environmental conditions are frequently opaque.

Second, even if environmental conditions are transparent, a variety of elements conspire against accurate perception of them by those in an organization. People tend to have idiosyncratic interpretations of the phenomenal world impinging upon them. They are known to selectively misperceive phenomena to accommodate their own bi-

ases. People frequently draw inaccurate images of organizational environments (Weick 1979). Where organizational adaptation might depend on a correct understanding of the causal sequences of particular environmental conditions, we can expect that an individual's causal attributions might lead to inaccuracies.

Third, because of their multiple hierarchical levels and communications up and down the hierarchy, organizations frequently suffer from impacted information: top-level managers responsible for making strategic and design decisions often do not have access to as much relevant information as employees lower down in the organization. Sometimes key people in an organization have access to all the information necessary, but they make poor decisions because of their own biases, bounded rationalities, and poor decision-making skills. Even if those in power, the dominant coalition, make the proper decisions, a host of implementation difficulties can impede their progress, such as resistance to change, intracoalition politics, and unexpected maladaptive outcomes of rational behaviors, as outlined by Rumelt (1987).

Competence loss. Many of the chapters in this book describe various kinds of incompetence. Some portion of organizational incompetence may be blamed on mistakes, stupidity, and panic. As must have been apparent in my discussion of life-cycle progressions, many previously competent managers of heretofore successful firms appear incompetent simply because they keep applying old cures to new problems. The loss in comps is a result both of people leaving and of the comps becoming obsolete.

Referring to the Harrigan chapter (Chapter 7), managers may adopt a mistaken turnaround strategy. Or, as Cameron, Kim, and Whetten discovered (Chapter 10), some managers fail to protect the technical core. As Staw, Sandelands, and Dutton argue in Chapter 5, managers may mistakenly rely on inadequate or irrelevant prior information. Sometimes managers do ill-advised things, such as the college president Chaffee (1984) describes who takes a pay raise while everyone else is asked to take pay cuts. Finally, imagine the firm attacked by a corporate raider whose management fights off the hostile takeover attempt by encumbering the firm with a huge debt in a stock buyback plan, or who gets rid of key assets in a "fire sale."

The list of ways managers can make mistakes is probably endless and quite random, given that there is no reason for such behavior to form a pattern. But organizations may suffer the effects of incompetence in more predictable ways. In fact, as Greenhalgh and Rosenblatt imply (Chapter 15), a positive feedback cycle often sets in. One of the effects of decline may be a systematic loss of competent people. As an organization begins to get into trouble and starts cutting back on pay raises, expense accounts, support staff, growth and promotion opportunities, and so forth, the highly qualified employees will leave the organization because they can usually find better-paying and more stable and promising jobs in more successful firms. The net result is that the proportion of relatively incompetent employees grows, so that the chance the organization will suffer from the effects of incompetence grows. As the number of poor decisions increases, the number of talented employees who will find work life better somewhere else also increases. Organizations dependent on external legitimacy and resource support for survival may find that once information about their decline leaks out, the sources of legitimacy and resources may withdraw their support, thereby hastening the decline cycle.

Conclusion

Strangely, organizational decline is the best thing that ever happened for those of us who draw on allogenic forces and natural selection theory to explain organizational form and function. Why? At present, the vast majority of scholars in micro- and macro-organizational behavior will accept almost without question the notion that managers prepensely create and implement strategies and

adaptations to push their organizations along the survival path. These scholars are frequently adamantly resistant to the ideas of natural selection and blind variation.

Attribution theorists distinguish between external and internal attributions of causality. Generally, they have found that people tend to attribute success internally ("I earned an A in physics.") and failure externally ("That S.O.B. gave me an F in math."). Because the field has focused principally on growth and success, it has been difficult for scholars to attribute causality externally. It was logical to believe that managers are the actors responsible for success and, further, managers and consulting clients wanted to believe it, of course. The task of switching scholars' thinking to ecological forces and natural selection should be much easier when the subject is organizational decline. After all, everyone will readily blame decline on external events! Later, after ecological theories explaining decline are established, it should be easier to get scholars to apply the frameworks to explaining growth and success as well.

Another insight that has become clear to me in writing this chapter is the importance of merging the ecological and population studies side of macro-organizational behavior with competitive strategy and industrial-organization economics. The ideology and methods of organizational development spread through the universities and businesses of the United States during the three decades after World War II, when the country was at the peak of its economic strength relative to competing firms from other nations. "Competition" and "survival" were not in the vocabulary either of scholars or business executives. Now, the ideology of competition has clearly gained much more currency. Whereas the current "hot topics" in the natural sciences are often driven by the creation of new instruments like particle accelerators, electron microscopes, radio telescopes, or space platforms, in organizational studies hot topics can be driven by prevailing economic forces. Right now, the United States feels the wind of foreign competition stirring up trouble for U.S. companies. It seems logical that many scholars and studies would draw upon the prevailing economic scene for both ideology and inspiration. The sooner academic departments focus on, and organize around, a merger of these fields, the more useful and insightful our field will be. (Maybe one of us will even become a White House advisor!)

During the decade since Hannan and Freeman published their seminal work, ecologists have focused primarily on applications of event-history and hazard-function analyses of organizational births and deaths. The approach has mirrored trends in theoretical bioecology. I should emphasize what may be a potentially significant difference between bio- and organizational applications of the Verhulst–Pearl and Lotka–Volterra equations. Clearly, organizational populations may decline due to the loss of members or competence or, conversely, strengthen as a result of gains in members or competence. Membership and competence may vary independently. Their degree of covariance may shift as a population, especially a synchronous one, moves from one life-cycle stage to another. Until ecological studies account for the potentially confounding effects of membership and competence, we should view their results cautiously. As I mentioned earlier, the likelihood that competing organizational populations may not achieve equilibrium status advises further caution over applications of the Lotka–Volterra equations. Of course, the many other reservations bioecologists and organizational scientists have about theoretical ecology also apply.

Most organizational-studies scholars still do not think in terms of the dynamics and effects of populations. Even in this volume — except for the chapters by Hannan and Freeman, Carroll and Delacroix, and Cameron and Zammuto — I see virtually no recognition of population effects. The field still is the handmaiden of practicing managers who want help in getting their particular job done better. The field is still driven, it seems to me, by consultants who get paid by practicing managers and who aim their intellectual insights at ideas apt to help in the personal consulting business. Unfortunately, populations usually do not hire consultants. Populations are abstract and imper-

sonal. Populations do not go out of business and fire people; only firms do. I would like to think I have made it clearer, if not clear, that little systematic understanding or explanation of organizational decline will emerge without a focus on population ecology. To do otherwise, that is, to focus on individual firms and individual managers, is to run afoul of the down side of blind variation — random, avoidable errors. What this means is that I do not think any useful systematic theory will come from most of the chapters in this book, because they are stepchildren of blind variation; that is, they are really studying natural selection (if they only knew) in an illogical way. They have captured one principle, blind variation, but they have missed the other three: selection, retention and diffusion, and competitive struggle. Given that blind variation exists, the only way — and I do mean the *only* way — to make sense of what is going on is to study populations in the context of competition, hence, by drawing on all four principles. Only then will our field begin to take on meaning. As Hayek (1978) remarked, "An age of superstition is a time when people imagine that they know more than they do."

References

Chaffee, Ellen E. 1984. "Successful Strategic Management in Small Private Colleges." *Journal of Higher Education* 55: 212–41.

DiMaggio, Paul J., and Walter W. Powell. 1983. "The Iron Cage Revisited: Institutional Isomorphism and Collective Rationality in Organizational Fields." *American Sociological Review* 48: 147–60.

Emery, F.E., and E.L. Trist. 1965. "The Causal Texture of Organizational Environments." *Human Relations* 18: 21–32.

Flamholtz, Eric G. 1986. *How to Make the Transition from an Entrepreneurship to a Professionally Managed Firm.* San Francisco: Jossey-Bass.

Freeman, John, Glenn R. Carroll, and Michael T. Hannan. 1983. "The Liability of Newness: Age Dependence in Organizational Death Rates." *American Sociological Review* 48: 692–710.

Freeman, John, and Michael T. Hannan. 1983. "Niche Width and the Dynamics of Organizational Populations." *American Journal of Sociology* 88: 1116–45.

Georgiou, Petro. 1973. "The Goal Paradigm and Notes toward a Counter Paradigm." *Administrative Science Quarterly* 18: 291–310.

Greiner, Larry E. 1972. "Evolution and Revolution as Organizations Grow." *Harvard Business Review* (July–August).

Hannan, Michael T., and John Freeman. 1977. "The Population Ecology of Organizations." *American Journal of Sociology* 82: 929–64.

Hayek, F.A. 1978. "The Three Sources of Human Values." Hobhouse Lecture, London School of Economics, London. Mimeograph.

Hutchinson, George E. 1957. "Concluding Remarks." Cold Spring Harbor Symposium on Quantitative Biology 22: 415–27.

Jurkovich, Ray. 1974. "A Core Typology of Organizational Environments." *Administrative Science Quarterly* 19: 380–94.

March, James G., and Herbert A. Simon. 1958. *Organizations.* New York: John Wiley.

McKelvey, Bill. 1982. *Organizational Systematics.* Berkeley, Calif.: University of California Press.

Miller, Danny, and Peter Freisen. 1984. *Organizations: A Quantum View.* Englewood Cliffs, N.J.: Prentice-Hall.

Pfeffer, Jeffrey, and Gerald R. Salancik. 1978. *The External Control of Organizations: A Resource Dependence Perspective.* New York: Harper & Row.

Pianka, Eric R. 1978. *Evolutionary Ecology.* 2d ed. New York: Harper & Row.

Rumelt, Richard P. 1987. "Theory, Strategy, and Entrepreneurship." In *The Competitive Challenge: Strategies for Innovation and Renewal,* edited by David J. Teece, pp. 137–58. Cambridge, Mass.: Ballinger.

Sabel, Charles F., Gary Herrigel, Richard Kazis, and Richard Deeg. 1987. "How to Keep Mature Industries Innovative." *Technology Review* 90: 26–35.

Singh, Jitendra V., Robert J. House, and David J. Tucker. 1986. "Organizational Change and Organizational Mortality." *Administrative Science Quarterly* 31: 587–611.

Stinchcombe, Arthur L. 1965. "Social Structure and Organizations." In *Handbook of Organizations,* edited by James G. March, pp. 142–93. Chicago: Rand McNally.

Weber, Max. 1947. *The Theory of Social and Economic Organization.* Trans. A.M. Henderson and T. Parsons; ed. T. Parsons. New York: Free Press.

Weick, Karl E. 1979. *The Social Psychology of Organizing.* Reading, Mass.: Addison-Wesley.

Williamson, Oliver E. 1975. *Markets and Hierarchies: Analysis and Antitrust Implications.* New York: Free Press.

Williamson, Oliver E., and William G. Ouchi. 1981. "The Markets and Hierarchies Program of Research: Origins, Implications, Prospects." In *Perspectives on Organization Design and Behavior,* edited by A.H. Van de Ven and W.F. Joyce, pp. 347–70. New York: Wiley-Interscience.

24

Organizational Decline from the Organizational Perspective

Alan D. Meyer

Organizational decline is approaching its tenth anniversary as an area of conceptual and empirical scholarship. The phrase began appearing frequently in the academic literature on organizations near the end of the 1970s. Rising bankruptcy rates, hostile takeovers, federal cutbacks, and taxpayer revolts soon underscored the practical importance of decline, attracted scholars' attention, and conferred the cachet of a "hot topic." Subsequent decreases in academic enrollments and funds kindled researchers' interest, provided firsthand experiences with life in declining organizations, and supplied convenient sources of data. For these and other reasons, several literatures began accumulating rapidly, albeit haphazardly, around the topic of decline.

The work collected in this volume attests to the diversity of the methodologies invoked and the vitality of the ideas expressed. Concepts and methods from anthropology, biology, political science, psychology, and sociology have been brought to bear on the decline phenomenon. Case descrip-

I am grateful for the contributions of Bill Starbuck, Paul Nystrom, and Paul Shrivastava.

tions of failing organizations have inspired speculative theories that have informed exploratory empirical work. Not surprisingly, much of the evidence currently available is preliminary, and many of the prescriptions currently offered are contradictory. Thus, in setting out to collect and organize a diffuse literature, the editors of this volume have undertaken an important task.

The objective of this chapter is to evaluate this body of work from the vantage point of researchers taking entire organizations as their principal units of analysis. My commentary begins by identifying some unique contributions that decline scholars have made to what is known about organizations. It goes on to point out some deficiencies and blindspots in the literature, and ends by speculating about productive directions for future work on organizational decline.

Contributions of the Decline Literature

Theoretical Contributions: New Paradigms

The decline literature has added considerably to what we know about complex organizations. But more significantly, it has changed how we *think* about them. The contributors to this volume have helped enlarge the repertoire of theoretical paradigms available for characterizing organizations.

Recall that when decline research came on the scene in the late 1970s, organization theory was dominated by static, mechanistic models derived primarily from observation of mature organizations during three post-war decades of economic stability and virtually uninterrupted growth. A few theorists tried to inject dynamic elements into their models, but their efforts usually focused on easing the strains and consolidating the gains of organizational growth and expansion.

Against this theoretical backdrop, developmental models of organizational creation, transformation, and decline stood out in bold relief. They redirected researchers' attention by assuming disequilibrium rather than equilibrium, emphasizing change rather than permanence, and establishing survival rather than goal attainment as the fundamental task of every organization. Because these models drew analogies to populations of biological organisms, they posed questions about how organizations begin and end, how industries evolve, and how interorganizational networks are constituted. Some of the gains were conceptual, such as highlighting the importance of historical and contextual features of organizations. Other gains were methodological, such as encouraging researchers to think much more rigorously than before about appropriate units of analysis, levels of measurement, and aggregation of data.

Our understanding of organizational environments benefited substantially from this early work. By identifying declining industries, impoverished niches, and outmoded strategies as alternate causes of organizational failure, the decline literature helped rekindle researchers' interest in the contexts within which organizations compete. Prior conceptions of organizations' environments had centered on the cognitive uncertainty that external turbulence and complexity created within managers' minds. But uncertainty was proving impossible to measure reliably because managers perceived their environments so idiosyncratically. Consequently, this line of research neared an impasse.

Decline theories revitalized investigations of organizational environments. They did so by portraying them as fields of clustered resources confronting the organizations inhabiting them with varying levels of munificence, competition, and interconnectedness. These models emphasized the multidimensional nature of environments, suggested new operationalizations, and alerted us to the possibility that certain organizational forms are better equipped to cope with the demands of a given environmental niche than others.

Empirical Contributions: Organizations as Ongoing Processes

Some of the richest work on the topic of decline examines the managerial actions and organizational processes triggered by it. We have learned that prolonged declines do not simply reverse the changes that accompany growth. Rather, new and different problems must be surmounted in order to turn around a declining organization. At the onset, decline apparently inspires top managers to centralize decisionmaking, which tends to undermine the quality of decisions and the morale of subordinates.

We have come to understand how critical stockpiles of slack resources become during periods of decline. Top managers confront hard choices: Should we consume slack resources to absorb the effects of decline, or invest them in adaptive responses that might reverse the decline? Some theorists, however, maintain that the critical problem is not managing resources, but managing ideology. Infusions of fresh ideas, they argue, are more apt to inspire turnarounds than are infusions of fresh resources.

In any event, we have learned that coping with decline generally requires solutions not contained in organizations' repertoires, and that managers' instinctive responses may exacerbate problems. Strategic reorientations are needed, but those who fashioned the outmoded strategies may defend them in order to retain their power. Thus, replacing top leaders can often be an essential first step in turning around declining organizations. These insights, along with others developed in the decline literature, have made vital contributions to our understanding of the interacting processes that map the trajectories along which organizations and industries evolve.

Finally, decline theorists have done their colleagues a great favor by articulating plausible explanations for why all organizations undergo periodic upheavals, and why these upheavals sometimes lead to their demise. During a period when U.S. businesses were chalking up the highest bankruptcy rates in history, most organizational scholars found themselves a long way up the empirical creek without a theoretical paddle. Fortunately, writers on decline came along to rescue us from utter irrelevancy.

Blindspots in the Decline Literature

The last section praised writers on decline for encouraging us to view surviving organizations as those that adapted to fit their environments, and environments as selecting those organizations fit for survival. This section, rather perversely, takes the decline literature to task for these same views, suggesting that it has obscured our ability to recognize organizations as social constructions, political arenas, and cultural milieus.

Regardless of whether organizations are viewed as the products of strategic choices, exquisite adaptations, or natural selections, biological analogies imbue organizations with a spurious aura of inevitability. Seeing organizations as endproducts of natural processes leads observers to assume that "what is" had to be, thus implicitly endorsing the status quo. This prompts us to overlook political and cultural causes of organizational actions and structures. Organizational scientists have been more prone to describing organizations' characteristics than to prescribing improvements. Perhaps this is because biological analogies have persuaded us that defects in organizations are self-correcting.

Biological analogies also tend to magnify organizations' tangible and concrete properties. But viewing organizations as objective entities leads observers to underestimate the extent to which their members collaborate actively in constructing and remodeling them. One result is that we fail to appreciate the degree to which organizations enact their own crises and instigate their own declines.

A social-construction view holds that environments stage ambiguous events. Some organizations do not notice them. Those that do interpret them idiosyncratically—perhaps labeling the events as opportunities in one case and as threats in another. Similarly, organizations observe their own performances, invent meanings, and seek to persuade external constituents to accept these meanings. Thus, decline may result from failure to erect convincing facades, to interpret performances elegantly, or to communicate the interpretations persuasively.

The social-construction view suggests some unrecognized conceptual and methodological difficulties for researchers studying decline. It implies that organizational declines are not objective, social facts. An ostensible decline may be a collective fantasy, a polished performance, or a conspiracy to unseat entrenched powerholders. In light of such possibilities, should retrenchments, turnarounds, exits, and acquisitions be lumped together as instances of decline? What about the recent corporate penchant for downsizing during periods of increasing profits? Are the organizations declining, growing, adapting, or merely sporting a momentarily stylish management practice?

The central issue here is that independent observers often cannot agree that a given organization is experiencing decline until the process has run its course. This is unfortunate, because processes that can only be identified by their endings can be easily investigated only in retrospect. Observing a sample of organizations longitudinally until a substantial number of them decline is a costly and tedious way to conduct research. On the other hand, selecting samples of organizations *after* they have declined is likely to introduce biases associated with sampling on the dependent variable, and biases associated with gathering data through retrospective reconstructions of decisions and events.

Directions for Future Research

Students of decline have invigorated organizational science. They have highlighted issues of theoretical and practical significance and challenged prevailing assumptions about organizations. But if decline researchers are to continue this trend, they may need to question some of their own assumptions. To facilitate this process, I will conclude by offering five alternative ways of viewing organizational decline.

- *View decline as maladaptation.* The publication of this book signifies the coming of age of organizational decline as a research topic. Isolating new areas of research sets them apart from their predecessors, identifies them as "hot" topics, and helps them gain a foothold in the marketplace for ideas. But as topics cool off, the benefits of isolation diminish and the liabilities increase.

  The empirical literature shows that declining organizations show symptoms of poor internal fit (between the organization's parts) and symptoms of poor external fit (between the organization and its environment). This suggests that it is reasonable to reconceptualize organizational decline as maladaptation. Treating decline as the deterioration of an organization's relationship with its environment should help assimilate work on decline into mainstream literature on organizational design and adaptation.
- *View decline as an opportunity.* The manager unlucky enough to find himself or herself at the helm of an organization drifting into decline is commonly believed to become increasingly isolated and impotent. However, this assumption obscures the opportunities that accompany crises. Decline focuses everyone's attention on survival and thus energizes the organization. It allows top managers to consolidate power and it legitimates unorthodox actions. Decline offers an opportunity for bootlegging changes that would meet stiff resistance if introduced during periods of stability.

  Managers and researchers might see these opportunities more clearly if they tried thinking of decline as a problem of *abundance,* rather than as a problem of *scarcity.* On balance, decline *increases* slack, at least initially. It yields a pool of idle human resources, produces excess manufacturing capacity, and releases other assets from utilization. Instead of laying off employees en masse, managers might ask how the energy and resources suddenly freed up from doing old jobs with obsolete technologies can be reallocated to foster innovation and bolster revenues.
- *View decline as a social construction.* If the set of potential causes of organizational decline is enlarged to include losses of shared meaning, commitment, and enthusiasm, then some different remedies are made available. Changing organizational languages, manipulating symbols, and staging ceremonies become potent means of effecting turnarounds. A conspicuous example is the leader who resurrects core beliefs, inspires new sagas, or inculcates values that update an organization's culture. A more subtle example is changing accounting practices. Accounting categories imbue organizational outcomes with arbitrary meanings by determining what is noticed, defining what is important, and interpreting what is happening. Their change potential stems from the fact that these properties escape notice — accounting data are usually considered literal, precise, and value-free.

  When William Anderson was hired in 1972 to halt NCR's slide toward bankruptcy, he announced that mechanical cash registers were obsolete, and he magnified NCR's already sizable operating losses by writing off $135 million worth of product inventories. By underscoring the gravity of NCR's financial crisis and blaming his predecessor for its occurrence, Anderson consolidated power. By emphasizing NCR's urgent need to enter the electronic age, the action heralded a strategic reorientation. And when demand for the purportedly obsolete mechanical products remained strong, Anderson's accounting legerdemain fueled NCR's comeback. Unfortunately, it is more common for leaders of declining organizations to change accounting practices in hopes of concealing the symptoms of decline than to undertake changes to signal routes toward renewal.

- *View decline as social progress.* Decline is commonly associated with failure and decay. A more upbeat approach calls decline the pivotal stage in a recycling process whereby old, worn-out organizations give way to young, vital ones. The evidence suggests that considerable quantities of human and financial resources are impounded in stagnant organizations. Dun and Bradstreet projected a modest 2.6 percent increase in jobs during 1987. But 75 percent of the newly created jobs will emerge in firms employing fewer than 500 people, and aggregate employment in firms employing 10,000 or more is actually projected to drop. Large, mature organizations provide unlikely settings for economic revival.

  In general, we have overestimated the social costs of halting organizations and underestimated the benefits. It may be instructive to remember that Henry Ford went bankrupt during his first year in the automobile business. Two years later, his second company went under, too. His third corporation, however, has done pretty well. Simply put, birth is usually easier than resurrection.

- *Do not ignore externalities.* Consider the following: In the early 1960s, top executives of a large corporation approved the construction of a plant that would enable a subsidiary making electric batteries to diversify into chemical manufacturing. Shortly thereafter, demand fell so sharply that the executives considered calling

off the project. But sacrificing the sunk costs would have embarrassed the executives, so they decided to complete the plant. After going into production, the plant immediately began losing money. Headquarters applied pressure to cut costs, left "nonessential" positions vacant, and watched employee morale deteriorate. After operating in the red for several years, production was cut back to 30 percent of capacity. Training and maintenance budgets were reduced, and interdepartmental antagonisms flared. The plant had virtually no continuity in leadership, since successions were taking place on the average of every other year. In 1980, corporate executives finally decided to exit. When they publicly announced that the plant was for sale, most of the remaining experienced employees resigned. The plant was shut down indefinitely in 1984.

In many respects, this case is typical. It includes some of the classic ingredients of organizational decline—escalating commitment to a failing course of action, a vicious cycle of decision centralization, declining morale, and tightening control—all culminating in the departure of the only people who might have turned things around.

What makes this particular decline unique is that more than jobs and invested capital were lost. The case describes Union Carbide's Bhopal plant. Its 1984 closure came in the aftermath of the most tragic industrial accident in history. An escape of lethal gas killed nearly 3,000 people and seriously injured approximately 200,000. About 2,000 domestic animals died and all the standing vegetation near the plant was destroyed. The chairman of Union Carbide's board of directors was arrested on criminal charges, and the corporation's image was irrevocably tainted.

Most of those studying decline have adopted a rather circumscribed, economic view of its consequences. Most have disregarded what are labeled "externalities" in economic parlance—costs borne by people located beyond the boundaries of the firm. The sad message of Bhopal is that before disappearing, declining organizations can create social and ecological catastrophes. Indeed, organizations can externalize costs even while they are building market share, hiring more employees, and earning handsome financial returns. How often do organizations export the costs of their decline? How many tons of toxic wastes have declining organizations dumped? How many workers have they unnecessarily exposed to occupational diseases?

The lesson is that a soundly designed, well-adapted organization is more than a means of boosting employees' morale and generating economic returns for owners. It may be our best hope for containing the potentially destructive consequences of complex organizations. Perhaps the greatest contribution scholars of organizational decline can make lies in teaching us that an effective, reliable, and humane organization is not a solution to reach, but rather an ongoing process to maintain.

25

Organizational Decline from the Individual Perspective

Larry L. Cummings

There is a natural tendency in most academic disciplines, including topical areas within disciplines, to become provincial and insular in focus over time. We tend to limit too narrowly what literatures, concepts, and findings we consider relevant to our interests. Consequently, we evoke concepts and paradigms that effectively hamper divergence. Of course, this process provides important functions of ordering, structuring, and partitioning a field of inquiry. Yet, these tendencies create myopia and inhibit the creativity and development of a field. They may even engender decline and intellectual death.

In this commentary, I will apply this reasoning to the field of organizational decline from the perspective of an individual level of analysis, meaning that the lens will be largely psychological. Occasionally the focus will draw upon a social-psychological perspective in order to enhance the criticisms of the existing literature and to offer suggestions.

My central argument is that the organizational decline literature has primarily used a macro-organizational perspective. Consequently, despite a few notable exceptions (see Chapters 14 and 15) relatively little research has examined how individuals interpret and react to organizational decline. Thus, a complete understanding of this topic must include a psychological orientation. This chapter is organized around four questions that will help incorporate the psychological perspective into the decline literature: (1) What is decline? (2) How is decline punctuated by time? (3) What is "organizational" about organizational decline? (4) What role should individual leadership play relative to organizational decline?

What is Decline?
Multiple Definitions and their Implications

It is important to distinguish among three different conceptualizations of decline when reflecting on the interaction between individuals and organizations in decline. These distinctions are important because different definitions of decline suggest:

- different psychological literatures relevant to understanding an individual's *interpretation* of decline;

- different individual stresses resulting from organizational decline; and
- different individual strategies for coping with the stress of decline.

I will make the case for each of these arguments after presenting three definitions of what an organization's decline might mean to an individual within the organization.

First, decline can be considered in relation to history. That is, an individual might perceive that his or her organization is declining when some critical resource (financial, human, physical) is less available to the organization and, thus, to the individual than in the relevant past. The concept of decline will be referred to as a *temporal comparative* framing.

Second, decline can be conceived relative to other organizations. The individual might ask: How is my organization performing (or behaving more generally, even on nonperformance indicators) compared to other organizations of which I am aware and that fall within my set of relevant comparisons? This framing will be referred to as *interorganizational comparative*. This second genre can be crossed with the first to yield comparisons among organizations across time.

Third, decline can be defined as *aspirational comparative*. Here, the relevant standard for the individual is how he or she construes that the organization *does* perform in comparison to how he or she believes that the organization *should* perform. This framing of decline might be expressed in statements like: "We failed to meet our goals, so we must be slipping."

Having introduced these three perspectives on decline, let me return to the consequences likely to be associated with these definitional distinctions. First, if an individual uses a *temporal comparative* framing to interpret decline, the relevant literatures for understanding that individual's interpretation are certain to be those on social reinforcement, behavioral modification, and punishment (Arvey & Jones 1985; Bandura 1977; Scott & Podsakoff 1985). This is because the referent for drawing inferences about the focus and causes of decline is one's own organization. This is similar to the use of self as a referent for personal decline over time. Most people, when using this referent, are likely to come to understand their organization's decline by examining what it has done inappropriately in its environment and by noting the consequences (negative or punishing in this case) for themselves and their organization. Furthermore, a constructive interpretation of decline within this framing is sure to lead to attempts to modify one's own behavior so as not to suffer negative consequences later.

An *interorganizational comparative* framing is apt to lead to perceptions of inequity or injustice concerning the allocation of opportunities and resources among organizations. Thus, the literatures on social inequity (Martin 1981), interpersonal injustice (Bies 1987) and relative deprivation (Crosby 1984) are useful in helping to understand an individual's sense of decline when using this framing.

An *aspirational comparative* framing implies that goal setting and feedback processes will be central to understanding how individuals interpret decline. If decline is characterized as a progressive and consistent failure to meet aspiration levels, then understanding how individuals interpret failure requires an examination of both how individuals set and react to goals (Mento, Steel & Karren 1987), as well as how they react to feedback and, if necessary, seek feedback to interpret failure (Ashford & Cummings 1983; 1985).

Not only are the meanings connected with decline likely to vary as a function of decline, but individual reactions are bound to be significantly influenced as well. For example, anxiety about personal skill obsolescence, ignorance of relevant knowledge, or feeling out of touch with key current issues are likely to result when the framing is temporal comparative. The perspective of the individual is of "being behind" and no longer individually competitive. Thus, stress is likely to be internal for individuals framing decline this way. Blame for organizational failure is placed on self. When the individual uses the interorganizational comparative framing, we observe frustration over the perceived inequity of resource allocations and unfair practices by competitive (or other relevant comparison) organizations. A sense of social, distributive injustice flavors the stress reaction, and blame centers on external agents as the likely causes of decline. Finally, when the framing is aspirational comparative, frustration and stress are often expressed by dissatisfaction with organizational leadership ("they" have unreasonable goals) and culture (this place is too mean and lean, is inhuman, is unreasonable).

Likewise the coping mechanisms that individuals use to deal with decline will vary with their framing. Using a temporal comparative framework, one probable, but under-studied, reaction is retrospective reinterpretation and denial. Much relevant literature suggests that when threatened with environmental decline, individuals cope by making an alternative "sense" of history or by denying the fact of decline. In addition, if denial and reconstruction of validity do not reduce the stress of decline, then individuals are known to shift to the constructive support of peer groups and to yield their definitions of reality to constructive confrontation (Trice & Beyer 1986). Along these lines, Harris and Sutton (1986) report that people who attended parting ceremonies, or wakes, held for dying organizations consistently told one another, "I guess this means it is really over." These authors contend that this feature of parting ceremonies serves an important function by helping members avoid or overcome denial about the impending fact of organizational death.

With interorganizational comparative framing, individuals frequently confront decline with fiercely competitive, even destructive, zero-sum bargaining. Their reactions to the perceived injustice generated by such framing can cause a rigidity of response that is destructive to the organization. The greater the perceived organizational threat, the more likely the rigidity (Staw, Sandelands & Dutton Chapter 5; Staw & Ross 1987). These typical reactions underscore the critical importance of emphasizing integrative bargaining, adaptability, and flexible thinking through leadership behaviors that inculcate cultures encouraging divergent

(versus convergent) thinking under conditions of decline. These somewhat unnatural actions enhance the chances of the successful turnaround of a declining organization. Finally, those adopting an aspirational comparative framework frequently cope by lowering aspiration or goal levels to adapt to the negative feedback associated with decline (Ilgen, Fisher & Taylor 1979; Taylor, Fisher & Ilgen 1984). Alternatively, individuals may well exit the organization at the earliest sign of decline, demonstrating lower expectations of what the organization can deliver, rather than shifting their aspiration levels downward. This represents a form of anticipatory or pre-emptive coping once the future of the organization is perceived as boding poorly for one's own future.

The temporal, interorganizational, and aspirational-comparative perspectives have largely been ignored in the organizational decline literature. Most studies in this area have treated the organization as a monolithic whole experiencing an objective fact labeled decline. Although most researchers have implicitly used a comparative perspective in their analysis, few studies have directly examined the interpretive processes used by members to make sense of, or cope with, their eroding work environment.

The meaning individuals attach to "organizational decline" varies considerably depending on the reference invoked in the comparison process. This suggests several new avenues for research on organizational decline. For example, it directs attention to the strategies used by high-level administrators to manage the sense-making process by focusing attention on comparisons that place the organization's performance (and their contribution to it) in the most favorable light.

This perspective also highlights the value of examining the interpretive processes engaged in by different groups in a declining organization. This is especially important in most large, complex organizations where subunits experience different levels of success. For example, how do members of a single declining unit in an otherwise successful organization, or of a single growing unit in a generally declining organization, frame their personal experience relative to the performance of the overall organization? How do they rationalize the conflicting evidence? Do they select referents that tend to maximize or minimize the discrepancy between the performance of their unit and the rest of the organization? Do members in an isolated successful department tend to minimize the disparity between their good fortunes and the misery all around them by arguing that their performance is only mediocre compared to their very high expectations?

A summary of the insights gained from explicitly examining this comparative perspective is presented in Table 1. It summarizes the interpretive processes, types of pressures, and personal coping mechanisms associated with the three framing alternatives.

The Periodicity of Decline

A central issue for understanding decline is how individuals punctuate decline by time intervals. Regardless of the definitional framing used, individuals are likely to vary in their temporal punctuation of a declining environment (McGrath & Rotchford 1983). Their reactions are likely to be influenced by their answers to such questions as:

- When did the decline begin?
- Is the rate of decline accelerating?
- Is the form of decline smooth, or is it represented by a jagged time line?
- Do periods of decline and recovery cycle rhythmically?

Table 1. A Comparative View of Organizational Performance

	Referent Used in Evaluating Organizational Performance	Individual Stresses Resulting from Organizational Decline	Individual Coping Mechanisms [1]primary response [2]secondary response
Temporal Comparison	Organization's previous performance	Anxiety regarding personal skill obsolescence Personal blame for organizational decline	[1]Personal denial and reinterpretation [2]Submission to peer group reconstruction of organizational history
Interorganizational Comparison	Performance of similar organizations	Frustrations over inequitable resource allocation or perceived unfair competitive practices Blame focused on external actors	[1]Intense bargaining [2]Agressive, destructive, competitive practices
Aspirational Comparison	Performance goal	Frustration with organizational culture and structure Blame placed on organizational leaders	[1]Lowered aspirations [2]Search for employment opportunities in better-managed organizations

Not only are dispositional differences among individuals common in their punctuation styles (Gupta & Cummings 1986), but it is also presumable that punctuations of decline may vary as a function of the level of analysis that the individual focuses on when interpreting decline. For example, institutions have histories and legacies that typically outlive individuals and even generations of individuals. Thus, time may proceed more slowly in institutions with long histories compared to the time frames used by individuals to pace their own development. (Similarly, the Roman Catholic church may measure time using much longer intervals than does the newly formed National Commission on the Study of AIDS.)

This perspective on the periodicity of decline expands our understanding of why very large, diversified organizations often suffer serious setbacks. In their chapter in Part IV, Nystrom and Starbuck draw attention to a particular pattern in the business-failure literature: spectacular success very often precedes massive failure. Their explanation for this type of decline is that managers in such large, very successful firms can easily become complacent about potential competitive threats or possible customer disaffection. This overconfidence makes them slow to respond to early indications of serious external problems. Recent criticisms of the U.S. auto industry in the popular press lend credence to this line of reasoning.

An interpretative view of organizational decline extends Nystrom and Starbuck's explanation in the following way. Managers in organizations producing stable goods that tend to evolve very slowly (e.g., automobiles) are predisposed to respond cautiously to early indications of serious problems. They are conditioned to think of change as a slow evolutionary process embedded in multi-year planning cycles.

This deliberate reaction to external challenges is compounded in sizable, very successful organizations by the tendency to minimize the significance of a recent period of bad fortune relative to the accumulated wealth of the firm. Emphasizing the relative insignificance of the drop in current earnings compared to total assets, managers have

little incentive to press for change. Managers are also likely to dismiss bad news by rationalizing that the firm is highly diversified and is, therefore, not dependent on any given source of revenue. Since there is little risk that the recent downturn in the sales of product X threatens the well-being of the whole firm, they reason, quick remedial action is not required.

This interpretive perspective is further substantiated in the example of the U.S. auto industry's response to foreign competition during the 1970s. Observers of the Big Three automakers during this period of rapidly eroding market share have noted that executives consistently downplayed the significance of declining sales by using only the sales of other U.S. auto manufacturers as their basis for comparison.

What is Organization?
An Interdependence and Positional Perspective

I have no intention of attempting to answer the above question. Indeed, there is strong precedent in the organizational-studies literature to sidestep this difficult issue. March and Simon (1958), for example, began their classic book *Organizations* by noting that it is more useful, and certainly easier, to give examples of organizations than to define them. On the other hand, I do believe that any analysis of how individuals react to organizational decline will be enhanced if two issues that stem from this question are taken more seriously in our study of decline.

First, there is considerable evidence indicating that the significant causal environment for most individuals in organizations is their proximal milieu (Pierce, Dunham & Cummings 1984). Thus, except in the case of the highest-level executives, it is not likely that it is the decline of the total organization that will capture the attention of the potential victim. Rather it is the person's job, department, or work unit that is the center of attention. The literature on organizational decline tends to take the macro-organizational level of analysis too seriously when attempting to understand individual reactions to change. What is effective, hardnosed coping to a senior executive is real job decline (or disappearance) to the lower-level, affected participant. Likewise, what is "strategic management of environmental decline" to the senior executive is opaque, abstract, managerial gibberish to the person "down in." The organizational decline literature needs to rediscover the old adage that the same event is seen and defined differently within the *same* organization as a function of one's focus and status within that organization.

Second, we need to take seriously the fact that most members of a declining unit are members of other units and organizations both on and off the job. Furthermore, it is unlikely that each of these units (jobs, occupations, communities) is declining simultaneously. So to understand reactions to the decline of a single unit (or even a family of similar units), we need to emphasize and study the proactive strategies that people adopt to view their total organizational space. For example, relevant studies should center on the shift of attention from work to nonwork as the work unit declines; on the shifts of attention and energy across parts or tasks within one's job as some tasks are de-emphasized by the organization, hence declining; and on the likelihood of shifts of attention by those who remain within a unit, subsequent to the exit of those victimized by a decline (Brockner in press).

In general, then, what is "organizational" about decline is that dwindling resources accentuate interdependence—between people, levels, units, and even organizations. Therefore, decline must be studied in a manner that takes this heightened interdependence into account. A study of the internal processes within a single declining organizational unit or level will tend to overlook a rich set of dynamics, including scapegoating, rivalries, jealousies, and coalition defections. It will also be insensitive to the social comparisons that various groups (e.g., engineers, middle managers, shop workers) engage in that influence top management's ability to forge a unified plan of action. In addition, they will probably not track the erosion of allegiance to the organization, reflected in the shift of attention to non-job factors, that precedes absenteeism and turnover.

What Role for Leadership? Floating in the Face of Decline

The directional perspective of this commentary has been to assume that the primary causal flow of interest is *from* organizational decline *to* individual reactions. Of course, the literature on leadership is rife with evidence and prescriptions concerning the reverse flow. While I do not intend to review that perspective here, there is a paradox, suggested in several areas of organizational behavior, centering on the effects of leadership on organizational effectiveness. The paradox is that leaders may well attempt to increase their significance to the organization to their ultimate detriment. One of the most thoroughly documented reactions to decline and threat of failure is a combination of denial, resistance, and struggle focused on the "enemy" versus diagnosis of the problem (see Chapter 5). All of these efforts to prevent decline generate counterforces, making the symptoms and by-products of decline even more painful. These actions and reactions, culminating in a downward cycle of dysfunctional rigidity, are well documented across several areas of knowledge in organizational behavior: the frustration-aggression syndrome, the structural impediments to creativity, the multilevel phenomenon of threat-producing rigidity, the dysfunctional escalation of commitment in the presence of decline, and behavioral freezing under conditions of severe punishment.

Management's natural reactions to a serious external threat are frequently not functional for the organization. Furthermore, what is functional generally is counterintuitive to the "take charge" style of management. To cope effectively with an organizational crisis, leaders may need to do the opposite of what their instincts, framing, and social reinforcement suggest. Namely, they may need to manage decline by "letting go." They may need to float, rather than swim against the current (Foster 1978).

By this I don't mean that managers should abdicate their leadership responsibility when times get tough. But it is evident from studies such as that reported in Chapter 10 that the commonly observed incessant struggling in anticipation of, and in the presence of, decline generally makes things worse. Managers tend to overreact. Scapegoating becomes common as key managers strive to shift the blame. They demand action for the sake of appearing to be in control. They engage the first plausible organizational response, rather than taking sufficient time to examine a variety of alternatives. In their haste, they cut off important sources of information and counsel. As a result, instead of fostering increased internal support and loyalty, the external threat actually fractures the organization into clusters of insiders and outsiders, haves and have-nots, informed and uninformed.

The floating metaphor is useful because swimming instructors stress that the key to mastering swimming is knowing how to float. Swimmers who are poor floaters panic easily. When their confidence is challenged by deep water or a big wave, they tend to fight the water rather than letting the water help them stay afloat. In teaching people proper floating techniques, swim instructors emphasize the importance of trust. Novice swimmers must learn to trust the water because the key to staying alive is working with, not against, the water.

Managers too must learn to trust the water in which they are swimming. At the onset of a crisis, managers need to realize that the key to staying afloat is working with, rather than thrashing against, their environment. Rather than clinging to traditional problem-solving practices and accepted solutions, they should seize the opportunity to engage more information, more constituencies, and more alternative solutions to problems.

What I have suggested here, then, is that by stressing the individual level of analysis, we can overcome a natural tendency to become myopic in our investigations of decline. We need to consider the individual's interpretation of, reaction to, and method of coping with decline by drawing upon literatures that have heretofore been ignored in decline studies. Specifically, as we become more precise in our definitions of decline, we can find informative psychological literature that is not usually reviewed by investigators of decline. Similarly, as we take temporal issues into account—that is, how long has the decline lasted; how long will it last—individual reactions to decline may be interpreted very differently. In addition, when we shift positional perspectives from, for example, the CEO's view to the individual member's view, interpretations of decline, and even the extent to which decline is experienced at all, may shift dramatically. Finally, effective leadership behavior in conditions of decline may mean counterintuitive behaviors, based on what we know from the psychological (but not necessarily the sociological) literature.

References

Arvey, R.D., and A.P. Jones. 1985. "The Use of Discipline in Organizational Settings: A Framework for Future Research." In *Research in Organizational Behavior,* Vol. 7, edited by L.L. Cummings and B.M. Staw, pp. 367–408. Greenwich, Conn.: JAI Press.

Ashford, S., and L.L. Cummings. 1983. "Feedback as an Individual Resource: Personal Strategies for Creating Information." *Organizational Behavior and Human Performance* 32: 370–98.

Ashford, S., and L.L. Cummings. 1985. "Proactive Feedback Seeking: The Instrumental Use of the Information Environment." *Journal of Occupational Psychology* 58: 67–79.

Bandura, A. 1977. *Social Learning Theory.* Englewood Cliffs, N.J.: Prentice-Hall.

Bies, R.J. 1987. "The Predicament of Injustice: The Management of Moral Outage." In *Research in Organizational Behavior,* Vol. 9, edited by L.L. Cummings and B.M. Staw, pp. 289–320. Greenwich, Conn.: JAI Press.

Brockner, J. In press. "The Effects of Work Layoffs on Survivors: Research, Theory and Practice." In *Research in Organizational Behavior,* Vol. 10, edited by B.M. Staw and L.L. Cummings. Greenwich, Conn.: JAI Press.

Crosby, F. 1984. "Relative Deprivation in Organizational Settings." In *Research in Organizational Behavior,* Vol. 6, edited by B.M. Staw and L.L.

Cummings, pp. 51–94. Greenwich, Conn.: JAI Press.

Foster, R.J. 1978. *Celebration of Discipline.* New York: Harper & Row.

Gupta, S., and L.L. Cummings. 1986. "Perceived Speed of Time and Task Effect." *Perceptual and Motor Skills* 63: 971–80.

Harris, S.C., and R.I. Sutton. 1986. "Functions of Parting Ceremonies in Dying Organizations." *Academy of Management Journal* 29(1): 5–30.

Ilgen, D.R., C.D. Fisher, and M.S. Taylor. 1979. "Consequences of Individual Feedback on Behavior in Organizations." *Journal of Applied Psychology* 64: 349–71.

March, James G., and Herbert A. Simon. 1958. *Organizations.* New York: Wiley.

Martin, J. 1981. "Relative Deprivation: A Theory of Distributive Injustice for an Era of Shrinking Resources." In *Research in Organizational Behavior,* Vol. 3, edited by L.L. Cummings and B.M. Staw, pp. 53–108. Greenwich, Conn.: JAI Press.

McGrath, J.E., and N.L. Rotchford. 1983. "Time and Behavior in Organizations." In *Research in Organizational Behavior,* Vol. 5, edited by L.L. Cummings and B.M. Staw, pp. 57–102. Greenwich, Conn.: JAI Press.

Mento, A.J., R.P. Steel, and R.J. Karren. 1987.

"A Meta-Analytic Study of the Effects of Goal Setting on Task Performance: 1966–1984." *Organizational Behavior and Human Decision Processes* 39(1): 52–83.

Pierce, J., R.B. Dunham, and L.L. Cummings. 1984. "Sources of Environmental Structuring and Participant Responses." *Organizational Behavior and Human Performance* 33: 214–42.

Scott, W.E., and P.M. Podsakoff. 1985. *Behavioral Principles in the Practice of Management.* New York: John Wiley.

Staw, B.M., and J. Ross. 1987. "Behavior in Escalation Situations: Antecedents, Prototypes and Solutions." In *Research in Organizational Behavior,* Vol. 9, edited by L.L. Cummings and B.M. Staw, pp. 39–78. Greenwich, Conn.: JAI Press.

Taylor, M.S., C.D. Fisher, and D.R. Ilgen. 1984. "Individuals' Reactions to Performance Feedback in Organizations." In *Research in Personnel and Human Resources Management,* Vol. 2, edited by K. Rowland and G.R. Ferris. Greenwich, Conn.: JAI Press.

Trice, H.M., and J.M. Beyer. 1986. "Charisma and Its Routinization in Two Social Movement Organizations," In *Research in Organizational Behavior,* Vol. 8, edited by B.M. Staw and L.L. Cummings, pp. 113–64. Greenwich, Conn.: JAI Press.

Selected Bibliography

The following references have been compiled to facilitate further study on the topic of organizational decline. Only references since 1980 are included. More extensive bibliographies on this subject have been compiled by David Whetten and Ray Zammuto, and information on these bibliographies is included here.

Behn, R. 1980. "How to Terminate Public Policy: A Dozen Hints for the Would Be Terminator." In *Managing Fiscal Stress,* edited by Charles H. Levine, pp. 313–26. Chatham, N.J.: Chatham House Publishers.

———. 1980. "The Fundamentals of Cutback Management." Paper presented at Second Annual Research Conference of Associations for Public Policy Analysis and Management, October 24, Boston, Massachusetts.

———. 1981. "Leadership for Cutback Management: The Use of Corporate Strategy." *Public Administration Review* (November–December): 613–20.

Berger, M. 1983. "Editor's Introduction." *Peabody Journal of Education* 60(2): 1–9.

———. (Ed.) 1983. "Managing Enrollment Decline: Current Knowledge and Future Applications (special issue). *Peabody Journal of Education* 60(2): 1–119.

Bibeault, D.B. 1982. *Corporate Turnaround.* New York: McGraw-Hill.

Biller, R.P. 1980. "Leadership Tactics for Retrenchment." *Public Administration Review* (November–December): 604–9.

Billings, R.S., T.W. Milburn, and M.L. Schaalman. 1980. "A Model of Crisis Perception: A Theoretical and Empirical Analysis." *Administrative Science Quarterly* 25(2): 300–16.

Bonazzi, Giuseppe. 1983. "Scapegoating in Complex Organizations: The Results of a Comparative Study of Symbolic Blame-Giving in Italian and French Public Administration." *Organizational Studies* 4: 1–18.

Buss, T.F., and R.S. Redburn. 1981. "How to Shut Down a Plant." *Industrial Management* 23: 4–9.

Cameron, K.S. 1983. "Strategic Responses to Conditions of Decline: Higher Education and the Private Sector." *Journal of Higher Education* 54: 359–80.

———. 1985. "The Paradox in Institutional Renewal." *New Directions in Higher Education* (March): 39–48.

Cameron, K.S., and D.A. Whetten. 1981. "Perceptions of Organizational Effectiveness over Organizational Lifecycles." *Administrative Science Quarterly* 26(4): 525–44.

———. 1983. "Models of the Organizational Life Cycle: Applications to Higher Education." *The Review of Higher Education* 6(4): 269–99.

———. 1985. "Administrative Effectiveness in Higher Education." In *The Review of Higher Education* 9(1): 35–49.

Cameron, Kim S., David A. Whetten, and Myung U. Kim. 1987. "Organizational Dysfunctions of Decline." *Academy of Management Journal* 30: 126–38.

Child, J., and A. Kieser. 1981. "Development of Organizations over Time." In *Handbook of Organizational Design,* edited by William H. Starbuck, pp. 28–64. New York: Oxford University Press.

Clark, R.E., and E.E. LaBeef. 1982. "Death Telling: Managing the Delivery of Bad News." *Journal of Health and Social Behavior* 23: 366–80.

Cornfield, D.B. 1983. "Chances of Layoff in a Corporation: A Case Study." *Administrative Science Quarterly* 28(4): 503–20.

Crespo, Manuel, and Jean B. Hache. 1982. "The Management of Decline in Education: The Case of Quebec." *Educational Administration Quarterly* 18(1): 75–99.

De Greene, K.B. 1982. *The Adaptive Organization: Anticipation and Management of Crisis.* New York: John Wiley & Sons.

Duhaime, I.M., and J.H. Grant. 1984. "Factors Influencing Divestment Decision-Making: Evidence from a Field Study." *Strategic Management Journal* 5: 301–18.

Filley, A.C., and R.J. Aldag. 1980. "Organizational Growth and Types: Lessons from Small Institutions." *Research in Organizational Behavior* 2: 279–320.

Finch, Wilbur A. 1982. "Declining Public Social Service Resources: A Managerial Problem." *Administration in Social Work* 6(1): 19–29.

Fleming, R., A. Baum, D. Reddy, and R.J. Gatchel. 1984. "Behavioral and Biochemical Effects of Job Loss and Unemployment Stress." *Journal of Human Stress* (Spring) 10(1): 12–17.

Folbre, N.R., J.R. Leighton, and M.R. Roderick. 1984. "Plant Closings and Their Regulation in Maine, 1971–1982." *Industrial and Labor Relations Review* 37(2): 185–96.

Ford, J.D. 1980a. "The Administrative Component in Growing and Declining Organizations: A Longitudinal Analysis." *Academy of Management Journal* 23(4): 615–30.

———. 1980b. "The Occurrence of Structural Hysteresis in Declining Organizations." *Academy of Management Review* 5: 589–98.

———. 1985. "The Effects of Causal Attributions on Decision Makers' Responses to Performance Downturns." *Academy of Management Review* 10(4): 770–86.

Ford, Jeffrey D., and David A. Baucus. 1987. "Organizational Adaptation to Performance Downturns: An Interpretation-Based Perspective." *Academy of Management Review* 12: 366–80.

Freeman, J. 1982. "Organizational Lifecycles and Natural Selection Processes." In *Research in Organizational Behavior,* Vol. 4, edited by Barry M. Staw and L.L. Cummings, pp. 1–32. Greenwich, Conn.: JAI Press.

Gilmore, T., and L. Hirschhorn. 1983. "Management Challenges under Conditions of Retrenchment." *Human Resources Management* 22(4): 341–57.

Greenhalgh, L. 1982. "Managing Organizational Effectiveness During Organization Retrenchment." *Journal of Applied Behavioral Science* 18(2): 155–70.

———. 1983. "Organizational Decline." In *Research in the Sociology of Organizations,* Vol. 2, edited by S.B. Bacharach, pp. 231–76. Greenwich, Conn.: JAI Press.

Greenhalgh, L., and R.B. McKersie. 1980. "Cost Effectiveness of Alternative Strategies for Cutback Management." *Public Administration Review* 40: 575–84.

Hardy, C. 1982. "Organizational Closure: A Political Perspective." Ph.D. diss., Warwick University, Warwick, England.

Harrigan, K.R. 1980. *Strategies for Declining Businesses.* Lexington, Mass.: D. C. Heath.

———. 1981. "Deterrents to Divestiture." *Academy of Management Journal* 24(2): 306–23.

———. 1982. "Exit Decisions in Mature Industries." *Academy of Management Journal* 25(4): 707–32.

Harrigan, K.R., and M.E. Porter. 1983. "End-Game Strategies for Declining Industries." *Harvard Business Review* 61: 111–20.

Harrigan, R.H. 1980. "Strategy Formulation in Declining Industries." *Academy of Management Review* 5: 599–604.

Harris, S.G., and R.I. Sutton. 1986. "Functions for Parting Ceremonies in Dying Organizations." *Academy of Management Journal* 29(1): 5–30.

Hirschhorn, L., and Associates. 1983. *Cutting Back: Retrenchment and Redevelopment in Human and Community Services.* San Francisco: Jossey-Bass.

Hoare, G. 1983. "Retrenchment Strategies in Mental Health: Lessons from the Private Sector." *Administration in Mental Health* 10: 259–71.

Hochner, A., and C.S. Granrose. 1985. "Sources of Motivation to Choose Employee Ownership as an Alternative to Job Loss." *Academy of Management Journal* 28(4): 860–75.

Hofer, C.W. 1980. "Turnaround Strategies." *Journal of Business Strategy* (Summer): 19–31.

Jick, T.J., and V.V. Murray. 1982. "The Management of Hard Times: Budget Cutbacks in Public Sector Organizations." *Organization Studies* 3: 141–69.

Kaufman, H. 1982. *Are Government Organizations Immortal?* Washington, D.C.: Brookings Institution.

Kimberly, J., and R. Quinn. 1984. *Organizational Transitions.* Homewood, Ill.: Irwin.

Kimberly, John R., and Robert H. Miles. 1980. *The Organizational Life Cycle.* San Francisco: Jossey-Bass.

Kinicki, A.J. 1985. "Personnel Consequences of Plant Closings: A Model and Preliminary Test." *Human Relations* (March) 38(3): 197–212.

Kolarska, L., and H. Aldrich. 1980. "Exit, Voice, and Silence: Consumers' and Managers' Response to Organizational Decline." *Organizational Studies* 1: 41–58.

Latack, J.C., and J.B. Dozier. 1986. "After the Axe Falls: Job Loss as a Career Transition." *Academy of Management Review* 11(2): 375–92.

Leana, Carrie R., and John M. Ivancevich. 1987. "Involuntary Job Loss: Institutional Interventions and a Research Agenda." *Academy of Management Review* 12: 301–12.

Levine, C.H. 1981. "Cutting Back the Public Sector: The Hidden Hazards of Retrenchment." The Third Inaugural Lecture, October 28, University of Kansas, Lawrence, Kansas.

Levine, C.H., and I.S. Rubin. Eds. 1980. *Fiscal Stress and Public Policy.* Beverly Hills, Calif.: Sage Publications.

Levine, C.H., I.S. Rubin, and G.G. Wolohojian. 1981. *The Politics of Retrenchment.* Beverly Hills, Calif.: Sage Publications.

Lewis, Carol W., and Anthony T. Lozalbo. 1980. "Cutback Principles and Practices: A Checklist for Managers." *Public Administration Review* (March–April): 184–88.

McEvoy, G.M. 1984. "The Organizational Lifecycle Concept: Approaching Adolescence or Drawing Near Death?" Working Paper. Department of Business Administration, Utah State University, Logan, Utah.

McKelvey, W., and H. Aldrich. 1983. "Populations, Natural Selection, and Applied Organizational Science." *Administrative Science Quarterly* 28: 101–28.

Meyer, A.D. 1982. "Adapting to Environmental Jolts." *Administrative Science Quarterly* 27: 515–37.

Miles, R.H. 1981. "Findings and Implications of Organizational Life Cycle Research: A Commencement." In *The Organizational Life Cycle: Creation, Transformations, and Decline,* edited by J.R. Kimberly and R.H. Miles, pp. 430–50. San Francisco: Jossey-Bass.

Miles, R.H., and K.S. Cameron. 1982. *Coffin Nails and Corporate Strategies.* Englewood Cliffs, N.J.: Prentice-Hall.

Miller, D., and P. Friesen. 1980. "Archetypes of Organizational Transition." *Administrative Science Quarterly* 25: 268–99.

———. 1984. "A Longitudinal Study of the Organizational Life Cycle." *Management Science* 30: 1161–83.

Milson, A., A.R. O'Rourke, G.A. Richardson, and H.F.A. Rose. 1983. "Strategies for Managing Resources in a Declining Resource Situation." *Higher Education* 12: 133–44.

Mingle, James R., and Donald M. Norris. 1983. "Managing Decline." *Phi Kappa Phi Journal* 63(2): 42–44.

Mintzberg, H. 1984. "Power and Organization Lifecycles." *Academy of Management Review* 9: 207–24.

Montgomery, C.A., R.T. Anjne, and R. Kamath. 1984. "Divestiture, Market Valuation, and Strategy." *Academy of Management Journal* 27: 830–40.

Nees, D. 1981. "Increase Your Divestment Effectiveness." *Strategic Management Journal* 2: 119–30.

Nottenburg, Gail, and Donald B. Fedor. 1983. "Scarcity in the Environment: Organizational Perceptions, Interpretations, and Responses." *Organizational Studies* 4: 317–37.

O'Neill, Joseph P., and Samuel Barnett. 1980. *Colleges and Corporate Change: Merger, Bankruptcy, and Closure.* Princeton, N.J.: Conference-College Press.

Petrie, H.G., and D.A. Alpert. 1983. "What is the Problem of Retrenchment in Higher Education?" *Journal of Management Studies* 20: 97–119.

Porter, M. 1980. "Competitive Strategy in Declining Industries." In *Competitive Strategy,* edited by M. Porter, pp. 254–74. New York: Free Press.

Quinn, R.E., and K. Cameron. 1983. "Organizational Life Cycles and Shifting Criteria of Effectiveness: Some Preliminary Evidence." *Management Science* 29(1): 33–51.

Rubin, Irene. 1981. "Preventing or Eliminating Planned Deficits: Restructuring Political Incentives." *Public Administration Review* (November–December): 621–26.

Schwartz, K.B., and K. Menon. 1985. "Executive Succession in Falling Firms." *Academy of Management Journal* 28: 680–86.

Scott, W.R. 1981. *Organizations: Rational, Natural, and Open Systems.* Englewood Cliffs, N.J.: Prentice-Hall.

Sharme, S., and V. Mahajan. 1980. "Early Warning Indicators of Business Failure." *Journal of Marketing* 44: 80–89.

Singh, Jitendra V., Robert J. House, and David J. Tucker. 1986. "Organizational Change and Organizational Mortality." *Administrative Science Quarterly* 31: 587–611.

Singh, Jitendra V., David J. Tucker, and Robert J. House. 1986. "Organizational Legitimacy and the Liability of Newness." *Administrative Science Quarterly* 31: 171–93.

Smith, K.G., T.R. Mitchell, and C.E. Summer. 1985. "Top Level Management Priorities in Different Stages of the Organizational Life Cycle." *Academy of Management Journal* 28(4): 799–820.

Taylor, Bernard. 1982. "Turnaround, Recovery, and Growth: The Way Through the Crisis." *Journal of General Management* 8(2): 5–13.

Tushman, Michael, and Philip Anderson. 1986. "Technological Discontinuities and Organizational Environments." *Administrative Science Quarterly* 31: 439–65.

Tushman, Michael, and Elaine Romanelli. 1985. "Organizational Evolution: A Metamorphosis Model of Convergence and Reorientation." In *Research in Organizational Behavior,* Vol. 7, edited by L.L. Cummings and B.M. Staw, pp. 177–222. Greenwich, Conn.: JAI Press.

Van de Ven, A.H., and W.G. Astley. 1981. "Mapping the Field to Create a Dynamic Perspective on Organizational Design and Behavior." In *Perspectives on Organizational Design and Behavior,* edited by A.H. Van de Ven and W.F. Joyce, pp. 427–68. New York: Wiley.

Volkwein, J.F. 1984. "Responding to Financial Retrenchment: Lessons from the Albany Experience." *Journal of Higher Education* 55: 389–401.

Warren, D.A. 1984. "Managing in Crisis: Nine Principles for Successful Transitions." In *Managing Organizational Transitions,* edited by J. Kimberly and R. Quinn, pp. 85–106. Homewood, Ill.: R. D. Irwin.

Whetten, D.A. 1980. "Organizational Decline: A Neglected Topic in the Organizational Sciences." *Academy of Management Review* 4: 577–88.

———. 1981a. "Managing Organizational Retrenchment: A Bibliography." Vance Bibliographies, P.O. Box 229, Monticello, Illinois 61856.

———. 1981b. "Organizational Responses to Scarcity: Exploring the Obstacles to Innovative Approaches to Retrenchment in Education." *Educational Administration Quarterly* 17: 80–97.

———. 1984. "Effective Administrators: Good Management in the College Campus." *Change: The Magazine for Higher Learning* (November–December): 39–43.

———. 1986. "Effective Management of Retrenchment." Working Paper. College of Commerce and Business Administration, University of Illinois, Champaign, Illinois.

Wilburn, Robert C., and Michael A. Worman. 1980. "Overcoming the Limits to Personnel Cutbacks: Lessons Learned from Pennsylvania." *Public Administration Review* (November–December): 609–12.

Zammuto, R.F. 1982. *Bibliography on Decline and Retrenchment.* Boulder, Col.: National Center for Higher Education Management Systems.

———. 1982. "Organizational Decline and Management Education." *Exchange* 7: 5–12.

Zammuto, R.F., and K.S. Cameron. 1985. "Environmental Decline and Organizational Response." In *Research in Organizational Behavior,* Vol. 7, edited by L.L. Cummings and B.M. Staw, pp. 223–62. Greenwich, Conn.: JAI Press.